A Celebration of Poets

California
Grades 4-12
Fall 2009

A Celebration of Poets
California
Grades 4-12
Fall 2009

An anthology compiled by Creative Communication, Inc.

Published by:

1488 NORTH 200 WEST • LOGAN, UTAH 84341
TEL. 435-713-4411 • WWW.POETICPOWER.COM

Authors are responsible for the originality of the writing submitted.

All rights reserved. No part of this book may be reproduced or transmitted in any form or by any means, electronic or mechanical without written permission of the author and publisher.

Copyright © 2010 by Creative Communication, Inc.
Printed in the United States of America

ISBN: 978-1-60050-334-4

FOREWORD

In today's world there are many things that compete for our attention. From the far reaching influence of the media, to the voices we hear from those around us, it is often difficult to decide where to commit our energies and focus. The poets in this book listened to an inner voice; a voice that can be the loudest of the many voices in our world, but to pay attention to this voice takes self-control. The effect of these words may not be far reaching, but to even make a small difference in the world is a positive thing.

Each year I receive hundreds of letters, calls, and emails from parents, teachers, and students who share stories of success; stories, where being a published writer provided the catalyst to a different attitude toward school, education and life. We are pleased to provide you with this book and hope that what these writers have shared makes a small but meaningful difference in your world.

Thomas Worthen, Ph.D.
Editor
Creative Communication

WRITING CONTESTS!

Enter our next POETRY contest!

Enter our next ESSAY contest!

Why should I enter?
Win prizes and get published! Each year thousands of dollars in prizes are awarded throughout North America. The top writers in each division receive a monetary award and a free book that includes their published poem or essay. Entries of merit are also selected to be published in our anthology.

Who may enter?
There are four divisions in the poetry contest. The poetry divisions are grades K-3, 4-6, 7-9, and 10-12. There are three divisions in the essay contest. The essay divisions are grades 3-6, 7-9, and 10-12.

What is needed to enter the contest?
To enter the poetry contest send in one original poem, 21 lines or less. To enter the essay contest send in one original non-fiction essay, 250 words or less, on any topic. Please submit each poem and essay with a title, and the following information clearly printed: the writer's name, current grade, home address (optional), school name, school address, teacher's name and teacher's email address (optional). Contact information will only be used to provide information about the contest. For complete contest information go to www.poeticpower.com.

How do I enter?
Enter a poem online at:
www.poeticpower.com
or
Mail your poem to:
Poetry Contest
1488 North 200 West
Logan, UT 84341

Enter an essay online at:
www.studentessaycontest.com
or
Mail your essay to:
Essay Contest
1488 North 200 West
Logan, UT 84341

When is the deadline?
Poetry contest deadlines are August 18th, December 2nd and April 5th. Essay contest deadlines are July 15th, October 19th, and February 17th. Students can enter one poem and one essay for each spring, summer, and fall contest deadline.

Are there benefits for my school?
Yes. We award $15,000 each year in grants to help with Language Arts programs. Schools qualify to apply for a grant by having 15 or more accepted entries.

Are there benefits for my teacher?
Yes. Teachers with five or more students published receive a free anthology that includes their students' writing.

For more information please go to our website at **www.poeticpower.com**, email us at editor@poeticpower.com or call 435-713-4411.

TABLE OF CONTENTS

POETIC ACHIEVEMENT HONOR SCHOOLS   1

LANGUAGE ARTS GRANT RECIPIENTS   7

GRADES 10-11-12 HIGH MERIT POEMS 11

GRADES 7-8-9 HIGH MERIT POEMS 97

GRADES 4-5-6 HIGH MERIT POEMS 239

INDEX 321

Fall 2009 Poetic Achievement Honor Schools

Teachers who had fifteen or more poets accepted to be published

The following schools are recognized as receiving a "Poetic Achievement Award." This award is given to schools who have a large number of entries of which over fifty percent are accepted for publication. With hundreds of schools entering our contest, only a small percent of these schools are honored with this award. The purpose of this award is to recognize schools with excellent Language Arts programs. This award qualifies these schools to receive a complimentary copy of this anthology. In addition, these schools are eligible to apply for a Creative Communication Language Arts Grant. Grants of two hundred and fifty dollars each are awarded to further develop writing in our schools.

Almond Tree Middle School
    Delano
        Sandie Barkley*
        Karen Mayberry*

August Boeger Middle School
    San Jose
        Brooke Herrington*

Bay View Elementary School
    Santa Cruz
        Jennifer Johnston*

Carden Academy of Santa Clara
    Santa Clara
        Gretchen Larese*

Carlthorp School
    Santa Monica
        Laura Bickel*
        Dr. Leslie Johnson

Charles Maclay Middle School
    Pacoima
        John Hanson*

Chinese American International School
    San Francisco
        Jake Sproull*

Corpus Christi School
    San Francisco
        Theodore R. Langlais*

Coyote Valley Elementary School
    Middletown
        Kathy Scavone*

Daniel Savage Middle School
    Modesto
        Sherry Chapman*

Dingeman Elementary School
    San Diego
        Leigh Morioka*

Eastwood Elementary School
    Westminster
        Kym Slingerland*

Foothill High School
    Palo Cedro
        Sharon Fernandes*

A Celebration of Poets – California Grades 4-12 Fall 2009

Gardner Street Elementary School
   Los Angeles
      Lisett Altmann Gunther*

Granada Elementary School
   Granada Hills
      Shelley G. Tenen*

Grant Elementary School
   Petaluma
      Mary Reynolds*

Heather Elementary School
   San Carlos
      Michelle Marino*
      Sheila Sevilla*

Henry Haight Elementary School
   Alameda
      Joan Braze
      Jessica Fisher
      Danielle Ullendorff

Hiram W Johnson High School
   Sacramento
      Marie Pearce
      Ms. Proudlove
      Barbara Tigert*

Huntington Park College Ready Academy High School
   Huntington Park
      Kelly Semlear*

Immaculate Heart of Mary School
   Los Angeles
      Allyson Alberto*

Isbell Middle School
   Santa Paula
      Mark Lopez*

Joe Walker Middle School
   Quartz Hill
      Brian Hurlburt*

John Adams Middle School
   Los Angeles
      Linda Bolibaugh*

Junipero Serra School
   Carmel
      Ellen Buckles*

Kadima Day School
   West Hills
      Jennifer Rutzen*

Lankershim Elementary School
   Highland
      Janet Parker*

Lincoln Elementary School
   Anaheim
      Janet Leslie*

Lindero Canyon Middle School
   Agoura Hills
      Carol Firestone*
      Rebecca Jones
      Sandra Porter

Lucerne Valley Jr/Sr High School
   Lucerne Valley
      Cindy Lazenby*
      Linda Schlenz*

Lydiksen Elementary School
   Pleasanton
      Linda Boveda*

Monte Vista Christian School
   Watsonville
      Janice Renard*

Ocean Air School
   San Diego
      Pam Martin*
      Carol Newberry*

Omega High School
   Richmond
      Ms. Zolly*

Orange Glen Elementary School
   Escondido
      Susan McKeon*

Poetic Achievement Honor Schools

Orville Wright Middle School
Los Angeles
    Ray Barbeau*
    John Wessels

Our Lady of Guadalupe School
Oxnard
    Christina Fernandez
    Amy Hallas*
    Carlos Lopez

Our Lady of Mount Carmel School
Redwood City
    Kelly O'Connor*

Our Lady of the Rosary School
Paramount
    Sr. Ellen Mary Conefrey
    Mr. Delgado
    Mary Frankart*
    Sr. Brigid Mary McGuire
    Sr. Mary Walsh, DMJ

Palm Desert Charter Middle School
Palm Desert
    Jeff Ball
    Nanette Davis-Kirchhevel
    Jennifer Roose
    Kristin Wagner*

Proctor Elementary School
Castro Valley
    Fanny Machado
    Bonnie Worthington*

Pulliam Elementary School
Stockton
    Mrs. Bolognini
    Mrs. Casenave
    Ms. Erlandson
    Ms. Hoang
    Mrs. Horn-Escoto
    Mr. Knipper
    Mrs. Mariani
    Ms. Moura
    Ms. Rizzuto
    Mrs. Wong
    Mrs. Xiong

Redlands High School
Redlands
    Joshua Murguia*

Richard Merkin Middle Academy
Los Angeles
    Brandon Bell*

Richardson PREP HI Middle School
San Bernardino
    Julie Doussett
    Emily Tauffer*

Ripona Elementary School
Ripon
    Kim Johnson*

Sarah McGarvin Intermediate School
Westminster
    Cindy Ribeiro*

Saugus High School
Saugus
    Brant Botton*

Shadow Hills Intermediate School
Palmdale
    Gerald Farrell*

St Francis de Sales School
Riverside
    Alissa Duarte*

St Francis Parish School
Bakersfield
    Bronny Bowman*
    Nica Underwood

St Helen Catholic Elementary School
South Gate
    Bernadette Windsor*

St Linus School
Norwalk
    Jennifer Muehlebach*

St Louis De Montfort School
   Santa Maria
      Cindy Hubbard*

St Martin-in-the-Fields School
   Winnetka
      Mrs. Hessamian*

St Mary's Chinese Day School
   San Francisco
      Patricia Lee Chan*

St Pius X Elementary School
   Chula Vista
      Guadalupe Vecchitto*

St Raphael School
   Santa Barbara
      Ms. Breton
      Diane McClenathen*

Tenaya Middle School
   Fresno
      Mrs. Franson
      Marie Meyer*

The Mirman School
   Los Angeles
      Veronica Gonzales
      Bonnie Muler*
      Wendy Samson*
      Tracy Walker*
      Marjorie Zinman*

Top Kids Center
   Monrovia
      Nicholette Espinosa
      Alicia Lopez
      Stephanie Mushik

University Preparatory School
   Redding
      Romney Clements
      Andy Hedman*
      Sarah Jepsen

Valencia High School
   Placentia
      Dana Leon*

Walter F Dexter Middle School
   Whittier
      Janay Hamrick
      Marjorie Lawrence

Language Arts Grant Recipients 2009-2010

After receiving a "Poetic Achievement Award" schools are encouraged to apply for a Creative Communication Language Arts Grant. The following is a list of schools who received a two hundred and fifty dollar grant for the 2009-2010 school year.

Arrowhead Union High School, Hartland, WI
Blessed Sacrament School, Seminole, FL
Booneville Jr High School, Booneville, AR
Buckhannon-Upshur Middle School, Buckhannon, WV
Campbell High School, Ewa Beach, HI
Chickahominy Middle School, Mechanicsville, VA
Clarkston Jr High School, Clarkston, MI
Covenant Life School, Gaithersburg, MD
CW Rice Middle School, Northumberland, PA
Eason Elementary School, Waukee, IA
East Elementary School, Kodiak, AK
Florence M Gaudineer Middle School, Springfield, NJ
Foxborough Regional Charter School, Foxborough, MA
Gideon High School, Gideon, MO
Holy Child Academy, Drexel Hill, PA
Home Choice Academy, Vancouver, WA
Jeff Davis Elementary School, Biloxi, MS
Lower Alloways Creek Elementary School, Salem, NJ
Maple Wood Elementary School, Somersworth, NH
Mary Walter Elementary School, Bealeton, VA
Mater Dei High School, Evansville, IN
Mercy High School, Farmington Hills, MI
Monroeville Elementary School, Monroeville, OH
Nautilus Middle School, Miami Beach, FL
Our Lady Star of the Sea School, Grosse Pointe Woods, MI
Overton High School, Memphis, TN
Pond Road Middle School, Robbinsville, NJ
Providence Hall Charter School, Herriman, UT
Reuben Johnson Elementary School, McKinney, TX
Rivelon Elementary School, Orangeburg, SC
Rose Hill Elementary School, Omaha, NE

Language Arts Grant Winners cont.

Runnels School, Baton Rouge, LA
Santa Fe Springs Christian School, Santa Fe Springs, CA
Serra Catholic High School, Mckeesport, PA
Shadowlawn Elementary School, Green Cove Springs, FL
Spectrum Elementary School, Gilbert, AZ
St Edmund Parish School, Oak Park, IL
St Joseph Institute for the Deaf, Chesterfield, MO
St Joseph Regional Jr High School, Manchester, NH
St Mary of Czestochowa School, Middletown, CT
St Monica Elementary School, Garfield Heights, OH
St Vincent De Paul Elementary School, Cape Girardeau, MO
Stevensville Middle School, Stevensville, MD
Tashua School, Trumbull, CT
The New York Institute for Special Education, Bronx, NY
The Selwyn School, Denton, TX
Tonganoxie Middle School, Tonganoxie, KS
Westside Academy, Prince George, BC
Willa Cather Elementary School, Omaha, NE
Willow Hill Elementary School, Traverse City, MI

Grades 10-11-12 Top Ten Winners

List of Top Ten Winners for Grades 10-12; listed alphabetically

Aaron Combs, Grade 12
Carroll High School, Corpus Christi, TX

Kellie Lenamond, Grade 12
Home School, Wills Point, TX

Jordyn Rhorer, Grade 12
Lafayette High School, Lexington, KY

Miranda Rogovein, Grade 12
Greenwood College School, Toronto, ON

Sydney Rubin, Grade 11
Cab Calloway School of the Arts, Wilmington, DE

Kyle Rutherford, Grade 12
Rosebud School, Rosebud, MT

Sara RuthAnn Weaver, Grade 12
Grace Baptist High School, Delaware, OH

Jessica Webster, Grade 11
Boyne City High School, Boyne City, MI

Abigail Yeskatalas, Grade 10
Avonworth High School, Pittsburgh, PA

Mariam Younan, Grade 12
Bayonne High School, Bayonne, NJ

All Top Ten Poems can be read at www.poeticpower.com

Note: The Top Ten poems were finalized through an online voting system. Creative Communication's judges first picked out the top poems. These poems were then posted online. The final step involved thousands of students and teachers who registered as the online judges and voted for the Top Ten poems. We hope you enjoy these selections.

Black Blankets of Stars

I am the heart that you never knew.
The question remains the same,
Was it suppose to be you?

No matter where life takes us, this feeling remains true.
So strong a change, nothing will remain tame.
I am the heart you never knew.

We look at the sunrise, light so true.
But for me, morning never came.
Was it suppose to be you?

We drive, time, in essence, is not an issue
Talking, in love, our voices carry no shame.
I am the heart you never knew.

The reality left us when the Santa Anas blew.
In this mess of fascination, are these truths or just a game
Was it suppose to be you?

The sun was setting, Night's black blankets of stars flew
Wind beating hard against our ears, but I heard you say my name.
I am the heart you never knew.
It was always suppose to be you.
Christina Chambers, Grade 10
Encore High School for the Performing Arts

Can't Give Up

What happened, how did this problem get out of hand
We're supposed to be friends, until the very end
And I'm sorry, for whatever I've done
How did we get this far, just to throw it away

You've changed, you're not the same anymore
You're not the friend, I used to know
Have you forgotten, of those nights we had
Staying up just to talk, just you and me.

What happened, you forced this problem to get out of hand
Now we'll never be friends, until the very end
It's useless, my words mean nothing to you
It's like you moved on, and won't look back

I'm up all night, twisting and turning
Remembering the times, we used to have
And now because of you I can't seem to sleep
'Cause whenever I do, I only dream about you

I can't forget, can't give up
On this friendship, that we lost
I'm trying, with all of my might
'Cause in the end, you know it's right
Ray Van Ness, Grade 11
La Serna High School

My Life

My life is full of ups and downs,
Most of the time it feels like a merry-go-round
I guess I'm no different from anyone else,
But in my mind I feel like I'm all by myself

I'm not sure which direction I should go,
At this stage in my life should I already know
So many places to go and things I haven't done,
I refuse to be held back any longer by anyone

I need discipline to take control of my life,
Work hard to reduce the stress and the strife
Is today the day I chose to do right,
Only I can answer that question because it's my life
Meerlin Cortes, Grade 10
Huntington Park College Ready Academy High School

The Sun

Red in fury, white in light
The hands of the sun give in to night.
Like on an artist's pallet the brush of air swayed,
Mixing the sky as the daylight doth fade.
How does thee change so swift?
How does thee drift and shift?
Yet with little heed paid from those below,
Those below cannot know.
The secrets of your intrigue cannot be found,
Not in the sky and not in the ground.
But those who look to looking liking see,
To those who dream to those who believe,
Your red fury is but a white light,
A white light that never gives to night.
Jacqueline Xu, Grade 11
Arcadia High School

On the Difficulty of Rhyming

Sometimes a rhyme has major stakes,
A make or break of a poem complete,
That may betray or at least deplete
That light through yonder window breaks,
For rhyming makes poetry rife with mistakes
And so many young poets, they try to beat
A rhyme scheme so complex — a difficult feat —
Into the eyes of the reader that ache.
But sometimes the rhyme does make the craft,
The mark of an expert, a paragon, it's true,
A rhyme that at one will be awed instead of laughed,
One that will be seen as great instead of daft.
But that is the difficulty of rhyming for you,
It's what makes poetry take more than one draft.
Dylan Spenhoff, Grade 12
Redwood High School

Feathers

When a love dies, can't a new one take her place?
Through the tears I've swallowed
When a dove flies, a new one doesn't have the same face
Through the years that followed
Footsteps in the sand blown by the wind left a trace
I can't bear it again tomorrow
Wish to see her again and be with her as we age
I fear for more of the sorrow
She's the ink in my every page

I should have been your soldier
The one to keep away the cold
To lend you both of my shoulders
Even when both of us grow old
To break away all the boulders
Even when our liberties are sold
But now I am smoldered
To remember how that story unfolds

A notebook written in love
Every sentence asking for repentance
Thank you for your acceptance
The story ends where another one begins as the feathers fall
Leonard Chan, Grade 11
Purple Lotus International Institute

Stay Strong

I wake up every day and do the same thing
Get up, get ready, BORING!
I drive down the same road every day going nowhere
It's pretty hard going from having everything
to waking up the next day and having nothing.

Life's pretty messed up right now!
Knowing that tomorrow's not a for sure thing.
How do I know that I'm going to have a place to live tomorrow?
How do I know if I'm being a good mom?

It's hard not having anybody by your side,
Telling you what you're doing wrong
Or even telling you if you're doing something right.

I can't keep living like this, I refuse to live like this.
I will give my daughter the best, that's my goal!
I'm just so confused I really don't know what to do.
I'm at a point in my life that I'm tired of being a nobody,
I really want to be a somebody.
Sometimes I even feel like dying.
But then I think of my daughter and can't take my life for drama,
I HAVE MY DAUGHTER TO LIVE FOR!
Angella Mascarenas, Grade 12
Omega High School

Someday...

The calming wind whispers softly through the Earth
The aroma of the morning flowers can be smelled far and near
The birds sing the song that never ends
And the chicks follow their mother hen chirping blissfully
Children hold hands and giggle harmoniously
The couple strolls down the path dreaming of tomorrow
The world is still for a moment and everything is serene
There is joy and glee in the air
There is amity and silence
And the world is a harmonious place
If there is peace one day, I pray
We'll see our world like this someday.
Jacqueline Lopez, Grade 12
Lucerne Valley Jr/Sr High School

Beauty Is a Smile

Beauty is in a smile but it takes a while
To figure out how it's in her braces that scintillate
Or in the great gap in his teeth.
Beauty is a smile so sincere it often accompanies a tear,
Like the smile of a father holding his newborn
Or the sudden change of scorn to admiration.
Beauty is a smile that makes a friend
That, in the end, is the best one that one's ever had.
Beauty is a smile that contains
Protection from the harsh rains of this world —
A helping hand and a kind word
Even when nothing's been said.
Sua Figueroa, Grade 12
Schurr High School

Sex and Violence

Polluting the minds of the young
Taking control of the old
Sex and violence is taking control
We are the ones feeding it until it grows
It's taking control of our lives until we burst and die
Our nation, our lives, our sins are under control
Of sex and violence.
Richard Coon, Grade 10
eScholar Academy

Diamonds

Darling dancers line up in the wings,
not knowing what to think.
Fear of messing up overwhelms their demeanor,
desperate not to damage the piece.
They dash across the stage,
their faces shining like diamonds for all to see.
Relief; they didn't dare to make a mistake.
Christina Mazzella, Grade 12
St Bonaventure High School

The Big Race

On a hot summer day, in Redding, California,
During a big swim meet, among tons of swimmers,
I warm up for a race.

Until the time comes, throughout the day,
Behind a starting block, next to the water,
I get ready to race.

Up onto the starting block, over the water of the pool,
Into the water as quickly as possible, off to the other end,
The race has begun.

Across the pool, sprinting at a fast pace,
Near the end of a race, hoping to win,
At the end of the race.

After a race, during a swim meet,
Ready to go home, with one race left,
I am as tired as can be.

Off to the snack bar, aside from everyone else,
Before you go home, inside your small van,
You must get some lunch.

Aimee Witherspoon, Grade 10
Foothill High School

Untitled

The sky will fall when the world ends, probably.
Everything else will fall too, probably.

Mothers will lose their children
When the world ends, probably.

Homes will be crushed by the universe and
Neighborhoods will collide, probably.

It won't matter where you come from
When the world ends, probably.

And everything you care about will be lost.
Most of us won't miss it…probably.

Grudges forgotten, washed away by the wind.
Our hopes and dreams too probably.

What are they worth
When the world ends? Nothing. Probably.

And when it's all over will Diamonds sparkle in emptiness?
It would be nice to think so, probably.

Diamond White, Grade 12
Encore High School for the Performing Arts

No Apologies

You may be mad at me,
but I told because I love you.
Your eyes tell me you hate me,
but I will not be the death of you.
You like it way too much
and I cannot witness the addiction,
I won't let you go through such
pain. I am not sorry for my decision.
I hope one day you forgive me.
You know I did it for the best.
I know one day you will thank me.
Your heart will still be beating in your chest.
I love you too much to see you go.
So please, let the pills go.

Amanda McKovich, Grade 11
Encore High School for the Performing Arts

Burning

To die in your arms would be a right fine way to go.
Forgive me, I'm not very good at this.
Don't ask me to explain, sometimes you just know
when a thing is right. When dreamless
sleep becomes obsessed
and prayers preoccupied
when thoughts become incensed
with everything you are — I start to think maybe I'm tied
to you. But then you take my breath away
and the panic sets in
as I scramble to hide the edges that have begun to fray.
Just wrap me in you, let me know I'm forgiven.
I'm perfectly content far past the point of no return,
we've set this fire and with you, I'll happily burn.

Chloe Madison, Grade 12
Encore High School for the Performing Arts

Behind a Smile

At a quick glance you see a happy young woman
But if you get the rare chance to see
Into the unattainable truth
Sad beauty and years of pain are secretly revealed
In her deep eyes you see her fear of being weak
You see her overall demeanor
Signaling her need to help
   Looking at her posture
You see her replacing her pain with others' needs

    You look at her and see someone new
    You see someone sad
    And someone hiding behind a smile

Ashley Cooper, Grade 10
Oakdale Charter High School

High Merit Poems – Grades 10, 11 and 12

Free Fall

Stand on the edge with me
Look over the side
Feel the rush of adrenaline
As we free fall through our lives
Together we stand, together we shall fall
I cannot complete this journey alone
Our memories support us
While our differences vanish
Together we shall stay
Your hand in mine
I was lost without you
But now you're leading the way
I have nothing left to fear
As we're falling through time
I wish for this to be endless
For this moment to withstand time
I came into this blind
But I've finally opened my eyes
You're all I want to see
I only need to know one more thing
Will you free fall with me?

Heather Adams, Grade 11
Desert Hot Springs High School

The Destination

Traces of a pattern,
Contain places to be found someday.
And if all goes as planned,
Forget the reasons to replay.
Find a route, follow through,
Then live along the lines still free.
But if the map becomes lost,
Go on, but travel lightly.
Don't rely on second chances,
That will not go anywhere.
Yet look not to first impressions,
That is hardly ever fair.
Live not for a destination,
Observe the journey ahead.
And if there is no arrival,
Carry on instead.

Jaimie Moran, Grade 10
Foothill High School

Four Leaf Clover

Finding a best friend
is like finding a four leaf clover
You look for one until
you've walked in circles
Often times it is very hard to find one
When you do
You cherish one forever
My four leaf clover is Damali Stennette

Dulcie Adhiambo, Grade 11
Saugus High School

Never Before

What is this feeling?
This feeling of anguish.
Whenever I catch sight of him, my heart throbs
Pounding relentlessly
As I sense time slows down with every glance
This feeling I've never experienced before
What is it?
Under what impression am I insisting on considering love?
It is an amalgam of emotions performing as one.
The breath of cold air I inhale wounds my affection with regret and distress.
Single tears stream downward
From the joy that I obtain in observing you from afar.
My golden eyes are glued to the back of your head,
As the wind crawls through my brown hair,
This compels me towards you
Whispering to me you are the one,
The one meant to be in my heart eternally.
Your figure fades away
As you walk deeper and deeper into the rushing crowd,
Walking further and further away from me
Leaving me here to love and love you more.

Kyla Alejandra Campbell, Grade 11
Alhambra High School

I've Fallen

I've fallen, gotten right back up
But when the sky keeps on calling
My life seems to deprive
A second option arrives for me to survive
Somehow I tend to thrive and my life seems to revive
Once again I feel alive
Somehow I tend to shrive
And change the lives of those whom are alive
To show them the meaning of life
And secretly conspire their perspectives on the meaning of love and life…
Sometimes it all feels as if it were a dream
Because when I try to please someone
The opposite waits for me
Man how hard it is to not understand what others expect for you
Why can't we all just fall and raise our heads and let life come through?
Why do we have to go through this pain and sorrow?
Love tends to hurt one another when we don't forgive each other on the day of tomorrow
Life seems to be harsh when we misjudge one another
Why? Why? Why?
These are the questions I asked myself when I was blinded and was once given light
And I come here once again to ask these questions because I fell once again…

Michelle Escobar, Grade 11
Maywood Academy High School

Masked Identity

The perfect life image
An imperfect life
To the eyes of peers
A spoiled brat
In reality, the family outcast
It all seems perfect
Electronics, clothes, jewelry,
You can't forget the perfect grades
It's a mask over your true identity
You feel hatred and sadness
Your thoughts misunderstood
"You are so negative."
It has been said so many times to you that
Your thoughts are kept to yourself
They are bolted down trying to get out
But too scared of those words
You only dare write what you feel
Hoping that this lifestyle ends
Just wanting to enjoy it because
You don't live forever.

Martha Morales, Grade 10
Huntington Park College Ready Academy High School

My First Talk

It was snowing outside, quick, eager
I don't know where the snow came from
I was shaking
The skaters went skimming round in a colored blur
Like painted horses
And then he came
His voice sounded calm and quiet
His arm was around my neck, so sweet his smell
He just made me happy, and I smiled innocently
I had never talked with a boy before, but that was great
It represented the significance of my coming of age
I expected to win
Warming, the moon hung just over
The houses around the rink
We walked toward him
He talked softly as we walked
I could feel my heart beating
The stars were around us
At that time I felt like I won a lot of money

Christian Mekuria, Grade 12
Hiram W Johnson High School

Windy Weather

Windy weather is like going 85 on
the freeway. The trees move side to side
while the leaves fall down
And move side to side and who
knows where they ever end up

Anthony Sanchez, Grade 10
Huntington Park College Ready Academy High School

Friends

We started out as friends who always had fun.
Then I got a crush and began calling you hun.
We've had our share of fights; you know it's true.
But despite the arguing, we still stuck like glue.

You see there's another guy, but we're too far apart.
Wish I could say it's a tie, but you have my heart.
You've hurt me before, but I couldn't stay mad.
I was even willing to introduce you to dad.

You made me feel things that were all new to me.
Every minute I spent with you made me feel so free.
What can I say, you were my first love.
There was only you, and no one else came above.

I understand that you just want to be my friend.
I just didn't expect you'd put "us" to an end.
I used to put on a smile to get me through the day.
Then I couldn't do anything but push you away.

To say I'm not sad would be a big lie.
Although moving on is hard, it's something I have to try.
Anything can happen, but it won't change how I feel.
Because one thing I know, is what we had was real.

Mayra Soto, Grade 12
Lucerne Valley Jr/Sr High School

One What? One O!

Graduation is finally here
Coming in as a freshman, leaving as a graduate
Adulthood is rapidly approaching, so much to fear
One what? One O!

Packing away pencils and reminiscing friends
Oh, how it went so quickly
Never thinking high school would come to an end
One what? One O!

Wearing a navy blue or white gown
Sitting in the scorching heat in the Bowl
Look around, not a single frown
One what? One O!

Walking across the stage with a goofy smile
Shaking the hand of past teachers
Receiving the diploma makes the ceremony worthwhile
One what? One O!

Grad Night is over, time to rest
Waking up tomorrow to the new life
My fellow graduates, I wish you the best
One what? One O!

La Dra Grissom, Grade 12
Redlands High School

High Merit Poems – Grades 10, 11 and 12

My Daily Life
Shoes are shattered,
So are laces missing.
School every morning,
It is not boring, but tiring.
Homework to be done with,
But parents still working.

Winds take the breeze,
Through the branches of trees.
Bunnies hop around the playground,
Like a party full of happy dancers.
The sky is blue, the grass is green,
But inside my body is pitch black to be fed.
Life is colorful,
But sometimes hurtful.

My loved ones are my strength,
My hated ones are my inspiration.
Day and night,
I stand to fight.
Through the struggle,
Of my daily life.
Edward Urtiz, Grade 12
Omega High School

Hectic
This time I'm done for.
All the time in the world…
Vanished like it was never there.
If I could go back?
No time.
Rush Rush Rush.
No time to waste.
And yet it all feels wasted.

I'm just eighteen.

How am I supposed to know?
Oh well.
All I have to look forward to
Is more of this.
James Frichner, Grade 12
Linfield Christian School

Blazing
Courage burns crimson.
Lighting human hearts,
Its blazing fire attempts
To brighten the gloom.

The flame glows strong
Like a beacon of hope,
A torch of lasting love,
It will never burn out.
Jason Kim, Grade 11
Saratoga High School

I Am
I am soft-spoken and gentle.
I wonder how you could look at me,
Straight in the eyes and lie.
I hear the faint tears in troubled souls.
I see what it takes to make it in life.
I am soft-spoken and gentle.

I pretend to be mean.
I feel strong and determined.
I touch the face of my crying mother,
I didn't mean to hurt her.
I worry that I'm going to be locked up again.
I cry when I make others disappointed.
I am soft-spoken and gentle.

I understand that it takes hard work and determination to make it in life.
I say that the past is the past, and I could never change it.
I dream that one day everyone could realize everything I have.
I try to make things right.
I hope I have what it takes.
I am soft-spoken and gentle.
Branden Gutierrez, Grade 11
Calaveras Hills High School

To Live Is to Die
To live is to die
for today is not a good day to live
for there is too much sorrow to be seen
there is not much to live for left in this world
and now there is very little to bear

This is the end of the line for us as we attempt to escape
we are prisoners of the darkness in the abyss that is the war
with no soul to live to tell what has happened to this world
all this I cannot bear to witness
the cruelty and evil that kills us all
only time will tell us how much we have left
how much longer will it take?

There is still time to stop the event from occurring,
with just enough to stop the catastrophic event,
the time limit is making everyone more and more claustrophobic by the second
until it sleeps, then the world will finally rest in tranquility
Ladislado Garcia, Grade 10
Huntington Park College Ready Academy High School

We All Make Mistakes
We all make mistakes
We all did things we regret and maybe been ashamed of
We all wished we could forget about our problems and let things go
But we shouldn't look back on things that happened that caused us misery
And life is like that it has its ups and downs and all we could do is keep looking forward
Evelyn Jaramillo, Grade 10
Huntington Park College Ready Academy High School

Meet Me*
Meet me on the dance floor,
we'll dance the night away.
Do what you want,
because tonight, it's all you.

Meet me on the dance floor,
we'll two-step a love song.
I'll steal your heart at
the final twirl of the dance.

Meet me on the dance floor,
I'll teach you the swing.
The room will be filled
with your happy laughter.

Meet me on the dance floor,
your love will be mine.
A dance and a smile
and I'll be yours too.
Samantha Hicks, Grade 11
Granite Hills High School
*Dedicated to Troy Smith

Bittersweet
Shuffling through amber photos
A box teeming with memory
Giggling notes and scribbled postcards
Passports filled with aimless travel
Nights spent on rooftops
Her eyes well and throat tightens
Words of a past life

Scrolling through forgotten files
A desktop saturated with office success
Impressive transcripts and deadlines met
Nights with caffeine and computer screens
His eyes glaze and mind wanders
Words of a lost life

They find the bittersweet hard to swallow
Trudy Vinson, Grade 10
Prospect High School

Halloween
Black-cats hiss
Witches fly
Blood drips
Vampires suck
Zombies awaken
People scream
Graveyards haunted
Maniac's ghoul
Ghosts boo!
Kids trick-or-treat
Andrea Zavala, Grade 11
Valencia High School

16 Years of Sorrow
Right now I feel abandoned
Right now I feel empty handed
Right now I wish I were someone else, somewhere else
How could you leave me speaking in stone language
Now, I will speak to you in blood language

As the thunder in my heart explodes
You will see rain drops pour from my eyes
When you wake day after day without the precious sound of laughter
You'll then see there is no before and after

Why did you leave me and mommy all alone?
Why did you leave us with such a heavy boulder?
Oh, I now know why...
March 27, 1993 changed your life

Right now I feel loved
Right now I feel that I am INVINCIBLE
Right now I know that my 16 years of sorrow is gone
Korina Serrato, Grade 11
CK McClatchy High School

My Existence
I am from a stack of nasty smelly clothes to never clean shoes
I am from big leafy trees to a jungle made out of grass
I am from ugly old cars to almost never seeing a new car
I am from a huge family that is always having a good time
To the memories of the loved ones that passed away
I am from my mom yelling "Pay attention!" to "Stop talking back!"
I am from my mom's super delicious posole to my gramma's tamales
I am from a house that has a lot of people to annoying rude neighbors
I am from noisy neighbors to screaming kids
I am from buying a lot of food to not knowing what to eat
I am from loud out going friends to never knowing what they will do
I am from playing outside to always having a good time
I am from the books under my bed
That have all my memories which never seem to end.
Maria Gonzalez, Grade 10
Valencia High School

Love Hurts More Than Hate
I thought that we would always last,
But I didn't think that our love would be stuck in the past.
And that is when I realized that what you told me was a lie,
And it hurts me even more from the inside.
Now all I have is a heart that is broken,
But the words "I Love You" are forever in my heart spoken.
Why did you come into my heart just to break it,
And your love was the only cure to fix it.
Now I can't stand the word love,
Because you just let it float away and above.
But there is one thing that I have learned after all our love has turned.
While I thought that our love was fate,
I realized that love hurts more than hate.
Roy Castro, Grade 10
Huntington Park College Ready Academy High School

High Merit Poems – Grades 10, 11 and 12

What Happened to Life?
Life…
Is it just a mission we are expected to complete,
or a journey we decide for ourselves?
How should we truly live life,
and how do we waste it?
An amazing gift placed in the palms of our hands,
and we cannot appreciate it for a moment.
What do we live for,
and how do we know it is worthy?
Do we live for him, her, or them?
Do we live without love,
or is it love that keeps us alive?
The lost art of morality trembles to the ground,
as terror of conformity rises above all else
What can we do to make a difference,
and would we be willing to make that change?
Krystal Smith, Grade 11
Saugus High School

Awakened
You are what you are
And what you are is like my shadow
Lingering next to me when life is at its brightest
And fading into the background
when darkness engulfs me

You are what you are
And what you are is like the moon
Enlightening me with your ghostly surface
But always keeping your distance

I am what I am
And what I am is like a bird
Dependent of you to survive
But now have grown up and can fly
Alberto Rodriguez, Grade 12
Azusa High School

Running Is My Retreat
My breath is running, my face sheer red.
My legs are weak, now they're useless.
The wind blows, hair swaying across my head.
Sweat drips down my face, I look like a mess.
Finish line close by, with each step of mine.
My body gets sore, as the heat gets worse.
Concentrate on running, past the wood pine.
Inhale oxygen, my lungs are the source.
Every time I run, the world passes by.
Running helps me solve all my troubles.
My choices seem to extend towards the sky.
Now walking uphill, with slow pace doubles.
Now I'm almost home, running down my street.
Finally here now, running is my retreat.
Brian Hechanova, Grade 12
Redlands High School

Forever
The very world would still be doing it.
Hoping to be correct.
You…you and the others would overthink, be pragmatic.
Be correct.
I believe the same as ever.
We'll open the deep and fall in,
There is no meaning to catch us.
That situation, destiny, it is
Today or tomorrow, or not the close future.
We wish for happiness, despite the world we'll hope forever.
I think we'll find that order of joy.
You say it will be tricky.
You see the small;
I tend to think about the universe,
It's endless deep embrace.
Let's think about being.
Let's think the end pragmatic.
Hope the end has reason,
Finds itself so deep it carries on forever.
It finds intrinsic hope;
It has no destiny to obsess over.
Marie Sbrocca, Grade 12
University Preparatory School

The Knock on the Door
We watch as her bubbly personality hides her fear.
We watch the growing distress she does not reveal.
Worry in her bright green eyes.
Worry in her bright red heart.
So many unanswered questions leave her waiting
Waiting for what?
The distance of the unknown does not move her.
No tears. No pain — yet.
A heavy pound on her front door awakes her spirit
No words, then only — "It's Daddy"
That was all that was needed,
to drop to their knees
to hold each other tight
to release the flow of tears.
We watch — helplessly, confused, motionless.
The sorrow in the air leaves us numb,
we watch the vacuum of despair replace hope.
Breathlessness.
How will she move on?
With the courage in her bright green eyes.
With the strength in her bright red heart.
Jessica Donyanavard, Grade 11
Saugus High School

The Ocean
Waves hit the water,
the sun hides in the ocean
and the wind's blowing.
Nestor Limon, Grade 10
Huntington Park College Ready Academy High School

You Are Perfectly Enough

Once a wreck and nothing more,
Sliced and broken there I was,
Hopelessly lying on the floor.
But as I began to pick up my strength,
There you were more brilliant than ever before.
You helped through my broken times,
And told me everything will be fine.
I listened and all was true,
Until the moment I began falling harder for you.
With a lot of talking and a lot of trust,
We became the two of us.
You're everything in and in-between,
With a brilliant smile beneath your teeth.
You really are my lucky charm,
Even though that is the corniest line.
But, in the end even if it all failed and died,
The feelings you give me are all I ever needed inside.
You're more than just any person,
But a person nobody can truly ever measure up to.
The one that gives that extra touch,
The one that makes seeing you perfect enough.

Rebecca Oronoz, Grade 12
Whittier Christian High School

War

Wars may change; for cause, for gain
But one thing remains the same — it never ends.
You can fight with words on padded seats
Lend the lives of our people to the ones who lie
Lend our money, our futures
To a cause without asking —
Unless you are asking for war?
You can fight with weapons in a desert far away
Shooting and burning, roasting and turning
With cold bullets and rich flames
For what gain? May I ask again?
It's not my war,
Nor my father's,
Nor my friends' —
Isn't it our land we're meant to defend?
Why gamble our money, our futures,
A means for an end?
Why not pay attention
To the will of we who watch helplessly?
Turn long enough, ignore the danger we pose,
And you might just face a war at home.

Ketti Schenck, Grade 11
Great Oak High School

I Just Want You to Know

Every day that passes, I feel that I love you more.
I feel thankful for the time we spend together,
I know and feel that you are my perfect sweet little angel.
I want to travel by your side…forever,
because I love you.
I just want you to know, how important you are to me,
knowing that you care and understand me,
that you trust and believe in me.
I just want you to know,
how wonderful it is having you as a lover,
knowing that you are always there for me.
There are those who are good friends,
and those who advise.
There are those who are lovable,
and those who are fun.
And then there is you,
you're all these in one and so much more.
I just want you to know,
that I know how wonderful you are,
that I care for you,
and that I'll always be there for you.

Johnny Esqueda, Grade 12
Artesia High School

In Love with Someone Else

I can't explain why it's him and not you,
But at the end of the day, babe, I just don't want to.
You see he's not a doctor and we always seem to fight.
He doesn't have the perfect body,
And sometimes he doesn't even treat me right.
So maybe you should go and find someone else
Who could treat you right and give you the world
That special girl
Someone who treats you like you treat them
Boy I knew there are plenty of women
Who would love to have a man like you.
But I'm in love with someone else.
Someone who understands the man you are
Because baby you shine so bright
And I would just dim your star.
If I could…could forget him, I would…please believe me
And I know what I should throw the towel in
But baby it's not that easy because my heart's all for him.
I know you'll never understand, that I'm in love with another man.
And I know it isn't right…
But I'm in love with someone else.

Larishia Kilgore, Grade 12
Omega High School

Beauty

I walk on the beach
Where the purest sea lays crisp and clean
Absolute beauty

Estefania Frayle, Grade 10
Huntington Park College Ready Academy High School

To Be a Leader

To be a leader,
One must first dream then act out,
Fulfillment is yours.

Jose Hernandez, Grade 10
Huntington Park College Ready Academy High School

High Merit Poems – Grades 10, 11 and 12

Untitled

Everything,
Nothing,
We are one,
And yet we are individuals,
We may seem important,
But we are not.

We are everything,
We are nothing,
And if we die
The world will go on.
Your death will not affect the world,
Will not affect what happens in the world,
Because we are nothing,
Nothing more then a dying cicada
Being pulled apart by ants.

And if you think that even when a butterfly
Flaps its wings affects things in the world,
Your wrong.
Because it's just an insect,
Which is just as insignificant as you.
Haley Barnett, Grade 11
Washington High School

What the Fairies Warned

Hear us, dear darlings:
Roses are Red
Violets are Blue
The Devil has horns
And Lilies do too
Demons they hide
In cute baby dolls
Concealing their whispers
In the Nightingale's call
Beware of the specter
Lurking around
It roams through the Cedars
Not making a sound
Sleep with one eye open
Dreading the Phantom
For He never rests
Once midnight has come
Smile those smiles
Sing gay songs
For They all are coming
And it won't be long
Magdalena De La Cruz, Grade 12
San Leandro High School

Dear Ostrich

Dear Ostrich,
You can bury your head in sand,
but the world still goes on without you.
Rikk Cavin, Grade 12
Eastlake High School

Generation Y

Dance little monster, dance on that barrier that separates you from insanity
Lovely don't fall, you wouldn't want to break your head
So your thoughts spill out on the dirty street paved with flies that never had a chance

Dear Queen of Past Requisites: There you sit on your throne of severed toes
Biting your dirty fingernails awaiting your pride to return

Vinyl hearts that love the same as platinum tin man ventricles fueled by oil
They don't beat — they tick.

Drip. Drip.

We taught our children how to set a time bomb so that they would get up in the morning
And love with limited capacity, robotically kiss us goodbye.

We're raising ultraviolet radiation
The future of our children blinded by high-capacity carelessness
Rational facts that rule out innocence

Would it take a stampede of wild dreams over our high-maintenance five-year-old sleeves
Corseted imaginations piled high with ingrown wires?

Look, partial advocate, theorize their thorn-covered feet
Rotting in your sleet colored dreams and allow your voice to run wild across their gazes.
Katie Brunner, Grade 11
Marymount High School Los Angeles

Transgenic Views

A world full of worlds not a planet, but of a place within
The current location and time where you may escape, not imagine
Although processed through dreams made not to life, but existence
In the space between spaces much like in your own mind resonance
Just in physical form, but adjacent to what you have never realized
As possible, where all is stable I believe where you are sent when passing

You may never destroy anything
Just reform it into what else is able
To be seen or not
It depends soulfully on perspective
What world you see it from
There is beauty in all, even to not live
All is different, including me and you
My eyes, to me, see what is true

Even if it's not to yours
This is where I will retain in my own view
Sad I must wait so long for this
To realize who I am too

What I am
Is here

Michael Whitley, Grade 12
Adelante Continuation High School

When I'm Gone

Whispers much too loud to be clandestine
You'd see the dark silhouette
Like a falcon trying to find its lost falconer
Girls in storybooks don't really exist
I've lost my voice, but did it ever matter?
Do you ever listen to your heart?
Mine only feeds me lies
I'm going to disappear, become invisible
Will you miss me when I'm gone?
Or will it be like now, moving too fast to see
I promise I'll miss you, it's not a lie
Will you remember our laughs and fun?
Leaves fall in the autumn months
Painted and written all over
It's burned at the edges
Ink dripping away, words lost in air
Safes filled with bittersweet memories
No longer lost in that happy dream
Awakened by harsh reality
I'll bid you farewell, maybe you'll hear
I'll miss you when I'm gone
Alex Bultsma, Grade 11
Whittier Christian High School

Death's Force

Death is force one does not see.
Its Nature a Reaper to be.
Why thee reap none know and
why thee deliver the final blow.
Death cannot be found as
death is strong all around.
For some death is a myth.
How could a force so sinister exist?
Death comes with an aura of dark.
An aura that seems to emit a hellish spark.
Some rise up with the power of light.
Only to fall to death's true might.
People try to keep death far from sight,
but memories bring back emotional fright.
You may run and you may hide, but
nothing stops death from reaching inside.
Noah Zubeidi, Grade 10
Visions in Education

Lost

In love that is lost.
Never shall be found,
Always will be sought.
Never shall be felt,
Always will be welcomed,
Never shall I have.
Always what I yearn for most,
My love that is lost.
Alexandra Razo, Grade 11
La Serna High School

A Purely Procrastinating Parody

White-crest pure pages sneakily snicker at my unsharpened unsure pencil
As that criticizing clock clicks away his weeping, wheezing breath.
Madrigals murdered by melancholic misery, mighty assurance annihilated.
Arrive the dearest death of healthy happiness!

Aloof dispassionate decisions darken the luster of my lucid light
As that worrying wind gives wings to the stronger, steadfast storm.
Cataclysms cloud the calamitous cognizance, corrupted mind made meek.
Run away, you risky, ruining repetitive repetitions!

Bloodletting letters and words scornfully skewering my poisoned potential
As deadlines drag my dilapidated death to dust!
Wiles wish away assuring actions, decisiveness defeated.
No! I will leave the barred barren brain, be clear of clichés!

Calm down. Calm down.
To free the mind is ever a task,
That we must throw away our mask
Of doubt and stress.
O! To only know to work
Without duress.
James Seifert, Grade 11
The Harker School - Upper Campus

I Am the Reaper

Have you ever felt a cold chill on a hot summer day?
Or a warm hand on your cheek as the cold wind blew?
Or that someone was watching your every move with the utmost importance?
Or an angry glare from afar when you're all alone?
These are a mortal's small signs of my world.
My world is neither heaven nor hell it is not on earth it is not alive.
Modern authors call them souls
these are the most accurate assumptions.
It is the part of humanity that lives after death

Most go to heaven
Few go to hell since even Lucifer needs his company
Most souls stuck in the middle world died quick tragic deaths
They are lost and confused and so full of envious hate of the living
My job is to persuade them to heaven or force them to hell
I have infinite shapes for I have to take the shape most comforting to the
Soul at hand.
I am from neither heaven nor hell,
I may have been human once, but I cannot remember that time
Yet I know what I am now
I am the Reaper.
Bryar McClellan, Grade 10
Bella Vista High School

High Merit Poems – Grades 10, 11 and 12

Invisible Lines

I search inside her hollow eyes,
And find that it is full of lies.
Everything she has ever known,
Has gone and left her all alone.
She doesn't know what to feel,
So she gets down on her knees and kneels.
She prays to God to end her pain,
And for Him to take away all the blame.
The fortress she once built so high,
Disappeared in the blink of an eye.
Intricate stories played out so well,
That no one could see she was going through hell.
From the outside she seemed perfectly fine,
But honestly she was crossing an invisible line.
Set to separate the real and the fake,
She wonders how much longer until she breaks.
Caught in a moment of give or take,
She finds herself fading away.

Brittney Maddox, Grade 10
Monache High School

Fighting for Life

Your embrace holds me tight
I'm fighting for my life with all my might
I can't stand having to go away
With you I know my heart will always stay
As they try to revive me from my unconscious haze
My mind puts all memories into a twisted maze
Looking up and barely seeing your horrified face
It becomes obvious this will be my last alive place
Reaching out to grab something to make me feel
The bullet is so deep that it could never heal
Never again I am able to speak what is on my heart
Consciousness is slipping away too fast, like a dart
Gripping to any last possible hope
The charts are quickly dropping down a dangerous slope
My brain starts giving up all around
I imagine your cries without hearing the sound
You will always be my one and only true love
I'm sorry I have to go now, but I'll be waiting for you, up above

Emily Fry, Grade 10
Foothill High School

Greed

Is want considered greed if other people need?
Is it wrong to feel happy while some kneel in sorrow?
How many people will die tomorrow?
While you think you have it bad, others have it worse,
And you just may have more money in your wallet or your purse
How can we be so self-centered,
While some are forced to starve with no dinner?
So while you're eating at your table,
Remember some remain unable.

Tawnya Rowland, Grade 12
Prospect Continuation High School

Heartless

I wonder what if I hadn't broken up with my girl.
I hear the wind blowing.
I see the clouds moving.
I want to make her happy.
I do everything to make her laugh.
I am lonely.
I pretend I am still going out with her.
I feel cold when she walks away from me.
I touch my heart.
I worry about her.
I cry every day.
I am lonely.
I understand what she feels.
I say everything to make her smile.
I dream my future to be her husband.
I try to get back together with her.
I hope I can still be friends with her.
I am lonely.

Xing Chen, Grade 10
Hiram W Johnson High School

I Am in Love with a Girl

I wonder about this girl.
I hear she has problems.
I see that she is sad.
I want to help her.
I do whatever I can to be close to her.
I am in love with her.
I pretend to look mad to get her attention.
I feel that she is someone I can talk to.
I touch her to see what she does.
I worry about her.
I cry from anger when I can't do something about it.
I am in love with her.
I understand her more every day.
I say that I don't feel anything.
I dream to be in her world.
I try to be with her.
I hope that she feels the same way.
I am in love with her.

Daniel Chavira, Grade 10
Hiram W Johnson High School

Alejandra

A mazingly cool
L emony yellow
E nergetic like a lion
J umpy around
A nnoyingly quiet
N erdy funny
D ecent and doesn't lie
R ocks like a party
A dorably nice

Ulises Castillo, Grade 10
Huntington Park College Ready Academy High School

Icarus

Dawn drowns out the moonlight,
Rooster out-yells the owl.
Girl wakes up, greets the day,
She says hi, hi, hi.

Girl stands in the doorway,
Stares at that orange glow.
Sees a hawk, watches it soar,
She asks, why, why, why?

The clouds thin out and melt away,
Letting blue sky shine through.
A breeze slips by, silky, smooth.
She sighs, sighs, sighs.

She thinks on back to Sunday.
Oh, how that old man was wrong.
He said no, no! You can't do that.
You lie, lie, lie.

She imagines she's on a mountain
She grows wings, she grows eyes.
She knows she can. She knows she will.
She's gonna fly, fly, fly.

Edward Gao, Grade 12
Redlands High School

Romeo and Juliet

So sad the way they die
They are in love and try, to fly
She acts dead but is only sleeping
As he's found beside her weeping

She waits and waits
Now it decides her fate
He doesn't get the note
That the love of his wife wrote

He tries to save his wife
For then she lost her life
She lost all hope
As he climbs up the rope

She looks so dead
In her bed
For then she finds a knife
After he loses his life

The knife now in her chest
They sleep for an eternal rest
Their love lasted forever
Now Romeo and Juliet lay together

Steffi Spencer, Grade 10
Lucerne Valley Jr/Sr High School

Troublesome Worries

I close my eyes and hope to wake
From what I seem to think is fake.
But when I look again I see
That *it* is still in front of me.
I mutter with a small, low voice,
Deciding on what be my choice.
Should I give up or should I try?
I choose to let out a long sigh.
The coming tasks will all be tough.
I know my time is not enough.
I need to finish, that I know,
But still I feel I work too slow.
My thoughts are dim, my feet are numb,
And everything just feels so glum.
Reluctantly I count the beats.
For energy, I eat some sweets.
I feel that I am close to done,
But really it has just begun.
And what is it that troubles me?
A game called Final Fantasy.

Tammy Young, Grade 12
Redlands High School

Fear and Love

Fear is at the heart of love,
Some would say
That one cannot love
Without first having feared
The one you call sweetheart.
But should it not be love
At the heart of all fear?
For what is fear but a threat to love?
When life is endangered
Is it not but a peril to the love of oneself?
And is not fear only but the chance
That you may lose that which you love?
If clear and present danger
Is to be a part of love,
Would it not be better to love despite fear,
Than because of it?

Kendall Cahill, Grade 10
Elk Grove High School

Baseball

Angels rock
Red sparkles
Players stretch
Fans cheer
Ralley-monkey jumps
Defenders catch
Home plate made
Fireworks burst
Team celebrates
People leave

Francine Ruiz, Grade 11
Valencia High School

Me

Looking through the window,
Reaching for the shooting stars.
Aiming higher than what I can achieve,
Trying to win it all.

Taking five steps ahead of time,
Ironically bogging me down.
Frustrations trapped inside my head,
My world is flipping out.

Where did I go wrong,
Wanting for the best of me?
Greediness blinding my head,
Why could I not see?

Backing up those five steps,
Ending where I used to be,
Instead of changing myself,
I should have stuck with me.

Stephanie Kim, Grade 11
Saugus High School

American Delusion

O! the unutterable pity
of living in a once majestic city
the angels
of what was,
blotted out by the greed and sin
of god's
Advancing Creation,
are held back

to stay hidden
behind the veil of the
American Flag

to fall short of the
American Standard

to be the forgotten wrinkle
on the face of the
American Delusion.

Elizabeth Monge, Grade 12
R K Lloyde Continuation High School

Boy/Girl

Boy
Handsome, lazy
Lying, selfish, acting
Jealous, mean — nice, honest
Behaving, respecting, loving
Beautiful, diligent
Girl

Khanh Nguyen, Grade 10
Hiram W Johnson High School

High Merit Poems – Grades 10, 11 and 12

Many Colors

Open that bag and look
all the colors that I took

A handful of joy
so sweet and delicious
the sacrifice is cavities
and becoming the biggest

Different packs
Different colors and flavors
There are so many to choose.

We don't have an age
Or a date to expire
To death do us part?
Yes, that I'd admire.

That everlasting desire
Chewing of the candy
Like a kid with sugar
Just plain and hyper.
Shontavia Miles, Grade 12
PAAL Campus

Learned by Example

You looked at me and laughed,
You told me I was pathetic.
And I just stared back,
Looking but seeing nothing.
My mind was elsewhere,
Seeing the previous six months.
Laughter, smiles, hugs, kisses,
Promises, dried tears, and the "I love you."
Those warm brown eyes,
The smooth gentle voice.
Those arms that held me tight,
The lips that brought me to life.
Now those brown eyes are cold,
The voice bitter and hard.
Now those arms push me away,
The lips are killing me slowly.
Someone asked me how I
Became so heartless.
I said that I learned by example,
As I watched you walk away.
Shelby Cron, Grade 12
Home School

Coloring My Hair

When I color my hair,
it makes me feel like a new day.
Blonde is like the bright sun
Red is like a rose
Black is like the midnight sky.
Andreah Foux, Grade 10
Vintage High School

My Memories

I am from baby food to Pro Club clothes
From PSP system in the afternoon to delicious orange flavor sodas

I am from an old red chair to a wonderful blue and black soccer ball
From a blue fast scooter to swinging baseball bats

I am from slick black cars to fast blue bikes
From nasty dirty parks to white building corporations

I am from a joyous cousin Caro to a marvelous cousin Ashley
From a noisy cousin Tito to my kind Aunt Ana

I am from God bless you to don't talk to strangers
From do your homework to don't be late for dinner

I am from shrimp flavor tamale to carneasade taco's
From barbeque ribs to sopes with chicken

I am from photo albums to video tapes
From boxes with secrets to my childhood memories
Brian Cruz, Grade 10
Valencia High School

Phoenix

Staring up at the night sky I wonder
Lying here amidst the grass I breathe in serenity
Dreaming of possibilities and then silence…
Quivering, I think of our creation
Who's up there, who knows?
The immensity of every life,
The simplicity of death
Yet the grandeur of stars propel me
Every waking moment children being born, lives continuing, despite others ending…
Is there rebirth? A judgment day?
Who will come with us, who will stay behind?
That decision unknown to us forever?
The immeasurable emptiness of knowing
The wind I take in, the taste of loneliness
The reality that time will someday be over floods my mind…
So instead are those bright tears thrown against a black canvas?
Tears cried for every loss
Realization costs too much,
But with love time can stand still and so the sky and I see each other,
But I can only see the world.
Maybelline Martez, Grade 12
Redlands High School

One Life

Out of the billions in the world
Millions in the US
Hundreds in my family
And the tens in my class
There's only one me and one life
Different from everyone ever in this world
Josh Hegwood-Kyle, Grade 12
Vintage High School

Tears

I have gone to a group home.
It's nothing like a sweet ice cream cone.
I had a lot of tears,
because I was overwhelmed with fear.
But now I am okay.
I will see my family another day.
Jason Maestas, Grade 10
Vintage High School

Sign Language Monkey
Yellow dresses flutter around
Why do I see them even still?

The salty wind wishes to be
Forever free within your heart

Guided by fate, cast into blue,
Frozen in red, leaving what nest?

The hummingbird wishes to be
Forever free within your eyes

Never alone so we are told
But always the truth is revealed

The grizzly bear wishes to be
Forever free within your mind

Always locked and split apart by
Conflicting soul with the key here
Felicia Travalini, Grade 11
San Luis Obispo High School

Senior Year
Panic is in the air
It would be easier if I didn't care
It's written all over my face
I wish everyone would get off my case
I feel like I'm the only one
There is no more time for any fun
Stress level's at its max
Boyfriend telling me to relax
The pressure is rising
Moving fast, not surprising
The struggle for survival
The battle between rivals
Losing myself
Predators using their stealth
As the prey all scatter
Your pride here doesn't matter
All regrets soon forgotten
Our hearts and minds broaden
The time is almost here
The end to our senior year
Nikki Orona, Grade 12
Lucerne Valley Jr/Sr High School

Cupcake
Like a shadow I crept slowly
Making myself unseen my
Target unknowing my enemy the same
Then I was in arm's reach I
Grab the cupcake and ran snickering
While my brother ran after me.
Cody Near, Grade 10
Vintage High School

No Real Name
My real name was stolen when I was ten and wanted to look in the playground.
My grandfather called me "Nena" and I was wandering outside the apartment building.
My name was on the concrete down the street when I was eleven.
My name was the dislocation of my thumb.
My homeboy called me "lil froggy" the nickname was passed down.
My name was good and funny but serious as well.
My cousin called me little one,
My name was always in the way.
My teacher called me intelligent.
My name was afraid of death.
My name was both Salvadorian and Mexican.
My name was daughter of Abdon who talked to me when I felt down.
My name was the laziness of an adult.
My real name is the freedom, the hope, the grace.
Elizabeth Martinez, Grade 10
Jane Addams Continuation High School

Potato Salad
My partna' went to jail.
Sad.
Wow.
Angry.
He robbed someone.
Blah.
He stole money and a phone.
I would feel like crap.
I wrote to him
I said, when you getting out?
I said, when you going to be
done with this shameful game?
You play, we are just going to live
our lives. When this sense of mind.
Makes me feel like crap when
You do these stupid things like
Rob someone. That ain't even
A person of guilt. Like it's worth it.
Don't do these stupid things.
Please get out of my shame.
Alex T., Grade 10
Sand Paths Academy

Where Fingers Meet Fame
Upon my hands the strings they lie
The tunes it sings will never die
Making its way into your brain
Can take away all of your pain
Steel string love affair through an amp
Up all night underneath a lamp
Melodies as thick as the soul
Can lift you out of your life's hole
But practice is what it will take
Because music you cannot fake
Scales its way to the top five
A fresh rock song that will survive
Mitch Grimes, Grade 10
Amador Valley High School

Eye Glasses
Constantly surrounding big round eyes
Held in place by a motley of colored frames
Feeling so cool on the face like ice
Hiding identity in shame.

Wherever I go I need your reflections
In order to see or else everything would
Be a mystery
If lost it would be a peril
You are the key for me
Constantly needed throughout eternity.

Although you get heavy
Making dents on the bridge of my nose
Itching my skin
With your wide brimmed pose
I can't help but to admit you were always
There for me
Through times of pain and suffering
Thanks to you I can see clearly.
Erin Rob, Grade 12
La Reina High School

Love or War
You can't have love
If you don't know war

You can't have peace
If you got no more

So stop running from the fight
And make victory
To end all the suffering and misery

Or better yet, end it now
For, you can make history somehow.
Mirna Hajjali, Grade 10
Options for Youth

High Merit Poems – Grades 10, 11 and 12

The Soul
Awakened by love, is the only time it comes out,
trying to break free from that evil of my own human flesh.
Escapes when love fills in, but my body is not satisfied;
it wants my soul back.
So this is why I wait until the end of time,
until I say goodbye
and goodbye to my own human skin.
Genevieve Crawley, Grade 12
Calvary Chapel High School

What Am I?
Here I sit, very still,
I see her through the windowsill

I gaze through my glossy eyes
Wishing only that I could cry

I wish I could move,
Or even make a peep
But I am only grateful
That I can watch her sleep

Things were so good
I thought the fun would never end
Then she grew into a teen
And I found a "different" friend

I promise to be more fun
The next time I come down
Until then, I'll wait here
Where I can be found

What am I?
I am a doll
Who will be there in the end?
When you need an old friend?
Brittany Bartholomew, Grade 12
Lucerne Valley Jr/Sr High School

Teeth vs Tooth
A sparkle within a cave
a tombstone on a grave
pure porcelain perfection
crusty corn-on-a-cob connection

a smile like when you first hear The Beatles
or perhaps a line of rusty needles
a row of parallel piano keys
a dash of bushy broccoli trees

the lovely fragrance of minty mouthwash
the stench of rotten onions and squash
brightly shining in the sun
all that's left is half of one
Hailey Hudson, Grade 12
Redlands High School

Watching. Waiting.
Watching. Waiting. For what?
For him to talk to me?
Only two conversations
since I met him.
Lasted only seconds.

Could I forget him?
Not important, right?

But I get a funny feeling
in my stomach
when I look at him.
My heart beats faster
at his name.
My eyes wander
to where he sits.

Can I forget him?
…No.

When will he talk to me?
When will I talk to him?

Is this feeling going away?
Or is it permanent?
Beatriz Alvarez, Grade 10
Bassett Sr High School

I Am From
I am from NYU
And 15 stories up Brooklyn.
I am from rainy winters
With some fried eggs cookin'
Curled up with angry cats
And twisting in the blankets.

I am from my bestest friends
And the movies that we'll make.
I am from the old pond with
Some heartbreak, Band aids, And books.

I am from the ocean
And the surfboard along with that.
I am from heated pools and big
Sweaters afterwards.

I am from the cult of Joss
With Buffy and Angel and Mal and Kaylee
I am from comic books and musty ink
And notebooks and pens
From saxophone and piano.

I'm from forever.
I'll always grow.
Susanna Sabin, Grade 10
Blair High School

Not a Day

There's not a day that passes;
When I don't think of you.
I may not say it
I may not even show it,
But trust me
You mean everything to me.
Everything I do reminds me of you,
Listening to a song
My eyes start to tear
Laying in bed; forgetting you're gone,
I wait for hours, for your arrival.
I may not say it
But I miss you dearly.
Weeks and months pass
Still no call waiting.
I love you, and
There's not a day that passes
When I don't think of you.

Ambyr Madison, Grade 10
La Sierra High School

Unfinished

This poem is unfinished —
it has something to say.
It's not like other poems.
It doesn't try to be the best
at rhyming
or flowing
or making people sigh.
If it did it might get caught
in a world of unclear identities.

This poem is not what
I thought it should be
when I started it.
It seemed to hold the key
to some great revelation.
but I found out it's like me —
still learning;
unfinished.

Caitlin Taylor, Grade 12
San Lorenzo Valley High School

A Better Tomorrow

Look for a new tomorrow
Because whatever's got you down
Might make you drown
Don't look back at the memories you had
You may do something bad
Instead look for a new day
You may meet a girl, by the way
But please don't just lie there in bed
Because you never know
Tomorrow might be a better day

Mario Flores, Grade 12
Maxwell High School

The Fear

I'm afraid that I will never live a life
so fulfilled and loved by my soul,
that I will never see magic
and live to tell a tale that great raconteurs would envy.
I'm afraid
that my once happiness will never come back,
but instead fade
and blur as if never once there,
and I'm afraid
that I will never steer clear of the traps and "deceivements" in my way.
I'm afraid
that I won't be able to stick to my likings,
the likings that something beautiful can majestically hold,
that I will be the first one to sink…or worse,
the second one that suffers.
I'm afraid
that I will never be honest in the eyes of myself.
I am afraid
that I will never have the mental stability of the person I pretend to be,
and my hands will be perpetually placed against my head,
ducked down in silent solitude.

Gloria Escamilla, Grade 11
Schurr High School

Blue Green Ocean

The oceans of Earth take on shades of blue, green, brown, and red
Beneath every shade there lies a world in which humans have only dreamed of
Mammals, and fish, plants and cells, all congregate to form one beautiful life force
The whale is seen to be the biggest of all
Lumbering smoothly around the great ocean hall
The shark slowly follows driven mad by hunger
Desiring and searching for some organic plunder
The Barracuda cuts through the blue, a bright silvery streak
It's as fast as the wind, but with grace and conceit
The reef formed by coral is teaming with activity
It is the home for fish families living with passivity
Their life is beautiful, but not free from troubles
Humans have made perfectly sure, to burst their little bubbles
Unless action is taken, and the oceans are saved
The oceans we know will be dried out, damp caves

Lee Menke, Grade 12
Redlands High School

Love Is the Best Thing in My Life

Love is the best thing in my life because of you
Without you my life is nothing
Every time I look into your eyes it's like looking into my future
And every time you look into mine you're looking into a life of love and happiness
When I see you smile my heart tells me I did good
And when I have that feeling I'm the happiest guy in the world
When I think of our future together I see you and me living our fantasies
And when I think of you my life is the best
So I just want you to know that you're my everything
And you will always be in my heart.

Lesley Ocampo, Grade 10
Huntington Park College Ready Academy High School

High Merit Poems – Grades 10, 11 and 12

Stories

I see the books
jump off their shelves
and telling me their tales.
Each book diverse.
From old to new
all talked amongst themselves.
The classic tales,
the old books said,
withstood the test of time!
The modern age,
the new argued,
will make the future shine!
As for me,
each book I see
were no better than the rest.
Stories told,
and tales to be,
I will always find the best!
Richard Wong, Grade 10
Abraham Lincoln High School

Autumn

A pocket of wind
Takes a leisurely stroll
Not hot, not cold
Not here, not yet
One leaf —
Tinged with tawny

Treetops court in rustle
Fresh air passes through nose
Cool, brisk, not yet biting,
Breezes dance and play

Leaves now bleed with emotion
Technicolor crimson and gold
Light of October,
Sunset of summer,
Autumn returns today.
Michael Lai, Grade 12
Redlands High School

I See You

sweat stained brow
creased with worry
because not all
problems go away
easily
and money doesn't grow
on trees
Aidan McCown, Grade 12
San Lorenzo Valley High School

My Buddy

Man, it is Mayne (cold) out here but you know, it gets like that,
I felt sad when I lost my buddy, my buddy was real close to me,
They took my buddy from me.
They said my buddy don't listen,
They said he was dangerous, when they took him I started to get mad,
but I stopped myself. I looked and said you're going to come home soon.

My buddy was by my side everywhere I went, when I went to get something to eat,
He went to get something to eat, he started to get hungry, so we had to eat.

I wrote my buddy and said, "What's up? How've you been? I miss you, buddy."
"I ain't seen you in a long time. What they talkin' 'bout with you?"
"I'm still holding up waiting for you to come home.
I be out there waiting for you to call and say, "Buddy, I'm home, I am home."
So I sit and wait for you to come home, my buddy."

We washed the car together
and got money together.
So I wait for him to come home.
Adrian Morgan Landers, Grade 10
Sand Paths Academy

Departure

I understand complex formulas
And the recipe for trees
She said and I
Remembered only her shirt
As we planted it in the front yard
Our shovels turning up the earth like cheap arterial clots and she said I
Don't want to part with it and I
Don't want to be responsible
I only want to sit and watch the news
And tell myself only once that
My shirt no longer smells of cheap vodka staining red vinyl seat covers
And I will tie back my sleeves
And get ready to work with my spade and shovel
When the whistles call our names
Parth Raval, Grade 12
Redlands High School

New Generation

I am from a big plasma TV to watching AVP
From molé and enchiladas to late night sandwiches
I am from fresh vegetables to storing water bottles
From dirty barbeque stands to cobwebs under chairs
I am from a quiet neighborhood to dark alleys where no one lives
From the shiny clean cars to shady trees that keep me warm
I am from my parents Francisco and Sugey to my brother Efrain
From my sisters Flor and Perla to my uncle Manuel
I am from tamales that taste like chicken to the Tacos my family loves to make
From the posolé that my mom makes during Christmas to delicious spaghetti with cheese
I am from a childhood memory to a toy box to remember the past
From the photo album to a new generation
Ariel Torres, Grade 10
Valencia High School

I Feel Like an Insomniac

Staring at the ceiling, what do I see?
I know the ceiling is there, but I cannot see him.
Dark wants to let me be free
But this disease that grips me like a tree
When her roots are unmoving and dim
Will not let me feel at ease

A curious light shining in the distance from my window.
No, it's just the moon, she never abandons my presence
As my impatience starts to grow
I start to think of the day that won't allow me to let go
Of all the stress going on in what is now my past

I'll think of something to make me feel like the end of a day is near.
I'll think that I am in Venice, upon a small boat in the river.
I see a shadow, and I think of my worst fear
No, it's only my chest of drawers, fooling me with his mirror.
Don't stare at the clock, it will only increase this fever.

How long will it be 'til dawn?
Will I fade into you before the sun shines bright?
These shadows that lurk and cause no harm
I am sick of counting sheep in the farm.
I just want to go to sleep and think of nothing but what is the night.

Veronica Sanchez, Grade 10
Huntington Park College Ready Academy High School

Kirgra

Kirgra black
Kirgra white
Kirgra dance on this snowy night
Move you feet to the beat of the drum
All until the rise of the morning sun

Kirgra day
Kirgra night
Kirgra howl with all your might

Sing the song of the gleeful wolf
Dance the dance of the happy fox
Spread your fingers as you spread your wings
Twist your body as you twist your scales
All to some avail

Kirgra me
Kirgra you
Kirgra lives in me and you
That one piece of our soul that dances and sings
Howling to the moon
Laughing at the wind
All so silently
Yet within

Iesha Isaac, Grade 12
Weber Institute of Applied Sciences & Technology

Thank God

I thank God that I am still alive
We all live in a crazy violent world
I pray that I will see the day and light

I also thank Him, 'cause I still have rights
Because of this I am in the twirl
I thank God that I am still alive

Even if I'm down I keep my pride
For it is my time to get out of the curl
I pray that I will see the day and light

Because of all of this, I love my might
I play with squirrels, and love pearls
I thank God that I am still alive

And my might helps me survive at night
And I know it's time to keep my rights sorted
I pray that I will see the day and light

For God is my helper and my life
I'm going to keep my life sharp like a sword
I thank God that I am still alive
I pray that I will see the day and light

Deion Calhoun, Grade 11
PAAL Campus

Peace and Serenity

I need peace and serenity.
A quiet and safe place.
A secret garden to which I hold the key.

My haven, my one sanctity,
where the metronome keeps a steady pace.
I need peace and serenity.

A place where I'm lost in infinity,
gone without a trace.
A secret garden to which I hold the key.

There I would spend an eternity,
drifting into space.
I need peace and serenity.

Relaxing, I sleep under a tree,
giving up chase,
a secret garden to which I hold the key.

There I would forever be,
lost in brilliant grace.
I need peace and serenity,
a secret garden to which I hold the key.

Jennifer Serrato, Grade 11
Encore High School for the Performing Arts

High Merit Poems – Grades 10, 11 and 12

The Indian
Branded by your diversity,
Bound together, only to be dismembered,
Born into a world abundant in dismay.

Sing, dance, be, the sorrow,
Sacrifice yourself,
Suffer in solitude.

Possess the power to be greater,
Prosecuted for your gallantry,
Persistent in finding your gambit.

Counting the crossroads,
Challenging your circumstances,
Conforming to cope.

Loathed for a secret magnificence,
Lugubrious, tired of being malleable,
Life long imprisonment, from the mordant men.
Raven Perry, Grade 11
Apple Valley High School

The Sea
He walks upon the seaweed-strewn deck.
The salty air assaults his face.
As he strolls, he remembers a time
When the sea was calm and the world
Was at complete peace.
Now all he sees are endless typhoons.
The roaring cannons of the ships
Fill his mind with terror.
As though the broken hulls
Of the ships have risen again.
To continue their foolish war.
But there is nothing left.
All was destroyed in the catastrophic struggle
For dominance.
With a sigh, he turns to walk away,
Not noticing as he starts to walk,
The golden rays that pierce the carnage
And boil away the layers of remorse
Buried at the bottom of the sea.
Colin Kerford, Grade 12
Blair High School

Every Moment…
Every moment of my life
I thank the Lord for everything
He gave me.
Every moment I look up at the sky
Thinking "What wonderful parents you gave me"
Not because I am forgetful but because
I remember what beautiful and amazing
Things you've done, but I don't appreciate it
Carmen Mendez, Grade 12
Omega High School

We'll Take the World
We'll take the world someday,
when our fathers before us are withered and gray.
The leaves may falter and fall,
but the tree still stands strong and tall.
They leave us the problems, the burdens, the pain.
We clean up their messes and erase the stain.
The stain that was left on a world so pure.
They came along, now we are the only cure.
We are the hope for a planet so broken.
We must say the words that were never spoken.
We'll take the world someday.
The debt we'll have to pay.
Look at your children and open your eyes.
Tell them what's real, tell them no lies.
They'll take the world sooner that you think,
an important part, a missing link.
They'll open a door, they'll start to mend.
Hold on, now, it's not the end.
Nicole Turner, Grade 10
Foothill High School

Don't
Why is it that when you don't
belong, you see what the others don't.
When you're alone, detached from the world,
where do you go? You don't.
Random trains of thought may take you
where you want to go, but usually they don't.
Do you ever feel alone in a crowded room?
I'd be lying if I said I don't.
When someone turns their back on you,
do they ever really come back? They don't.
If your backwards is your forwards,
then when others conform you don't.
When your past is your present,
where lies your future? Do you know? I don't.
I know I said I'm happy, I'm not.
I know I said I love you, I don't.
Feel like I'm wandering through a distant woods.
Where do you belong when you don't?
Mariah Woods, Grade 12
Encore High School for the Performing Arts

My Grandma
I remember the sweet smell of the food she used to bake every day
I am an unhappy girl that used to live with her
And always the big smile on my grandma's face
I feel lucky to have her with me
And how significant she is
I always appreciate her care and love
When I hug her my heart pounds slowly
I'm eager to see her again
But I remember my beautiful country and its sweet smell and
The innocent girl I was
Heidi Galisia Tellez, Grade 11
Hiram W Johnson High School

Life's a Long Road

Life's a real long road,
Many mistakes are made,
It may just be a big load,
But we can all change

What will your life bring you?
What decisions will you make?
Some people are successful,
Some people are big fakes.
We all have a purpose,
That's what God meant for us.

We live down that long road
Our whole entire life,
We can be filled with pleasure,
We can be filled with strife.
We can be filled with love,
This is our big long life.

'Cause life's a yellow brick road,
Each giant step we take,
Determines where we will go,
In God's big giant game.

David Goodman, Grade 10
Riverside County High School

That Time of Year

Christmas is that time of year
When family and friends gather.
A time when there is no fear
And everyone would rather
Be together and share their love.

Christmas is that time of year
When each one tells the other,
"Merry Christmas to my dear"
When everyone's our brother.
We are together and share our love.

Christmas is that time of year
When children's eyes are shining.
They know that Santa's time is near
And in the malls they are lining
To share Santa's love.

But Christmas is that time of year
When we really should remember
That the Savior's birth is really here
On this special day in December.
He came to share His love.

Annie Morrell, Grade 12
Mater Dei High School

Death Clock

Maybe days
From my own demise
Should I just sit and wait
Or should I open up my eyes

All these thought
Pollute my mind
Am I to stand idle
and wait for death to take me
Or am I to run against
and fight it away

What has caused
This grim train of thought
Is not my own demise
But the demise of others

All along, I sit and think
Not noticing that
All that is valuable
Is leaving me behind
In a cloud of worry and confusion
All is well
'till the death clock chimes.

Kaitlynn Pecka, Grade 11
Valley High School

The Light Calls You

Walk away into the gentle light
Warm and comforting, akin to the night.
Don't turn around, nor fear regret
You owe no one any debt.

Free from a constricting embrace,
There is a new world for you to face.
No weights upon your shoulders ride
Now is the time to turn the tide.

As years passed by you fought so hard,
And your heart, I know, was marred.
Your time was like a river, swift.
It swept you up, then left you adrift.

Now you are to find peace at last.
Don't fear the unknown, for it too will pass.
In that Eden above you are sure to thrive,
And below I'll keep your memory alive.

Your time is gone, as tears fade in the rain,
But with your passing eases your pain.
And for you, I will be strong
Hoping to join you in years along.

Brianna O'Leary, Grade 12
University Preparatory School

Shattered

A sudden slip and I'm falling,
Through the air.
A sudden glance and she's calling,
"Oh no, you'll break — !"

Tumbling, soaring, leaping,
Through the air
I'm on the ground and it's seeping,
Seeping through my hair.

Over my head and all over me,
Slipping through the cracks of my fingers.
Finally, finally free
Of its confines, the body of water.

She dries my fingers
With a white bathroom towel
And yet the feel lingers
As the towel soaks with it.

I'm lying on the floor,
So I rise, and survey
What was once a glass of water.

Tamara Takeshita, Grade 12
Alameda High School

I Will Rise Above…

I will rise above
his comments and criticisms,
his discouragements and put downs,
his hatred and jealousy.

I will rise above
by making myself:
harder, better, and stronger,
than before.

I will rise above
by staying calm and composed,
and uninfluenced by his opinions.

I will rise above
but not boast or brag,
but show him I am able,
without his help.

I will rise above
not with vengeance or retribution,
but with proof that I can become
what he can only dream to be.

Shannon Valdizon, Grade 12
Redlands High School

The Grand Facade
Do you know me?
Can you tell
What lies beneath the surface,
Who is really the rebel?
Be careful what you promise me,
I will twist it to suit my intent.
I have no mercy for you,
So do not expect it
From someone who is Hell-sent.
An angel on the outside,
Devil through and through.
Do not come to me with your problems,
I cannot fix you.
Anger will bubble beneath
But, smiles are all you see.
You'll never open your eyes
Because I know you are blind to my deceit.
So walk the path my feet have trod.

You'll never truly understand.
You'll never see behind my grand facade.
Naomi Cahn, Grade 10
Kehillah Jewish High School

Beautiful Psyche
Beautiful Psyche
Full of passion
Your beauty was a curse
For Beauty herself resented you
And sent her son Love to punish
But No!
Love had fallen under your spell

Placed in a secret marriage
Your curiosity would hurt you
You turned to Beauty for help
She only put you through torture
Curiosity again came and brought pain
But Love came again to save you
Adam Massimiano, Grade 12
Redlands High School

The Owl
Oblivion is my world as I dream
I will never be just like you it seems
A world has been created in the base
Of my mind, stars illuminate the place
My bed is a cloud that carries me there
A small child again, I leap on a dare
Once in the night world where I go to play
I black out the troubles that plague my day
At night there is just stars, nothing is foul
In this world I am free; I am an owl
Alexandra Sysol, Grade 11
Grossmont High School

I Look Out My Window...
I look out my window, the leaves are changing.
Summer has left me and fall is just beginning.
The tree outside my house once a lush green, now
appears on fire; red, orange, purple, and yellow.
They dance in the wind as they wait to fall.

I look out my window, the leaves are gone.
Fall is over and winter has begun.
The sky is filled with gray clouds, the trees are naked and empty,
and the wind is cold; I shiver.
Snow blankets the lawn, fresh and untouched.
The wind blows through the trees, the wind blows through the streets,
the wind blows through the city, waiting for spring.

I look outside my window, the snow has melted
and spring has finally come.
The birds fill the air with song, the flowers reach toward the sunlight,
the leaves begin to sprout from the branches.
The tree outside my house, once dead, alive again with blossoms.
The air is fresh and new; the sun bright and warm;
a new beginning has come.

I look outside my window, the leaves are changing...
Alyssa James, Grade 12
Redlands High School

Walking Wounded
Why do you hide behind that mask you wear so well
Pain deep within silently screaming
Wishing to be dealt with somehow, your heart aches with heaviness profound
Wanting to be rescued but deceiving the ones all around

Why do you linger in those dark rooms of your life
You're walking wounded trying not to show it; suppressing your hurt with so many drugs
Hoping for a relief in return; relief so temporary leaves you craving more
Destroying a destiny that has so much more in store

Your life slowly slips away
Denying the danger that's at hand; pride so elevated
Afraid to let your guard down; your emotions like stone
How will this heart ever mend

Stop pretending, stop defending like everything is alright
I can see your anguish behind that disguise
I can feel your pain just from looking into those eyes
Eyes; like a window to the soul that is burning out wondering if it will ever be saved

Why do you hide behind that mask you wear so well
Pain deep within, silently screaming as you die from the result of your own living hell
Esther Lopez, Grade 11
San Pedro Sr High School

I'll Be Here Forever

I spot a beauty far away from me,
realizing that I finally found her.
Despite all of the uncertainty,
my mind was in a blur.
You were there in the open, no one by you to hold,
all the love that would never stay,
and all of the stories you've ever told,
disappeared quickly in the fray,
and leave you stranded in the cold.
I run to you in open arms,
hoping to hold and love you soon,
as the essence of you're being,
reminisces with the moon.
You tremble and you stutter,
your body is filled with fear,
emotions start to flutter,
but don't worry I'm here.
I'll hold you forever,
my love is an abyss,
our hearts will endeavor,
by that one special kiss.
Spencer Ortega, Grade 11
Saugus High School

Soccer Miracle

You wait for a great moment, and that moment arrived.
The fans are nervous, all you can think of is the end of the game.
Throughout the game there is faith and prayers to God.
At the same time you feel proud of your country's effort.
It has been a long journey for every player.

The journey is almost over and your country is losing
The game and a feeling to show that they can.
You wait for a miracle, that miracle never came along with
The already lost dream of being champions. After the game
On the field you see the devastated faces of the team who had
A dream. Some of the players even have tears in their eyes.
All you can think of is "work, struggle, fight, and play hard
On the field for nothing." But there will be more soccer
Games to win and to prove people wrong who didn't believe.
Yadira Hernandez, Grade 10
Huntington Park College Ready Academy High School

The Heart's Black Knight

The Black Knight, as bright
As the sun, enters the blood stained field
In the darkness of war, he is a light
To those with no blades, he is a shield
He is their arm and fist
He blockades a tyrant's flame
For without his defense, they would not exist
That is the Black Knight's true aim
Although his armor is dark as night
His heart is pure as light
Miles Nossett, Grade 11
La Serna High School

Jason

Today will be the first year without you here,
We try not to shed any more tears,
To be strong,
So that we will be able to move on,
Your life was barely beginning,
At the same time it was ending,
God wanted you home because that's where you belong,
Watching down on us with a smile on your face,
With the angels in heaven,
And the big golden gates,
Memories we will remember,
Laughter we will share,
Our love for you will always be here,
Till that day when it comes,
When we will all be one,
A family again and this time it won't end,
You will be there, and we will be here,
Living life and shedding no more tears,
We will never forget you Jay,
How could we?
Our love for you is eternity.
Jasmine Perez, Grade 12
Prospect Continuation High School

Just Love

I need you here by my side
To help, to hear, to see, to guide
You cannot leave cause you know I am in need
For someone who can help me grow this fragile seed
The seed of love
To help me know
That I could live in affection
and not all alone
I could watch you forever
Until I die
I could watch for hours as time passes by
Please stay I need you now
I'll love you forever that is my vow
Come stay and spend eternity with me
And together we will live in perfect harmony
Jasmine Raymundo, Grade 11
Providence High School

So Many Things

So many things I want to tell
If only you knew that I want to yell
So many emotions, so many thoughts in my head
I don't know where to start
So many things I want to say, things that come from the heart.
If only you knew I was misled
By the feeling I can't express
This makes me stress
The fact that I love you
Which I want to pursue
Luis Soler, Grade 10
Huntington Park College Ready Academy High School

High Merit Poems – Grades 10, 11 and 12

One State of Mind
Passion, Heart, and Intensity, he said,
Will take you anywhere you wish
As long as you believe that the finish,
Is the most important part of the race.

Passion, he said, is pure love
While you run in never leaves
And when you walk it unweaves,
But when you are unvarying, it's constant.

Heart, he said, is the power within
To use your fire to succeed
Allowing your skill to be a deed
For those who never had the strength.

Intensity, he said, is that great energy
Found within your emotional connection
That pushes you in a positive direction,
So you can win the fight, take the heat.

She replied to his words calmly saying,
"I've come this far and touched the stars,
Seen the worst and come in first, so
Thank you Dad, for showing me right."
Kimberly Micheletti, Grade 12
University Preparatory School

My Skateboard
My skateboard can help me ride.
Just down the street we glide.
My skateboard can take me places,
And there we see many faces.

My skateboard has four wheels,
To help me get up steep hills.
My skateboard can be really fun.
We skate all day in the hot sun.

My skateboard gives me many falls,
Sharp turns and running into walls.
My skateboard can grind on rails,
Board slides, nose grinds it never fails.

My skateboard can do an ollie,
And oh yeah his name is Polly.
My skateboard does a bunch of tricks,
But be careful of running over sticks.

My skateboard is my best friend,
I and he will ride to the end.
My skateboard will one day die.
'Till then we shall fly.
Brenton Haynes, Grade 12
Riverside County High School

I Do Not Hate You
I do not hate you, I really don't
He only saw you, never noticed me
How could he
You were perfect
I do not blame you

You made him happy
It's all that mattered
Even though my heart shattered
He loved you so, it made him smile

You broke his heart
It was inevitable
He was breakable
You took his smile
It broke my heart

His heart remains yours
I crave it so, yet it hurts to know
You make his heart beat
When I could never

I do not hate you
I simply can't
Cristina Patlan, Grade 11
Christian Brothers High School

Once Upon a Time
Once upon a time there was a marriage
Divorce
Once upon a time there was love
Hate

Once upon a time there was kindness
Cruelty
Once upon a time there was truth
Lies

Once upon a time there was peace
War
Once upon a time there was friendship
Acquaintances

Once upon a time there was joy
Sorrow
Once upon a time there was perfection
Sin

Once upon a time there was light
Darkness
Once upon a time there was normality
Change
Melanie Gaston, Grade 11
Saugus High School

What I Feel
I don't know what to feel,
I just don't know what is real?
It feels like a wheel,
Because I don't know how to steer,
My life is going crazy.

I just don't know what to do,
I've got to let go and tell you.
My life is out of line,
I don't know whether I live or die,
Because of my mistake.

I want to know what others might say.
Say to my life and pain,
Should I give up or fight?
Tell me how it feels,
To have the wheel spinning

Tell me what to do,
And I will thank you.
When I let you know,
I just don't know how to feel
But this feels real.
I understand how to be real.
Justin Dennis Wagner, Grade 11
Riverside County High School

The Night You Left
The light shines across the
Reflection of the pond,
And the visions of our
Lives together stream before us.

Your face flashes before my eyes,
And our past blinds me.
The fact that you left
Scars me for life.

Silence sweeps around us,
And the colors of the night
Are visible to the love
Of our eyes as they glance together.

I imagine the memories
With the rain drenching my cold face,
And the city lights
Shining into your perfect eyes.

I feel your embrace even though
It was only a dream of the night
When you were taken,
Away from us to a better place.
Kezia Howard, Grade 12
Redlands High School

Dwelling

remnants of my past
come back
to haunt me

wounds long forgotten
are cut
and reopened

a crestfallen angel
knowing not
what I desire most…
the burning of your soul
or the yearning of your hold

contemplation drags me
into an abyss
of darkness…
a rumination
of unwanted recollection

Teresa Ortiz, Grade 11
Schurr High School

The River

The river keeps a flowing
Faster than I'd like.
Feelings of yesterday float along
The bird has learned a brand new song.

The river keeps a flowing
Boiling hot with hate.
I stick my feet in…and burn
I wonder if I'll ever learn?

The river keeps a flowing
Rapids strong and fierce.
I struggle not to let go
I really must let him know.

The river keeps a flowing
Why can't I do the same?
Even when that river is gone
I'll still be stuck holding on.

Jocelyn McMahon, Grade 12
San Lorenzo Valley High School

Beauty

Beauty
Confident, energetic
Laughing, smiling, joking
Fair, happy — disappointed, sad
Looking, depressing, wanting
Jealous, proud
Ugliness

Phuc Tran, Grade 10
Hiram W Johnson High School

In Memory of a Ballpoint Pen

We are gathered here today
To put a dear friend away
In that circular coffin it shall lie
Until Wednesday when the trash man may take it, I cry
O the unwritten words that die with this cherished tool!
To those who swear by Microsoft Word: You are all fools!
What other device would give its very blood so selflessly?
At the flick of a wrist, all too willing
Doodles, essays, no matter how drilling!
We should all be ashamed for the ink we have misused
Crossing out sentences we have abused
Idly sketching hearts or flowers to keep ourselves amused
Surely the legacy of this great device is not to be confused
Every one of you can surely remember
Sleep deprived nights with homework, ready to surrender
But who never left you, even when the pet parakeet had gone to bed?
That ever present ball point pen, ink flowing red
For your death my history notes are to blame
Now we can only hope your brothers in the value pack can live up to your name.

Lilly Clew, Grade 10
Whittier Christian High School

Daddy's Little Girl?*

— Thunder strikes —
I don't think he ever really cared
I know he tries his best
I cried so much, every day
He makes my life so great
I tried to escape, he held me back
I am always helped to fly
I grew up too fast; raising the man I called "Dad"
He wants me to grow up slow, like "Daddy's little girl"
I left the pain; it wasn't hard
I'm home, welcomed with open arms
I hold no grudge
Because he raised me well.
— Sunshine follows —

Devon Maier, Grade 11
Grossmont High School
*A comparative poem between my biological father and my stepfather

Magnificent

The gentle wind rustled the birch trees,
And the leaves sparkled in the dazzling sun.
Everything was still, except for the faint singing of a bird.
The cumulus clouds above were as white as linen,
And formed accidental figures that contrasted the azure sky.
The sun, projecting warmth and light, shone upon the harlequin grass,
As well as my face.
The vibrant shades of the flowers, mixing into the other,
Reflected the glorious season.
As I lay motionless, absorbing the beauty around me,
I felt a tingling sensation.
And at that moment, I knew I had reached my spot of serenity; I felt complete.

Aleks Stasiuk, Grade 12
Redlands High School

High Merit Poems – Grades 10, 11 and 12

The Life of a Penny
The penny is lonely.
It languishes under couches
in between car seats
in the back of our wallets
and the back of our minds.

The penny is jealous.
Never glorified in a coin toss
worth less than every other coin
it longs wistfully
for the silver luster of its counterparts.

The penny feels unwanted.
Credit cards make them obsolete,
parking meters don't accept them.
When the poor mother fumbles for her pennies
at the front of an endless line
the penny is ashamed that it is a nuisance
and wishes it was never created.

I wonder
are there any pennies in our midst?
Richard Chung, Grade 10
Harvard-Westlake School

Man's Successor
Iguanas, so noble and carefree
They run through God's green pastures
And bask in the glory of their achievements.
Iguanas don't discriminate or start wars,
They are too preoccupied with eating insects.

Iguanas, the ideal man
For they enjoy life and all of its pleasures,
And value even the smallest insect.
Iguanas fight when they have to,
But usually try to abide by peace.

Iguanas, the perfect creature
For they encompass all that life can offer.
The only creature that iguanas need to learn from are,
Other iguanas.
Denis Geary Lopez, Grade 12
Redlands High School

A Fool's Dream
His hand softly brushed against my cheek.
The thought of it takes my breath.
He looks at me with his deep hazel eyes.
On his lips waits a kiss so soft, it may weep.
I wake, realizing my fantasy is foiled by a dream.
A dream, crushing my perception of reality.
Tomorrow brings a new reality
Tomorrow brings a new dream.
Geena Bakotich, Grade 11
La Serna High School

Granada
Boys, their skin flecked like worn canopy. They watch
The good soldiers, in starched white uniform,
Pockets pressed and
Sleeves cuffed.

The rain tiptoes across cobblestone, past
Forlorn alleyways, vacant cinemas. There,
Violins yawn across rooftops. Goat hooves clack
Like teeth.

Mothers, they watch too, the soldiers in their
Waxed black shoes. Their
Pretty, scarred faces.
They swat the flies suspended
On rice paper wings.

Nuns walk like whispers, lisping epitaphs
Of the eternal and internal.
The ghosts of Granada and their hail Mary's,
Cadillac's engine snarling like the vagrant mutts.

Rosaries strike chests,
Barreling fog grates the horizon.
A soldier lights his cigarette and
Washes the sky with his gaze.
Sayre Quevedo, Grade 11
School of the Arts Alternative High School

Love Sick
One day you'll love me, the way I loved you,
One day you'll think of me, the way I thought of you,
One day you'll cry for me, the way I cried for you,
One day you'll want me, but I won't want you.

I said release my heart, please,
Put it back where it used to be.
I can't go on much longer,
You're the one who does the torture,
I'll never hurt as good again.

Out across the endless sea,
Is where you are and I longed to be.
Yet nowadays I cry constantly,
And I know that I shouldn't be.

I remember those words you said to me,
So sweet, so clear, so vividly.
Yet now I realize they meant nothing,
So worthless, so mean, so misleading.

I said release my heart, please,
Put it back where it used to be.
I can't go on much longer,
You're the one who does the torture, I'll never hurt as good again.
Jessica Silvers, Grade 12
La Jolla Sr High School

I Wanna Be Black
I wanna be black, How black? So black.
Black enough so that when these words touch,
They leave fingerprints on every soul.
I wanna be black; like Africa
Like thick hips and full lips
Like single mothers with tight fists
Like Friday's fish and grits.
I wanna be black. Black enough to take a stand
Black enough to lend a hand
Be a keeper to my brotha man
Uplift a sista like no other can;
Like Oprah.
I wanna be black. Black like impossible dreams,
Black like coffee with no cream
Black like silent screams
I wanna be black. How black? So black
Black like the struggle
Black and anonymous enough to chase my goal.
Hawk it down like the elusive thing it has become.
Black and unending, Black and relentless, Black and unyielding.
Michael Washington, Grade 12
Woodcrest Christian School

Always and Forever
The warmth of your embrace,
full-bodied and safe like the sand.
Light glimmers on that vivid blue,
a deep ocean of glances.
Soft kiss lined with those white pearls,
the happiness they reveal.

Aquatic bliss with you by my side,
flowing with the tides and
capturing coral pinks and kelp emeralds.

Tides come and go
as we lay on the warm sand,
the sunlight fading over the amber horizon.
Chills from the cold,
concealed with passion.

Days end and yet I still have you.
The ocean breeze echoes,
always and forever.
Lauren Katz, Grade 12
San Lorenzo Valley High School

Scream
S ilences all over like a lonely road
C racks of laughter
R oar of the beast
E veryone in sudden dismay
A iming for fear
M orning never seems to appear
Gabriel Ramirez, Grade 10
Huntington Park College Ready Academy High School

Mirror
You see me, I can't see you
All I see is what is reflected in front of me.
I see what you see,
You see what you want to see,
Not always not never but sometimes.
You see happy you see mad
But yet you keep coming back.
Big or small I don't care what we see,
All I want to see is what reflects from me.
I wish I could see the real you,
You wish you could see a model reflected from me to you.
You come to me for advice but yet I can't speak,
All I can say is words reflecting from me.
Edgar Barba, Grade 12
Omega High School

January 20, 2009
Clumsy, comatose
In the grips of a frosty dream
Out the door; the clock strikes four
Blood turns to ice

Crushed between Scarecrows and Tin Men
Pennsylvania Avenue seems like Oz
Remind me again what the Lion asked for?
Home with a click of those ruby red slippers
Where's Glinda when I need her?

A glorious morning on that Yellow Brick Road
Melts our chill with hope of a Wizard unveiled
Kelley Villa, Grade 12
St Joseph Notre Dame High School

Rush Hour
Dark and hard, slick with rain
Concrete and asphalt stretch as far as the eye can see
The constant rush of cars washes over me
Like the waves of an urban ocean
The taillights wink and twinkle
Like pieces of sea glass in the moonlight
The blaring horns sound
Like the call of the gull

Despite the tumult
I find peace.
Jesse Swatling-Holcomb, Grade 12
St Joseph Notre Dame High School

Popcorn
Popcorn
Buttery, delicious
Soft, greasy, bumpy
Yellow, roundish, creamy, salty
Crispy, noisy, crunchy, pleasant, extraordinary
Marlen Quintero, Grade 10
Huntington Park College Ready Academy High School

High Merit Poems – Grades 10, 11 and 12

A Chance in Life
The sky is above my head
The ground is below my feet
The world is waiting for me
To make a big change in my life

I sight so many stunning creatures
I took a chance and come out of this egg shell
I'm not afraid to speak out
I'm not afraid to search for my own destiny

My life is a part of me
My dream is what I need to create
I seek in the beauty of me
All need is I

My eyes is what I need to see
My ears is what I need to hear
My nose is what I need to smell
My mouth is what I need to taste
My body is what I need to balance

Here I come
Out of this pink rose
Going on a journey to seek the world
The world is waiting for me

Jennifer Lysaythong, Grade 11
Hiram W Johnson High School

Another Chance
Hello there the black in the distance
Destroying everything like you're not persistent
Your name is Addiction you can be a hurtful thing
You hold onto a person like a tight ring

You hurt the people who hate you the most
You just try to boast
Especially when the person is one I love
It's almost like a huge shove

You're the voice inside their head
Are you trying to make them dead?
You cannot take the life of those who are devout
So they try to live it out

You make us lose the ones we love
And every time it makes it harder to let go of
We live with these feelings for the rest of our lives
Until we suddenly strive

I'm lucky he got another chance to make it right
But it has been one big fight
He looked with hope for the highest power
So he could live again without cower
He found God

Caitlin Lopez, Grade 11
Saugus High School

Grama Rose*
My whole life you have been with me,
Always showing me what was right,
Together the whole world we did see,
Never did we fight,
I always loved to be with you,
To me you never lied,
Showing me what I should do.
Sadly now you have died.
With family by my side,
Grama you will never be forgot,
All the days and night I have cried,
The love you showed us can never be bought,
By my side are my friends,
To help us stay on task
Your name and values I will defend
Along with every day a happy mask,
You will always be in my mind,
You were smart,
All around me you I will find,
Always in my heart,
I love you Grama!!

Patricia De La Mata, Grade 12
Cathedral Catholic High School
In loving memory of Grama Rose M. Diamond 1922-2009

Different Me
When people look at me they see her,
when I look at me I see him.
When I am happy, that's just me.
When I learn it's me, but it used to be her.
How come I have to be a part of them?
Why can't I just be me and me only?
Would I be the same or would I be different?
Sometimes I ask myself why,
I am different. Well, Sometimes, I am
Bright and sometimes I am not
And sometimes I am cold and sometimes
I am warm. When I am in the light
I change to someone and it's never right
I just want to be me and that's
Who I'll try to be.

Waltanisha Ennon, Grade 10
Sand Paths Academy

Stolen Sentiments
When I was a child, my memories flew from me
On the wings of a dream that resembled a nightmare.
Now that I am older,
I am trying to retrieve those stolen sentiments.

As I stretch my hands to the clouds,
I feel my memories within reach.
But then, when I am just about to grasp them,
A malicious wind comes and blows them away.

Melissa Young, Grade 10
St Patrick-St Vincent High School

Lone Wolf

I'm the Lone Wolf, the leader of my own pack,
I live to survive on my own,
Living in my own world that I control,
living day by day, night after night,
I control my future no one else.
My motto is "live alone, die alone,"
been living like that for as long as I've lived,
don't trust anyone who ever comes in your way,
isolate yourself from everyone else,
the only one you need to trust is yourself,
I'm never sad nor happy,
I'm the Lone Wolf, the leader of my pack.

David Moreno, Grade 12
St Bonaventure High School

I Am Who I Am

It's our memories that keep us coming back for more.
Hold onto everything that made us smile.
You talk about me like I'm not there.
I bet you don't know what I'm all about.
I will speak for myself.
What you see isn't all I am.
There's so much you're missing.
If you cared you would listen.
I'm not sorry for who I am.
Take it or leave it.
I am who I am,
and who I am doesn't need your approval.

Brianna Cuadra, Grade 11
Saugus High School

The Creator

My creator is like God and Satan
I've never met him but I hear stories about him.
He has made my deliverer happy but then,
stabbed her in the heart and back.
He is my creator but he is inhumane and evil.
My creator is not my loving dad,
but my heartless father.

Tyler Salinas, Grade 11
Vintage High School

Invader

I don't care if
N o one lives or dies,
V ital instincts help me
A venge my nemesis.
D amaging the world, I am an
E verlasting ruler
R ising from darkness, I shall be victorious

Jossimar Porfirio, Grade 10
Huntington Park College Ready Academy High School

Foggy Feeling

Foggy feeling, feeling good
Lost in thought, but more in gaze
Sounds are jumbled, my voice just mumbles
Dreamy feeling, like a haze

With a friend, we complete the scene
Realizing our minds are free
But lost in the moment
The lights are a lure

Following vibes which ring on "C"
The sounds resonate
Light turns things to brass
As we drive on the freeway of Chi

Daniel Aviña, Grade 12
Redlands High School

Memories in Song

It is written by a stranger,
yet you feel their pain.
The beat moves through you,
each note making another hair stand on end.
The instruments move together,
the artist's voice moving up and down.
Each time you hear the song,
it reminds you of a certain day,
a certain person,
a certain moment.
Each song hits a different emotion.
It can make you feel comforted, loved, lonely, joyful, or wild.
It does not matter which, as long as it touches you in some way.
Music is powerful, music is special, music is life.

Chelsea Herrmann, Grade 12
Redlands High School

Peace and Love

P eace
E very day
A t any time
C hanges people
E motionally

A mor as easy as it sounds
N o one really knows how to express it
D elicate to your heart

L ove is complicated
O ver all it brings
V ictory for
E ternity

Andrea Martinez, Grade 10
Huntington Park College Ready Academy High School

High Merit Poems – Grades 10, 11 and 12

Come Find Me
eyes big and searching; as my hands and fingers shake
my feet stay bolted to the ground, eyes to the ground in shame
    it's the ocean crashing, a blank stare at the sea
      the salty water matching those, that fall down my cheeks
closing my eyes, breathing it in
the smell of your skin
    of just you
      water falling from slippery rocks
        the sweet smell of the dew, on the daisies in the garden
take a breathless swallow, of water I thought
I would never see; in the desert — out of reach
    taste the salt of a secret sea
      a sharp whisper in my throat
      cutting through the air
      "come find me"
the seagull crying sweet tears, into dark tangled hair
the cold hard surface of metal
never soft, never warm
    closing my eyes listening, to the trees rustling
      the bittersweet taste
of longing.

Ash Lee Williams, Grade 12
San Lorenzo Valley High School

Fairies
Fairies course through the skies of my mind —
    Fairies that take forever to find.
They hide in the cobwebbed corners of my brain,
    For centuries that's where they have lain.

I try my best to awaken their flight,
    To resurrect their beauty and might.
But they still lie sleeping in paralyzed splendor —
    Yet even there they are a wonder.

Take flight my lovelies! Be free once more!
Stop hiding behind a closed and locked door.
Awaken and shower the world with your glory!
Awaken and add life to my long dead story!

Alaina Simpson, Grade 12
Valley Center High School

Love Is
Love is a cloud
Love is a dream
Love is a feeling
That nothing comes in between
Love is a wishing well
A fountain of youth, a hard feeling
Love will see through
Love is a fairy tale
A dream come true
And I found love where
I found you

Jose Angel Reyes, Grade 10
Huntington Park College Ready Academy High School

I Love…
I love it all…
I love the smell of your clothes
I love the sound of your voice
I love waking up in your arms
I love how you still give me butterflies
I love how I smile when I think about you
I love how when I'm with you I can't see anyone else
I love the feeling I have when you're around
I love the sparkle in your eyes when you look at me
I love how you make my day better without even trying
I love the shivers you send up my spine with the slightest touch
I love you

Angela Gerlach, Grade 12
Prospect Continuation High School

My Family Is a Broken Home
My dad is the broken garage door
Staying isolated for help and never changing bad habits
My brothers are the flickering light bulbs
Always annoying everyone
My mom is the decomposing base
Trying to hold the family together
But falling apart herself
And I'm the broken door hanging on by a single hinge
Still trying to deal with everything but about to fall apart
My family is a broken home
But to fix it
It wouldn't be MY family

Alex Pacheco, Grade 11
Saugus High School

Giselle
G orgeous
I ndependent like a wolf
S oft like a rabbit
E xpressive like a puppy
L ikable to all
L oving
E xcellent as a sister

Jazmin Banuelos, Grade 10
Huntington Park College Ready Academy High School

What Is Love?
Love is the absence of yourself
It is not greedy
Nor does it envy the other's wealth
Love is love even in death
Love is not afraid to love deeply

It is forgiving
It does not have regrets
It is always giving
Never hides the real meaning
It does not reject

Jonathan Martinez, Grade 10
Huntington Park College Ready Academy High School

My Name

My real name was rubbed off my lips
When I was nine and wanted to cry.
My brother called me baby
And I ran to the playground
To jump in the sand.
My name was on the cake on my night stand
From Clarence C when I was thirteen.
My name was the damage by my ear.
My sister called me beautiful.
My name was Chicken do-little
That ate meat and just that.
My cousin called me goofy.
My name was Who did this.
My best friend called me Loner, but cool.
My name was Hahaha.
My name was Big hair.
My name was Giant who walked over everything small.
My name was Little girl who eats markers.
My real name is the Ocean, the Sky, the Sun's Earth.

Taurean Wade, Grade 10
Jane Addams Continuation High School

Little Dream

Every day, I go looking for you in the deep of my chest
Open my body to the stars' inspection
I offer you to the moon, tell them that out of you
Man extracted the dream.

Little dream, to you I go running
Little dream, to you I go running with a telescope of bronze.

And they cannot separate the mark of your eyes from my flesh.
They cannot as they cannot separate words and dance and time
From the drunken tide rising forever, escaping the sea.

Little dream, little dream
From my throat you sound like a tall tale
But you are not meant for words.

Little dream, to you I go flying
Little dream, to you I go flying with wings of bronze.
Hide me in your naked flatland.

Yaul Perez-Stable Husni, Grade 11
School of the Arts Alternative High School

Leopard

L eaps super high
E xtraordinary eyes
O versized cat
P atches on its back
A ll so cute
R eally adorable
D angles like a monkey on that tree

Brenda Garibay, Grade 10
Huntington Park College Ready Academy High School

Untitled 13

Portraits painted dazzle untouchable white walls
Sculptures sculpted scattered across picturesque lawns
People wander amongst such simple wonders,
    crafted by hands no different from their own
The hands that swing along
    that hold the childrens'
        that hide in pockets
These hands are no more special from the two
    that held hammer and chisel to the marble
        paintbrush to canvas
The fingers that twirl the girl's hair
No different in shape or form than the fingers that
    molded the clay
        that pressed the button to capture the image
Framed and on display for its brilliance
Yet when all is said and done
All eyes are the same
As they stand back and admire

Brooke Helm, Grade 11
Saugus High School

A Better Place

Imagine a world full of peace
A world without discrimination
A world without hate
A world truly united into one nation
Imagine a world without racism
Where the color of your skin didn't make a difference
Imagine a world without war
Where there are no soldiers dying
No reason to be fighting
No loved ones crying
Imagine a world where there is equality
Where no one lives in poverty
Imagine a world full of happiness
A world without drama
A world full of respect
Where kids get along with both daddy and mama
Imagine a world without stress
Where everyone's life isn't such a mess.

Samantha Alvarez, Grade 12
Prospect Continuation High School

Some Things Just Don't Go Away

I'm tired of being let down
I can't depend on anyone to stick around
No one will ever stay
Keep your mouth shut
Because I don't believe a word you say
No I won't ever be okay
Everything that's ever went wrong is constantly on replay
The memories refuse to go away
And that's the one thing I wish wouldn't stay.

Sarah Barnett-Magdaleno, Grade 10
Sunset Continuation High School

Love

Love is not always what you expect,
because sometimes those three words you can easily regret.
Jocks usually play with girls feelings
but some girls try and find the true meanings.
In this battlefield of love some words can be misunderstood
unlike the little train I think I can what about I think I could.
Love is what someone can most desire,
but I am convinced that you are a liar.
Love is not always something tragic,
it can also be abra cadabra magic.
The most important resource of love is company,
but trust me you cannot buy a relationship with money.
I am blind towards the person that makes my world go round
I have to be careful and trust the one that I have found.
When I am with you I swear my heart skips a beat
and when you talk to me and smile you lift me off my feet.
I can honestly say that I love you so,
but can you please say it back because it's time for me to go.
Rosa S. Villegas, Grade 10
Huntington Park College Ready Academy High School

The Love of My Life, Not My Husband or Wife

I'm in love — oh yes, I am
Not with a woman or with a man
The love I've found is of a different sort,
For I've fallen head over heels for my sport
Can you guess what it is that I love so much?
I'll give you a hint — you must have a good first touch
Shooting, dribbling, and passing are the fundamental components
But I assure you there are some brutal moments
Like when a player kicks you in the face
Or you're so beat up, you need a brace
A cut, a bruise, a black eye, a sore muscle
But you can't let this affect you — keep up your hustle!
Sweat on my brow and blood on my knee
Oh the sweet smell of victory fills me with glee
Have you guessed it yet? Have I made myself clear?
My sport requires you to have no fear
All right — I'll tell you in case you don't know
It's soccer and no, girls don't play slow
Courtney Mera, Grade 12
Redlands High School

My Best Friend

My best friend's name is Lola.
She is special for me because we have been together for 7 years.
With her, I remember the traditions and cultures
Important to my life.
When I feel angry, she makes me happy.
When I am in school or at work,
I always think about her because she is beautiful.
She is my baby, and I love her with all my heart.
My best friend is my guitar, Lola…
Jovanny Avila Ortiz, Grade 11
Hiram W Johnson High School

Chasing Hearts and Breaking Dreams

I see the most private of things,
day in, day out, rush in, blackout
I mostly view a young, pretty thing swallowed in lust,
with heart strings pulled and wound,
who's bound to discover the effects of heartache somehow
Her naive innocence doesn't deserve
all of the boys who are objects closer than they appear,
this makes her want to break us into a thousand sparkling gems,
chasing hearts and breaking dreams,
day in, day out, rush in, blackout
The hopefully luxe dresses that premiere in front of me,
the beautiful yards of fabric I only see,
we spend our time together waiting for that one charming guy,
who is nothing more than pleasing to the eye
His reflection never visits me, his face never visits her,
he's making her chase him and breaking me,
I am a mirror that sees what she sees
I'm losing her — the fading glow,
I gain her — her days spent alone in her haven, my home
her reality is not my own,
day in, day out, rush in, blackout
Caitlin Belardes, Grade 10
Prospect High School

Love vs Hate

i thought i loved you,
but then you hurt me,
you broke my heart,
but i don't understand,
it doesn't make sense,
i've heard it was me,
me that was the problem,
just 'cause i didn't want my parents to know,
that makes me mad,
that makes me hate you,
but why,
'cause you hurt me,
you broke my heart,
but then i still love you,
but i don't know if you love me,
do you,
or do you not,
why me,
why not someone else,
why does my heart get broken,
why
Amber Brownell, Grade 10
Weber Institute of Applied Sciences & Technology

Basketball

One pair of Nikes.
An old jacked-up basketball court.
Finally a ball.
Eduardo Rojas, Grade 10
Huntington Park College Ready Academy High School

The Horse and Rider

What you have taught me my silent savior
I have learned to hear your whispers
To understand your gentle impulsion
We are partners

I feel safe with you
And with my deepest faith I trust you
We embrace a bond to last an eternity
We are partners

Going through it all
Through the happiness
Through the pain
We are partners

Only you could be so strong
Yet so gentle
That is you
My horse, my partner

Sara Shier, Grade 11
Saugus High School

Life

We are all just civilized savages;
Seeking satisfaction through
intricate plans and fulfillment,
but burning with animalistic
desire nonetheless.
Once that burning flame of
passion has been quenched,
what then?

Life is meaningless.
We are like dogs striving to
complete tasks solely
for the stimulation
it provides.
An empty, unimportant life.
Pointless goal of survival.
A pointless existence,
a meaningless existence.
Life is meaningless.

Elizabeth Conklin Walker, Grade 10
Bella Vista High School

Positive/Negative

Positive
Truthful, sure
Convincing, agreeing, expressing
Confident, hopeful — harmful, attitude
Divorcing, affecting, staring
Dark, poisonous
Negative

Juan Prieto, Grade 12
Hiram W Johnson High School

The Beginning

I awoke on a cooled lava rock and was puzzled by this new world.
The sky was soot black and the magma,
Piping hot and glowing with an ominous crimson red,
Flowed around me, filling crooks and crannies with its glorious essence.
A voice, deep with the new land's wisdom, boomed overhead.
It spoke no language
For it was the beginning of all languages.
On impulse, I looked down at myself to observe my bare body.
With an odd instinct that no other animal possessed, I attempted to cover myself
Using the only material that was available:
Fluid black lava that fell from a newly created cliff.
It did not burn me, nor did it cover my skin with rage ridden blisters.
All it did was stretch around my body,
Not at all sticky and comfortably warm.
By yet another command of the world, the conscience of my nature filled my mind.
Fierce determination danced in my eyes.
It was then that I stood for the first time.
I deemed myself a name that could only belong to me.
I turned my perfectly unique face to the sky
And, with my voice rugged from its first use, whispered,
"I am human."

Kristen M. Mesa, Grade 11
Schurr High School

No Real Name

My real name was why did you do that when I was mad
And wanted to disappear from this forsaken life
My friends called me disappointment and I just
Forgave and forgot after hours of shedding tears
My name was the only thing being talked about
My first girlfriend called me the never changing hard headed person
My name was the young confused charity case
My homeboy called me his idol
My name was really Mr. Regret
My name was the name I want to erase from my past
My name was not Alejandro but HIM
Who does what he did without a clue of what I'm feeling inside
My name was a long story from the past
My real name is successful, the child my parents always wanted me to be
The child who grew up and realized right from wrong

Alex Murillo, Grade 10
Jane Addams Continuation High School

The Thought of You

I could never get you off my mind from the first day we met
The moment we kissed is one I'll never forget
You swept me off my feet by just being true
And now being in your presence is all I want to do
If you continue to be my companion, my partner and my one and only friend
I'll continue loving you till the very end
Somehow when I'm around you I can't find the right words to say
And whenever I do so, you manage to take my breath away
Ever since you left me you turned my world upside down,
Whenever I hear people call your name it's just so hard not to turn around.

Karly Bueno, Grade 10
Whittier High School

High Merit Poems – Grades 10, 11 and 12

My Cold Day

Stacks of papers were
dancing around the room.
The wind was mad,
and it shoved me down.

I needed something
to hold my skin,
so my shirt hugs
me around my body.

The ocean waved at me,
and I waved the ocean back,
the ocean made me happy,
and would never be snappy
to me because the ocean's nice.

The cookies fell apart
because their inner heart
cannot live any longer,
I wanted to do something
to repair them but I'm
too late for that.

Rayson Hong, Grade 10
Abraham Lincoln High School

Red Sky

The mountains were very tall,
But they will never fall.
There was fire spilling in the sky,
It was almost like red dye.

They battled till the very end,
Flapping their wings out of their dens.
Scratching one another with claws,
Nearly snapping each others' jaws.

The fire now turns to smoke,
However they still provoke.
These deadly beasts fill the night,
The dragons continue to fight.

Racquel Chagoya, Grade 12
Lucerne Valley Jr/Sr High School

Music

Head bangs
Gangsters rap
Feet tap
Hair sways
Hips touch
Fists pump
People mosh
Singer roars
Fingers snap
Crowd screams

Gabrielle Romero, Grade 11
Valencia High School

Flashback

As I lay my head to rest for the night, I wake up sweating almost every night.
A 17 year old boy shot in front of my house,
Visions surround me when I'm out and about.

Never knew that saving someone else's life comes with death.
The killer robbed my family members' life, now he is charged with theft.
To lay internally bleeding in front of a church,
Praying God would save you, instead of seeing death.

A little girl, 13, is at summer camp,
She has an 11 year old sister enjoying her summer there too.
As two, they go back home from the best summer camp ever,
To find out their brother has been murdered,
Everyone cries, tears fill the house, nobody was around.

All we know is our brother didn't die on the scene, he lived six hours later.
Mom is losing her mind in the time being.
We found out the young boy was killed on August 14, 2006
And that his name was Aubrey Abrakasa,
From the news to the newspaper, we never could forget,
The story we heard when we got back from the best camp ever.

Lavett Williams, Grade 11
Sand Paths Academy

I Am Looking for a Sign

I am going to look for a sign
Only if you give me love, will it help me out
In this cold world, I need your heat
I need to know if you really love me
I don't live with lies in my heart
I need to know if you are for real
I am not up for games and lies
A strange love is what I feel for you
Being here with you is something new
Give me your soul, where our souls could dream
My eyes can't hold it in any longer and I cry
I love you, I feel something very different for you that is indescribable
And am still here by you, lost for your love
Because I can't live without you
Let's make a good change for both of us
Please, make a true promise and grant it
Do it for our love
The only thing I ask is for you to change and be true for us…

Aticza Arreola, Grade 10
Huntington Park College Ready Academy High School

Time Travel

Back to the past with no regret
The essence of cosmic visions erupt profoundly
Past flashback visions blazing timelessly into gravity echoing in your darkest fears
Remembering a glance of the past, haunting your mind endlessly
Waiting to go back to the beginning to erase the future

Jasson Garcia, Grade 10
Huntington Park College Ready Academy High School

Too Many Strings

Too many songs, too many memories, to be left behind.
Too many nights, too many soul ties;
Too many thoughts of her that purge my mind.
So much sight of truth to share lies.

Not enough words for fantasies to be described,
An abundance of destiny of lives intertwined,
Imaginings beyond which an asylum can prescribe,
And nothing to allow love's grasp to unwind.

Though emotions are as violent as a storm,
My bond will not fade, it will not die.
The moments with her are still warm,
I am captivated, yet my heart is free to fly.

Other motivations or joys cannot compare,
She is my bright sun;
Without a deterring glare.

Jeffrey Andre, Grade 12
University Preparatory School

Hate

There's something inside me twisting and turning
My thoughts and emotions silently burning
Each night I lay in bed aching in pain
Everything I did was all just in vain
I live in regret from so many fears
Of love and hate; it brings nothing but tears
Trampled heart burning soul
Deep inside dark as coal
All this hate is seeping through
It sat in my head and constantly grew
All the mistakes and neverending lies
Grow and grow as my body rapidly dies
Pushing it in I try to survive
The hate is shrinking, beginning to die
In the end I finally fell
On the small things I no longer dwell
There's something inside me twisting and turning
My thoughts and emotions no longer burning

Hannah Crawford, Grade 11
Academy for Careers and Explorations High School

Love Is Beautiful

I ncredible

L ong lasting
O ne time
V ivid
E motion that can never break, like a hard rock

Y oung lovers will always be together
O nly happens once in a lifetime
U nbreakable

Nadia Villa, Grade 10
Huntington Park College Ready Academy High School

Layered

Love; a hypnotic spell only to us,
blindly slipping to a high deception.
In pure ecstasy; we were in disgust,
to have surrendered to imperfection.

How could I have fallen to a coma?
To be entangled in its lies and sins.
To resign to you, what awful karma!
To fight a doomed battle, whom no one wins.

Is there a peachy side to this abyss?
To see an intoxicated mirror,
one that adores me with an earnest kiss.
Unmask what made us blind; you'll see clearer.

Was it worth being in love? Scarred and sore?
No, but I wouldn't mind falling once more.

Anna Le, Grade 10
Abraham Lincoln High School

Soul's Sonnet

Sweet songs fill the air
As light breaks through the clouds
Her presence so powerful
Her beauty so radiant

Blood rushes through my veins
Like a black stallion in the night
Never stopping, always hidden from sight
And here is where my heart pains

Because it shall never be
For as light and dark cannot be together at one time
So also is the fate of my beloved and I

And thus, I live in the shadow of Hand's harsh decree
Never catching a glimpse of day's break
Always alone in the deadness of life

Alexander Ramsey, Grade 11
Whitney High School

Never Say Never

Never…
Never say never, when you don't believe
Never say never, when you don't see
Never say never, when things don't go right
Never say never, if you don't see the light
Never say never, things will be okay
Never say never, I'll come find you today
Never say never, the darkness will end
Never say never, hope is right 'round the bend
Never say never, the monsters will hide
Never say never, love will change the tide
Never…

Katey Fielding, Grade 10
Foothill High School

Thing to See

I will open the world that I never saw
I will leave the world I already saw

I wonder if the people will see the ways I do,
Because there might be more things they saw.

More fear comes as I see new things,
But I will be brave and see what I never saw.

I won't try to regret from finding out the real truth,
Because new things were learned from the thing I saw.

Dreaming about the things I have never seen,
Because those are something I never saw.

Things that can be seen are never limited,
And that is why I will find things I never saw.

Unlike the others, who only believes at what they have already seen,
I will never ever limit myself from what I already saw.
Aram Jang, Grade 10
University High School

My Mask

My mask is strong,
It hides me from the world.
It divides so I don't have to.
I let it cover me like a blanket
So that no one can see
What's underneath.
Things go wrong
But I take it all in stride,
Or so it seems.
My mask doesn't change,
Or does it?
It appears to be constructed of strong steel,
But really it is the flimsiest covering there is.
Cold and hard on the outside,
But so soft and delicate on the inside.
That is the way I have built my mask.
A smile can change the world,
But it can also keep the world at bay.
My happy front keeps the world
From seeing the broken parts underneath…
Brandi Sealander, Grade 12
University Preparatory School

Mother

M agical moments like in a fairy tale.
O bstacles in life
T alking about problems
H elping always and forever
E njoying life together
R eady for the world
Elizabeth Medina, Grade 10
Huntington Park College Ready Academy High School

Alienated

I feel I've been alienated
my pride has been destroyed, alienation

I feel empty inside
complete and total alienation

Only feelings I have
anger, sadness, false happiness, alienation

My heart is heavy, my throat is knotting
you stare in my eyes and see nothing, alienation

A horrible frown across my face
I feel like an alien

You tell me all is well
to just go with the flow, alienation

Jared, you said come and join us
come and join the alien nation
Jared Paris, Grade 12
Encore High School for the Performing Arts

Sister

My dearest sister
and it's you,
How I think of you
and it's true.
There's is so much I'd like to say
but things get in our way.
Maybe we don't see much of each other
but it's always one thing or another.
My dearest sister,
and it's you.
Don't ever forget that
I love you.
Don't forget all the good times
that we share.
Don't forget I love you
each and every day.
My dearest sister
and it's you.
Don't be blue,
just remember that I love you.
Rebecca Chaqueco, Grade 12
Huntington Park College Ready Academy High School

The Meaning of My Name

F ierce like a bear with lots of hunger
A mazing like the sky
U nique like the ocean
S ensible like the wind
T remendous as an almighty god
O utstanding like the sun shining upon us
Fausto Beltran, Grade 10
Huntington Park College Ready Academy High School

Kiss

Because as into her eyes I stare,
the moon casts its glare.
Her cheeks, red, plump, flush.
Her lips, more than, beyond lush.

As our lips approach their destination,
as our noses graze, subtle hesitation,
a feeling of uncertainty ensues.
We, two lovers are lost on what to do.

Do we proceed to kiss?
Indulge momentary bliss?
A union of one lip to another,
waiting lover to waiting lover.

Or

Let the precious moment fade
Levy the overbearing cascade.
Is it all right to venture into the gray?
Let the emotions out to play?

Adrian Navarro, Grade 11
La Serna High School

Your Dreams Are Not Yours by Accident

You sleep and enter a place of darkness
Your head fills with welcomed images
You smile and swim in your joy
Wait.
Perhaps there is an onlooker
A puppet master in a sea of dolls
Manipulating those sweet mirages
Your smile is matched with the lurking
You awake with bright and loving images
You welcome the images
And embrace reality with a new spirit
But in the shadows is a figure
A figure that just waits in the shadows
Waits until you need a push
Holding the strings taunt
Your dreams are in his hands

Brenna Butler, Grade 11
Saugus High School

My Life Flashes Once Before Its End

My life flashes once before its end;
It thus far sees its end
If perpetually betrayed
A last limit to me,

So mighty, so inconsolable to enamor.
Like its distressed insolence.
Escape is but inevitable,
And all we hear is turmoil.

Rosa Alexandra O'Campo, Grade 12
Fontana High School

Forever and Always

Broken down, shattered on the ground,
You were there to turn my frown up-side-down.
When my skies were gray and my clouds would rain,
You would promise me the sunniest of days.
When my heart would ache and my tears weren't fake,
You were by my side, accepting my next mistake.
People would walk out of my world;
They would leave me stranded, mangled, and blue.
But you were always there for me, making sure I could still move.
While the world would inflict pain, and my life would go down the drain,
You were right there next to me, helping me find my next epiphany.
I just want to apologize, not being there for you,
Was the worst thing I could do.
Now I am yours, one hundred percent for sure.
I only wish we had more time so I could prove to you my rhyme.
My love for you will only grow, though time will fight and memories will reunite,
The love I have will still be in sight.
Miles apart, but minutes away,
My heart will shake with every intake.
Look over the sea and through the trees,
For I will be there, waiting.

Emily Wright, Grade 12
University Preparatory School

I See You Everywhere

There is not one day that doesn't go by and I don't think of you,
There is not one time that you are not out of my mind
See, it is really hard to get you out of my mind, when I see you
I see you every day, I see you everywhere, there is not one single day,
That doesn't go by without me thinking of you, there is not one single day,
That doesn't go by, I see you
I guess it is because, I see you every day in school,
I don't really know if what I see is love,
But I don't want to lose you now that I've seen you…
See, I have to leave right now and I don't know when I'll be back to see you again
I see you every day, I see you everywhere, there is not one single day,
That doesn't go by without me thinking of you, there is not one single day,
That doesn't go by, I see you
Let me know when it is gonna by you, boy you got something to prove
'Cause I got to make sure, that what I am seeing is really you
Let me know when it is really gonna be you
Let me know that I am gonna be all right
Because I don't really know what I'm seeing is really you
I see you every day, I see you everywhere, and there is not one single day,
That doesn't go by without me thinking of you, there is not one single day,
That doesn't go by, I see you.

Kathy Cortez, Grade 12
PAAL Campus

High Merit Poems – Grades 10, 11 and 12

Regret Runs Rampant
Pondering upon perceptive problems
perhaps possible to prevent,

I continue countering confusing
conclusions creating contradiction.

Dutifully I discover dreadful doubts
deftly defining democracy.

Finding fantastic fundamentals for
fixing frequently fractured failures,

I incidentally inquire independently,
ideas implicating ironic indecision.

Tragically, time ticks tediously
turning taunting temptations

To tomorrow.
Emily Johnson, Grade 12
San Lorenzo Valley High School

A Day at the Boardwalk
Sitting in the driver's seat,
holding the wheel tight,
Smiling at the shout of glee,
as our destination leaps into sight.

Hearing the screams of the passengers,
as the roller coaster drops.
Looking out across the horizon,
when the ferris wheel reaches the top.

The haunted house to the left,
that is the most fun at night.
There is a distinct smell of candy corn,
coming somewhere from the right.

The day's been fun but long,
now it is time to go home.
"Proceed through the parking lot,
and please do not hit the cones."
Houston Howard, Grade 12
Redlands High School

Timeless Soldiers
Timeless soldiers marching by
Timeless soldiers no one knows why
Killing enemies
Their master they will appease
Guns and swords
Dukes and lords
Each to be defeated in time
By the timeless soldiers walking by
Emma White, Grade 10
Foothill High School

Hurdling with Style
Leap from the earth, hurdle to the floor.

One, the mind shuts off. Two, the feet react. Three, the body snaps.
Three steps. It's the only way.

I do not feel the body. It is not numb; it lacks existence.
One, nothing. Two, sustain. Three. the body snaps.

The wind bleeds across the enemy in the path; it strikes now.
It touches the figure to my left, to my right, and all those behind.
It does not touch me; it never touches me; it cannot touch me.

One. Two. Three.
I cannot think; The mind has no speed.
It will not happen this time; it's second nature. The mind sleeps now.
No it's first. It must be first.
Feel the rhythm and let the body go.

One. Two. Three. The body must not let the mind see. One, two, three.
Hurdle. One, two, three. Leg, up and forward. The other, follow but stay close.

Right arm, lead the way, be the key. Left arm, shut the door.
I fall behind, sink away, begin to feel the world again.
One. Two. Three…four. It's over. I lean. He leans, far ahead.
Another battle my existence is confirmed.
Nicholas Lee Kebbas, Grade 12
Redlands High School

Veritum Dies Aperit
Time flows, runs, struggles through quicksand.
It moves quickly, creeping through the days
Running out slowly.

Grains of seconds, minutes and hours
Litter the desert of time, of days of months of years.
Time is never enough, yet more than we need.

It steals form us happy times, good memories and youth
It grants us wisdom, content and refuge form old wounds.
Time is eternal, but for us, it runs out.

Feelings change, love is discovered, people are forgiven babies are born;
Wars are started, friends grow apart, people die, love fades…
We all cry, because Time is passing too fast.

But as we look back, we realize how much we've changed.
What we've learned, what we could have done better.
But we also realize the Time is a gift, and
That without the changes, the knowledge and the mistakes,
We wouldn't be who we are today.

Time is a gift,
And Time runs out.
Valerie Taber, Grade 12
Redlands High School

Lioness

sweet lioness
majestic being with the sad eyes
sublime and wonderful
they have all been deceived
skittish? sweet lioness
they can't hurt you
strength is on your face
they can't love you either
scream to them dear girl
use your roar; it is louder than those eyes
swallow them whole
eventually they will hear you
such imperfection
in such a beautiful creature
does it scare you?
dear lioness yes it
scares me
what a tragic feeling dear
sister
don't overthink it
they will hear you
Caitlin Alexander, Grade 12
Mills High School

Reality Takes a Break

I'm on a journey, never ending
Voices sound and time stands still
My mind falls victim to imagination
More and more as I climb the hill

I reach a point where I must rest
Yet my mind continues the climb
Reality takes a break as well
Replaced by rhythm and rhyme

I reach the top and get that feeling
Of joy, of peace, of bliss
I leave reality far behind
It, I surely won't miss
Cody Christiansen, Grade 12
Redlands High School

Trucks

Keys turn
Engines roar
Tires squeal
Smoke flies
Tahoe's lifted
Suspensions colored
Chrome shines
Paint sparkles
Horns honk
Trucks displayed
Timothy Rangel, Grade 11
Valencia High School

i know she's always there

i don't know why he's taking her
my thoughts aren't clear
the trumpets blaring that she says she hears
no one can see them except her pair of eyes
this is something i despise
for she's going away and here i'll have to stay
left with the windows that she looked through
and the spoons she used to cook stew
although in reality she will be gone
she'll never be far like a deer and its fawn
we have to look at it optimistically and unselfishly
because her time here is done
and from her great smiles i know she had fun
forever in our hearts she will lie
and i did promise her that i'd try not to cry
as these pieces of this puzzle come together and bind
and with hours and time
the loss of my grandmother will settle in
in the minds of her children and their kin
we will always miss her but she will always be a great and special part of me
Andrea Gonzalez, Grade 11
Whittier High School

The Winning Shot

On one hot, humid, hectic day,
I was invited to play in a basketball game.
It was really hot and I had rather not,
but graciously made my way to the court.
The court was made of black asphalt,
which seemed to be as hot as the red hot embers of a roaring fire.
The game began and I had the ball in my hands.
I passed it along to my friends down the court.
I ran towards the hoop, my feet shifting and scooting.
The ball was passed to me and I could clearly see the shot to be made.
I went for the shot, ready or not.
As the ball left my hands, my hands hung high up towards the sky.
With the sun in my eyes, I couldn't see if I had made the shot or not.
It was the winning score, if I made one more.
The ball circled the hoop,
like a vulture circles its prey.
I jumped to my feet,
to see if my shot was complete.
It went in!
I had done it again!
Kyle Logan, Grade 10
Sierra Charter School

Pain

I like crying in the rain,
Because nobody knows my pain.
When you stare into my eyes you
Won't see a thing.
But if you stare deeply into my heart,
You will find a story of my life.
Abigail Perez, Grade 12
Omega High School

I Fell

I fell, and looked at him
And thought, Oh why won't you help?
He just stared
And I then felt
If not him, then no one else
…Would ever help.
Kevin Vasquez, Grade 10
Ann Sobrato High School

Sun and Moon

I'm in the world
of two eyes.
One eye brings warmth
to my face, life to nature,
light to all creatures,
making about three billion friends.
The other eye
brings new life
into me,
lights up some
of the darkness
to tell everyone
it's time to go to sleep
except the nocturnal,
who wake up
and have fun.
This eye
reveals it has company
with millions and billions of gems.
We are never alone.
The sun and moon — my eyes.

Maricela Cespedes, Grade 12
Schurr High School

The Clock Bleeds On

Fingers smell like orange —
The descending sun.
Eyes strain to open —
The vast purple sky.
Ears hear the pulse —
The blood that stirs.
Dry tears —
Feel no more my skin.

Lonesome moon ignites
As tick tock twelve o clock
The clock bleeds on.
Disconnect no more —
My soul is fate.

Andrew Yang, Grade 12
Crystal Springs Uplands School

The Spider

Precarious
mutual and
unlikely
existence.
Dangerous
spider in my window —
help me
don't hurt me
and
I won't hurt you.

Cece Castaneda, Grade 10
St Bonaventure High School

A World Without Music

Without music our world would be plain.
We would not be able to sustain through the pain, and still keep sane.
I am not saying our world would not have sound;
rather, we would be bound to the sound
of the plain world we live,
bound to the sounds of a world that doesn't give.
A world without rhythm and lyrics to hear;
for we are not deaf, but blind in the ear.
We do not see the true beauty and art;
of a world that is detached from us, a world far apart.
I am thankful to be able to live in a world where music is taken to heart.
Where people can convey ideas and thoughts through the sound of their voice;
that mutually coincide with a rhythm, beat, and genre of choice.
A world where joy and laughter can be found,
by the strum of a guitar, or a soothing jazz sound;
an expression of emotion, another way out,
a world we can go to in a time of misery and doubt.
In times where we can feel all alone,
music can be our release, our comfort, our home.
Music is a world that has developed in society,
and it is this world I am glad that is a part of me.

Nicholas Koenig, Grade 11
Valley Christian High School

I'm the Same as You

I'm me and being me
Makes me just the same as you
It feels so hopeless sometimes
The music
The games
The food
The drama
They're all so hopeless
I want a car a horse a laptop a ring
Just so hopeless because they all say
I'm me and being me makes me just the same as you
They all get drunk
They all party hard
They all do what they want to do with the only authority
Their own Judgments
Their own lives
Their own temporary satisfactions
No looking forwards or backwards just running because they just want to
Maybe that's why people are dying in nations beyond our comprehension
Maybe that's why the voices of others are suppressed because of me
And the fact that being me makes me just the same as you

Talar Malakian, Grade 12
Crescenta Valley High School

The Day All Love Stood Still

The day was as a dim winter night.
The trees whistled along with the cool
breeze that came about.

Daddy, with his jet black
hair, used to help me laugh away
pain and fear, sitting in the front
room among all our family. He
would tell me about his childhood.

The day started the way it usually did.
I got up to find Daddy and Mommy and that's
when the atmosphere changed. The house felt
as if all the oxygen had been sucked out of
the house. I heard screaming and yelling,
back and forth, first Mommy then
Daddy. The yelling became louder.

I began to cry and tug on Daddy's shirt. Daddy finally
looked down at me with tears in his eyes.
Daddy knelt over, kissed me on my forehead
and walked out the door slamming it behind
him. I ran up to my room and I crouched
behind the door, curling myself into the smallest shape possible.

Tamara Washington, Grade 10
Woodcrest Christian School

Somber Solitude

I am alone,
The faint smell of your long, flowing hair
Lingers upon the empty sweatshirt.
This pitiful substitute for you cannot extinguish the want.
With my face buried in this cloth,
Memories of our moonlit embrace,
Our last night, dance in my mind.

We are there, it is dusk.
The mellow night sky.
I hold you as close as I can,
Locked in this twilight farewell.

Hand in hand, united,
We amble through the remnant shallows,
Of the ocean tide.
The reflection of the moon and
The glow of the dark water lights our melancholy good-bye.
A loving kiss and she is gone.
In her place, I hold a faded sweatshirt.

I am alone.
So I bury my face into the memories
And sob gently of her Absence.

Troy Wollman, Grade 10
Vasquez High School

Memory 87 — Mistakes

We seem to run away from our mistakes,
From the morning miracles we escape,
But we see nothing for others' sakes

From death to ashes we make coffins and ashtrays,
To avoid time and cleanse the world faster in many ways,
We seem to run away from our mistakes

We worry about our happiness being taken away,
So we let our brothers die at night during the day,
But we see nothing for others' sakes

We worry about their mistakes and we take the fault,
And they run while someone bleeds in the asphalt,
We seem to run away from our mistakes

Later we feel content, but disappointed,
And as they rejoice they hold up high the old school joint,
But we see nothing for others' sakes

As life goes on the mistakes we made make us tougher,
and we see those who made us cry…suffer,
We seem to run away from our mistakes,
But we see nothing for others' sakes

Enoc Garcia, Grade 10
Eco Academy High School

Memories

I am from my little brother's soccer shoes
To my older brother's Jordan shoes
From my pink flowery backpack on the couch
To my two dogs leashes on the kitchen chairs

I am from my clothes hanging on the washer
To my dad's GT bike on the rack
From a brown round table
To white patio chairs

I am from Loara St.
To many colorful blossoming flowers
From a light blue playground
To multicolored benches

I am from my older brother Abel telling me "Get out of my room!"
To David my little brother running around the house
From a mother that will help you on your homework
To a father that would take you anyplace you want

I am from my mom saying "Do you have homework!"
To a teacher telling me "Lorena you are a good student."
From my aunts saying "You are a very nice girl."
That's how these memories live in my world.

Lorena Garrido, Grade 10
Valencia High School

Nature and You

Sitting on a bench,
Looking around,
At the young faces
Smiling and laughing
Making life so bright and enjoyable

The flowers here and there,
Bringing beauty to the place,
Making it so lively and lovely too
In soft wind tossing their heads,
Making life so colorful

Listen to the music
Of water in a fall
It's so sweet
And makes you so calm
Making life so peaceful

Walking by the sea-shore
With silence all around
But the noise of the waves
The vastness of the sea and the breeze
Making life so relaxing and comforting

Junaid Saleem, Grade 12
Redlands High School

Life

Life is valuable and priceless
Life is short.
Don't spend your whole life sitting at a
Desk working.
Go do things with your life.
Go on adventures.
Don't spend you life in a box you
Won't live a good life.
If you spend you life in a box you
Wont' have fun.
Do things with your life while you
Are alive.
Have fun, go on adventures.
Life is short so have fun while you
Are alive.

Angela Altman, Grade 10
Vintage High School

Who Am I?

I am me,
I do what I need to succeed.
I fill my life with determination,
all in order to achieve my station.
Though it may be rough,
I will remain tough.
By living my life to the fullest,
I can become the greatest.

Neil Verma, Grade 12
University Preparatory School

Tears of Yearning

Each time I hear this sweet melody
Another look to the past
To watch the eyes of another child cry for their mother
The loss of innocence her only theme
To watch the clouds of heaven finally open
Another soul enters this world a dimension of pain and suffering

Each time I hear this sweet melody
Another look at myself as that child filled with tears
But I don't cry for my mother my tears don't yearn for family
To feel my heart from your distance
Is unimaginable and unattainable just plain impossible

Each time I see me cry
Faces of familiar people pictured crying and distraught
Wonders of how they look with salt water drenched faces
Red, blotchy and broken
Are we all really that different?
We, the pain-filled, regardless of type

Each time I see you cry connections are unblocked feelings unleashed
Floods of tears from mine mesh completely with yours
Our voices reach up to heaven we all cry the same sweet melody
Hungry for love and acceptance

Teresa Silva, Grade 12
Washington High School

Feel Good Generation

Do you know how it feels, to be stuck in scenes behind the reels?
The things we see aren't as they seem, we're "Feel Good" kids and that's our theme.
We're forced ourselves to find the cure, to take away our pain for sure,
So take your hit and come inside, will society always make us hide?
From every truth and all the lies, we'll kill what's left of their surprise
To feel what isn't real. I know that we haven't died, but left them all behind.

Because as we dive deeper and the drugs reach the core,
Now we're all full-time sleepers, but are we "Feel Good" anymore?
Are we worn out for life? will this always be our strife
Or can we break away? Does it pull us down, drag us in
Or will I stay astray? Because I'll never win, not again.

We've fallen "Feel Good Generation," I wish we had the explanation
For why we're falling down the path, and how we've seen the aftermath
Of everything we've ever done, the things we youth just see as fun.
To everything we'll ever feel and every scene behind the reels
That leads us to our final keel, we're not "Feel Good" and that is real

Don't ever be dependent, stuck on an addiction
Your world will be much better, keep away from self affliction
Repeat the story's header: "Feel Good Generation"
Is that the way to go and simply waste your education
I pray to God that now you know.

Bijan Shoushtarizadeh, Grade 12
Huntington Beach High School

The Plot

Anguish and frustration fill the stage
The characters take their place
The plot thickens
And so does my sorrow
It cannot contain my heart's depravity
A back is stabbed
Who did it?
The lady with nothing to lose
The gardener with malice
Or the quiet rage that leaps from
The flames of the book
The victim
Wanting to scream but falls to
A silent cry
The waiver that something is askew
In this puzzle are two empty spots but left are
Two wrong pieces
It is never satisfied and only goes
Back to the beginning

Adeola Adeyeye, Grade 12
Redlands High School

Eye of the Storm

The morning,
It sows new beginnings into the lives of the lost.
It sews strangers together who run into each other at the cafe.
The fog,
It lies heavy and hard on one's shoulders.
It lies and tells you that you know better, that you know what to do.
The wind,
It paws at brave walkers' hair.
It's pause creates a time to catch flying thoughts.
The rain,
It brews the sharp smell of the asphalt road.
It's bruise is seen as a mud puddle in a wide-open field.
The storm,
It led to destruction and pain.
It's lead consequences were written in stone.

The end,
It brakes lives, hopes, dreams, futures.
It breaks my heart.

Caitlin Nadalet, Grade 12
Redlands High School

Thinking of You

I'm thinking of you
with joy and pleasure
remembering times
I'll always treasure

when I think of you
my heart is light
you're a special person
a sheer delight

thoughts of you cheer me up
whenever I'm mad
I'm always happy
when I think about you

I think of you often,
in the fondest way
I cherish you more
than I ever could say.

Gabriela Gonzalez, Grade 10
Huntington Park College Ready Academy High School

Downpour

When the sun shies away
And the clouds consume the blue
Windows shut their eyes
And windshields will wave at you.

When the cold creeps up your back
And the wet finds your socks and shoes
Goosebumps travel your arms
And your teeth will sing to you.

When the frost eats away at windshields
And the raindrops knock on your door
Lightning dances around
And thunder will get angry with you.

If the sun finds its way,
And the clouds scamper away,
A rainbow will jump over you
Screaming in reds and yellows, greens and blues.

Hannah Tavakoli, Grade 12
Redlands High School

Nature

Wild as you can see
The perfect gift of nature
Misty mornings of nature's cycles
Cherry-blossom assuming in spring
Spring's first, winter's last
Temperatures rising, snow days later
Arctic ice sheets thicken
The rich life of nature.

Carmen Reyes, Grade 10
Huntington Park College Ready Academy High School

Sound

Tap tap tap go my feet
When I listen to the beat
Shaking my booty left to right
And start to dance to the music
Moving with all my might
Even though I am sick
Finding someone nice to meet
In this irresistible heat

Gina Ramirez, Grade 10
Huntington Park College Ready Academy High School

High Merit Poems – Grades 10, 11 and 12

Family

Family is extremely important
It represents love and care
Love and Care must be the center of the family
Parents must be beside their children
And should never abandon them
Money is just a paper and not the center of everything
One family means One team
Everyone must work and cooperate with each other
Everyone has a part that they must accept
Children must Obey and
Never Deceive their parents
Parents should understand and give guidance to their children
Family is about understanding and supporting each other
Family should not judge one another
They should respect every member and be patient with one another
There is no such thing as a Perfect Family
Family will never turn away and can never fade away
Family standby together and pass through
Hardships and Obstacles in life
Family will last Forever
Family is Pride

Ma. Ariane Quizon, Grade 11
Saugus High School

A Comfy Chair

I am from a comfy chair
To laying down on a cozy bed
From playing a video game
To playing outside
I am from playing soccer in the street
To eating delicious enchiladas and a cold drink
From talking to my friends
To buying flaming hot cheetos
I am from sitting in a beautiful chair
To where I see snails stuck on a wall
From where I sit by an old tree where my friends talk
To a park were I play hand ball
I am from playing a video game at a friend's house
To watching a movie at my house
From driving my uncle's car
To staying there for a time or even staying over
I am from buying chips at the liquor store
To going to a party
From walking home
To sleeping in a soft bed
This is how I grew up

Cristian Medina, Grade 10
Valencia High School

Bird and Hunter

A bird flies high up into the sky.
It swerves, it sings, it shrills, it cries
It does not see the hunter stalking it
It does not feel the target on its face
Nor does it hear the gun's click
It is innocence, it is life,
It simply knows joy and happiness.
It has no strife.
Bam goes the gun.
The bird is down
Falling, falling
Unto the forsaken ground.
What has it done to deserve this fate?
To be itself?
To be innocent?
To be content with life
Precipitates a death date?
The hunter goes to pick up his prey,
Crying out what he has won this day.
Innocence, youthfulness, and life all is ended.
Because man will not let the bird live its own way.

Jasmine Gerritsen, Grade 10
Schurr High School

Stuck

Stuck, lost, not knowing which way to turn
surrounded by flames, but yet I don't burn
no people, no homes, no buildings, no streets
just me and my life in the hands of my feet
which way do I turn? where do I go?
no sun, no moon, no clouds, no snow
just covered by the wetness of the rain
but it don't seem to affect the flames.
young girl out here with no one in sight
no tears, no frown, no fear, no fright
staring at life right in front of my eyes
stuck in a circle of deceit and lies
nothing makes sense, it's all just a blur
but she doesn't realize everything is in front of her
thinking dang, this is all I'm about
I'm stuck in a predicament where there is no way out
no one is here, it's just me and myself
no clothes, no shoes, no hair, no health
where is the way out? which way do I go?
am I just gonna sit here and die slow?
why is this here? why is this me? I wonder if I'll ever leave.

Deja Davis, Grade 12
PAAL Campus

It Appears at Night

It appears at night
And shines beside the moonlight
Floating high above

Sergio Zataray, Grade 10
Huntington Park College Ready Academy High School

The Sky

Sun is very hot,
Clouds are very white like snow,
Leaving the sky blue.

Victor Castillo, Grade 10
Huntington Park College Ready Academy High School

The End

Down the sunset goes again.
Oh, how I wonder how many of thee can I see,
this horrible ache pain,
just won't go away.

Every second,
Every minute,
the clock ticks faster,
but yet I'm getting slower.
I'm a shattered glass bottle,
that won't be able to get fixed.

That yellow light
seems like it's getting a little too bright,
is getting closer and closer.
When I see another sunrise,
I wonder how many of thee can I see.

I wonder how many sunrises I still have.
The flowers are drying,
the river is crying,
and the story is ending.

Vivian Chiu, Grade 10
Abraham Lincoln High School

Here*

Even though you're not here
I know you're always watching,
Always making sure nothing bad ever happens
I miss you, I wish you were here
Since you're not,
I'm glad you're up there
You are always on my mind
You are always in my heart
No matter what, I know you're always watching over me
You always said I was "destined for greatness"
You always knew I would achieve in life
I know you will see me walk across that stage
I know you will be proud
You always said, "You will be someone in life,"
…and I will be…
You always knew my strengths and weaknesses
You always told me my strengths would "prevail"
You were right
Thank you for not giving up on me
You will always be…

Leticia Cespedes, Grade 11
Schurr High School
*In loving memory of my great grandfather Tomas Cespedes

Rain

Spilling on the land
Clear water drops from holdings
Of thunderous clouds

Anna Ascencio, Grade 10
Huntington Park College Ready Academy High School

All I Can Hear

All I can hear is the clomp of my boots,
the drops pouring down
hitting the leaves on trees,
dripping from the roofs.

Pitter patter, pitter patter.
This is what silence truly is.
Thunder rolling off in the distance.
I'd love to hear this for the rest of my life.

My shawl protects me,
until I must stop under an overhang.
It is like I am on dry land,
and the street in front of me is a vast lake.

A waterfall cascades in front of me —
but it is only a stream of water leaking off the roof.
All I can hear is the fresh juices of mother nature.
All I can hear is true beauty.

Desiree Ferguson, Grade 12
California High School

We All Have a Soul

We all have a soul at times
times of definite understanding of what just is
honest opinions of extraordinary features that surround us
infinite secrets, feelings, thoughts, explorations
beauty illuminates off the most simple things
the coloration of the sky or a friend passing by
just look at what beauty a smile brings
We all have a soul at times
but then it can escape us
problems after problems persist to come knocking on your door
when all you are looking for is way to get your soul back
back to where it belongs
but we focus on the worries regrets right and wrongs
sometimes we forget the beauty or silence…
…So when you awake and shake dreams from your hair
remember attitude is a choice
so let us rejoice in the coming of our soul
and the unity we share
because we all have soul at times

Raymond Flores, Grade 12
Encore High School for the Performing Arts

The Beauty of Our Love

Your hair is as black as the beautiful night
Your eyes look like two stars shining from above
Your smile is as beautiful as the sunset
Your skin is as soft as snow
And when I'm with you all my troubles go away
When I think of you I smile and wonder where you are
Our love is like music to my heart
That beats softly and transmits energy to my soul.

Zaira Luna, Grade 10
Huntington Park College Ready Academy High School

High Merit Poems – Grades 10, 11 and 12

Eye of the Storm
I've found a way to sleep without closing my eyes
I'm dead to so many around me
I always fall asleep under a cold black sky
Trying to find someone who likes me

I've been the one on the team who gets picked last
I've been the one that feels hurt
I've been the one who regrets what I never had
I've been the one that's sorry

The rain was pouring down on my knees
I need my closest friends to shelter me

In the eye of the storm
A warm winter blanket
All I need is right here with me

My heart tells me what my words just won't
Everything's fine right now
I'm with my friends
In the eye of the storm

Andy Brooks, Grade 12
Redlands High School

Like a Flower
Dreaming,
of the time where I may pursue my passions,
of a world with ambition,
of a life without restrictions.

Hoping, that I may drop these weighty chains of responsibilities
in exchange for true freedom of expression.

Wanting,
to slip into my own shoes
to create my own path
to leave my own legacy.

Waiting,
like a flower late to bloom,
I too am waiting for my time:
the year, the month, the day, the hour
where I blossom to my full potential

Knowing,
My time will come.

Kaylin Mahoney, Grade 11
Saugus High School

My Beautiful Island
I was born on a beautiful island of Samoa
It is very good, you will never feel bored
I still remember it in my heart
Especially our traditional culture, which is so hard
The way you sit, and the way you stand
I am so happy to teach others in the way we talk
Nobody would believe that it is so innocent
That is why tourists feel free to visit it
My father is proud to be a real Samoan person
Because God is our foundation
Our island depends on tourism for most of our income
We need money to build up our families
Luckily my parents and family are ok
After the tsunami that killed a lot of people
It makes me feel angry.

Tuileva Tuigamala, Grade 10
Hiram W Johnson High School

My Little Sister
My little sister is just two years old
When she smiles her little
Chubby cheeks stand out
She acts all crazy and hyper every day
Claudia eats a lot but she loses it
Because she runs all the time
What makes me laugh is her little jokes
Or has that evil laugh
She sings, gives kisses, and says hi to everyone
What really bothers me is when she cries a lot
And has no patience whatsoever
When I'm feeling down she always puts a smile on my
Face because she says crazy stuff that I can't understand
Even though she is a pain in the butt
I still love her as my little annoying sister she is today.

Rafael Villa, Grade 10
Huntington Park College Ready Academy High School

My Poetry
You are my poetry,
the reason for my passion.
Submerged in the waves of your arms,
your words consume me.
Your eyes, piercing.
Your smile, the rays of the sun;
your touch, a delicate breeze caressing my cheeks.
Ardent and amorous,
the joy of my soul,
you are my poetry.

Ariana Braga, Grade 11
St Joseph Notre Dame High School

Nature's Beauty
The sweet scent of her perfume.
Her beauty, as almost rude to stare.
Her arms always stretched out as if to give a hug.
She is always still to make sure to preserve herself.
Her body sways with the wind.
Not to be touched by a human hand
Because of how delicate she is.
She shines more with the rain
And adores the sun.
Nothing can compare to a flower.

Katrina Gutierrez, Grade 12
St Bonaventure High School

Alone

I'm alone
In my own thoughts
And in my own world.

I'm alone
I shout in anger and rage
When the woman I love doesn't know I exist.

The pain of being alone
Is tearing me from my family.

The pain of being alone
Is making me think about you even harder.

Christian Vazquez, Grade 11
Omega High School

Is Love Real?

That fluffy feeling inside
That makes us smile when we think about it.
That sense of "we belong together"
This is what we call love?
In a world full of broken hearts
People of all types with tear-streaked faces
Thought they knew this feeling
But all they know now is the pain
This so called "loved" caused
Our anger inside has us asking
A single question we always thought
We knew the answer to
Is love real?

Samantha Borda, Grade 10
Foothill High School

Why???

Use me like an old rag
I am the one who was there
For you when it really meant it, the
One who you told all of your secrets to.
So when we went to high school
You changed to another person as if you
Don't even know me so now when you need my help
Tell me why should I even help you when
You keep ignoring me and only talk to me when
You want me to do your project so just give me one
Good reason why should I help you?:

Juan Cabral, Grade 10
Huntington Park College Ready Academy High School

No True Friends

In this world there are no true friends
There are only back stabbers
They say that they are your best friends and they have your back
But sooner or later they will turn on you
So you can depend on yourself and only yourself.

Miguel Oliva, Grade 10
Huntington Park College Ready Academy High School

Cross Country — XC

Cross country abbreviated at times as XC
Is the sport I consider to be about me
Yet the reality is that it's about the team
Hearts are pounding, crowds are cheering
All the girls at the start line fearing
Hearts beginning to pound harder, faster, waiting to hear the shot
BOOM!! the race has begun
We're all racing, giving it all we got
Competition is tough, but this is our only shot
Pushing ourselves to the highest potential
Knowing that each and every girl is essential
The race is done
We have all won

Ericka Aguado, Grade 12
Redlands High School

Trouble

Trouble is all around you
You try to move forward
But the problems get in your way
Hoping the issue is gone
So you won't feel bad, and unhappy
But trouble is a part of life
Even though we try to avoid it
It always finds us and follows us
So we feel bitter, like fools
I see people in conflict
I feel angry and sick
I am nervous when I'm around the investigators
Luckily I'm not in trouble now

Binh Tran, Grade 10
Hiram W Johnson High School

Free

Keeping yourself from trying gets you nowhere
But if you try you just might
Many no's lead to one special yes
And that yes will be your success
Which will lead you to a life you won't regret
Because in everything you tried your best!
No matter what
You have to try
To get where you have never gone in life
Your effort will be your success
And the world will be in your hands.

Nancy Dominguez, Grade 10
Huntington Park College Ready Academy High School

Music

M otivates
U nites nations
S ka
I ndescribable
C an adapt to any situation

Miguel Torres, Grade 10
Huntington Park College Ready Academy High School

Love*

You are on your way up golden steps,
While I am wiping tears that I have wept.
You are in God's berth,
While I am serving out his purpose here on Earth.
I love you more than you ever will know,
And I will join you when God deems it so.
I still turn around and think you are standing next to me,
A guardian angel you must be.
To help me make decisions between right and wrong,
And encourage me with your smile all day long.
I never understood why the doctors said you had a bad heart,
For you loving heart and compassion really set you apart.
O, why did your heart have to fail?
I would have given all I have to cure your Earthy ails.
No longer will you sit by the fire and talk with me,
But in my memory, you will always be.

Erica Soultanian, Grade 12
Oak Park High School
*Dedicated to my grandfather

Teardrops

A teardrop for ever break we have had
Every crack that has weakened the poor heart
Leaving a river on the dirty ground
Why are you tearing our great love apart

A teardrop is just like a breaking sound
It's like I am being shoved into darts
Losing what we had is making me frown
Why are we turning our love into hate

Love troubles in the heart of the younger ones
It is like you are trying to break me
You are nothing but a painful sticker
I sure am not your divine property

You broke the trust that I had within you
Can't we be a happy couple of two

Jamie Fowler, Grade 10
Lucerne Valley Jr/Sr High School

Reality

When you fail
You feel you lost your trail

You get off the road
And you feel you want to explode

You want to cry
But you feel so dry

Open your eyes
And take this advice

Try again
Or try another lane

Continue your life
Because this is reality

Liliana Nunez, Grade 12
Weber Institute of Applied Sciences & Technology

School Deja Vu

School is so much fun
Nervous knowing my school days are almost done
Committed, I still rise every day like the sun
But before it even begun
My school's day already done
Thinking on the past
Going wow it went by so fast
Years later, I can't remember the first day
Like reading your favorite book and forgetting the first page
Impossible to remember where it all started
Now regretting never striving to be the smartest
Well now my futures bleak
Now I'm burning every day like California's heat
I feel my high school years were taken
Sorrow for my friends mistaken
Slump, with a mugged feeling
While I was in school they were drug dealing

Keith Moorman, Grade 12
Redwood High School

Things Come and Go

Things come and go —
It's so hard to say goodbye.
Just the thought of you leaving
Makes me want to cry.
Things come crashing down
Til there's nothing left
To see, to do…
Everything I do reminds me of you;
And when I'm in need,
There is on one there
Who can make me smile
Like you made me smile.

Tiffanie Lazos, Grade 10
Huntington Park College Ready Academy High School

Ashley

My heart feels like a plump of clouds,
your yellow hair swing lightly,
and your body strong and fragile.
My mind feels half dead and half alive,
when it comes to a lady that had inspired me,
my heart lifts with a light cloud underneath
and my body floats to an unknown world,
of where my minds run through great and amazing ideas.
Your smile lingers in my mind, loving a woman like you,
waking up every day and smiling
as the sun lights our morning,
saying "I love you, My Beloved."

Armani Nguon, Grade 12
PAAL Campus

And I Loved It
In the forest by the sea beneath the sky,
I did lie while the crickets did cry.
I saw the trees sway in the wind,
The shadowed emerald on soft and sturdy brown,
The quills lay on the ground, flew through the sky,
They caught my eye, and I loved them,
The grove alive in night's breeze, and I loved them.

A while went by then the sea did catch my eye.
It tossed and turned and crashed upon that mighty bluff
Which held me high above the chaos.
The moon's face bounced off the tidal surge.
It waved and swayed and breathed
Its salty breath through my locks, and I loved it,
The way it glistened and rose, trying to meet my eyes, and I loved it.

Again time passed and I did spy the glimmering of the sky,
The twinkling dance on blue canvas.
Amazed at the promenade going on beyond my reach,
I again felt a surge of emotions in my chest
Yet somehow different and unknown.
It caught me with its unpronounced beauty, and I loved it.
It kept me with its existence, and I loved it.
Brenton A. Reasin, Grade 12
Mater Dei High School

Changing of Years
Unknown atmospheres and foreign spaces.
Everyone in view is larger, better, superior.
Searching for a single familiar face from the previous year,
Classes with peers and becoming accustomed to the next four years
In an instant the first year is over.

Starting to be accustomed to the school,
Hallways and pathways become recognizable again.
Doing homework late at night with the help of others.
Getting your act together when grades really start to matter.
Right when you become adapted to the year, it is over.

Possibly the most important year of high school arrives.
Tests, late nights, tests, prom, tests, one step closer to graduation.
Studying takes over your life more than ever,
As you worry about getting scholarships and getting into college.
As soon as you believe the year starts, it is over.

The best year of your high school career arrives.
Getting into colleges and maintaining grades,
Laid back classes with torrid teachers.
As everything culminates to this final moment of graduation,
It is only the beginning.
Jeffrey Cabanez, Grade 12
Redlands High School

Lyla Rose
Nobody understands why
I see the light
So brightly through the covered, cloudy sky.
It gets me through the days,
When I see her face.
All else might be lost
But I have found
Something, which is so sweet, so dear and so profound.
I love her dearly, I love her so.
She is no man in which I supposedly need.
She is simply my niece, Lyla Rose.
Need no one else because although she can only crawl,
She would never let me fall.
Chelsea Ovanessian, Grade 11
Saugus High School

Misunderstood Man
The tale is not widely known
About the misunderstood man who resides alone
Somewhere far away he stands
This oh so lonesome misunderstood man
I walked for years in search of him
When all my prospects seemed so dim
I searched and searched
But no one seemed to understand
My obsession with this misunderstood man
Today I gave up trying to find
What all along was inside my mind
Today I found out where he stands
This oh so lonesome misunderstood man
Courtney Van Buren, Grade 10
Henry Sr High School

Like Father Like Son
I see the love a father and son share
I hear their joy and care within the air
I see them bond, and this isn't fair
'Cause I feel a pain that I cannot bear, inside my heart
I truly know my father and I have grown apart
I don't have a father
And this keeps me bothered
Yet this is the truth
Cause' I haven't seen him for a year or two
This pain I feel is indescribable
Just like he was unreliable
Like father, like son is just a lie
It just reminds me of the nights I cried
Brandon Judulang, Grade 10
Monta Vista High School

Finishing the Race
Running so quickly,
Never daring to look back,
Finish line ahead.
Sarah Hutt, Grade 10
Foothill High School

High Merit Poems – Grades 10, 11 and 12

Fire*
The New Sun could free the sky,
The pleasure in heat wonders why
A pretty face could feed the soul,
But what one flame makes it whole
Fire as Far as the Eye can see,
Loving Life has come back to me
Yesterday seems to dim, despite
Today's blistering light
The anticipation is killing me,
Combustion can be on any degree
Fire as Far as the Eye can see,
Loving life has come back to me
As I stop to think,
Ashes fall and sink
As I wait and see,
The smoke fades but bleeds
As she approaches, I notice in full,
It's hours worth of thought that She had stole
Fire as Far as the I could see,
Loving Life
Loving, Living has come back to Me…
Armando Figueroa, Grade 12
John H Francis Polytechnic High School
*Dedicated to Isabel Ozaeta and Daysi Roxanne Nerio

My True Love
Love means I can't live without him,
I get butterflies beating in my stomach,
I forget how to breath when he walks by,
No one can describe my timeless attraction,
His words flow from his lips like a dream,
This wonderful person never puts me down or ever counts me out,
He thinks of us as equal as two sides of a coin,
One is not more important than the other,
He thinks I could not have looked better with no makeup on,
I will never forget my first love even if he is lost,
I miss it like nothing else I have ever felt,
It's like not being able to feel anymore,
I will cry until my eyes go dry,
But when he comes back that is what makes it the best feeling ever,
When he does he will never deserve me, yet never leave me,
For he has realized what it is like to be without me.
Elizabeth Stamps, Grade 10
Foothill High School

My Hidden Gift
I'm giving it to you today,
The thing I guard the most,
Tuck it away and cast it not astray,
Or I will be as a ghost.
Carefully I'll place it in a box,
Only you can open my small token,
You have the only key to all the locks,
It will always be yours — even when broken.
Paige McMath, Grade 12
University Preparatory School

The Choice
A young man is sitting alone,
A white room, filled with silence.
He sees two buttons on a wall.
One allows him to forget his past.
The other releases him into the future.
He must press one, only one.
His memories have been good to him.
Memories have haunted him.
His past was sweet.
memories filled with many regrets,
The future is frightening.
The future is unknown to him.
His age passes over time.
A choice has not been made.
He walks away from the wall to the other side of the room.
Year are wasted, decisions are left unmade.
He blinds his vision and presses a button by random.
His eyes finally open.
There is only one button on the wall.
Johvani Vegar, Grade 12
Redlands High School

Masquerade
Dancing so swiftly
The unknown faces
Moving at once, quickly
Twirling in an unbound circle

Those eyes I see
Behind the mask
Speak to me
In an ancient rhyme

We dance 'til the midnight hour
our spirits filled with glee
The night filled with magic power
I see the dawn, breaking the spell

We mourn the night's farewell
The magic of the night
It seems, I soon befell
To the dancing in this wondrous masquerade
Maria Sandoval, Grade 12
Esparto High School

Winter
It's the snow that tells me I'm thinking of you
And it's the sun that makes my soul decay
It's the hail that tells me I'm missing you
The storm of our lives blows me away
I've got ice running down my wrists
And frost melting on my eyes
I'll take the darkness of our past
And paint the white cutting through the sky
B.L. Shies, Grade 12
Mater Dei High School

Selfish Friend

I would take a bullet
To save a friend.
I would jump in front of a friend
If a knife was descending upon them.
I would surrender myself
To save my best friends.
I am selfish.
Death is much easier
Than living with the pain and despair
Of a loved one's death.
I would suffer for weeks
If a friend died.
But if I die instead,
I'll cease to care.
I won't care if you cry,
Well not that much,
As long as I don't have to be the one in pain.

Natasha Stepanova, Grade 10
Bentley School

Love in September

There is only one special month to me.
Just the perfect weather in September.
When my day of birth comes to be,
The month that I will always remember.

Not cold, nor hot, the weather is just right.
Summer season is about to end,
Fall is like the rush of the ocean; sky still bright.
September is just like my best friend.

It is my favorite month of all,
Weather is just hot and cold at the same time.
Every time this month comes, it's almost fall.
I've been waiting for this month for a long time.

Month that I enjoy the last of summer.
A month that will be enjoyed forever.

Pinky Wong, Grade 10
Abraham Lincoln High School

I Walk the Path of Illusions

I walk the path of illusions
Have I been asleep?
I walk with confusion
There's nothing to see
I'm blinded by the light
I think I'm flying home tonight
I apologize for no farewell
I am not sure if I shall return
Please have no fear
I will forever be here
I will protect you as you sleep
I'm not far, but closer than you think.

Joselyn De la Pena, Grade 10
Huntington Park College Ready Academy High School

The Intertwine

Words breath a new
Lyrics kept in the mind
It is only a few
Who know the depths of the musical bind

Tunes that continuously ring
Sounds that are constantly made
Give others the willingness to sing
Never in life will it ever fade

But at times there are those
Who try to take away one's expression
However one's own heart knows
They can never take the feeling of affection

That music and person hold
Together and forever they are each other's mold

Sophia Tran, Grade 11
Covina High School

Thank You

When you feel like the whole world is crumbling around you
and everything in your life leaves you like the morning dew
you know that you will always have someone by your side
to go up and down with you through the life ride
I don't know why it always happens to me
but I know that You are the only one that can set me free
I live every second and every minute for Your glory
to praise You and to tell my kids the same story
You saved me from this terrible place
so that one day I will see Your glorious face
oh I live my life for You
thank you for making me new
You changed my life
and rid me of my worldly strife
You deserve everything
from every grain of sand to every human being
Thank You

Caleb Pilarski, Grade 11
Saugus High School

Small Joys

Skipping through the frozen section on a hot day
With a free stick of honey from the market
Baby's first steps
And a loud sneeze in class
Inside jokes
And melting popsicles
July nights
With Sparklers and candles that don't blow out
Tight embraces
And valentines between friends
Small joys, poke their heads out throughout the day
Sprinkling their delight in every which way.

Patool Afanan, Grade 12
Redlands High School

High Merit Poems – Grades 10, 11 and 12

I Am
I wonder about my future
I hear the beating of my heart
I see people laughing
I want to be healthy
I do what will make me strong
I am a tiny girl

I pretend to study more
I feel headaches sometimes
I touch my forehead
I worry about my family
I cry when I'm alone
I am a tiny girl

I understand what I have to do
I say I will get a good job
I dream that my wishes come true
I try to do my best
I hope I can do everything I want
I am a tiny girl
Binh Gip, Grade 11
Hiram W Johnson High School

Blue and White
The pushing and roaring
The way you move
Calm one second then angry the next
So big and full of life
Blue and white from the outside
Colorful in the inside
Unique creatures you hold
Beautiful and amazing swimmers you keep
Treasures you find
Eyes you open and amaze
Minds you make wonder
Homes you destroy
Lives you have changed
Ruling Earth every second of the day.
Stephanie I Olvera, Grade 12
Redlands High School

Take Me Away
Looking into this old antique mirror,
I see the reflection of exhaustion.
Crumbly, wrinkled pale skin,
I'm a shattered window from years ago.

Admiring that painting of the little girl,
O, the sight of luxury!
How I wish it was the olden days.

Dawn-to-dark, sunrise-to-sunset,
How much longer do I have to wait?
'Till the spirit would take me away…
Stephanie Chen, Grade 10
Abraham Lincoln High School

Trapped
As if in a dream, a child is sitting in a chair.
She is being stared at in every direction,
A man is talking to her,
Her hands are sweaty and sweat is dripping down her forehead,
Her body is tense and she can't relax,
She closes her eyes and tries to answer all of the questions,
She feels the pressure build up as she cries,
She feels a pounding in her heart as she speaks,
She feels weak and scared,
She talks with this passion about things that have happened,
She hears everyone talking and feels trapped in this chair,
Everyone is looking at her and she breathes heavily,
She gets the chance to finally leave the chair after numerous hours,
And realizes that as if this were a dream this child is me,
She weeps and cries with loved ones,
Knowing that everything that has happened to her will never go away,
For she will always be trapped with the memories.
Victoria Cairns, Grade 11
Valley Christian High School

I Try
I have been told I would not graduate
But I try
I have been told that I would never get a job
But I try
I have been told because of my background nothing would become of me
But I try
I have been told that I would not go to college
But I try
I have been told I'm not smart enough
But I try
I have been told I would never do anything successful for myself
But I try
I have been told many things but I learned that it does not matter
What people say as long as you believe in yourself
I learned to deal with people's negative comments
But to me it goes in one ear and comes out the other.
Liliana Santana, Grade 12
Omega High School

The Year
Pop-pop-pop! January explodes with people popping bottles to celebrate
Bang-bang, mu-ahhhh! February shoots with Cupid's hugs and kisses
Ouch…hurrah! March pinches with leprechaun's luck
Crackle, hop-hop, drip drop…April hatches eggs with bouncing bunnies in the rain
Crunch, crisp, AAHHH! May dances with chips and Mom's hot salsa
Splash, splash! June dives into lots of pool parties with Dad's barbecue
Ka-boom, pow-pow-pow! July blows up with fireworks and 90 degree days
Chop-chop! August rushes into end-of-summer-days sales
"A, B, C…1, 2, 3" September counts up all the days 'til the first day of school
"Trick or treat!" October spooks into Halloween
Gobble, gobble! November cooks up turkey and special thanks
Ho, ho, ho! December frosts the milk and cookies left for Santa
Tiffanee Zamora, Grade 11
Bell Gardens High School

I Was Only Five…

I was only five…
When he used to hit her…and she would cry…
But when she cried…we cried too…
But there was nothing I could do…because I was only five…
They would always argue…and fight…
I was only five…
I didn't know hitting someone was such a big deal…
I couldn't help heal her…I try to help her…by yelling, "Stop!"…
But I was only five…then she left…
I want to tell her…I'm sorry for letting him hit you…
But I was only five…what can I do?
She was very kind and smart…she had a great heart…
She's the most gorgeous person I have ever seen…
Even the bruises on her face couldn't make her ugly…
But now all we can do is dream…about her gorgeous face…
She was so special to me…
I couldn't helped her…maybe she would've stayed…
But she left…for good…
And I was only five…
Her name is Maria…

Marielle Viray, Grade 12
Omega High School

I Am

I am a person that wants to do well.
I wonder if I'm going to graduate this year.
I hear people always fighting.
I see myself with no escape from anything.
I want to graduate from Milpitas High next semester.

I pretend that I'm all right when I feel down.
I feel like nobody cares.
I touch my rose and it reminds me of my lady.
I worry that one day I'm going to die.
I cry when someone close to me dies.
I am a person that wants to do well.

I understand a little why we came into this life.
I say that everything is going to be good.
I dream about having a nice life.
I try to make things better when they are not.
I hope that life goes well with my family.
I am a person that wants to do well.

Anthony Padilla, Grade 12
Calaveras Hills High School

Smiles

Sometimes it takes a while,
to form your kind of smile,
but once the frown is reversed
it takes away the worst of the cursed.
So, ladies wipe those tears off your face
and put a smile in its place,
because today is just one of them smilin' days.

Abriana Griffith, Grade 12
University Preparatory School

I Am

I am a teen with a lot on his mind.
I wonder if I will ever graduate.
I hear people telling me to do something with my life.
I see everyone becoming successful.
I want a high school diploma.
I am a teen with a lot on his mind.

I pretend words don't hurt, but they really do.
I feel like my family is counting on me to graduate.
I touch my diploma every time I think about graduating.
I worry someday I won't have my mom there for me.
I cry when my mom and dad always fight.
I am a teen with a lot on his mind.

I understand that not everyone lives forever.
I say live life to the fullest with no regrets.
I dream someday I will be happy with my wife and kids.
I try giving my mom the respect she deserves.
I hope I graduate this year.
I am a teen with a lot on his mind.

Paul Rodriguez, Grade 12
Calaveras Hills High School

A Lifetime of Training, and the Training of a Lifetime

Although practice makes perfect, no one can be
I've learned about teamwork and even about me
Meeting friends from all kinds of places
Seeing people, players, and new shining faces
I have no social life, and am always with the team
Sometimes all my homework makes me want to scream
Without volleyball these last four years
My life would be incomplete and I would be in tears
My time as an athlete can never be topped
And my life as a volleyball player will never be stopped
I met new people and experienced life
And it wouldn't be as meaningful without all the strife
Missing out on fun and average teenage things
Has prepared me to enjoy what the future brings
Making it to playoffs is definitely my goal
As well as playing the next division with my team as a whole
Only two years left at this place, Saugus High
And then on to my life as Stanford's right side
Our years together have been lots of fun
Now it's time for college at Stanford, my number one

Kristen Nystrom, Grade 11
Saugus High School

Irving

I ntelligent as Albert Einstein
R espectful in every way, usually
V ictorious against others, most likely
I ndependent, has
N ever been
G reedy since second grade

Irving Juarez, Grade 10
Huntington Park College Ready Academy High School

High Merit Poems – Grades 10, 11 and 12

The Little Garden

Bordered by a white fence,
Flowers in full efflorescence.
The sun awakens and shines through,
Like crystals, settled on all, the morning dew.
My hair tussled by a gentle cool breeze,
Flowers rustle and giggle from the flirty tease.
Bees not yet up, I don't hear their familiar bumble,
The clumsy pit pit put each time I stumble.
As my feet squish the rocks they stir no commotion,
Only supporting my steps with pure devotion.
Humble rose buds staring at the bloomed in vain,
The thorns they shield their innocence from pain.
Fluffy hydrangeas circumscribed about the edges,
Every so often there are intricately trimmed hedges.
The scene comes to an end, its time for the next part
Silence takes its leave, the days about to start.
The little garden emerges from its deep sleep.
Birds serenade their loving tweet tweet.
Splish splash from the birdbath, two white doves,
I smile and whisper to all, "Good morning my loves."
Caroline Dang, Grade 10
Mission San Jose High School

I Am

I am an independent and respectful person.
I wonder if I will ever get a chance to open my own barbershop door.
I hear the cash register open.
I see money falling into my hands.
I want to be successful.
I am an independent and respectful person.

I pretend that my worries went away.
I feel I have a strong future.
I touch my barbershop's light switch.
I worry that someday my dream will come crashing to an end.
I cry tears of happiness.
I am an independent and respectful person.

I understand if I work hard I will achieve my dream.
I say work hard in what you believe in.
I dream of everyday struggles to make me a more powerful person.
I try to be the best person I can be.
I hope for the best and forget about the past.
I am an independent and respectful person.
Eric Salazar, Grade 11
Calaveras Hills High School

Soccer

S occer spirit
O vercoming obstacles
C razy 8
C reative like an artist
E nergetic
R estless respectful
Ricardo Mares, Grade 10
Huntington Park College Ready Academy High School

I Am

I am outgoing and charming.
I wonder if my brother is looking down on me.
I hear his voice at night.
I see and imagine my brother in the house.
I want my brother back.

I am outgoing and charming.
I pretend that my brother is there.
I feel like I am left without him.
I touch my brother.
I worry about my mother.
I cry to show my mother my feelings.

I am outgoing and charming.
I understand what my mother goes through.
I say bad things to my mother, but I am sorry.
I dream of being a rap star.
I try to do well in school.
I hope I graduate.
I am outgoing and charming.
Maurice Ross, Grade 12
Calaveras Hills High School

I Am

I am trustworthy and caring.
I wonder if the violence will ever stop.
I hear a voice telling me what to do.
I see a world full of miserable people.
I want the war to stop.
I am trustworthy and caring.

I pretend like I am happy when most of the time I'm not.
I feel the pain that my loved ones feel.
I touch the hearts of other people.
I worry that hatred is going to spread all over.
I cry that my family is falling apart.
I am trustworthy and caring.

I understand that violence will never stop.
I say that only God can stop the violence.
I dream that one day people will believe in me.
I try to do well in school.
I hope to go to college and prove people wrong.
I am trustworthy and caring.
Rafael Arreola, Grade 10
Calaveras Hills High School

Crying

C auses are so many
R ips the heart right out of the soul like petals from a flower
Y es, could mean happiness
I n a way it's good
N othing should impede this feeling
G iving you a sense of being a true human being
Ana Bahena, Grade 10
Huntington Park College Ready Academy High School

I Am

I am wise but helpless.
I wonder if the icecaps will stop melting.
I see the polar bears drowning and dying of hunger.
I want our careless world to stop.
I am wise but helpless.

I am everything yet nothing.
I wonder if wars will ever stop.
I see a new generation of rage and violence.
I want an unreachable peace to come.
I am everything yet nothing.

I am high and low in this world.
I wonder if stars are fake sometimes.
I see my life as a test to prove myself.
I want to know everything there is to know.
I am high and low in this world.

Jesus Barrios, Grade 10
Calaveras Hills High School

Narcissus

The boy up ahead walks the same way each day
Walks so carefree and never will stay

Though I'm clearly around him he never will see
The Echo that follows his warmth and his glee

This blackened archangel whose face haunts my dreams
Without him I won't be content as it seems

Oh give me just one taste of heaven divine
Let me cease being Echo and let him be mine

This gorgeous Narcissus corrupted by darkness
And turned to a hell god beneath my gaze

He's stolen my heart and locked it away
For this he remains Narcissus of chains

Taylor Gilstrap, Grade 12
Lakeside High School

Sleeping Always

For once in my life
I would like to sleep the whole day
So I don't think of problems
Think of school
Think of homework
I would like to sleep
Not to stress about what is due the next day
To run away from all problems
To dream the unimagined
Or to see something unimagined
Or to see something unrealistic
To sleep and feel refreshed.

Joshua Franco, Grade 10
Huntington Park College Ready Academy High School

The Unfailing

You're not just my friend
You're not someone I just met

You're someone special
Sent from above and put in front of me
Though I can't see
Though it's blinding

When I forget, you are there to remind me
When I am in pain, you make me feel better
Though I am in pain and I forget
Though I can't see and it's blinding
You are there to comfort me

When I begin to fall, you are there to catch me
When I am bored, you want to play a game I hate
though we are far apart you're all I can think of
Though we are together, I still miss you

Though you are not with me now
Our love is still pure
No one to break our strong bond
We are one and always will
We belong with each other
We'll love like no other

Shannon Arwine, Grade 12
Lucerne Valley Jr/Sr High School

The Calling

Echoes of an elusive world are calling soft to me,
"Choose well sweet child
Your time ensues,
Your path unfixed is free."
How can I know so lost so young
Too close at hand to see?

Frozen in fear this rising duty
Whispers forth on separate winds,
For walking West instead of East
A different sunset,
Another end.

I linger here in the embrace of you my guardian
And with or naught either assent
Soon face mortality.

The future's sloth incessant march
Runs swift by season's turn,
I'll breathe once more, I'll forward stride
Still weary of a fledgling's pride.

I vow that any maelstrom fierce won't break me or my will,
Although my soul is malleable
My courage leads me still.

Severine Richardson, Grade 12
Washington High School

High Merit Poems – Grades 10, 11 and 12

(This One's for You) Can't Get You Out of My Head

Your hands draw hearts on mine
I can't take my eyes off of yours
That smile, that black dress
Can't get you out of my head.
Sometimes know you can only love me this way
There must be a reason
Were we meant to be together?

Hand in hand
Forever means forever
You'll be in my heart and I'd be in your
Keeping me laughing
Your hand drawing hears on mine
Your smile your eyes your lips
Perfect
That warm soft kiss
That little smile
No wonder I can't get you out of my head

You're always on my mind
You're always in my heart
And you're the only one who can love me this way

Ivan Guerrero, Grade 11
Robert F Kennedy High School

Momma

Momma was an angel,
And she will always be,
But she was in a lot of pain,
So god set her free.
And even though home,
Is where I want her to be,
God is taking care of her,
And is watching over me.
Momma always cared, she never let anyone down,
That's why everyone loved having her around.
She was a loving person, and every one knew,
That's why when she passed we didn't know what to do
So now to this day, we stand around and pray,
That god is taking care of her,
Each and every day.

Korrena McDaniels, Grade 10
Center High School

On Dreaming

Languid reconnaissances scattered as diaries.
Perpetual entourages of shapes and ideas,
desperate for form and recognition. They
shrink in the shadows of the mind, proving
illusive to the ever-musing dreamer — inebriated
intuition of the frugal consciousness.
Lost in the seams of the streams, where water
flows through the earth and shapes the
contours of perception.

Colin Rosemont, Grade 12
Agoura High School

Elegy for the Living

This is my elegy for you
you're dead to me
like Sunday morning
lazy day burning
in your heat,
in my hearts
pounding
you don't know
how honesty feels
let me in
why can't you
how can anyone care
when you don't
nothing went through,
you can't feel love,
you can't feel love
when you have a cold heart
you're drowning in lies
you can't move on
if you're not dead to them,
on a hot afternoon
I can feel your lies
bee-eee-eat
you don't know how to
fix it without a needle
lost in three months time,
you're full of self pity
you can't find truth when
you can't move on

Carly Vollers, Grade 12
San Lorenzo Valley High School

Ode to My iPod

My iPod,
like a mini radio,
I just like the fact
that I can bring you
where I want, when I want.
I can't resist taking you
if I see you on the bed,
just waiting for me to put on your headphones
as you whisper those gentle
melodies in my ear.
I see many others in the Apple Store,
all lined up and looking much more attractive and appealing,
but don't worry,
they don't give me the feeling that you do.
I love your smooth sensor pad and your slim texture,
but sometimes,
we just have to move on and meet new people.
I'm sorry, it's not you, and it's not me.
It's the new iPod Nano.

Chris Ma, Grade 10
Abraham Lincoln High School

The One I Love

The one I love with all my might
The one I'm thinking about tonight
The one that helps me do my things right
The one I dream of when I sleep at night
The one I think of when I hug my pillow tight
The one that makes me happy when she comes into my sight
The one I'm not giving up without a fight
to "The One" that changed my life.

Raul Rosas, Grade 10
Huntington Park College Ready Academy High School

Poetry

Poetry is putting your feelings down on paper
Hoping others feel the same
Poetry is speaking out loud
Without a sound said
Poetry is a way to calm down
When your thoughts keep going
Poetry is saying, "I love you"
With more than just words
Poetry can say, "I'm sorry"
Hoping to be forgiven from the heart
Poetry is reading the words
That give you feelings
Poetry is the way I speak aloud to you
Without one word from my mouth

Yesenia Guillen, Grade 12
Yosemite Adult High School

Happiness

Happiness is something you cannot find,
Yet it should be something you will search for.
Things like happiness cannot be confined;
Everyone experienced it before.
Happiness is like seeing a rainbow
In the middle of a terrible storm.
Happiness is like seeing the bright stars glow
With a love: close together, snug, and warm.
We should all share our happy encounters
To prove to the world that we are not sad.
We add a single click to the counter
That shows to the world that we are all glad.
Happiness isn't something you always get;
So when you are happy, never forget.

Stephen Trinh, Grade 10
South Hills High School

The Rainbow Seasons

Red leaves fall from the tree,
I pile them up as high as my knees.
Orange pumpkins line the streets,
I see them as I go trick or treat.
Yellow grass begins to show,
And the sunshine starts to go.
Green decorated trees fill the room,
With a star on top and a train that zooms.
Blue puddles line the street,
The water splashes and tickles my feet.
Purple flowers bloom in the light,
And turn to floaties when the pool feels just right.
The seasons come like colors of the rainbow,
Look for them and watch them grow!

Kylie Bender, Grade 10
Foothill High School

Standing on Faith

Everyone looks from left to right,
Not knowing which to choose.

Some people turn from side to side,
And they don't know what to do.

A mass of people,
Insecure,
Start following the crowd.

Is it best to take that path?
Go with the group and walk with them?

Not if you're going to choose what's right.
What's right for you may not be for them.
You can stand strong without following the crowd,
And don't let them change your mind.

Instead, take a giant leap of faith.
Go on the path
That you're supposed to make,

And hope on.

Taylor Brass, Grade 10
Horizon Charter School

Off to Never Land

I just want to escape
To a place where the people never betray
Life's always ready to play
Where curiosity rules
And you never have to go to school
Where souls would bend with mirth
And we could be more than we're worth

I just want to run away
From true sadness and fake smiles
Leave the mail to stockpile
Forget you and the pain it brings
All those horrid feelings
No reminders of your face
Or the heartache to erase

I just want to leave
Pretend I was never here
Off to witness what's beyond
The brimming lights of the city
To have them blind me with the pureness of the carefree
And with a skip and a swirl
I want to play with the "big bad world"

Olivia Brayan, Grade 11
University Preparatory School

High Merit Poems – Grades 10, 11 and 12

Dawn and Dusk

Dawn is like a new beginning,
A fresh start you might say.
Dusk is like the end of a book,
Much to the reader's dismay.

Dawn is young as a dimpled, cooing baby;
Dusk is mature as an elderly man.
Dawn's phosphorescence is like a rainbow;
Dusk's like a dull stone that is pale and wan.

The dawn is like the budding seed of a pear;
When it breaks, the transparent mist and dew it wears.
Reinvigorating as the sun;
Dawn sprouts and looks upon the world in salutation.

The dusk steadily steals from the day shining light;
Like a thief, it creeps discreetly into the night.
As evening melts away,
Nature turns to slumber without delay.

Between the two, I favor dawn;
Though dusk is needed for the cycle to go on.
Jessica McCallum, Grade 12
Redlands High School

The Other Side

For every 'yin' there is a 'yang,'
For every song there is one who sang,
Every story has two sides,
Every diary has one who confides.

For every great victory, a loss,
For every gigantic tree, a small green moss,
For every death, there is a birth,
And for every sadness, there is mirth.

Not everything is as it seems,
And one has to identify reality from dreams,
For every one awake, be sure to count the snoozers,
And when congratulating the winners,
Be a good sport and don't forget the losers.
Ryan Loughrey, Grade 10
Foothill High School

Forever

My love for you would always stay,
the way you love me would run away,
I always thought this could be forever,
look at it now we were never meant to be together.

Days went on thinking of you,
just seeing that I couldn't be without you,
so we went back together,
hopefully this time it would last forever.
Priscilla Garcia, Grade 10
Huntington Park College Ready Academy High School

Beautiful Dream

The moon rises and fills the sky
with an eerie light.
Shadows dance upon the ground,
and the music of the forest is all around.
Suddenly my soul is awake
and I feel more alive with each breath I take.
Everything seems to blend
into a beautiful dream that doesn't end.
I'm at peace and I have no fear
when all that I hear
is the harmonious hoot of an owl
and a lone wolf's howl.
As I lie beside a stream
and gaze up at the twinkle and gleam
of the bright jewels above,
I'm filled with true peace, happiness and love.
Heather McGrath, Grade 12
Paradise Sr High School

All Me Baybee

If I were a color
I would be as blue as the clear, sunny sky.
I am a circle that is not yet complete.
A walk in life, which has a destination
A lion's roar, loud enough for the clouds to hear
I am a song left unfinished and unheard
I'm like infinity, I never stop going
A black Lincoln MKX, with an engine that doesn't turn off
I'm a new shiny, bright lamp with lots of ideas
I am a pizza with extra toppings
I am a flute playing a low, sleepy lullaby
A mountain with a never-ending top
A girl with so many fears they could kill her
I am
Indescribably, unpredictably
ME!
Destiny Tiffee, Grade 12
Prospect Continuation High School

Compare and Contrast

One speaks English, the other speaks Chinese.
One lives in a house, the other lives in an apartment.
One's already adapted, the other needs to adapt.
One has "everything," the other doesn't.
One pays workers, the other gets paid.
They are so much apart,
Yet,
They are both citizens,
both share the same but different law.
Yet,
One has wealth and power,
and the other only has rights —
that will not be taken away...
Hopefully.
Dandan Chen, Grade 11
Alhambra High School

In the Waiting Line

The wind serves as a vessel, transporting the leaves, parallel to the birds in constant motion.
But, I can take no flight of my own.
They say my flight will take off soon. I've been on the waiting list far too long.

I've been watching the planes land and take off for years now —
But the Pilot doesn't think I'm ready to leave.

I wander around the airport to pass the time. It gets old. All of it.
Change is constant here. New people arriving and departing.
New languages I've never heard before. I want to be one with the change. I need a change of scenery.
But first I have to make the change within myself.
I'd rather switch airlines and find a way out. The Pilot won't let me.

The beautiful becomes the ugly.
That's what it means to be depressed.
I open the shades of the waiting room and try to enjoy the sun,
Try to appreciate the people I hate, try and love the sounds I called noise.
That's what it means to make an effort.
I close the shades of the waiting room and bury my head in my hands once more.
That's what it means to relapse. Again.
I keep checking the boards for my flight. It's not listed. I'll have to be patient.

Gunita Singh, Grade 12
Palo Alto High School

My Mother Weeps and I Don't Know Why

My mother weeps and I don't know why.
When I see my mother weep, I feel a stab through my heart because there's nothing I could do to stop her tears.
Every single one of her tears has the value of a diamond to me.
There are not many mothers out there like mine.
My mother is like a piece of gold thread in a stack of hay,
It's hard to find.
I love my mother more than anything in the world.
She's done so much for me and has gone through a lot to help me.
She's the reason I want to be successful in life.
She taught me to never give up on my dreams and to keep going no matter what happens in life.
But when I see my mother weep and there's nothing I could do, I feel as if my world breaks in half.
As if it were a sunny day and suddenly dark clouds come and conquer the beautiful warm day.
There is a story behind her tears and I don't know what it is.
If I could give my life for hers I would do it in a heart beat.
My mother weeps and I don't know why.

Andy Lopez, Grade 12
Dunlap Leadership Academy

In the Midnight Hour

Tears flow from my eyes and appear on my face like little streams washing down my cheeks. Tonight, is one night where I wish for nightmares. I wish for anything that will take my mind off the news I've just gotten. Something to ease the emotional, physical and mental agony I suffer from. Suffering because of a loss that isn't completely a loss. More of a movement. The movement of someone into a new stage in life where I'm nonexistent to them. I'm now in the past just a memory, a memory trapped in the back of their mind, forever put to rest, never to be resurrected. I cry because I have become invisible. I have been wiped away from the memory of the one that I love. I cry because I'm supposed to be happy but instead I sit here, weeping, eyes red, face hot, head pounding, heart shattered into a million pieces like broken glass. I cry because I used to wish nightmares away but now I'm wishing for them to overtake me, for them to bring me to a world where everything is horrible just so when I wake up, I won't suffer as much. I cry because I let myself. I used to be the girl that cried for no one, now I find myself shedding tears like a young child when they don't get their way. I cry not only because I've lost my love, but because I've also lost myself.

Marshanna Valrie, Grade 11
Gardena Sr High School

High Merit Poems – Grades 10, 11 and 12

Memories of Past

It's only been days
But it feels like decades
The road that I once crossed
Crosses me no more
Neither does the flame of inspiration.
Tattoos label the skin
But a portrait makes
Them say ah...
Denying what is real
Is like walking in snow barefooted
When a rumor is spread
It's already halfway around
The world while the truth
Is still tying its shoes.
Lessons and mistakes are meant
To be learned from, also
Checking your life twice
For there are some that stay and some
You never get a chance to say
Good-bye
Oscar Gonzalez, Grade 12
Omega High School

I Am

I wonder when the problems can be gone
I hear people talking
I see a cat running
I want to be a teacher
I am a student

I pretend to do my work
I feel happy when I do funny things
I touch my heart
I worry about Dad
I cry when my uncle doesn't listen to me
I am a student

I understand my sister
I say "I love you" to my mom
I dream of buying a big beautiful house
I try my best
I hope my family is happy every day
I am a student
Mei Mei Su, Grade 11
Hiram W Johnson High School

Light/Darkness

Light
Necessary, bright
Radiating, beaming, flashing
Gentle, luminosity — nebulous, shadowy
Blinding, hiding, dimming
Mysterious, secret
Darkness
Ana Mecalco, Grade 11
Hiram W Johnson High School

Every Time

Every time we blow out the candles,
The sparks between us still light up my sky.
Every hello brings good-bye, and it takes part of me.
I pretend I don't think of you, you don't mean a thing to me.

But I still try so hard to breathe when you come around.
They all know the effect you have on me, everyone but you.
It doesn't matter how much I try to make it go away
It would seem that love had its own way.

Every time, once in a while I'll dream of what we could be
Ever since that day with one smile you took all of me
With the warmth of your hand I knew where I should stand
And I want to know why with you I seem to be able to fly.

You should know you're the only one for me
I understand, I know I'm not the only one for you
I hope every time she looks at you she'll see what I see.
While I'm stuck writing these words hoping they'll mean something to you.
Ericela Ruiz, Grade 11
Connecting Waters Charter School

Tale of a Greek Goddess

The goddess of spring is what she is called
A paintbrush to paint flowers is what she hauled
The cheerful, radiant daughter of Demeter
No goddess could be any sweeter

The young goddess soon caught Hades' eye
To the Underworld he took her, where she couldn't see the sky
Her outraged mom brought droughts to the land
To have her daughter returned is what Demeter planned

Unfortunately, the young maiden ate a couple of pomegranate seeds
While the girl stayed with Hades, nothing would grow, not even weeds
When returned to her mom, flowers would shoot up from the ground
The story of Persephone is well-known all around
Keren Reimann, Grade 10
Lucerne Valley Jr/Sr High School

The World at Peace

The world would be a perfect place:
If the wars across the world ended
If the wars within a country were halted
If the children of third world countries stopped dying
If men of different races saw each other for what is on the inside
If women stopped trying to better their appearances
If children were taught to share and care from birth
If people just loved their spouses and worked their problems out
If people stopped caring about artificial happiness and more about genuine happiness
If people put an end to killing one another and focused more on embracing each other
If man stopped seeing money as a thing of value but more as just a piece of paper
If man was just himself and did not worry about impressing others
The world would be a perfect place if EVERYTHING WAS AT PEACE.
Daniela Pakro, Grade 11
Saugus High School

My Clementine

I looked out the window, saw her coming inside. My heart just jumped a mile high.
But her face was stone, and I don't know how this goes.
Without a word, she leads me up, up the stairs, to my room, close the door shut.
She turns to me, and says the word: "Goodbye."
That's the girl, that's the girl. She says the word, she says the word. I'm now alone, now alone.
Will you die? Will you die? When the one you love leaves you there.
No explanation, black hole inside. Will you die? Will you die?
Now his heart is filled with fear. Alone in the world, I'll miss you dear.
Paralyzed, there's no disguise for the pain, the hole deep inside.
That's what she's like, my Clementine, so goodbye.
That's the girl, that's the girl. She walks away from my open arms.
Her shoes leave stains on the carpet floor. She pauses just as she reaches the door and says,
"Will you die? Will you die? I know you don't need me to be with you.
And this is something I have to do.
Will you die? Will you die? You can survive when I'm not by your side 'cause my loving you was a lie."
That's the girl, that's the girl. Then he makes his way to the cupboard.
And he pulls out a rope. Do you know what he plans to do?
Will you die? Will you die? When you've lost the world, when you're in the dark,
And you've lost everything you had. Have you lost everything you have?
With the rope in his hands, did she understand how much she meant to him?
Did she know that she was keeping him alive?

Kimmi Ligh, Grade 11
La Serna High School

Untouched by Man

Untouched by man the limbs of Mother Nature protect all that is hers
    And those who wish to embrace it are treasured and its meaning is heard
If only all would listen, smell, touch, and taste the fruits of knowledge it has to offer
Our world would unfold and the secrets behind the power of nature would be revealed
In defense to the destruction of industry and greed, the deep penetrable branches reach
Far beyond what any man woman or child could ever teach
That is the simplicity and beauty of life and truth that lies deep within the layers and roots of ancient life
Those that we neglect during everyday routines
Whose moss is laid upon its aching trunk that carries the burdens of man
Truth is what we see in the evergreen forests, the wonder, glory, and awe
    It's what we hear in the wild birds' morning songs
    It is the taste of its ripe fruit delicately rejuvenating the pores of our tongues
It's the smell of the ageless serenity that is thrust upon our senses
It is the appreciation of life at its best a transcendental ecclesiastic
An understanding of what peace truly is at heart
The power of the simplicity and wisdom in nature

Citlali Alvarado, Grade 12
Cathedral Catholic High School

A Glimpse of Me

My favorite place isn't near or far, but a place that's very familiar. I have an infinite amount of love for this home, and I would go there every day if I could. It's not over the rainbow, it's not where the sun meets the Earth, but it's a place where the rainbow glows and a place where the sun always shines. This magical place is my grandmother's house of course. Never in my 16 years of living have I ever come across a place better than this. However, it's not the green grass or the myriad amount of avocados her garden produces that attracts me to such a wonderful place, but it's the way it feels like home and when I walk through the front door the aroma filling the room pulls me in and wants to never let me leave. It's also the way my grandma looks when I walk through the door, the wide smile bearing over her beautiful face, it makes me want to throw my arms around her and tell her I love her. This place is very special to me and a main part of my life. Without it I would be incomplete. You'll never know how much love and joyfulness one house, one place, could have on this big Earth, until you've been to grandma's house.

Nicole Farquar, Grade 11
Grossmont High School

Where Are We

Traveling, Traveling, searching for yesteryear.
Looking for the times of peace, of love, the times of joy, and happiness.
Trying to find the good in people that once existed.

Looking for the representing in our representatives.
Looking for a hint of what we were. Looking to find the leaders of old,
For certainly there is still a Washington, a Jefferson, a Lincoln, and a Wilson.

If there be not these than what are we?
Are we left with nothing but Buchanans, and Nixons, Clintons, and Jacksons?

Surely we are not so lost that we cannot get back to the beauty that was our country.
Surely there are still leaders who are able to lead.
Surely they will come, maybe not today, and maybe not tomorrow.

But in our darkest hour, they will rise, rise like eagles, on wings of love.
Love for country, love for neighbor with malice towards corruption and hatred toward conflict.

Surely we will find these in our search, but are we willing to work hard and struggle long for the answer we seek?
Or will we continue to settle for sloppy seconds?

It is in our hands.
Search how you will, and I will search as I must, for that hint of yesteryear.

Ryan Tucker, Grade 11
La Serna High School

Get Up!

In life we get turned down for dates, we get rejected for help, but remember get up. When we fall down after we realize that someone has pushed us, remember get up. When we fall before we reach our goal, remember get up.

Yes, in life we do get rejected, but remember get up. Yes, we do get turned away, but remember get up. Yes, it's good sometimes to weep over a loss of a loved one, but remember get up. Yes, it's good to weep over the loss of a girlfriend or boyfriend, husband, or wife, but remember get up.

When you fall down, thinking that this is it for you, remember get up. Jesus fell. He fell many times, but remember He got up. Yes, Jesus died on a Friday, but remember that Sunday, He got up. Yes, Jesus was tempted, but He remembered to get up.

Yes were going to fall, feel bad for ourself, and wish we could just cry our heart out, but remember get up. Yes we're going to have some bad days, but remember get up. Yes we're going to have some sunshine and some rains, but remember get up. Yes we're going to have some heartaches and pains, but remember get up.

So, after you fall remember get up. Let's get up and tell somebody else remember to get up.
Remember get up!

William Brothers II, Grade 10
Salesian High School

Memory

Fifteen years old, in school on U.S.A.
Somehow, I just miss her a lot even though it hurts, but I just want to be with her.
It's like everything is nonmalleable without her.
I don't know, but it was a totally new, different feeling without her.
My heart feels more empty inside every moment, ever hour, every day I just want to be by her side.
I can't focus on anything, I can't think of anything beside her.

Cai Vang, Grade 10
Hiram W Johnson High School

My Favorite Place

It was snowing, inches and inches fell on the ground
It was my favorite time on the year
It's called winter
Long drive to get there, but we finally made it
Mammoth here we come
We have our boards, boots, bindings, luggage, and warm clothes
We are ready for snowboarding, my favorite sport
And three days with my family and friends
Finally, we arrive and we finally step and sink in the inches of snow
How I love the beautiful white powder and the freezing wind blowing in my hair
And seeing my breath in front of me
Night finally arrives, sleep is near
Getting ready for the eventful day tomorrow
Fall asleep, then all of a sudden I hear the alarm
Quickly getting ready, mountain here we come, one long day of boarding on the fresh powder
The slopes close and we head back to our cabin.
All of a sudden, a snowball fight occurs
Before I know it, it's over and time to go
Another great vacation

Lauren Correa, Grade 11
Saugus High School

Dreams

My dream is clear as a crystal,
I envision being on that stage with the crowd cheering for me and only me,
People scream like in horror movies and cry like in sad movies,
All because my lyrics relate to them.
To know that I made a difference in someone's life like that and helped them through a tough time,
Truthfully makes me want to cry with happiness.
I get on that stage every night and give it my all because when I was in that crowd's position that's what I expected
So I will give my fans nothing less.
My voice gives people chills like nails on a chalkboard but in the good way,
Music has always been a part of me but to live it like all my idols have,
Is the real dream.
Some say I play guitar, piano, maybe even a little drums and I sing,
They question how I ever achieved a goal as high as the sky.
And I have to reply:
"If you dream it, go for it! Don't let anyone ever get you down!" Because,
That's what I've always been told,
And to everyone who ever said I couldn't, look at me now.

Alayna Will, Grade 11
Grossmont High School

Sounds of Music

What is that sound? Is it a string quartet? Or oboes warming up? No, it is the sound of a youth symphony playing Brahms. I have played violin in youth symphonies for the last three years and it has been a memorable experience. Youth symphony is both educational and fun. I learn about music while making friends and enjoying playing music. However, youth symphony it has its up and down, like when we haven't practiced and the conductor gets mad at our section. But all the bad times are made up for when during the concert we play all the notes correctly and enjoy what we play. I especially like youth symphony when I get to play a famous song or a song that I like. Probably the most memorable part of youth symphony is the conductor. He is usually strict and funny even when he doesn't mean to be. But even though he yells at us, gets angry often, and criticizes us, we know that he just wants to make us better musicians. And after being in the symphony a while, it feels like a musical extended family. Youth symphony is a social event which revolves around playing classical music. I love it.

David Ascencio, Grade 11
Valley Christian High School

High Merit Poems – Grades 10, 11 and 12

A Window Reflecting a Mirror

A stumble, never intended to happen, is the moment you fall in love.
You thought you knew what love was, what it meant to care about someone,
But then you realize that you spent your time in love with love,
And caring more for caring than caring for another person.
You discover more about yourself from him than you would have alone.
You know how to feel close to someone and trust in their words.
You don't love him because you need him; you need him because you love him.

You notice the little things, the way he talks, smiles, shares secrets, and loves.
He sees through a window into your being and notices the mirror shining back,
That he is your everything and without him you wouldn't be who you were today,
Forever changed by the way he holds you in his arms,
And how he wipes the tears from your face calling you honey, baby, sweetheart.
Then tickling you until a grin suddenly appears like a rainbow after a dark storm,
Knocking you onto the floor and laughing as you almost hit your head, but stopped by his steady hand.

From all that he has taught you, from the steps you both took
From strangers, to friends, to close friends, to best friends, and beyond,
You will never regret anything that you have learned,
You will cherish the memories and live life to the fullest,
But wherever that may take you, he will always hold a special place in your heart.

Alexis Dubin, Grade 11
Saugus High School

A Starry Night

A starry night it was, cold yet warm in his arms
As I looked up to see his perfect smile, with his dimples on both sides, and the little giggle he made when he looked at me. I stared at him, and the smile on my face grew.
A wonderful picture perfect moment it was.
Just a quiet moment it was, under the stars, under the bright moon, with the wind moving through us. No words were needed, not at all. I knew what he was thinking, and the smile faded.
His eyes looked concerned, and a smile faded, but one giggle changed that. The smiles were back and a giggle swept every few seconds. The hug never moved the hug they kept was nice and tight.
Not wanting to let each other go, not wanting to leave each other's side. As she was scared of losing him if she let him go. She not wanting to be hurt again, trying to trust him, but scared to get hurt. Trying not to fall, wanting to take things slow. Feeling all these things in one night
One guy, one girl, just hugging, talking, giggling, having a wonderful time just being around each other
As they stand under the stars, and under the bright moon.

Caitlin Bryan, Grade 12
Valley Magnet School

From Boys to Soldiers

Time seems to pass by, and as it passes by…
Days get colder and they get older
And no longer are they considered boys but are considered soldiers
Thrown into a world of love and hate
Pain and depression, different views and regression
But they as men, as boys, as soldiers, are viewed to stand tall
To have everlasting honor and without flinching, wait for roll call
And if you are too weak to become a soldier, you become nothing, a fading memory, an average joe
No honor, no praise, nothing but a boy, who couldn't be a soldier, and never could grow
The days get colder and they get older
And they will grow and find out if they are a boy or a soldier.

Desiree Lindsay, Grade 12
Williams High School

Night Light

Midnight envelopes all;
Silence hangs over me
As too restless rounds

Of projects, deadlines,
Labs float in my mind,
Prevent me from sleep.

As I lie, teeth clenched,
The luminescent moon
On this dark night shines

Through my window,
Wipes my mind clear
Of numbers and letters.

As I drift off, I thank
The crescent for relief
From gloomy thoughts.

Angeline Lee, Grade 12
Saratoga High School

What?

They call it peace of mind,
Piece of my mind,
Pieces undefined.

And it's only closed eyes
Seeing an open mind.
The villains fighting the crime.

And it's a touch of unsteady ground.
A touch of barrier-breaking sound.
The square fitting a circle's round.

And it's only temporary,
Only momentary,
To fit this permanent role.

They call it peace of mind,
Piece of mind,
Pieces undefined.

Katrina Calaustro, Grade 12
Redlands High School

Let Me

Let me die, let me fade, let no one know.
I will go to the land of pure white snow.
Let me be saved from my sinners course.
He will save me but not by force.
Let me go to see his power.
Where he shall fill each passing hour.
Let me feel hope and joy.
I will be like a little boy.

Charles Lambert, Grade 10
Mountain View Academy

The Girl from Yorba Linda

I am from the old grandfather clock and antique medicine cabinet
To the smell of cinnamon raisin bagels and hazelnut coffee creamer.
I am from a custom built playhouse and horses
To pink and yellow roses
To a tetherball pole and a saltwater pool.
I am from dirtbikes racing up and down the street to the loud untalented band next door
To people walking their dogs at night and the hot guy named Danny across the street.
I am from great grandma riding elephants to Grandma Dotty with all the latest fashions
To Grandma Sammy and Gi-Gi.
I am from mom and dad always saying "What goes around comes around"
To "Act like a lady."
I am from watermelon ice cream and rice-a-roni
To baked ziti and New York cheesecake.
I am from the memories in the streets of homeland
and Harvest Valley Elementary School
To photo albums and a Vans shoe box on the top of my closet.

Taira Pehrson, Grade 10
Valencia High School

Coach

Playing soccer for one who is so wise will soon be coming to an end
The last two years with you have been such a success, this is hard to comprehend
So before I depart I would like to thank you
Because you are the only coach who believed in the team and stayed true
You have lead us to many successes
As for your knowledge of the game is contagious
Drills, practices, running, and games is all part of the sport
You pushed each player, thank you for the support
Playing under your leadership has been an honor
As I grow on and continue to play, your words to a defender will be remembered, "delay"
I will miss everything about such a strong team you made
It is quite sure that I will not forget a moment I played
When I move on to the college level I won't forget your words of wisdom
And how you counted on me to help the team with my knowledge
I can't thank you enough for my last two years
But I want you to know that as a player, you helped me grow

Danielle Mabie, Grade 12
Mater Dei High School

My Life, My Choices

In life, everyone has at least two choices,
that have either good consequences, or bad.
But in my life,
MY choices have, and always have, a negative consequence.
I tried my best to make everyone happy,
but I ended up making them want to hate me…
Every day, every hour, every minute, every second,
my choices keep on hunting me like a bounty hunter, and torturing me,
like a mad scientist will do to his test subjects.
And every decision I make hurts everyone I care.
Throughout my whole life,
I've noticed that I have three choices, or what I like to call "doors,"
and only one leads to a good cause.
But years will have to pass until I get that door and make everyone happy…

Jonathan Gonzalez, Grade 10
Huntington Park College Ready Academy High School

Honesty

For it is unspoken,
The truth of our lives.
That we still seek,
Happiness within lies.

But if the truth were to be told,
Could our lies ever unfold?
Does the man we have become,
Have the courage to stay and not run?

Could we exist in this existence,
As we are truly meant to be?
If all was honest and pure,
Instead of lies to endure?

But Alas! Man will never know.
For we seek comfort in our lies,
And the lies and lies of others.

So this world in which we currently live,
Can only those who lie survive.
Diamante Smith, Grade 11
Mojave Sr High School

Werewolf Transformation

Spine twists
Ribs crack
Shoulders bend
Hands extend
Face stretches
Teeth grow
Hair sprouts
Heart races
Body warms
Tail wiggles
Werewolf crawls
Howls heard
Pain excruciating
Fingernails sharpened
Kelsey Martindale, Grade 11
Valencia High School

Softball

Slugger hits
Pitchers throw
Fans cheer
Coaches yell
Knees bleed
Umpires choose
Winners celebrate
Defenders dive
Offense dominates
Losers cry
Joclyn Camarena, Grade 11
Valencia High School

True Joy

Being materialistic doesn't make your life wealthy it's an illusion
not gold but golden plated wood
the epiphany that realizes our identities are
not reflections of our price tags
but our morals, emotions, and characteristics our family and friends
the commencement of our evolution
end of something, start of something new
we evolve but we also pollute
minds, perspectives, environments
but this cycle of life is all repetitive
we inspire individuality on this identity tree
there is no need for antidepressants
love can be our natural dopamine rush
re-cultivate the values of past days
when money wasn't everything
and lives just survived from the closeness of their families
materialism can't make you happy
enjoying life can
love can
family can
these are the true fulfillment in life
Semaj Earl, Grade 10
View Park Preparatory Accelerated Charter High School

Daphne and Shaggy

Flightful crows all follow in suit; a phalanx of black feathered fiends.
All the lonely people pause to stare
Then, falsely recognizing those birds as examples, follow in suit as well.
"Where has the sanity gone?" I cry, as the souls of those I once knew
turn grayscale and transparent.
The vibrant tints and liveliness fade into the darkness.
Complete strangers kiss, yet it is not theirs to blame as their icy hands intertwine.
"Do I hear any more bids?...
Sold! To the unknown, near the empty abyss within society's soul."
But the secret is…love isn't to be sold,
or tossed away as a hand-me-down, or even forced in the least.
Who cares what those clones have to hardly articulate regarding such a hot-button issue?
No one is that powerful, as to question the steerage of my heart's journey.
So what if Daphne loves Shaggy? Ironic it may seem, maybe even a little bizarre.
But when true love is founded, deeply embedded within the stubbornness of us all,
no queries are to be asked, no comments made regarding this uniqueness.
Just simply quiet your chi and let it be.
Fred will live and continue with his crime solving career with his old pal Scooby Doo.
Velma, a tad confused, will still run her mystery novel shop,
while the redhead and the "Shagster" defy all laws of attraction,
breaking every single rule, truly taking on the persona of "mangy, meddling kids."
Chloé Hamilton, Grade 12
Garces Memorial High School

Sugar Pills

Sleep little dear, placebo? Take one or two, you're looking ill.
Call me in the morning, when you've had your fill.

Take her hand, but follow naught, can't remember times forgot?
What? Throat too dry? Have some Lethe to calm your mind.

Take my hand, but lead the way, life may last just one day.
Amaranthine dreams lie just between the seams.

Read between the lines and you will find it's a miracle we're still alive.
Stay in the moment, stay in the bliss. First thing's first, read my lips:

Step 1: Lean in, kiss. Sugar lips?

Gum drop, sugar pill. "Doctor please! I'm feeling ill!"
Placebos like apples, a mouthful of knowledge, the Arariel pill.

Overdosed and comatose, the Nephilim child wakes a slumbering, shoot-to-kill kind of good will.
And yet she smiled with closed eyes! Your Honor, the defense rests!

The smell of burnt flowers reminds me that my heart's a pyre. Come warm yourself by my fire.
The smoke is choking…just one more sugar pill — fall asleep — you were never ill.

David Takehana, Grade 12
Redlands High School

Last Resort

All the friends lost, all the hard work being done, all the disappointments made
Nothing matters
Alone in one room, surrounded by mirrors
My depressed curls obtain body and begin to flow with my body
My mind is at ease, allowing my brain to rest
My body listens to whatever the music tells me to do
How to move, when to turn, when to move faster, and when to move slower
My instability, gone. My clarity, returned
Every frustration I ever had, released. Every weight put on my shoulders, lifted
No one can remove me from my mirrored room and relaxed state of mind
And when the music halts, I fall to the floor
Just lying there… Processing my state of mind
As I think, the horrible thoughts are no longer there
As I dream, the horrid dream no longer exists
Listening to my heart beat loud and strong in confidence
My conscience remains at ease and I am ready to face the world
No one can interrupt my state of serenity
I wait until I catch my breath before I walk out of the mirrored room
I turn off the lights
And lock the door, leaving all that was wrong to evaporate within the power of the lyrics of my favorite song
Still playing, repeating, waiting for my return, to save me from myself.

Liann Wang, Grade 11
Saugus High School

Earth

So many things that nature has provided us with but nobody takes into consideration. We go throughout the days without thinking about the environment and the beauty of nature. The earth is paying the consequences for damages we have done and it is unfair. We need to protect the earth and aid it from what we have done to it.

Annabell Silva, Grade 12
Fontana High School

Remember?

Remember soft footsteps from behind, being lifted up by strong arms.
Remember the never ending kisses.
Remember not paying attention to anything because we couldn't wait to see each other again?
Remember little stares here and there?
Remember a million songs, and holding each other while love songs play in our ears.
Remember tickling each other until we ran out of breath and gave up.
Remember our fast beating hearts.
Remember dancing in the rain, and cuddling in the winter just to keep warm?
Our cheeks and noses bright red from the wind.
Remember looking at the sky?
Remember frozen fingers on your face, cold laughter.
Remember voices on the phone? Prank calls?
Remember yelling, screaming, fighting, your angry face, and the tears in my eyes?
Remember crying yourself to sleep, staying up all night and thinking of one person only.
Remember making up a thousand times?
Remember forgiveness?
Remember never, never forgetting?
Remember you? Remember me? Remember love?

Norhan Altimimi, Grade 12
Chaparral High School

With Everything

I thought of so much I could write about, yet I did not know where to start.
I thought of miracles, when you believe, but I'm just going to let it come from my heart.

I believe we have so much potential, we have soo much to gain.
Yet we cannot reach our limit, until we try with *everything*.

We're going to face some hardships, there'll be obstacles in our way.
But if we try with *everything* in us, we'll live to see a brighter day.

Even if you think you're all alone, DO *EVERYTHING* to stand!
If you fall yet can't get up, *don't give up!* There's a helping hand!

Seems like it's always two steps forward, three steps back, yet you feel you're not gaining ground.
There's a still small voice that says, "*Don't give up* my child, my angels are all around!"

If everyone around you quits, just pray and keep standing strong.
For if you trust in God with *everything*, my friend, you will *never, ever* go wrong!

Brittany Smith, Grade 12
River City Christian Academy

Mirrors

I dreamt of a room filled with mirrors. All were elevated, straight and seemed to glisten, illuminating a mesmerizing, yet harsh glow. I began to see my reflection in each mirror, different in each. I saw dizzying beauty, radiance, poise, grace, intelligence, and esteem reflected in every mirror. Each mirror held a treasure that I hungered to behold. I turned away from the sheer splendor of the mirrors, dismayed, and revolted with myself. I could not, and never would, be able to mold myself into the image that the spectacular mirrors displayed. I meandered aimlessly towards the furthest wall. An empty frame stood on the last wall. The structure was old fashioned, wooden, and stood true. Curiously, I put my fingers through the frame, the edges sparked like a fiery current. I withdrew my hand, and ran towards the dauntingly beautiful mirrors. I threw my hands out before myself, and flung the dastardly mirrors to the insane depth of darkness behind it. The splendid shards of glass fell and looked like menacing stars in the impenetrable darkness. With a decisive swift boldness, I turned my back on the beautiful mirrors, and plunged into the lone mirror. The frame shone with immeasurable warmth in hue and tone, golden humble tones. The lone mirror now possesses a beauty all its own. It holds love and vibrancy, all woven into song.

Niamh Mercer, Grade 11
Apple Valley High School

2012

The Mayans said the world is going to end in 2012,
I think they could put that book back on the shelf,
That's when their calendar ended,
But ours is extended,
They think it's going to be the end of civilization,
But to us, we will still be in the same location,
Are there any facts in their calendar at all?
I don't think so because it's too small,
They're trying to end our world early,
It won't end soon, but eventually surely,
What man or woman wrote this calendar anyway?
Would you believe them if they stood in front of you today?
I don't believe Mayans' calendar or beliefs,
When Christmas come in 2012, people will still be buying wreaths,
I'll still open my presents that year,
I will open them and think of the future with no fear,
I've been on this Earth for 16 going on 17 years,
You think on that day I'll be sitting shedding in tears?
Now way, I believe there's only one who knows what lies ahead,
If you think it's the Mayans, then in 2012 you will be dead.

Salvador Castro, Grade 12
Lucerne Valley Jr/Sr High School

We Are a Paradox

We're so different that we're the same
Every time I see you, my heart starts jumping
Being with you is like being somewhere
Where there is no tomorrow,
No tomorrow but there is hope that someday
We'll fall in love with each other
However, until that day, we will learn
How to be the same.

We are so different that we're the same
We don't have anything in common
Except the fact that we like each other
That's why we are a paradox
We contradict each other's style
Moreover, we have different dreams,
Dreams of being together is our desire
Nevertheless, there is only one way we'll get there
That is if we're together forever
We'll get there, we'll get there
That's why we are a paradox.

Elizabeth Alvarado, Grade 12
Fontana High School

Sunset

S low as a snail
U nder the clouds
N ear the beach
S ight of an orange light
E ye glance over
T he beauty goes away

Yesenia Ake, Grade 10
Huntington Park College Ready Academy High School

The Fright

Every day there is a different fright,
Will this house burn down tonight?
When I was young the world seem a different sight,
Today this world seems nothing alike,
I am begging to see the truth,
When will death come down for you?
So to which god do I pledge my allegiance?
When I see men, the only thing in my mind,
How long will they survive?
Seems death reaches from the corners nearly anywhere,
All you can be is a sheep and beware.
Never did death shine so bright,
Do I pray to Buddha or Jesus Christ?
Tell me who I am,
I am running out of time,
Everything just does not seem in line,
Death doesn't have a face
It attacks without leaving a trace
How do I fight back when there is no one there?
So how is this any fair?
And doesn't anyone care?

Edwin Salgado, Grade 12
Sierra Vista High School

Infinity Lost

The air whistles through these empty places,
empty spaces, forgotten faces,
while the silence, deafening in its solitude,
underlines the absence of the love,
the loss of the life
that the wind, whistling through
the forlorn trees, acknowledges
and sings of.
A haze fills the mind
that can't comprehend
the changes, so permanent, and the words
unsaid, unheard, never to be
released from the confines of the soul
that is doomed to hold them forever.
The broken, deteriorating autumn leaves whisper of
what once was, dancing their eerie dance,
swirling memories into the foggy midnight moon,
illuminating a tale of misery,
never before seen, that, with hope, remains unparalleled
for eternity.

Ridhima Vemula, Grade 11
California High School

Basketball

Basketball the game.
Rubber and sweat.
Ball, guarding, rim.
Round, crowd, shot clock, scoreboard.
Bounce, squeaks, chanting, buzzer, swish!!

Everett Tucker, Grade 10
Huntington Park College Ready Academy High School

Changing

I am from new to old
From stick figures to animation
I am from looking at art to making art
From hearing to being heard
I am from small portions to big opportunities
From lost to found
I am from pencil and paper to paints and canvases
From black and white to different colors
I am from a trashy complex to a clean street
From ignored to loved
I am from the same to being my own
From love to a broken heart
From a broken heart to love
I am from forgiveness and happiness
From many laughs and many friends
I am from kindness and friendship
From family to friends
I am from me…

Matthew March, Grade 10
Valencia High School

Cheerleader

Redlands!
I can hear the crowd roar
As I run on the mat to the first formation,
The adrenaline pumps through my veins.
The cheer starts.
I walk to my first stunt,
A partner stunt.
I can feel the power in my body,
I can feel the energy portrayed through my smile.
Then, the music starts screaming from the stereos.
The team works it from head to toe.
Girls get thrown in the air up and down, left to right.
The jump sequence is next.
Our throbbing legs make a perfect toe touch.
We still have the power to perform our last techniques.
The music stops in our final pose
And we run off the mat in an excited blur.
First place, here we come!

Caitlin Cox, Grade 12
Redlands High School

Beauty Is…

Beauty is not pouty lips or curvy hips
that can disarm anyone with a flick of the wrist.
It is not big arms that can cause harm
to anyone around them that will not conform.
Beauty is a kind heart that will do its part
in starting a change for the world.
It is a benevolent soul that helps others
and their mothers survive each other.
Beauty cannot be bought.

Alison Wexler, Grade 10
Corona Del Mar High School

I Am

I am a loud and determined person.
I wonder if I can go back to high school.
I hear loud voices telling me I can do it.
I see all my people outside waiting for me.
I want to graduate on time with all my classmates.
I am a loud and determined person

I pretend to have my dreams come true.
I feel like my life has a path.
I touch my heart and my dreams
I worry about if I am going to go back to the high school.
I cry when people tell me I can't.
I am a loud and determined person.

I understand I don't get what I want. It's okay.
I say my dreams will come true.
I dream my life will be a good successful life.
I try and make all my dreams come true.
I hope for MHS to accept me back.
I am a loud and determined person.

Erika Ortiz, Grade 12
Calaveras Hills High School

One Click

Standing among the grassy fields of generations to continue
I stand alone in the corner of the touchdown
With one hand on the camera
The other hand upon the lens
Zooming in and out seeing all the action as
Players rush, catch, tackle, block, jump, yell across to each other
Both crowds roar out songs and chants
The coaches shout out plays with hands
Trainers stand beside at the moment's notice
I stand alone in the corner of the touchdown
One play, one catch, one run is all I need for the picture
It is not as easy as it looks
What is seen through the eyepiece is too late
What I click while the play is going on is too early
What I click when I foretell the future is all up to luck
That one picture comes when all is silent for that one play
That one play that would decide either a win or a loss
It just happens that the play just ended with no gain for either side
Here it goes again all over
In overtime

Sunny Huatran, Grade 12
Redlands High School

It's a Nature-Like Thing

Rainforest
Fresh, natural
Soft, bumpy, wet
Amazing, relaxing, peaceful, natural
Birds, water, trees, joyful, buzzing insects

Maria Ramirez, Grade 10
Huntington Park College Ready Academy High School

Reason and Rhyme of Season Time

In spring, the trees and flowers shed their sleep
and join the celebration of new life.
Kaleidoscopes of colors bright and deep
entice forgetfulness of worldly strife.

With summer come the sweet and luscious fruits
that were but once the innocent fleurets
upon the lips of trees' sun-kissed shoots
grasping at the loftiest turrets.

Autumnal tide brings forth orange and green,
for this is when Demeter sobs and grieves.
And silver zephyrs whistle in between
the spindly branches, loosening their leaves.

And then comes winter; this is last of all.
The time of frosty white and restful pall.

John Paul Beall, Grade 12
Redlands High School

I Am the Air

For what is promised is that I shall die
If it's God's will, the breeze won't waken me
In peace, the dirt is where my heart shall lie
Where I'll reach for your hand to hold onto me

When you look at the flowers, that is I
When you feel the winds, that is my touch
When you look at the ocean, look through my eyes
When you hear the birds singing, don't pull the clutch

For I am in the world living with you
When you inhale, I am the air you breathe
The two footprints behind you is your clue
Beyond me is the air, though I'm beneath

For as long as the eye of heaven shines
And one day I will die, still you will be mine

Jazmine Rhodes, Grade 12
PAAL Campus

A Selfless Girl

When I look into her eyes, I see hope for me and her smile lights up my world, but the day she cried I thought my life was over, until I discovered my courage and bravery and made her happy again.
She made me free; warm inside every time she looks at me she made me wonder if she was an angel from heaven or a princess from a fairy tale.
When I hear her sing and see her dance she's like a carefree spirit looking for the perfect soul mate to spend eternity with. She's never selfish, she thinks of others before herself when someone is upset, she will try and succeed to make that person happy again.

Eric Ceballos, Grade 11
Vintage High School

disappearances

disappearances in the forest
are commonplace, because if the wolves live in the walls
then goodbyes are everyday evil
and if you drive until you run out of road,
eventually you must arrive at a place
where everything ends.

there are no letters from home:
I am alone and alive, and to drive
until you run out of road
is to open an envelope warm with familiar handwriting
but to find that there is no sweet light
to see by.

all streams empty into the sea.
all paths lead to a place where there is no more road.
I am alone and alive.

Caitlin Powell, Grade 12
San Lorenzo Valley High School

I'm with You

You are never alone
For I'm always here
Holding you in your thrown
Keeping you from your deepest fear

I'll hold you high
Above all your pain
With my wings, you'll fly
Only love shall you gain

Take a breath
I'll hold you close
Far away are you from death
No kiss from said black rose

For you are my life
Let me be your wife

Erin Coughlin, Grade 11
Encore High School for the Performing Arts

World

World of wonder,
So much beauty
Hidden from our eyes
Valleys covered in shadows
Light against darkness
World of wonder,
Rise and conquer
Stop at nothing
Finding the fallen
Poorest of the poor
The most vulnerable
The forgotten faithful.

Evelyn Vargas, Grade 10
Huntington Park College Ready Academy High School

High Merit Poems – Grades 10, 11 and 12

Ticker
It was orange,
A bright tacky shade of happiness
That caught my eye with its uniqueness
Plastic and cheap,
I held it in my palm without knowing where to put it
It belonged nowhere and everywhere
Without sticking out, it refused to fit in
Unclassifiable and irresistible,
It reminded me of autumn —
The smell of spice, the taste of cider
The feelings of warmth

It was orange
And it was your heart
And though people took for granted its vivid shade,
I treasured it.
Alexandra Terzian, Grade 12
Mount Carmel High School

At Peace
At beach, near sun's soon goodbye, I listen
So calming I can hear the guitar's voice
Imagine a world, no ocean glisten
Fortunate are we, knowing we have choice
Live life tropic shore, wild nature floor

Again, the guitar's soft strum, wind breaking
Ocean waves roll over sand, wanting more
Evening now, moon rise dark awaking

Yet, still I stand, bright horizon no more
Voice of music no longer, world sings now
Sound of waves crashing, can't help but adore
I drift away, the world, its broken vows
A moment in time, can't help but savor
I just wish I could save some for later
Katy Fetters, Grade 11
Huntington Beach High School

Midnight's Love
Once upon a midnight hour
A love so sweet for my heart to devour
We danced under the October Blue Moon
And wrapped ourselves in a stardust cocoon
One pink candle, white sage and rose oil
We exchanged secret love vows on sacred soil
I am the moonbeams, and he the sun's light
He aligns my chakras and turns my aura ivory white
I cradle his soul while he caresses my heart
Like an artist to his muse we must never part
Forever lost in the reverie of two visionaries
A world full of wood nymphs, dryads and fairies
Once upon the dawning sun
A pair of lovesick artists whose tale has just begun
Elmast Kozloyan, Grade 10
Schurr High School

Enrique Iglesias
E nergetic as a bunny
N o one could love him more than me
R ich as a bank
I mportant as the president
Q uick beats my heart when I see him
U nique
E verything has to do with him

I love him with all my heart
G orgeous
L ovely like a rose
E verything he does is wonderful
S exy as a model
I nteresting as reading poems
A lways in my mind
S weet as candy
Kassandra Martinez, Grade 10
Huntington Park College Ready Academy High School

The Burden They Bear
With the weight of the world on his shoulders,
He crawls across the sky.
Carrying the planet along its path
As other worlds pass by.
Heavenly bodies led by heaven's hosts;
Led in a celestial dance.
The planets are guided around the sun;
Around their sun they proudly prance.
Their great sun they follow is called a star
And many stars fill heaven's space.
Each star with its own circling planets,
Put in their predetermined place.
They forever move and never tire,
Each holding their galactic gem.
The great march of the planets
And the beings that bear them.
Robert Barnett, Grade 12
Heritage Christian School

Betrayed
Can't hold it anymore, it has to end!
The heartache inside that cannot be stopped.
Leaving me out, I try my best to blend;
friendship we had is about to be dropped.
HATRED and ANGER, sadness and distress.
The pain that you caused, had made me wonder,
repaying me with an ache on my chest.
You have been as frightening as a thunder.
Words you said, has been printed on my skin,
always repeated, never forgotten.
Trying your best, but you may never win.
Leaving me here alone to be rotten.
Extremely angry but I still forgave,
learn to forgive and forget and behave.
Joyce Liu, Grade 10
Abraham Lincoln High School

Page 83

My Life's Story

I come from the early morning sounds of my moms playing Ramona Yala and Golden oldies
To cleaning gloves and the sound of a vacuum that seems to be passing by my room every second
To the aroma of bleach and Clorox circling the house looking for a way out
From the green yellow plants that seem to look as if they were rooted at the seam
And broken bricks with cracks in the wall that just happen when one of us gets a little too out of control
To water hoes being sprayed to feed the starving plants and the rust smell of the water
To my own miniature mini pool.
From a place that kids are always out, running around screaming and crying their heads off with scrapes and bumps as proof
To being scared just to step out of the safety of my own sanctuary
From a mom that knows what's right who always does what she has to and never puts her self before her kids
To a dad that just disappeared as if he was never there to begin with
To my beloved sisters Lisa, Louisa, Linda, Holly and my beloved big brother that I love so much, words can't even describe
From my mom saying the same thing over and over again like a broken record "Don't talk to strangers"
"Look both ways before crossing the street" "Don't talk back," "Pore estupita" "That's what you get"
To "no's" and "maybes"
From the sweet smell of arose con leche
To the spice salty smell of chile reaños
From video cameras with special moments of my family to pictures in tattered and ripped up albums
This is where I came from, where I was brought up, who I am and how I came to be.

Joanna Nunez, Grade 10
Valencia High School

Opening the Window

Inside my house it's humid and hot, my boss is a jerk, work's not what I thought.
Each day I wake up to lies and deceit, to dishonest people who walk on the street.
They say they're your friends without any doubts, we got your back but what all about.
Some rumor that has it that came from a hater, no trash talk now you can save it for later,
When I go walking down away, they go running their mouth, being free, living in peace something they don't know about.
Don't dwell on events, you cannot control, these are some things I would like to let go.
I open the window and take a fresh breath of air, I think to myself, I am happy, I am here.
I care for myself, but not conceited at best, I will work to be better, until the day comes to rest.
The future is like what I want most, swimming and fishing all down at the coast.
With family and friends and fun in mind, I know the future will be a good time.
I am joyful and proud of all my earnings, for all that in the past, I have stopped hurting.
A new step in life, another breath to catch, a baby born, a life begins, an egg begins to hatch.
It holds a group of individuals, that may look normal to us all, but tomorrow won't be like today, these people hold the ball.
We are all the future now, and it is up to us to win, night has risen, snow has fallen, I close the window again.

Adam Boyer, Grade 12
Prospect Continuation High School

Forever Flowing Fearlessly

The rushing water flows past everything it meets
Over, around, or under the obstacles that block its way
The water rumbles and trembles underneath my feet
It seems as if the water has a message to the world it wishes to convey
The enormous power of the water does not harm, but simply washes everything away
It holds no prejudice, no anger and just drifts down to an unknown place
The path it takes is the easiest, and it seems to have no hurry
Forgiving those who scar her, and continuing on her way
The hardest thing for man is to turn the other cheek, but the water just continues and flows, flows, flows
Until one day she reaches the open ocean
Filled with possibilities, but just blending in for now
With the most important responsibility — nothing — but everything
More patience than anything just going along her way.

Paige Piper, Grade 11
Saugus High School

Trees Are…
Trees are the wood,
The wood is the desk,
The desk is a stage,
Events unfold.

"Roots

A tree is the pencil,
The pencil is a tool,
The tool will be used,
A word will be written.

To

Trees are the paper,
The paper is a canvas,
Put pencil to paper,
The tree is art.

Branches"
Collin McGrath, Grade 12
Redlands High School

Underneath an Empty Sky
Underneath an empty sky
In the deep sea I want to die
For she sucks twisted bones clean
To drift below to sights unseen
Far beneath the roiling churning
Waves to where my heart is yearning
To be. In the inky night
They dream of rising to the light.
Up above the crashing roars,
Sweet sirens call from desert shores
And for just a simple price
Do promise me a paradise.
Buried faces in the sand
Stare so blindly up at me and
So I wait here, day by day,
With heart of stone and feet of clay.
Erzsebet Vincent, Grade 12
Redlands High School

Football
Players stretch
Helmets placed
Ball kicked
Fans cheer
Feet run
Whistle blows
Coaches scream
Athletes catch
Game ends
Team celebrates
Joseph Guerrero, Grade 11
Valencia High School

A Horrific Tale of History
As it starts the bombs burst
What happens is the worst
Millions of people are dead
Two alliances blood is shed

While this cold war is on
The war efforts are strong
Italy and Japan do wrong
By joining the enemy making him strong

Meanwhile the harbor is bombed
When it's over waters are calmed
While many soldiers are hurt
Nurses do their best work

The enemy does his best to dominate
We do our best to kill this hate
And politicians debate and communicate
What we do with all this hate

Now the destruction is done
And it's all up to fate
Now I will communicate too
This is the horrific tale of World War Two
Dakota Gochenour, Grade 10
Lucerne Valley Jr/Sr High School

I Once Knew You
I once lived a fairy tale —
Simply left me breathless,
Falling "too deep, too soon,"
But eventually, the memories faded —
Gone forever.

You shut me out of the world,
Left me to stand alone.
Caged animals are unleashed
As the corner of our eyes meet —
I see no soul
But a passion for rage

I still chase yesterdays with remorse —
A riot with no voices.
The silence must be broken,
Too relentless to bounce back
The boomerang that slipped away.

It's time to let me go,
To let me live my life once again
Awakened from a horrid nightmare,
Finally in the reality of my destiny,
My "happily-ever-after" without you.
Victoria Hernandez, Grade 11
Schurr High School

I Refuse to Say Her Name
I refuse to say her name.
This hallowed history haunts me
Eternally.
So I should reject
But the strength of hope,
Of renewal,
Will pull me back again.

So I refuse to say her name
For the pain she causes is
corrupting.
I want to reject
But the fear is like traveling into
The abyss
Too afraid to take action.

So I refuse to say her name,
But doing that is punishment equal to
Tantalus's
So I refuse to say her name
But it is ultimately depressing
To reject the person you love.
So I refuse to say her name.
Bryan Nunes, Grade 12
Hanford High School

Veteran's Life
Heat of the jungle,
full of blood red leaves.
I walk looking scared.
Mines, trip wires, swamps.
My life was danger.

There laid a victim,
foot struck the mine spring.
Smell the burn and string.
I went to aid him…
However, he already died.

I've saved many people,
as the field medic.
The sudden guns fire,
I was called to aid.
I was getting tired.

The M16's rust,
jeeps turn into dust.
I am a med kit,

almost out of supplies.
Ryman Ruan, Grade 10
Abraham Lincoln High School

My Color Defines Me

Can you guess who she is?
She is dark as dove chocolate
Her teeth are white as white mint
Her hair is soft as cotton
Her eyes are the eyes that can see right through you
Her hands are scarred with hard labor
Her feet are swollen with misery
But yet she is stronger than an ox
Can you guess who she is?
She cares for her young as a bear does for her cubs
She is hated for the color of her skin
She is the threads that holds everything together
She is who she is and nothing can change that
Can you guess who she is?
She is the flower that blossoms on a sunny day
She is the ray of sunshine on a cloudy day for her color defines her in many ways
As a result she is judged as a book is judged before it is read
She is not wanted with open hands
She faces trials and tribulations but she knows that God is on her side
But in her mind she knows that the end is not the end for her, it's only the beginning of a new life.
Can you guess who she is?

Lejon Hicks, Grade 11
Fresno High School

Expansion (Graceful Expansion)

Flowing through the swarm of naïve intelligence,
My hair glistens in the sunlight as I subtly look from side to side.
The faint fabric of my ensemble flutters against the sensitive skin I have grown to adore.
(Faintlyfreelyfreedom) escapes through my toes; lightly through my fingertips.
Bumps and skims of the rush surrounding me
Rushing, rushing, the rush of (Subjects, exams, education, dance, money, family)

STOP. BREATHE. ESCAPE.

Catch my eye and I turn away. Catch my attention, but I'll go astray.
On to my next destination; always moving, always going, and always wanting more.
No one will get in my way as I fulfill the title bestowed upon me.
Sleep deprived until sunrise, I'll move back through the swarm of adolescent brilliance.
I'll remember the carefree movements and concerned expressions that have embraced my environment for all these years.
A single entity braced for society, breaking through. I am breaking through.

Destiny Aragon, Grade 12
Redlands High School

All the Same

Black, White, Asian, Hispanic, Indian, or mixed color doesn't matter, people are the same on the inside. So why must we be so judgmental? We say that people are all equal, but that's a lie. People are still excluded, treated differently, and discriminated against. But why? We're all so alike, and yet so different. But is that really a bad thing? We're all different for a reason. Life is excruciatingly miserable and difficult for most individuals, and it all happens because they're different.
It's pathetic!
All of these people being so judgmental and looking down on others as if they're superior, it's a false kind of power, like hiding behind a mask, formed from nothing more than hate. Remove your masks and your plastic smiles, open your eyes and see each other as the equal beings you're meant to be.
Because in the end of it, we're all the same!

Bonnie Jean Marks, Grade 12
Riverside Preparatory School

Identity Crisis

I feel like a monster, but in actuality I'm just a condescending, cynical parasite who has issues with her father.
When it rains?
I feel as if I'm a hurricane passing through, leaving a typhoon of misery in every threshold from my hunger pains.

some people, think I'm funny.
some think, I'm insane.
some think I'm weird.
that's fine with me, as long as they don't think that I'm plain.

I'm glad they can think something of me, 'cause I can't.
I'm just among you, knowing, waiting, watching, taking in, digesting and spitting out — I kind of haunt you.

You wouldn't even know I was a poet,
If I didn't drop lines that showed that, every consonant, every vowel, is drenched in style. rolls off my tongue.

next time you feel sorry for me?
next time you think I'm frail 'cause I'm young?
don't, because I feel nothing for you but sickness.
wow, I guess I know who I am after all.

Valerie Stroud, Grade 10
Creative Learning Center

Who Are You Teenager?

Who are you teenager, what have you done to me?
To that girl that was filled with laughter. So careless and so free.

Who are you teenager, to make me feel this way moody, sad, frustrated, and more confused each day.
Who are you teenager, tell me why do you hide the confidence and love that I used to feel inside

Who are you teenager new hormones raging each day I feel so insecure and unloved now with my body quickly aging.
Who are you teenager please I need and want to know will you help me find my dreams as I learn, change and grow.

Is that you teenager showing me how to care for so many hidden pieces inside me I never knew were there. Is that you teenager playing a young woman's part maturing body, changing body, you're always a child at heart! Is that you teenager helping me to see that I am unique, special, beautiful in my own way and so glad that I'm me again. Is that you teenager showing me all the love and compassion for others I once had inside me. Dear teenager thank you for letting me be my true self again.

Veronica Ramirez, Grade 10
Sierra Charter School

What Be Thy Trade?

What be thy trade? What be thy school of thought? What dost thou do? What treasure hath ye bought?
In the realm of honor, grand; duty for the king. Risking life and limb in war, as thy blade doth sing.
Be it love for thee thine brother, or for lord or friend. Be it for thy fellow man, or glory in the end.
Nobel, strong this trade must be, fighting for what's right. This, my friend, oh could it be? Be thy trade a knight?
What be thy trade? Have thee husband or wife? What is it that makes ye work? What dost thou do in life?
Traveling long upon the road, dancing to the happy beat. Playing with the friendly fiddle, bringing joy to all ye meet.
Play ye lute, or sing ye song, culture be thy flair, bring good spirit to thy cohort, share thy song with care.
A skill like this be heartening, and friendship be thy card. Art thou this, which hath been named? Be thy trade a bard?
What be thy trade? Where does thou journey lead? What be thy will and value? What be thy humble creed?
For the generation yet to have thy full force come in spring, giving knowledge to thy student, for many a thing.
When thy student must be learned, who giveth thou the truth? Preparing them who have not known, and giving aid to youth.
Knowledge be thy one true trust thou giveth a younger creature. Are ye able, be this thee? Be thy trade a teacher?
What be thy trade? Be it in ye family tree? Be it for thy friends ye knew? What is it thy trade be?

Nathan Eroles, Grade 12
Pacific Coast High School

Liberation

Imagine my heart divided from the truth
That book's covered with kindness why don't you open it and take a look
Escape from the body watch it on the outside look in
It's appalling but the audacity of satisfactory
Represents what words teach you and one fourth percent of what most people will preach to you
Breathe! Take a step back and look at me
Are you telling me that no one knows what's going on these days and it's free?
That truth hurts and this is WE I opened my eyes so that I could see;
See who's been trapped inside their selves to long. Put some love where the hate don't belong.
Maybe the world destined to be forsaking well what about the syntax of the worlds rotation?
Maybe we should turn Thanksgiving into Thanks-taking.
I started putting the pieces to the puzzle to
Make them dream about the world's liberation of minds.
The finest lesson is learning that the lime light lies.
Imagine my heart divided by its roots
My tears are a gift proud to say that they aren't for you!
Love is complexity I dare you to quote it.
My minds a necessity the words of a poet
Think about the word legacy internally and not because I wrote it.
The heart of a soldier listens because she told it.
Sad to say in confusion she wrote it her words drift deep still in the words a poet.

Darion Baskerville, Grade 12
Natomas Pacific Pathways Preparatory School

Day Dreaming

I close my eyes as the daydreaming begins, holding me close to your chest whispering in my ear "I love you" smiling so big as I say it back,

As you touch my lips I blush, as you hold me, my heart beats out of my chest or it seems like it, my head on your chest hearing your heart beat smiling more and more on every beat, you kiss me again with your hands on my hips and my arms around your head,

In a flash we start to dance looking in your eyes I smile more, dancing looking into each other's eyes as we are together at last.

Gliding across the dance floor, my eyes so bright and blue I kiss your cheek with no worries at all as you continue to smile, I kiss your lips softly and gently as a tear rolls down my cheek as the happiness grows more I touch your cheek softly with a twinkle in my eyes.

I open my eyes and smile and see you they're standing in front of me smiling you take my hand and hold me tight as you whisper in my ear "I'll never let you go"

Autumn Fox, Grade 10
Palo Verde High School

Friendship

F or me friends are unforgettable and were made to stay
R emember people are not always what they seem
I t's incredible that some people are telling you stuff but they don't mean what they say
E verything happens for a reason and is sometimes harder that what it seems
N o one can ruin your soul or your friendship no matter what they do
D on't pay attention to the people who mind because they don't matter and the ones that matter don't mind
S ay and follow what you think is right in your heart
H ow difficult is life and the message it tells us but
I t is just a part of life we don't have to understand
P eople come and go but real friends stay in your memories and your heart

Tania Ochoa, Grade 10
Huntington Park College Ready Academy High School

High Merit Poems – Grades 10, 11 and 12

Time to Fly
Petal wings kiss the faithful sky
Flying flowers, gifts from God
Sparkle like the moon's reflection on a secret pond
Heart opened wide to memories
Magically gliding from blossom to blossom
Never rush, take the time to remember
Lord's hidden message from above
Tiny presents of true blessings
Lucky charm, a loved one in heaven
Sweet angels sent form dreamland
New life and old, together as one
Hope and love brought to us from paradise
So silent, speaking only to God for closure
Fragile reminiscence gone all too soon
Effortlessly comforts the sorrow
Never forget, little butterfly, never forget
Shannon Addison, Grade 12
St Bonaventure High School

Desired Love
As my heart shattered
Broke piece by piece
All seemed like nothing mattered
It was broken with ease

As the fire of my life was almost put out
All of my actions gone to waste
Like a lonely lost scout
For survival, he has to hold on and brace

Lonely I was as a cloud
Until I looked and stared at your eyes
Knowing my love at first sight is not allowed
But when we both look now after a year
My feelings for you makes me not to shroud
Hoping your love for me wants me to be near
Andy Garcia, Grade 10
Huntington Park College Ready Academy High School

Music
The sweet, lively tune dances through the air
Embracing my body with every sound.
My favorite songs are alive and beating
Keeping me alive just like my heart does.

I cannot grasp every word, but I try.
I try to listen and also to learn,
To learn its true meaning and to cherish,
To cherish and wish that it never ends.

From soft simple sounds to those of pure chaos
It is all graceful despite the lyrics;
It is all graceful despite the sounds.
This sweet sound envelopes me and my soul.
Michael Cortes, Grade 12
Redlands High School

I Am
I wonder why I fell in love like this
I hear her talking about me
I want to make her happy
I do all I can do
I am lonely boy

I pretend to not look at her when she talks with some guys
I feel sad and jealous when she is talking to other guys
I touch my heart
I worry I will lose her someday
I cry why she did that to me
I am lonely boy

I understand what love is now
I say please don't leave
I dream of her every night
I try to tell her don't leave
I hope she will be happy in the future
I am lonely boy
Hing Vong, Grade 11
Hiram W Johnson High School

I Am
I am clever and quick when it comes to things I like.
I wonder if this will help me get far in life.
I hear my name getting bigger in the world.
I see myself making it to the top.
I want to make it to the top.

I pretend I will make something out of myself.
I feel that it will be a hard road to finish.
I touch that top of the mountain.
I worry I will fall to the bottom.
I'll cry if I ever lose it all.
I am clever and quick when it comes to things I like.

I understand that I have to be the best to make it to the top.
I say that one day I will make something out of myself.
I dream that I will be on the top of the world.
I try to keep getting better at what I do best.
I hope that I won't step on others to reach my goal.
I am clever and quick when it comes to things I like.
Miguel Sandoval, Grade 12
Calaveras Hills High School

Football
F urious as a bull
O ffense
O verpowering like a lion
T ackle
B litz
A lliance
L eader
L oser
Bryan Reyes, Grade 10
Huntington Park College Ready Academy High School

My Baby

Her birthday is coming.
Barely one year old.
I feel like just yesterday I was in the hospital.

She caused a lot of pain.
9 months of looking and feeling different;
A big beach ball looking thing in front of me.

She was so tiny.
Also so soft her body so light.
Tried so hard to move her head.
She was looking around looking at her dad.

Now she jumps moves, and does funny noises.
She goes burrr, or lur lur lur.
When she gets excited she dances.
When she hears yay she claps her hands.

She looks so cute in her little pink shoes.
Her clothes are pretty pink.
She is like an unblossomed rose;
That will keep getting bigger.

I love my baby.
She's my world.

Sabrina Lizama, Grade 12
Omega High School

Hurt

December is here, the weather is cold.
And you're still not by my side.
Days passed by, months disappeared.
Feelings forgotten.

So many words not said,
Too many mistakes made.
The words I love you, no longer mean a thing.
I'm sorry.

The way you were.
The things you've said.
The sweet smell on your clothes, the warmth of your touch.
I miss you.

My heart beats slowly, slower, paralyzed by pain.
Shattered like broken glass, it still and will forever ache.
You stole my heart and smashed it, neglecting my feelings.
You've hurt me.

I have forgiven you, but never forgotten.
The pain you have inflicted.
I love you, but I can't take it anymore.
You've lost me.

Maria Canela, Grade 11
Omega High School

The Moment

As you wake up and you take a fresh breath of air,
You know that a new day has started,
But still your mind wonders about
Yesterday and tomorrow.
If only you could think about today.
Living in the moment is like
You were to be hopping from cloud to cloud.
Or as if you were to smile like the sun.
Perhaps your eyes are like diamonds because,
Every kiss begins with kay's.
But our day doesn't end there,
As your heart starts pounding like a race horse
Trying to win its first race,
You realize night is starting to fall,
And you ask,
Is this a new moment or is it still the same?
As you lay down to close your eyes
Like a tired baby,
You wonder will tomorrow bring me
Joy or sorrow
Like yesterday or is it just by the moment!

Jamesa Roberts, Grade 12
Omega High School

Forever Young

It's hard to ponder what will be
As life progresses on
The doubt that follows certainty
As new discoveries awaken
While roses grow and bloom to show new colors
Life goes by employing wonder
Forever young we yearn to be
But pray for wisdom's surplus
Forever young we hope to stay
Grace lighting the path ahead
It's hard to say what will occur
As soon as you lose track
Of hopes and dreams and progress
Forever young holds back
Together we stand conscious
Of all that does surround
Through rain and shine, we triumph over problems
Seeking purity within each sliver of glass
Shines back a new reflection
Changing shape and consistency
With each year's passing

Chelsea McKean, Grade 12
San Ramon Valley High School

The River

Calm flowing river
Crystal clear, blue and clean; full
Of swimming fishes

Alexa Sanchez, Grade 10
Huntington Park College Ready Academy High School

The Dream That Never Ends

I find myself alone, the world is plain and gray.
I search for someone, anyone, who would know my name.
As I run through the streets, I see no one around. Once I turn a corner, I hear a deafening sound.
I looked around and saw no one in sight, then a car turned the corner and turned on their searchlight.
They asked who I was, so I gave them my name. They said, "He's on the list…escort him to the train."
We arrived at the train, I was thrown in a boxcar. As I looked out the window, all I saw was a solitary star.
A voice behind me said, "Baby, they got you too?" When I turned and saw who said that, my skin turned cold and blue.
I looked at her and saw the bruises and scars. She told me cryin', "It was the guards."
It was time for revenge; at that moment, I cared not for my life. As I searched for a weapon, I luckily found a knife.
I walked to the doors where there stood a guard. In an instant, the knife in my hand, made contact with his heart.
He somehow acquired his gun and let out a shot. I knew at that moment that I was sure to get caught.
The door opened as guards flooded in. They emptied the boxcar; the situation looked grim.
They asked, "Who killed this guard? Who's committed this crime?" It's as though his voice froze the hands of time.
I was about to step forward when she said, "Baby no!!" My last words to her were, "I'm sorry, but you must let me go."
I said, "It was me!" It came out so calmly. That's when they began the killing spree.
One by one, the prisoners fell. It's as though on earth, there was hell.
Then all that remained was my wife and I said, "Don't! Pease!!" When I uttered these words, their fire ceased.
They asked if I wanted to save her and I screamed yes. They said, "Too bad…you can't clean up this mess!!"
They stood her up and they took aim. Before these events, I never knew of such pain.
The word I heard was the word, "Fire!!" I heard shots and, with my eyes closed, I called them liars.
As I opened my eyes, I saw my wife on the floor dead. That's when I realized that this was a dream that would never end…

Kevin Sanchez, Grade 11
Anaheim High School

I Was Trying to Describe You to Someone

I was trying to describe you to someone the other night.
About how when we met you were much smaller and
with eyes much brighter and it was years ago in lifetimes behind.
I was trying to describe you but I couldn't
at least not the way I describe other more orthodox figures. I tried.
I tried to describe you as theme music. As the opening credits of *Amelie*
where everything is written in gold print and is all so familiar but whatever way you twist things it all comes out in French.
I was trying to describe you as heavy air left cut-up on the mixing board overseen in the song
or movie like the moment in *Easy Rider* where Peter Fonda all in the adaptations of his
Captain America says "I never wanted to be anybody else" like he says every time and how every time we try to believe him
I try to describe your mind as the last call in a midnight diner as the waitress behind an all blue freckled counter
or the poppy-seed between her two front teeth. The diner that nobody ever tries too hard to find,
but where everyone goes when they don't want to go home
I try to describe your eyes as moment Illuminated as after diving into the water
your toes needles of a comb, your hands brush strokes eyelashes forced finally apart as you ONE TWO THREE HANDS UP!
feel into the moment as how I would look up frozen in whirlpools of evergreen smog because it dances just like you dance
and it traces a labyrinth in the water overhead and there it is
what you would have never known if you hadn't opened your eyes and looked up
I was trying to describe you as if in the act I could sew you to the sky
pin you up there like the immovable hero and let the ash from your cigarettes
fall like snow and let your heartbeat sound thunder and always have you above so I would never have to leave you behind.

Reya Hart, Grade 11
School of the Arts Alternative High School

Warmly Colorful Love

Warmly, colorful love,
Warmly, colorful love is God's Word,
Warm, tender, comforting, words of wisdom "heb.chokmah"
The two edged sword of lively promises of knowledge.

Alicia Ann Vandenibos, Grade 12
Shasta Valley High School

Can I Keep You?

Life is for living, I live for you
Dreams are for dreaming, I dream for you
Hearts are for beating, mine beats for you
Angels are for keeping, can I keep you?

Rosendo Valencia, Grade 10
Huntington Park College Ready Academy High School

The Sparrow's Curse

If I were but your flying sparrow,
I would not hold a dove's grace.
My feathers would be weak and humble,
my skin the texture of lace.

I would whither high, and sometimes low.
I wouldn't be one to hide.
I may have never reached your gods,
but at least I'd know I tried.

If I were but your flying beauty,
what retribution brings,
You could crush me like a hawk.
You could break my wings.

You might think me innocent,
how I wish that it was true.
But power is my sinful desire,
to acquire it I betrayed you.

You once may have loved me,
despite my ungraceful wings.
But now all is hatred, that is what my justice brings.
I am not your flying sparrow,
but please don't pierce me with your arrow.

Caitlin Burke, Grade 10
Foothill High School

The Sorrow Filled Day

The wind is just a disguise for thee,
You are the wind,
You are the sea,
You are the world to me.

Although not in human form, I know that you are there.
As a bird, as the sun,
Watching over me.

It is true, I shed a tear in a mere while,
When we parted, my heart stopped,
Tears flowing down my cheek,
The tears turned into a pile,
Then I began to weep.

I have learned to live like this,
It has been a very long time,
Since your soul turned into mist,
That faithful day I cried.

When I cried,
Not of normal tears,
Yet blood from my heart.
You left my heart and then that blood,
Had to do me part.

Selena Peterson, Grade 10
Pacific Coast High School

untitled

you were somebody i wanted to hold,
you were somebody i wanted bad,
now it's so hard to let go,
something perfect we could have had,
but now my heart lies in ashes,
there is no savior for me now,
i feel me coming to an end,
i feel me falling to the ground,
there is no doubt i'm going down,
i'm all alone,
no not one soul creeps around,
now there's nothing,
no not love,
we are broken,
in the end you'll pay for what you've stolen
you lifted me up just to watch me fall,
now as I lay you to rest i kiss you once and say goodnight,
for this is the last time i'll hold you tight.

Hector Soberon, Grade 11
Robert F Kennedy High School

Faith

Our lives are spent in circumspect
We should script each page with care,
And wonder if the words we say
Are written down somewhere to keep account list
We forgot the past things we've spoken of.

So I prefer to choose my words by wrapping them in love and care.
For little words are measures of the faith that we let grow.
Our daily satisfactions come in the degree of it we show.
Believing isn't what we are it's something that we do,
Practiced whenever things go wrong to help to get us through.

Faith is more than getting past those things that cause us fear;
It also knows in good times that we have friends that are also near
And likes to have communion with each person day to day.
Faith is more than wish and want
It's also what we say and do that's faith.

Robert Estrada, Grade 12
Riverside County High School

Guilt

Guilt
If guilt was a color,
It would be as black as a dark abyss.
If guilt was a taste,
It would be just like bitter medicine.
If guilt was a feeling,
It would be like a mouse gnawing at your insides.
If guilt was a smell,
It would be like the depressing smell of autumn leaves.
If guilt was a sound,
It would be your conscience screaming at you.

Corey Walters, Grade 12
Prospect Continuation High School

Golden

I reach for the stars and land in the sky.
I touch a cloud and miss the moon.
I soar over lakes, rivers, trees, and seas.
I fly next to the birds and the bees.
My imagination allows me to be free.
Free from hate, free from adversity, free from stereotypes of who so many choose to follow.
See I am unique, See I am different.
Yes, I get ridiculed for being honest, I get ridiculed for being opposite, I get ridiculed for being me.
Me? Who is me? Other than being described as coming from a he and a she.
I guess me is this greater force inside of myself because I sure don't see it.
As I look up into the skies, I realize that different is fine, I realize that unique is actually cool and
living life as golden as a sun that shines on a warm day, is exactly who I want to be.
Free spirit? YES!
That is why I reach, I touch, I soar, and I fly.
Want to know the key to success? I just told you…
Be yourself, be you, be an outcast, be confident, dare like me.
Me, me, me that is all I want to be.
I am pure, I am golden.

Nia Franklin, Grade 12
Mater Dei High School

What Used to Be

He use to say I love you, and showed me he cared
but now by the way he reacts I wonder if the sparks are still there
he sometimes gets me mad
and to even it out he can make me sad
he tries to fix things by saying to me you need to grow up and start acting your age
that doesn't really fix anything it only builds more rage
he use to give me kisses and hugs every day
now it's only when things go his way
he use to cuddle with me every night
now instead the cuddling turns into a fight…
but what can I say I'll always love him he is now part of my family and I wish he could care enough to see
and be able to tell that I sure do miss what used to be…

Sabrina Compton, Grade 12
Tulare Adult School

A Hole

Doing something I hate is like falling down a hole,
Every time I walk down a street.
I know it is there, yet I can't help but fall.
I know what to do to avoid it.
Yet I can't help but walk into that hole,
Every time I'm there.
Eventually, you get used to the hole,
Eventually the hole becomes familiar.
Then, even when I manage to walk around it,
I can't help but feel like I have to fall in it.

I hate falling into that hole,
I hate myself for falling into that hole,
Every day of your life,
But no matter what,
The next day I'll be falling down that same hole.

Cameron McClure, Grade 12
Redlands High School

Burn House

I possess, within this congested cavity called "body,"
lungs no longer sanguine from the times of ripe childhood.

I have been ambushed
by an exquisite fragrance saturated with
such sweet bedlam.
How carelessly you vitiate my lungs.
As if I could simply exhale all this warfare.
Then, you became malignant.

A crevice.

While inside, I sleep next to it
to draw in at least a whiff of what dwells somewhere behind
this place so
soiled with traces of you.

Samantha Montemayor, Grade 12
James Logan High School

Our Last Bond

I go there every summer,
Back to that special place.
It is not hard to remember,
That brilliant smile on your face.

I go there every summer,
Back to that one great memory.
It is not hard to remember,
The way we felt so free.

I go there every summer,
Back to our last bond.
It is not hard to remember,
That you are now gone.
Shea Tinsley, Grade 11
Saugus High School

How Soon

How soon I forget your love
Why do I worry alone
Why do I wait so long
To call out for your mercy
When I know I need your touch
Just to touch your robe
Just to see your face
Smiling down on me
When do I remember
To call out your name
Sometimes I need to shout
Out your name
Pick me up and hold me close
For you belong to me and I to you.
Aaron Mitchell, Grade 12
University Preparatory School

When the Dragons Came

the dragons came
they took me away
this happens every night
while in my bed, i stay

the sea nymphs sang
and the pigs flew around
all of this was happening
without making a sound

the beanstalks grew tall
the ogres stayed in their lair
then the wizard sent me back
without misplacing a hair
Lauren S. Elledge, Grade 10
Rio Americano High School

Life Is a Seed

Many years had gone by
and I wonder how many are left,
but none seems to get better.

Every single day,
the road seems longer,
more and more difficult to reach.

My way is not the way anymore,
steps and stairs are not my way,
the elevator is more like it.
It can never be the way it was.

Life is a seed.
Growing each and every day,
little by little,
everything fades away.
Cindy Chen, Grade 10
Abraham Lincoln High School

Opposites

Lethargic
Passive, lazy
Slacking, debilitating, oversleeping
Comatose, apathetic, goal, aim
Reasoning, encouraging, thinking
Purposeful, intentional
Motivated
Charlie Lopez, Grade 12
Lucerne Valley Jr/Sr High School

Journey Above the Clouds

I lay underneath the endless stars,
To mesmerize the work of gods,
I journey above higher than the clouds,
Guided to a mythical fantasy.

I am embraced by greatness,
And this feeling lasts an eternity.

Here I am,
Playing in the moonlit ponds of Nymphs,
Soaring up Pegasus's wings,
Basking in the sunlight of Helios,
Sporting alongside Zeus,
And dancing with the beautiful Aphrodite.
Shoumyo Dewan, Grade 12
Redlands High School

Transitions

Innocence,
The beauty of a child,
Laughter,
The soul's way to smile
Patience,
The virtue we desire
Romance,
The feeling of being entire
Happiness,
The reason to live
Tranquility,
The way life begins
Innocence
Madeline Altieri, Grade 11
Saugus High School

My Personality

I'm delicate as a rose
Yet dangerous like its thorns
I have a temper like a bull
Big and strong with the sharpest horns
I have my times when I feel depressed
So be careful, you have been warned.

I like to be happy most of the time
But if you make me sad I will get revenge
I will make a fire in my soul
Then release it out and make you singe
I will at least get my hopes back up
Maybe it will let my self-esteem be avenged.
Brittney Lawrence, Grade 12
Redlands High School

Isolation

The closest thing to a tomb
is sitting here in my room,
locked behind a big white door
dying on the hard wood floor,

feel this darkness in my soul
can't take it losing control,
from here I can see the shore
but locked up, I'm so much more,

lying here my brain half dead
dying, bleeding, full of lead,
like a rat inside a maze
escaping in a light blue haze.
Alan Munoz, Grade 10
Whittier High School

Grades 7-8-9 Top Ten Winners

List of Top Ten Winners for Grades 7-9; listed alphabetically

Gemma Bush, Grade 8
Dominion Middle School, Columbus, OH

Heather Kinkade, Grade 7
East Marshall Middle School, Gilman, IA

Sasha Kogan, Grade 7
Public School 334 Anderson, New York, NY

Hayley Lange, Grade 7
Mater Dei School-Nativity Center, Sioux City, IA

Colleen Maher, Grade 8
Our Lady Star of the Sea School, Grosse Pointe Woods, MI

Coralynn Nydokus, Grade 9
ES Laird School, Lloydminster, SK

Addie Pazzynski, Grade 9
Waynesburg Central High School, Waynesburg, PA

Taylor Thornton, Grade 9
Shepherd Jr High School, Mesa, AZ

TJ Wells, Grade 9
Cardinal Spellman High School, Brockton, MA

Joanna Zou, Grade 8
West Jr High School, Columbia, MO

All Top Ten Poems can be read at www.poeticpower.com

Note: The Top Ten poems were finalized through an online voting system. Creative Communication's judges first picked out the top poems. These poems were then posted online. The final step involved thousands of students and teachers who registered as the online judges and voted for the Top Ten poems. We hope you enjoy these selections.

My Sister

She is a nightmare.
Her hair is static.
She stomps around
Like a giant.
She roars
Like a bear.
She soars
Like an eagle.
And then
Returns to her den.

Jack Clark, Grade 8
Junipero Serra School

Holiday Cheer

Christmas time is for holiday cheer,
Not for old, grouchy reindeer,
Receiving and giving too,
There will be more than just food,
Having fun is what it's all about,
No one would be happy if you were to pout,
Magic dust will fill the air,
I just hope that you will be there,
'Cause Christmas time is for holiday cheer,
Not for old, grouchy reindeer.

Rebecca Caldwell, Grade 7
Long Valley Charter School

Christina

C reative
H ard-working
R eaching out to friends
I nto sports
S pecial
T idy
I nteresting
N ice
A wesome

Christina Horton, Grade 7
Lucerne Valley Jr/Sr High School

Teardrops

Tears flowing down my cheeks
I can't stop them
and I don't know why
they are unstoppable
It's all so confusing
I can't talk to anybody
because nobody understands me
Tears turning into teardrops
and I can't stop them…

Marcela Alvarez, Grade 8
Corpus Christi School

Wishful Thinking

I am going to miss how his hazel eyes sparkle in the sunlight
And it pains me to know that soon he will no longer be in my life
I am going to miss his rosy cheeks when he smiles at me
And the way his laugh fills me with glee
When he says goodbye to me that final time I will not be able to breathe
Then he will look at me sorrowfully and I will beg him not to leave
I wish he knew about the butterflies that he always makes me feel
I'm trying not to show my tears but they are hard to conceal
It hurts to be away form him for so long
And even though you might think this wrong
I love him and that is all that matters
And if he ever stopped being my best friend my heart would shatter
He means the world to me and now that he has left
My heart is aching and I am feeling bereft
I would give anything to have him by my side forever
He is the best friend I have ever had whatsoever
I just want him to know how much I ma going to miss his smiling face
And no matter how long he is gone still no one could ever take his place
Every morning when I wake up he is going to be the first thing on my mind
And every day I am going to wish that one day we will once again be closely intertwined

Olivia Furano, Grade 8
St Rita School

Wavering

Usually I see the lies behind people's eyes
But when I see you I see a wall of dark blue
I'm slowly chipping through the wall hoping to see it all
I hope you will break the wall for me so you will let me see the power of we
But I was wrong I can't believe it took me this long
And now I realize that I wasn't looking for your kind of eyes
Now I have to wait and see what's in store for me
Slowly walking away I look for the pathways that are the right ways
And slowly regaining the lost hope I come to a slope
Now I stand wondering if I can land over this slope with my small hope
So I can stop the wait
And walk away with faith

Lorraine Gail Cortes, Grade 8
August Boeger Middle School

United States Military

They risk their lives for us,
To know that we are safe.
They leave their families home,
To fight for their freedom.

They know that when they leave, that every hour might be their last.
They have to wear camouflage, to hide from the enemy.
They see things that should never be seen, and witness what can happen.
They put themselves in harm's way, because they love us and our country.

They are the United States Military,
And they are honored to serve us and our country.

Daniel Anderson, Grade 7
St Francis Parish School

High Merit Poems – Grades 7, 8 and 9

Winter

I can feel winter coming
It's starting to get cold
Everyone starts running
Before the jackets get sold

The snow starts to fall
Little kids drink hot cocoa
They all start to scream
I swear they're going loco

The snow goes away
And we all feel sad
I wish it would have stayed
But we had fun while it lasted

Alexa Allison, Grade 8
Long Valley Charter School

Beautiful or Dangerous?

Porcelain;
Can be beautiful,
And mysterious
Crystal clear
Or intricate
It's so fragile
Disasters can be caused
By just one wrong move
And you'll only get hurt.
Who knew something so beautiful,
Could cause so much pain?
So, is it beautiful?
Or just dangerous?

Beatriz Paredes, Grade 7
Immaculate Heart of Mary School

Snowboarding

Up the chair lift,
Down the slopes,
Through the trees,
To get to the bottom,
Off the jumps,
Getting air,
Awesome tricks,
Cheering me on.

Cody Hurtado, Grade 7
Willma Cavitt Jr High School

Day and Night

Moon
Crescent, round
Shining, hoping, expecting
Romantic, mysterious — energetic, strong
Burning, lighting, heating
Hot, big
Sun

Serghei Civirjic, Grade 9
Hiram W Johnson High School

The Meaning of Patriotism

Late winter, stormy, and cold.
Patriots hide from sleet and rain.
Many with no garments…many with no belongings.

Washington the wise commander,
Helps the soldiers gain freedom from King George the third.

The continental wars.
Harsh, and bitter.
Many vanished. Gone forever, while others risk their dear lives.

Majors…Captains…Generals…Soldiers.
All dedicated to their country.
Like a family — all brothers and sons,
Stand next to each other with no fear of the redcoats. Fighting on and on.

Many battles have been lost,
Soldiers lay dead on the welcoming ground.
Harsh it is to see a friend die right beside you.
The pain eats you away inside, but strong you shall stay.

Many were lost in the continental wars,
Taken into a black hole.
But in the end, something great is gained.
The Independence of America.

Diana Hernandez, Grade 8
Richardson PREP HI Middle School

The Routine

Awaking to a new bright day, the feeling was dry.
For every morning was the same routine, I ask myself, "Why?"
Struggling awake, I pulled myself together,
From the bed that was compiled by gods, with fine gold-laced leather.

I took tedious steps to the room of rest,
And stuck that toothbrush in my mouth; coating my teeth like a vest.
The water was icy cold, splashing on to my face.
It pained and writhed, but this was the routine; one that I cannot replace.

Tromping down the fiery steep stairs,
I smelled the same old bread; I almost cried to tears.
Why couldn't I have something else to eat?
Even something off the street, would be a better treat.

Even though this pain was unbearable, I forced myself to march;
Marching to the prison of education, one that's shaped of an arch.
At last! I reached this building of tyranny while falling upon my knees,
"Thank God I have finished this blasphemy routine, it feels like a disease."

But as I glare upon this school, there was no one to be found.
Where has everyone gone? This silence was profound.
Pondering for a moment, realizing to my dismay,
Today; this day was Saturday.

Justin Lee, Grade 9
Irvine High School

The Beach

The sun shining on the sea,
The sound of the crashing waves and
Seagulls flying in the sky,
The fresh air
Of the salty sea —
It's a paradise!
A creation of God
That He made for us
To enjoy.
Thank you God!
Thank you for this wonderful
Gift!

Stephanie Cervantes, Grade 7
Corpus Christi School

Poetry

What do you think?
What do you feel?
What emotion are you experiencing
Right now?
Are you sad?
Happy?
Upset?
Excited?
Let the world know
And feel the heartbeat
Of your emotion,
Too

Maria Garcia, Grade 7
Corpus Christi School

Love

Love is a feeling,
Not something you know,
Not something you state,
But something you show!
Love isn't just there,
You've got to create it,
Invent it! Relive it! Appreciate it!
Love, although is great,
There's something you must know,
It never stays, it comes and goes.
Love, oh, love.
How bitter-sweet the taste.

Brandee Clark, Grade 8
Our Lady of Guadalupe School

Holidays Here

When snow starts falling down
I feel that the holiday is near
the birds then make a chirpy sound
that can be heard so clear
remarking that I want to say
Happy Holidays to all

Mai Nguyen, Grade 7
Sarah McGarvin Intermediate School

The Game

Every day we wake up we begin a new day
Its filled with hurt, happiness, and pain
But this is life, and that's the name of the game
The aim of the game is to succeed
To accomplish a goal that most of us can only dream
We all want to make it we want to win
We all want to have happiness until our very end
In every game there is only one winner
Whether it be the skilled veteran or a first time beginner
There's no difference in this game of life we play
There can only be one who makes it to the top
So give it you've got and never ever stop
To win the game people are willing to lie, cheat, steal, and even kill
Sometimes making you numb where it's hard to feel
Just because you cheat doesn't mean you'll win
For those cheaters and thieves the honest player will be your start and your end
They'll be the ones to succeed
In every game there are
People with motivation and passion
Others who take the easy way through
With that being said "Which one are you?"

Jessica Robinson, Grade 7
Orville Wright Middle School

Missing

I know that I'm not perfect but who really cares?
I've always gotten what I wanted just until now
I somehow got over it, 'til the day I noticed something strange
About myself of course, I felt like if I was missing something
But what was it? I was the only one who knew what it was,
But why can't I figure out what it is?
Can somebody please help me?!
Then one day I wondered, did I finally know?
Did I finally figure it out? Was it something that I've felt before?
So what was it? Was it love? Was it you?
I can't believe that I still haven't figured it out!
But the question that remains the one that I still ask myself,
The one that I wonder about is, did I really know what I was missing?

Jesenia Sablan, Grade 8
August Boeger Middle School

The Missing Smile

The cold autumn morning bites at my cheeks.
Another day, another walk…so dull it can be.
The smile…that small wonderful glow.
It makes my heart overflow.
The cutest curly haired girl, tucked into her stroller.
The walk takes a new life, a reason to smile.
Now the smile is gone, as it has moved to Chicago.
What I took for granted was the highlight of the morning.
Gone, gone, never to come back.
Now I realize the thankfulness that I lack.
That smile, oh that smile…and that cute little girl who gave it to me.
That smile will bring me a wonderful memory.

Emma Hager, Grade 8
Carmel Valley Middle School

High Merit Poems – Grades 7, 8 and 9

Winter
W arm gingerbread cookies
I gloos made of snow
N ice cozy fireplace
T eeth-chattering weather
E xtraordinary snowflakes
R ed cheeks and noses
Nicole Sims, Grade 7
Willma Cavitt Jr High School

Prejudice
prejudice is but a word
an evil word, but only a word
the only thing that matters is if people
are against or for it
if no one is with it
then who is against it?
Rachel Rodewald, Grade 8
La Reina High School

Chained Heart
The door to my heart is closed up tight,
Waiting for you to knock.
Someday you'll bust it open,
And I don't need anything else.
I want to believe in tomorrow.
Christopher Chiong, Grade 7
Corpus Christi School

People
There are people around us every day.
Some are bad and some are good.
Some people love, help, and guide you.
Others can break your heart or harm you.
Over all the good side is winning.
Lauren Torrez, Grade 7
Our Lady of the Rosary School

Cake
Vanilla frosting white as snow
On carrot cake like a sponge
With a center full of strawberry filling
And at the bottom is the best
Because chocolate cake makes up the rest
Kyle Lasater, Grade 8
Long Valley Charter School

Hockey and Nature
Hockey is like nature
It's fun to watch
It gets crazy too sometimes
You never know how it ends up
But it is always fun
Daniel Grimaldo, Grade 8
August Boeger Middle School

Dreams
Dreaming noisily in my sleep,
Sinking deep into the ocean or counting sheep.
Fighting monsters or flying high,
Running from giant spiders while crying out, "Oh my!"

Riding my beautiful stallion down charming roads,
Using my magic staff to turn villains into toads,
Being crowned queen for my courageousness,
Beaming as the village howled, "Hail young warrior maiden!
For you destroyed evil and all of its wickedness!"

Sprinting frantically down the spooky wood,
Looking behind me for that horrible creature in a hood,
Going stiff all over, I barely make out an, "OH NO — "
I try to gather in my courage, as I face my greatest foe.

There are many strange events that occur in my dreams,
Pleasant dreams that are full of happiness, or nightmares full of screams.
I wake up, panting, and the only noise I hear is my father's soft snore,
Once more, I drift off to sleep and yet again, reality becomes no more.
Hannah Carlson, Grade 8
Granite Ridge Intermediate School

Rosaline
It was a kingdom far away from the sea, lived a princess by the name of Rosaline
She had everything, and everything except one thing, which was the love of her dreams.
She looked and looked, but never found that dream.
But looked again, but this dream couldn't be.
It was a slave who worked for the king, who was the father of Rosaline
It was love at first sight that brightened every night,
they were happier than anybody could have been.
The king couldn't see this dream, but sooner or later someone had to see
They told the king about the hidden love the king was furious and said, "This can't be."
The king said, "I cannot believe you lied" so Rosaline began to cry.
The king sent Rosaline's love away and said, "you better stay away."
Rosaline cried for days because she needed her love always.
He escaped to be with his Rosaline
and said, "I love you and we're meant to be."
But it wasn't his decision or hers it was the kings.
The king had seen them together and the man was gone forever
That meant he was murdered and Rosaline stayed alone
She cried and cried and decided to go on her own
But she would never forget that one thing,
which was the love of her dreams.
Emely Barranco, Grade 8
John Adams Middle School

Anger
Anger is like a red fire, growing hotter by the minute.
It is as bitter as garlic.
It is as loud as a fire alarm growing stronger and stronger, until you can't take it anymore.
It smells like melted metal.
It's more terrifying than watching flames approach the place you call home.
And it makes me feel like I am seeing everything I love, slowly disappear…
Dorrin Akbari, Grade 7
Monroe Middle School

A Heart Frayed

Each throb echoes with pain
And the burden of that pain
Gushes out of my eyes
As blood as clear as water
Oh how I wish it would end

But a heart frayed
Has yet to mend
And only takes a long (time)
But when it has (mended)
It dreams anew
For another love to seek

Mahnoor Saleem, Grade 9
Santa Susana High School

The Hill

At a place
where the weather's great.
Where I can be me
where I can be free.
The quiet peaceful hill

Way up high
in the morning sky.
A place to have
a place where things get done.
The quiet peaceful hill.

Catherine Almaraz, Grade 8
Richardson PREP HI Middle School

Clouds

Loss of words
You look to the sky
You watch as life passes by
Like a cloud in the sky
Different emotions overcome your face
Happy or sad it's new every day
Constantly moving, where do you go
An unknown adventure you'll never know
A blur or a haze
Like a bird or a plane
Lost in the afternoon sky

Danyelle Robinson, Grade 8
Shadow Hills Intermediate School

Memories

M aking something happen,
E ver remembering it.
M aking a memory,
O r forgetting them forever.
R un away from the truth you know,
I t's going to come after you.
E very turn, it's after you,
S o keep your memoires true.

Druthi Srirama, Grade 7
Carden Academy of Santa Clara

Halloween

It was a Halloween day.
I was a princess and my brother was Batman.
I a princess almighty.
Wanting everything neat and tidy.
My brother Batman,
Bossing everyone around using the excuse "because he can"

I asked him if he had any good ideas about what to do.
Then a mischievous smile on his face grew and grew.
Using a juicy secret as bait he led me to the patio roof.
He told me he was Batman, I said I needed proof.
He said if I jumped he would save me.
I looked at him in doubt and thought how bad could it be?

For about ten seconds we flew
After those ten seconds I said "few."
He ended up going to the hospital with my mother.
While I was left to go trick or treating with my father.
The number of candies increased by the coming of each door.
My taste buds were with rich with sweetness but inside I felt poor.

I visited my brother and he took all my candy, a smile made up for it all.
I guess having more brother than candy is better after all.

Crystal Herrera, Grade 8
John Adams Middle School

The Same Thing Is Overrated

I'd like to admit that I'm different,
Of course no one is the same if you think about it though,
If I as dumb or stupid I would pursue to fit in,
It sucks to be alone but not to be by yourself,
Open the window and you'll see something new,

What you could be if you break out of that stale, old boring clique,
I need to follow no one other than me,
Two minds are better than one but what if those two minds
Just tend to repel and count for zero when they're together,
Oh, I'm surprised,
I'm surprised you've never changed; you don't go on for more, do you?

Pale, stupid dolls who stay so still,
Let's just come back to your heart,
Crawl down deep in your dreams and pull yourself back to reality,
Because do you really want this? Are you happy with yourself?
The sun is coming down so what will you do?
Please if you're smart you'll stay away,
Normality, insanity no more different than those who stick together,
Don't think you can't wander,
It's not up to anyone but you,
But you, only you so break free!

Hugo Garcia, Grade 8
Richard Merkin Middle Academy

Skate

learning new tricks,
going new places,
going fast down the street,
playing other people skate,
landing your tricks,
missing tricks and getting letters,
winning contest,
looking for stairs,
doing tricks off the stairs,
going off switch,
taking four tries to land it,
kicking and pushing to go
getting tired, sweating,
people telling you to get out.
security chasing you
hopping over fences
catching my breath,
running scared,
didn't get caught,
finally home,
free at last.

Joshua Silva, Grade 8
St Helen Catholic Elementary School

Challenge

Keeping grades high
Study hard
Pay attention in class
Passing tests and quizzes
Read lessons over
Focus on the lesson
Getting diplomas
Behave in class
Try to pass lessons
Staying in honors
Keeping grades high
Passing tests
Finishing all assignments
Complete projects
Doing neat work
Not talking in class
Focus on the teacher
Go along with lesson
Doing the above
Key to success
Doing an excellent job!

Jorge Serrano, Grade 8
St Helen Catholic Elementary School

Skies

Beautiful vistas
Blue, red, orange, pink
Lovely sights
Wondrous

Neftali Duarte, Grade 7
St Martin-in-the-Fields School

Forever Lasting

Though memories are made,
They eventually fade away,
Leaving not a trace,
Seeking old dreams,
Tracing bad doubts,
Chasing time,
As it disappears,
Vanishing in thin air,
Spreading through,
The world,
Finding new means,
Of hope and renewal,
Within our,
Hearts.

Tu Pham, Grade 8
Leroy L Doig Intermediate School

What Shall We Do

If we meet a bee
What shall we do?
Have it make honey
For Winnie the Pooh.

If we meet an octopus
What shall we do?
Have it find shells,
Shades of ocean blue.

If we meet a squirrel
What shall we do?
Give it some food
So it can chew, chew, chew.

Savannah Macias, Grade 7
St Sebastian School

Love

When the world is against you
When you want to drop out
When there's so much to do
And you just want to pout

When you want to sigh
There is hope for the lost
Though the debt seems so high
Love comes at no cost

In times of despair
Then you can find
That love's always there
Just keep that in mind

Greg Sanders, Grade 9
Faith Christian Jr/Sr High School

Herbie

Bright snow legs are what he has;
With all the things he likes to scratch,
If he ever seems cranky or in a foul mood;
It may be a sign that he is low on food;

The sneaky devil, thinks he's king,
With his loud collar bell going ding, ding;

He always seems in a hurry;
With his big head soft and furry,
There he goes, scurry, scurry,

That's my cat Herbie, we love him dearly;
He is the best, as you see clearly.

Hailey Garza, Grade 7
Joe Walker Middle School

Dogs Being Abused

They are your best friends,
They are good pets,
They are great companions,
They are good to have.

They are at the pound, scared,
They may be abused,
They may be killed,
They may be attacked.

They may be dogs,
Does that mean we have to hurt them?
Think of them as your children.
Will you abuse them now?

Jesus Santoyo, Grade 7
St Francis Parish School

An Almost Perfect Dream

The moon's gentle light,
On a starlight night,
A lullaby for sleep,
Peaceful, quiet, deep.

A dreaming place,
Your imagination roams free,
Unlocking with a golden key,
At your imagination's pace.

Your dream is like a movie,
And you're the star of it,
It may come in wild or gentle scenes,
The emotional ocean lit.

Kira Wessels, Grade 7
Orville Wright Middle School

Ode to the Night Sky
Night rode over the city,
In dark blue and purple waves
The stars came out of hiding
Like guilty, cautious knaves,
Each pinprick of light
A reflected sight,
Or light from a distant sun,
Every being of late
Could change a planet's state,
Even I could help or harm,
The face of the glowing sky,
Where gods are said to live on high
Pours upon our world light and dreams,
And so I wish to preserve these stars
To save their beauty seen from afar
As the day chases them away.
Alex Kromrey, Grade 8
August Boeger Middle School

Friends
Gotta like my friends
Crazy as they are
And the drama that follows
Just gotta drown it all with the fun
And remember
That they are still my friends

There are many ways to describe them
From crazy to kooky
But the way they are described best of all
Is as my friends

You gotta live with their mistakes
Get around their problems
And get back to what counts
That they are my friends
Ryan Knott, Grade 8
Temecula Valley Charter School

Don't Burn Down the U.S. Flag
Do not burn my flag
My flag stands for many things
Do not burn my flag
For my flag my country sings

Do not burn my flag
My flag waves in the sky
Do not burn my flag
My flag makes people cry

Do not burn my flag
My flag makes people free
Do not burn my flag
It means a lot to me
Hudson Hartley, Grade 7
St Francis Parish School

The Holy Spirit
What did He mean?
I don't understand.
Although He's unseen,
He tells me to stand.

I get off my knees,
And feel a great warmth.
I look towards the sky,
It's like a great hearth.

I see tongues of fire,
But not from the Earth.
As they cover me,
I feel a great mirth.

The Spirit's within,
The power's not gone.
Although He's unseen,
His love still moves on.
Emily Gu, Grade 8
St Anne Elementary School

Parasite
A stout, massive tree,
Rising to be strong,
It meets a green ivy,
That prepares to do it wrong.

Gradually sapping strength,
To sustain their healthy growth,
Fighting at any length,
To the detriment of both.

Of green ivy and stout tree,
The hungry leech prevails,
The tree will no longer be,
But the ivy's plan fails.

With its life source gone,
As with the tree,
Unable to move on,
Survival cannot be.
Garrett Splinter, Grade 8
Joe Walker Middle School

Wondering
Sometimes I wonder why
my head is always in the sky.
I think of things like hams and yams
that makes me think of jam and lambs.
Once I forget all about junk
I begin to picture a glowing monk.
But I still wonder why
my head is always in the sky.
Serina Leung, Grade 7
St Mary's Chinese Day School

Let Go
I'm afraid of what You're going to say
Scared of unsaid feelings
The last thing I want is change
Yet here I am, kneeling
Confusion interrupts my thoughts
Relaxation is a myth
Countless wars need to be fought
And I'm falling into my own abyss
Lord, would You open my eyes
And let me see?
Would You open my heart
And let Your Spirit come to me?
I need to let go,
Fall into Your arms,
Feel Your love
Wash away my scars
I need to let go
Sarah Mighell, Grade 9
Joshua Springs Academy

Facade
A laugh
A smile
A giggle,
A grin,
And then a sigh.
A happy facade made up,
just to show the world outside.

A sob
A scream
A whimper,
Silence,
And then a sigh.
A broken heart,
A tear stained sheet,
No shoulder on which to cry.
Chelsea Boyd, Grade 9
Oakmont High School

Day and Night
Day comes and day goes
Just like the night
It comes and then goes.
The sun is what makes
Us wake up every morning
Its sparkling light
Heating our faces.
While the night puts us to sleep
With its white and bright moon
That lightens the dark streets.
The sun is beautiful but
The moon is, too.
Which one is better for you?
Marisol Gonzalez, Grade 8
Almond Tree Middle School

High Merit Poems – Grades 7, 8 and 9

Good/Evil
Good
Nice, polite
Caring, respecting, sharing
Decent, strong, bad, destroyed
Deceiving, poisoning, killing
Hurtful, lie
Evil
Ricardo Rodriguez, Grade 9
Hiram W Johnson High School

Death
It is mysterious, the unknown
And you must experience it for your own
Although you fight to flee from it,
Some people claim to know a bit
Through religion and psychics,
The false and the true,
You never know when Death might hit you
Koby Otsuka, Grade 7
Sarah McGarvin Intermediate School

On the Raining Day
The sky turns gray,
birds flew away.
The winds blowing hard.
Rain falls to the ground.
The sounds like cracking.
Down yonder slowly rumbling.
It's on shaking.
Huy Bui, Grade 7
Sarah McGarvin Intermediate School

Babies
whining and crying
and pooping everywhere
making my mom get white hair
making my dad
who sweeps up the mess
get madder and madder
with every time my mom frets
Mayson Lasconia, Grade 7
Sarah McGarvin Intermediate School

Thoughts on Escher's Relativity
Never ending staircases
People with no faces
Colors black and white
Will they ever escape?
A jail cell?
Black as can be
Doesn't seem peaceful to me.
Keionna Tucker, Grade 7
Tenaya Middle School

Alzheimers*
There is a disease,
so ugly and sad.
When you say the word
it makes you feel bad.
If you've seen a loved one affected by it,
the person you knew
is taken from you
bit by bit.

My great, great grandma doesn't always remember my name
and even though it angers me
I don't want to give her the blame.
When she acts so hurtfully,
I have to remember she isn't the same.
The one that was loving and sweet,
who gave me a smile and a treat,
is still inside it's true,
but her mind doesn't always let her heart
tell her what to do.
Sierra Christabel Stefani, Grade 7
Sierra Charter School
*In loving memory of my real Great, Great Grandma Oline Neubecker

9/11/01
I heard the planes before they were seen
The moment of impact let off a deafening sound
I heard the screams and turned around
The buildings and people falling down
How bad the pain must have been to those unfortunate
And brave women and men
Flames seething
Rubble crushing your bones
If you were above, whom were those left below?
The moment those Twin Towers did fall
Silence was given by all
I never did know how loud silence could sound
Until that fateful day
The pain was deep to those who saw, but there was a small light at the end of it all
Our nation became one just for a moment
Goodbye to the people whose lives were lost
To the men and women who remained brave and loyal to the end no matter what the cost
To whom have lived through that day
Be grateful it wasn't you
But never forget who saved and still saves you
Olivia Shipherd, Grade 8
Ripona Elementary School

Skateboarding
The best thing for me to ride is a skateboard.
I like the thrill of landing a new trick like a kickflip, varial, or shove it.
There are so many tricks to remember.
I wish I was as good as the other professionals.
When I grow up I want to be a professional skateboarder.
My favorite sport is skateboarding.
Christopher Reyes, Grade 7
Lucerne Valley Jr/Sr High School

Abortion

Right now a baby has died of abortion
They did not have a choice
They couldn't live their lives
They did not have a choice

They could not go to school
They did not have a choice
They could not have friends
They did not have a choice

Their precious lives were thrown away
They did not have a choice
No one could ever see their face
They did not have a choice

They could have done great things for the world
We will never know
They did not have a choice
Why is their life less important than yours?

Katherine Morton, Grade 7
St Francis Parish School

Tales of a Grieving Brother

I wish I had a brother.
A family member like no other.
Someone who has fun with me,
But who also understands me.

If he was older he would help out.
If he was younger, I'd put him on the right route.
It wouldn't matter if he was adopted or biological,
Just someone, anyone would be logical.

Being an only child has its perks,
To many, this way of life really works.
But what would it be like,
Just to have someone to like what you like.

I was supposed to have an older brother,
A family member like no other.
Why did he die in the womb,
That soon became his tomb?

Ryan Lopez, Grade 8
Richard Merkin Middle Academy

Brothers

B ugging us all the time
R eady to get us siblings in trouble
O pting to reduce us to rubble
T alking to no end
H aving the world captivated by their charm
E asily getting their way
R eady to fly away
S triving to be a disaster

Neha Tibrewal, Grade 7
Carden Academy of Santa Clara

Thoughts on Edvard Munch's The Scream

The person is having difficult times in his life right now.
Many thoughts are rushing through his head.
The water appears to him as it is swishing, swirling,
splashing, waving, whooshing, and is discovering its way
through the land.
The sun's bright light is reflecting off the disturbing water
and reveals colors of orange, yellow, white, and just a
touch of sky blue.
The person unveils a scream that is completely silent to let
out all of his emotions.
But yet the people walking on the bridge hear nothing,
only the thoughts that are moving through their minds.

Savannah Guerrero, Grade 7
Tenaya Middle School

My Life

My life is always full of trouble and bitterness.
When I'm at home I feel uncomfortable
But when I go outside the house, I feel honest.
Sometimes I try to escape that feeling when I'm at home.
I try to yell so loud to make that anger go away.
No matter what I do, I always fail.
Only when I hang around with my friends I feel relaxed
I feel like giving up everything I have
At that moment I see everything around me is so beautiful
And everything I smell so sweet
That's the only chance that I can appreciate everything I have done
And just say to myself thank you I made it.

Trung Nguyen, Grade 9
Hiram W Johnson High School

2012

The clock goes tick, tick, tick,
As time goes by everyone prepares themselves.
In hiding, they wait. Wait for the end.
However, some believe they will live longer than
2012 and will survive, they believe that the
Mayans were wrong. Is this apocalyptic date
A hoax? Will the polar shift really happen and
Disrupt our ways of life?
We'll have to wait. Only time will tell if the
Planets align, if the Earth burns like a
Torch, if the stars fall, if everything quakes
And aches our souls, if darkness arrives.

Robert Nicks, Grade 8
Richardson PREP HI Middle School

I Love...

I love the things you tell me
I love the warmth I feel in my heart when I hear your name
I love when you smile
I love the way you speak when we are on the phone
I love the way you tease me, and say that you don't mean it
But most of all, I Love You!

Lizet Martinez, Grade 8
Corpus Christi School

The Closet Downstairs
In the dark
is a good place to hide
even though
it's the first place they'll look.

In the dark
the ceiling's too low.
Ow!
Maybe I should stop growing.

In the dark
we have all of
our camping supplies,
but how about a flashlight?

In the dark
I hear a thump and —
AAAHH!
Oh, it's just my foot.

In the dark
you can't see
the creepy creatures
and they can't see you.
Macarena Blando, Grade 8
Richardson PREP HI Middle School

Bitter Apples
There once was an apple tree,
Who started off as a seed,
Into the life of the free,
And a heart full of deed.

Full of healthy evergreen leaves,
And bittersweet tasting fruits,
There are times that I grieve,
Which into the sunshine, I'll dispute.

Like a dream under the shade,
With the silent growing grass,
My memories will never fade,
That I don't want to surpass.

To the gentle whispering wind,
Right beside the moaning seasons,
Who knew I haven't sinned,
There are many untold reasons.

With a swoosh! down it goes,
A loud — poof! — and a — phew! —
I looked down in sadness for those,
For the tree was now in view.
Nataly Rosales, Grade 8
John Adams Middle School

Ocean
Cyan, but Lavender
Green, but Blue
Tiny clear bubbles
When I push my hands through
Can't hear my breath. Can't hear you
Silence. Stay still muscles frozen
But relaxed. What am I in?
Nothingness
I can't remember
I can't feel
I close my eyes.
Close my fists.
I can't catch anything
Because there is nothing there
Blink open
Swirling aquamarine
White foam
Shake back to life
Heart pumps
I remember
Come up for air.
Claire Locke, Grade 7
Arcade Middle School

Championship Challenge
Adrenaline pumping
a cheering crowd
awaiting start
nonstop running.
Working hard
playing rough
juke after juke
goal after goal.
At half we rest,
drinking water
strategizing for next half,
there it starts.
Playing hard getting hurt
don't stop, keep going
leaving our hearts on the field.
Another goal
crowd cheers
playing defense
blood and sweat.
The whistle blows
Champions Forever!
Daniel Zaragoza, Grade 8
St Helen Catholic Elementary School

Bear
B ig
E normous
A ttack
R oar!
Justice Torres, Grade 7
Lucerne Valley Jr/Sr High School

Fly Away
I take flight
In the ink dark of night
Fly, fly away

The wind rushing through my hair
As I soar through the air
Fly, fly away

Then I notice with fear
I'm leaving everything here
Fly, fly away?

So I slowly descend
And decide not to end
And not to
Fly, fly away
Maddie Frank, Grade 7
Willma Cavitt Jr High School

Mystery
To me it's a grand mystery,
Of what had happened to me right now,
To many it is ancient history,
To me it is still foul,

It had impacted many events of my life,
It can be good or scary,
Though it cuts like a scythe,
And is always merry,

Surely I could get some help,
Or I could fail,
Sometimes I whelp,
But never hail,

Can you guess what it is?
Anthony Nguyen, Grade 7
Sarah McGarvin Intermediate School

Dogs
Trained to be dangerous,
Trained to be vicious,
Dogs are only doing what they're told.

Some people teach their dogs
These things,
To boost their ego or power.

Trained to protect,
Trained to defend,
Dogs are helpful.

To cause greater peace,
We should teach our dogs to be nice.
Lamarr Mattison, Grade 8
Richardson PREP HI Middle School

Another Day, Another Breath

Watch the sun set,
And the moon peek out,
The past slips away,
The future sneaks up.

When something starts,
Another thing ends,
The circle of life,
Goes around again.

For us to live, so peacefully,
Sacrifices must be made,
For our today,
They give their tomorrow.

Lives to be remembered,
For our days go on,
The beginning of another breath.

When something starts,
Another thing ends,
The circle of life,
Goes around again.

Kaitlin Hearn, Grade 9
Marysville Charter Academy for the Arts

Kuro Dog

My dog was so great and wonderful to play with
Who wouldn't want a dog so graceful
He played and he licked
Kuro, the only dog I had to play with
There was no other dog so perfect for me

His time has passed and I loved him so much
He never did anything wrong in the household
He wanted to do the best that he could
He could never do anything so, so bad
Kuro tried his hardest to make our life easy

He didn't want to do anything else but play all day
His chew toy and ball were his favorite toys of all
Kuro would drink water all the time
SPLASH!!! his face went into the water like a torpedo
he would have his face as wet as the ocean itself

My dog, the best pet a family could wish for
He was like the sun, would warm you up after a cold night
Kuro would love to jump and run
He always wanted to help us out
He will always be with my family and me

Brandon Mears, Grade 8
Walter F Dexter Middle School

Nighttime Bane

Upon the grassy hill sat I,
eyes shimmering up at the star dotted black,
the ivory light reflected from the sky,
the cold-snipping wind pushing gently at my back.

"What have I more to desire?" whispered I
my voice in; out with the breeze
Than to gaze upon this, midnight sky,
and join in the rustling bane of tree's

For far has this tenacious, young one, traveled
Fought, and shambled upon many a-frights,
Just to hear the singing,
to join in with the banging
to stumble, in one of these scarce winter nights.

"For all the evil I have dealt, (upon a very weary day),
It pales in from nature's small token,
that I ask, who can spend, if you may?"
For a infinitesimal freckle was she,
upon this grassy hill
and yet, surely, no other being could be
the one to hear the rusty trill.

Jamika Eichelberger, Grade 9
El Toro High School

Challenge

Running a marathon is hard to do.
If you fall behind, you try to follow through.

Exercising all day and night,
you try your hardest.
If you lose it's ok
at least you did your best.

You train for the big day
and you are excited to win.
You run with a smile on your face.

You don't have to be nervous
because people are with you
throughout the way.

You hear people cheering
and screaming your name in a distance.
The finish line is only seconds away.

Once you get there you feel victory
because you know that you
accomplished your challenge that day.

Samantha San Diego, Grade 8
St Helen Catholic Elementary School

High Merit Poems – Grades 7, 8 and 9

My Daddy
In my heart forever,
because we were always together.
His laugh, his smile, his personality,
I know how big his love was for me.
I will love him forever,
as if we were together.
I will remember the image of his face,
He will never ever be replaced.
Brianna Borunda, Grade 8
St Francis de Sales School

Around the World
I haven't been around the world
Or traveled to the moon
For the pain and suffering
I've seen in small, wide, empty rooms.
For the awful things that I have seen,
I must see every day.
For scars made in my mind
Will never go away.
Dean Moss, Grade 8
Lucerne Valley Jr/Sr High School

The Game We Play
I'm always there,
but you run away.
The mad sky throws a storm
on the middle of May.
You come back,
and I don't care.
Everything starts again,
the game we play.
Cristina Gaytan, Grade 9
Charter School of San Diego

Postseason Dreams
First half success, first half history
Second half resiliency, second half ending
September closing, October approaching
Emotions run high, playing to the fullest
One game at a time, 110 percent
Support the team, be the tenth man
Postseason dreams
Are you in?
Luis Wright, Grade 8
Corpus Christi School

Fun Day
Remember that day we went to L.A.
We had so much fun smiling in the sun
We said Hi to Mickey, and Minnie too
We laughed so much when we saw Razoo
I never thought I'd get to say,
Just how much fun I had that day.
Natali Ochoa, Grade 8
Isbell Middle School

That Hero of Mine
Finding away upon this dream, looking at you is all it seems
Wondering and hoping someone will find me
That hero of mine, I'll give my heart to thee
The one that I love and the one that loves me

That hero of mine will fight and fight until he rescues me
And that hero of mine so kind and so sweet
I will be so happy when we meet
As I sit all alone, just wishing I could go home

Finding myself in darkness and disbelief
In the night you act like a thief
Taking me away from that darkness and disbelief
All I know is, that would be such a relief

But until that day and that hero of mine
Comes to save me, I am next in line
Coming closer to my death bed, and nothing not anything is to be said
In the ground no happiness is found
Margie Santos, Grade 7
St Martin-in-the-Fields School

So Did I…
I run after you — you run after her
My story is strong
But still my part unheard
We had a thing once
But now it's all gone
I don't know what happened
Don't know what went wrong
I sit and ponder day after day — and think about why our love
Went away

You were a crush, maybe something more…
But it seems you don't want me anymore…
I laugh — I cry — I say goodbye — because you're just another guy
I didn't cry — just stood strong — because I figured life *will* go on
You said you loved me — I guess you lied
But hey…

So did I.
Breshana Picho, Grade 8
August Boeger Middle School

Halloween
H appy Halloween!
A dorable costumes.
L ittle kids run, while parents chase them.
L ots of candy!
" **O** ow!" screamed the kid after his tooth came out from the chewy candy.
 W alking up and down the streets
" **E** ek!" said the scared kid
E verybody dresses up
N ever forget parents like candy too, so hide it
Shelby McPhail, Grade 7
Willma Cavitt Jr High School

Challenge

Trying to be the best
making all the baskets
shooting and scoring under pressure
being the best that I can be
always try my hardest
trying to get over losing a game
beating the other team
trying not to scream
listening to what everyone has to say
trying not to fall
but always stand up tall
being the best player I can be
juggling with school
getting the good grades
graduating with my class
keeping everyone satisfied
getting through the good and bad days
while trying not to cry
making my parents proud
making my family proud
making myself proud.
Justine Manjarrez, Grade 8
St Helen Catholic Elementary School

Working Is Hard

Working is hard
while doing other things
like washing the clothes and the
dishes at the same time
Working is hard
when people give you many things
to do when you have plans and
you can't do them
Working is hard
when you are too tired and lazy
after a long day; it's a real pain
Working is hard
after you are told to relax,
it's hard to be active
after relaxing for a while
that's harder
Working is hard
when you don't want to work
or do anything
Working is harder now
because I work hard.
Mark Garcia, Grade 8
St Helen Catholic Elementary School

End of the Road

Love is like a road
it has sharp turns
it sometimes has accidents
but it will always have an end!
Edward Rivera, Grade 7
Immaculate Heart of Mary School

Someone

All she ever wanted
Was someone to offer
A shoulder to cry on,
Or someone to help take
All her fears away.

Someone to hold her tight
And tell her everything
Was going to be all right.

Someone to wipe
All her tears away.
Someone to help her
When she falls.
Someone to be there
When she needed them
To answer her calls.

She only wanted someone
To be there for her
To help her be herself.

Someone who cared enough
To save her from the hurt
She was causing herself.
Lindsey Murillo, Grade 8
Holy Family School

Music

Music is a huge part of my life
It gets me through the rough times
Uplifts me in the good
And it's a way to express how I feel
When I'm not sure how to put it in words

Music is what can ease my mood
Whenever I feel the need
I can listen to my iPod
And just lose myself
In the words that I am hearing

Music is what I connect to
When I strum my guitar
And feel the rhythm in my fingers
The power of the instrument
Surges through my hands

Music is what I feel
As I put my heart on the dance floor
The lyrics, tell me the story
The beat tells me the emotion
My heart tells me how to portray it

Music: a way to express myself
Kari Roberts, Grade 8
Park View Middle School

Jack*

There's a horse named Jack
Who lives in a field of green
With the sun gleaming on his back
It's a sight that must be seen!

If you pass by his field
Be sure to look on in
All your troubles will be healed
Go tell all your kin!

When he runs
It's an amazing sight
Under the sun
It looks like he's in flight!

Just remember that horse named Jack
In his field of green
With the sun gleaming on his back
It's a sight that must be seen!
Justine Garcia, Grade 7
Monte Vista Christian School
*Dedicated to my cousin's horse, Jack.

Friendships Gone Wrong

Promises broken,
Secrets spoken...

Friends come and go,
Some for a reason,
Others for a season...

No more laughs late at night,
All our memories are gone,
Out of mind and out of sight...

The tears I couldn't take,
I guess our friendship was just fake...

But, do I give up on friendship?
Of course not;
That's not who I am...

I'll just keep looking...
For that one special friend.
Samantha Menchaca, Grade 7
Walter F Dexter Middle School

Roses

When roses bloom
The air smells like perfume
I love when roses grow red
Until their petals shed
Roses start with seeds
You can never confuse a rose with a weed
Amanda Chacón, Grade 8
St Francis de Sales School

High Merit Poems – Grades 7, 8 and 9

Friends Are Playful
Claudia is my best friend.
She is in my happy-loving heart.
I hope this never ends.
Claudia and I do not want to stay apart.

She is in my happy-loving heart.
I feel glad when I am with her.
Claudia and I do not want to stay apart.
We are both in this together!

I feel glad when I am with her.
We love to play fun games.
We are both in this together!
To me, Claudia never blames.

We love to play fun games.
We love to play Sorry!
To me, Claudia never blames.
We can play it, especially when the sky is starry.

We love to play Sorry!
I hope this never ends.
We can play it, especially when the sky is starry.
Claudia is my best friend.

Mira Wolman, Grade 8
Kadima Day School

My Butterflies
Butterflies, they come and go;
No one sees them, so no one knows.

When you're near, they start to flutter.
And when they fly, my heart does sputter.

I love them enough to let them fly
But the day they leave, is the day I'll cry
And if I'd cried until today
Would they love me enough to stay?

I cannot say they will not leave,
But if they do my heart will grieve.
And if I grieve will you stay?
To take this painful grief away.

You did not stay, and then I cried
Today's the day I watched them die.

My butterflies, they came and went
Because of them, my love is spent.

I thought our love was never ending, but then you set them free
From now own we'll be gone forever, my butterflies and me.

Sarah Harris, Grade 8
Joe Walker Middle School

Secrets of Pacific Ocean
S eaweed extending monumental height
E lectric eels hiding in the rocks
C oral reefs containing many mysteries
R ockfish blending into the reefs
E nglish sole swimming in the ocean's sand
T he vast pacific blue
S eahorses wound around sea grass

O tters breaking their clams on their bellies
F lying fish jumping and soaring out of the water

P uffer fish inflating for protection
A ngelfish with their beautiful colors
C hambered nautilus floating up and down in the depths
I slands formed by ancient volcanoes
F latfish hiding under the sand
I sland kelpfish roaming through the reefs
C lownfish hiding in the sea anemones

O ctopus ready to strike
C opper band butterfly fish with their amazing stripes
E paulette shark swimming for a meal
A balone clinging to the rocks
N urse sharks swimming in the oceans shallow bottoms

Cameron Morrow, Grade 7
Arcade Middle School

Pocket of Fear
The roller coaster is a loud and exhilarating song,
The thrill is like an electric shock.
Don't be scared, stay strong,
The track is ticking like a clock.

The thrill is like an electric shock,
The seats jump up and down in delight.
The track is ticking like a clock,
Sit down before the seats take flight.

The seats jump up and down in delight.
The adrenaline is pumping like fuel.
Sit down before the seats take flight,
Be brave like a knight in a duel.

The adrenaline is pumping like fuel,
The speed is as fast as a rocket.
Be brave like a knight in a duel,
Let the fear run out of your pocket.

The speed is as fast as a rocket,
Don't be scared, stay strong.
Let the fear run out of your pocket,
The roller coaster is a loud and exhilarating song.

Talia Gnessin, Grade 8
Kadima Day School

A Slice of Pizza
Pizza is delicious when you take a bite of it.
It has a lot of mouthwatering toppings
Such as supreme, pepperoni, cheese,
Ham, pineapple, and more.
You should try it
Sometime.
Tasty!

Braydon Clark, Grade 7
Lucerne Valley Jr/Sr High School

Life/Death
Life
Happiness, bright
Laughing, playing, dancing
Peace, love, dead, disgusting
Crying, uncaring, hating
Sadness, dark
Death

Harley Gibson, Grade 9
Lucerne Valley Jr/Sr High School

Summer/Winter
Summer
Sunny, hot
Swimming, vacationing, fishing
Beaches, lakes, cold, snow
Sledding, freezing, cooling
Ice, hail
Winter

Alberto Barbosa, Grade 9
Lucerne Valley Jr/Sr High School

soccer/basketball
soccer
fun, mental
running, kicking, stopping
ball, pass, stop, run
shooting, screen, dribble
hard, physical
basketball

Armando Apodaca Morales, Grade 7
Our Lady of Guadalupe School

Soccer
S hoot! Score!
O ffense or defense?
C orner kicks!
C leats are needed!
E nergy is required!
R eady to play?

Pranav Nagarajan, Grade 7
Carden Academy of Santa Clara

Why Us?
When one thinks about life, one thinks about life on Earth.
But why?
Why does only Earth have life?
Why were humans given the gift to think about this?
Why was this burden placed upon us?
To realize why we are here?
To discover what we are supposed to do?
Why hath The Almighty placed us upon this Earth?
Who put us here?
Are we on a mission?
Are we test subjects?
Or perhaps the most puzzling question of all:
Are we human, or something else?
Can we be more than we already are?
Will we be able to think beyond the constrictions of rationality and logic?
Why were we put here?
What are we to do?
Why us?

Cole Phelps, Grade 8
Isbell Middle School

In Memory of My Great Aunt Rosie
It happened all too quickly
My mom said it was her last night
My parents raced around and left my brother and I in confusion
In the night, we drove to say goodbye
Into the cold, plain hospital we walked to face sorrow
My mom's eyes on the verge of tears, and everyone silent and still
I asked, "Is there anyway we can go see her?"
And soon I saw her laying on a bed
The mechanical sound of her ventilator was the only noise made
She looked as frail as ever, and I held her hand to say goodbye
For five long years she fought,
Her body soft, skinny, and bony, her face tired, drained, and weak
My grandma tells her in tears, "Sis, say hi to Papa for me, and Mama. Don't leave me!"
After a long wait, the priest arrived and we all prayed
Then I left, turning my back as the ventilator plug was later pulled
My dad says moments before her last breath, she twitched her eyes as she saw Papa
And someday I will see her again, happy and rested, with Papa and Mama

Nicole Peternel, Grade 8
Monte Vista Christian School

Darkness All Around Me
Every day seems to make me cower
Like falling off the tallest tower I feel so different inside and out
It makes my life spin which all I see is darkness.
It takes a while to come around but darkness is all I found.
I feel my eyes won't ever open and there is nothing I can do
But sit and wait for the light to come and show me where to go.
I try to get out of whatever I'm in but I fall from four to ten.
If I find myself an exit to get me out of this tight space maybe I can teach
Others how to run the human race.
But when I see the darkness all around me I look to
Perseverance as my key.

Patrick Ortega, Grade 9
Riverside County High School

Abuse

Every day dogs are abused
Without doing a thing such as eating shoes
They are left there without any defense
While they are beaten again and again.

Dogs whimper and yelp
As pleas for help.
They sit there in sheer terror
Anytime someone gets near.

Sometimes they are left in the cold
With no one to hold.
No food or water for days.
If they go to the pound or the SPCA
They will be put down in three days.
Breanna Gonzales, Grade 7
St Francis Parish School

Masquerade

Porcelain-painted faces entire
Dance the days away,
Play off the grief,
And hide their tears
With carved smiles,
And pretty little lies…

They beckon me to join them.
No — I will not;
I am not fond of this dance —
That same mask
Worn by everyone else.
I'd sooner dive into Atlantic,
Or walk on fire — feet bare,
Then be without my eyes.
Mariah Edwards, Grade 8
Richardson PREP HI Middle School

Grandma's House

I dashed
Out the window,
Around the corner,
Under the tree,
Up the mountain,
Into the water,
Below the branch,
Through the bushes,
Around the pond,
Near the creek,
In the cave,
Down the mountain,
Over the snake,
Up the stairs,
Into Grandma's house.
Ryan Slater, Grade 7
Monte Vista Christian School

Love

Love.
It's in the air,
It follows us,
Everywhere.

It makes us smile,
It makes us frown,
It makes us laugh,
It makes us feel down.

"Love," sometimes I say,
"Go away."
"I don't want to play today."

But it's impossible,
Without a doubt,
To live without,
This funny thing called,
Love.
Shannon Laub, Grade 9
Irvine High School

My Nightmare

In the night,
I lie awake.
I get lots of nightmares,
But I knew they were fake.

I sweat all over,
And I cry in my head.
A killer tracks me down,
And I wake when I'm dead.

Screaming and kicking,
Feeling fake pain.
My heart pounding hard,
With my blood as the rain.

My eyes finally widen,
Feeling so scared.
I stop screaming and realize,
It was just my nightmare.
William Ochoa, Grade 8
Richard Merkin Middle Academy

Life

I walk down the street
The wind blowing in my hair
I see old memories
I realize the past
I stare at the sky
Watching the clouds float by
I feel like I'm moving with them
Watching my life fly by
Christine Garrett, Grade 8
Shadow Hills Intermediate School

Bai Bai

Bai Bai,
Rabbit,
White as snow
Soft and furry
Magnificent creature
Creation of God

Friend
Delighted when you are happy
Mournful when sad
Always there for you

Companion
With you everywhere
Through every hardship
And struggle

Death
Forever in your heart
All the fun
Disappears
Into the midst of the past

Waiting for you to come and play
Heaven
Christopher Pang, Grade 7
St. Cecilia School

Challenge

Life is full of
many challenges
that people
try to overcome

You get tired
and frustrated of
trying and failing
just keep on trying

Eventually you'll
get it right
when you do you'll
feel very satisfied

Once you accomplish
your goal you feel
like rejoicing and
celebrating

Grab some friends
celebrate your accomplishment
do what it takes
to be happy
Life is full of many challenges.
Diana Capilla, Grade 8
St Helen Catholic Elementary School

Don't Hold Back
Live your life
Laugh with all your heart
Don't hold back
You're not the only one
For some day God will come
And everyone will whine
"I wish I would have lived my life"
So live life to its fullest
Laugh till you cry
Live every day like it's your last
And remember, don't hold back
Karissa Gasper, Grade 9
Lucerne Valley Jr/Sr High School

O' Summer
Summer approaches;
All the children are cheerful,
And run off to play

The silent, warm breeze
Adorns the scent of flowers
Across the meadow

Each passing day, is
Fall closer another day
O' Summer! Farewell
Tinarpan Ghumman, Grade 7
South Lake Middle School

Stars
Whenever I gaze up
At the stars
A great feeling of peace and security
Overwhelms me.

To me the stars are God's angels
Staring down at me
With watchful gaze
Always looking after me
Wherever I go, never leaving me
Out of their sight.
David Martinez, Grade 8
Corpus Christi School

When I Think About You*
When I think about you,
my heart overflows with happiness!
When I think about you,
I always think about your flawless
dark brown eyes, smiling with kindness.
Although you have passed on,
I will always love and remember
you until the end of time.
Veronica Jardeleza, Grade 8
Corpus Christi School
*Dedicated to my grandpa 1936-2006

I Am
I wonder if I could see the sky.
I see people shouting.
I see undead.
I want to be alive.
I do nothing in my kingdom.
I am a devil.

I pretend to be human.
I feel lonely.
I touch fire.
I worry about my underground.
I cry every day.
I am a devil.

I understand what they say about me.
I say that I want to play.
I dream when I sleep on my bed of persuading the undead to follow me.
I try to make people leave God.
I hope someday they will know who I am.
I am a devil.
Doua Vang, Grade 9
Hiram W Johnson High School

Proud Red, White, and Blue
She rolls back and forth in bed, iPod on full blast, trying to block out the world, thinking of how much she loved to see him in that dark green and navy blue, and all she could do was cry herself to sleep, but then there he was when she went to sleep always telling her it would all be ok, and when she woke with tears running down her face she knew it wouldn't. She walked around school, through the hallways, quiet, but screaming on the inside, everyone staring, she's holding back the tears knowing that she had no one to watch out for her or to stand up for her and tell her everything was going to be ok. As she ran to the bathroom eyes filling with tears, everywhere she looked as she ran all she saw was his face staring back at her with that red, white, and blue. Everyone knew then that no matter how much she said she hated him and wanted him dead that if he was dead then so was she. But now he is gone and all she can think and say is how proud she is that he is again now part of the red, white, and blue that he has always belonged to.
Brooke Lindee, Grade 8
Coronado Middle School

Abortion
Abortion is murder
Abortion is selfishness
Abortion is cruel
Abortion kills

Why is it legal to abort an unborn baby, but illegal to murder a person?
Same thing.
Why do pregnant teens have no compassion for their unborn child?
Selfishness.
Why do parents throw a life away like it's no big deal?
Cruelty.
Abortion kills; period.
Ashley Purviance, Grade 9
St Mary's High School

High Merit Poems – Grades 7, 8 and 9

Which Way

It was a gorgeous day,
I took a stroll in the woods;
Then I lost my way,
I would try to get out if I could.

Something tried to grab me,
I thought I saw a face;
I felt something wet, smooth, and icy,
I need to get out of this place.

Then I arrived at two trails,
One went left and the other right;
I knew in choosing I would fail,
I would be here all night.

One could lead me to my doom,
I would never again see the light of day;
The other could lead me to my welcoming room,
Where I could laugh and play.

I took the left trail which made my stomach churn,
When I was correct, then I knew I couldn't lose;
I think that I will soon return,
Wait, which trail did I choose?

Katie Bear, Grade 7
Joe Walker Middle School

Frozen in Time

Nine-eleven,
Completely unexpected,
The whole nation was affected,
Because the day had come,
Where an innocent man may die for his only son.

A dark and gloomy day indeed,
As the firefighters searched for a beating heart in the debris,
There was a ray of hope on the soul-stealing ground,
Patriotism was all around in the air,
So that our country would band together and care.

The soaring downfall of planes,
A mother's cries of sheer pain,
Screams of the ambulances' sirens,
People praying like there's no tomorrow,
Tears and tears of fear filled sorrow.

The day was devastating,
With so much heartbreaking,
But courage was apparent on the ground now hallowed,
For respect was filled in the man that followed,
My heart goes to that passionate hero,
And his fighting soul that now rests on "Ground Zero."

Maci Christian, Grade 8
Ripona Elementary School

Tears and Smiles

Tears are like a river
They look like rain
Sometimes makes you shiver
It makes you take the pain

They look like rain
Rain turns into smiles
It makes you take the pain
Through many miles

Rain turns into smiles
Smiles make you friends
Through many miles
When friends break your heart and the smiles end

Smiles make you friends
Everything you go through makes you stronger
When friends break your heart the smiles end
That makes the friendships last for longer

Everything you go through makes you stronger
Sometimes makes you shiver
That makes the friendships last for longer
Tears are like a river

Ronnel Azizollahi, Grade 8
Kadima Day School

My Name Is Daniel Band

My name is Daniel Band
I go to Kadima, our school
By going to this school I know my education will expand
And by going to this school I know I will not be a fool

I go to Kadima, our school
I love its food too, it is very tasty
And by going to this school I know I will not be a fool
They give lessons slowly, not like ones that are very hasty

I love its food too, it is very tasty
Our school is very fun
They give lessons slowly, not like ones that are very hasty
I give in all of my work fully done

Our school is very fun
The yard is very green
I give in all of my work fully done
They have the best teachers I've ever seen

The yard is very green
By going to this school I know my education will expand
They have the best teachers I've ever seen
My name is Daniel Band

Daniel Band, Grade 7
Kadima Day School

Happy Ignorance
I perch myself on the cold asphalt
Cold. Bitter. Angry.
Is this all I am capable of?
Simply grumble at this harsh world?
I do nothing, though.
Who am I to alter this cruel reality?
I speculate at the wonders of human corruption
Some may call me a hypocrite, but my view is unscathed.
I hold up my sign more, though I know better.
"Spare change?" I utter, words seldom beneficial
People do not acknowledge me.
Cynical, I get up and gather my few belongings
As I stuff my nickels and pennies into my hat — a voice.
"Here you go, mister!"
I turn, dumbfounded.
A small girl, holding out a $5 bill and a lollipop.
She placed them in my hands, and skipped along.
My eyes tear, admiring her pure innocence
I have a newborn hope for humanity
Christian Cendana, Grade 8
August Boeger Middle School

Gigi
Gigi is my favorite dog
She loves to go and play in the fog.
She loves to dig and make a mess
but hey that is why she is the best.
She loves to chew on squeaky toys
my mom is who she annoys.
She's my best friend in the whole wide world
She definitely is my favorite girl.
My dog is a shameless beggar
she's going to be like that forever.
She is the cutest puppy I have ever seen
no one thinks she is mean.
She is definitely favored more than me
but I respect that because she is keen.
When she is ill she sleeps in the sun
instead of having lots of fun.
But either way I love her to bits
even when she raids the first aid kits.
Gigi is my favorite dog, she is the best of them all.
Katie Beasley, Grade 8
Monte Vista Christian School

Ode to a Soldier
You risk your life to save ours
When you leave your home you are filled with hope
When you fight for our country you act strong
But inside you are filled with terror
People should stop and think about you but they don't
So I do
Thank you for all you do to save our country
Because freedom isn't free
Oriana Montiel, Grade 7
St Francis Parish School

Santa Claus
Plump rosy cheeks,
Button nose
And eight tiny reindeer,
Once a year he comes to town
Turning all those frowns right around
With bows and ribbons hanging from his sleigh
Children's dreams grow every day
Gleaming with joy he shouts with holiday cheer
"HOHOHO MERRY CHRISTMAS!"
Jean Sue Murry, Grade 7
Long Valley Charter School

The Truth
Truth can hurt us
The truth can save us

Most of us are afraid of it
We turn our back to it
Deny what is needed knowledge
We hide the fact that the truth is too hard to take in
It's a reality check
That can make us or break us
Amanda Geldert, Grade 8
August Boeger Middle School

My Life
My life has been out of control
I have ups and downs with no control
suddenly when I'm happy I'm sad
when something good happens it turns bad
I feel dizzy riding this roller coaster
I'm going to blow up like an over heated toaster
the only time my life stays happy is with my family
so now I want to be with my family to live happily
Neftali Arevalo, Grade 7
Isbell Middle School

Heartless
She talks about everybody, including her so-called "best friends."
She tries to act cool, but she can never do it.
She acts like a baby in front of adults.
She never seems civilized.
She thinks she has many friends,
But what she doesn't realize is…
They don't even like her.
Justin Perez, Grade 8
Corpus Christi School

Friendship Will Always Last
I love you with all my heart.
Even though you might not be there,
I know that nothing will tear us apart.
You are the happiness in my life, I hope you can see
Because our friendship means everything, everything to me.
Jennifer Tram Nguyen, Grade 7
Sarah McGarvin Intermediate School

High Merit Poems – Grades 7, 8 and 9

Life
Life is like a pencil with no eraser.
When you make a mistake, you can't correct it.
When you try and scratch
things out, it makes it look worse.
When you give your drawing to someone else,
they might treasure it, or rip it to pieces.
Sometimes, your drawing looks like a huge mess,
so you try and throw it away and get a new paper,
trying to focus on the new
paper and forget about the old one.
When you make your drawing perfect, some
people may get jealous and mess it up.
When you try and erase
what they did, you make it worse.
When you find a good friend,
they can help you make your drawing look better.
When you find someone that you love, your drawing
may look beautiful for a while,
but sometimes they can mess it up.
Life is like a pencil with no eraser.
When you make a mistake, you can't correct it.
Kayla Roberts, Grade 8
Arroyo Seco Jr High School

Everlasting Summer
Summer lightly falls in a dream,
Shining the sky of golden seas;
Forbidding spring's deathly sky screams,
It glows out a sight never seen.

Distant hills draw out their scheme
While soft breezes rehearse their waves;
Streams widen their mouths to a glowing beam
As nature weeps at spring's grave.

All is well 'till an hour or so,
When shadows curtain the summer stage;
But not far off in a mile or so,
Summer still roars in rage.
Niki Vaghjiani, Grade 8
Joe Walker Middle School

My Life
My life is like a broken record
that keeps repeating itself.
Every day I wake up, I change to go to school.
I give a kiss to my mom before I leave
I get in the car and off to school I go.
I get to school I go to all seven classes.
I walk home with my little brother.
I eat, do my homework watch a little TV
I eat dinner and off to bed.
And every day the broken record keeps
repeating itself.
Alondra Medina, Grade 7
Isbell Middle School

Ifs and Ands
Wish upon a star. Will your dreams go far?
Will they stay inside your heart, or shoot the world like a dart?
Dancing in the heavens,
Or singing like a god,
Shining a light on destiny,
Or following your heart.
Whatever you do, Try. Don't sit and die.
Show some action and demand,
Make a fist with your hand.
Writing a beautiful song,
Or making a piece of art,
Floating or falling, stalling.
Lots of ifs and ands,
Life's like a bunch of rubber bands
Tangled up in the world somewhere,
So we've got to love and care.
Your life's an hour glass or a crystal ball,
When you're scared do you hold
Your favorite doll?
Wish upon a star. Will your dreams go far?
Will they stay inside your heart or shoot the world like a dart?
Jules Coppock, Grade 8
Chico Jr High School

Reaching the Top
The wind I feel, hitting my face
As I promise myself to always be safe
I won't look down or I'll fall
I will keep climbing this mountain
Until I reach the top

I won't let a rock slow me down
I'll reach the top, no matter how
It's cold out there, I know
But this is not enough to stop

The wind blows harder and harder every time
I hold myself very tight.
My old clock mark's midnight
But I won't sleep this night.
Anayeli Montano, Grade 8
Charles Maclay Middle School

My Life
My life is a struggle it has ups and downs
I've been through many things I have lost count
I've been through things here I've been through things there
I feel that I'm spreading my pain everywhere
Every tear expresses my pain
Wondering if you were here things might have changed
With so many problems and so many thoughts
Wondering what I should do and what I should not
Life is difficult life is hard
Taking the chance of everything like a game of cards
Vanessa Sanchez, Grade 8
Richard Merkin Middle Academy

Stairway to Heaven
Starting off was easy
Everything was still beauty
Skipping up the stairs without any nightmares
Along the way
You get delayed
By a whirlwind
Feeling chagrined
Slower than last time
You climb encountering a giant wave
You do not cave
Dirty and tired of the things just transpired
The flood then came
Setting you aflame
Feeling the absence of your innocence
The final trial
Deems if your are able
Surviving the earthquake
You live to see the daybreak
Reaching the top, drenched and charred
Knowing the reward was beyond imagination
The gift was more than a fortune
Carmen Luk, Grade 8
St Anne Elementary School

A Week on the Mexican Riviera
We sailed away on a luxurious ship,
To Mexico we went on a summer trip;
Mazatlan was the first port at which we docked,
The poverty all around us had me shocked.

Cabo San Lucas was our next stop,
Its beautiful beaches were over the top;
Puerto Vallarta was our final destination,
The scuba diving was quite a sensation.

We dined and danced the week away,
Another week I would have liked to stay;
Finally our cruise came to an end,
With a sad heart I had to descend.
Kavya Shivaram, Grade 7
Joe Walker Middle School

Thoughts on Edvard Munch's Painting The Scream
A man on a bridge
Screams for a reason.
People walk right past him
Not giving any attention or comfort.
The man is crying for something,
For help, a family, a friend?
Screaming like a lonely wolf howling in pain,
Is the man we see.
Why is this man screaming with such fear?
Is his scream a fear of rejection, or maybe it is a scream of
Fear itself.
Kyle Tomlinson, Grade 7
Tenaya Middle School

The Ride
The morning was cold and brisk,
And I went alone anyway, knowing the risk,

I traveled up, to embrace the terrifying cliff,
I made it up the mountain, it was very swift!

The bike rumbled and my trip was ALMOST a success,
Until that rabbit crossed the road, and I hit that cactus!!

As I brushed off the thorns and dirt,
I looked at my broken arm, wondered where else I was hurt!

I got back on and rode right back,
I was in so much pain, I thought I'd have a heart attack

When I got back home, my mom flipped out,
"What has happened to you while you were out?"

"Long story mom.
You should never travel alone,
Unless you have your cell phone!"
Ty Marsh, Grade 7
La Mesa Jr High School

Thoughts on Edvard Munch's Painting The Scream
The painting, "The Scream"
Is very beautiful and mysterious.
The man in the painting is screaming with fright.
Maybe even with pain.
It seems like he's had enough
With whatever kind of stress he's had
And just let it out
With a huge scream.
The people in the painting walking on the bridge
Don't recognize how the man is screaming.
They walk by as if he doesn't even exist.
The colors in the painting are amazing.
Orange bursts with a mixture of yellow and orange.
Colors so realistic that I can imagine
Myself watching this sunset.
Alexia Areola, Grade 7
Tenaya Middle School

My Bedroom
My bedroom is messy like a pigsty.
It is quite a sore for many an eye.
There's stuff nearly everywhere, especially the floor.
It's almost impossible to open the door.
It's truly a mess, the state of my room.
I've tried everything, such as vacuum and broom.
And — oh! What's that smell?
With so much stuff, I cannot tell!
But the debris just will not go away.
I guess it can wait for some other day.
Stephen Williams, Grade 8
Carden Academy of Santa Clara

First Visit
It was my first time there
And all I could do was stare
AT the wonderful landscapes
Of my home country, Guatemala.

We put our things through the scanner
In an orderly manner
Got into the seven-forty-seven
At the time of eleven.

I finally arrived there
And smelled the air
It smelled of green trees
And the hot summer breeze.

I walked on the steep, rocky terrain
Also witnessed the violent rain
And indeed I did see
Lots of my family.

Finally, after four weeks
Adventures and treats
I came back home
And wrote this poem.
Jorge Morataya, Grade 8
John Adams Middle School

My Future
I walk down the aisle with my team.
It feels like a beautiful eternal dream.
At my sad and happy graduation
Night with my big, supportive family.

First day of my long eternal class,
And it feels like time doesn't pass.
Feels like lots of years, years, years
And years are passing by very fast.

After four long years of college,
I have gained a lot of knowledge.
Fast forward four more years,
One final graduation ceremony

Finally, I become a vet!!!
And help a very needed pet.
Help a cute little needed puppy,
That is very sleepy, hungry, and grumpy

It's been such a long road,
In accomplishing my goal.
Finally I find myself where I dreamed
And I feel a great sensation.
Mireya Perez, Grade 8
John Adams Middle School

Maybe
Looking down at the ground
As I walk these lonely streets
Now as I look up
I see the sky, clear and blue
I smile and look ahead
Nobody in the distance
I look all around, side to side,
Behind me
Still nothing…
The grass is green and fresh
The air is cool with no breeze
Yet, I keep walking
Not sure what I am looking for…
But maybe, just maybe
I'll stumble upon something.
Rachel Hoops, Grade 8
Stepping Stones Program

Shadow
As she sits on the sidewalk
With her head to the ground
A sign hangs from her neck
That says she'll pay to be found.
It then becomes night
With not a peep
But a fright
As she cries herself to sleep.
Tears fall from her eyes

As the sun begins to rise
With nothing to feel but fear.
Today's another day
She puts her sign on and persuades
As her shadow lingers on the sidewalk.
Taylure Ruggeri, Grade 8
Palos Verdes Intermediate School

Blank
Here and there the Earth is still.
Nothing to see.
Blinded as the bat?
Maybe.
From the lake in the horizon,
From the river on the mountain tops.
From the clouds on the heavens.
Life is blank.
Nothing to leap for.
Everything's blank.
Blazing in the silver is the sea.
And a silvery radiance spills.
Where the moon drives royalty.
So I walk by with no smile.
For life is a tragic trial.
Abel Fekadu, Grade 7
Orville Wright Middle School

Nights with My Cousins
Secrets in the night,
Sneaking on the laptop
Surfing the Internet in the dark,
The laptop's glow is our only light.

Secrets in the night,
Swapping stories of school
Feigning sleep in the gloom,
Whispers left, right, and from the floor.

Secrets in the night,
Taking out the camera
Flicking on the "night" setting,
Stealthily snapping funny pictures.

Secrets in the night,
In the little bedroom
Cannot see a thing,
But we giggle and titter
Secretly in the night.
Melissa Chen, Grade 8
Richardson PREP HI Middle School

Up, Up, and Away
Up, up, and away
I know it's going to be new
You're going away
I know it's hard for you
You had sickness
But you overcame that fear
I'm holding your hand
Crying, tear after tear
I'm going to miss you
My most beloved friend
We had so much fun
Now it's time for an end
Having you
Was my best gain
Laughing in the sun
And hugging in the rain
We were together
Day by day
But now your eyelids are closing
You're going up, up, and away
My Pham, Grade 7
Sarah McGarvin Intermediate School

Water
I love water
One day it took my breath away
Crashing down in big powerful waves
How it saved my best friend Dave
Floating away and pushing him back
I love water.
Jesse Vazquez, Grade 8
Long Valley Charter School

I Am

I am a hardworking and proud Latina
I wonder if I will go far and live my dreams
I hear the stereotypes and negative comments around me
I see myself accomplishing all my goals
I want to be successful
I am a hardworking and proud Latina

I pretend to ignore all negative comments I hear
I feel proud of who I am
I touch and hold the keys to success
I worry if I'll achieve all my goals
I cry when I'm on the stage graduating
I am a hardworking and proud Latina

I understand that there will be obstacles in my way
I say, "Come on, show them that you can!"
I dream of making a difference in this world
I strive for the doors of success
I am a hardworking and proud Latina

Maria Nolasco Ramirez, Grade 8
Roseland Accelerated Middle School

See You Again

When I feel like my world is crashing down
I look to you to turn it around
Down, down, down I go you say get back up and try again!
You make me smile every day
So please best friend don't go away

I've known you what seems like my whole life
You make my day go by as fast as a train
You live so far away
Lets spend another day!
Please best friend don't go away

When I come to visit from afar
We do crazy things because that's who we are
We laugh more than we can possibly breathe
I have your back through everything
Now it's time to leave
We cry as we say goodbye
Goodbye until next time my best friend.

Paige Myers, Grade 8
Palm Desert Charter Middle School

In Escher's Bond of Union

The faces on the picture
Look like they're together;
Bubbles are around them and they look depressed.
But, then again, they look like there's nothing on their mind,
And they might be happy.
Maybe they love each other.
We'll never know.
Escher makes us guess.

Brianna Phillips, Grade 7
Tenaya Middle School

The Longest Wait Ever

Standing in the line only to wait, wait, wait
It's hot, hot, hot, dry. If only I had a drink
It's worth it, right? Standing, waiting, waiting, waiting
It's worth it, any minute
Any moment we'll move
Waiting, waiting, waiting, hot, hot, hot
I just have to find out. Must wait
I just need to know. Just maybe
Hot, hot, hot, waiting, waiting, waiting
Is it possible for this to take so long?
But it's worth it, right? I have to know
Waiting, waiting, waiting. It's worth it
Conversations. Just one. Somebody?
My turn…no, I'm sorry…not possible
Twenty seconds done. Finally we are there
To change my brother's class
And find out we can't change it.

Emily Duncan, Grade 7
Monte Vista Christian School

My Passion

You're the person that takes my breath away
You're my passage to my gate
You said you'll stay
And you promise you'll never be late for our date

You're that girl with that great smile
You're friendly and funny
If you weren't with me I might have been in denial
And you're also my sweet honey

You can fix whatever I break,
And you're always kind to me
You'll always be true to me and not a fake
You're also affectionate, even people I don't know, can see

I'll never let you go
And I hope you'll always know

Jeffrey Julian, Grade 8
Almond Tree Middle School

A True Friend

A true friend is someone special.
Someone who is always there for me.
Giving me advice to help me keep up with the world.
A true friend is there for me in the good and the bad times.
I know this true friend is there somewhere.
Friends say I am lucky to have a true friend.
Then I reply it takes a friend to be a friend.
I smile and say today is not yesterday.
A true friend smiles to me when I am down.
Tells me jokes when I have a frown.
A true friend is someone who keeps me with the in crowd.
That's what a true friend is someone such as these things.

Mitzi Torres, Grade 7
Isbell Middle School

Temptations*

Soft throat, temptations overcome.
I love you ever so, but how long must this last?
My longing, my thirst. Soon, this must pass.
Come with me, take my hand,
see what I am forced to be.
You turn away, I understand, then slowly you turn back,
on your knees you beg, you want to be with me,
just like me, an immortal soul.
Your love is so strong, you are so willing,
what can I do but agree?
With your soft, soft throat at my lips,
you utter a quiet moan
as the burning takes over your body.
Through the minutes I wait,
through the hours I wait
until you awaken to a beautiful new place
full of amazing sights you never knew.
Now we look into each others' eyes
because behind the red tint
of the short-lived bloodlust haze
is the beautiful person that is mine for eternity.

Amber Jones, Grade 8
Palm Desert Charter Middle School
**Inspired by "Twilight" by Stephenie Meyer*

My Home

Where life grows, and people play
People laughing, and adults screaming
A dog will come to be fed I will feed it
That was my house in Rialto

There's a gourmet kitchen inside
With a fort around every corner
Equipped with a queen-size room
That was my house in Rialto

Attached to two prince's rooms
Lava colored carpet just waiting to boil
Pearly colored tile that glistened with sunlight
That was my house in Rialto

Meihki McNeill, Grade 8
Richardson PREP HI Middle School

Snow

A white frozen tear from the cloudy sky
A white dot standing out from a pure black sky
It's a blessing from the heavens
It is so soft and cleansing
But cold at first touch
Then it starts melting as you hold it
In your warm, warm, palm
Turning to water
And then filling me with joy
I use the snow as a playful toy

Peter Tran, Grade 8
August Boeger Middle School

My Room

Big but small,
It's where my pictures cover each wall,
It's where I can rest my eyes,
Or at night I look out my window and see the star lit sky,

It's where I can go to be alone,
It's where my dreams never end,
Or it's a place to hang out with a friend,

It's a place where each wall knows my secrets,
Big ones and small,
When I'm sick,
It's there to comfort me through it all,

It's a place that had all memories,
Happy and sad,
It's a place to go when I'm mad,

Some people see it as a room,
But I see it as my kingdom,
It's a place where I can close my eyes and count some sheep,
A place that helps me sleep.

Brianna Amador, Grade 8
Daniel Savage Middle School

The Fierce Dragon

Dragon piercing through the water
As if shooting a target
So desperate to get those fish as if they were the last.
Beak as sharp as a brand new razor blade
Wings as good as baby birds
Dragon as big as a whale
Fish as scared
As if a gun was pointing towards them
Water as dirty as
Fish guts pored into a bucket
So many bubbles as if it was a hot tub
Fish as big
As a car wheel
Dragon's eyes glowing
Like a moon in a dark night

Jordan Rubio, Grade 7
Daniel Savage Middle School

Hacker

People call me a hacker.
As I am the first person arriving to P.E.,
Yenyen cries, "Hacker!"
My violin skills are so crazy…
Too crazy, people imagine a hacker.
In any game involving the brain, I use a unique strategy,
So useful, people think I cheat!
Do I really have these crazy abilities outstanding the average…
…or am I the Hacker!

David Phung, Grade 7
Sarah McGarvin Intermediate School

Water

I'm sitting in the grass
It's raining
I think about my life
The struggles I faced were challenging
Sometimes they seemed impossible to overcome
Just thinking about them makes me ache
I try to hold back my tears
But some escape from my eyes
I never liked to cry
I wipe them away
I think about the past few months
Sleepless nights
I would lose control of my anger
I yelled at my best friend
Then I realized that she just cared about me
As I sit here on the grass
Absorbing the past events
My face is wet
I wonder
Where is all this water coming from
When it stopped raining hours ago?

Montana Villamil, Grade 7
Corpus Christi School

Thinking About You…*

I woke up at night…and slept in the morning…
    Thinking about you…

I rode my shirt…and put on my bike in the rain…
    Thinking about you…

I combed my teeth…and brushed my hair…
    A little confused but I don't care
Untucked my work…and finished my bed…
    And laid my head

To sleep…
Thinking about you…

Martin Jimenez, Grade 8
August Boeger Middle School
Modeled after the Nikki Giovanni poem "I Wrote a Good Omelet."

Seasons

On an Autumn day the moon would rise,
the sky would sing and the leaves would fall,
between and afar sadness is spread,
sleepiness is brought upon,
because this season is not so fun,
people seem to have more fun in winter,
winter is here let the children cheer,
with lots of fun, playing in the snow,
we hear the sounds of everyone's joy,
oh Christmas is a time of joy in the year,
seasons Greeting with peace and happiness.

Kevin Nguyen, Grade 7
Sarah McGarvin Intermediate School

She Walks with Me

An angel walks beside me,
I sense her presence every day,
she helps me through life's ups and downs,
and whatever comes my way.

She guides me down the road of life,
and lights the darkest road,
she picks me up and carries me,
when I cannot bear the load.

She helps to ease the pain I feel,
she mends my spirit, too.
She holds my hand and shelters me,
she also gives me courage and strength.

She speaks to me with words of love,
and she listens to my pleas,
she was sent here from the Lord above,
she gives a peace I feel deep within my heart.

So that leads me to believe.
An angel walks beside me.
I feel so blessed every day,
that the presence of this angel,
will never go away.

Joshua Garcia, Grade 8
St Martin-in-the-Fields School

My Little Sister

She's a two-year-old angel
or maybe a terror
she can be very spoiled

Her favorite show is *Spongebob Squarepants*
she cries if I change the channel
and throws a fit if I turn it off

She is very sweet
she puts away stuff without
being told
once she brought me my
stuffed rabbit while I was
sleeping

She stays up later than I do
she can't brush her teeth
she bites the brush instead

She knows her alphabet and animals
if she sees a cat, she says "cat!"
if she sees the letter S, she says "S!"

My little sister is a terror
but is really lovable

Johanna Contreras, Grade 7
Isbell Middle School

Class, Class

Class, class.
Numbers, elements, verbs, kings.

THIS letter represents THAT number and
THOSE letters spell out a number.
THIS king helped THAT scientist, mathematician
Discover THIS quality of THAT element.

She's making N cookies for Y friends
And she needs X cups of sugar
And her math grade is dropping by the minute
And she can't figure out
How many teaspoons of vanilla she needs.

And he doesn't have any
Baking soda or clay or friends
So how can he finish his project?
Where's his excuse?
So his science grade just got lowered.

And so, they're failing and crying
And their [parents'] dreams are dying
And it's all because they couldn't get that A
So they didn't make it to Stanford
And she isn't even pretty enough to marry a doctor.

Zoe Hu, Grade 8
Herbert Hoover Middle School

Epitaph for a Young Maiden

Here a pretty maiden lies,
Once sweet and fair, a lovely lass —
But because of Death, this star is gone —

No more to stand, before the glass,
And curl those curls, so they will last,
All day to frame her pretty face —
But! Young men no more foller her lace
And the country weeps, over Lady Lea.

Once more did Death ring his toll
And take this lass, loved by all,
Forevermore, not to return again,
Though may she be mourned! Now, like then;
The country weeps, over Lady Lea.

She was the light, in the dark
The heaven, placed on Earth,
An angel, if there ever was such,
To bless all those she met.

Yea, no one will ever forget her face
The chaps that loved her, the folks she'd met
And now malicious Death has taken her life,
The country weeps, over Lady Lea.

Hannah-June Bigler, Grade 7
Reformation Lutheran School

Can It Be?

Can it be that we're so heartless?
As we watch our babies die,
Can it be that we're so heartless?
That we don't even cry?
We talk about how bad this is,
And sing a very sad song,
We talk about how bad this is,
Yet, carry on like nothing's wrong?
I think it very heartless,
That when we hear of those who care.
I think it very heartless,
We suddenly cry out in despair!
We know about what we're doing,
Yet, none of us even try,
We know about what we're doing,
Yet, when we hear of it we deny???
Well, denial doesn't help them,
Because they're the ones who die!!
Well, denial doesn't help them,
They never got a chance at life.
If you are EVER faced with this choice…say NO!!!

Natalie Moss, Grade 7
St Francis Parish School

My Family

I love my family
A family is something very special you can have
My family and I have been through a lot together
We argue, we fight
But then we become really good friends
Yet they still care about me
And show lots of love towards me
We celebrate our traditions
We get together and have lots of fun
My family is very important to me
They are a big part of my life
They never put me down
They always cheer me up
I care for my family
And without them I don't know what I would do

Amparo Valdovinos, Grade 8
Isbell Middle School

Escher's Bond of Union*

It all starts with one ribbon with stars all around.
Blackness as far as the eye can see.
But they don't care about anything except each other.
They are attracted to each other for reasons we may never know.
Stars all around.
Round they swirl.
They come out of nowhere and are everywhere
Without them, there will be no sense of distance,
No sense of place.

Zia Anwar, Grade 7
Tenaya Middle School
*Inspired by Escher's Bond of Union

Sweet Angels

Don't you worry,
Sweet little angel
It will be all right
So just trust in me
Close your eyes
And count to five
Don't you worry
Sweet little boy
It will be ok
Just close your eyes
And count to five
Don't you worry
Sweet little girl
It will be
All right
Just trust in me and close your eyes and count
To five
Just close your eyes and to
God's eyes we are sweet
Little angels

Alex Arias, Grade 8
Our Lady of Guadalupe School

I Am

I am a dreamer and a wisher,
I wonder why life is so complicated,
I hear ocean waves in a seashell,
I see every memory of my past,
I want pictures of my future,
I am a dreamer and a wisher.

I pretend I am older than I am,
I feel some things in life never make sense,
I touch my face against my pillow after a long day,
I worry life can be too short,
I cry when others are put down,
I am a dreamer and a wisher.

I understand life is what you make of it,
I say that dreams are wishes your heart makes,
I dream I could paint every sunset,
I try to open more doors in life than close them,
I hope I can make a difference,
I am a dreamer and a wisher.

Hannah Davis, Grade 7
Willma Cavitt Jr High School

Beautiful Beloved

If my love should fade away like a shadow in dawn's light,
then surely my heart's death was in vain.
For the image of society's burning rose,
is enough to cause my beloved pain.
The phantom rain will not wash away my tears,
nor bring forth this angel of mine from up above.
Fake smiles and tales of the deepest happiness,
is still not enough to cover the feelings of this broken love.
Lying under the Moon Maiden's great shine,
I face bravely and anxiously against the await,
to kiss again, the wings of my beautiful beloved,
and watch the heavens open, telling of a dreadful fate.
I see him now, his halo glittering in the image of my mind.
My heartbeat lifting the Earth's ground.
His eyes so deep you feel the universe is living there.
His breathing in the night, the only everlasting sound.
The gates of Heaven suddenly close its welcome,
no longer allowing my angel back up above.
I look into the universe of his eyes,
grateful to the skies to let me keep my beautiful beloved.

Olleanna Stabler, Grade 8
Walter F Dexter Middle School

Dare to Like School

Oh no, it is Monday
Again, that means there is school today.
I don't want to
But I know I have to.
I wish I could stay home
And play games alone
Until my thumbs
Became numb.
Yet that is not positive
For us, it's destructive.
Our intelligence is a gift, and we better put it to the test.
We are capable of so much if we combine work and rest.
School may not always be fun,
But it is meant to fund
A bigger and brighter future
For us to some day nurture
And give something positive to society.
Let us be grateful and not let anxiety
Overcome us, for we have
An opportunity to thrive.

Rene Mendoza, Grade 7
Our Lady of Guadalupe School

First Place

I shift, I slide, I steer, I fly
The jumps are cool but I'm too shy
My gear is cool, my moves are tight
I do a move and it's just right
When I ride my quad, I love to have fun
The crowd is cheering I must be number one!

Heather Fraser, Grade 7
St Francis de Sales School

Thoughts on M.C. Escher's Bond of Union

What I see in this picture
is a man and his wife who were tied together, but now
she is gone forever.
And now the man is lonely without his wife.
But he still has memories about them together when they
were younger.

Brittany Maldonado, Grade 7
Tenaya Middle School

High Merit Poems – Grades 7, 8 and 9

Nothing
My thoughts are like clouds of fog
I can't make out what's right or wrong
Trying to figure out myself
As I'm walking on the shore and find a shell
Don't know what to do 'bout this
So many feelings that are controlling me
I don't think I will ever feel
A happiness I'm doubting is real
Consumed in my misery
I forget how to live
But when I look into the world
I'm wondering if it's better to return
To a life where people fabricate joy
Or to remain as I am
In my state of numbness
Where nothing can hurt me
Because everything I know is real
And all I know is nothing.

Angel Piña, Grade 8
Our Lady of the Rosary School

Mother
Life, it seems so different without you here
It's like I have forgotten all the years we had together
There's emptiness inside me
Longing to be filled by your love and care
I wish you were here, because I wouldn't dare
Live another moment without you
Unfortunately, things happen that we cannot prevent
Now in my heart there lies a dent
Trying to rid the pain
But there's just too much that time cannot erase
You were always there for me
And I was always there for you
You made everything better
Now your absence has torn my world apart
I am so frightened and confused
All I can do is keep you on my mind
Pretending you are by my side
Just like the good old times.

Brooklyn Slagoski, Grade 7
Walter F Dexter Middle School

I Am Myself
I wonder if I will graduate from high school and college.
I hear when my parents talk.
I see in my future what is going to happen.
I want to study hard.
I do whatever I can to get success in this place.
I am myself.
I pretend to be stupid.
I feel that I'm alone.
I touch my heart.
I worry if I'm going to pass my classes or the cahsee.
I cry because I see how hard and difficult it is to get good grades.
I am myself.
I understand what learning is about.
I say "What can I do."
I dream to be more perfect.
I try my best.
I hope my wish comes true.
I am myself.

Jessica Thao, Grade 9
Hiram W Johnson High School

I Am a Dragon
I wonder if I will live long.
I hear humans saying, "Catch him!"
I see hunters searching for me.
I want to fly away.
I do what makes me feel safe.
I am a dragon.
I pretend to be friendly.
I feel miserable.
I touch the cave with my wings.
I worry if people are scared of me.
I cry when I burn fields of food.
I am a dragon.
I understand nothing about heroes.
I say to myself "Be strong."
I dream about being caught by the ones who walk on two legs.
I try to be helpful.
I hope the universe understands me.
I am a dragon.

Meng Vue, Grade 9
Hiram W Johnson High School

Edvard Munch's Painting The Scream
To me
It seems like he is sad,
That he lives in a world where no one can
Hear him or see him.
He is acting as if people are avoiding him.
He has his hands on his face and is screaming and crying,
But still, no one can hear him.
How would you like it
If people can see you,
But they just walk right past you and not say anything.

Rodney Banks, Grade 7
Tenaya Middle School

The Notebook Between Two People
They didn't agree on much
In fact…
They rarely agreed on anything
They fought all the time
They always challenged each other every day
But…
Despite their differences
At the end of the day
They had one thing in common
They were crazy about one another

Carina Balderas, Grade 8
August Boeger Middle School

Pizza

The cheese globbed
Mindlessly in the center,
Leaving the thick warm crust isolated.
Thin tangles of melted mozzarella
flowed down the sides,
Exposing hot, steaming tomato sauce.
Pepperoni, veggies, or pineapple —
All would have suited my growling stomach.
I inhaled the savory smell,
Ripping a piece of pizza off with my teeth
And gobbling it down.
Grease dribbled down my chin.
I wiped it away with a waiting napkin.
When I got to it, the crust
Crunched under my bite.
The crumbs fell to the plate.
The doughy middle overwhelmed me
As I closed my eyes and bit down again.
When I opened them,
I saw the box was almost empty.
Too bad. I could eat pizza forever.

Bridgid Elliott-Pope, Grade 8
Palm Desert Charter Middle School

This Boy

The thought of you and me
Have you ever thought of what we could be?
Your smile, your laugh they brighten my day
They make me smile in every way.
We walk the halls like it's no big deal
But is what I'm feeling actually real?
You're cute, you're sweet
You make my heart skip a beat
There's something about you I can't get out of my head
It's like you're tied into my heart like a piece of thread
How you feel about me
Is still a mystery
But you and me
Were the perfect fantasy…

Madison Scott, Grade 9
St Mary's High School

To My Brother

Hello little bro, how was your day?
I guess mine was pretty okay.
Hey, I know I haven't been here for you at all,
When you had troubles I wasn't exactly the one to call.
But now I want you to know that I'm here,
And if you need something I'll be listening near.
To me, you're my twinkly star,
Every day you shine brighter and brighter so I know you'll go far.
I think about you every single day,
And I've been wanting to say,
I love you Junior…

Martha Gonzalez, Grade 8
Richard Merkin Middle Academy

I Run

I run to live,
I run for speed,
I run to shun the pain and sadness that I feel and see.
I run to climb to the heavens above,
And I run be with the ones I love,
The ones that are no longer with me,
Whose shadows went from gray to clear,
The ones I myself, can never draw near.
I run for guidance and run to be free,
from the never ending thoughts of civil rights and slavery.
People seem to ask me a lot, why I run so fast,
Is it a hobby,
Or something in your blood,
Am I just someone whose energy can last and last and last
I always tell them it's just in my blood and I'm not lying
No I'm not at all, but that's not the main reason at all.
I run to live.
I run for speed.
I run to shun the pain that I see.
I run to the side of me that is unclear.
But I run to ease the pain that grows near and near.

Makeda Gayle, Grade 7
Orville Wright Middle School

Music Isn't Just…

Music isn't just the words spoken through our lips.
It's the secrets you should never tell in friendships.
Music isn't the type of thing you once loved then lost.
It's the soon to be lifting line that should be crossed.
Music isn't the mindless singing of an unwritten song.
It's the sound of a world of which you should belong.

Music isn't just the crack of a tree tumbling to the ground.
It's the wood of the tree itself as seen in hardbound.
Music isn't the noise of the rain on your roof at night.
It's the angels singing in your dreams with great delight.
Music isn't the smell of old leather bound books.
It's the sweet scent of musical taste in your song writing notebooks.
Music isn't just…words.

Alexandra Forte, Grade 9
Palm Desert High School

Reflections on Edvard Munch's The Scream

I noticed a man covering his ears,
But I think maybe he did that because he feels
Really lightheaded or hurt.
His head hurts more than he thinks.
His feelings are full of pain and anger…
Emotions are building up into screaming and fear.
He struggles…trying to scream for an answer
But
The couple behind him walk on by
As if he has not a reason for happiness,
And like…he is a part of nothingness.

Joshua Juarez, Grade 7
Tenaya Middle School

High Merit Poems – Grades 7, 8 and 9

My Family
My family is fun and loving.
We are always happy and cheerful.
My dad is tall and strong.
My mom is smart and pretty.
My brother is young and innocent.

We like to play
And dance.
We sing and
Talk about things.

Sometimes we
Go to the movies.
Sometimes we
Stay at home.

My family is
Very important to me.
Cesare Clubb, Grade 8
Park View Middle School

Daddy Where Are You?
I never thought this would happen to me,
But it did and was as weird as could be.
I ignored it and had to argue,
I said it couldn't be true.
Then it was the day,
I met him and didn't know what to say.
It was fun for a while,
And he even knew how to make me smile.
But why did he choose them over me?
I was as nice as can be.
I listened to why he wasn't there,
And played with that teddy bear.
My mom said he had to disappear,
Then it became all clear,
That he did not want or love me
But he wanted his other family.
There I was hurt badly,
And left again with no daddy.
Brianna Ramos, Grade 8
Walter F Dexter Middle School

This Is My City
San Francisco is my city
where I learn and grow.
San Francisco is my city,
filled with all the people that I know.
San Francisco is where my dreams begin
and where I learn to make them true.
San Francisco is where my life starts
and the good things I will do.
San Francisco is my city,
where I leave my heart!
Catherine Rose, Grade 7
Corpus Christi School

Animal Cruelty
What is animal cruelty?
Hurting and abusing animals
Is animal cruelty.

What is animal cruelty?
When we don't care,
When pets are forgotten
Is animal cruelty.

Why do we abuse animals?
People think hurting
God's creation is "fun."

Is animal cruelty right?
Absolutely not! Animal cruelty
Is killing God's creation!

What is animal cruelty?
Showing animals exactly what
They don't deserve: hatred.
Amanda Armstrong, Grade 7
St Francis Parish School

I Am Soul
I wonder if people see me around
I hear other humans' voices
I see myself with them
I want to feel important
I do what I can do to show I'm there
I am soul

I pretend that I'm happy
I feel alone in this world
I touch so many hearts
I worry for others' futures
I cry when I lose someone special
I am soul

I understand I can't help
I say some words that I regret
I dream to someday have a good life
I try and find the way
I hope to be seen here
I am soul
Yazaira Garcia, Grade 9
Hiram W Johnson High School

Shadow
I am chased here and there
to and from everywhere
I am only delaying the inevitable
running from my shadow is impossible
I will never escape
because my shadow's reach is great
Thien Pham Nguyen, Grade 7
Sarah McGarvin Intermediate School

Monte Vista Christian
M y school
O ver the mountain
N ext to the ocean
T he best school around
E ducational

V ery nice place
I ncredible teachers
S mart students
T errific food
A wesome athletes

C hapels
H orses
R eal good classrooms
I ndividually cared for
S ongs for worship
T he smartest students
I nsanely huge
A n exciting place to be
N eat and clean
Andrew Cosimano, Grade 7
Monte Vista Christian School

Love Seeps Through the Walls
Love seeps through the walls
Of this place I call home.
Like a single solar ray
In an April gloom.

Love seeps through the walls
Of this four walled sanctuary.
When all my imagination takes flight,
Like a dream on a hot summer night.

Love seeps through the walls
Even when everything inside it
Wants to hate.
But the magical leak seeps through again
And we remember to forget.

Love seeps through the walls
Of this place I call my soul.
And it's love, I guess,
That builds the place I call
Home.
Olivia Flores, Grade 8
Richardson PREP HI Middle School

Autumn
The leaves change colors
From green to orange or red
And fall down from trees
Catharine Chiu, Grade 7
St Mary's Chinese Day School

I Am

I am a beautiful girl who loves to be involved in sports.
I wonder if I will ever be good enough to play college volleyball.
I hear the crowd roaring when I make a good play.
I see professional players playing on television.
I want to be successful in volleyball.
I am a beautiful girl who loves to be involved in sports.

I pretend to be a professional.
I feel the pressures of being a young lady.
I touch my cousin that now is in Heaven.
I worry that the kids in high school will scare me.
I cry when my sister cries.
I am a beautiful girl who loves to be involved in sports.

I understand that life is difficult.
I say that one day I will go to Heaven.
I dream that one day I will be a great children's doctor.
I try to help other kids learn what they need to learn.
I hope that I will be very successful in life.
I am a beautiful girl who loves to be involved in sports.

Courtney Kelly, Grade 9
Lucerne Valley Jr/Sr High School

The American Flag Still Stands

With the sun filtering through the debris,
Finally some were free,
There was a ray of hope in a mass of chaos,
Even though many lives were lost.
We all had to help others,
Just because we were all brothers.

The screams of the sirens racing by,
The soaring of the planes flying high.

Emotions like devastation and fear,
Wondering if any help was near.
Thankfully many were brave, and because of that, many were saved
Bodies full of terror,
So much destruction you could not bear.

When the worst came it was up to us,
To not give up, but to have trust.
Thanks to our nation holding hands,
The American Flag Still Stands.

Kaitlyn Galeazzi, Grade 8
Ripona Elementary School

Obstacles

Obstacles are not so easy
As a matter of fact they make me feel uneasy
I think of them throughout the day
Wondering how to get them out of the way
When I am all done facing them
I feel like a new, sparkling gem!

Amanda Rodriguez, Grade 7
Our Lady of Guadalupe School

Winter

Winter is full of fun,
Summer is full of sun,
Winter is cold,
And summer is bold,
But winter I love the most.

In winter you get to wear long sleeves and long pants,
Thick sweaters and gloves for your hands.
In summer you can play outside and go on bike rides,
And go play in pool the next day.

In winter you get to bake.
Muffins, cupcakes, or cakes.
You can bake pumpkin bread which no one does dread.

Still, winter I love the most.
You can make a great Christmas toast,
While opening presents which I like the most.

Andie Bonette, Grade 8
Palm Desert Charter Middle School

To Learn to Forgive*

I am Cole Matthews. I am very angry.
I see the spirit bear it licks up my spit.
I hear the spirit bear.
I feel like alone wolf scared and afraid.
I am Cole Matthews angry and mad.

I dream of the spirit bear and my mauling.
I worry about Peter's health.
I want to help Peter.
I hope Peter gets better.
I am Cole Matthews. I am learning to forgive.

I understand I was wrong when I beat up Peter.
I try to dance the dance of anger.
I say I am sorry and I fell like a wolf pack strong.
I touch the Spirit Bear's fuzzy coat.
I am Cole Matthews. I learn to forgive.

Alan Borelli, Grade 8
Palm Desert Charter Middle School
*Inspired by "Touching Spirit Bear" by Ben Mikaelsen

The Undiscovered

The once undiscovered has now been discovered
Thirty-two exoplanets,
outside of our solar system
The undiscovered alien worlds,
Found by advanced technology

The so-called super Earths,
Many times the size of Earth,
Can be found outside of the solar system
Alien worlds.

Andrue Wells, Grade 8
Richardson PREP HI Middle School

High Merit Poems – Grades 7, 8 and 9

Flying Zombies

Sixteen hours, no breaks nor sleep
Dreaded dragging hours slowly pass by
Working, flying all day long
Once more my strength seems to die

Long haul flight left to do
Oh, how I long to sleep tonight
Yet, I cannot — I need to stay awake
In cockpit the copilot turns on the light

In this light we talk and check up on traffic
While passengers laugh, play and sleep
Oh, how I long to take one more nap
A short little nap, not even deep sleep

We sneak a nap
First me then him
We break the rules once more
Oh, how I long to sleep — even if it's dim

I hope we win our right to sleep
For this job is way too cruel
Only eight hours outside of this plane
Isn't enough too win, nor fight this duel
Jackie Gamez, Grade 8
Richardson PREP HI Middle School

Is Winter Coming?

The leaves are falling,
The flowers are blooming,
The sky is not bawling,
Yet winter is calling.

The birds are chirping,
The sun is shining,
The frogs are burping,
Yet winter is lurking.

The grass is green,
The sky is blue,
No clouds to be seen,
Yet winter is keen.

The ducks are quacking,
The squirrels are shopping,
The bears are packing,
Yet winter is lacking.

The days are long,
My sleeves are short,
In the air there's a song,
Yet winter is wrong.
Sierra Zeiter, Grade 9
St Mary's High School

Midnight Frights

The sun rises, dawn is here
Chasing away, midnight fears
The sun goes up, the moon goes down
Gazing at the sky, some people frown
People go, off to work
The children just, stay home and smirk
The sun shot up, noon is here
Lunch for elders, and our peers
The sun begins its slow descent
Half a day, came and went
Many people lounge and lay
Waiting for, the next day
Loiterers, wait for their lunch
Or maybe dinner, just a munch?
Six-twenty-three, the people say
Onto their beds, they'd go and lay
Two hours later, the clock has struck eight
The bustling streets, now hold no mate
Now silence joins, the moon at night
Welcoming back, the midnight frights
Joseph Park, Grade 8
South Lake Middle School

But Most of All…

I like many things to name a few
I like the different things I do
I like the times I go for a walk
I like being with my friends just to talk
I like 7th grade and going to school
I like swimming in my pool
I like to shop at the mall
I like to play volleyball
I like playing different sports
I like wearing my lime green shorts
I like eating chocolate cake
I like living by Folsom Lake
I like the winter to play in the snow
I like to learn how to sew
I like reading in my room
I like pretty flowers when they're in bloom
I like the ocean with my toes in the sand
I like dancing to a rock and roll band
I like so many things that I can see
But most of all…I like being me!
Mary-Frances Hansen, Grade 7
Willma Cavitt Jr High School

Sock Monkey

Once a sock with stripes
Now a toy with life
Once a needle with thread
Now a pair of eyes
Once green and blue and white
Now a striped monkey
Kayley Hall, Grade 8
Temecula Valley Charter School

Sunflower

I remember the day we planted them.
They were just seeds, so small.
I wondered, "Would they ever grow
To be anything at all?"

We watered them with showers of blessings.
They were nourished by the Sun.
Then, one day, they started to grow
And they blossomed, one by one.

The first seed blossomed into trust.
The second seed bloomed with love.
Another seed blossomed into admiration.
Yet, all were blessed from up above.

I remember the day we planted them.
The seeds were all so new.
We waited and watched, and wondered,
And, from them, something grew.
Victoria Dragun, Grade 8
Palm Desert Charter Middle School

Trophies, All for Me

32 and counting
Atop my shelf
32 and counting
All for myself

32 and counting
Collecting dust
32 and counting
Will never rust

32 and counting
Brand new smell
32 and counting
All earned well

I may die
But my legacy won't
32 and counting
The bronze, silver, and gold
Arick Cohen, Grade 8
Richardson PREP HI Middle School

Bouncing Ball of Love

Bounce, Bounce.
Love is like a ball;
It is very colorful,
It comes in many
Shapes and sizes,
But if you drop the ball,
You're dropping your chances,
Of playing.
Kayla Guzman, Grade 7
Immaculate Heart of Mary School

Heart Broken
Put all my faith into your heart
Hoping that nothing will fall apart
blinded by love you took my sight
At first false warmth
Made it all right
But your heart turned cold
All in one night
Now I'm wondering
How it all, went wrong
And how our loved turned out
To be the lyrics to this break-up song
Swallowed by pain and loneliness
I drown in this new darkness
But my love will revive
All it takes is a little bit of time
Ashley Manjarrez, Grade 7
La Mesa Jr High School

No Puppy Love
Dogs are beaten every day
They do not get to play
Fighting is what they are made to do
Which is not cool

The owners beating them
Fighting their own kind for no reason
Dog fights all over the world
When they win they get nothing
Just their lives

They have no life
Just to fight and stay alive
But when they die
The owners do not care
Alex Smith, Grade 8
Richardson PREP HI Middle School

Moms
Moms are like popcorn
Popping in the summer days
Fun, nice, and lovely
Is mostly their game
They clean up messes
Like a tide washing up a shore
Moms make sandwiches
For their kids
Everyone likes them so much
They want more
Moms like sweets
More than anyone
Moms are like the sun
Rising and helping everyone
This is why moms are the best!
Cristina Fekkes, Grade 7
Junipero Serra School

We All Love Them
We all love them
They comfort us when we're sad
and make us happy when we're mad
Some are fuzzy, others puffy.
some are hairy and others scary
No matter what they look like;
ugly or nice, we will always
love them, through the good and
the bad.
They don't care how you look,
or if you listen to music or read
a book.
They don't seem to mind if your hair
is straight or curly.
They don't pay attention to whether
you're a tomboy or if you're girlie
All they care about is the love you
give them and the love they give you.
So give them love and care for them fondly
because they will do the same for you too.
Denise Hernandez, Grade 7
Isbell Middle School

Living
In green pastures
Where childhood plays,
And teenager years
Disappear within days.

That is where I lived.

In violet shades
Of a deep blue sky,
Clouds swoop and swirl
And birds come to fly.

That is where I live.

In daydreams of a future unknown,
Where love is one and I have grown.
Together, what will become of us,
And will the end become unjust?

I wonder then, where shall I live?
Tiana Ramirez, Grade 8
Joe Walker Middle School

Waiting
Waiting, here with open arms
Waiting, for you to run into them
Waiting, for two to be one
Waiting, calmly, I'm in no rush
Waiting, for your touch
Waiting, for you, never going to stop
Tiffinee Derby, Grade 8
Shadow Hills Intermediate School

Insanity
My perfect world couldn't be better,
It's where I today remain,
It's a place of no emotion,
A place where no one goes insane.

For this place is beautiful,
Nothing ever feels bad,
You are always happy here,
You will never again feel sad.

But yet they call me crazy,
Sometimes even insane,
For there is a down side to this place,
In your eyes it might be dead.

Why is this you ask?
Well, because sadly it's all in my
HEAD!
Brenna Orr, Grade 8
Shadow Hills Intermediate School

The Hamster
I am but a pet
A hamster that's all wet
I've fallen in my dish
I have just one wish
I am out of food
I find it quite rude
As the fleas bite my skin
And I grow so thin
He feeds me bird seed
Yet I cannot fly if I need
I plot an escape
But the broken cage is covered in tape
I'll never get out
And I hide my snout
My failure has me pity myself
While the dog sleeps free below the shelf
I wish to be
Oh so free
Jonathan Allen, Grade 7
Monte Vista Christian School

My Aunt Nini
I miss my Aunt Nini, for that's her name
I think it's cool, but others think it's lame
She is so very far away
even farther than you can say
On the little island of Guam
that's where she has settled on
It is a beautiful place
yet it doesn't put a smile on her face
She won't be back until next year
that's why every night I shed a tear
Jada Reintegrado, Grade 7
St Francis de Sales School

The Life of a Rose
I am a rose
Yet a very damaged rose
The wind has torn my leaves
And my color has faded

Others have broken my stem
Since I've been picked and played with
I am a rose who has grown thorns
Without the support of my dozen

I am simply a rose
A very faded and harmed one
I am a rose a sign of love
Who gives a sweet breeze

You who has me in your hands
Take care of me
For I have suffered
And need someone
To share my laugh and sorrows
I am a rose a damaged one who needs you
Karla Cuevas, Grade 8
John Adams Middle School

Space in Love
Space is an empty place
So very large and vacuous,
Ever-changing
And unexplored

It's like the empty space
That reside in my heart
Waiting to be discovered
By someone that can love
And can love you for what you are
Whether that's an empty space
Or a shooting star

This sacred place
Has been torn down
By love's true natured ways:
An endangered trace
Desiring love,
Never sweet, never nice
But it will be with you; even in this
Dark, dark space.
Thomas LiVolsi, Grade 9
University Preparatory School

Moon
The moon in the air
Shines golden of pride up there
It gleams in darkness
Christian Romero, Grade 8
St Francis de Sales School

Life
Full of surprising things
Life
Not always a wonderful place
Life

Is sometimes bad
Can go off track
Send messages without a plan

Can be scary
Life
Sometimes bright
Life
Remember not to put up a fight

Life
Kasey Berry, Grade 7
Long Valley Charter School

A Broken Heart
My beloved Sidney Lee
My heart belongs to thee
My beloved Sidney Lee
Listen to my plea
My beloved Sidney Lee
My heart must shine with glee
My beloved Sidney Lee
Please o'please love me
My beloved Sidney Lee
Don't let me lie here for all eternity
My beloved Sidney Lee
Let both our souls be free
My beloved Sidney Lee
Please don't leave me
My beloved Sidney Lee

Giovanni Daniel Ruggiero, Grade 7
Monte Vista Christian School

Laugh
Everyone needs it
Without it, life hurts
It never is painful
Like having dessert

It does so much for us
Without doing anything
It's nothing fancy or expensive
Like a nice diamond ring

It's easy to get
And worth all the while
Just a simple laugh
Can make anyone smile
Natalie Pederson, Grade 7
Nobel Middle School

By My Side
You were by my side.
Always.
And now the distance between us,
Will drown us in memories.
That day,
When we said our goodbyes,
My heart nearly stopped.
It raced to find an answer.
What changed?
It might just be me,
But it's something more.
And without you by my side,
My world would end,
And my heart would ache.
You were by my side.
Always.
And now the distance between us,
Will make our heart farther,
And farther,
Apart.
Jessica Garcia, Grade 8
Roseland Accelerated Middle School

Heartbreak
In this particular moment,
I feel the connection between
You and me
This bond we have is just unbreakable,
Your lips are attached to mine
Your arms around my waist
And your whole body
Close to mine
I swear I can feel your heart beat
It's beating so fast,
Yet so gently
Time is running out
And don't have much time
To be with you.
As a call approaches I ignore it.
I wanted to be in your arms and continue,
But you decided it was wrong
I begin to feel tears in my eyes
I understand why you did that,
But still, it breaks my heart
Lizzette Aguilar, Grade 8
Richard Merkin Middle Academy

Six Flags
This is the best place ever
If only I could stay forever.
There is so many rides to choose
after all you have nothing to lose.
The best is surely the "X2"
it always makes me go "Woohoo!"
Justin Waterman, Grade 8
St Francis de Sales School

Death

Death,
Death will come,
Indeed, Death shall come,
To me, to me,
Oh can't you see?
Clear as a day,
Come if it may,
As it takes my last breath away,
It pulls me into the darkness,
And leaves me senseless,
As I float, I think of a way out,
Always full of hope,
But deep down — is doubt,
Oh! What a dope!
Thinking about the day under the warm sun and the clear skies,
But they're all filled with lies,
False hope and false dreams,
My tears fall down in giant streams.

Caroline Hang, Grade 7
Ramona Elementary School

I Am

I wonder if I could be a better person.
I hear my voice say that I have a heart.
I see how nice it is to have a cup of coffee.
I want to go to all my classes and be healthy.
I do my own job.
I am myself.
I pretend to know you.
I feel like I am getting there on time.
I touch my dark hair.
I worry about my class work.
I cry along.
I am a champion.
I understand the teacher's feeling.
I say I am having an awesome day.
I dream about driving a car.
I try to help myself and be successful.
I hope my wishes come true.
I am a wrestler.

Vichai Chang, Grade 9
Hiram W Johnson High School

The Protective Dragon

As I look at the art I wonder if dragons do exist
Do they fly
Or are the wings just for looks
Are they evil
With the horns they look evil
As they rap around the statue
They look as if they were protecting it
The longer you stare
You feel like
You smell fish or lizard

Enrique Macias, Grade 7
Daniel Savage Middle School

Martin Luther King, Jr.

Without him I would not be here.
This is something very clear
My mom and dad would never meet
If racial jokes he did not beat.

He's my hero, he's my friend
Even tho' he does not blend.
He's black and stern and very bold
But he would not want to see you cold

He twisted through many knots and ties
But came out victorious through all his tries.

"Love is the only force capable of
transforming…" a crow into a dove.

This means love is the only cure
For hatred, and to make things pure.

So Martin Luther King is my hero and friend.
I owe my life to him to the very end.

Christopher Honda, Grade 7
Monte Vista Christian School

Cherish Life

war there is nothing good about it
people die people cry
we are fighting over stupid things
is it really worth it I don't think so
there are thousands of troops out there
that risk their lives every day
they live in horrible conditions
they don't have the things we have
where they are today
they wake up every morning
thanking God they made it through the night
while we wake up not thanking God
but whining because we have to get up
and go to work or school
all the little things we take for granted
they cherish all the time
we talk about our friends
while they may never see theirs again
its sad to think they are out there
risking their lives every day while we are here
not even thinking how lucky we are to be alive today

Selina Martinez, Grade 8
Isbell Middle School

Love Story

Love is like a book.
Each chapter is a continuation of your story.
A missing page is not just another less page to read…
…but you and the book itself are not complete

Kaela Uy, Grade 7
Immaculate Heart of Mary School

Accomplishment

To achieve the prosperity of accomplishment, what you seek, relies in the accomplishment of:
Fears,
Goals,
Hopes,
And dreams.
You must breathe honesty,
Portray the act of determination,
Moreover, believe that seeking will always get you far.
You must adventure in crevices of knowledge you would never need or want,
But accomplishment is everywhere,
In your mind, when you don't want to grow, but you do.
That is accomplishment.
In your heart, when you don't want to risk and take the plunge, but you jump.
That is accomplishment.
In your eyes, when you think you can't reach your goal, but you succeed.
That is accomplishment.
To achieve the prosperity of accomplishment, what you seek, relies in the accomplishment of,
Yourself.

Dylan French, Grade 7
Harvest Park Intermediate School

Reflection of Guilt

While the roaring flames begin to smolder though the smoke's stench seems to pause
Guilty not, is our Mother Nature for man is the true cause

Your walls no longer offer shelter, no more does a damaged roof sit aloft
Your weary frame has grown much lighter and many grieve for all they have lost

Your timber no longer does twist or splinter, through the haze your walls cease to melt
Now each clear, clean, crack shows truth even after, its damaged face may whisper whose guilt should truly be felt

For whomever received the harm are now nowhere near as full of sorrow
As those responsible for all alarm, who now feel the heat down to their marrow

Their no longer quiet and cruel violence, caused more than a mere abode to be lost
The blaze of truth inside the throbbing conscience may claim their every sense at a severe cost

Your melted glass serves as a mirror for a true reflection, for the accountable now is justly charged
For they now know their full true intention, and thus, have been duly scarred

Mac Colquhoun, Grade 8
The Mirman School

A Time Lost in Time

The white snow is a blanket of frost laid politely over the brush, the wolf sings in harmony with his pack.
The rabbit scurries gracefully across the ocean of white without a trace.
The deer stands still like a tall evergreen in infinity of white and green.
The trees wait for just the right breeze to reveal their dance of longing.
When the bear sleeps it is one with the world outside its own,
not knowing at any moment it can be awoken into a place never recalled in his memories.
The white snow lies there waiting to be embedded by a single touch.
The icy surface stands still while screaming signs of safety for those who are not wiser.
The owl lies perched never wanting to be disturbed until the waterfall of black covers the sky.
The child asks himself what is this time of peace while still in awe looking around the house of white and unseen.
His question will go unseen for this is a time lost in time itself.

Stephanie Lugo, Grade 8
St Francis Parish School

Music

Music is my life, my heart, and my soul.
I love listening to my favorite song.
Listening to music makes me feel whole.
When I'm rocking nothing seems to be wrong.

Yes, my first love was my first stereo.
It was crazy awesome and a bright red.
My mom would yell, "Turn it down!" I'd yell "No!"
My poor, poor stereo; it is now dead.

Music has taken a huge toll on me.
A world without music would be nothing.
Just music alone helps me think clearly.
When I hear a song I can't help but sing.

Without my iPod I could not survive.
Without music I would not be alive.

Kimberly Medina, Grade 9
Lucerne Valley Jr/Sr High School

Spring

Spring marks the start of baseball season,
The snow is melting the ground is thawing,
The groundhogs venture out with good reason
I take to the park to start my drawing

Valleys of flowers pop out of nowhere
Colors fill the landscape with no boundaries
With shape and size and colors so rare
All while the new leaves begin to crown trees

The children are eager for Easter time
Chocolate eggs and bunnies in baskets
Hear bells at the church beautifully chime
Egg hunts and picnics and naps on blankets

In the warming sun the rain drops glitter
Spring brings a peaceful end to the winter.

Adam Garcia, Grade 9
Lucerne Valley Jr/Sr High School

Love

Love, is it really a thing or is it just
made up for mortals to keep a
generation line?
They say our hearts are full of love, or
is it just to keep a pulse?

A soul. Is that what produces love?
Is there really such a thing as a soul?
There may be.
They say when you die your soul
walks the Earth.
Do you walk the Earth with your love?

Dani Garman, Grade 7
Los Molinos Community Elementary School

Ode to My Father

I thank you my father,
For you make me laugh
When I'm about to cry.

I thank you my father,
For you always know what
To say and do to make me happy.

I thank you my father,
Because there is always one special soccer game
When you allow me to sit in your favorite chair.

For these reasons I thank you my father,
For you are the best dad anyone
Could ever ask for.

Thank you.

Bianka Sanchez, Grade 8
Richardson PREP HI Middle School

I Am Xavier

I am Xavier
I see hurting in my family
I hear crying from my brother and sisters
I feel scared
I am a shy person but smart person

I dream of getting a better life
I worried I wasn't going to live a successful life
I want to get A's in every class
I hope our family gets better
I am a shy person but a smart person

I understand life is hard
I try to not be mad
I say that life is better for me now
I touch my PSP every day after school
I am Xavier and I am a shy person but a smart person

Xavier Wesley, Grade 8
Palm Desert Charter Middle School

Do You Realize?

Drugs are something bad for you
They will kill you and that's so true
People get high every day
But don't realize what they'll soon pay
Many people get high for fun
It's just like a kid playing with a gun
People most likely end up the same
Always end up in death's aim
Substance abuse is very scary
You never really know what life carries
Families have to deal with deaths each day
Would you like them to worry about you that way?

Corina Little Turtle, Grade 8
Isbell Middle School

High Merit Poems – Grades 7, 8 and 9

Summer

Summer is my favorite season of all
My friends and I carve the hills by the pier
We jaywalk with boards and try not to fall
New friends go away and old ones come near

My grandmother's awful cooking pains me
The family is good and so is the heat
Like all you touch and ev'rything you see
But the fire season starts, what a treat!

At home, nothing ever really goes on
Life goes on as usual and I stay bored
I stay home and watch the tube, it turns off
In a house with no doors, I stay ignored.

Doing my chores just for something to do
Being lethargic there's nothing that's new

Dereck LaGuardia, Grade 9
Lucerne Valley Jr/Sr High School

Books, Books

Books, books I like them all;
From the start of winter to the end of fall
From Sherlock Holmes
To garden gnomes,
Books, books I like them all.

Books, books are fun to read;
With wizards, witches and other weird things.
They can be large or they can be small,
But I don't care I enjoy them all.
Books, books are fun to read.

Books, books I like them so much;
That's why I couldn't go with you to lunch.
A series of three or a series of twelve,
I'll take both off the shelves.
Books, books I like them so much.

Brandon Rudney, Grade 7
Joe Walker Middle School

The World Within a Child's Hand

The world within a child's hand
Tells a story all its own;
Unique in every way.
Each individual crease and crevice is you.
So show your beauty; the beauty from within.
As only you can.
Take your time;
When you're given the chance, look at a child's hand.
What story do you see?
Often, we do not acknowledge that
GRAND
Once was so very small.

Jessica Palacios, Grade 7
Tenaya Middle School

I Am

I am a girl living with a sick mother,
I wonder if there will ever be a cure
I hear the worry in her voice
I see the pain she goes through
I am a girl living with a sick mother.

I pretend she will get better
I feel sadness when she cries of pain
I touch her to let her know I'm there for her
I worry about her future
I cry when no one's around
I am a girl living with a sick mother.

I understand that there is nothing I can do but,
I say I will help her
I dream of a doctor with a cure
I try to be optimistic
I hope that it will go away
I am a girl living with a sick mother.

Autumlace Grasman, Grade 8
Park View Middle School

Fun in the Snow

One day in the snow
    As the wind stopped to blow
Out in the snow went I,
    Austin, my cousin, and I.

What we did, we started to dig
    Deep in the snowdrifts big
He on one side, and I on the other
    Till we met in the middle and saw one another.

Then out went we, and started to dig
    And make our hole more big.
We made more tunnels, but in
    Came the cold, we couldn't win!

That night we were in for a surprise
    For the temperature's rise brought the tunnel's demise.
The tunnel was great, but better still
    The making of poetry with memories fill.

Collin Vis, Grade 7
Heritage Christian School

It's Almost Over

It's almost over, graduation is near
this is something I have always feared
I do not want this year to end
because I'll miss all of my friends.
The memories we have will always last
because they sure were a blast.
We are in eighth grade and we think we're cool
so we try really hard to not break the rules.

Katie Vahl, Grade 8
St Francis de Sales School

Without You

My tears are flowing for you
As my mind wonders and heart beats
My body is nothing without you
As the wetness of my cheek begins to dry,
And my thoughts weaken and try to forget,
I feel like nothing without you.
The beats within my chest were real,
Something that no one will ever steal
Where there is nothing without you
But as I try to forget you more and more,
My body grows weaker and begins to wear
My mind floats, and rises to react
I know I am nothing without you.

Yvonne Ramirez, Grade 8
Richard Merkin Middle Academy

Save the Animals

The animals that we love
like any pet or the doves
are still among us.
If we pollute,
they will die.
If we don't,
they'll survive.
Do you want them alive?
I do.
You can join in too:
Save the animals,
one day they'll save you!

Samantha Bueno, Grade 7
Walter F Dexter Middle School

My Friend and I

My friend and I like to play soccer
When we play we feel happy.
We are on a soccer team
And we always win
We speak Spanish.
We smile at the people
A lot of times we get a gold medal
To wear on our jackets.
My grandpa goes to watch us play.
I hear him whistling.
When I get good grades,
The school gives us a scholarship.

Nieto Jesus, Grade 9
Hiram W Johnson High School

Igor*

I ntelligent
G reat
O utstanding
R emarkable

Claudia Rodriguez, Grade 7
Lucerne Valley Jr/Sr High School
*In honor of my big brother

Life Is?????

Life is a fantasy.
You can get better at it with nothing to worry about.
But the real truth is that no said life would be easy to do.
Life is like a fairy tale.
You can dream about anything you like.
But no one will promise that all your dreams will come true.
Life is a joke.
You can laugh at anything you think is funny.
But no one said everything in the real life would be funny all the time.
Life is like a house.
You can live your life like if there's no tomorrow.
But the real truth is that you never know when is your last day of living.
Life is love.
Everything in life has a connection with you loving someone or something.
But no one promised that someone or something will love you back the same way you do.
Life is life.
No know knows what's going to happen next.
Everything in life is unexpected.
So get ready because any moment your life can end just by one blink of an eye.
Life is reality.

Kelly Mendez, Grade 8
Richard Merkin Middle Academy

My Best Friend!!

You've been my best friend since eight years ago
I remember when you came up to me and said,
"Hey, my name's Marvin and I was wondering if you wanted to be friends?"
I just laughed and said, "Yeah, my name's Lupe by the way."
Ever since that day we're inseparable
I know I can come to you for anything at any time
You're always there with me when I have good and bad times
You're the main person who brings me up when I'm down
You can put a smile on my face even if I'm sad
Even though we sometimes have our "fights" I know that we're still friends
You may be crazy, weird, cool and funny
But YOU WILL ALWAYS BE MY BEST FRIEND!!

Guadalupe Conde, Grade 8
Richard Merkin Middle Academy

If Love

If love, were a color,
It would be the lightest shade of pink.
If love, were a noise,
It would be the gentle laughter of a bunch of kids.
If love, were an animal,
It would be the softest little kitten
you hope dearly to keep by your side.
If love, were a feeling,
It would be the cold, crisp mist of rain,
on one of the most hottest days of the year.
If love, were a sound,
It would be the gentle whisper of you saying "I love you forever,"
and if it is true, I will whisper "I love you too and I'll never let you go."

Kassandra Ortiz, Grade 8
Roseland Accelerated Middle School

Through It All

Sometimes you just can't stop the pain,
And it stings when open wounds feel the rain.
Being dropped down, having no sympathy,
Days go on and you continue to face your enemy.
You want to run away; getaway from it all,
But the further you go, the further you fall.
Being drowned out by the memories of your past,
You worry, realizing how long this can last.
Now everything's really starting to fall apart,
And you wish you noticed sooner, back at the start.

When the day ends, right before you go to sleep,
You stare at the ceiling and silently weep.
Remembering the way things used to be,
And it kills you inside as you begin to see.
How much better things were then,
Compared to how terrible they are now.
Goodbye to sorrow,
Here comes tomorrow.

Chanel Nye, Grade 9
Chino Hills High School

The Day of Pride

It was a chaos-like day
Everyone was trying to find their way
Soon there was a shot heard around the world
And that started disorder around the globe

Lexington, the beginning of divorces in the colonies
Soon were the history of the nation
Paul Revere and William Dawes alarmed with distress
Risking their lives to build a creation

A few town people lined up like boats
And were shot by merciless redcoats
The merry redcoats marched to Concord
Eager with indifference to conquer

The Americans forced them to retreat
And they with no choice did not get a treat
The Americans accomplished victory
And with pride created history

Lily Hernandez, Grade 8
John Adams Middle School

Where I'm From

I am from a family of responsibility.
I am from a family that cares for me.
I am from people where religion is deep.
From ancestors that were beat.
From family members of high college degrees.
From jocks that cannot be beat.
I am from brother and cousins that sure can eat.
I am from family that loves me.

Kenneth Smith, Grade 8
Bret Harte Middle School

The Loss of My Uncle

The days without you are lonely,
The nights without you are cold.
Even though you are gone now
That burning passion will never be old.

Sometimes I cry myself to sleep at night
Just knowing that you are gone, but it makes
Me feel better knowing that you are peacefully at home.
Your body lies at rest now.

It's harder than I thought,
Just knowing you are
Gone for good and thinking it's all our fault.
Time will take its curse now,

For there's nothing left to do.
Just always remember uncle that I still
Care and that I will
Forever love you.

Emigdio Solis, Grade 8
John Adams Middle School

Grandma

bright and loving
Grandma can put a smile on anyone's face
she is bright like a star
shooting through the night sky
she is loving like the sun
warming the world and promoting life

calm and vibrant
Grandma brings joy to everyone she meets
she is calm like a river
cool and soothing healing the worst of wounds
she is vibrant like a flower
blooming in a meadow where worldly thoughts
are all but a distant memory

Grandma
has compassion, wisdom
and
memories to last more than one lifetime

Emily Woodward, Grade 7
Junipero Serra School

My Memorial of Mrs. Kimbirk

The day I met Mrs. Kimbirk, she scared me quite a bit
She was the type of teacher who was fun but very strict
You could tell she loved art dearly, clearly that was true
New memories were always happy, they were never blue
She always had a big smile on her face
She will never be replaced
Mrs. Kimbirk, her happiness so sweet like pie
I'll never forget the day that she died.

Maureen Roberts, Grade 8
St Francis de Sales School

A Beautiful Memory
Sometimes you remember miracles
You remember memories from when you were an infant
Your beautiful cradle where you would dream
Remembering back then, someone used to call your name
Sometimes at night you would hear voices
Some sweet and quiet
And sometimes a beautiful melody

You remember looking at the sea
Its vast waves and strong winds
You would look into the sunset
Waiting for the voice to call again

Watching the sea, you hear a voice
You think it's coming from the sea
And then you hear a beautiful melody

You're sitting at the ledge of a rock
Listening to the beautiful melody
You search and search
Yet you can't find the source

Virgille Factor, Grade 7
Corpus Christi School

Christmas
Christmas is that time of year,
Where it's filled with Christmas cheer.
All those Christmas cards that have been sent,
Show how much your family's love meant.

Remember all your Christmas joys,
And all those little toys?
Remember all that Christmas food,
And that music that puts you in the mood?

The magic mysteries,
The toy victories,
The questions of Santa Claus.
Think of the joys you have, and pause.

Ashley Harvey, Grade 7
Joe Walker Middle School

Can't Live a Day Without Music
I can't live a day without music
me with no music is like macaroni with no cheese
when I listen to music it takes me away
away from the drama
away from it all
when I have stress
all I do is pop in a CD and it all goes away
if there was no such thing as music
I don't know what I would do
I can't live a day with out music
what about you?

Nicole Villarreal, Grade 7
Isbell Middle School

Love
He looks at me with his
soft brown eyes,
Oh so sweet like a lullaby.

He talks to me only in class,
but in the hallways he walks right past.

He flirts with me
and has a constant tease,
but somehow it puts me at ease.

His smile brightens my day,
his laughter tends to my heart,
his face is perfection
as if it was Van Gogh's art.

I know we will never be together,
but my heart will be his forever,
he is the T-shirt I can't have,
the car I can't drive
but I will always love him every day I am alive.

Madison Wada, Grade 8
Joe Walker Middle School

A Blank Paper
A blank paper
Is like a newborn baby
Its mind is young and empty

As the baby gets older
Its mind will be filled with thoughts, memories, and ideas
And so will the paper
Those memories could be written by pencil, pen, or sharpie
It can be erased forever, blocked by whiteout, or stay permanent

That paper can only hold so much
So only fill it with things that you truly need
Don't waste it on bad memories
Erase it, or block it, just don't make it permanent
And keep life simple and happy

An Pham, Grade 8
Roseland Accelerated Middle School

Edvard Munch's The Scream
A man screams upon a bridge letting
His emotion out but
No one else can hear
People stroll along not coming to the end yet
The man has hit the end, but
They haven't reached that stage.
The sunset in the background
Casts a glow on the water beneath, yet
No comfort is given to the man.
I haven't felt that stage yet have you?

Madison Mendoza, Grade 7
Tenaya Middle School

A Day at Six Flags

It was toward the middle of May
we were going to Six Flags.
I thought it was going to be a fun day
we went inside and took off our rags.

We had finally arrived everyone was happy, even me
then we had a problem to solve right away.
We had to find a parking space near a tree
it was full with little cars, it was going to take all day.

We waited in line to enter; I said hurry up if you may
we bought the tickets and got in.
I started to scream HOORAY!
Then they threw my ticket into the bin.

I went on every ride in Six Flags.
I went on roller coasters, water rides, and game stands.
They had to stop a ride because of a rag,
stuck in the rail, we went on to eat, I ate in the sand.

It was already six and we had to leave,
we went in the car and away we went.
They said let's go, and believe,
that next time we have no doubt,
we will be back to Six Flags.

Christopher Zavala, Grade 8
John Adams Middle School

Explore Your Heart

Explore your heart
Each heartbeat tells you, "You're still alive."

Open your heart
Don't let it be harmed
Listen to the words it speaks
For your heart shall never lie.

Lead yourself on the path to believe in.
Follow your heart.
Then you'll know you've got the power
In your mind and your soul —
The tenderness of your heart
Is a sign of a passion
To love —

A passion to believe.
Explore your heart,
Your heart leads you on the right path
To show you're more than just your exterior
Appearance

Explore your heart, listen to the words it speaks,
Don't let it be harmed,
For your heart shall never lie.

Jocelyn Alvarez, Grade 7
Corpus Christi School

My Sea

Sweeping currents, taking off from the sea.
Swaying, churning, bubbling,
Waiting for us to see the mystery hidden behind it.
Foaming, rocking, and lapping at the shore.
My sea, find me.
Find me while I'm swimming.
I lose myself to thee.
No thoughts or worries.
Just me and you.
Climbing this mountain,
You are always there for me.
Watching my back, making sure I don't fall off the edge.
But you help me back up when something knocks me down.
I look down and see the sea that helped me.
You help no matter what situation.
But now I must leave.
But I will come back.
I could never leave you permanently,
But I will see you soon.
Thank you, for helping me stand up when standing was hard.
Thank you.

Alexandra Cruz, Grade 8
Temecula Valley Charter School

Halloween Night

Trick-or-Treat comes late at night.
Going alone gives such a fright.
Monsters may not be in sight
You'd better be careful, or they'll bite.

You come home tired and ready for bed.
But not so fast, you have night ahead.
Scary dreams and nightmares galore
That will make you scream with so much horror!

The morning comes, you cannot wait
You lie in bed, not dead but awake.
To know you've survived, but with a fright,
Can you survive a Halloween Night?

Sara Martinez, Grade 7
St Sebastian School

Life

Today our life is filled with sorrow.
Because of all the little children who will die today and tomorrow.

These little souls have no way to fight.
Against those people who want to take their lives.

They are all just like me and you.
They're just tiny and in the womb.

I am very against those who want to kill God's children.
And those who do if I were you I would ask to be forgiven.

Bridget Boylan, Grade 7
St Francis Parish School

The Almost Perfect Day

Clouds are drifting through the sky
I can see their silver lining
A daisy chain around my wrist
Petals intertwining

The sun is starting to fall
But the air is still warm from the day
A crimson leaf falls into my lap
But I don't blow it away

I don't think a perfect day exists
But this one's pretty close
Content and peaceful and happy
As the sun sets by the coast
Janessa Greig, Grade 7
St Cecilia School

The Shining Star

There is a star
lighting our way.
It shines through
the night.
The shining star is always
with us.
It will guide
us when we
are alone.
It shines with
the moon
and it will
always shine in
you.
Jemm Magaling, Grade 7
Corpus Christi School

Different

We live in a world that's different.
People are constantly changing.
They change their hair and eyes
Sometimes as a disguise
They don't like what they see.
Since it's not who they want to be.
The world is so cold
It's hard to feel bold
When you live in a world like this
You always fit in
No one ever listens,
It's hard to feel good
You wish that you could
In a world that's different.
Joseph Guajaca, Grade 8
Shadow Hills Intermediate School

Puppy

There's a puppy sitting on my foot
My leg is feeling numb
I really shouldn't be nasty
And kick it up the bum

But, it's so loving, I have no choice
I just have to let it sleep
So, I'm momentarily paralyzed
And lost the use of both my feet

And now the other puppy arrived
So appealing and enchanting
They get so loud and shrill
That I lose my sense of hearing

And then she jumps onto my lap
And rests her head upon my arm
Further 'paralyzing me'
With her captivating charm

And so, each day I spend my life
Like some disabled fool
Thank you God for inventing the puppy
I didn't know you could be so
CRUEL!
Justin Manwarren, Grade 8
Monte Vista Christian School

Nana and Tata's House

At the house on Sixth Street —
Cookies, tortillas, tamales, menudo,
Salsa, pots, pans, goodies and treats
Fill the kitchen with wonderful smells.

At the house on Sixth Street —
Decorating for Christmas each year,
Listening to Christmas carols, and
Putting up Nana's "pride and joy"
Christmas village.

At the house on Sixth Street —
Feeding Tata's many lovebirds,
Helping water the garden,
And picking the best grapefruits
Off the grapefruit tree.

At the house on Sixth Street —
Barbecue outside with
Grilled chicken, carnita, beans,
Rice and tortillas, even my Mom's
Delicious spaghetti.

I have many memories made
At the house on Sixth Street.
Roberta Salgado, Grade 8
Richardson PREP HI Middle School

Challenge

Waking up in the morning
doing homework
doing work and chores
doing class work
not talking during class
not playing in class
trying to beat a team
not getting in trouble
trying to do the best
doing a perfect job
reading a whole book
always doing what you being told
doing the right thing
being good at a sport
winning a game
not bothering other people
trying to be smart
trying to help other people
cleaning after people
studying for test
and type of work.
Aldo Rayas, Grade 8
St Helen Catholic Elementary School

School

It is my last year of school
Time is passing by quickly
And I will soon be in high school
It will not be easy though
I will have to work hard
I will have to face many obstacles
I have to do all my homework
Have to do all my projects
And have to do all my tests
I will have to improve my behavior
Participate a lot more than usual
And show much more effort
I'll have to learn new lessons
I'll have to learn new procedures
And learn new skills
I have to do my best
I must study my hardest
I must not let myself down
When the time comes to graduate
I will say good bye to friends and teacher
And say good bye to St. Helen School.
Alexander Amaya, Grade 8
St Helen Catholic Elementary School

Love Is Like Fire

Love is like fire, it burns
and stings. It leaves a
mark in your heart, that
you can't wipe out or heal.
Ashley Torres, Grade 7
Immaculate Heart of Mary School

Ode to My Cleats

My cleats are old
But I love them so
My Mom wants them sold
But I told her no
They have duct tape all over the place
But they're mine and people need to —
Back out of my space
Old, black, brown, and beaten up
My cleats have been through a lot of stuff
The spilt Gatorade they see
And even all the sunflower seeds
The fast pitches that I catch
and even the girls sitting on the bench
I love my cleats ever so much
Even though they look like they're worth two bucks
My cleats are very close to me
They're like leaves on my tree
The beat to my heart
And the song in my soul
My cleats are the best
And always help me reach my goal

Raylene Chairez, Grade 8
August Boeger Middle School

Hand

The world within a child's hand
Holds the lines of your life.
There are scars, cuts, and marks of all kinds.
Hands that were there to write this poem,
Hands that held on to my first bike,
Hands that held onto my dog when I came home.
All of the lines on your hand…symbolize YOU.
Your hand can be written or painted on,
It can wear jewelry.
Hands can sign and make friendships,
Hands get things from up high and from down low.
GOD wanted us to have hands.
I don't know why,
But, I'm glad we have them.

Esmeralda Caballero, Grade 7
Tenaya Middle School

Ode to My Bed

My wonderful bed,
You mean so much to me.
You are always there after a long day at school,
You don't mind when I jump on you or leave you a mess.
I love when you sit there and wait all day
For me and you to meet again.

When I lie down and pull over the covers,
You give me comfort and I know I'll be fine tomorrow.
As I walk in my room,
I see you there waiting for me and another night to share.

Annabell Benjamin, Grade 8
Daniel Savage Middle School

Christmas

Everyone longs for this time of year
It's when parents lose money,
But children are happy for getting their favorite toys
The kids believe there is a man whose name is Old St. Nick
He brings them toys and lots of joy for the holiday every year
On the night of Christmas Eve
While the children are asleep,
He sneaks in through the chimney
And unloads his bag of gifts
Then places them under the Christmas tree
For those kids who still believe
The children awake on
Christmas Day and rush over to their tree
They expect the best of Christmas gifts
And their stockings filled with candy canes
And those who misbehaved expect the worst
That is hard black coal
So we know their New Year's resolution
And that is to obey
Or they won't get a special gift
Like the others did that day

Shayla Garcia, Grade 7
Isbell Middle School

Reflections on Edvard Munch's "The Scream"

What looks like a bridge over water if you fell in you would be stuck
because the river would never let you go
The bridge is also under a sky that more resembles a sea of lava
But even stranger than what was above or below the bridge was on it
For standing on the bridge was a man
Who may be going crazy
For this man seems to be screaming
At a tone that could be heard all over the world
Yet no one seemed to notice
They just went along with their own business
They just avoid this man and his odd act
What could be scaring this man?
Could he be insane?
Or just threatened?
He may even be tapping into forces more powerful than himself.

Gus Krider, Grade 7
Tenaya Middle School

The Joys Life Brings Through Others

The joys life brings through others
can be friendship.
It can be a hug.
It can be a handshake.
It can be a friendly letter.
It can be a nice compliment.
It can be a kiss.
It can be an invitation to a party.
It can be a flower giving attention.
All of these things are some of the joys of life.

Jesse Garcia, Grade 7
Our Lady of the Rosary School

My Furry Friend
Caring cat at knees
Rubbing against my legs
Purring very soft

Clever cat hunting
Slyly slinking in the grass
Catch the bird of prey

Playful cat on ground
Chasing rope around the floor
Catch the rope kitty cat

Curious cat claws
Pawing red yarn on the floor
No more string to paw

Cute cat in my arms
Fuzzy ball of happiness
Soft, furry, loving
Vicente Sandoval, Grade 7
Monte Vista Christian School

A Rainy Day
Oh how I wish that it could stay,
Forever as a rainy day,
With lots of water coming down,
From the sky onto the town.

Wherever rain falls on my face,
Turns into my favorite place;
It is always so exciting,
Just as long as there's no lightning.

One way I can always tell
That rain is coming is the smell;
The smell of moisture in the air,
When it rains it's always there.

In the hearth a fire blazing,
On the couch my body lazing;
When the rain comes to an end,
I wait for it to come again.
Ian Martinez, Grade 7
Joe Walker Middle School

Life
Life is easy
Life is pain
We love it,
We live it,
We don't truly
understand it,
Things happen
for a reason.
Nathalia Padilla, Grade 7
Our Lady of the Rosary School

forbidden love
the time you took my
frostbitten hands in yours
and held them against your face.
the darkened days soon
to come as depressed clouds
showered the earth in rain.

my silky hair
sprawled aimlessly
across the bed.
a soft, feathery kiss.
three words never
to be spoken again.

the chains hugging
me tightly, letting
me go no further.
the pain hidden behind
the vacuous hazel eyes.
the mask of lies and deceit.

forbidden love
never meant to be
but already past.
Olivia Hsieh, Grade 9
Milpitas High School

The Taste of Fruits
I love fruits so much
They taste so good
I would eat a whole bunch
Fruit is a delicious food

They taste so good
All fruits are very sweet
Fruit is a delicious food
The food I love to eat

All fruits are very sweet
Fruits are very delicious
The food I love to eat
And are also very nutritious

Fruits are very delicious
They all have a great flavor
And are also very nutritious
One that I savor

They all have a great flavor
I would eat a whole bunch
One that I savor
I love fruits so much
Toby Winograd, Grade 7
Kadima Day School

Winter
Snow is coming
Flakes are falling
Winter is getting near
Carolers singing
Santa's bringing
Presents and good cheer
For all the little girls
And all the little boys
Everyone believes
In family and some joy
If I had the choice
If I had to guess
I would have to say
That Christmas is the best.
Riley Clark, Grade 8
Long Valley Charter School

Rain
I've only felt so little of it
But I just love the feel
How cool the dripping water is
It is a gift from God
The look of water on the concrete
Drip, drip

The splash when a car zooms by
Like a roadrunner on the ocean
Splash
When you first know it arrives
Saying, "Look! I'm here!"
You rush out the door and stand there
Oh how I love the rain.
Devyn Stoebe, Grade 8
Palm Desert Charter Middle School

Rain
She sat by her window
And stared out into space
As she thought of all her frustrations
Tears ran down her face

Then it began to rain outside
And then began to pour
So she stood up and ran outside
As her temptation grew more and more

She wanted to stand in the rain
And let it wash all over her
So when she took those first few steps
It rejuvenated her, right to her core
Audrey Wong, Grade 8
Carden Academy of Santa Clara

High Merit Poems – Grades 7, 8 and 9

Hello Goodbye
Hello. Why do I love you? Why can't you?
When I see you I run out of words to say
I love what you do. You're amazing
You make simple things amazing.
I never want to hurt you, never want to see you cry.
I never want to lie.
I curse the day that I was born, born to be with you.
I hate you, but you know that's not true.
I love you but is it true? I have waited too long.
The hardest part in life is letting go.
I can't, I'm tired of waiting.
But I can't forget all the special moments we have had.
Together. My heart and soul are in pieces.
They can't be repaired, I am scarred for life.
I forgive you, but I hope you know you are losing me.
As a friend I'll be there, but who knows?
Are you losing the joy and happiness in your life?
What is your answer? Yes? Or no?
Your pick, it's your turn to choose.
My life is wasted, only you can bring me to life.
Sadly you notice nothing. Goodbye.
Enha Renderos, Grade 8
Centers of Learning

Why Don't They Understand
There are many ways to explain
How I feel about you
But here are the most important two
I love You, I fear You.
I can truly say
I've never seen You before…
But I've felt You
Some people don't understand
They don't want to understand
Other people say they believe
Do they really?
They never show they do
You show Yourself in many ways,
Just not physically
One of those ways is by using me
And I'm glad You do
Some people see it
And again they don't understand
I wait and wait for You to come
To show Yourself and for people to see
And maybe then they'll believe…they'll understand.
Crystal Rojas, Grade 8
Centers of Learning

The Big Wave*
His family gone,
He will never be the same.
Sadness consumes him.
Micayla Perez, Grade 7
Tenaya Middle School
*Inspired by Jiya, in the novel The Big Wave

Love
Is love true, can it ever happen?
Can a love for a thing cover that dark spot in your heart?
Can anyone fall in love at first sight?
Is love just hormones or is it real?
Can it be fake or play?
When somebody says they love you what does it mean?
Will they be with you forever?
Will they take their affection away?
Is love just a game or a play?
What happens when the person you love loves someone else?
Will you cry or try to die?
Does love cause pain and suffering or a life of joy and loving?
It's confusing and I don't understand…LOVE
Angelo Peters, Grade 7
Orville Wright Middle School

Summer
As more downpour falls along the window,
I'm missing the sun,
And looking for the rainbow.
The dark clouds seem cemented in the sky,
They must carry all the tears I cry…
Missing the warm, sunny days.
Loathing the cold, hours of gray.
So many seconds, filled with memories,
Going with friends to see the new movies.
Why is it that summer goes by so fast,
When I want nothing more than to make it last?
It must be that time flies when you're having fun,
But why must that mean summer is done?
Brandy Bowman, Grade 7
South Lake Middle School

Wind
What does wind have to do with love?
Wind blows into different directions
Left, right, up, down, and everywhere around
It is very unpredictable
From a gentle, cool breeze
To something deadly enough to kill you
People say there is always an end to everything but
There is never an end to wind
It's just the way of life
Amber Ocampo, Grade 7
Immaculate Heart of Mary School

No Matter How You Turn It…in Escher's Relativity
No matter how you turn it
It always makes sense
All the people have stiff backs
That are straight up and down.
There are lots of stairs
In the house that go in every direction.
No matter how you turn it.
Dallas Cline, Grade 7
Tenaya Middle School

Oh How Sad

Oh dear one please
don't
Cry
But it's okay now there is
more to come
It's okay that Roxy
isn't here
With us
Because now she will
watch over us
Along with our old
Family
And Friends

Heather Tortorice, Grade 7
La Mesa Jr High School

The Café

A café at night, bustling with people
Some at the tables
Some on the streets
Above in the buildings
Most people slumber
While down on the streets
Some are left to wonder
The streets are stone
And the sky is dark blue
The stars are bright yellow
A waiter waits on tables at the café
While people chat and gossip
As the night goes on

Alyssa Canada, Grade 7
Daniel Savage Middle School

For What Reason?

Gunfire shots going round and round,
the American flag down on the ground.
For what reason?
Our beautiful flag that flies through the air,
is burned to ash, thus treated unfair.
For what reason?
They show us this for some reason,
all I call this is treason.
For what reason?
All the insults they will throw,
why they show this I will never know.
Out of all of this I ask,
for what reason?

Kelsey Turner, Grade 7
St Francis Parish School

Words

Words are fun and cool.
Words are hard to comprehend.
All things have a word.

Gavin Lin, Grade 7
St Mary's Chinese Day School

To My Mother

That one day I felt the coldness of the world I was scared and I felt alone
I was being held by cold hands I cried, not knowing how to feel
When the hands let me go I felt an unusual warmth I felt my first warmth
It came from you, Mom do you not remember as you held me dearly?
I was not scared anymore I felt loved, and cared for
As I looked up at you, I smiled as you held me close
My tears didn't stop, but I knew I was safe
The big men, wearing blue and white grabbed me and took me away
I looked at you, as they took me away
You were still smiling, so I knew I was safe you filled me with love, and kindness
As I looked at you, I knew you were my mom
That day I was born, you took my heart you still hold my heart you hold it dearly
I know you are the one I love
For you are the first to love me completely and you still love me.
After I came back to you, I always felt happy those times I cried
I may have cried for food, or warmth but I always wanted YOU
Please mother, love me forever just like that day you held me.
Please, don't ever leave me without your love, or even without you
I can smile, but I might never be happy.
Your love is what counts. For you may be mad at me
Or be tired of me but you shall forever love me.

Jessica Garcia, Grade 9
Castle Park Sr High School

Veteran's Day

Mommy? Why do soldiers jeopardize their lives?
"They want to save their country.
They don't play,
They save.
They might have fear, they might have tears,
But the crying of mothers when war is over, is worth all those years.
Shuffling of soldiers' feet, silence while hearing your heart beat, faster and louder.
No worries, just family, freedom, and victory.
They just want to win against those ugly beasts.
With all their hardships and pain
Sometimes they'll drive each other insane
But depression and complication is worth a fortune
When these tall big men will win once again.
And in the end all you see, is marching marching
For independence."

Vanessa Damian, Grade 8
Ripona Elementary School

My Parents

My parents the ones who love me.
The parents that cared about me when I was sick.
The parents that stayed up with me until I stopped crying.
The parents that would sleep with me when I would have nightmares.
The parents that bought me a bike and showed me how to ride it.
The parents that would make me happy every time they'd come home from work.
The parents that gave me my first present for Christmas.
The parents that would give anything to see me happy.
The parents that love me.
The parents that I love now and for the rest of my life.

Claudia Magana, Grade 7
Isbell Middle School

High Merit Poems – Grades 7, 8 and 9

Donuts
Donuts are tasty
Donuts are small
They beat other foods
They beat them all

When I see them
I get so excited
I ask my mom
If I can buy it

I like to buy the box of sevens
It's like I own a piece of heaven
*Justin Tran, Grade 7
Sarah McGarvin Intermediate School*

Jax
Silver sound, quick as light,
Jax is always up for a fight.
Forehead wrinkled, he runs around
Looking for his ball…
But nowhere to be found.
Love in his eyes, curled up with bliss,
I can't help but give him a big wet kiss!
When he licks the screen door,
I start laughing, but I don't know what for!
It's Jax I adore, he is so clever.
He'll be in my heart
Forever and ever.
*Justine How, Grade 7
Junipero Serra School*

Deep Breath
When I get irritated,
Annoyed, angry, or furious,
I blow up.
I scream, I yell,
I give attitude,
And I don't stop.
But it always ends one way —
Me, in trouble, crying.
I've been through it
So many times before.
But now I found my secret:
Just take a deep breath
*Samantha Geronimo, Grade 7
Corpus Christi School*

Lies
You should never lie,
It makes people's hearts die,
Like an arrow through the chest,
It makes such a mess,
The more lies built,
There will be more guilt.
*Dion Fong, Grade 7
Sarah McGarvin Intermediate School*

Cole Matthews: A Change*
I am Cole Mathews
I see Peter Driscal bloody and beaten to a pulp
I hear Peter begging for mercy
I feel flames burning inside me
I am foolish and changing

I dream about Peter wondering was I wrong for what I did
I worry about Peter how bad is he what happened to him
I hope Peter will forgive me for what I've done
I am foolish and changing

I understand what I did was wrong
I try to tell and make peter see that I've changed
I say to myself that I'll never go back to that foolish deceiving Cole I was
I cry when I remember how ignorant I was
"I am Cole Mathews and I'm foolish and changing"
*Eric Gomez, Grade 8
Palm Desert Charter Middle School
Inspired by "Touching Spirit Bear" by Ben Mikaelsen

A Panegyric to the Greatest
Oh how great you are, you are the best, by far
From the elegant east to the wild west, you are known to impress

From your fertile farms an your crowded cities, to your big buildings and your towering trees
We're always guarded and we stand, united

When Columbus found you, you were just as new
As the growing technologies that are valuable like our vast allies

It's astonishing how your cities reflect the many races that over time collect
You are known as the great melting pot because of all the hoping immigrants you got

Lady Liberty stands so tall, showing freedom for all
And an elegant mountain with faces can be seen from many places

Represented by the great bald eagle, America, you truly are so beautiful
*Harry Tenenbaum, Grade 8
The Mirman School*

My Teddy Bear
my teddy bear is my favorite thing
its been with me my whole life
I dragged it across the room when I learned to crawl
I held it close when I was scared and waited
and cried when my mom put it in the washer
it stayed with me through thick and thin
it was my safe place when my parents fought
and when my dad moved out it went with me back
and forth to my moms to my dads and I held it
close with joy when my dad came back to my mom
so even though its raggedy and old my teddy bear will always be my favorite thing
*Felicia Rubio, Grade 7
Isbell Middle School*

Where Poetry Hides for Me
Poetry hides
In my family,
Poetry hides
In my heart
Poetry hides
In a special person in my family;
He was always there for me
And relieved me when I was mad
And his name was Dad.
Angel Rivera, Grade 7
Tenaya Middle School

Whirlpool of Lies
Can't find my way out
Spinning, spinning
What was this even about?
Swirling, swirling
Thrown around and around
Like a cobweb in the breeze
Around and around
Just caught…
In the whirlpool of lies
Aislynn Cetera, Grade 8
Shadow Hills Intermediate School

Broken Heart
I can't watch this anymore
The tears in my eyes are about to pour
My heart is broken once again
All I want is for this to end
I was really hoping he wasn't the same
As all those others who put me in pain
I guess sometimes you really can't tell
Until they break your heart as well
Kyleigh Roberts, Grade 7
Palm Desert Charter Middle School

The Evil Thing
I hear the moans and groans in the night.
The sounds and noises give me a fright.
I hear footsteps but no one's there.
I walk a little faster right into its lair.
I'm face to face with this evil thing.
It throws me back with a fling.
I start to think this is all a bad dream.
It's not and he smiles really really mean.
Kiona Campos, Grade 7
St Francis de Sales School

Fall
The trees look very beautiful
The trees colors are red and orange
Fall is my favorite season
Vanessa Ochoa, Grade 7
Our Lady of the Rosary School

What Happens?
What happens when life is over?
When everything is stopped by either getting shot, stabbed,
Or being at the wrong place at the wrong time
Does everything freeze? Or do you start a new journey
Your actions determine your destiny either Heaven or Hell
All decisions you've made all your actions have you been forgiven or forgotten?
What happens when death comes?
Will you be granted happiness or pain for the rest of eternity?
Will you start the journey pain free with the people you love
Or painful with the people you hate
What happens when death awaits you?
Do you have a feeling in your gut? Or does it just happen?
Do you really see your life in a few seconds? Or do you just see pitch black?
Death or more like a nightmare, a nightmare you can't wake up from
Where you can't go back and change anything
A nightmare where you can't tell your loved ones thank you again and again
Where you can't go back and say sorry for your mistakes
So why hold grudges when death can come at any time
So what really happens when life is over? When death comes
When death awaits you? That really is up to you
Elizabeth Waner, Grade 8
Richard Merkin Middle Academy

O Police Car
O Police car! A beautiful police car! Our wonderful days have been lost,
My babyish hands would roll your wheels, and make noises of your exhaust,
My small lips would make noises of your beautiful, blue engine,
But having lost you forever and on, my heart has been hit with a cannon.

O Police car! A beautiful police car! How long will our separation last,
I want to hold you, and roll you around on a floor made of glass,
I cry out tears that spell your name, for you will not be forgotten,
But having lost you forever and on, my heart has been hit with a cannon.

O Police car! A beautiful police car! I have tried to find wherever you are,
Please hear my plea for I cannot sleep, for you are my favorite car,
Your beautiful parts glamorous in every portion,
But having lost you forever and on, my heart has been hit with a cannon.

O Police car! A beautiful police car! You have left me all alone,
My life went from happy to sad, and a completely different tone,
I remember the days when we had a lot of fun, while bringing a lot of action,
But having lost you forever and on, my heart has been hit with a cannon.
Raajan Raj, Grade 9
Irvine High School

Earth
Earth is a home for many different species.
It provides shelter for them.
There is no other place like Earth.
It provides water and food.
Maybe that's why they call it Mother Earth.
With out it we wouldn't survive. But humans don't appreciate Earth.
We humans have to take care of Earth because it's our home.
Alan Millan, Grade 8
Isbell Middle School

Fall

Fall is my favorite season of all
I enjoy the Thanksgiving holiday
I enjoy the awesome sport of football
I play out in the yellow leaves all day

In fall the weather outside is just right
When we are on fall break we hang with friends
On Halloween the kids play in the night
On this very night elks are in their dens

Volleyball is one of the best sports played
The weather is not windy; it is nice
That was the best spike I have ever made!
My mom makes the best pie called pumpkin spice

My volleyball team and I go running
Yes, we get happy when fall is coming

Gloria Bell, Grade 9
Lucerne Valley Jr/Sr High School

Summer

Summer is my fav'rite season of all,
The blue birds in the tall trees are singing,
You can hang out with friends and have a ball,
And no annoying school bells are ringing.

Motorcycle riding is very fun,
Visiting family is my fav'rite thing,
Chilling with friends in the burning hot sun,
We just got over fun amazing spring.

Enjoying swimming at the beach is fun,
Spending most of my summer with kin,
Now that school is all over with and done,
I very much enjoy it when I sleep in.

Summer could be one of the best seasons,
If you have fun for all the right reasons.

Samantha Morrisette, Grade 9
Lucerne Valley Jr/Sr High School

Life Is Like an Elevator

life is like an elevator,
what with it's ups, down, and in-betweens,
the ups are short but sweet,
the downs are as suffocating as a low flying cloud,
the in-between nothing but a fleeting feeling,
life is always switching floors joined by new people
who take you where you wouldn't have gone before,
with your decisions wavering you wax and wane,
mood goes up, rests in the middle then comes back down,
life is like an elevator so enjoy the ride,
but remember it's okay to jump every once in a while,
just to stop your movement and catch your breath.

Nicole Carlon, Grade 9
University Preparatory School

My Club House

Hurry! Take a look
Come and play with me
Let's show who we could really be

Hurry! Take a look
I hide and laugh
While they are seeking me

Hurry! Take a look
We're sharing secrets now
You want to join?

Hurry! Take a look
Time is passing by
The fun is coming it's almost over
Let's just pretend that in our world, it doesn't have to end
  Hurry! Take a look

Raquel Holmes, Grade 8
Richardson PREP HI Middle School

My Mother

When the dismal clouds fill up my mind
She is always there like a ray of sunshine
Destroying the darkness and replacing it with light

She is elegant and graceful like a princess on the outside
But she has a strong heart and mind
And is always ready to face anything life throws at her

She is like an angel
Selfless in every way
Always giving all her time and effort to others

We sometimes fight over silly things
And it tears me apart
We are always there for each other
Cheering each other on
And patching up each other's mistakes

Kendra Calhoun, Grade 8
Junipero Serra School

The Way It Used to Be

All I can do is remember you
and all the times we had
now we're drifting apart
once my best friend
now a stranger I don't know
I hope we can go back to the way it used to be
when we would tell each other everything
how we would laugh about nothing
we were as close as sisters
now we barely talk
I hope that one day
we will be as close as before

Hali Dinh, Grade 7
Sarah McGarvin Intermediate School

Thoughts on Edvard Munch's The Scream

Where the lake meets the sun in the sky, and the bridge that overlooks the lake
There stands a person who looks terrified and is screaming for dear life.
But the people on the bridge walking away from screaming person, look relaxed, calm, as if
they are enjoying the sunset around them.
They aren't showing any signs of trying to run to the screaming person, or trying to get help.
No, they're just walking like he's not there, like he doesn't exist, like he's not screaming for his
life and not terrified out of his mind.
Maybe,
They are trying not to notice the person, because it might remind them of
The difficulties in their lives and they want to ignore those things as long as possible.
It looks as if the screaming person sees something that no one else can see,
Or maybe he's screaming because of something horrible he did.
He's just so frightened and no one understands him, or understands what kind of things he is
going through.
He's just screaming for someone to come and help him, to save him from the world around him,
or to save him from himself.
I think there is a screaming person in all of us at least once in our lives —
A time in our lives when we erupt like a volcano because no one 'gets us'
or understands how we feel when we really need them to.
Don't you think so, too?

Domanique Contreras, Grade 7
Tenaya Middle School

The Ten-Minute Run

"Timer's on," said the P.E. teacher, I started to run and tried to go farther.
This was a lap about 3/4ths of a mile, as I became tired, I stopped for awhile.

This was the most difficult task of the day. I noticed I was walking and time was wasting away,
So, I started running and ran 1/4ths of it. I was so tired I wanted to quit.

"I need to finish!" I told myself. I accelerated and passed by Michelle,
And in a minute I was already halfway. The halfway time was 3:58.

"Oh no!" I said, "I need to get under 9 minutes to pass!" Thinking of a way to speed up, I cut through the grass,
Doing what ever I could to go faster. I could see my obstacle and it was getting closer!

It was a steep hill, as tall as Mount Everest, In order to pass, I needed to go my fastest.
My feet climbed up the never-ending hill, "I don't think I can pass; I think I'm going to be ill!"

I can see the end and the teacher calling out the time. She yelled, "8:15, 8:30, 8:55!"
I need to run, there's only 5 seconds left to finish! "8:59!" she called out my time, my energy started to diminish.

It was over, I passed the ten minute run, in the end it was fun.
I needed to say my prayers, because I passed without a second to spare.

Sang Yoon, Grade 9
Irvine High School

You Came

The stars in the sky made from God above You came down here to give us love You taught us Your word and Your word only, You died on the cross for us to live You were put in a grave for three days only and rose again you showed yourself to all of the disciples You talk to us then and You talk to us now, many die and go to heaven little die and go to hell all have sinned and fall short of the glory God, the first and most greatest command is this, love the Lord your God with all your heart all your soul and with all your mind, God loves you and me and he always will

Nick Smith, Grade 8
Sierra Charter School

Lakers

They shoot the ball into the hoop
and they play as a group
Kobe Bryant makes the swoosh
without even a single push
Everyone is cheering them on
for the Lakers to win until dawn
We're almost there to win the game
we won they lost what a shame
we all had fun that's all that counts
There's smiles on everyone's faces
and no pouts.
Priscilla Mercado, Grade 7
St Francis de Sales School

Respect

I'm black you may be white
but please, let's not fight.
We are all the same, I claim.

Respect each other
as you respect your mother.
Respect someone's culture
as you respect the American soldiers.

If I'm not mistaken,
respect is not something to be fakin'.
Walanda Flowers, Grade 7
Orville Wright Middle School

An Unpredictable Moment

Life is unpredictable
it happened so quickly
yet it was so unusual
for I was in shock
and ran to the room swiftly
noticing the chill down my spine
the moment was like a book
a beginning, a middle, and end
my life felt like the end
yet I shall not be overwhelmed
for life is unpredictable
Anthony Diep, Grade 7
Orville Wright Middle School

Life

It is a privilege
you don't get a second one
it can last years or even seconds
don't let it go to waste
just imagine never being born
or life after death
it makes you think
what it would be like
if you never had one
Sacramento Zamora, Grade 8
Isbell Middle School

Writer's Block

I am writing this poem for Herrington's class
If I do this thing right I think I'll pass

Sitting here with writer's block
Writing nothing only staring at the clock

It's 8:02 with nothing to do
Can't watch TV 'cause my dad's blasting on guitar
So loud that you can even hear it from afar

Can't go on the internet 'cause Mom's on the computer
Wasting her time going on Facebook and Twitter

Wanna listen to music but I can't
Because my headphones are broken
I hear reruns on the TV and want to watch it
Even though I've already seen it — and all the words were already spoken

My house is so boring, no time to myself
Not even in the cold — boring — morning.
Ethan Hernandez, Grade 8
August Boeger Middle School

We Are Like Leaves

We are like leaves.
Not because of weight or color of skin but because of our struggle in life.
There are the leaves on branches just going through life like nothing,
Then there are the leaves atop and below them.
The ones on top are on big strong branches
They don't even have to try to hold onto the tree.
Then there are the ones below.
They are on twigs and have to try really hard to hold on.
Many don't make it.
But then there are the ones that stay on
and the tree grows
and soon they are on the top.
So you see we are like leaves.
Tristin Duarte, Grade 7
Daniel Savage Middle School

Beauty Is

Beauty is.
the crash of waves on a rocky shore…
in the whispering of the wind through the treetops…
in the cold, crisp air on the top of a mountain, under the swaying pines…
in the gentle breeze, sweeping up golden maple leaves over the sidewalk in the fall…
in the long, crystal-clear icicles thawing after winter…
in a trickling stream that broadens into a roaring waterfall…
the sight of home after a long, tiring journey…
in a radiant sunset on the horizon every evening…
in the expanse of blinking, silver stars, twinkling high above the Earth…
in the darkest depths of a cold heart…
in a flash of hope, a helping hand, a bright smile…
Beauty is.
Samantha Tsai, Grade 7
Lindero Canyon Middle School

Sunny Days

Sunny days
Warm outside
The breeze is gentle
Smiles are contagious
Laughter is present
These are happy times
Times that are rare but memorable
Worries seem to float away
With every passing sunny day

Eryn Jones, Grade 7
Orville Wright Middle School

Thoughts on Escher's Relativity

In this beautiful picture
I see
People with no names
And
No faces
Walk stiffly up and down staircases
Carrying things.
Others are just hanging around.
What do you see?

Isaiah Graves, Grade 7
Tenaya Middle School

Teddy Bear of Eternity

LOVE is like a TEDDY BEAR.
It keeps you warm during those
cold endless nights. Your security
when you are scared or frightened.
It's your extra hug when you are
feeling sick or down. Your cuddle
buddy during those scary movies.
Most importantly, your friend for
all time sake!

Allison Basa, Grade 7
Immaculate Heart of Mary School

Drumline

I hit the drums so hard to hear the beat
the loud rhythm in the summer heat.
One, two, three, four I count to start
all the drummers hit their part.
We practice to improve our skills
and beat the competition at the next drill.

Anissa Quintero, Grade 7
St Francis de Sales School

Manny

M orning person
A lert
N eat
N ice
Y oung

Manny Rodriguez, Grade 9
Lucerne Valley Jr/Sr High School

The Baby

I walk through the valley, there I hear cries
Cries of a baby
Baby I don't see,
I keep on walking there I found the baby
In the bush between darkness and light, it was a girl
I pick her up she closed her eyes and mouth
She looked three month old,
"Poor Baby, Poor Baby" I cried to the darkness
I took her home put her in a crib, next to the fire so she can warm up
But when I cradle her, she is still cold
I pray to my God for her to be healthy again
But she is still so cold,
Next day I hear cries, I awake from a deep sleep
I go to the cradle the baby still sleeps
I look outside it's almost winter,
Christmas my favorite holiday
I look at the baby again,
She is awake, looking at me with her big brown eyes
She opens her mouth to say something, I pick her up from her crib
She said "Mom, Mom, Mom, Mom, I love you."
I kiss her forehead and called her my daughter from the gods.

Sara Toussaint, Grade 8
Heritage Digital Academy

Past Memories

Memories swirl in my head of a time long gone by.
I start to remember them all and I begin to sigh.
They started to get pulled up, when I've pushed them down so far.
What I refused to acknowledge, and tried to let fall apart.
Finally they take over, the beauty and the pain.
The friendships that seemed would last forever,
All my losses and gains.
I remember the day I was new and made so many friends.
Fast-forwarding through the scenes, I watched the happiness end.
I watched the girl in white gradually turn to black.
I watched the continuous pain and suffering,
Now it all came back.
Truth back then seemed to rule, now lies are all I hear.
Where bright hope once lingered it just had to disappear.
My life is sunny rays of hope eclipsed by bitter shadows.
The shining sword in my hands was a knife in the back from my foes.
I relived that perfect life, two years old but an eternity away.
My hands are outstretched, grasping; why did it all have to fade?
White to gray, gray to black, so remains my way.
I stood up and faltered, not ready — never ready — for another day.

Avneet Khurana, Grade 8
Lindero Canyon Middle School

Feelings

I never knew that feeling sad would ever hurt as much as it hurts right now.
I am sad, mad, and rarely am I ever happy.
Sometimes I feel as though it will never end,
but someday it will when I meet my true love.
That's when the sadness and the madness will go away.

Pauline Truong, Grade 7
Sarah McGarvin Intermediate School

The Fruit of My Labors

I dream of taking you from your throne, thinking that though you are greater than me
I wish forever to have you as my own, my sweet, pristine apple on top of the tree

My purpose in life is tough to reach, too, this goal is as you are, held up quite high
From here I feel I have one thing to do, I must climb up great rocks to the sky

You will be worth my strenuous ascent, the fruit of my labors, the prize of my toil
The shining bright star for my life I have spent, up from the bottom, reach peak from the soil

Just as I reach you, I attain my desires, I lunge out with courage to catch what is mine
The purpose for living, like you, is acquired, My efforts push me to the grand, holy shrine

Although I have dreamed of you all these years, time and time again, in my mind it is painted
It haunts my soul, my greatest of fear, what if you, my apple, are tainted?

You and my dreams share much of my mind, the beautiful goal at the end of the road
And my lovely fruit with its thin, red rind, to you and my dreams, my heart truly is owed

Andrew Friedman, Grade 8
The Mirman School

My Saturday Morning

I woke up on Saturday morning feeling the soft breeze through the window
The sweet uplifting smell of bacon drifted into my bedroom
From that moment on, I knew it was going to be a miraculous day
I got out of my bed and made it adequately
My mom strode into the room and told me breakfast was ready
I quickly took a warm, relaxing shower and hurried into the dining room
My breakfast was five pancakes stacked up with two extra greasy pieces of bacon
I devoured it in two minutes flat, then took my completely empty plate to the kitchen sink
I thanked my mom, then went to brush and floss my teeth
Then I sat down and read silently by myself on my cozy beanbag for an hour or two
After that, I went down to play with my baby sister, she chased me all around the house
I went to my shed and took out my three-wheeler, my brothers and I went drifting down the driveway
At about 11:00 am, my dad and I played catch with the football
Then I played fetch with my dog Kenzie who runs with all her might and leaps to grasp the ball
When Kenzie was bringing back the ball, my mom called us in for lunch; it was the end of my morning
I knew I would look forward to next Saturday morning, but I had to wait a whole week

Lucas Porter, Grade 7
Monte Vista Christian School

Mr. Roller Coaster

Everything moves so fast. When I'm getting ready for something to approach, then suddenly it's the past. I'm cruising along and everything's fine. I hit a bump in the track that signals me to stop the ride. People climb in and out of me. Some happy, exhilarated. Some sad, gloomy. Years pass. Traditional and unshiny, few are attracted to me. That furiousness appears when that one special, gentle old man is riding and I come to an abrupt halt, shaking with anger. I lose him, he never returns. Now, I feel lonely too. I move slowly in circles, around and around, dreading the day that I leave this sacred ground. Noises and lights alert me to the end of my "coaster" days. As it begins to rain, I rust and cry for help. But those onlookers only watch with joyful faces while I am removed.

My junkyard is close and I see a young girl run to my empty space in my home, the fairground. She sees it is vacant and I watch as her eyes fill with tears. She sulks back to her grandmother.

My metal has become a fun-house, with small children just like the little girl running through me. I see a familiar face, that of the sweet child, but wrinkly and pale. Ah, I remember those days, and can only wait for the cycle to begin again.

Delaney Niehoff, Grade 8
La Reina High School

The Destruction of Miracles

Man has made many discoveries of significance over its short period of existence
But too many simple miracles are tainted by man's unforgiving persistence

Broken are the boundaries that protect nature's gifts, every last piece, analyzed until its death
I hope that humanity never sees the day when wholesomeness takes its very last breath

Our boundless curiosity turns fantasies into reality, that glowing star you wish upon is just a raging ball of fire
We crush their dreams once children are old enough, leaving them with nothing but the facts to admire

Our hunger for knowledge is like an endless abyss, every day, digging deeper without any regret
So I commend those that are still mysteries, these unknown treasures that remain a silhouette

But despite imagination prying its way through every secret, some still live perfectly untouched, unconsumed
Like the enigmas of the ocean that rest deep below the ground, and those preserved pieces of history that still in their tombs

The vast continuity of the marvels in space, and other life forms which thrive on planets afar
Regardless of the questions that we constantly ask, I hope the cloak of mystery will keep them from harm

Yes, man has destroyed so many unrefined wonders, but children — stop those remaining from being torn asunder

Bree Iskandar, Grade 8
The Mirman School

The Last Year

For the last time, the key turns, the windows shut, and the door to knowledge closes forever.
The classroom, empty, a place for good friends, old teachers, and times no one will forget.
The lifeless markers lay on the dented tray, longing to only be used one more time.
Colorful and cherished memories on the whiteboard erased; gone forever.
The cold hard desks are silent, motionless in the darkness, patiently waiting to again feel the comfort of a lively room.
The windows, imperfectly clean, have streaks of tears crying out for the sun to shine through them and light a path in the lingering darkness.
The linoleum floor, once full of clutter and safe under a paper blanket, now sparkling for no one. The remains of our reflections can be seen etched in the floor, reaching out; calling us to return.
The big table, the teacher's territory, sitting on the floor now forced to wait in isolation for the arrival of reassurance to know it will once again feel needed.
Within the room, the walls and ceiling reflect the ideas that have rested there; the ideas that gave us the confidence to portray our best as we moved forward.
Bad memories lurking in the corners are whispering thoughts spoken about past discussions, striving to make us regret having been in this now vacant, inert room.
The doorknob, familiar, oxidized, quiet with fear, hangs on the door like a wilted flower that has shed its beauty.
The door, never to be opened again, stands there, as if the world is ending, as if it has lost everything.
Every second, every moment.
Every memory of the last year.

Samantha Pitti, Grade 8
St Rita School

Ode to a Soldier

Dear Soldier,

You stand out there while I'm back here safe and sound. We don't even think about you even though we should. We hear about you dying do we care? We hear about a star dying and it's all over the news but don't you think you are just like a star and if you die it should be on the news? Guess not! I would like to take this time right now to say thank you, and that I'm thinking about you even if no one else will.

— Abby Hulsey

Abby Hulsey, Grade 7
St Francis Parish School

You Say It's a Curse

you say it's a curse,
you loving me so,
holding me tight,
not wanting to let go,

I'm moving away
don't want you to wait,
it's not fair to you,
to watch me walk away,

when we get older,
who knows what will happen,
live our lives now,
and we'll see what will happen,

we can be friends,
and write to each other,
and make great decisions for one another,

so you say it's a curse
but remember our times,
it's time to let go and say goodbye.

Adriana Freiling, Grade 9
Hemet High School

Illusion

love isn't love,
it's just an illusion.
makes us feel different,
changes our thoughts.
it doesn't exist
'til the day we found it.
then all hopes are lost.
you're head over heels,
the cycle begins again.
it keeps repeating
'til the day we give in…
we finally found it.

Lizette Ibarra, Grade 8
Shadow Hills Intermediate School

Green Bird

Have you ever heard:
The tragic story of a bird
In her great big nest
With her big puffy chest…
It was 12 o'clock
And she was being stalked
By a big scary hunter
Who looked much like a football player
With his big scary gun
The hunter amend his gun
And he saw the family
And he let them go.

Aliquon Ross, Grade 8
Palm Desert Charter Middle School

Rainbow

After every rainy day,
Comes the most beautiful sight;
Ooohhhhs and Aaaaahhhs,
Not the slight sign of dismay.

Every head is turned,
To see this wondrous sight,
To look and see the rainbow's light,
The colors so nicely patterned.

Soon the colors fade,
Ever slowly melting,
The sky, slowly is grayed,
Until the next raining.

Taylor Densing, Grade 7
Joe Walker Middle School

Pathway

Life's like a road,
which way do you go?
Being yourself, the way you feel right,
or like your friends, just follow the light.
Don't be afraid to show who you are,
when you make your own choices,
it takes you quite far.
Your friends could be nice, happy, or mean.
But if you're yourself,
you can wear your own jeans.
So ask yourself now,
not if, but how,
you can be just yourself
And no one else.

Hailey Webber, Grade 7
Arcade Middle School

Shadow

I have a dog
Who has it all
She chases cats
And runs after rats
Dives in a pool just to get cool
She likes to play
Every night and day
Sleeps on my bed
And doesn't shed
She throws her ball
But not very far
She likes the car
And loves to go far
She hates the vet she's my favorite pet

Ryan Weberg, Grade 7
Monte Vista Christian School

Ballet

Pointed toes in every step
Passion in every turn
Graceful with every movement
That's the kind of dancer I am
A love for ballet burns up inside me
I dance around the house
I leap around every corner
With a turn to enter every room
Ballet is beauty beyond compare
Ballet can calm you down
Ballet can cheer you up
Ballet can express emotions
That's why I love ballet
I love going to the ballet
Lifts and glides make me smile
Ballet is peaceful
When I'm happy I can't help but dance
It's in my blood, I'm made of dance
Ballet lifts my spirits
I can't stop thinking about it
Ballet is my talent, and I will use it for God

Ashley Burdick, Grade 7
Monte Vista Christian School

Love Problems

My heart is
In a complication
Every time I see her
She's like my temptation,
My desperation
And I can't even speak right
With her in a simple conversation
It feels like in my heart
There's a laceration
So deep with
So much aggression
Feel like between me and her
There's segregation
This is must be
The work of
Predestination
Since my fate is like
Circumlocution
So basically we come from
Two different worlds of
Love and compassion.

Justin Ng, Grade 9
George Washington High School

Our Earth

Our Earth is so big,
We must all take care of it.
God created Earth.

Jaimie Ramos, Grade 7
Our Lady of the Rosary School

I'm Afraid I Just Might Fall

I hide up above as the monsters fight,
Please don't pull me down.
I want to be able to say "good night,"
But sadly, you can only mumble with a frown.

They yell and battle and punch the walls.
The cracks are easily seen
I wish one day, and one day soon,
The world could stop being so mean.

The black hole opens, I twist and fight —
Fighting to stay sane.
But it pulls me closer, makes it harder to breathe,
And then it calls my name.

It wants me to have a breakdown,
To cry and scream and sweat.
But I refuse, I refuse, I refuse.
I am trying to forget.

I must forget the pain,
The sorrow among them all.
I want to fight, and never stop,
But I'm afraid I just might fall.

Maya Litvak, Grade 9
Irvington High School

Flying

Mammoth is the best place to be
The coldness sings to me, I love the weather
When flying down the mountain, I feel free
My friends and family get to be together

The coldness talks to me, I love the weather
Riding down the mountain as fast as race cars, going wild
My friends and family get to be together
When we snowboard, we are never mild

Riding down the mountain as fast as race cars, going wild
Sailing south in a split second
When we snowboard, we are never mild
We do tricks and rack with one simple beckon

Sailing south in a split second
We wonder what will await
We do tricks and race with one simple beckon
We get up quickly, on our behalf

We wonder what will wait
When flying down the mountain, I feel free
We get up quickly on our behalf
Mammoth is the best place to be.

Dana Leonard, Grade 8
Kadima Day School

My Cousin Jr.

My cousin Jr. was so dear
I always loved when he was near.

He was always so crazy
I don't think he was ever lazy.

When June 26th came
The day turned out really lame.

There were so many flowers
People cried for hours.

It all happened so fast
When his life came to pass.

I couldn't believe what had just taken place
It was scary to think that I would never again
see his face.

He was everybody's best friend
And they all loved him till the end.

It broke my heart to see him go
But I will always love him so.

Ariel Ygloria, Grade 8
St Francis de Sales School

Little Things

The little things comfort me every day,
We snuggle and wuggle around,
They make me feel happy, all smiley and gay,
And fill my mind with joyous sound.

The purple things I like so much,
The spiny things tickle my feet,
The yellow things laugh, tell jokes and such,
The orange things like to eat.

Oh what fun are the little things!
Cuddling snuggly with me,
They realize what fun this brings,
And they go on a little thing spree.

And what may you ask, are the little things?
A key, a blanket, a golden chain,
A pot, a pan, some apron strings,
Random things that vanish my pain.

So whenever I feel lonely or sad,
In the day or in the night,
I just take out my little things,
And they make me feel all right.

Sarah Spivack, Grade 7
Arcade Middle School

High Merit Poems – Grades 7, 8 and 9

A Beautiful Sound of Nature
An evening and shining day
The sun bursting out
Deer, squirrels, and rabbits resting down quietly
Birds chirping loudly in their nest
The waterfall pouring down peacefully
Leaves on the trees falling off gently
Wind flowing in the sky
Bees and butterflies flying around
Flowers are shifting right to left and left to right
What is it?
Nature
Sound of Nature
Nisha Nair, Grade 7
Daniel Savage Middle School

Berries Blast
Blueberries are a fun delight with every little bite,
It could be small and sour or it could be gushy and sweet.
Everyone loves to snack on blue blueberries, like who wouldn't?

Strawberries are red spotted fruits related to berries,
They make delicious strawberry smoothies, ice cream, and Jell-O.
Juicy strawberries are another one of my favorite fruit.

Raspberries are hairy, but taste really delicious.
I describe raspberries as little red berries in one.
This is the last ingredient in this berry blast poem.
Melinda Leung, Grade 8
St Mary's Chinese Day School

Young Love
It is often burning with fiery passion
A fierce desire for one another
Like a fire that cannot be stopped

Burning deep with romantic fury
Bursting into flames of intimacy
Mesmerized by each other's touch

Yet…
Brilliant and Beautiful
Kaitlyn Seaman, Grade 8
Los Molinos Community Elementary School

Cars
Cars cars everywhere you see cars
Red cars, blue cars old cars new cars
They come in different shapes and sizes
They have tires that spin round and round
They come and go just as they are found
They do not speak but they can turn around
They don't mess around like circus clowns
They get us to where we need to go
And that is why they are so good in the snow
Austin Miller, Grade 8
Temecula Valley Charter School

Come and Go
Memories come and go — but soon fade away…
Called, "I make you laugh a lot. Happy New Year!"
Texted, "I like you. — can't live without you."
Messaged, "I wanted to take you with me, to my dad's."
Shouted, "Want to get with me!"
Hugged, "You look beautiful."
Mumbled, "Let's dance."
Whispered, "I want to be with you forever."
Wished, "To hold you in my arms."
Dedicated, "That song is ours. I meant it."
Answered, "I would marry her."
Joked, "I'm your dork."
Smiled, "I love you too."
Laughed, "Let's go fly. Me and you."
Wrote, "Hi Baby…I love you. — Psycho."
Sighed, "I'm sorry." Asked, "Can I be with you today?"
Yelled, "I said we're friends!"
Replied, "I like her as a friend."
Complimented, "Congratulations! You look nice too."
It is whether you decide to cherish them,
With no hatred because memories come and go.
Desiree Avila, Grade 9
La Serna High School

The Golden Dragon
The golden dragon flies high and low,
Bringing gifts of peace to those you know,
The dragon flies but is never seen,
Except by one, its only queen.

The most beautiful woman in all the land,
So beautiful every bachelor offered his hand,
But the queen said no to everyone,
The dragon was her shining knight, her light and sun!

The dragon would come to her night and day,
To watch her sleep, have fun and play,
But one night, to the dragon's despair,
An angry bachelor came within her lair,

And in the midst of night there was a frightening scream,
Never again would the queen awake from her dreams,
Centuries have passed and the dragon still flies,
Snaking along the western skies,
Looking for one with gifted eyes.
Michael Murdock, Grade 9
Pacific Coast High School

Experience
Experience the world while you can,
Experience the world before it is too late
Time passes by like how water rushes over the falls
Before you know it, it is too late to go back,
Too late to change.
Davina Le, Grade 7
Sarah McGarvin Intermediate School

Challenge

Ballet is hard
moving to a higher level
achieving your dream
succeeding to move up
trying not to get injured
that's a challenge
trying to impress teachers
trying to get better
don't miss a class
try to take many classes
not getting distracted
do many parts in shows
get good grades to continue
go to professional shows
ask questions
staying in shape
stretch at home
leave any distractions away
try your best
love it no matter what
and act like it's the last day.

Erika Espinosa, Grade 8
St Helen Catholic Elementary School

Soldiers

Soldiers risk their lives
every day, they leave families
every time to protect our lives
they stay in their camp not
knowing what will happen and
when they'll come home. They
stay up all night praying that
God will protect them so they
can go home again. They don't have to
leave but they do to protect us,
some men come home or wait in
airports to see their firstborn son
or daughter, to hold them for the
very first time. After that holiday
they have to leave once again.
If it weren't for them we couldn't
stand up and say "I'm proud to be
an American," we are alive and we
wouldn't be if it wasn't for our troops,
so thank you Soldiers and all that
you are doing.

Ciara Whitehead, Grade 8
Ripona Elementary School

I Always Forget

I always forget
what I have to remember.
I'll think about it
all the way through December.

Daniel Prado, Grade 9
Vintage High School

In My Own World

In my own world
Raised and lived
Learning right from wrong
For I have been here so long

In my own world
Having fun
Breathing fresh air
And loving to dare

In my own world
I eat
I sleep
Without making a peep

In my own world
Not living alone
But now I'm happy
With my family

Paul Salazar, Grade 8
Richardson PREP HI Middle School

Family Trip

Thinking about camping
Thinking about family
Going on a huge trip
With the whole family tree
We get to the car
The cousins start to stack
They shove me from the front to back
They jacked my PSP®
And snatched all my snacks
Thinking about camping
Thinking about family
Tons of junk food
Takes my grumpy mood
Elbows in my face
People stealing all the space
I start to see the moon
Thinking that I'm doomed
They stop the car, we are there
I'll never do this again, "I swear"

James Bruce, Grade 7
Long Valley Charter School

The Glance

All it takes is one glance,
just one, then I'll take your hand.
The day you let go, my heart will be cold.
Just one glance, that is all it will take.
But if you do leave, please don't forget,
all the memories, whether good or bad
because they wouldn't have happened
if you didn't glance.

Jennifer Lopez, Grade 7
Walter F Dexter Middle School

Guitar

Playing
guitar
is awe-
some!
I love
to play
it every
time I go home.
It calms me down.
There are many types of
moods one can express
when playing guitar. Every
time I play, I feel extremely
happy, or feel like a
rock star!

Richard Johnson, Grade 7
Lucerne Valley Jr/Sr High School

Death

Death happens every day
every hour, minute
every second, of the day and night

Nobody can stop it
there's no cure,
no way of knowing when it comes

Death happens
in a blink of an eye.
Death goes around and around

You hear about it
talk about, but you never know
when death will come to your life.

Carol Marcelo, Grade 8
St Helen Catholic Elementary School

The Scream

A burst in the brain
A skip in the heart
The terror held within

The heated rush
The pounding beat
That only madness can begin

The trembling hands
The shaking knees
That cannot be ignored

No one can remove
The pain and fear
That the silent scream bore.

Madeleine Garza, Grade 7
Tenaya Middle School

Nature's Love

When a tree bears a fruit,
That new fruit has a meaning to life,
A new life,
It has evolved from its primordial times,
To the new outside world,
It realizes how happy and bright it feels.

There is color surrounding the roads,
Each color a bit different from the one beside it,
The red gives authenticity,
The orange gives long last,
The yellow gives joy to the change.

The first snow,
It's cold,
But it has a sense of cheer to it,
One snowflake may not be recognized,
But several more will.

Bright, colorful arrays of lights glide across the Arctic sky,
Each color is something new,
A feeling, characteristic or a bright, happy smile,
Bringing joy to your heart.

Danielle Sormann, Grade 8
Horace Ensign Intermediate School

The Lost and Found

The greedy iceberg bites the ship
tearing off chunks of metal flesh
digging into its insides
the ship yawns
slowly laying down to sleep
in the watery depths below eternally.

The unmanned submarine
roars to life
euphoric to be in the water
its blinding yellow eyes
penetrating the suffocating darkness of the deep
searching for anything
anything at all
finally its glowing gaze falls upon the ship
still sleeping.

Slowly sinking
into the groping sand
enveloped in clinging algae
gradually waking to the bright searching eyes of the submarine
the tiny yellow beast rumbles with joy
happy to have done its job.

Jennifer Smart, Grade 8
Carmel Valley Middle School

Family

Family is a big puzzle
Every family member is a piece of the puzzle
When you detach one from it
There will be a hole
And the hole is a member fighting against the force
And that piece will feel like there is nothing
When they leave

Family is a big puzzle
When you tear a piece
It is hard to put back together,
but it is possible to fix it
And if you don't fix it fast enough
It will ruin your puzzle

Family is a big puzzle
When it gets stuck together
You can't get away
And when it stays and doesn't have something pulling it
It will look amazing
And if you don't fight against the force
You will have the best life,
But if you do you will regret it

Cassie Hanafi, Grade 8
Richardson PREP HI Middle School

The Dream for Fame and a Better Life

This feeling, this sudden urge of motivation
A dream that cannot be caught
Filled me with great irritation
Wishing to be recognized, wishing to be known
No more! No more would I be a mere clone!

I go outside, look around all my surroundings,
And a nightmare is all I see
Gangsters tagging, kids smoking
Failures is that all they want to be
Is that as well what they see in me?

I wonder to myself, who am I?
Am I like everyone else, the same?
Would people remember me when I die?
All these thoughts that came,
If only I had glory, if only I had fame

No I will not live in this shame
I will no longer be the same
No more will I live in this nightmare,
No more will I live in this insanity,
It's time I made my dream into reality.

Christian Barreto, Grade 8
John Adams Middle School

Little Spoiled Dog

He yips and barks at the slightest thing, his collar is studded like a diamond ring.
He thinks he's bigger than the Great Dane, Little spoiled dog.
He sits by the fire in his owners lap; his fickle ways gives everyone a great laugh. He is a little spoiled dog.
He goes on long walks to the doggy park; He thinks he is really smart. He was trained by the master of the art. Little spoiled dog.
He goes to the finest pooch parlor in town, he thinks all the other dogs look like a clown, and he eats the finest food around. He is a little spoiled dog.

He wears clothes better than any humans I know, he is never made to go outside in the cold. Little spoiled dog.
His vet is the nations very top; He even gets a doggy lollipop. What a little spoiled dog.
His teeth are pearly white; his owner swears he'd never bite. Such a spoiled little dog.
And if you should see that little dog, you had better treat him like a God! For his temper is legendary, or so I'm told, for he is a little spoiled dog!

Audrie Ford, Grade 8
Heritage Christian School

The Truthful Lie

I think I saw a hummingbird by the apple tree.
I didn't say another word as it spoke to me.
"Little girl, little girl. Why are you working? Come sing, dance, and twirl, and stop your lurking."
I shook my head and replied, "I can't procrastinate. I'll stay in bed to finish up, even if it's late."
"But it's very sunny outside, don't you see? Just for five minutes, please, spread some glee?"
I stood up to sigh but I ran outside to enjoy the beautiful day, but the sly bird went in to eat my homework away.
My teacher asked for my homework, and my head was going to burst.
But I rose up to say, "Can I please justify myself first?"
"What foolishness! What nonsense!" she cried when I finished my story.
"Get out of my classroom while you still have your glory!"
A lesson for me to imply is always tell the truth and never a lie.

Bianca Padilla, Grade 8
Walter F Dexter Middle School

Suburbia

the houses are like daylight through glass
colors against a pale blue canvas
as the sun slowly moves down the horizon it rests on the shoulders of a man with a hose
the sun makes the man's neck red and sticky and beads of sweat fall down his neck like mercury on a cold day
the water from the man's hose feeds the walls that protect the man's fortress
    soon the sun illuminates the short blades of grass surrounding the homes like oceans of green
they shiver in the light breeze even though they are in the warmth of the sun
and as the world darkens the houses become blank silhouettes against the dark hole of night and the grass stops shivering
and the man is already asleep
and the sun does not move down in the sky
because once the sun goes down nothing moves in suburbia

Owen Thomas, Grade 8
Chico Jr High School

No One Is the Same

When I dream, I dream of you.
When I awake it feels as if I were still dreaming, because everything reminds me of you.
I see the sun that lights up as bright as your smile was.
I smell the shampoo, the one that I would smell as the air would run through your hair.
As I would sit down to look at the stars, they would remind me of that sparkle you would carry in your eyes.
The only thing that I would never be able to compare is what you had inside.
Nothing that's alive could ever be compared to who you were inside.

Jessica Avalos, Grade 8
Palm Desert Charter Middle School

Happy Birthday

It's been 14 years since the day you were born.
You've made many memories, learned a lot, grew a lot, cried a lot, but also smiled and laughed a lot.
You've seasoned 168 months. Enjoying 56 winters, springs, summers and autumns as they passed.
You learned to love each season despite its natural flaws, just like how I've learned to love you.
730 weeks went by, and you accepted each new one as it came.
Whether it be sunny ones, rainy ones — dark ones or bright ones,
Because every new week meant a new start.
You've pulled through 5,113 days. Welcoming each day as it came by;
Blowing out candles and making wishes on your birthdays, having faith that each year will be better than the last.
You've gone through 122,721 hours, treasuring and making good memories to last.
Meeting new people and loving old ones; especially those whom have learned to love you back.
You've spent 7,363,282 minutes, most of them, smiling.
People are happy around you, because your happiness is so contagious.
But it's hard not to be when your smile shines so bright.
441,796,964 seconds flew by that you spent reminiscing,
But never dwelling or regretting. Always moving on, knowing that time won't stop for you.
Your heart has beaten 530,115,840 times. Beating fast and slow,
As it learned to forgive and forget, and loving like it's never been hurt.
It's too late for anyone else to steal your heart now, because from now on,
It will always beat for me.
Happy Birthday.

Thucdan Ton, Grade 9
Oxford Academy

I Am From

I am from average — one single ray of sun through a crystal door,
a drip drop in a rainstorm, a dusty forgotten book in a library corner.
I am from a popsicle stick cross — one in twenty naive voices praising the one who died for their sins,
the simplicity of right and wrong, the sweet thirst grape juice leaves after flat bread in a narrow pew.
I never had "that time when I got first place," or "back in the day I was the best of the best."
I was the one in second place.
Not the best. Not the worst.
I am from innocence — the warmth of four bodies sharing a grunting couch,
a sapling sheltered by its progenitor, the crisp, newly washed sheets still lingering of "All" detergent.
I am from following — one in a hundred shedding leaves in autumn,
The sheep. Never the shepherd.
A cloud influenced by the slightest heavenly breeze.
I am like a caterpillar — cradled in the security of a cocoon.
awaiting the right time to take responsibility, to take charge.
I may be from average, but average does not define me.
I may be from a flimsy stick cross, but that is not the edge of my understanding.
I may never have epic stories of my past, but that doesn't mean I can't create them.
I may be from innocence, but I can't change my past, nor do I want to.
I may be from following, but that has only given me insight on how to lead.
A world lies before me — cold, brittle and rigid,
awaiting a mason audacious enough to engrave her legacy.

Hayley Bennett, Grade 9
La Costa Canyon High School

Life

No one makes it out alive so live your life to the fullest. Life is something you should never take for granted and never wish you were without it. Always appreciate what you got and think of the less fortunate, they barely have a place to stay and maybe they won't eat today. Never give up and try your best and never live life with regrets. Forgive and forget enemies from the past and keep looking forward and don't look back.

Nayra Perez, Grade 8
Isbell Middle School

Christmas Time
Christmas time is when
it snows all the time
and snowmen you build
come alive.

Christmas time is when
you eat yummy cookies
and hot chocolate that
fills up your little tummy.

Christmas time is when
you decorate a tree
and hang up lights
for everyone to see.

Christmas time is when
Santa comes down your chimney
and you unwrap gifts
with your family.
Aubree Virgen, Grade 7
Walter F Dexter Middle School

Alone
In a black shadow,
Hides your timid face;
Searching for a light,
In this dark place.

In a deep hole,
Buries you shy self;
Looking for a hand,
Where no one helps.

In a roaring crowd,
Covers your faint voice;
Seeking out someone,
Who will hear your choice.

In this hopeless world,
You're not on your own;
I'll be your friend,
You'll never be alone.
Apeksha Singh, Grade 8
Joe Walker Middle School

Tick Tack Toe
Tick Tack Toe
Should I be an X or an O?
My turn must be first,
but if worse comes to worst
I can play to tie.
So I can make them cry.
My X must be in the corner in order to enter
my winning move that will be in the center.
Gabriel Phun, Grade 8
St Francis de Sales School

Why Can't We Fly?
Why can't we fly,
High up in the sky
With the birds and the bees,
Way up past the trees?
Try as we might,
We still can't take flight,
Up there in the sky
So high.

Planes and balloons,
Pelicans and loons,
Have all the fun
Soaring while we just run,
Around all day
On the ground.

Maybe planes
Can take us up high.
Maybe we can fly in them.
But it's still not the same,
If only the day came,
The day that we could fly.
Rachael Barron, Grade 8
Joe Walker Middle School

Colors
They are what we see every day,
and they are colors.
Colors give the world excitement,
from black to white
all colors are bound to excite.
Even when you go to school,
all of the colors are colorful and cool.
Colors put the world at its height,
without them there wouldn't be any life.
From pastel to neon,
they are all beautiful to me,
just look around and you'll see.
Destiny Rubio, Grade 7
Isbell Middle School

The Garden
Big bright flowers purple and blue,
Looks like it rained
The wind also blew. Flowers all over
Orange and yellow,
They are as long as a big tall fellow.
Big bulky bushes
With flowers on top, they are so big
They can almost pop.
They are as fluffy as a cloud
White and gray,
When the wind blows the flowers sway,
Then blow away…
Gabriela Galvan, Grade 7
Daniel Savage Middle School

Creating Deep Rifts
The seagulls fly overhead
The waves rise in the air
Traveling in flocks
The crash into the rocks with no care

Traveling in flocks
Fish swim through the sea
They crash into the rocks with no care
They see a shark and flee

Fish swim through the sea
Not a care in the world
They see a shark and flee
Up in the air the foam is hurled

Not a care in the world
Seaweed slowly drifts
Up in the air the foam is hurled
Creating deep rifts

Seaweed slowly drifts
Traveling in flocks
Creating deep rifts
The seagulls fly overhead
Sam Shpall, Grade 8
Kadima Day School

The Little Deer
As flowers bloom in red and white,
The baby birds start to take flight;
And in the meadow down below,
One little deer desired to know,
How winter changes into spring,
And why all the birds like to sing.

All alone in that peaceful place,
He looked around for his mother's face;
Nothing to see but grass and trees,
So into the forest he went to seek;
And in the forest all alone,
He cannot seem to find his home.

After hours when hope seemed lost,
And it appeared he paid the cost;
Deep in the forest he heard a sound,
And couldn't believe what he had found;
He found his mother between the trees,
Laying in flowers enjoying the breeze.

As flowers bloom in red and white,
The baby birds start to take flight.
Samantha McKim, Grade 7
Joe Walker Middle School

Shackled Allegiance, to the Flag

Disasters in the nation. Is but only nature's rage?
We are not a blind people. Yet as a whole, young of age?
Mountains may come crashing,
cities swept to sea.
Shed tears, we find brevity,
and can come together peacefully
'Tis but a mob mentality.
But positive in its nature.
Is it not sad in prospect?
That we can summon all this power?
Unstoppable in unity,
we thrive in our selflessness
But in all our capability,
we crawl through these lives
I pose — has no one kept their sight?
Alas. Some have, yet does the mass remain blind.
But to enlighten. Oh the panic it would cause
'Tis a devil, we've conjured,
but choose not to see.
He blinds us with his blizzard.
And we empower him, to make it warm.

Bryton Horner, Grade 9
Irvine High School

Individualism

Beauty is individualism.
Who we are is our own individual.
No one can tell us how we should be,
We shouldn't fake who we are, in order to be accepted,
Otherwise we really aren't,
And the end result, is that we are hypocrites.
Love, happiness, generosity, makes us who we are.
But hate, sorrow, loneliness, greed, and the thirst for acceptance
Also claws its way to label us as individuals.
Hold your head high, and know,
That the true beauty lies within,
And doubt and the need to fake your way to acceptance,
Should be neglected.
For if we have to become hypocrites, to be accepted,
We are not accepted, we are only neglecting ourselves.
So love who you are, be grateful of who you are,
Be proud of yourself, know that you are beautiful,
And remember, that you are special,
Because you are an individual,
An individual, who is one with themselves.
Be happy and proud, that you are you.

Lucy Zhuang, Grade 8
South Lake Middle School

The Weeping Willow

The weeping willow's graceful fronds
Sweep across the glassy pond
As much as a millennium has gone by it seems
Since he was a small sapling by a stream
With a great forest behind him, full of life
Where he was free of worry, free of strife
But no more does the stream's water flow
A great resort on the mountain now blocks the snow
No more does the forest sing its song
Its lush green foliage now is gone
His stream, now a still pond, was taken by nature's foe
Who destroys the earth and pretends not to know
The willow looks up and prays to the sky
Why can't anyone hear him cry?

Allison Deoudes, Grade 8
Monte Vista Christian School

The Moon

The Moon is Earth's older brother
It sits in the dark midnight blue sky
As it looks upon its younger brother
It slithers around Earth twenty four seven

As the Earth evolves, it visits the Moon
Not once but twice
First in July 20, 1969
Then bomb it with a missile September 2009

It lies in the sky, silent once more
No longer looking upon us
We hope the very best as soon we will return
To make a man-made moon base to become its friend once more.

Robert Rendon, Grade 8
Richardson PREP HI Middle School

Fourth and Two:

Fourth and two;
Patriots attempting to get the first down
All is hyped.
The ball is hiked to the quarterback.
The pass is away,
The catch is made,
But he's behind the line.
They turn it over to the Colts,
The goal line was within reach;
The Colts score the game-winning touchdown.
New England goes home empty-handed.

Avery Manley, Grade 7
Tenaya Middle School

Good-Bye

Saying good-bye is so hard.
Especially when they drive away in their car.

Not seeing them feels like forever.
We barely talk sometimes never.

They never write, they never call
We haven't talked since last fall.

You hope that you'll stay friends.
And hope it's not the end.

Kassandra Aguilera, Grade 7
St Francis de Sales School

Hope

She was more, than just another pet.
She was a part of the family.
She won my heart —
With her beautiful, hazel eyes.
She knew my call,
for her to eat.
She would play with the blue yarn.

But no matter where she is —
She will always be in my heart.
A heart,
That will always be hers.
Hope will always help me through the tough times.
Her memory will live on with me.
Not even when I part from this world,
I will never forget about her.

Rosa Garcia, Grade 8
Richardson PREP HI Middle School

This Cold World

What kind of world am I in,
This world is full of pain and sin,
Cops are corrupted,
Young girls are getting abducted,
Families are separated,
And bullets have penetrated,
Wars won't stop,
And no one trusts cops,
What kind of world am I in,
Where 15 year olds are going to the pen,
Where governments care more about building prisons,
Instead of helping children,
Why must people suffer,
While others get supper,
What is the solution to these problems,
No one knows we just got 'em.

Francisco Yanez, Grade 9
Freedom Community Day School

Ode to Ginny

Ginny the guinea you are so round
you are so plump and perfect, you weigh a pound
You scurry, you waddle, you jump and you purr
but what I enjoy most is petting your fur
Ginny I think I shall never see
a guinea as furry and soft as thee
The mohawk that you wear
makes people stop and stare
The trail of pooh that you leave
may be my mother's new pet peeve
You talk, you chew, and throw things about all night
And when I wake up in the morning
Your home is a frightful sight!
Welcome to the family!

Natalie Cowlishaw, Grade 7
Arcade Middle School

Perfect Is Not What I Seek

You have one life to live
You need to believe yourself,
You exist in this world for a reason,
You exist for me.

You're beautiful no matter what anybody says.
You're the most shining star I see,
You're the light that shines my way.

I can say I love you every day
A perfect body is not what I need,
A pretty face is not what I seek.

A kind heart is what I want
A loving, caring, and honest girl like you,
I had been waiting for so long till this day.

Allen Lysaythong, Grade 9
Hiram W Johnson High School

Shining Flower

Shining flower,
Your petals are filled with beauty.
As rain falls down, you still stand tall.
But everyone's dream shall shatter and eventually you'll fall.
You sit alone in a meadow,
Awaiting patiently.
You wait for a friend, true.
Though one might never come,
You still have you.

At night you are lonely and cold.
The moonbeams come upon you.
Beneath the petals of hope,
You cry silently but alas you don't cry of fear or joy.
You just, well cry
Because you are a shining flower.

Jennifer Phan, Grade 7
Sarah McGarvin Intermediate School

Escape

The barren domain where we are encased;
Through ticking time will lay us to waste;
The map through this maze must be drawn in haste,
Lest the dropping sands touch bottom of vase.

Lurk in our hearts do glee and sorrow,
Don't slumber long, for we leave on the morrow,
Let dawn touch the hills, then leave your burrow,
And come has the time to part from this furrow.

Our chests are high, our ships are vast,
And we follow our blood red compass;
Shackles unbolted free is our mass,
And salvation reigns o'er us at last.

Niket Kulkarni, Grade 7
Joe Walker Middle School

High Merit Poems – Grades 7, 8 and 9

My Dreadful Day of Middle School
Today is my first day of middle school
And I don't really know what to do
I am walking through the halls in this brand new school
Looking for my classes makes me feel like a great big fool
Everyone in my class has already made friends
I just wish they could lend me a friend
Any friend I wouldn't care
Now I am in the front sitting here alone
Trying to pay attention
But I just keep feelin' redemption and more redemption
From the clock going tick tock when will it all end?
A girl came and asked me "What's your name?"
"Audrey" I said in shame
"The name is Melly" she said, and she was wearing a t-shirt
That looked like jelly
Then she said "Wanna be friends?" I surely replied "YES!"
My troubles were over,
And I didn't even need a four leaf clover
"I made a friend!" I said
The next day I got up and said "member Melly?"
Which made me stronger than strawberry jelly!

Audrianna Gomez, Grade 8
John Adams Middle School

Last Moments
Oh how I know it's my last moment,
The last time I'll take a breath on Earth,
The things that fly through your mind,
As you watch people crying,
All the embarrassing moments you've had,
All the memories you have,
Flashing in your eyes like a movie,
I know I will never sing, smile, or laugh the way others do,
Because I am dying inside,
My heart crumbling,
My eyes blurred with tears,
I know I'm not the only suffering,
The cancer patients,
The poor,
The homeless children,
They're all so strong,
But I am weak.
My eyes close,
And I bade a silent good bye to the world,
And let myself be shut out of the world of life,
And into the world of darkness.

Tiana Gong, Grade 7
La Colina Jr High School

I Am
I am the wolf that howls at the moon.
I am the hawk that flies by day.
I am the stallion that gallops at night.
I am the tiger that is the king of the jungle.
I am the bees that make the honey.
I am who I am,
And no one can change me.
For I am strong.
I am brave.
I am loyal.
I am like that of a good guard dog, protective, and bright.
I love with all my heart.
I am who I am.
That is all that I can be.

Tucker Cadle, Grade 8
Franklin Sr High School

The Sky
During the day the sky is so blue
Its color is true
The puffy clouds float high
like a bird in the sky
The sun, very yellow and bright
Like its opposite the moon with white light
At night the only light so bright and bold
although it is very old
Its image so crisp and so clear
even though it is not at all near
The stars at night shiny and small
that you can't see them all
The darkness a big thick black sheet
so perfect and neat
Without the sky and all that is hold the world would be incomplete

Jacob Arroyo, Grade 7
Monte Vista Christian School

Memoir
It started on June 21, 09
I said I liked you and you said you do too
It just took three words to say
Three hours to explain
And now a whole lifetime to show
You said forever and you promised
I said I don't know
I'm only thirteen and perfect couples are only in fantasies
You said to trust you and I said I will
It's been 7 months and I know you still love me
And I still love you

Jessica Escobar, Grade 8
Richard Merkin Middle Academy

Dads
Dads with their warm hugs and big smiles
Are like the sunshine when it is raining.
They are big teddy bears.
They comfort us when we are sad and
They hold our hands when we are scared.
Dads do what's best for us even if we don't like it.
They pick us up and dust us off when we fall and
They help us to do what's right.
Dads are like warm summer days.
Dads are the best.

Amber Clark, Grade 7
Junipero Serra School

Everyone Else

So odd,
that,
unless you are ill,
no one will bring you any flowers.
Unless you yell for help,
no one will notice your troubles.
Unless you cry,
no one will care.
No one will be sympathetic.
Unless you say you are moving away,
no one will come to visit you,
and,
unless you die,
no one will forgive you.

So forgive them.
bring them some flowers,
show you them care,
and,
visit them just to show them you know they are there,
and,
you won't be like everyone else.

Kiana Panbechi, Grade 8
South Lake Middle School

Contentment

The old woman said to the little boy
"Listen my child and listen well,
for now I shall tell you a story that some others tell.
It begins with a boy, not older than you
who was so kind and so sweet yet miserable too.
You see he wasn't content, no not at all
and in his room grew a stack so big and so tall.
It was full of things he wanted no more,
'Please give them away!' his mother would implore.
But the little boy was greedy and refused to give in,
until his mother did not buy him a thing.
He then realized the wrong of his ways
and gave each of his toys till he had nothing with to play.
The boy felt happy and even better…
The weight was off his chest and he had done his best!"

Yassmin Mostafavi, Grade 7
Carden Academy of Santa Clara

Beautiful Day

It's a very good day.
Nobody's around and it's quiet!
You can hear the movement of the water.
The flowers growing from the ground.
The splashing of the fish jumping.
The trees growing strong and good.
There are not that many flowers.
But they still look pretty.
One tree is growing different from the others.

Katelyn Smith, Grade 7
Daniel Savage Middle School

The Day

As the day grows near
We will soon start to fear
It's the end of our time at St. Francis
We sure had a lot of fun at those dances
I know we will go our separate ways
But we will always remember the good ole days
Soon we will say our goodbyes
I will try my best not to cry
Friends like these come around so rarely
I will always try and treat them fairly
I'm really going to miss the people I've come to know
It's sure going to be hard to let go
This year's going by so fast
I just need to take a step back to relax
I still can't believe we made it this far
Hey, it actually wasn't too hard
The day we've been waiting anxiously for is near
It's graduation day there will be no fear!

Mikala Mendoza, Grade 8
St Francis de Sales School

Can It Be True?

You told me you would love me forever and always.
And my heart finally accepted it.

Then I couldn't believe you would be the one
To break your vow of love.

Thinking that our love would last
always made me so happy,

Until the day you said,
"We're done."

Depressed until this day,
I still can't believe you did this to me.

I drew creative works of art about you and me,
But I guess it was never meant to be…
Gone is such great beauty.

Allison Balocating, Grade 8
Corpus Christi School

Violence

She falls to the floor, peacefully without a sound;
Screaming and screaming for one more round.
Sweat was dripping from her face, and she knew it was real,
She was only human; that's how it was supposed to feel.
Fists clenched, she gets to her feet;
Wondering, will she get beat?
Her opponent was laughing until she turned red.
Losing was something she would surely dread.
"I give up," was what formed on her lips;
Her match was over, and she'll never regret this.

Megan Tran, Grade 7
Sarah McGarvin Intermediate School

Dream

Dreams are hopes for the future
wants of the mind
only dreams
unless you make them worth something
with continuous actions
faith and perseverance
things that make every second count
you can make it possible
it is truly up to you whether or not
to take that ability and power
and make something of it

Sierra Howard, Grade 9
Natomas Charter School

The Pain of Losing a Father

Once I had a dad and
Once I thought he
Was gone, but
(It was very foolish of me)
Then once,
We went to the hospital —
All of my bad thoughts
Of my father came to mind
Then one day
It all came true

Jennifer Molina, Grade 7
Corpus Christi School

Faith

We tried our best
to work it out.
Our best didn't seem
good enough.
You went your way
and I went mine.
But for some reason,
FAITH
is bringing us back
to where we started.

Allan Guintu, Grade 8
Corpus Christi School

Contentment

I took a train to the North,
And all I found was sadness.
I took a plane to the South,
And all I found was slavery.
I took a bus to the East,
And all I found was crime.
I took a boat to the West,
And all I found was death.
Then I realized for the first time,
I was happy where I was.

John Sullivan, Grade 9
Lucerne Valley Jr/Sr High School

Softball

Home runs, strike outs, and outs. Good sportsmanship, catcher,
Pitcher, sweat, dirt, fields, bases, bats, gloves, and balls.
Getting yelled at, attitudes, and the coaches.
Teams, all together, lose, win, and tie. No I in team,
Together till the end, lose together; win together, all in it together.
In it to win it, that's how the sport is played.
Most importantly have fun. Infielders, outfielders, offense, defense.
Might get hit with the softball, shake it off.
Take one for the team. Be strong.
Swing the bat, keep your eye on the ball,
Run the bases, slide at home plate. Home run! Triples, doubles,
Singles, or even walks as long as you get on base you're happy.
The umpire calls it "Strike three, batter out" It's okay
You'll get it next time. Keep your chin up. You feel sad,
You feel as if you let your teammates down. Unsatisfied and unaccomplished.
Hit a home run, and you are the happiest person in the world.
Strike out an you feel depressed. Teammates are sad.
You let them down and your coaches.
The pressure never ends. It's on you as you practice and play.
Teammates depend on you and coaches. Only You.
You feel as if you do something bad the whole world is mad with you.

Lizbeth Diaz, Grade 8
St Helen Catholic Elementary School

Waking Up in the Wrong Moment

Day burns into night, ashes are falling down the sky,
Millions of small sparks coming down, burning your soul,
Making your eyes close, and making it hard to stay awake,
Your whole body collapses, but your mind is wide open,
And your soul is free, everything changes once you've awoken,
Fantasy has become reality, an unexplained sighting,
And everything you imagined is right there in front of your eyes,
It is devastating? Is it what you've always wanted to have?
Or is this just a dream? A stupid dream that makes this seem real,
It's hard to think when the moment you've been waiting for,
Where you want to know what's going to happen next,
And the most shocking thing ever, turns to darkness, ten seconds later,
Your remarkable eyes open, daylight has taken over night once again,
And everything is shining so bright, so ordinary
And real, and all you can do at that point, is think about it…

Nancy Lara, Grade 8
Richard Merkin Middle Academy

Bond of Union

A man a woman; we don't all agree,
We could say a child and a man
But then again we don't all agree.
They are unwinding, drifting away. Is their marriage over
Are their thoughts unwinding?
That is what I think and that is what I say. They are leaving each other in
Space where it never ends.
Did they belong together…is that why they're tied?
Is their marriage over…are their thought drifting away like a light feather?
Who knows, nobody knows, but then again we don't all agree.

Michael Rodriguez, Grade 7
Tenaya Middle School

Since You Left*
Since you left our lives
We've been missing you here
More and more every day.
Since you left,
It's been quiet without you
Here in our lives.
Since you've been gone,
There's nobody to call my hero,
Only you.
Since you left,
Everyone has been bothering me
Because you are gone.
Since you left the world,
I never go to sleep
Without thinking of you.
Since you left,
When I look at pictures of you
I cry.
Since you left,
My life will never be the same.

Kyle Veloro, Grade 7
Corpus Christi School
*Dedicated to my father 7/11/1977-10/23/2009.

My Mom Is a Heart
My Mom is a heart
She is always there for me
Through good times and even the bad times
She pumps her love to me

She keeps me alive with her kindness
Also, with her indomitable strength
She gets me through the tough times
Like a heart throbbing during a marathon

Just as the heart is a major part of the body
She is a major part of my life
I wouldn't be here without her
Because she is my heart; I shall always be with her

Connor Denier, Grade 7
Junipero Serra School

This Girl
When I saw this girl
She looked so beautiful
I expected to be with her
When I saw her at school I nervously went up to her
My heart was pounding like it never did before
When I went to talk to her she looked at me and smiled
When she and I were together I was very happy
When she kissed me I was very shocked at how it felt
It was very calm and sweet
It was the type of love I always wanted
When I felt her lips they were so soft

Pheng Lee, Grade 9
Hiram W Johnson High School

Biking Down Rustling Oaks Dr
Sweat drips down my face
As I vigorously pump air into my tires.
I brush the dust off the seat
With a ragged, old towel.
Five minutes later I breeze down the driveway
Wind whistles through my ears
And I shiver while waving with stiff fingers
As a neighbor spots me from a ladder.
He's putting up Christmas lights.
Kids throw footballs while moms read on the porch
The wind blows the stench of fertilizer,
And I crinkle my nose.
My wheels crunch over dry maple leaves.
Like a snail leaves a trail of slime,
My bike traces the road
With water and soap suds
From someone's car wash.
I round Old Carriage Ct. and
A last reserve of energy
Pushes me up the driveway
And into the garage.

Beverley Loo, Grade 7
Lindero Canyon Middle School

Where Poetry Hides for Me
Poetry hides in the chambers of my heart.
Poetry hides deep in my green eyes.
It hides in my room where I sleep.
Poetry hides in the saxophone I play.
It hides in the drawings I make.
Poetry hides in the clothes I wear.
Poetry hides when I go swimming.
Poetry hides in the glasses I wear.
Poetry hides in the new converses I got for my birthday
Poetry hides in the words that I write.
Poetry hides everywhere in my body.
Poetry hides in my mind where I think.
Poetry hides in the things I use and love.
Poetry hides in my ears where I listen to what I have to say.
Poetry hides in my dog that I love.

Briana Taylor, Grade 7
Tenaya Middle School

Dreams
All I'd remember was a part of my dreams
Little I remember and know what it means
Suddenly I'm flying high up in the sky
Next I'm in a room with familiar faces walking by
Some dreams are sweet, some of them are not
But mostly I know that they're strange a lot
Even though all my dreams have no meaning
I just love to lie down and happily be dreaming
That's why at night I rush quickly to bed
I just can't wait to have dreams in my head

Christine Tran, Grade 7
Sarah McGarvin Intermediate School

High Merit Poems – Grades 7, 8 and 9

Desire, the Devil

Desire works its way slowly into your heart
And then one day you wake up
And all your soul wants
Is that thing, that person, that feeling'
To be able to relive that moment
Over and over forever
Until you grow so old that your lungs hurt to breathe
Or to have him always with you
Always whispering with you and holding your hand
Always there, glued to your hand and heart
You know he will never leave
Or what's more —
To be known, to be recognized
To have an effortless wealth
Everything you want:
Eternal love, eternal glory, eternal money
Desire is the devil
Bringing hate, heartbreak, war
Yet every day we speak of what *we* want
The death of us will be our desire

Zaynab Malik, Grade 9
University Preparatory School

I Miss You

The sky is blue, and so I am
Oh why, oh why did you have to die?
I lay there on the shore, doing nothing
When you were out there suffering.
How could I just leave you out there,
When I loved you so dear?
You were my father, you still are
But now you are only in my heart.
You saved my sister; well at least you tried…
But don't worry she is fine.
That day when you drowned,
A marine came by and helped her out.
I feel guilty, not doing a thing.
I was two; I didn't know what was happening.
I wish I could have known you better,
I miss you like a bird to its feather, but MORE!
MORE I SAY!
I miss you more than a child to its blanket, or a dog to its leash!
I miss you like a little girl misses her father,
Because it is true, I am your little girl, and I DO miss you!

Brielle Reynolds, Grade 7
Arcade Middle School

I Am

I wonder where all the Hmong people are.
I hear my relatives crying.
I see a lot of white spirits flying.
I want to support my life.
I do what is necessary to help my grandpa in the war against Laos.
I am Hmong.

I pretend not to care about my cousins.
I feel sad for my culture and people.
I touch the sky of my heavenly eye.
I worry what will happen to me in the future.
I cry when I am about to get shot.
I am Hmong.

I understand what the elders try to tell us.
I say words to make them happy and smile.
I dream about my mom who left me alone.
I try to tell my parents that I am happy to be their son.
I hope I will get a better life.
I am Hmong.

Tommy Vang, Grade 9
Hiram W Johnson High School

I Am

I wonder what I can be in this story of my life
I hear the birds sing every day
I see the rainbow after the rainy sky
I want to help others
I do whatever I can to improve myself
I am a reader

I pretend I can fly
I feel wonderful when I am in the sky
I touch the clouds gently
I worry how my tale will end
I cry when I do the wrong thing
I am a reader

I understand what my plot needs
I say in a low voice to the writer, "I have a wish"
I dream I can be a worthy character in this chapter of the earth
I try to show my best effort
I hope I can be what I intend to be
I am a reader

Yen Ngan, Grade 9
Hiram W Johnson High School

Planes

Boom! A sonic boom fills the air.
It shakes the windows and ruffles your hair
There must be a plane above
Flying as peaceful as a dove
They are very important to the world scene
Where would we be without this flying machine?

John Gorder, Grade 8
St Francis de Sales School

Nature

Bright skies, cold winds.
Hot days, bored kids
Raining cats and dogs a plain vision of fog.
Feeling kinda lost, but the mind is already gone.
Flowers bloom, but will die soon.
Dark skies guided by the moon.

Gabriel Hernandez, Grade 8
Shadow Hills Intermediate School

A Girl and Her Horse
The sound of him calling you,
You know he is always there for you,
Your hearts will never be separated.

You love that being next to you,
He loves you back.
A girl and her horse,
A never-ending love.
Audrey Montgomery, Grade 8
St Francis Parish School

Marred
My tears are spilling over,
Drenching a sodden land,
Through the night awaiting dawn,
Where rays of light shall take my hand,
Justice I do seek thee,
To right the rotten core,
For innocence and truth both slain,
The white lily, now stained red.
Halie Carton, Grade 9
Academy of the Redwoods

Live
Laugh your heart out,
Dance in the rain,
Cherish the moment,
Ignore the pain.
Live, laugh, love,
Forgive and forget,
Life's too short to be
Living with regret.
Marissa Zosimo, Grade 7
Our Lady of Guadalupe School

An Unknown Love
It dwells beneath my stubborn skin
Hidden below my feigned indifference
Mixed with emotions; I try to conceal it
Lest you might see I am feeble and weak
I must be the last to break this vow
A silent vow of our secret love
Which you, nor I, know does exist
Though we're both raptured in its dark kiss
Chanel Bayard, Grade 9
University Preparatory School

Softball
Swing, catch, run
Softball is lots of fun
Hitting the ball with all your might
Running the field with your team
Trying to score and put up a fight
Swing, catch, run
Sabrina Soriano, Grade 8
Shadow Hills Intermediate School

September 11, 2001: America Forever Scarred
September 11, 2001:
That day was the day the Twin Towers fell
So many innocents were killed, so many families broken
Terrorists were cruel, horrifying…terrible
Had so much nerve to dare attack our country
America forever scarred

September 11, 2001:
There were the screams of sirens
Cries of pain and agony from the crash of the first tower
Sobs from those who had lost
Then, as the second tower fell, shocked silence
America forever scarred

September 11, 2001:
Even through those dark hours, our resistance to be destroyed never faded
We, America, knew we had to fight together
Patriotism united us all
Our flag was raised
Our heroes never stopped working to save lives, and the stability of our country
The flame of this great nation flickered, but never went out
American forever scarred, yet healing
Gabby Brow, Grade 8
Ripona Elementary School

Where Poetry Hides for Me
Poetry hides in my favorite songs that make me dance all day.
Poetry hides when I see my old bear with all the memories still there.
Poetry hides of when I see my old bike in the dusty garage.
Poetry hides in the old house that I was raised in.
Poetry hides in my first Barbie doll that I still have today.
Poetry hides in the halls I walk every day.
Poetry hides in the church I pray in every Sunday.
Poetry makes me imagine the setting in my *New Moon* book.
Poetry hides by my old dance shoes.
Poetry hides when I'm with my family.
Poetry hides in all faces that you see in the street every day.
Poetry hides in love.
Poetry hides in all of your brothers and sisters.
Poetry hides in all the teachers that taught me so much.
Poetry hides everywhere.
Sarah Redmoon, Grade 7
Tenaya Middle School

Last Summer
I remember that night at the beach
Hearing the waves crashing, the seagulls chirping,
And us laughing. I loved the way you gave me butterflies.
When you held me tightly in your arms, it felt right. After that night,
I never stopped thinking of you. Weeks later, school started and I noticed
You weren't the same person I knew. There were rumors about you; you dated
other girls. I was so confused, lost. I didn't understand. You stopped talking
To me. I was so depressed. I wish I could go back to that night…
Last summer.
Analise McFarland, Grade 7
Lucerne Valley Jr/Sr High School

High Merit Poems – Grades 7, 8 and 9

Flowers Are Like Knowledge
A scenery as blue as the sky
Yellow flowers as yellow as bumblebees can be
White textures just like snow on a frosty morning

Nature's winds going briefly through the leaves
Sounds like voices upon the meadow trees
As I lay there quietly and still
I feel a breeze like a ghost, water flows
Through the flowers just like nature is my desire

As the day grows
I dare to know flowers are like knowledge
When you water them they grow
Karina Albor, Grade 7
Daniel Savage Middle School

Life
Life is like a roller coaster
You will have your ups and downs
When someone you love dies
You feel like the world has stopped
Although you might have downs
Some days you'll have your ups
Your life depends on how you live
Do you live life to the fullest?
Or do you look at the half glass half empty
Many people live life like they don't care
But that can get them in some serious trouble
If you want to live life to the fullest
Just pay close attention to how you live
Paola Torres, Grade 7
Isbell Middle School

Colors
A color can mean many things.
Black can mean a bad day or a day of sadness
Orange is a happy color to all
Blue, the saddest of all colors, is a bad day for you and me
Red, passion and love, is the best kind of love in the world
The one we want, but sometimes can't have.
A rainbow is a happy color
Because it comes after you cry your eyes out.
Colors are nice. That is why we have lots of them around.
Michelle Leiva, Grade 7
Immaculate Heart of Mary School

Makeup to Me Is an Art Form
Makeup to me is an art form
the way the eyeliner brush makes its way across the eyelid,
it's like the way an artist's brush paints its canvas.
The way the eye shadow pains the eyelid with color,
It's like the way a person colors the sidewalk with chalk.
The way you elongate the eyelashes.
It's like a flower growing and reaching its full potential.
Shelby Cox, Grade 9
Vintage High School

Childhood World
In my childhood I remember
Playing under the trees.

In my childhood I remember
Hiding under the table when I was in trouble.

In my childhood I remember
Pretending I was a doctor saving lives.

In my childhood I remember
Running around the kitchen.

My home was my childhood world.
Crystal Mendez, Grade 8
Richardson PREP HI Middle School

Love
Why do people confuse love with hurt?
They say love hurts and I'm not going back to it
They say they were foolish to go down that road
But loves is that one feeling that makes you forget
About the sadness in your life even the fact that
You flunked your biology final exam and when you
Get home your mom will be waiting
Love makes you day dream about that one person
Every minute — every second
And hurt is simply that one feeling that makes you cry
Yourself rivers day and night wishing this was over
Hurt is an experience which we learn from
And must move one and leave the pain behind
Mayra Torres, Grade 8
Richardson PREP HI Middle School

Memories
When I look at the sky,
It reminds me of your beautiful eyes
And every time I think of your smile,
I always remember the past, seeing you walking down the aisle.

We may be away and apart,
But your beautiful spirit never leaves my heart
Your soul may have ascended,
But we'll be together again, when my life has ended.
Mark De Guzman, Grade 8
St Martin-in-the-Fields School

Zombies
Zombies are undead creatures of the night.
They come out and scare people with all their might.
There favorite day is Halloween.
Because it is their day to be very mean.
They lurk in the shadows all night and all day.
They jump out and make people say,
"Oh no, it's a monster!" and run away.
Jamie Alaniz, Grade 8
St Francis de Sales School

That Special Day

All the girls are busy with their looks,
while all the boys are throwing away their books.
The girls are looking for their shoes,
as the boys just go and watch the news.
The girls are all putting on their make-up,
as the boys are still in their room dressing up.
All the mothers cry saying, "I'm so proud of you."
While only some friends get to say, "I'll see you soon."
Everyone is finally ready,
and everyone is thinking, "Just take it slow and steady."
As the first person walks down the aisle,
everyone in the room stands with a smile.
The people walk down with nice dresses and nice suits,
then the mothers say, "They're all so cute."
Finally for the moment we've been waiting for since May,
here it is, Graduation Day.

Michelle Nguyen, Grade 8
Carden Academy of Santa Clara

The Path of Life

Like an endless road, miles upon miles.
Faces change, but what stays the same is smiles.
Roads may differ, paths may part.
Blows are stricken to your heart.

It's one big race, we're all working for the final prize.
Waiting for a new competitor to arise.
Smells of sun, skin and fear.
One may shed many a tear.

Started in a mother's womb,
Ended in an empty room.
Love and Laugh.
Peace and Wrath.
This endless road may seem dire
But this is just the path of life.

Alley L. Madison, Grade 7
Los Molinos Community Elementary School

At Christmas

At Christmas
I see big Christmas trees with shiny lights
I hear presents being opened
I smell chocolate cookies and gingerbread
I taste chocolate cakes and pretzels
I feel the Christmas spirit
At Christmas
I see Rudolph on the roofs
I hear snow falling from the sky
I smell candy canes
I taste hot chocolate
I feel the snow on my hands
Christmas is a special holiday for the whole world.

Miguel Piña, Grade 7
Our Lady of the Rosary School

My Dog

My dog is a beagle.
He's better than a seagull.
He likes to run around and play with his ball.
His birthday is in the fall.
He likes it when you pet his head and body.
If you make him scared he might go potty.
He's happy when he wags his tail.
Maybe I'll teach him to get the mail.
He loves to get in the trash and make a mess.
Getting into trouble is his best.
He's not too smart or clever.
He'd look real good in a sweater.
He's black and white and brown all over.
He's super cool but he can't roll over.
I love my dog, I always will.
When it's hot outside he sits and chills.

Andrew Burdick, Grade 8
Monte Vista Christian School

Bacon

Bacon is good for breakfast or brunch
But it is even better in a BLT lunch
It lies on your plate, next to eggs or rice
And as a side, it is especially nice
It can be soft or hard or crunchy or chewy
Leave it too long and it can get quite gooey
Whether wrapped around shrimp or in little tiny bits
Bacon is versatile, no matter how it sits
When I cook bacon in just the right fashion
It's easy to tell makin' bacon's my passion
It comes from the butt of a pig its true
You eat snails an frogs, so that's nothing new
Bacon has protein and yes some fat
But it sure tastes better than possum or cat
However you serve it, let there be no mistaken'
My favorite food is definitely bacon

Kai Paresa, Grade 8
Monte Vista Christian School

The Scream*

A guy is screaming,
Nobody seems to care,
Nobody stops to help,
Something tragic is going on,
Maybe he was robbed,
Maybe he was late for something,
Maybe he's dying,
Maybe he's trying to warn everyone,
To warn them of danger that is ahead,
No one knows except for the man,
The man who screams,
The scream of the soundless scream.

Francisco Antonio Tapia, Grade 7
Tenaya Middle School
*Dedicated to Edvard Munch's "The Scream"

My Life
Sometimes I suffer,
Sometimes I enjoy.
Sometimes I wake up,
And find a new toy.

Sometimes I work hard,
And earn what I get.
Other times I procrastinate
Or even throw a fit.

Little times I'm lonely,
And dream about this life.
Many times I'm with friends,
Who save me from this knife.

All the time I know,
In my heart it says.
Never will I tell —
But it's my life, you'll guess.
Frances Abalos, Grade 7
Cope Middle School

What a Mess!
Time is running out!
Hurry, the guests are coming!
Clean, clean, clean!
Oh my, what a mess!

Wipe down that counter!
Go sweep the floor!
Pick that toy up!
Oh my, what a mess!

It is five to six!
People are on their way!
We are almost done!
Oh my, what a mess!

I can finally see the floor!
The counter is practically shining!
Knock! Knock! Knock!
I am really glad that is over!
Neena Moore, Grade 8
Richardson PREP HI Middle School

Mystery Girl
When I first looked in your eyes
It was like winning the Nobel Price
I was thinking of what to say
Though that night I prayed
If she was my love
That would be enough
Now as I lay in my bed
I was thinking what I should've said
James Mazzuca, Grade 7
St Martin-in-the-Fields School

Challenge
On my challenge I want
To be a better, smarter,
And knowledgeable guy

I am a person that's a
Little shy, and I am a
Little good at spelling

And when I am in PE, I am
Doing some yelling, I'm good
At participating in school mass

But I do much better when
I am doing one of my favorite
subjects religion, during class

The only thing I don't want to
Be is a guy who is a fool
When I am in school.
Daniel Salas, Grade 8
St Helen Catholic Elementary School

Loneliness
Everyone has deserted me
No one seems to care
Now I walk alone
How much of this shall I have to bear?

I am left in this world of emptiness
But I am not alone
My shadow keeps me company
And helps me find my way back home

Slowly, my shadow starts to fade away
The darkness is taking part of my soul
My shadow starts to split in half
Both halves are sucked into a deep hole

I start to cry, alone in the streets
Left in this homely mess
It's like it's been the end of the world
Left in the shadows of loneliness
Rachelle Tanega, Grade 7
Corpus Christi School

Dragonfly
Long, skinny, blue
Flying and fluttering in the breeze
High, between, and above the trees
Soaring, looking for a place to settle
Finally finding a great big meadow
Green, soft, wet, and dry
This is where it chooses to die
Dragonfly
Tria Slate, Grade 7
St Martin-in-the-Fields School

Trees
A tiny seed bursts
Beginning a strong new life
Rooted in the soil

Growing in springtime
After weeks now a sapling
Stronger every day

Months then years pass by
Watching over the forest
Towering above

Swaying in the breeze
I hear gently flowing leaves
Whispering my name

Now old but wiser
Broken branches from harsh winds
Bare without its green

Life is now complete
Heavily drooping over
Yelps with one last cry
Lacey Umamoto, Grade 7
Monte Vista Christian School

Muscle Cars
Camaros, Mustangs, Plymouths too,
The old ones are better than the new.

They're cool, they're fast,
And from the past.

Don't leave them out to rot and rust.
Taking good care is a must!

Wash them, wax them, buff them out.
They make the girls scream and shout.

Treat them good, they're not to trash,
If they're nice they are worth more cash.

I'm saving money every day,
In hopes that I can someday pay

For the one I want the most
The coolest one on this coast!

As you can clearly see,
Muscle cars are made for me!
Steven Souza, Grade 7
Monte Vista Christian School

Moms

Moms are   busy
Moms are   caring,
she brightens your dull day
by being the sun, she loves you,
she works really hard to keep
the house running, so
respect her, care
for, but most
of all love
her!

Mashal Yaseen, Grade 7
Carden Academy of Santa Clara

Remember

Remember when we talked on the phone,
And we talked for hours?
Remember when we hugged,
When you were sad?
Remember when we kissed,
And we fell in love:?
Remember when you moved away,
And we broke up…?
I will remember you, wherever you go.
Will you remember me?

Christian Rose, Grade 8
Corpus Christi School

Eyes That Cry

Turning myself numb
After something has gone wrong
I tilt my head back
Look up at the sky
My eyes only slits
A grim smile on my lips
A chuckle and say
"Why should I cry?
I knew this was coming
The pain hurts. I must stop crying."

Ana Monjaras, Grade 9
Santiago High School

Love Everywhere!

Love shows passion.
Love shows compassion.
It shows you.
Explains what you do.
You have a heart,
If you do your part.
Keeping best friends' friendship,
And your family's relationship.
Love is here and there.
Love is everywhere.

Marissa Yu, Grade 7
St Mary's Chinese Day School

Why Now

You left my mom crying day and night
Never seeing her smile always worried
You don't know how much things happen
You won't be there when I get sick to tell me you will be fine
You won't be there to see me play my soccer games
You won't be there when my mom is having trouble
You won't be there to give me advice when I need it
You won't be there when I shed a tear
You won't be there to tell me how was your day
You are not there when my brother needs someone to tuck him in bed
You are not there to tuck us in and say sweet dreams
You won't be there to say have a good day at school
You won't be the person telling my mom if she needs help
You won't be there to sing me happy birthday
You won't be there to tell me "Good job"
So why now?

Vanessa Barcenas, Grade 8
Richard Merkin Middle Academy

Step

Have you ever seen me cry,
or a tear drop from my eye?
Have you ever witnessed my pain or thought my love was a game?
You see me and you, we could never be the same.
Not now not ever!
I always thought we'd laugh forever.
Until that day reality changed us.
Rearranged our paths and separated us.
Don't stop me now listen to my story!
I thought I loved you but, I've just realized that my pain is because of you!
Your someone who effected my heart
and put my life to a whole new start.
If you haven't seen my tears or haven't witnessed my pain
then, I think that's what you want
because you now know that we could never be the same…

Miriah L. Billberry, Grade 8
Delta Sierra Middle School

A Day in Middle School

I wake up at a quarter past six, and sleepily poor a bowl of Trix.
I then get dressed and comb my hair. I drive to school without a care.
At cross country practice, I run countless laps. Then school closes around me like a trap.
History, science, English, math, my day is just a worn in path.
Straight after school, I catch the bus, it's here on time, now that's a plus.
Soon as I'm home, it's off to soccer, I run on the field, almost hitting a walker.
Practice goes on for hours, then home, and it's time for showers.
Dinner on the table straight away, oh shoot, it's meatloaf day.
I start my homework at seven sharp, it's spread around me like a tarp.
I crawl into bed around 9 o'clock, so exhausted, I can't even talk.
Now this, for me, is an average day, tomorrow I'll wake up, and it will all replay.

Carmen Lyon, Grade 7
Willma Cavitt Jr High School

The Seasons

The year begins in a cold wet winter,
As it rains and snows we gather by the fire,
But soon the air gets warm,
Flowers bloom and bees buzz as new animals are born,
As the year goes by the air gets hotter,
School ends and people swim in the cold ocean water,
As autumn begins we get the nice cool breezes,
The kids dress up for Halloween,
And get excited for Trick-Or-Treating,
People get ready for the holidays,
They shop and cook and wrap for days,
As we go back to the cold wet weather,
A new year begins and the seasons will start all over again.

Allysa Barrett, Grade 8
Chico Jr High School

Rose Gift

A rose is like a gift of love
So bright and red like a heart
It seems like magic when you glare
But only happens if you care

When time goes by it starts to dry
Turns brown and ugly with the sky
By morning only thorns are there
Which hurts to see the love ain't there
You think love ain't a fairy tale
Tears fill your eyes when nothing's there
Then months go by a bloom is there
Your rose is back and love is there

Consuelo Langarica, Grade 8
Los Molinos Community Elementary School

Rain

The sound woke you up this morning
It is soothing
The pit-pat against the window pane
Slowly lulling you back to sleep
Then jumping with fright when you hear the thunder
There is no choice but to get up
But the chilly air keeps you from moving from the covers
So you lay in bed listening to the rain
Thinking of the wet day ahead

Lily Marmolejo, Grade 7
Mayfield Jr School of the Holy Child Jesus

Friends

F riendship is like a second family
R emembering the memories that you shared
I nfinite nights of fun
E veryone gets along
N othing is kept a secret
D istance is hard
S leep overs are a key to friendship

Sakthi Ponnuswamy, Grade 7
Carden Academy of Santa Clara

Summer Day

I was sitting outdoors enjoying a wonderful summer day
As the birds were out to play
The smell of the flowers is so very sweet
As we listen to the birds go tweet, tweet, tweet
The butterflies dance across the green grass
As I sit and wish the day would not pass
The wind was whispering back at me
As the cats were swinging from the tree
The dogs lay sound asleep
As they soak up the summer heat
The sky is so blue
It sparkles like brand new
The wind chimes make a wonderful sound
As my family and I gather around
An occasional butterfly stops to say hi
As we sit and dream, the day goes by

Nichole Banovac, Grade 7
Monte Vista Christian School

Life

Life can sometimes be difficult,
especially if your family isn't united.
Some people aren't fortunate,
many of them live in an orphanage.
Life is a very special present,
and some people don't value it.
We only get one shot at life,
so we should be wise on how we use it.
If you are involved in bad things,
you might be saying good-bye to your life.
Part of life is having a family,
at least that's what's important to mostly everybody.
So please nobody be a fool,
value your life and you'll be cool.
Like I have said before,
we only get one shot at life and no more.

Rudy Soto, Grade 8
Isbell Middle School

Music

Music is like a friend who is always there for you,
Pop, jazz, R&B, and country too
Whenever I listen to my favorite tune
It's always in my head the whole afternoon

At the dances I love to sing
With my friends while we dance in a ring,
I've always got a tune in my head,
During school, swim practice, and even in bed.

I love to listen to meaningful songs
Put them to music and I'll sing along!
Music is in my heart and my soul
And I know I'll never have to let it go!

Shweta Tatkar, Grade 8
Carden Academy of Santa Clara

Creation

Every stroke was brushed with care,
Every mark was made with love,
Every line held a deep passion,
It was his masterpiece.

Every move showed her incredible grace,
Every leap was full of control,
Every twirl was spun with delight,
This was her dream.

Every shot was thrown with held breath,
Every jump was like his goals,
Every point was earned with joy,
He loved his sport.

Every day was filled with hope,
Every night was filled with prayers,
Every second was noticed for its value,
This was the fight for her life.

Every person was formed unique,
Every personality was created its own,
Every feature was perfect,
He knew what He was doing.
He saw what He had made and said that it was good!

Faith Hughes, Grade 8
Joe Walker Middle School

The Day That Changed Our Lives

The screams of sirens,
And people running down the street.
Implosions heard off in the distance, then silence.
Prayers being made by millions of people,
Hoping everything will be okay.

Courage comes up on those who try to save lives,
But many are lost.
Families are horrified by losing loved ones.
Honor goes to those firemen, policemen, paramedics,
And pedestrians who helped that day.

The flag still flying high above us.
A ray of hope in a mass of chaos,
The look of patriotism in one's eye.
Bright sun filtering through the debris.
We are fighting for what's right.

Although it took a matter of seconds to fall,
The thousands of lives that were lost,
Left families heart broken, for a lifetime.

Why, why us, why now?
What will this prove? Nothing
Can't we just all get along?

Courtney Sheppard, Grade 8
Ripona Elementary School

When He Came Home

There is no way I could describe
I never stepped beside
The idea of death
His one last breath

I kept believing that it would not end up to be
How everybody expected him to see
Everyone and everything would change
In the eyes of his battlefield range

He arrived when I thought he was gone
I could not have doubted him when he showed up on the lawn
His eyes patched with black leather
And a colleague on his arm, just in case he fell like a feather

It was when he walked through the door
When I felt that I needed him more
My soldier, my hero was here
All he could do was hear

My voice, was comfort to his ears
I felt like I heard cheers
When I saw him for a moment, it was no chore
I hugged him, and cried, my husband, my soldier, my hero,
    was blind and back from war.

Isabella Gantman, Grade 8
Kadima Day School

Who Am I?

Who am I?
I'm the person you love to hate.
I'm the person you start to like.
I'm the person you will never forget.

Who am I?
I'm the girl that's too shy to talk.
I'm the girl that will make a fool of herself
just to make you laugh.
I'm the girl that isn't perfect.

Who am I?
I'm a teenage girl that's a wannabe adult.
I'm a teenage girl that will walk the line but never cross it.
I'm a teenage girl that isn't fully there.

Who am I?
I could be your girlfriend or your worst nightmare.
I could be your dream girl or your enemy.
I could be the nerdiest girl or your best friend.

Who am I?
I'm everybody and nobody.
I'm everything you want to be.
I'm just me, myself, and I.

Abbygail Whitlock, Grade 8
Ripona Elementary School

High Merit Poems – Grades 7, 8 and 9

I Remember
The day I never thought would happen.
I remember everything that happened and the pain.
As I remember everybody's faces sad and crying.
It seems like it wasn't enough time.
Wishing you were still here with me.
All I have are memories.
This helps me be strong and never give up.
I will always remember my sister's death.

Rosalinda Martinez, Grade 8
Isbell Middle School

Death, We Only Fear What We Don't Know!
Yet fear is what makes us feel alive.
Familiarity breeds comfort,
The unknown breeds doubt.
Will this be your last sunset?
Will you ever eat ice cream again?
Will you ever feel the way he makes you feel right now?
The uncertainty keeps us on a rim.
Sharp, living, in suspense, and at the edge of possibility.

Natascha Czekaj, Grade 8
Walter F Dexter Middle School

The Sound of Color
Silver is high-pitched, high as the sky.
Red is loud, BANGS BOOMS! Louder than explosions.
Pink is like water drops,
Getting s l o w e r each second.
Yellow is a storm twirling all the world.
White is so plain, just no sound at all.
Blue is mellow, a sweet symphony.
Feeling the sound is all you need.

Hojun Kim, Grade 7
J L Academy

Nature's Beauty
Nature is beautiful in many ways
The sky is like a lake that gleams and shine brightly
The land is a everlasting green field
The ocean sway around like it is trying to reach somewhere
Nature is so beautiful
But only if you look closely
That you will see this beauty around you

Angelique Nguyen, Grade 7
Jordan Secondary Learning Center

Island in the Sea
Island in the sea, a heart of independency,
Freedom that is vested, not trying to be bested
A clock that's untimely, complete and totally free,
Percussion that protested, sound gone untested
A heart that none can see, one that is let be
A bird that has nested, a soul that has rested
Island in the sea, alone but not lonely.

Joey Tansey, Grade 8
Palm Desert Charter Middle School

The Mayan's Calendar
The Mayan's calendar ends,
On that date December 21, 2012
They believed that on that date
The world would come
To a destructive end
The Mayans were an ancient race,
That live today in Guatemala
Their calendar was made long ago,
Maybe around 600 AD
All we know is that is ends,
On that date December 21, 2012
No one is sure how it will end,
Or even if it will end at all
People say it could end in many ways
Like a big disaster, meteorites, and even black holes
But then again, it might not end at all
But just like the day it might just reset
But if it is the end,
It will be a tragic day
All we can do, is have no regrets
And wait…till 2012

Rafael Nunez, Grade 8
Richardson PREP HI Middle School

My Family
My family is mine
My family is beautiful
My family is small, but grand
My family is small, but not too small you see
Or we wouldn't be in harmony
My family of sisters, brothers, nieces, nephews, cousins, and more
Some I know and some I don't know as well
My family of older
My family of younger
Some play bingo
Some play tag
That doesn't matter as long as they're with me
Even if they don't know me so well
They love me
And I love them too

BridgeAnne d'Avignon, Grade 7
Monte Vista Christian School

Reflection on Escher's Relativity
Normal and peaceful activities happening
Yet so confusing
Stairways being used everywhere
Leading to somewhere
The unknown
Faceless beings, about to their regular jobs
Nothing stopping them from accomplishing their goals
Up, down, left, or right
Like a puzzle made upside down
Which staircase should you take?

Ravi Aulakh, Grade 7
Tenaya Middle School

Drifting Apart

You are always together,
Leaving me alone.
Whenever we're together,
I feel I don't even
know you any more.
You changed into a person
I don't even recognize.
Our friendship's drifting apart
like leaves scattered by
cold winds.

Rheanna Ostrea, Grade 8
Corpus Christi School

Volleyball

V ery competitive sport
O utside hitter
L ibero
L ove to dive for the ball
E nthusiastic all the time
Y elling out "Mine!"
B locking
A ttacking
L istening to your coach
L oving your teammates

Stephanie Sam, Grade 7
Carden Academy of Santa Clara

Sunsets

All the time around dusk
Night begins its arrival
The sky streaks colors of all
Red, orange, and pink too
Making the night sky
Like a natural light show
It's hard to believe
That this happens almost every day
But most people don't notice
But I do…

Miguel Lopez, Grade 8
August Boeger Middle School

Life

It can be sweet
Or it can be sour
You can be happy
Or you can be mad
You can be quiet
Or you can be loud
You can be bored
Or you can have a ball
You can be you
And that's honestly all.

Tyler Oliver, Grade 8
Long Valley Charter School

Night Stalker

He waits by the window — waiting for his love
She's out in the distance
He can see her and can't wait to bathe in her beauty
Slowly creeping out the window
Hoping that she doesn't see
Her beauty illuminates the streets as the night falls upon him,
The stalker knows he can never have her…
She's impossible to hold down.
She doesn't know he even exists — she's too good.
He tries to reach out for her
So they can finally get to know each other
But — she's unreachable.
She walks with the stars
She shines just like them
She's desired by all the men
He's the only one that seems to try to make something out of nothing
Strangers into lovers — unknown souls into soulmates
Time is running out — he has to do it now before he loses his chance
He calls out her name, but she continues to shine away from him
The *beautiful moon* is now gone…
She left him, and now he must return to grieve for another day.

Caridad Barocio, Grade 8
August Boeger Middle School

The Little Girl with Big Hopes

Who would cry for the little girl cold in the winter's night,
Who would cry for the girl frightened of the far away light,
It is I that would cry,
Cry myself to sleep thinking that one day I might be,
The little girl that cries inside of me,
As much as I try,
I just rather cry,
Wishing I could fly,
Somewhere far away,
If someone would have known how I feel inside,
Knowing that I wouldn't want to be here alone,
I just rather it not be shown,
But we all have our fears,
Our day would be near,
That one day the time could be near we all should do something for nothing.

Ms. Specialjoy Alexander, Grade 8
Charles Maclay Middle School

Christmas Tree

Christmas tree, oh Christmas tree, oh how you would not cooperate
Because you insisted on leaning, you finally met your fate
Now you are down in the cold, dark basement
And mom brought in a beautiful replacement
Your replacement is adorned in splendor, even though it's a lender
It stands tall and straight, it's definitely not your mate
You just had to, lean, lean; lean until you were a pile of green
I hope you now find peace in the county dump; we will try to forget your thump
When you hit the floor and went soaring out the door
Now you are no more.

Clint Barsi, Grade 8
Monte Vista Christian School

Heroes

When it comes to a hero, there's only one
He doesn't wear capes and can't lift a ton
He can't fly or run at the speed of light
He doesn't dress up in boots or long tights
He doesn't turn green when he gets mad
He doesn't start a storm when he gets sad
He doesn't have three blades hidden in his hands
He doesn't have indestructible internal glands
He doesn't have spider powers, yes that's true
But hopefully he lives inside of you
He can be found deep within your heart
And each day he lets you have a brand new start
He sacrificed himself on a cross for us
and when He did He didn't complain or make a fuss
When you say his name the world is filled with glee
In my opinion, Jesus is the only hero for me!

Jordan Mazza, Grade 8
Monte Vista Christian School

Present

Early floods sail up the plateau
and swifts over leaving fresh scent
reaching up the high arch where man may rest
while scanning the careless waves
The dew mashed over the walls
and meant it like any subliminal sightseeing

Winds purge noises sound and sweet
but no more mysterious to the warm car
but they still have yet to see moonlight
As the sun long ago departs

The moon and arch so crescent
makes good for a poem
bring back the recent past
And clarify what clouds my mind.

Fernando Ballesteros, Grade 8
Charles Maclay Middle School

Don't Know You

I just met you
and I barely know you.
I wanted to get to know you,
but I decided too late.
I know I can't do anything about it now,
now that you already have someone,
someone who is lucky to be with you.
Maybe you're not what I think you are,
maybe you're only what I wish you were,
but maybe you're what I've always hoped.
It doesn't matter anymore.
I guess I'm better off not knowing you at all,
Because I just don't want to get hurt once more.

Roni Nievera, Grade 7
Corpus Christi School

Animal Harm

Look at me I'm a cat
But not only that
I'm an experiment in a cage
I have so much rage

But you, you keep giving me needles and pain
All for your research will you find your fame?

I had a home on the streets
But that has been taken from me
I'm a true, harmless, and loyal feline
But look inside me, my heart is dying

Look at me I'm an elephant born in the wild
But that was when I was only a child
Now, I'm being trained to follow my master
Tied by chains to make the learning go faster

Those chains broke my leg so my master forgot me
What's left of me now? Nobody wants me
Now, I'm at a freak show where everyone sighs
Because beside them is an elephant who has no more life

I'd like to be fed, bathed, and loved
But that wasn't the case you sent me up above

Kelly Lauren Muller, Grade 8
Richardson PREP HI Middle School

Teenage Love

So, there is thing called 'teenage love'
The type of love that means the world
A hit and miss
The type of love that makes you want to wake up,
And dance at midnight, singing, doing twirls

So, there is this thing called 'teenage love'
A feeling like no other
When you lock eyes for that split second
Forcing yourself to look away
Then you realize,
That's your best friend's brother

So, there is thing called 'teenage love'
They say it's so great
You don't want to fall asleep,
Because life seems better when you're awake

We have all had a 'teenage love'
Even though they broke your heart
You never thought you left your feelings so far
The breakup was hard, wondering why he left you
You never noticed what happened behind closed doors
No matter how bad it may hurt, we never forget our first.

Krystal Nzeadibe, Grade 8
William B Bristow Middle School

The End

Never hope for the end, for the end will come to you,
Through sleep, through thoughts, through speech.
You cannot avoid it, no matter if you hide,
Run, flee or become another,
It will search until the day it shall…
Envelope you in its arms!
Strangle your thoughts! It will find the most precious one!
It will drain you of hope! It will whisper to you…
You then wince! And hide from it,
You know it will find you — wherever you hide,
You do not wish to hear the whisper,
That hideous whisper before you pass…on.
You hear it, you think,
You open your mouth, yet the words never come out!
You panic! You prepare to scream!
Your words haunt you! They —
You hear it! You heard it!
You forget everything!
However, the whisper…
…The whisper…
The whisper of death.

Amanda Pinski, Grade 7
California Montessori Project - Shingle Springs Campus

Where I'm From

I'm from Forever 21 v-necks, jean shorts, scarves
Listening to Taylor Swift on the drive
Dancing to Lady Gaga
I'm from a house like all others
"Clean up your room" no pools, no jet skies
Love and care is all I need in my house
I'm from cruising once a year
Mexico, Canada, Panama Canal
Dark Friday shopping at 4 a.m.
"I shop, I drop, and then roll to the next store"
I'm from "Eat Fresh"
Homemade macaroni and cheese with hot dogs on top
From orange chicken and broccoli beef
Friday morning trip to Jamba Juice
I'm from a reality TV family
Watching *Big Brother* three nights a week
Voting for my favorite on *So You Think You Can Dance*
I'm from the comfort of forgiveness
Knowing that I will be with Him soon enough
Strengthening my faith one day at a time from Philippians 4:8
I'm from "everything happens for a reason"

Kelly Coson, Grade 7
Grace Lutheran School

Ice Cream

ICE CREAM, it takes you to your HAPPY place,
but the longer it's exposed to heat, the faster it MELTS away.
It is smooth, creamy, but sometimes CHUNKY.
ICE CREAM. There are no 2 flavors that taste the same.

Pamela Ygrubay, Grade 7
Immaculate Heart of Mary School

Smudge

My dog, Smudge, has floppy ears,
Colors on his body look like smears,
Two colored eyes, blue and brown
It's really trippy when he stares you down,
When you think the cold has you in defeat,
Smudge plays "Slippers" on your feet,
When he wants attention, he will root,
Under your armpit, it's so cute,
I can smell impending doom,
Smudge can really clear the room,
Someone can drown, when he drools,
Smudge can fill a swimming pool,
Smudge can burp really loud,
You can hear him in a crowd,
Smudge destroys his toys way too quick,
Maybe we should give him a brick,
As an Aussie, he likes to grin,
At tug-of-war we try to win,
I love everything about him, except his breath,
It's like receiving the Kiss of Death.

Derek McFate, Grade 7
Monte Vista Christian School

The Hikers

The water bangs and crashes
The hikers pass ignoring it
The beautiful volcano is covered in snow so quietly
The hikers ignore the magnificent sight
The sharp rocks look fierce, just waiting for a fall
Whoops!
Someone slips…but no fall
The hikers ignore the near death experience
The slip
The fall
The rock
The death
The wind yanks the boat to the sharp rocks
It tips
It crashes
It burns
The hikers continue walking while ignoring this tragedy
We…are like this
We…ignore
We…are the hikers in this world

Cheyenne Collins, Grade 7
Daniel Savage Middle School

Friends

They're always there when you need a hug.
They make you laugh and give you love.
Sometimes they make you mad and start to bug.
When they act weird and silly I just shrug.
They're always there when you call.
Ready to catch you if you fall.

Laurisa Sanchez, Grade 8
St Francis de Sales School

Dancing Is Life

Dancing brings joy, passion, soul to the stage.
Can make people cry or light up their face.
Dances are as good as how much love and heart you put in them.
We don't just make friends, we create a family,
They suffer, cry, and bleed right along with me.
I hope I'll never have to tell them good-bye,
We've made memories that will never die.
Every time I fall I come back around,
I'm hoping to capture the perfect sound.
Music is beauty that comes deep from within,
I let the world see what I have hidden.
Never say never, you can do anything,
If your hearts right, your mind will be free.
Dancing is energy, through time and through space.
Never let any movement go to waste.

Stephanie Hernandez, Grade 8
Palm Desert Charter Middle School

Are You Listening?

There are many choices out there.
So are you listening?
I've tried to help you all along.
So are you listening?
It's time to change and get a better life.
So are you listening?
If you don't want my help, then I'll walk away.
So are you listening?
Because this is what you need to hear.
If you're not listening, then I can't help you.
So are you listening?
It's time to take a stand in your pride.
So are you listening?
I can't help you anymore if you don't want to hear me.
Good-bye.

Sammy Sullivan, Grade 7
Lucerne Valley Jr/Sr High School

The Truth That Lies Within

When you speak
Are you yourself or a natural alibi you created —
This is your mask.
The mask prevents you from being your true self.
This mask is made from all of your lies.
Lies for good and for bad
Selfish lies
Hurtful lies
Lies to protect others and lies to protect something you care about.
Your mask feeds off these lies
Until
You can barely tell the truth.
We all hide behind these masks
Because we all lie…we can't control this aspect
All we can do is use it.

Russell Adjei, Grade 7
Tenaya Middle School

Inspiration

My blessed muse, whisper in my ear,
All of the secrets I long to hear.
Are star-crossed lovers never meant to be?
My personal muse whisper the answers to me.
The world unveiled I may never see,
If my muse doesn't open the door for me.
I have become solely dependent on you,
To take your leave, I give you your cue.
My cursed muse leave my ear,
Your toxins I no longer care to hear.
I was made by someone's creation,
To be my own blessed inspiration.

Taylor Partin-Majerus, Grade 8

Promise Me

Promise me that you'll be true
No matter what I say to you
Promise me that we'll be together
Today, tomorrow, and forever
Promise me that you'll catch me when I fall
Through thick and thin, throughout it all
Promise me that you won't go away
My heart will stop, memories will start to fade
Promise me that you won't forget the past
Cherish each moment, make it last
You'll always be my one true
I promise, I promise, I promise you.

Janine Lano, Grade 8
St Francis de Sales School

The Sky

The bright blue sky shining like a star
The bright yellow sun beating down its rays
Then clouds come blocking the sky
Turning the sky gray,
Rolling like if it was a ball down the street
Dropping their big balls of water
Making puddles and puddles of water
Animals waiting till it stops, others enjoying every minute of it
Then it stops
Animals are happy others are sad
And the sky is bright blue again
And the sun shines again

Astrid Salazar, Grade 8
Palm Desert Charter Middle School

Love

Love is a gift from God
to spend time with our family and friends.
Love is happiness.
It may be difficult to find its true meaning,
but the true meaning will always be in one's own heart.

Elsa Orozco, Grade 7
Our Lady of the Rosary School

I Am

I am Andrew Grindeland
I see my family and friends
I hear the waves crashing down like thunder
I feel the wind going across my face like a tornado
I am joyful and happy

I dream that one day that I will become something important
I worry that one day I might become a recluse
I hope that one day I can skydive
I am joyful and happy

I understand that school is mandatory
I try to be as helpful as I can be
I say that I can touch the stars
I touch the sand from the beach
I am Andrew Grindeland I am joyful and happy

Andrew Grindeland, Grade 8
Palm Desert Charter Middle School

My Friend?

I know you're with me all the time,
but sometimes, you don't act like a real friend.

You insult me,
but say "just kidding" at the end.

You slapped my face really hard one time,
just because I said something wrong.
I don't even know what to say to you anymore.

We shared secrets and we promised not to tell anyone.
But one day YOUR friend knew MY secret.
I had really trusted you…

Can I still trust you after what you said?
Or should we still be friends after everything you've done?

Erika Olazo, Grade 8
Corpus Christi School

My Heart

When I was born,
I came out shouting, crying, whining, and tearing up.
In front of me I saw a person:
Her eyes watering with joy.
I am set in her arms,
And suddenly
I am calm.
When I looked up
I realized
She was my mom.
She had a beautiful face;
A face I knew would love me forever.
And it still does.

Arianna Bratton, Grade 7
Tenaya Middle School

My Dad

My dad is unique;
He glows like the morning sun.
He knows how to have fun.
He laughs and plays with all his family,
And he is jolly like Kris Kringle.
When one of us does something bad,
He doesn't yell and doesn't get mad;
He helps us understand we did something wrong,
So we can be good people all our lives,
I love my dad very much;
I never want him to leave.
I'm glad I have a family for eternity!

Laura Latch, Grade 8
Junipero Serra School

Music Is Awesome

Whenever I'm sad, there is something that cheers me up.
It's music, music is awesome!
Songs tell me to be stronger and face all my problems.
The melodies are beautiful, and the words are inspirational.
The artists express how I feel when I'm sad,
But real life love is different,
It's part of your heart.
Love cannot be expressed through notes and rhythm,
While music may give you an idea of love,
Love is more like the wind,
You can't see it,
But you can feel it all over.

Xian Yin, Grade 9
Hiram W Johnson High School

Why Can't We Be Friends…Again

We used to be best friends…
really tight, close best friends.
We used to tell each other everything,
every little detail —
We shared even the most unimportant things.
I miss our old memories and the fun times we used to have.
Where did all those go?
Down the drain?
Why did we throw it away?
Just for a fight?
Why can't we be friends again?

Alice Saidawi, Grade 8
Corpus Christi School

Lego Mindstorm's First Lego League

There once was a boy with some bricks
He programmed them to do all kinds of tricks
When he looked at the screen
He saw he scored two fifteen
All with one simple click

Alec Schardein, Grade 8
Park View Middle School

Michael O'Toole

I am Michael O'Toole.
I see kids as they go from class to class.
I hear my teachers as they teach me.
I feel the wind as I ride up to my friend's house.
I am a teenager I am Michael O'Toole.

I dream of getting a college degree in criminal justice.
I worry about my brothers and sisters and how they are doing.
I want to be smart and have a good education when I grow up.
I hope I do well on my test.
I am a teenager I am Michael O'Toole.

I understand that if you work hard you will succeed.
I try my best.
I say that I will be well educated and I mean it.
I touch my pencil as I begin the test my first step to an education.
I am a teenager I am Michael O'Toole.

Michael O'Toole, Grade 8
Palm Desert Charter Middle School

Sanctuary

Here is the society of light,
Bright, calm, and open to the sea.
A place I will go without a fight,
Somewhere perfect just for me.

In my place I see all,
With my ever-changing eyes.
I ignore those who seek to fall,
Into the arms of their demise.

My place will live until the end of time,
Always changing to fit the owner's needs.
Someday my children will read this rhyme,
Then they will run to this place at all speeds.

The numbers of places like mine may vary,
Still, this place is my Sanctuary.

Marissa McTaggart, Grade 8
Encore High School for the Performing Arts

My Sister

As I wake up in the mornings,
I think about my sister.
I am her only example.
I wonder if today I will set her a good example.
I want the best for her
And I love her.
She sometimes gets on my last nerve,
But I deal with it.
I know she sometimes hates me
And I sometimes hate her too.
However, I must help her through life.
My sister is my sister and I love her no matter what happens.

Yesenia Garcia, Grade 8
Isbell Middle School

A Fading Friend

You were a special friend to me.
We shared secrets,
And we would always talk to each other.
We didn't hate or lie,
We were friends who helped one another.
But now, since you've been talking with someone else,
Rather than me,
I feel left out…
You barely talk to me,
But if I try to talk to you,
Your other friend would just disrupt me.
Your friend seems so mean.
Maybe I'm jealous, but
I don't know what to do.
I think our friendship is going, going, gone.
I feel so sad.
I thought we were friends forever,
But it seems our friendship is fading fast away.

Janessa Madarang, Grade 8
Corpus Christi School

World War II

The stillness of the night,
As the planes fly overhead,
Who else will be taken by these deadly spheres,
Everyone's heart pounds as they hear the "hum" of the engine,
Heads are throbbing, people are panicking, when will it end?

Fear pulses through the veins of the innocent spectators,
The tension, the urge, and will to be quiet and motionless,
Why, why, why me,
How could this possibly solve anything,
But it is not all bad…

The hope for freedom, and relief when the war is over,
The day our veterans finally come home,
The unity the war brings to the nation,
The freedom to finally be won,
Only then will our hearts finally be filled with triumph!

Sienna Starck, Grade 8
Ripona Elementary School

When I Open My Eyes

When I open my eyes I see what you can't see
When I open my eyes I see one true way
When I open my eyes I see Love around me
When I open my eyes I see a white dove representing peace
When I open my eyes I see the wonderful colors of Peace
When I open my eyes I see the Spirit of God in me
When I open my eyes I see white wings protecting me
When I open my eyes I see the blessings of God all over me
When I open my eyes I see a small gold crown
With my name representing my Honor and Glory
Open your eyes wide and see the wonders of life

Maria Espinosa, Grade 9
Weber Institute of Applied Sciences & Technology

You and Me
I had to be honest with you and me
I had to clear my feelings
Afraid to let go of you
But you make me feel uncomfortable with your words
Sad to look at you in the eyes
Nervously I had to tell you
Shaking I said goodbye
Quietly I looked for your reaction
Crying I tasted my tears
Slowly I turned and walked away
Now thinking about you makes me cry
I hardly talk to you anymore
I suddenly look at you and miss you
Finally know what I feel for you
I am happy to know that you are happy

Griselda C. Santoyo, Grade 9
Hiram W Johnson High School

Christmas
Christmas is my favorite time of the year,
Especially when Santa and the reindeer appear;
In my house the aroma of cookies drifts in the air,
It makes me want to eat them everywhere.

My stocking is filled right to the top,
And I hope that day will never stop;
There is an angel at the top of the tree,
It reminds me of the story I heard when I was three.

The story is about Jesus Christ who was born on Christmas Day,
He was placed in a manger that was full of hay;
He was born to save us when we fall,
All we have to do is call;
And that is why Jesus is the greatest gift of all.

Kate Moody, Grade 7
Joe Walker Middle School

Thoughts on M.C. Escher's Bond of Union
Love and compassion
All wrapped up
They are blinded from the rest of the world
Only them, only those two
Lost in one another's eyes
Gazing with love and compassion
True love is there
There's no separation
They share the same thoughts
They leave humanity behind
Out into space
They trample
They have not transportation
But by love they carried
Such strong love.

Samantha Swan, Grade 7
Tenaya Middle School

Of Fields and Flowers
Have you ever slept beneath a starry sky?
Heard grasses murmur and breezes sigh?
Or smelled a lily all in white,
Fragrance sweet and petals bright?
Consider the fields and flowers that grow,
These that create an earthbound rainbow…

But the beauty of these simple things we often fail to see,
When caught up in the busy world of I, myself, and me.
Can you imagine a world bereft of flowers, grass, and sky?
I am sure, if this occurred, our hearts would break and die.
So don't take flowers for granted — admire their vivid hues!
Go take a walk! Go climb a tree! Go sing, and dance, and muse!
Take every moment captive and give every day your best,
Rejoice in nature's bounty and live your life with zest!

Teal Speece, Grade 9
South Sutter Charter School

Storm
Somewhere in the distance
Somebody
Will be standing
Looking up at the same sky
And letting the rain kiss their face.

I wander along the meadows
Deep in my own thought
Brushing my hand along the tall grass
Tiny pearls and diamonds tickling my fingers.
Clouds rolling by
Begin to rumble.
The sweet scent of earth
Surrounds,
Buries itself deep down.

Sara Clausen, Grade 9
Woodbridge High School

Where Poetry Hides for Me
Poetry hides in my journal lying on my bed.
It hides in my two little cousins' smiles.
It hides in my brother's beautiful green eyes.
Poetry hides underneath the flesh of my grandpa.
In the front yard where all the trees and bugs are.
In every single dust bunny under my bed.
Poetry hides in all the folds of each blanket in my hall closet.
It hides underneath the pupil of my eye.
It hides with my mom's teeth when she smiles.
It hides in all of my fiction books filled with adventure.
It hides underneath my baby cousin's drool.
It hides will all of my memories.
It hides with all the tears I've shed with joyful moments.
It hides in all of my favorite books.
And at last it hides inside of me.

Mariah Massey, Grade 7
Tenaya Middle School

Night Animals

Owls hoot while soaring
All the day animals are snoring.

Bats flutter around in search of food.
Raccoons' food searching way is rather rude.

Badgers tunnel through the ground
Wolves make a dreadful howling sound.

Foxes trample through the night.
Watching a Jaguar kill is a disturbing sight.

Mosquitoes may carry a deadly disease
Skunks feed on mice, beetle, and flees.

Owls, bats, and wolves alike,
They all must do their own fight.

Huda Khwaja, Grade 7
Home School

I Am Kody

I am Kody
I see the blue sky
I hear dogs barking and birds chirping
I feel the cool wind on my skin
I am an eighth grader

I dream that there will be world peace
I worry the world will come to an end
I want a clean environment
I hope to succeed
I am just a boy

I understand no one or anything is perfect
I will try my best
I say always work hard, play hard
I touch the world because it will always touch me
I am Kody just an eighth grade boy

Kody Punt, Grade 8
Palm Desert Charter Middle School

Best Friends

I'll stand by your side,
Even if you have cried.
I'll never leave you alone,
And help you out when you don't know.
I'll help you fight your fights,
And help you out at nights.
I'll never leave you out even it we are mad,
And I will help you out when you are sad.
I'll always have your back in good or bad,
And I will never leave you because you're the best friend I ever had.
I'll be there until the end,
Because you're my best friend.

Perla Aguirre, Grade 8
Richard Merkin Middle Academy

A Puppet on Strings

As I choose my words carefully
And explain them with strength
I am easily shut down
With that six-letter word

"Enough" is what I hear shortly
As I try my best to improvise, I am quickly sent away
Why is this happening?
I'm old enough to make proper decisions

Everything seems to be controlled for me
And I just don't understand why
As I shut the door, I feel as if
My hands are behind my back and my legs are tied together.

As I mentally try and free myself
I feel TRAPPED
I lie sprawled upon my bed
Thinking the past incident over

As I tighten my fists and clench my teeth
I feel as if I am a puppet on strings.

Sarah Abughrib, Grade 7
Corpus Christi School

Home Is Where…

My family is.
the warm feeling of love and free-spiritedness
memories cherished and never forgotten

home is where
I dance around my bedroom
music playing
me smiling
memories never forgotten

home is where
you watch the Christmas tree being put up
shiny stars and dreams of presents and family
memories never forgotten

Jessica Ritchie, Grade 8
Richardson PREP HI Middle School

Death

As you look at the world through your eyes
It's like a movie; it must end at some time

You never know when the game is going to end
Or if the sun will stop its shine

I guess it's God's way of saying it's your time
It's not like you can say goodbye or goodnight

Death is just a part of life

Braelynn Gasper, Grade 7
Lucerne Valley Jr/Sr High School

Beneath the Stars
Looking at the bright shining stars in the sky
We are always hoping the light will never die.
Each of those stars is a truly magnificent sight
With their gleaming lights which are astonishingly bright.

Zooming swiftly across the endless space
Shooting stars look like they are playing an exciting game of chase.
Soaring through the dark night sky
Watching them dart over you and I.

Lying on the ground with not a soul around
Not even a tiny cricket makes a sound.
Gazing up into the universe
Into the galaxy we immerse.

From where we lie
Looking into the night sky
I see the diamonds glistening in the reflection of your eye.
It makes me happy to hear your captivated sigh.

For we see that the wonders in the universe above
Make us think about the people we know and love.
Oh how I wish we could soar amidst the stars so high
To be surrounded by them till the day I die.

Kevin Amarasekera, Grade 8
St Martin-in-the-Fields School

Basketball, the Most Amazing Sport Ever
Basketball is very fun,
It is the best sport,
Not as much in the sun,
Jacob has the best court.

It is the best sport,
It's also fun to watch,
Jacob has the best court,
Lakes are so amazing, whoever plays them it's a mismatch.

It's also fun to watch,
Whoever does not like basketball has an issue,
Lakers are so amazing, whoever plays them it's a mismatch,
I'll be more than happy to provide them with a tissue.

Whoever does not like basketball has an issue,
It is a great experience to go to their games,
I'll be more than happy to provide them with a tissue,
Many of the players get to the Hall of Fame.

It is a great experience to go to their games,
Not as much in the sun,
Many of the players get to the Hall of Fame,
Basketball is very fun.

Nima Natanzi, Grade 8
Kadima Day School

Hand in Hand
Sunshine sweeps across the room
lighting everything in its path
people helping people
makes our hearts shine like gold
mother nature verses human nature
makes global warming and the earth is going insane
gangs, violence, drugs, and weapons
make our cities and towns unsafe
people cheating on each other
make us feel useless and helpless
movies and music showing kids bad stuff
it makes us think it's right
BUT NO
hand in hand
we can make this a better place

Victoria Huynh, Grade 7
Sarah McGarvin Intermediate School

The Sun
Shining over me so beautiful and strong,
Helping the plants grow and giving us food
Bringing us life to move along!

Glowing so brightly and giving us heat,
You made the world the way it is now
The wonderful land under our very feet!

All of the Earth's trees and flowers,
Made by you and your shining light
Leaving us wondering what is your next power!

Sadly the story of the great sun ends,
When the moon rises and the sun falls West
At daybreak the sun awakens and rises again!

Brandon Tracy, Grade 7
Joe Walker Middle School

Aphrodite's Song
The sound of laughter floating in the breeze
Nine young maidens dancing through the trees
Aphrodite's song sounds very sweet
As she slaughters with a cold heat

Just one look, an enchanted smile
To pull you deep into denial

She will lure you into her fortress
Look at her a good young murderess

She came and rose out of the sea
And reigns with terror on you and me

Shelby Brown, Grade 7
St Francis de Sales School

High Merit Poems – Grades 7, 8 and 9

This Is America

What's happened to us, oh America? Sweet America
Once the land of the free,
and opportunity.
Such a promising seed,
now a forest of weeds.

What's happened to us, oh America? Dying America
The people's voice is long gone
how can this nation succeed?
Democracy is replaced,
by politics and greed.

What's happened to us, oh America? Our America
We're a nation under God,
let's change; now or never.
Restore our great country,
righteousness forever!

What's happened to us, oh America? Beautiful America
We must work fast to clean,
the corruption unseen.
From sea to shining sea.
bring back democracy!!

Matthew Tsai, Grade 9
Walnut High School

Skimboarding

I jumped on my board;
I felt the wind blow past me as I soared.

As I moved faster and faster,
I prayed to avoid a disaster.

Turning out the sounds of laughter and cries of the sea,
I focused on my board down in front of me.

All of a sudden, I felt my feet slip;
I hit the sand hard after I did a flip.

I pushed myself up to gasp for air.
I held up my head and shook my wet hair.

I looked for my board down on the beach;
I sighed with relief when I saw it was within reach.

Determined to never give up, I jumped back on.
I caught five waves before the break of dawn.

It was the beginning of a perfect day;
I wouldn't spend it any other way.

Luke Brown, Grade 7
Monte Vista Christian School

A Year's too Long

When death comes by,
You wave hello and goodbye;
The presence of those who have gone,
Remain a simple memory, remembered at dawn.

The sweet feelings of the past
Are known to never last,
Though their lives have come to a halt
You must remember it was no one's fault.

A year's too long
But the memories remain strong

The comfort and the console,
Can never heal the broken soul;
Not even the warmest smile,
Is worth anyone's while.

A sunset comes around,
A new day is crowned
Looking up to the sky,
When death comes by;
You wave hello and goodbye.

Ifeoma Ufondu, Grade 7
Joe Walker Middle School

Fish of the Sea

Deep in the sea,
I wish I could be

Swimming with the fish
Tails moving, "Swish, swish, swish."

Tuna, Sardines, and Trout
Swimming with salmon in their own special route

Schools of fish swimming side by side
With the current like a carnival ride

The smallest fish
So timid and shy

The mighty shark
In the ocean dark

You can only wonder from what great source
The waves receive their great force

While walking away I see
One last glimpse of my beloved sea

McKenna Pahl, Grade 7
Monte Vista Christian School

Ode to My Room

O my dear room, you are so great
You are my only escape
You are my sanctuary of solitude
Such a peaceful place
You are my fortress of safety
So calm and serene
The greatest place for a teen
In my room are the tears I've cried
And everything I hide
No one knows the secrets you know
You are the only one who knows the traits I don't show
You are the only one I trust
Because I know you won't tell
Just how many times I really fail
You are freedom to me
I can do anything
O dear room you will always be there

Nicole Cohea, Grade 8
Daniel Savage Middle School

The Thought of Sports

Sports is not just physical,
It's also mental.
The rush you feel
When your chances of scoring,
So mighty so powerful so nice.
You feel as though noticed like
All those animals in the rain forest:
Oh, that great and wonderful feeling.
That smile on your face when the
Crowd cheers for you,
Just wanting to scream from your excitement
Just like Buddha when he became enlightened.
The joking around when you hear that whistle sound.
Oh, the sweet smell of victory.
The surge you feel when you know it's over,
You jump and clown.
Oh, that sweet smell of victory.

Isaac Alarcon, Grade 7
Our Lady of Guadalupe School

The Highway

the highway is fast
there are many turn offs
my life is a highway
it is fast
and has many turn offs too
there are shortcuts to take on the highway
in my life I will take shortcuts that I might regret
the highway goes on forever
that is how long I am going to live
unfortunately you get off a highway
my life will end
but until then I will live free on the highway

Franchesca Espino, Grade 8
Isbell Middle School

The Best Dog

Matza Ball
O, you big brown mutt
You make me smile
Even if I have the biggest frown
I hold you
I cuddle you
Your bark annoys me,
But your lick adores me
Your soft fur feels like a blanket to me
And your sharp nails are knives to me
You big brown nose looks funny to me
Your big floppy ears make me laugh
And last, but not least those eyes make me love you,
I have felt this way since you were a puppy
Till now
Eight years later
You are the best dog I could ever of asked for.

Andrew Gonsalves, Grade 8
Daniel Savage Middle School

Slavery

Is America not the land of the free?
Is it not the land of opportunity?
Aren't all races supposed to be treated equally?
Then what's up with slavery,

You mistreat them in so many ways,
You beat them until they bleed,
You make them do your hard work and labor,
So why not lend them a favor,
Put yourself in their shoes,
Now you choose,

Is America not the land of the free?
Is it not the land of opportunity?
No, this is America,
The land of opportunity,
So set them free.

Tyler Matthews, Grade 7
Orville Wright Middle School

Memories

Family visits
friends go
seasons change
people pass away
but memories are here to stay
some memories are of people from the past
or about current friends, teachers,
or people that have left us
sometimes I wish people were still here
and maybe that things hadn't changed
but one way I know I can remember the past
by the memories that are here to stay

Laura Solis, Grade 7
Isbell Middle School

High Merit Poems – Grades 7, 8 and 9

Sorrow
Sitting by the lake,
Under the shade,
With guilt and sorrow taking over the day.
People make mistakes,
Everybody knows it's true,
Then why does mine feel like it's overdue.
I hurt a good friend,
And I don't know why,
But now all I do is sit and sigh.
I tried to make up, I begged all day,
Yet for some reason the guilt won't go away.
My hope is almost gone,
I try to bring it up with a song,
But I still know I did wrong.
I don't know what to do,
Yet all I can do, is make up with you.
But till that day,
I won't laugh, I won't play,
So I'm sitting by the lake,
Under the shade,
Waiting, just waiting till that special day.
Karim Sharif, Grade 7
Willma Cavitt Jr High School

Remember
I remember my love
I remember the day
She went away
She told me lies
That I did not buy
So many lies
I wanted to die
So I said goodbye
But why, why did she lie
I liked her so
I remember how
I fought for you
My heart big as the moon
I mistook how little you cared
I remember your eyes
Twinkle in the twilight
By night we kissed
Now those days I miss
I remember the bliss
You gave to me
Remember me and I'll remember you
Jessie Hernandez, Grade 8
Our Lady of Guadalupe School

A Friendship
Friends are forever,
Friends are love and support you.
They also give hugs!
Beverlyn Law, Grade 7
St Mary's Chinese Day School

October
The night I used to stare at has been broken
Now it's blanketed with clouds
Thundering with lightning and rain
I miss it
I miss them
Their souls have gone
Their minds conquered
He claims it's not real
Yet he says it mocks us
It's easier to pay no mind to his words
It's affected him
He doesn't know it
I wish it was over
That he'd come back
Where's my sky?
Hannah R. Thompson, Grade 8
St Rita School

Dream
Soft eyes
Skeptical ears
Long flowing mane
Galloping through a field
Long strong legs
She whinnies as I approach
Quick flick of the tail
Gentle nuzzle
Takes a treat out of my pocket
Peaceful and soothing touch
Tickles as whiskers brush against my arm
Playful
Relaxing
The clip clop of hooves
A beautiful horse
Madison David, Grade 7
Monte Vista Christian School

Sun
Fills up the blue sky
Bringing light to the whole world
Warm and hot and bright
Makes everyone warm
Created on the fourth day
Like a ball of light
Clears out the gray clouds
Can be dangerous to skin
Brings heat to the air
Sometimes makes you sweat
Helps trees and flowers to grow
Makes me real happy
Comes out in the spring
And comes out in the summer
Hides in the nighttime
Molly Cortese, Grade 7
Monte Vista Christian School

This Is My Country
This is my country,
Sweet land of liberty.
This is my country,
Land of the brave.

This is my country,
Where we sing and dance.
This is my country,
Where hope and love thrive.

This is my country,
The land of adventure and awe.
This is my country,
Land of untold secrets.

This is my country,
Where the wild animals roam.
This is my country,
Land of the free and home of the brave!

O, this is *our* country.
Kyle Haffermann, Grade 7
St Francis Parish School

My Brother and I
The place me and my brother
Could do anything we wanted
We could run and play
Without a care in the world

The place me and my brother
Would always get hurt
But wouldn't even care
We would just keep playing

The place me and my brother
Can be alone and play video games
Where we can sit and watch TV
The place where we skate

The place where me and my brother
Can have fun
Where we can be ourselves
We can do anything
And not get in trouble
Is my mom's house
Austin Tabor, Grade 8
Richardson PREP HI Middle School

The Moon
Seizing with her light
When all there is is darkness
Watches as night falls
Selena Garcia, Grade 8
Almond Tree Middle School

Oh, the Work
Oh the work it
Would be,
To walk up and down
The dirt bumpy path,
As you're wearing big
Hats and long dresses,
You must get tired,
Carrying heavy things
Up and down the path
Protected by the grassy
Mountains,
Oh how I wish I could
Be as strong as you are,
Where would the world be?
Without people like you?
Nowhere
Oh, the work!
Madison Farris, Grade 8
Daniel Savage Middle School

Defiance
Fire
that will freeze
the sun

Ice
that will sear
the darkest sea

Wind
that will create
an everlasting foundation

Stone
that will weave through
all others

Nothing is or is not
Sandra Vadhin, Grade 8
George Ellery Hale Middle School

Empty Bags
I've never experienced happiness,
I thought buying the clothes I want
Would make me happy,
But no,
I always feel emptiness,
Inside me,
Wanting something,
But not knowing exactly,

Now I know you can't buy happiness,
It comes from within,
I had to learn it the hard way
Daniela Guido, Grade 8
Roseland Accelerated Middle School

Unwritten Love Letter
I like the way you talk,
the way you smile,
the way you walk, and
the way you say my name.

When lunch ends and we go to class,
you say good-bye
and I smile and laugh,
and my classmates tease me.

They think we'd be cute together;
I say we're just friends.
But what if this was forever?
What if?

I like the smell of your hair,
the happiness in your eyes.
Maybe someday I will dare
to tell you that I like you —

— just the way you are.
Jennifer Fang, Grade 9
Irvine High School

Challenge
Sitting on that two wheeled contraption
Being held behind,
How scary it was
I had fear all over my mind.
As I started down the field,
A slow and steady pace
It be as if I were riding on a stallion,
Peaceful and full of grace
As the breeze blows my hair
As I watch, the world passes by
As if it had wheels
Riding to the contrary side
I thrust on the pedals faster
I try to balance myself
It was quite a challenge
I stopped up at the end of the path
As I looked at the floor,
A smile grew on my face
I turned back
Off the distance was my dad
He waved, I had done it!!!
Karina Ornelas, Grade 8
St Helen Catholic Elementary School

Bright Stars
Light in the dark.
They sparkle all the time.
They are like glow sticks in the dark.
White stars.
Michael Ng, Grade 7
St Mary's Chinese Day School

The Leaves of Autumn
The leaves of autumn
Begin on a tree.
They slowly fall,
Along with others,
With the wind blowing them
Any which way,
Until they finally reach the ground,
Silently resting and decaying.
While others cover and join them.
People walk past them,
Ignoring them, avoiding them.
Everything is cold,
Everything is windy.
All you know
Is that the
Leaves of autumn
Are on the ground,
Dead and silent.
Sophia Ynami, Grade 7
Corpus Christi School

Football
Football is a very
fun sport. You can meet
new people when you
play against them,
and you can
have fun while you play the
sport. You can work up the
skills you were never good
at. You can learn to catch
better than you ever imagined.
You can run faster than you
ever thought you could.
If you play foot-
ball, you will
soon learn
that you
have skills
you never thought you'd ever have.
James Gonzalez, Grade 7
Lucerne Valley Jr/Sr High School

The Old Willow Tree
The old willow tree speaks
Using words no other can compare
The tree sways through the breeze
Gentle, kind, happy and loving
That happiness turns to sadness
She becomes weaker and weaker
With pain at each thought
Soon there is nothing left
All that remains
Is her broken hearted soul.
Gabriella Georgedes, Grade 8
Buchser Middle School

High Merit Poems – Grades 7, 8 and 9

The Tragedy of 9/11
Thousands of lives were ended by evil,
Innocent people who have died from terrorists
Who hijacked an aircraft and changed the world,
No one to stop this tragic incident from occurring.
And now these men who changed the world,
Have destroyed the Twin Towers in the city of New York.
This conflict has ended, but never forgotten,
Through the world and future that is yet to come.
Beatriz Romero, Grade 8
Richardson PREP HI Middle School

Faded Copy
Sometimes I feel like a faded copy
nobody could stop him but everyone could stop me
I always hear what people say
that he's better than me in every way
only one thing I have the upper hand on
but if he tried it he'd probably beat me
I can't compete with him but I'll always try
I'm not a faded copy
Rene Perez, Grade 8
Richard Merkin Middle Academy

Basketball and Me
Basketball is one of the greatest pastimes.
People sometimes play it to get stuff off of their mind.
The best part of basketball is playing with your friends.
When you play with your friends the fun never ends.
I've been playing basketball since I was six years old.
It's really easy as many people have been told.
I've won many trophies and medals over the years.
When I was little I only wanted basketball as my career.
David Benitez, Grade 7
Our Lady of Guadalupe School

Artistry
Art is a part of me that fills my heart with great joy,
by letting my eyes and arms explore.
As my eyes dance across the page,
the movement of the lines soothe while the colors boom
off the creation and enter my senses.
It displays moods and gives a feeling of curiosity,
as if it were wanting to be observed.
Miriam Camacho, Grade 9
Patriot High School

Gone too Soon
Life is a gift,
It can go away at any unknown time,
You left us so soon,
You were gone in a quick second,
The joy you brought to people,
And the love you gave,
Will *always* be in my heart, till my last given day.
Sarah Alvarez, Grade 8
Our Lady of Guadalupe School

Wildfire
The fire crackles and rushes
The animals run far away
It rolls over the land and burns bushes
Faster faster they run
But it's no match for this savage beast.
One, two, three pine trees fall.
The fire eats it all as a feast.
Soon nothing will be left.
Gray smoke fills the air.
Firefighters spray water on the glow.
Does the one who start these fires even care?
Spreading, spreading!
An unfortunate young doe falls behind
Fire takes over the path
The deer is now confined.
Fire is now everywhere.
When it's past, animals come out of hiding
They seem to be crying.
The forest is slowly subsiding.
Katrina Crosby, Grade 7
St Martin-in-the-Fields School

The Black Rose
I see my love lying under the moonlight.
I lie down beside her.
Gently, I kiss her lips,
but she does not respond to my act of affection.
Her skin is pale and as cold as the late January snow.
Nervously I touch her heart.
It hasn't a beat!
For my love is…dead.
Tears flow down my face.
Angrily I shout to the bitter night sky.
My sharp cry rings through the forest.
During my sobs of grief, I glance to her hand.
In her lovely hand lies a black rose.
Somehow, within its gloominess, there was beauty.
Curiosity takes over me and,
I begin to reach for the rose.
Gently, I grasp the rose.
While admiring its beauty,
I fade to sleep…
Ben Romero, Grade 8
St Martin-in-the-Fields School

And the World Goes on By
Day by day,
Night by night,
I sit here staring in the fading light.
I am lost in my own imagination,
Not knowing or caring what is going on in creation.
I am in my own little world.
I wait and I wait for something, someone to pull me out of my daze,
So I won't sit here mesmerized in my world for day upon day!
Samantha Reichenberger, Grade 7
Willma Cavitt Jr High School

Life

The painful memories of my bro,
Haunt me every day,
Memories of him make me sad,

The painful memories of my bro,
Makes me cry sometimes,
Hurts me to think of them,

The painful memories of my bro,
I wish you still were here.
Ricardo Cintron, Grade 8
Richardson PREP HI Middle School

Ode to My Little Brother

My little brother is an angel at heart
As little as a squirrel
But big inside
My little brother is my life…
His smile is as bright as the sun above
He is the only one I love…
My little brother is #1
Stand tall and never falls
He is like the waves are to the sea
My little brother is like me
Andres Sandoval, Grade 8
August Boeger Middle School

Beauty and Pain

Blue rose so abnormal
Red rose so common
One of the sky
One of the blood
Though they appear different
Both are connected by
Every small similarity
both with drawing fragrance
Both with sticking thorns
Both loved by all
KaSea Cirincione, Grade 7
Arcade Middle School

Phases

I don't believe in name.
I don't believe in face.
I don't believe in fame.
I don't believe in race.

There's a rhyme and reason.
There's a fall from grace.
There's a thing called treason.

It's written on your face.
Angelica Palencia, Grade 8
Charles Maclay Middle School

Thoughts on Escher's Bond of Union

A man or woman find a way to tear apart
To see their future in a new world
Breaking apart then coming back together again
Feeling all of our souls filling up above
Going to a place of peace.
To see all as who we really are…
To tear apart what we were
To feel a new world that begins…to feel a new start.
But to miss
What we had remembered…what we had from the lives that had been missed.
Anthony Rocha, Grade 7
Tenaya Middle School

Ode to a Soldier

You fight for our freedom.
Yet, nobody loves you.
You get shot and lose blood.
But people don't care.
They are too interested in their lives.
But you die for theirs.
I am here to tell you.
That I care, I love, I try to appreciate you more.
I salute you Marines, Navy, Army, National Guard, Air Force, and Coast Guard.
You fight for our freedom.
Samuel Perez, Grade 7
St Francis Parish School

Where I'm From

I am from hanging out with friends and throwing parties on the holidays
I am from having Barbeques and family reunions
I am from books and magazines open on my bed
From listening to music while doing my homework
From fried catfish, French fries, and Caprisuns; from laughing with
my mom about what happened at school that day
From mom saying, "You never know until you try" and Grammy saying,
"The sky is the limit."
I am from spending my whole life in Alameda and then moving to Oakland.
I am from crying on my mom's shoulder and talking to her when I need to
Chabree Keil, Grade 8
Bret Harte Middle School

Soldier's Heart

Sounds of gun shots the fight has begun
Soldiers running, hiding, and crawling trying to find safety
Men and women screaming, "help me,"
Cries for help and shrieks from bombs exploding
Planes flying over holding the flag that we know as home
Finally the soldiers have come to a finish with no one missing
The day has been fought and lives have been saved back at home
We will always remember the soldiers that fought for us and the heart
They must have to fight for our lives every day
Patrick Nelson, Grade 8
Ripona Elementary School

High Merit Poems – Grades 7, 8 and 9

Gone Away
Loved you with all my heart
It was like a piece of art
Creating it bit by bit
Awaiting to see if it's really legit
You said it, the three words that meant it all
It was really the least
Having to see every bit of it split
Ai Luu, Grade 7
Sarah McGarvin Intermediate School

Love/Hate
Love
Strong, romantic
Caring, trusting, attracting
Special, unforgettable — angry, dislike
Destroying, killing, suffering
Madness, fearless
Hate
Cinthia Laguna, Grade 9
Hiram W Johnson High School

A True Friend
A true friend is important for everyone,
especially someone who has been hurt,
someone who has lost themselves,
or someone who always feels alone.
A true friend cures the hurt,
helps you find yourself,
and is there so you won't feel alone.
Asalia Arauz, Grade 7
Our Lady of the Rosary School

Boyfriend/Girlfriend
Boyfriend
Handsome, strong
Loving, holding, walking
Responsible, smart — sweet, hardworking
Playing, kissing, dressing
Beautiful, interesting
Girlfriend
Will Yang, Grade 9
Hiram W Johnson High School

Monster
Mysterious sounds come from the cover
Ogre-like face on three of its faces
Neglected for years because it's a horror
Snake-like tails, he has six
Ten heads, it's mutated
Even bigger than the stories say
Raging with anger for being alone
Alexander Apitz, Grade 7
Carden Academy of Santa Clara

The Coming of the Tide
As raindrops glisten on a dark windowsill, I remember times gone past
Of another land, another place, the place I truly belonged in
But I was taken away, to never return
From the place I thought I should be
And now the forgotten laughter rings in the air
Lost thoughts, hopes, and dreams now crushed
Lie scattered everywhere
Not a whisper stirs the air
No breath of breaking dawn
The forest hides in ever darkness, shielding those who ran astray
No joy, no tears, no hopes, no cares
On a forgotten island in a lost ocean sea
An empty void
Where nothing but your darkest fears remain
And in this place of misery I find myself once more
So many miles away from where I belonged before
Surrounded by misgivings, and doubting every word
Dragged in by the pulling of the tide
And taken out to sea, where I can no longer see land
And so my friend I ask this thing of you
To pull me back to where the darkness cannot grow
Kate Iida, Grade 7
St Rita School

As I Prayed
The wind is thrashing violently all around me.
Yet I am not afraid.
Everything around me is tumbling down.
Yet I am not afraid.
A sound like that of a freight train follows shouts of terror
as certain death creeps towards me like a cat about to attack its prey.
Yet I am not afraid.
As everyone is scrambling to get away
I get on my knees and pray.
I know that God will protect me as I am kneeling there alone.
When I finally get up and look around, everything is still.
The beastly tornado has left this town and disappeared into the sky
as quickly as when it first came down.
Once again I get down on my knees thanking God for keeping me safe as I prayed.
Nicole Colangelo, Grade 9
Lucerne Valley Jr/Sr High School

As Spring Turns to Fall
I am sitting here feeling as if the seasons are changing
from the bright summer to the breezy fall.
I see bushes and trees making shade for the people who are enjoying the life of this park.
As the leaves change color and fall to the soft soiled ground
the wind pushes the leaves to their new journey.
I see this place as a relaxing rejuvenating place to get away.
The leaves leave their prints on the sidewalk as a human would in the soil.
The flowers bring joy to the many people who walk past them.
I watch this beautiful flower sway in the morning breeze.
I here the wind whistling through the trees.
I sit on this bench listening to the sounds of nature hoping to come back again.
Katelyn Martin, Grade 7
Daniel Savage Middle School

Homestyle

I played
I walked my first steps
That house
I fought, cried, loved
I have hugged
Spent time with loved ones
Seen pets come and go
That house
I would hide
And fly away
That house
Stay there when sick
Stay inside when cold
Go outside when it is hot
Come from school to
That house
I would run away when scared
I would always love
That house
I will always know
That house
Leonard Ayala, Grade 8
Richardson PREP HI Middle School

My Bedroom

The long hot school day is over
my eyelids start to fall
I think about the summer
when this won't happen at all
I go to my place of solace
rewarded with some sleep
with my wooden pterodactyl
hovering silently above me

My bedroom is a sacred site
filled with the sound of silence
everything in here is just right
the bed soft as the sky
the lights as bright as the sun
but the real thing that catches my eye
is the book collecting I've done

This is my fortress of solitude
my special place to be
free to finally rest from a world
full of insanity
Samuel Louis Kushell, Grade 7
The Mirman School

M.C. Escher's Bond of Union

Two coiling faces,
Connecting with each other,
Man, wife, together.
Martin Gonzalez, Grade 7
Tenaya Middle School

Where I'm From

I am from a land of freedom and peace.
I am from a place where I am loved and taken care of.
I am from multitudes of family who I love and care for.
From a place where children are taught the right things.
From a place where multitudes of cars surround me like trees.
From a land of opportunities.
I am from a place of laughter and siblings.
I am from a place where music like "High School Musical" are loved.
David Uyong, Grade 8
Bret Harte Middle School

Clouds

Oh! To sit upon the clouds
To see the world
As little ants
Crawling by
When rush hour starts
To look upon the cities
When every kitchen light
Is a glow in each window
When the moon is bright in the sky
To see the sun rising on the sea
And the waves crash upon the shore
Before a soul is awake
To watch the fish
Swim up the rivers
When the sun is high
To see the preschoolers
Swinging on swings
And coloring in their books
When their parents leave them
And when I'm there
It's you I want standing by me
Bella Alejandro, Grade 7
Monte Vista Christian School

Snow

I wake up one morning,
Excited to play,
I look out my window,
To the cold winter's day.
I see the white snow,
Laying there on the ground,
I think to myself,
What a wonderful sound.
So quiet and peaceful,
So close to touch,
Yet as soft as it is,
When I step outside
It will go 'CRUNCH!'
The most wonderful place,
In this wonderful town,
Is the one you can be at,
Up, down, or around.
Haley Rosenthal, Grade 8
Monte Vista Christian School

The True Enemy

I blame
All others for my woe.
I can say that it is they
who spur my anger on,
But will I ever know?
Who is the true enemy?
Who makes my dreams implode,
Who holds down my wings,
Will I ever know?
Who is my true enemy?
A flash of lighting strikes
Sending a spark into my brain,
The true enemy,
Not her, not him,
But me.
I am responsible for my woe,
Spurring my own anger on,
Causing my dreams to implode,
Holding down my wings,
But now I know.
That I am my own true enemy.
Nicole Cohen, Grade 7
The Mirman School

My Family

My family is best
They are always there for me
Especially when I am stressed
As other people can see

They are always there when I need to chat
I love to talk to them
They like to wear hats
My family's like a perfect gem

Sometimes, my family has a bad day
They can get really mad
My family tries to find away
So we can all be glad

I couldn't ask for a better family
I love them all infinitely
Jolly Mae Mercado, Grade 8
Almond Tree Middle School

The Lonely Boy
It was afternoon
Kids were playing —
Happy and having fun, when …
Crying…They heard
Someone was crying …
Someone was unhappy…
It was not one of them.
Curious, they looked around.
Everywhere they checked,
Getting closer to the sound,
Yet so far from seeing someone.
No one…They saw
No one crying,
No one in need of help…
Then each one left to go home.
Empty…I saw
The playground began to empty…
And there was only me
The Lonely Boy
Crying
Roland Theo P. Capulong, Grade 7
Corpus Christi School

You and Me
You've got a smile
You can see from a mile
You've got a dream
You say is too extreme
You know you would never reach it

You told me…

Just know I'm here for you
Whenever you're blue
I'm the shoulder you can cry on
I'm the shoulder you get tired on
You're the one I've always wanted
You have that sweet sensitive side
Never let anyone tell you otherwise

You make me laugh
When I want to cry
You'll never say good-bye
You'll always be by my side
Emily Sarale, Grade 9
St Mary's High School

Reflections on Escher's Bond of Union
In their time in space
Two souls roam helpless
Trying to break free
But can't find a way how.
If they actually put their minds together,
They'll find a way.
Chandler Hosepian, Grade 7
Tenaya Middle School

Starvation
Starvation
Desperate people and weak children
Running tears
Full of fear.

Typical days
Dead cattle and rotting corpses.
Too late to save
Hyenas eating the frail.

Near Djibouti
5,000 tons of food daily,
Vanishes.
Magic.

Among victims
The throbbing thought comes
"Live the next day,
Or hibernate forever."

Starvation
Around the world
Revolves around us
With inevitability
Each and every moment.
Archibald Lai, Grade 8
Richardson PREP HI Middle School

Love
Magic surrounds us;
Every day it's around,
Tinkling so thus;
It's making this sound.

Bells fill the air;
Chimes mingling,
My heart beats faster
Than a bell's dingling.

New snow falls down;
As if to say,
Starting over now;
Approving this day.

Old ones end,
New ones begin;
What's round the bend?
Perhaps a sin.

This love's just beginning;
Right here, right now,
When does it end?
I don't know now.
Bethany Mahan, Grade 7
Joe Walker Middle School

The Sun
I love the way,
The sun doth shine,
And someday,
It will be mine.

It understands,
When to be bright,
And when to let the moon,
Show her light.

It gives me warmth,
And comfort too;
It gives me mirth,
And won't make me blue.

I love the way,
The sun doth shine,
And someday,
It will be mine.
Mackenzie Murphy, Grade 7
Joe Walker Middle School

Scattered Thoughts
Rising from the depths
of a darkness unknown,
confusion lurking in your mind.
Not a sensible thought
in your consciousness
to remind you what to do.
You wander aimlessly,
seemingly lost,
a lone soul abandoned
in the blazing desert.
You try to understand,
but the answers do not come.
Your state of mind
shattered
a broken mirror
you cannot pick up
the pieces until
the darkness lifts.
Gregory McKay, Grade 7
The Mirman School

My Secret Hideout
My secret hideout
It's so quiet; it's so fun,
I go in there when strangers come
No one really knows it's there

My mom's closet
Behind the clothes
I go in there when strangers come
My secret hideout.
Leylani Quintana, Grade 8
Richardson PREP HI Middle School

Purple!!!!

Purple is the color I love
Purple is the color I dream of
Purple is the latest fashion
Purple is the color of passion
Purple is the color of glad
Purple is the only color they should have
The color of me
The best you see

Amanda Williams, Grade 8
Richard Merkin Middle Academy

The Bad Ways of Betrayal

She is walking down
the wrong path of
darkness and shadows.
Animals scurry past with fear,
the wind howled a warning,
but still she is going.
No one to stop her
from the bad ways of betrayal.

La Tricia Edmondson-Gooden, Grade 7
Orville Wright Middle School

Snow

An innocent color,
Covers the ground.
A sheet of silence,
Omits all sound.
A numbing pain,
A dull sensation.
A scene of wonder,
A sudden elation!

Iris Wu, Grade 8
Holy Name School

Courage

Courage is skydiving for the first time.
It is like fighting a shark in the ocean.
It is a baby learning how to walk.
It is as bold as someone giving a speech.
It is the smell of great pasta.
It calls out to you, "Don't go!"
It is more fearless than a badger.
Courage is freedom.

Daniel Olvera, Grade 7
Monroe Middle School

The Lost Soul

When a soul has lost its way
The soul always travels for days.
It never stops for anything.
When the soul travels it sees many things.
The soul never takes a break.
A soul can be as clear as a lake.

Aman Sanchez, Grade 7
St Francis de Sales School

I Try

I lie in my bed with tears hoping you might hear my fears.
But you don't.
I stand in the lonely hall hoping you might help with all my problems.
But you don't.
I sit upon the wooden chair hoping you might stop and stare at me.
But you don't.
I try with all my might so you can see what I fight for.
But all I get in return is just a solid burn you placed on my heart.
You just don't understand it's hard to be the girl that I am.
O.K. ma'am?
All I hear is you yell and scream.
Why do you have to be so mean to me?
You lecture, you fight you ignore my right and it hurts.
You can't see that all I do is try to impress you.
You put a burden on my heart before I could even start to explain.
I am human and not perfect and at the end of the day it doesn't seem worth it.
To try to give you what you want
I end up failing and it hurts you a lot.
I try.

Sierra Lucey, Grade 8
St Cecilia School

I Am

I am the shaggy, straw colored, furry maimed Cowardly Lion.
I wonder what it would be like to be "The king of beast like Matasa"
I hear to be the king is only to have courage.
I see myself filled with tears like a wave crashing in on the shoreline.
I am the scared, four legged, brown-eyed Cowardly Lion.

I pretend that I am brave like King Arthur.
I feel unreasonably fearful.
I touch the fear I face.
I worry that I am ashamed of never being the king I should.
I cry almost all the time especially when I met the God the Wizard of Oz.
I am the big eared, sixteen clawed, furry-neck-like-a-fur-coat Cowardly Lion.

I understand great bravery is needed.
I say ROOOarrrrrrr.
I dream of not being embarrassed of my fears.
I try to only stand up to the courage that lives inside of me.
I hope that courage means acting in the "face of fears"
I am whiskery, big teethed, big-nosed Cowardly Lion.

Trent Mossino, Grade 7
La Mesa Jr High School

That One September Day

As we watched in horror a jet came and hit one more
It hit so hard we closed our eyes
We made our prize that they would all come out alive
Still hoping the man up high would grant our prize
But our prize was not granted because many died.
As the first one fell floor by floor it hit the ground and was there no more
As many died on that tragic day it will go down in history as
"That One September Day."

Eric Jarvis, Grade 7
Willma Cavitt Jr High School

High Merit Poems – Grades 7, 8 and 9

Skating
Skating is fun, skating is cool,
It gives me something to do after school.
The better places to skate are far, so we get a ride,
When we get there we power-slide.
360-flips are hard, 360 tricks are kicky,
And after doing a bunch they can be tricky.
When we get to the stairs, we kick flip the four
And we compete, to see who can do more.
We bring a camera along to film a line,
We see who is talented like Einstein.
With the sun on our backs we get real hot,
We go grab some water, we drink a lot.
After a while, we start to get tired,
To get a ride home, a phone call is required.
"ET phone home," is what we say,
My mom can't hear us, because she is listening to reggae.
She calls us back, we get a ride,
We do our last trick and we wait by the curbside.
Sebastian Santander, Grade 7
Our Lady of Guadalupe School

I Will Always Be Here
You're not alone, together we stand
I'm right by your side, know that I'll take your hand
When it gets quiet, and it feels like the end
just know I won't let go, because I'll fight and defend
Just hold on, hold on tight
give me your best strength, give me all of your might
Don't let go, just stay with me
I'm here for you, stay and you'll see
Please listen when I say I believe
because nothing's going to change our destiny
Just stay strong, we can make it through
keep holding on, I'm here for you
Everything I do for you I give my heart and soul
that's all I ever wanted, that's what I wanted you to know
Your words are the ones that get me through each day
these are the words I think of when I pray
I will always be here, with you forever
and nothing will separate us, not now, not ever
Taylor Ramos, Grade 8
Coronado Middle School

War
War is filled with hatred and sorrow
With lifeless soldiers lying dead on the floor
To wounded soldiers brought through the paramedic's door
Would you be willing to serve your country?
At a high risk of not coming back at all
To watch your comrades come and fall
You will be watched by your enemies
By land and sea
I know it's hard to say good-bye
But make sure not to die
Joseph Garcia, Grade 8
Isbell Middle School

Glory Beach
The royal blue waters churn as the sun breaks the dawn
The gulls wake and sing their song of paradise while
The slight breeze sweeps the coast flat
The ocean grows alive with exhilarating life

Sweet salty air livens the coastline
Flowers stir out of their peaceful sleep and
Paint the trees with brilliant color
Sun rising to its mighty place upon the sky

The bold Pacific warms in the rays of light and
The deep's mysterious wildlife opens up as a world unknown
Wildlife roams around the beach in search of food
Little sand crabs come to the surface as the tide washes in

Serene as cars are boisterous, nothing could disturb the tranquility
Away from the city and din, the earth comes to a halt
The changing sky grows to gold as the sun sets under the horizon
Away goes the heat so the sea can rest for another awe-inspiring day
Ruby Zalduondo, Grade 8
The Mirman School

How It Would Feel
When I sit and think
I wonder how it would feel
To live life on the brink
And how it would be
To be someone other than me
Richer than my wildest dreams
Cash growing from the trees
Or poorer than a mouse
Who could only dream of owning a house
Or sadder than an emo
Who only listens to screamo
Or wild like a cat
If you can handle that
Or slow like a slug
Just staring at a bug
Or faster than a car
In which I could go far
But I already know how all these things could be
Because all of these things are me
Jenna Cadwallader, Grade 7
St Martin-in-the-Fields School

Drifting Away
You were my sister, you were my friend
I knew this thing we called friendship wasn't pretend
Best friends forever that's what we used to say
Now all our memories are drifting away
So sad to say we're moving on
But in my heart the old you will never be gone
Things are different, people change their ways
But I promise you I'll always stay the same.
Briana Palencia, Grade 8
St Francis de Sales School

You
You always brighten up my day!
You're the one who
Makes me smile.
When I'm sad, you
Find a way to make me laugh
You complete me.
Without you,
I would be nothing.
Without you,
I cannot live, because
You are my world,
My everything,
And you are my lifeline.
You are the one I will
Love forever. You are
The only one who holds
The key to my heart.
Three simple words…
I love you!

Belle Nguyen, Grade 7
Corpus Christi School

That Special Someone
We go for a walk on the beach,
Just you and me,
We have our feet in the sand,
As we watch the sea.

The next day we are on the phone,
Just you, me, and some friends,
You ask me out,
I wanted this day to never end.

I see you at school the next day,
You talk to me in the hall,
We have a great time,
And you take me to the mall.

As you can see it is going well,
I loved the time we spent,
But it is getting late,
And then we went.

Jessica James, Grade 8
St Martin-in-the-Fields School

The Colors of Nature
Green
Green leaves dance in wind
Like emeralds they glimmer
They jump and shimmer

White
Mexican poppies
Their petals reach for the sky
Bees race to find them

Red
Waiting to be picked
Juicy red apples taste sweet
Dripping with flavor

Brown
Gnarly native oak
Branches stretching to the sun
Brown acorns falling

Rozene Enloe, Grade 7
Monte Vista Christian School

Simplicity
Portions of pleasure
Guilt gone askew.
Is this what life
simply means to you?

Pain, sorrow, and shame
experience every day
Hate, betrayal, and disappointment
have been gone through the same way.

But beauty and elegance
also go astray.
And affection and kindness…
Understanding it's hard to say.

Is life all that worth it?
Or is it a limited view?
I suppose this is what life
simply means to you.

Steven Dao, Grade 7
Sarah McGarvin Intermediate School

First Cry
A new soul,
enters the world,
whole and pure,
a rose unfurled.

A short sweet cry,
pierces the air,
a baby's song,
a baby's prayer.

Great yearning,
and simplicity,
a mysteriousness,
fills the soaring plea.

Flowing love,
for a polished pearl,
much thanks and joy,
because it's a girl!

Zehava Dalia Nadler, Grade 8
Yeshiva Rav Isaacsohn School

Hidden in My Room
Hidden in my room
I sit all day,
And no matter what happens
I try to stay

Hidden in my room
I do what I like,
Listening to music
Without a fright

Hidden in my room
I turn on my computer,
I download more music
Wishing I did it sooner

Hidden in my room
I can be me,
And nobody can change
How I can be free.

Nakia Blackwell, Grade 8
Richardson PREP HI Middle School

I Wonder
I wonder what it's like outside,
Outside beyond the sea
Does our world and another collide?
Of course that couldn't be.
And if two worlds did collide,
What would happen to me?
These questions fill me up inside
Oh boy, oh golly gee!!!

Delaney Englert, Grade 7
St Martin-in-the-Fields School

The World Within a Child's Hand
A child's hand is something
That means joy
Happiness and holiness.
A child's hand is
Something we can learn from:
Something that adults
Can study to find the
Power of youth again.

Dylan Logan, Grade 7
Tenaya Middle School

Golf
Look at the little ball go.
The game has started now watch the show.
I hit the golf ball with my golf clubs.
Oh no! It has landed in the shrubs.
Next it lands on the green and hits the pin.
It rolls back and goes right in.
I have finally won the game!
Now the other golfers are filled with shame.

Jason Perez, Grade 8
St Francis de Sales School

High Merit Poems – Grades 7, 8 and 9

Abraham Lincoln Freed the Slaves
Abraham Lincoln freed the slaves.
He signed the contract, he was afraid.
He was forced to sign,
Shaking and sweating.
He was afraid.
Abraham Lincoln had a slave himself
That he did not want
to give away, to the world that
Waits for the slaves — the free slaves.

Abraham Lincoln freed the slaves.
People were against him.
He did not like it. He was afraid,
But he was also brave.

Abraham Lincoln freed the slaves.
This time he wasn't afraid.
He was sad but he knew he did the right thing.
Free the slaves. He made history.
Alexa Garcia, Grade 7
Orville Wright Middle School

Jackie Robinson, The First Black Baseball Player
The first black baseball player
is one of the best.
The first black baseball player,
is better than all the rest.

To him it didn't matter,
if you were black or white.
To him it didn't matter,
because he knew he would win the fight.

He made a difference,
he did something nobody dared.
He made a difference,
Even though some people didn't care.

He showed the world,
it didn't matter if you were black or white.
The only thing that mattered,
was making the world right.
Matt Steindorf, Grade 7
Willma Cavitt Jr High School

Your Special Day
You are now to become a wife
And this is the day you have dreamed of all your life
As you say those famous words "I do"
You cry a tear of joy and happiness too!
And when you kiss the groom
A smile comes to you
You know you're with the one you love
When your special day is done.
Andrea Ramirez, Grade 7
St Martin-in-the-Fields School

At My Nana's House
Red lipstick, oversized flower dresses,
Long pearl necklaces, dressing up like movie stars,
At my Nana's house…

On the long swerving path, almost flying,
Caught by Tata with his bikes
At my Nana's house…

Jumping into the air,
Hiding in the dark corners, time's up,
They've come for the jumper
At my Nana's house…

Seven or eight of us in five seats,
Across the street we go,
Our junk food trips
At my Nana's house…

A place to be me,
A place where I have many memories,
A piece of my heart will always be,
At my Nana's house…
Arianna Yepez, Grade 8
Richardson PREP HI Middle School

Untitled
Battling my own mind
Makes tears run down my face
Peace is what I can't find
I want to escape this place

The echoes of my screams still travel through the walls
My heart screamed in agony
For I have lost all
I curse this tragedy

Which made the darkness devour my soul
And the sadness consume my eyes
Life has become an empty hole
Where only misery lies
Stephanie Gonzalez, Grade 8
John Adams Middle School

Fall Is in the Air
Fall is in the air,
The leaves falling everywhere.
Plants changing colors really shows,
The feeling of dew on your toes.
Apples and cinnamon tickle your tongue
Crickets at night make a wonderful hum
The crunch of leaves as you walk,
Smelling fragrances of pumpkin pie as you talk.
Turkeys fluttering here and there,
Fall is truly here.
Austin Sobon, Grade 7
Smith Flat Charter School

I Am Your Marine
I wonder what it will be like to be a marine.
I hear the ocean weaving.
I see the sun shiny as your pretty eyes.
I want to hear you call my name.
I do want to love you.
I am in your dreams.

I pretend to be your bodyguard.
I feel my heart in love.
I touch the silkiness of your heart.
I worry about you.
I am your marine.

I understand I miss you too much.
I say there is no one like you.
I dream about you.
I try to do my best for you.
I hope to be your lover.
Rafael Pena, Grade 9
Hiram W Johnson High School

Struggling with the Opposition
His antagonist,
Not a physical adversary
Although he wants
To strike it down forever
Domineering from within,
The voice inside
His mind and heart.
Binding him with insecurity
A covert force
Impelling him
In unforeseen directions.
He tries in vain to escape
This momentum,
Yet it wins the battle
Over body and soul
Keeping his spirit
Trapped inside
Once again.
Erin Lee, Grade 7
The Mirman School

The Hitter
When the pitcher throws the ball
He takes aim and gives it his all
The hitter swings with all his might
Hoping the ball takes a very long flight
The ball takes off with a crack of the bat
He runs so fast he loses his hat.
He runs to first with a big stride
If the play is close he will slide
If the fielder makes the out
Back to the dugout with a pout
Ana Yuliana Ceja, Grade 7
St Francis de Sales School

The Moon Is Glowing…
The wind is blowing
The waves are crashing
The moon is glowing
The sea foam is splashing

The waves are crashing
The wind is cold
The sea foam is splashing
The sand is gold

The wind is cold
The sand is warm
The sand is gold
There is going to be a storm

The sand is warm
The clouds are dark
There is going to be a storm
The trees would splinter if not for their bark

The clouds are dark
The moon is glowing
The trees would splinter if not for their bark
The wind is blowing
Rebecca Roland, Grade 8
Kadima Day School

Snow Pearl
Snowflakes gently falling from the sky
I stick out my tongue and it falls in my eye;
Snowflakes fall oh so much harder,
I think to myself O my, O my!

I go to bed dreaming of all the fun
We're going to have without the sun;
I awaken sleepily in the morn,
To the smell of gooey cinnamon buns.

Bundling up to prepare for the day,
"Don't forget your gloves," Mom will say;
I scamper quickly out the door,
Getting ready to play, play, play!

I wonder what I'm going to do first,
I pick up some snow to quench my thirst;
I see a large snowman off to my left
I gave him a kiss with my lips pursed.

The snowman needed a girl,
So I decided to give it a whirl;
I rolled three big balls of snow
She needed a name, I gave her Pearl.
Brianna Thrasher, Grade 7
Joe Walker Middle School

Girls
I know I am a girl
But who cares girls rule
Boys think we stink
Just because we like pink
I say we have power
Even though we like flowers
Some like sports
Many get A's on their reports
Lots have friends
Many like the latest trends
All of us are loved
Like we were sent from above
We can be as rough as a boy
And we give each other great joy
We are women, female, and girl
Hannah Brown, Grade 7
Monte Vista Christian School

Cats from the Past
Cats
rolling and rioting
kittens are frightening
first they cuddle then bite
scratch, attack, fight
they harass the old cats
'til they're worn out
and fall asleep in piles
on TVs and in mom's files
while listening to stories
of "Practical Cats"
and studying longevity
and trying on names
fit for Eliot's,
Rumpleteazer, and Macavity
Jasmine Melancon, Grade 9
Hemet High School

My Room
My secret place where
I play with balloons and
Only share with you

My secret place where
We make a fun house and
Only you can come inside

My secret place where
You can feel right and take
Off on an imaginary flight

My secret place that place
I call my room and have
Fun playing with you
Karla Pahua, Grade 8
Richardson PREP HI Middle School

High Merit Poems – Grades 7, 8 and 9

A Reflection on Edvard Munch's The Scream
Oh no!
I cannot be heard.
The people behind me have no thought of my existence.
I am out of place.
The straight and narrow bridge,
Strong but soft waters
An exciting but peaceful sunset.
I do not belong
With all this stress and pain painted into me.
All these scared feelings dwelling inside me;
Wouldn't you think that I
Would be some place that has
No words, that is dark and cold,
No feeling, no heart
Isn't that where I belong?
Wouldn't you think so?

KeJae Gattison, Grade 7
Tenaya Middle School

Nature's Moods
Nature is full of different moods
Such as when a flower blooms
The trees grow taller
The grass gets cut smaller
Birds build nests upon the trees
Flowers are pollinated by honeybees
The water is warmer and so are the days
Nature can be described in many beautiful ways
Summer is leaving, the leaves are falling
Leaves are changing colors for fall is calling
The trees are becoming bare
Animals are inheriting more hair
Winter has started, snow is falling on the ground
Since nature is asleep at this time there is not much sound
Nature is beautiful and has great meaning
Because God made it and there is no other reasoning

Kelli Graham, Grade 7
Monte Vista Christian School

If Only…*
If only the world wasn't in pain,
If only we all weren't so vain.
If only we all could see far true,
If only our friends weren't sad or blue.
If only the world wouldn't cry,
If only we all would never die.
If only there was no sadness,
If only our days were filled with gladness.
If only the world wasn't corrupt,
If only we wouldn't interrupt.
If only you could ever see,
If only the difference would come to be.

Katarina Ivanovich, Grade 7
Monte Vista Christian School
*Dedicated to all who have needed help in the past years and now

I Remember…
I remember moving into the house full
with awaiting dreams…
I remember unpacking and
organizing everything in place…
I remember sleeping the first night
and awaking the next morning…
I remember the first party, the first holiday,
the first family reunion…
I remember our first fight and
our first love moment…
I remember our good and bad times,
our ups and downs…
I remember all the moments we had on our most
memorable house, my house, my family's house,
the Duke's house…
But I mostly remember my old house.

Maricela Duke, Grade 8
Richardson PREP HI Middle School

Blizzard
The blizzard was fierce.
I was getting tossed around by the wind.
Snow was whizzing by my face.
I felt like it was burning my skin.
I was getting numb.
The arctic breeze was covering my body.
I could barely move.
All of a sudden the wind pulled me off the ground and
into the air.
Then I saw black.
I screamed, I struggled,
I was being sucked into a black hole!
Then I opened my eyes.
I was staring at the ceiling.
I felt relieved.
Then I rolled over on my pillow and fell back asleep.

Maddie Schmidt, Grade 7
Monte Vista Christian School

After Every Song*
I opened my bed and folded my eyes
After every song
I played with my phone and called my dogs
After every song

I watched my couch and sat on my TV
After every song
I changed my hair and combed my clothes
Somewhat confused but whatever…

I fluffed my head and laid my pillow
After every song…

Ysabella Garcia, Grade 8
August Boeger Middle School
*Modeled after Nikki Giovanni's "I Wrote a Good Omelet."

Christmas Time Is Here!

The gust of the wind in the winter air flows by like a fly,
In the cold, damp air,
The cars drive on by.
The snow falling on the streets,
The children laughing in the snow,
Makes the whole wide world start to glow.
Christmas time is finally coming,
Birds chirping and carolers humming.
Wrapping presents under the tree,
Lighting the fireplace for the family,
And cozy slippers for me!
Grandma bakes some gingerbread cookies,
Bubbling up some crispy cocoa,
"Grandma, can I have one, pretty please?"
The night of Christmas Eve,
The children gather grandma's cookies and milk for Santa to eat,
Say their prayers and go to sleep.
"Christmas!" Children run to the tree,
Open up their presents,
And become filled with glee.

Carolina Chernyetsky, Grade 7
Arcade Middle School

The Championship Race

Waiting on the starting line for the shotgun to blow,
BANG goes the gun, here we go!
Here comes the first turn, hang on tight,
The leader is still in my sight.
Passing guys, here and there,
Some people think it just isn't fair.
There's a rock in the middle of the trail,
Hold on for dear life, I just might bail.
Down on the ground, the bike on top of me,
How do I get out? It's stuck on my knee!
Pick it up and start it quick,
Before I throw a fit.
Lost some time, it's no big deal,
Just got to get back on the wheel.
Catching first place, here I come,
This race is far from being done.
One lap to go, the race is winding down,
If I don't win, I'll upset the whole town.
To the checkered flag with a smile on my face,
From the start, I knew this was my race.

Connor Tustin, Grade 7
Arcade Middle School

People, People, Please

War is the most common of all problems,
But it is the way to handle things.
Though this war comes from human beings
People, people, please

War is what causes pain
Though the other team sleeps in vain
People walk and live like zombies
People, people, please

War is the center of depression
The sadness that sweeps through a town
With the thought of a loved one living downtown
People, people, please

There is no medicine for war
So please shut the door
As I sleep I come aboard
The thought of a peaceful world with no war
People, people, please

Luke Routhieaux, Grade 8
Richardson PREP HI Middle School

Mommy

Mommy
   Smells as sweet
   as a flower
   in mid spring
Mommy
   Looks graceful
   as the willow tree
   moves gentle in the wind
Mommy
   Sounds gentle and kind
   her voice a peaceful lullaby
   that makes me drift to sleep
Mommy
   Feels soft and squishy
   her soothing hug
   I never wanted to let go
Mommy
   My one
   and only
   first love.

Sierra Hancock, Grade 8
Los Molinos Community Elementary School

Two Heads Drifting…in Escher's Bond of Union

I see two lovers
About to kiss.
They're dancing in space.
They don't care if people see them because they're in love;
Spirals
Just drifting away.

Jason Berry, Grade 7
Tenaya Middle School

Reflections on Escher's Bond of Union

This drawing looks like
A father and son in space
Looking at their lives going on without them;
They're connected together, while looking sad at each other.
Trapped in space,
They look down and see other people having fun in their lives.

Brendan Daddino, Grade 7
Tenaya Middle School

The Unfortunate Accident

On my way back home on a rainy day
I had found myself with nothing to say.
Silence filled the car
My dad raced to go on far.

Silence suddenly disappeared
As a loud noise caused me to cover my ears
The sonic boom came from the outside
But immediately put in danger our own lives.

There was a screeching of tires that came our way
My dad didn't notice until it was too late.
We were hit by a truck
And that was not the end of our bad luck.

We turned to our own bloody death
Until we came to a giant stop
My dad unconscious was kissed by death
Then came the carnivorous cop.

My crying eyes were consoled by my mother's love
I no longer felt the need to sob
Because throughout the tragedy
I still had my family.

Elmer Portillo, Grade 8
John Adams Middle School

Describing You

The sun may shine that star-glazed sparkle,
The waves would crash softly upon the shore,
But none compare to you
With your dazzling eyes staring, staring…evermore.

Not a minute passes when I think of you,
Your voice whispering in my ear,
I anxiously await to see that face
Right now, right here.

When you're close I feel complete,
Like nothing can conquer our love,
Invincible against dangers outside,
And envied by those above.

No matter how many times I look at you,
I always gaze in awe,
To know you're forever mine,
Fills me with warmth I can't recall.

You, by my side,
Is a picture I adore,
For nothing compares to you,
With your dazzling eyes staring, staring…evermore.

Claire Chen, Grade 9
Irvine High School

Days to Remember

where we met;
we learned the alphabet
years full of joy
will not be destroyed

friends that I made
together we played
we had a good time
learning to rhyme

I was so glad, as glad as a first time mother
nothing could make me mad
but days of glory
are only part of my story

to friends I waved
to stay was what I craved
days of tears,
now filled me with fears

remember I will
it makes my heart ill, like a fish with no gills
but now that they're gone
I'll have to move on

Vanessa Verduzco, Grade 8
John Adams Middle School

An Only Child

Being an only child,
You have to be responsible,
You have to be mature,
And you always have to be first.

You will be the responsible one,
The one who leads,
The one who can't count on someone older than you,
Other than your parents.

You will be the mature one,
The one who acts like the adult,
The one whom adults judge as the oldest,
Yet also the youngest.

You will always be the first one,
The first one who goes to school,
The first one who goes into changes,
And the first one who always gets in trouble.

Those things will never be the same for the second child,
Because I will be the leader,
I will be the adult,
And I will always be first.

Anabell Gimena, Grade 7
Corpus Christi School

Little Black Shoes
little black shoes
ever since I got you
on that Christmas morning
I had cherished you
I would wear you every day
'til your color will fade away
even though you would start to tear
I still wore those little black shoes
but one day came
when I threw you away
bye bye little black shoes
Alexia Romero, Grade 8
Isbell Middle School

I Miss You!
All the times we had I miss them
I was blind to see I had you there
Foolish and dumb I miss you
You are always in my heart
I want you to know
I should have spent more time with you
But I didn't and now you're gone
Thick and thin we've been through
But all I have is an old picture of you
But what I'm glad is that I can still say
Is I love you and miss you a lot!
Karina Mejia, Grade 8
Richard Merkin Middle Academy

Don't Worry
No worry my friend
I will lend you a hand when you need one
We can stand together forever
No matter how tough life gets
If someone has hurt you, don't worry
Never let anyone make you feel bad
For who you are
Stay strong,
Don't worry I will be there for you
Soon we will be set free
So until then you can lean on me
Sarah Sigala, Grade 8
Isbell Middle School

The Beauty of a Puppy
Puppies are nice and cuddly,
beautiful and gorgeous.
They eat and drink,
sleep and play.
They like to dig holes to hide a bone
and make a dirty mess.
They get sweaty and start to smell,
but are still loveable after all that fun.
Boy, I wish I could have just one.
Carina Maldonado, Grade 7
Our Lady of Guadalupe School

My True Friend
At school there was a group of girls and guys
Who always had to make me cry
They made my preteen life so horrible
That I found it very unendurable
I had a best friend but in the end
She left me all alone
By then there came another girl
Who never made me cry
Instead together we stood against all the girls and guys
But then she too left me cold and dry
My heart ached and I cried
Would I ever find a friend so true who would love me and not leave me alone
But then came a girl from the group of girls and guys
Who never ever made me cry
But instead comforted me
She was nice and encouraging
I never found another so friendly
And she was the reason why
I dried my eyes and never cried
Because in the end she proved to me she was, is, and will always be
My best and only true friend.
Samantha G. Karis, Grade 9
River City Christian Academy

Stop, Think, and Thank
You always say to yourself as you pass by field workers
I'm happy I don't have that job, or I wouldn't want to be them
But, do you ever wonder what it would be like if we didn't have them
We would not have fresh fruit or vegetables
So next time, Stop, Think and Thank
When you put your garbage out to be taken away
Do you ever wonder what it would be like without those people
Our streets would be even worse than they are now
They would be cluttered, smelly and gross
So next time Stop, Think, and Thank
Sometimes we take things for granted
We don't think about what our lives would be like without the people doing
the jobs that no one else wants to do
So next time you see someone working to help make our lives easier just
Stop, Think, and Thank
Cydney Parker, Grade 7
Monte Vista Christian School

I Am From
I am from "There's no food mom" "Well make a potato!"
I am from John 3:16 "For God so loved the world that he gave his only begotten Son
That who so ever believeth in Him shall not parish but have ever lasting life."
I am from trying to be different but not make a statement.
From Christmas get togethers, Thanksgiving eating, and birthday wishes.
From freedom, yet captivity in my own mind.
From go here, go there, be this, be that, he's that, she's this.
From you're smart, don't cut your hair, and eat your dinner.
I am from friends getting me through everything. I am from family and God that's there through anything.
Jade Belvin, Grade 8
Bret Harte Middle School

High Merit Poems – Grades 7, 8 and 9

A Night in the Woods
I stare out the window, what do I see,
The full moon glistens in the pitch black dark,
Millions of little stars surround me,
Far away, I can see the scary park

The night is so cold, it gives people frights,
Feels like the night is trying to swallow me,
To survive, I will fight with all my might,
From far away, I could see the black sea

I feel like it's only the beginning,
When will this crazy nightmare ever end,
Now my poor head is crazily spinning,
This harsh pain will take a long time to mend

Alone in the woods, I look at the sky,
Alone in the woods, I wish I could fly.
Nina Hoang, Grade 7
Sarah McGarvin Intermediate School

The Warmth Within
Water leaks from the grieving clouds,
Everyone seeks shelter, forming crowds

Me? What do I do? I jump and play,
Not taking any chance to waste this fun, wet day

It began as a sprinkle, but now starts to pour,
Filling the air with a deafening roar

I dance, I splash, and I laugh in the rain,
Not caring at all if people think I am insane

The final drops fall from the sky like morning dew on a leaf,
The duration of the rain was all too brief

I am now drenched in water and soaked to the skin,
So what? I am happy and warm within
Christina Ngo, Grade 7
Sarah McGarvin Intermediate School

Can We?
Can we honestly say,
We think about how lucky we are
And how fortunate we are?

Can we?

There are many days that we get mad,
Just because we don't get something we want.
Can we deny that we don't do that?

Can we?

Honestly, we can say that we,
Think, pray and hope that the soldiers
Who sacrifice their lives for us are okay.

We can!
Samantha Courtney, Grade 8
Park View Middle School

Save a Heart
Puppy mills
Large-scale dog breeding operations
Among these pups are illnesses, disease
They're treated without care,
Those poor puppy mill dogs

Do not get grooming or exercise
Miss out on treats and sometimes even the sun,
Most will live in fear of humans,
Others will die young
Out of those poor puppy mill dogs

All this began after World War II
Help stop this, end this crime
Consider not buying puppies
Instead adopt,
And mend a broken heart.
Alice Gamez, Grade 8
Richardson PREP HI Middle School

In Edvard Munch's The Scream
There are two men walking casually on a boardwalk,
Pretending like nothing is happening.
The water beneath them flows very intensely.
There is a man on the boardwalk screaming with all his strength.
He has a very scary expression;
His eyes are bulging out.
But, still, the two men don't appear as if they heard him.
The sky looks very intense, almost exactly like the water.
But what really bugs me is
If the sky and water are reacting to the screaming man,
Why don't the others hear him?
What was this screaming man looking at?
Nahom Benyam, Grade 7
Tenaya Middle School

Touch
I constantly hear the same things in my head
If they are on too long, I soon die instead
I feel soft ear wax with my extended hair
The sounds of notes fill the air
I am in great health when my battery is charged
By your touch a part of me becomes enlarged
With different sounds that come from out of me
Different languages you may seek
By the click of a button
You can change all of me

iPod
Katrina Pacheco, Grade 8
August Boeger Middle School

Page 203

Just Imagine

When I am alone,
boredom is my kingdom,
and laughter is my throne.
I go to this place,
just to escape
my hectic everyday life.
What is this place that is absent of strife?
My imagination.
Here, I can create my own nation.
Full of peace, and disdain for war.
Where neighborly people call upon your door,
just to say hello and good-bye and leave you with a smile.
Where you are free to go about, acting like a child.
With no discrimination,
an absence of all segregation,
and a loving family for all.
Come and see for yourself
the wonderful wealth
that imagination can provide.
Just imagine.

Brianna Miller, Grade 8
Vaca Pena Middle School

The Grand Canyon

Beauty of nature's canvas
Just like a painting.
The rain comes down hard
As I drift off to sleep
My head clouds with dreams
That the Grand Canyon will flood
With water without damaging any of its beauty.
I would be able to climb into a submarine
And look around in its glorious beauty.
When I awake
The water from my dreams has diminished
And the painting is restored.
The Grand Canyon is there.
I reminisce in the beauty of my dream.
The magnificence of it is overwhelming.
I can see the Colorado River.
I look into the canyon.
The Grand Canyon is overwhelming.
The real-life painting
Painted on nature's canvas.

Lauren Julius, Grade 8
Coronado Middle School

BMX

When you hit the jump, and are in the air,
You do a flip without a care.
But, when you are on your way down,
That's when your heart starts to pound.
When you land and are surrounded by your friends,
All you want to do is go again.

Kyle Vaughan, Grade 8
St Francis de Sales School

Love

I always wonder why I love you so much
Even though you treat me bad
I want to forget about you but I just can't

It makes me cry when I think about our
Past because I know that our past
isn't going to happen again

You're the reason why I can't last in relationships
Because I think to myself what if
he breaks my heart like my first love did and if I
ever get an opportunity to forget about you believe
me I'll take that opportunity in a heartbeat

Jasmine Ortega, Grade 7
Los Molinos Community Elementary School

Watercolor

Watercolor is cool as regular painting
It is incredible and beautiful
It's as fun as drawing and coloring
some as detailed as the ones in a museum
watercolor is watery as sodas
It is when you use water and paint together
It's fun to do, just painting in pictures
watercolors are so beautiful
looks like 3-D
It feels like when you do watercolors
you're good as an artist
an artist is good at different types
of painting but I think watercolor is the best.

Maya Alves, Grade 9
The Westview School

The Beat in My Soul

The tune in my head, and the rhythm in my soul,
An alternative beat, to a suspending drum roll.
Each stroke makes a difference,
A flurry of sounds,
The flow of the music, in my head, all around.
My sticks hit the hi-hat, the tom and the snare,
Adding a fill every here and there.
My hands and my feet, working in sync,
When I play the drums, I just do, I don't think.

Jessica Kwok, Grade 8
Carden Academy of Santa Clara

Thoughts on Escher's Relativity

It looks mysterious;
Like so many questions.
It's different, it's sideways,
It looks awesome,
The stairs go up, down, left, right
So many questions I want to ask
It's like a crossword puzzle you can never solve.

Brianna Gonzalez, Grade 7
Tenaya Middle School

Leaf

It's coming down. gently patting the soft grass on top of hill.
it's coming down.
Up goes her babies as Mother Nature delicately blows.
little time does it have, oh what little time.
until it becomes like the rest…
whoosh! fragile parts hear their last sound.
hears the last soft mourn of their mother nature…
now.
others are coming like before.

Christina Kim, Grade 8
Windemere Ranch Middle School

Family

Friends come and go
Family will always be there for you
Making sure you'll be fine
Family will love you every day
They will be there on the hardest times
When you're laughing and when you're crying
So love them every day
Say you love them as much as they love you
Don't forget to say thank you for what they do for you every day

Sofia Camargo, Grade 7
Our Lady of Guadalupe School

Eve of Heart

She watches sky,
clouds tumble by.
Pastel smears reflect in her eyes,
She dances in circles.
Pale blue heart flutters,
time begins to speed,
She falls with no emotion.
As stone she shall exist,
Forever she shall cease dancing.

L. Ortega, Grade 8
Oliver Wendell Holmes International Middle School

Ode to My Room

My room
My sanctuary
A place where I relax
A place where I kick back
Where my imagination runs free
Like a squirrel in a tree
Where my dreams grow and my wonders flow
Where I laugh and play
And be myself in my own way

Fernanda J. Gonzalez, Grade 8
August Boeger Middle School

I Am a Tree

I am a tree
I am strong and open to others
Strong forces may try to take me down
I will always stand firm and bend without breaking
The fruit of my branches helps civilizations grow
My trunk is strong but my will is stronger
My actions speak louder than my words
I am a tree

Alexander Okamoto, Grade 8
Palm Desert Charter Middle School

Special

A lot of people stand out for the many reasons
But if you are just you,
You will stand out for the best reason
And that is because who you are on the inside
Not who you are on the outside

You are special because you are you

Evan Snell, Grade 7
Willma E. Cavitt Jr High School

The Race

Swim faster and faster
the pain, the joy
oh god help me
help me get through the race
the race of life, the hardest one we'll ever take
yelling and cheering by the ones you love
do what you can: trust…relax

Rose Wyse, Grade 9
Foothill High School

Life

The sand between my toes
Feels like a happy ending
To a long happy life

The breeze in my hair
Feels like an old friend
Waving and saying hello

The water against the rocks
Feels like a loved one
Saying goodbye

The rain from the clouds
Brings back happy memories
That I once shared

With the last beats of my heart
I look back on my life
And think to myself….
What a wonderful life

Elizabeth Harmer, Grade 8
Walter F Dexter Middle School

The Sun

Look up in the sky
Look up very high
You see what gives us light
The sun is very bright
Sometimes I wonder if it will go out
Like a candle
Getting smaller, smaller, and smaller
Gone

Marissa Dempsey, Grade 8
Our Lady of Guadalupe School

Nature

Gardens are colorful and beautiful too
mountains are big and rocky too
the world is green and blue too
nature is AWESOME
rain is nice too as it falls on your face
nature is fresh
as fresh when you take a shower
nature is GREAT!!!

Monica Castellanos, Grade 7
Sarah McGarvin Intermediate School

Love Story

I wrote your name on my hand
But I washed it away
I wrote it on paper
But I accidentally threw it away
I wrote it in the sand
But the sea washed it away
I wrote it on my heart
And it will forever stay

Alex Le, Grade 7
Sarah McGarvin Intermediate School

Him

His smile overwhelms me —
  Whatever mood I'm in!
His voice is like a song
  Of love that lasts forever.
His eyes are so beautiful,
  Like the sunset in the sky.
Whenever he's with me,
  My heart floats in deep Heaven.

Rheanna Ostrea, Grade 8
Corpus Christi School

Noise/Silence

Noise
loud, scream
yelling, talking, laughing
cry, argue, read, write
quiet, still
silence

Jessica Angel, Grade 9
Hiram W Johnson High School

Backwards

The corners of my mouth sink into my face
My world goes black and my memories begin to erase
My legs shake underneath the body I am dragging around
I force my lips shut until I am forever unable to make a sound
Every day is exactly the same, and I am so sick of losing this game
Every word I stutter is burning me empty, my past still tempts me
Gaping holes take over my soul, destructive thoughts are taking control
I am lost in this world, dying to find my purpose
There's so much to this nightmare than what lingers on the surface
Dreadful moments pass through cluttered brain waves
And I am unable to feed the addiction my mind craves
I suppose it's best that I throw my old self away
And wait for my impulsive fantasies to decay
But it seems as if the more I wait, the more destruction I generate
I suppose I'll simply have to hang around for my fate
But my future lies in these dreams I create
I'll rise to my feet and stay strong, I'll do my best to prove everyone wrong
I'll do everything in my power to avoid relapsing
I'll stop myself from ever collapsing
I'll stay breathing and hang in there
And hopefully find the pleasures of inhaling air.

Yasmine Kahly, Grade 9
American High School

The Shadow

If I am still alive tomorrow,
the shadow will lurk towards me.
If I am filled with sorrow,
it will come closer until I've taken my final breath.

Every day I mourn of how things could've gone between us,
but in the morning it's gone again.
It could have been the shadows in my dreams at night,
but in the end it's hopeless.

Although I try to capture it with my mind set before me,
the shadow finds a way to interfere with everything I have left.
My moments of memories were gone before my eyes,
but nothing could make me forget the way I worked to get its attention.

Mindy Chang, Grade 7
Sarah McGarvin Intermediate School

M.C. Escher's Relativity

The four corners of the world,
In their good times and bad times,
The relativity of us all,
In the game of survival on planet Earth,
Fighting,
Loving,
Killing,
Caring,
The human beings not paying attention or giving respect to others,
And the ones that do give respect and care are not seen hidden in time,
But we are all related in some way.

Jacob Kovacevich, Grade 7
Tenaya Middle School

Teenager?

The daggering looks that can kill
Peers pushing you against your will
Telling you:
Choose a side! Choose a group! Choose a path!
You're thinking:
I'm not good enough, not quite smart enough...
They're not *proud* enough
Telling yourself:
Keep pushing, keep going, do better, do more
You wish everyone's expectations would hit the floor
You want to break free through the door
You just can't take it anymore
Adulthood is calling, responsibility is mocking
All you hear is:
Grow up, get up, do better, do more
Stop fooling around
You want them to see, to appreciate what you've done
How far you've come, but it's never good enough
Their patronizing haunts your every thought
You want out, and they just don't get it.
They say troubled teens, I say troubled parents.
Monique McDaniel, Grade 8
Chico Jr. High School

Rhapsody for a Nobody

Oh, my dear Nobody —
May I call you that, sir? — If sir you truly are.
I long for your embrace in the absence of your being
And to smile a welcome home as you return from a long day's
wrestle and tumble through life.
My sweet, sweet Nobody
Is your voice ever but a whisper in my ear?
From a distance you seem so near; yet zooming in —
Lovely Nobody —
You were never even here.
I feel your hands gently sliding into place between my fingers
Lighting afire my heart with your heat.
Oh, my dear Nobody,
I am dissatisfied with but a mere pair of hands to hold onto.
I pray to God, each night I do,
If he would tilt your world just this angle towards mine
Into an entanglement of Forevers; we could be ensnared,
My precious Nobody,
I will find this face of yours; as you begin to unmask mine
One day, some day, we shall be Mr. and Mrs. Somebody —
If only for ourselves.
Catherine Tsai, Grade 9
Temple City High School

Music

I love music
You can express yourself with music
Music is also entertaining
Music is something everyone can enjoy

I love playing instruments
The conductor hands you a variety of music
You play music written by people all over the world
Everyone has a preferred music style

Music is also a form of art
Schools put music as a fine art in their curriculum
I enjoy music
There are different types of music to fit everyone's style
Silvia Romero, Grade 8
Park View Middle School

Mom's Room

Children laughing at play
Mom and Daughter bond
George Lopez making us laugh
That was mom's room

A pointless conversation
Mom running out of patience
My ears are ringing of this
I can't stop thinking of it
That was mom's room

Hugs and kisses from mom
Now that you're gone it can't be the same
I miss you dearly I want you in my arms one last time
That was mom's room
Melanie Perez, Grade 8
Richardson PREP HI Middle School

This Is About Edvard Munch's Painting The Scream

The water is colorful; with blue, white, and orange.
The colors seems smashed to each other.
Two guys are walking toward The Scream.
The man screaming looks like he is scared, so scared.
Maybe, because of the two guys walking by.
Maybe, the man screaming has bad dreams.
This painting, is so painful and colorful,
That is just
Screams
At
You.
Adrianna Contreras, Grade 7
Tenaya Middle School

Ode to the Sun

How it brightens the day just right
Nothing can compare to the beauty of its light
The perfect morning
Into the perfect day
Through its childish play
Like a god waiting to rise
But too great for the human eyes
Afraid to say our last goodbyes
As we watch the light of our day
Sink into the ocean's bay
Christa Cruz, Grade 8
August Boeger Middle School

My Best Friend

You were there for me when I needed you the most
You made me laugh when I was down
I just want to take a step back
And reverse the hands of time, do it all again,
Form the day we first spoke,
The day we shared our first laugh…
We share so many memories
From all the many parties
Where I covered your face in cake
To our minute-long handshakes
And our trick-or-treats on Halloween —
But now we come to our present year,
Knowing that our graduation is near,
The many hugs and tears that day…
I just want to thank you
For being one of the persons I'll never forget.
You're like a brother to me —
The kind of friend
Who'll stick through to the end

Kevin Pineda, Grade 8
Corpus Christi School

My Family

My family is what matters to me most
They help me when I'm down
They take me on vacation and let me ride around
They are very loving with everything that they do
It's always a pleasure to see them
I love them dearly, with all my heart
And I will love them as along as I live

My dad takes me to ride my dirt bike and to surf
I thank my dad for teaching me how to do those
He surfs with me and rides with me, and teaches me everything cool
My dad is great all around and can never let me down

My mom helps me with my homework
She teaches me how to cook and how to use the stove
When I'm sad she will make me something great
She does my laundry all the time even when she is sick
My mom is great and my dad is great
That's why I love my family more than anything

Thomas Lerouge, Grade 8
Park View Middle School

School

You go to school, learn, be successful.
Pay attention,
Your work won't be as stressful.
Did I forget to mention?
Not everyone in the world has it as easy as we do.
Get a bad grade.
So, you get a redo.
Don't let the opportunity fade…

Elliot Wong, Grade 8
St Mary's Chinese Day School

I Am*

I am Garvey,
I see the good in everyone,
I hear the sounds of good kids,
I feel the need to help,
I am honest and trustworthy.

I dream of the world being good,
I worry of the kids who do dreadful acts
    like a raccoon raiding a trash can,
I want to lend a hand to all those in need,
I hope for world peace in all nations,
I am supportive and apprehensive,

I understand anger of kids,
I try to show kindness like a brother and sister,
I laugh at anger of kids who don't care,
I touch kids hearts in ways unununderstandable,
I am honest and apprehensive.

Garin Mesarch, Grade 8
Palm Desert Charter Middle School
*Inspired by "Touching Spirit Bear" by Ben Mikaelsen

In Memory of Grandma

Suddenly my world was becoming gray and sad
Your life came to an end
I didn't want to believe it but I couldn't let it go
Rest in peace and be with God, look after me

Your life came to an end
I will love you forever, don't ever leave
Rest in peace and be with God, look after me
You'll always be in my heart, there to be my guide

I will love you forever, don't ever leave
You've taught me so much, I will never forget
You'll always be in my heart, there to be my guide
That day you had to leave, my heart had fell to pieces

You've taught me so much, I will never forget
Suddenly my world was becoming gray and sad
That day you had to leave, my heart had fell to pieces
I didn't want to believe it but I couldn't let it go

Holly Luong, Grade 9
Irvine High School

The Faces in Escher's Bond of Union

The faces
Look like orange peels.
At the top
The faces look connected to each other.
Maybe, they are related,
Possibly, they are best friends.
It looks as if the world stops
When they "bond" their "union" of friendship.

Milca Gutierrez, Grade 7
Tenaya Middle School

High Merit Poems – Grades 7, 8 and 9

America
America, land of the free,
and most pleasing to me.
America is great and strong,
with this I can never go wrong.
If you doubt it, just wait and see.
Timothy Tsang, Grade 7
St Mary's Chinese Day School

Thoughts on Escher's "Bond of Union"
Together bonded,
Through thick and thin to show how
To love your friends
Saraé Madron, Grade 7
Tenaya Middle School

Thunderstorm
The loud thunder roars,
And then the lightning flashes.
Rain slowly falls down.
Tiffany Ye, Grade 8
St Mary's Chinese Day School

Escher's "Bond of Union"
Together as one;
Nothing can break them apart —
Tied close by a string.
Genessa Sandoval, Grade 7
Tenaya Middle School

Escher's Bond of Union
Two heads connected
Son and father held by strands
Floating in a dream
Joshua Tanuwijaya, Grade 7
Tenaya Middle School

Slippery Like a Fish
Love is like a live fish,
Once you think you have it,
It swims away.
Kathleen Escusa Reyes, Grade 7
Immaculate Heart of Mary School

One by One
Flowers are growing
Shining brightly in the sun
Blooming one by one
Leore Oren, Grade 7
Kadima Day School

Paper Heart
My heart like paper,
Fragile and sensitive,
Will bleed if broken in two.
Marielle Juinio, Grade 7
Immaculate Heart of Mary School

Grandfather
It was three sad months ago when the doctors detected
That my grandfather had stomach cancer.
In the hospital Bed lay my grandfather away.
It was sad and depressing seeing him lay away in the hospital bed.

He was a man well known and well respected as well, everyone trusted him.
I still don't understand why this tragedy happened to him.
It was sad and depressing seeing him lay away in the hospital bed.

During the summer came the day of his birth.
Since he couldn't go anywhere for his birthday the celebration came to him.
The whole family pitched in to help rent the Mariachi for him.
It is a day that no one in the family shall ever forget.

He sang and sang until he could no more…he even sang from the bed were he lay away.
His singing made it seem like he wasn't sick at all.
That moment was so magical but it wasn't made to last forever.
Two weeks later he got very ill.

A day or so he got ill and passed away.
It was the afternoon of August 16, 2009.
The whole room was silent all you heard was BEEP! BEEP! BEEP!
It was sad and depressing seeing him lay dead in the hospital bed away.
Viviane Blake, Grade 8
John Adams Middle School

Where Poetry Hides for Me
Poetry hides
In the beach with the waves going up,
It hides in my phone when I text,
It hides in my favorite songs, when I listen to them,
Poetry hides in me when I'm watching TV and get ideas,
It hides in a tree house when I'm alone,
It hides in my room, when I'm doing my homework,
Or, next to the fireplace, on a rainy day.
It hides when I dance and hear the rhythm,
It hides when I'm camping in the forest, or when I go to my cousin's house and have fun.
It hides when I'm playing my favorite sport with energy or when I'm watching
A football game and hope our team wins.
It hides in the pizza that I'm eating when I'm focusing on the flavor.
It hides when I'm hanging out with my friends and having fun.
It hides in me when I'm running and feel the wind.
Mahmoud Musleh, Grade 7
Tenaya Middle School

In Escher's Relativity
There are crazy stairs that go around in different diagonals.
There are faceless people that walk on the stairs
Upside down, sideways, and the right way.
There is a man with a bowl of food and a woman with a bucket of water. I see
What looks like a thief carrying a sack on his back, and two people holding hands walking.
There is a man in a secret room and a couple of people looking down on the rails.
There are so many things to look at in this drawing, even if we don't know
What this drawing is trying to say.
Angel Molina, Grade 7
Tenaya Middle School

I Weep

E nergy waves
L aughing through my brain.
E nticing it to wander,
A round the land which is my own.
N ever will someone else enter
O r even understand, the
R egion of my fantasy, my own little land.

N ear my heart
I nteresting thoughts swirl 'round,
C ivilly waiting for me to write them down.
O ver and over they say their part,
L osing themselves in sound.
S o, I listen eagerly, acting like a clown.
O h, listen to place where my thoughts are born!
N ever let them be smashed, or broken apart and torn!

W here is gone my savior now?
E ven lost or killed?
E verywhere I turn to look
P eople shout through stares.
S ilence remains my only peace.

Ella Nicolson, Grade 8
St Cecilia School

R.I.P. Tia Chuya

We had some good times together,
But it's too bad your time was over,
Your son misses you,
You will always be in our hearts forever,
It's never been the same without you,
Making us laugh and helping us with our problems,
Your daughter had a baby,
And her name is Kaylee,
I know she made a mistake,
But she didn't have a mother to guide her,
We will always have you in our hearts,
We will never forget you,
Rest in peace Tia,
We will always love you.

Arturo De La Torre, Grade 8
Richard Merkin Middle Academy

Volcano

My outside is hard and brown
Inside is red, orange, yellow and mushy
The scent is like burning coal
Or burning fire
The explosion of red, orange, yellow shooting in the air
Caboom! Bang! Bang!
A river of fire
Harden like a rock
Still very hot
I create new land

Tina Mistry, Grade 8
August Boeger Middle School

He Gave Me a Better Life

He was my friend
Whom I could depend
We had laughs, cries, and he finally told me goodbye.
Before he did it, he told me it was okay.
Because I was going to be with my Father today,

It came so fast
I couldn't scream, but I did bleed.
He said it was a blast

I was so worried
I felt the dirt hit my face.
I couldn't breathe
But everything was now okay.
I finally saw the light
Today

I am fine
My Father says that I can no longer feel the pain, I felt
But now I worry for the others
That man will do the same
Without any shame.

Jada Umpierre, Grade 9
St Mary's High School

Ode to Spring

The trees whisper silently
As the wind passes by
Gently weaving the flowers.

The moon looms above
Casting crystal shadows on the water.

Vast meadows sigh
As the rain falls softly
And the clouds roll by
Holding caskets of water.

A young bud sprouts out of the sod
Stretching its tired limbs from a deep slumber.

Snow shimmers as the forest awakens
And rivers trickle.

Flowers shed an aura of light
And the air hums with life
Once again.

Sara Clausen, Grade 8
South Lake Middle School

Nature

When I look at the moon and stars I feel sad
When I look at the green grass I feel relaxed
When I look at the sun I feel tired.

Andy Winn, Grade 7
Sarah McGarvin Intermediate School

High Merit Poems – Grades 7, 8 and 9

The Blood-Red Scarf

As I walked in the dark
I saw something small and sleek
I ran into the woods after the thing
That went into the creek
It was really a scarf, that I had seen before

There I was, back in time
To the place that seemed so sublime
When my sister ran into the creek
But soon after it will seem so bleak
She fell into the ice-cold creek
This is when it turns so bleak
She never resurfaced the water
In my mind it seemed a step behind a slaughter

Now back to the present
Where it isn't very pleasant
I saw the scarf fall next to the creek
Where my sister's fate was so bleak
The very same scarf my sister had worn
The very same day she was reborn
Into a life anew, without her blood-red scarf

Josh Wheeler, Grade 8
Los Molinos Community Elementary School

My Winter Dream

I've always wanted it to snow,
Like freezing, cold ice you know.
My yard will be covered in a blanket of white
And all around a world of lights
With a Christmas tree as tall as a redwood
And ornaments so colorful that it'd look good!
Angels decorated and floating all around
With people's voices singing with a beautiful sound.
Me, impatient for Santa to come
With a sack full of toys like dolls and a toy drum.
The snowflakes dancing and falling from the sky
And all nine reindeers dashing by
Oh! My winter dream will come true as I sleep soundly,
No, but wait, I live in Orange County.

Leilani DoLe, Grade 7
Sarah McGarvin Intermediate School

Love and Soccer

My love for soccer is the same for my love for you,
Hanging out is the same as playing a game,
Saying you love me is the same as making a goal,
Telling secrets is the same as learning a new trick,
Never letting you go is the same as never giving up my cleats,
The ones I use to help me just like you help me,
You are as perfect as the perfect pass I did,
When you support me it is just like the cheering crowd,
I want that first place trophy,
Yet I still have a long way to go.

Sharleene Hurtado, Grade 7
Our Lady of Guadalupe School

Live, Love, Life

Live by what you believe
Live by how you think things should be
Live on what you know is right
Live
As a shining light

Love the one who is unloved
Love the one who rules from above
Love the one who is the third wheel
Love
The one who's heart needs to heal

Life is what we need to preserve
Life is something we don't deserve
Life is within me and you
Life
Gives us the strength to make it through

These three L's will be your guide
On how to live your days by and by
Whenever someone does you wrong or gives you strife
Live, Love, Life

Gracie Gullen, Grade 8
Monte Vista Christian School

Western Skull-faced Rattleworm

A Western Skull-faced Rattleworm,
The face of a dragon and the body of a worm.
Its wings are almost as tall as a
Normal human being.
It's red, jewel looking ovals on
Its wormy body,
Are as shiny as if it was a real jewel.
Its fangs are as long as your legs and head.
Its flesh is as hard as concrete and rock.
It lives underground, hunting for prey.
But eating bugs in the ground is just the beginning.
At twilight and morning, it comes out of hiding to feast
On cowboys and trailers.
That is the life of a Western Skull-faced Rattleworm.

Jeremiah Stucker, Grade 7
Daniel Savage Middle School

Holiday Times

The smell of **C**andy canes are in the air
lots of **H**appiness everywhere
Figures of **R**eindeers and cooks with spice
snow and **I**ce make the weather nice
Kids stay up late when **S**anta is near
decorating the **T**ree with no fear
Children are **M**errily dancing with glee
making the **A**dults happy as can be
Christmas is about **S**haring the gift of life
with your whole family all through the night

Emily Lerias, Grade 8
St Francis de Sales School

Mom

She is strong as a tree in a windy storm day
Her presence has strength with no words to say
She can heal your pain with a hug and a smile
This woman is so gentle and mild
When you are down and out
She makes that pout inside out
Which makes you laugh and forget what you were sad about
Her love for God has taught me well
Trails and tribulations are not so tough now
Her words of wisdom are always profound
She never ceases to amaze me
I'm always astound
Her heart so gentle
Her love so strong
Add it up together
You get my wonderful MOM

Angela D'Souza, Grade 9
St Mary's High School

What Happened in Edvard Munch's The Scream

What I think happened
Is that the man has either seen something terrible
Or heard something terrible.
Whatever he has seen or heard
It must have frightened him so much
Because he screams with all he has.
If you take another look at the painting, the two men
In the background have not a thing wrong with them.
If you look at the expression on the screaming man's face
It looks like he just ran 9 miles without stopping.
The sky looks like it's on fire and just about ready
To come and set the whole place aflame.
The river looks like it's mad at something, too.
That's all I see in this painting, but I'm still left with
Unanswered questions.
What happened in Edvard Munch's "The Scream"

Jaziah Cooper, Grade 7
Tenaya Middle School

The River

Snow falls down
Everyone is freezing
Birds Fly around in the sky
I look everywhere you look, its white
To some people its magical but,
To me its pain cause your freezing
Then something catches my eye like a crystal
I walk towards it
It's a river
I feel myself reach for the water
I stop myself
Is it cold?
Frozen
Maybe even warm
I dare myself
It's cold, But not frozen quite yet, but it will be soon

Emma Letson, Grade 7
Daniel Savage Middle School

Twin Towers, 911

Proud and Tall they are standing
Not knowing what would happen
Within it there was life
And it was taken away
They stuck a knife in our lives
And destroyed it all
And we watched it fall
What was standing Proud and Tall, is now ashes on the ground
Souls were lost on that tragic day
But we did not give up
But rather stood together as one
We grieved not
For we are stronger than ever
Oh, on that tragic day that our Proud, Tall towers fell
But we grieved not
For it brought us closer together than ever

Diana Peña, Grade 8
Charles Maclay Middle School

Ode to My Hands

From birth my hands have been there
To death my hands will be there
They have helped me with everything
From crawling to standing
From holding to throwing
From making noise to silencing
They help me with daily tasks
They help me with extreme tasks
Some hands are pure, but mine are damaged
Must wait to be replenished
But until that day
I will have my hands
And they will never be replaced

Adrian Gomez, Grade 8
August Boeger Middle School

A Stormy Day

The clouds roll in like an army
The day turns as dark as gray
And it turns cold like space

Then the rain falls
As if the army has opened fire upon you

You seek shelter like a snail would from the sun
The chill from the wind
Feels like needles poking your skin

Then the storm turns silent like the night
And the warmth makes you feel alive again

Garrett O'Hara, Grade 8
August Boeger Middle School

Barack Obama

Tears and shouts of joy are what was heard
On the night of November fourth, two-thousand eight
In the city named Chicago
The most important event in U.S. was being held

Born in one of the most beautiful places in the world
Honolulu, Hawaii, on August fourth, nineteen sixty-one
So many obstacles in his life, but he didn't give up
He managed to pull through

He announced his candidacy for president of the U.S.
Emphasized the issue of ending the Iraq War
Selected Senator Joe Biden, of Delaware
As his presidential running mate

Yes! It turned out to be he won the debate
Finally now after a long time there was going to be change
"HOPE" is what he exclaimed
Hope that everything will go just great

Now there is a man, that proclaims to be able to change
And fix all the mistakes we've made
From the east to the west
He is the man believed capable of making a difference

Stephany Ortiz, Grade 8
John Adams Middle School

Dreams

Dreams are like stars
They're bright and everybody wants them
Sadly though, they don't always come true
Like is what happens to a girl named Emilie

She dreamed of being loved by a Renaissance man
A man who would love her and stay by her side
And no matter what put a smile on her sad gloomy face
For a man like that could only bring happiness to her life

Not only did she dream of love but also of marvelous things
Marvelous that could make all of her sadness go away
Sparkling jewels to shimmer and jingle around her neck
Things like that is what she longed and adored

Dreams are just fantasies
Is what Emilie soon found out
She found out her dreams would remain in her head
Remain in her head and only come true in her sleep

Her dreams were like streams on which she could travel
When she forgot dreams she had nowhere left to travel
Therefore stayed put where she was and never reached those dreams
Those dreams she called stars

Gabriela Garcia, Grade 8
John Adams Middle School

Friendship Forever

It was one of the best friendships ever
Two young kids ages four and five
A boy and a girl
We thought it would last forever

We would, run, skip, laugh, and play
Not caring about the time of the day
We were very happy together indeed
Like two puppies not caring about their breed

As time passed our beautiful friendship stopped to grow
We began to slowly grow apart
It was sadly very true
But those memories would remain in my heart

One average day the terrible announcement was made
He confessed he was moving away
The news made my smile go away
I cried, nothing could console me and aid

We both cried to say good-bye
I knew I would someday see him again
One last hug and smile without a replay
In my heart he will always be

Juckilin Tellez, Grade 8
John Adams Middle School

A Love Story

If she falls will he catch her
In his arms or will he
Ignore her and leave her behind?
Will he notice that girl also known as me?

The girl smiles, laughs, and cries
Just hoping for a glimpse of his eyes
Will he notice her if she dies?
Will he notice that girl missing the girl also known as me?

He notices her but not in the way she desperately needs
He screams at her to go away
To never come back 'cause he won't stay
And so she begins to see they were never meant to be

Depressed she begins the slitting trying to numb the pain
The cuts get deeper and deeper yet the pain is still the same
By the end of the year she is pitied and hated
So she vows to never fall again

Years come and go and the girl has still not fallen
The scars on her wrist never forgotten
She is not the same fool she once was
No, she is not the same

Emely Mayoral, Grade 8
John Adams Middle School

A Friend

A friend that lasts a lifetime,
Always stands by you,
When no one else does.

A friend that lasts forever,
Wouldn't rather be anywhere,
But with you.

A friend that always helps you,
Can't be happy,
When you're not.

A friend that is always there for you,
Guides you every step of the way,
And waits for you to catch up.

A friend that is true,
Is your savior and guardian,
In your darkest hour.

A friend that is gone,
Is another angel in the sky,
Never forgetting you.
Anisha Singh, Grade 8
Joe Walker Middle School

Guilt: A Heavy Load

Heavy burdens, stored inside,
Prime to burst at any time,
She looks for forgiveness,
But there's no one to forgive,
No one but herself

Heart beating, racing,
Pulsing, pounding,
Longing for release,
Wanting so much to be someone else,
Searching, searching for some place to go
Finding everywhere her enemy lies

Her heart has sunk,
She has created
A load that cannot be lessened,
Trapped inside,
Seeking in vain a way out

Still to this day
From now to the end
There will be those faults
Heavy loads in her heart
Carly Miron, Grade 7
The Mirman School

Lost

I'm not sure what I feel,
But I wish all my pain would heal.
Knowing that you are my every thought,
Realizing that love can't be bought.
Acting with so much fear,
Trying to hold back every single tear.
Covering it all with laughter,
But in the end, I'm dealing with it after.
Beating myself up inside,
Broken heart, so broken I would cry.
While crying myself to sleep,
I finally got some time to think.
Not knowing how to tell you,
Not knowing what to do,
I honestly think that I'm in love with you.
Mya Blanks, Grade 8
Shadow Hills Intermediate School

Birds Over the Soft, Cool Ground

Birds fly gracefully
Showing their colorful wings
Through the dark night's sky
In early morning
The birds go hunting for worms
In the soft cool ground
Flying toward their nest
To care for their hungry young
Like all parents do
The babies jump high
Then start to fall toward the ground
They flap their wings hard
Then glide through the air
Flying through the deep blue sky
Watching their mothers
Garrett Cooper, Grade 7
Monte Vista Christian School

Time

They move so slow
Like little white cottony bunny tails
Clouds surround by the deep blue sky
I wonder why
I wonder how
So many shapes
So little time
They look so close
Yet so far away
It looks so serene
To be up there
I reach out my hand
To grab those cotton fluffs
And bring it back down
Empty
Surya Baraiya, Grade 9
Hemet High School

Best Friends

Every time I think of you
A smile's on my face
You have cleansed my soul, white clean,
Left without a trace
You listened to me when I'm down
You lift my spirits off the ground
You always know just what to say,
Even if it hurts
You always help me up when I'm
Pushed down in the dirt
Even when I make mistakes
You treat me just the same
I wouldn't trade you for all the world,
Or even fame
For if I lost your friendship I
Would do more than just sigh
Nothing in the world would help
Not even if I cry
Don't you ever leave my side,
For I will forget all my pride

Nothing can replace you.
Audrey Shepherd, Grade 7
Arcade Middle School

The Beach

It was one hot summer day
We were getting all excited
Beach towels, a barbeque, food to cook
An ice chest filled with sodas
We ran to the beach
Taking
   Off
     Our
       Over
         Clothes
           As
             We
               Go
We
  Dove
    In
      The
        Water
Cool, clean, pure wonderful water
"Come and eat!" we didn't want to
The sand was hot it burned my feet
Franky Maisonet, Grade 8
Glen Edwards Middle School

Alone

Sitting on a bench
My eyes, staring all around
But my body, still
Edan Evenhaim, Grade 7
Kadima Day School

Drip Drops
Rain drips and drops
It flips and flops
Falling, pouring, showering
From the sky to the ground below
Drops
Alyssa Ortega, Grade 7
St Martin-in-the-Fields School

Uninvited
the dog keeps barking
protesting the silence.
but the silence is still there
sitting between us
uninvited.
Barbara Montano, Grade 8
St Jerome Catholic School

Video Games
There once was a boy named Jose
who played video games the whole day
He moved to the side
On an incredible ride
And found he was stuck in his game
Jesse Juarez, Grade 7
Sarah McGarvin Intermediate School

Me
They ask me
"Are you this?"
"Are you that?"
I say,
"No, I am me"
Jaclyn Kayfez, Grade 9
Vintage High School

Rabbits
Rabbits
They are fluffy.
They have furry tails.
They hop around on their two feet.
Mammal.
Kevin Lee, Grade 8
St Mary's Chinese Day School

The Little Guy
Tucker
Adorable, grey
Heehawing, stomping, jumping
Always ready for fun
Donkey
Victoria Margaret Slusser, Grade 7
St Martin-in-the-Fields School

Beauty Is…
Beauty is many things.
Beauty isn't the shape of your ears, or nose.
Or whether your voice is sharp and noisy.
Nor is it the thickness of your arms, legs, or stomach.
It isn't even the color or your hair or skin.
Beauty is in the eyes of your mother and father.

Beauty isn't the size of your rings or the amount of bracelets you wear.
Nor is it measured in the sweaters you own and the shirts you style.
Or even in the glasses that are put on your face.
People won't even measure your beauty by the brand of shoes on your feet.
Beauty is in the eyes of your friends.

Beauty isn't a picture of a mountain range or a photograph of the forest.
It isn't a new car you bought or the plane you ride in.
Nor is it a perfectly styled haircut.
Beauty is in the eyes of the beholder.

If all this I say is so, then why do we spend hours prepping our hair?
Or choosing what shirt and sweater go together perfectly.
We even fuss over the paint we put on our nails.
This is because we feel that we must look good in everyone's eye.
Ryan Quevedo, Grade 7
Walter F Dexter Middle School

A Dozen Roses for You
The first rose holds the joy that's in my heart today
The second are the feelings that I feel every day
The third rose is the sunshine that circles around me when you're near
The fourth rose holds the shedding of every joyful tear
The fifth rose is the appreciation I have for you
The sixth rose is the patience in your heart for me at all times
The seventh rose holds the care I give so full and free
The eighth rose holds the love you give so much to me
The ninth rose is to forgive when I am wrong
The tenth rose is to say thank you for choosing me to love
The eleventh rose is for your smile, brightening my days
The twelfth rose is to say I love you each and every day
Another dozen roses, a dozen reasons shared
Love and friendship with you
Who I know has always cared
Dianna Nguyen, Grade 7
Sarah McGarvin Intermediate School

Life Lessons
I ask myself
Was this meant to be?
Why did it happen to me?
Yeah, maybe it was meant to be, to prove myself I could tell them I love them
Yup, life lessons are hard and we never know how many are we going to get
After this hard life lesson I can finally tell my family "I love them"
My first life lesson was hard but I survived
Always going to be marked on me and thankful I learned how to say I love you
Because I never know how close I can be to death
Veronica Mendoza, Grade 8
Richard Merkin Middle Academy

Faith and Hope

Sitting alone in a room of despair, those who could help just don't seem to care
They've left you alone to struggle from the ground, can't quite come clean and turn this around
Your whole life in ruins, your heart bound by chains, your mere existence like living in a grave
And whenever you rise, you're pushed right back down, you can't stay steady on this hard, beaten ground

Still no surrender as you struggle to the end, your courage like lions fighting against men
When your weakness shows, their strengths shine through, as their one source of pleasure is tormenting you
Just as you've given up and you can't seem to try to resist any more, that small voice inside
Says 'hold on there, it won't last long, sooner or later, you'll feel like you belong'

Throughout all of this, you're standing alone but you don't give up; you still have your hope
And faith there to guide you when you cannot speak, you will be tough, though you think you are weak
Hope and Faith both should be kept in mind, though others will abandon you time after time
With faith and hope, you'll never go wrong, when you feel confused, like you don't belong

Faith will be there in the blackness of night, when you're full of worry and trembling with fright
With no one to guide you or tell you what's wrong, faith will be there, always singing its song
Then Hope will take over — shining her light, and that's when you know that you'll be all right
For whenever Hope's here, she washes away the troubles that you thought were here to stay

Christine G. Bradshaw, Grade 8
The Mirman School

The Best Present of All

Late in the year always comes that time again
When the weather is cold and windy, and every house has decorations up
Everyone rushes out to find gifts to give for the winter holidays
And you think to yourself, "What will I get for Mom? Dad? Grandma?"
But even more you think, "What will *I* get this year?"
So you write down your wish list and always bring up that game set you want or the pretty, pink shoes
As days pass by, and time is whisked away, you become more and more anxious
And soon, you are setting out Mom's homemade sugar cookies for Santa
On Christmas, you get the game set and yes the pretty, pink shoes plus more
However, you are still disappointed that you didn't get the earrings you asked for
Even though you know you shouldn't be
Later, you go out to lunch to celebrate the occasion in your fanciest dress
As you leave, you see an old homeless man on the corner shivering in his threadbare clothing
You start to say something but nothing comes out
But then, he smiles his toothless smile at you and says,
"Have a Merry Christmas!"
And that's when you realize, you don't need the earrings or any of the other gifts
You just received it all in one smile from someone who has nothing
And it was the best present of all

Brooke Kessler, Grade 7
Lindero Canyon Middle School

Hard Times

You never know when you can trust anyone until you have really met them.
When I feel lonely he always tries to comfort me
When I need help on something I can always count on him no matter how tough it gets.
When my grandpa had died he was by my side
he told me that everything is going to be okay because he will always be with me.
Then one day my parents came up to me and told me my cousin had passed away now I feel lonely and sad. He was the only one
I had ever trusted. Until this day I still remember the last thing he had told me: "I will always be there no matter what happens."
Now I know why he kept on telling me that. I really miss my cousin he will always be in my thoughts.

Veronica Perez, Grade 8
Isbell Middle School

The Perfect Couple

And there we sat, beneath the dim lunar glow,
We were perfect for each other, she and I,
We held each other's hands, and so,
We promised never to say "Good-bye."

"Before we move on; before we advance,
I must first sorrily confess,
That within this loving romance,"
I have not been of truthfulness,

"Though it may sound awkward,
Though it may not be pleasant, however,
Please just understand,
That my love will be here forever."

"What is it, my darling? What is it, do tell.
Why do you have so much gloom on your face?
Is there something in me that does do repel?
Please tell me, please tell me under this dark bittersweet place."

Staring at me forlornly, she put her hands to her hair,
And looked at me with such a great sigh,
As she pulled off her wig, she said, "I must share,
I'm sorry to say, I'm actually a guy."

Kenny Chen, Grade 9
Irvine High School

Song of the Singer

Rustle of wind-swept grass,
Shivers of cowering mice,
Buzz of insects, trickle of a stream
Subtle sounds in the silent dark

Almond, ivory eyes, ashen, shadowy fur,
Needle-like claws, fangs of lethal life
Earthy scent of dust,
Of sharp pine, and musty dirt
Of fragrant flowers, rotten leaves

Eerie cry of the devil, gift of mother earth
Silent prowling of danger,
Singing the wondrous song of death
Muzzles tilted to the radiant moon,
Silver sparkling in the light,
Sapphire eyes glowing in the dark,
Howling the cry of the hunt

The meal has been eaten, peace is restored yet again.
Beasts lie down for the night, pulling on the soft veil of sleep
Until sunset calls to wake, when the chase will begin,
The question rises once more,
Who will live, who will die, only fate can decide.

Tiffany Zheng, Grade 8
Dorris-Eaton School

Tough Reality

I keep off my shades 'cause the world's dark enough.
People bake with no shade as girls strut their stuff.
Cars roll. Leaves fall, and children play.
Someone stole. Police call. Bodies in the bay.

Take some time, and look past the surface,
'Cause while your life is going oh so perfect,
A mother wonders if this world is worth it,
As her kid sits in the other room watchin' Kermit
Innocent with Elmo and *Sesame Street* dreams.
People wave hello as war victims scream.

Terror fills eyes, and warmth fills hearts.
Winter days with a homeless man pushin' his carts.
Goin' through the garbage, passin' the stink,
Seems a new fear comes with each blink.
So I soothe the senses with a mix of pen and ink.

I write about this stuff 'til my hands bleed.
I tell stories out loud cause some can't read.
Hand out. Some beg and plead.
Third-world kids. Food and rest in dire need.

So, I sit back and think…"Man, who cares if I succeed?"

Cameron Neimand, Grade 8
Chaminade College Prep Middle School

Lonely Melody

Playing the piano is something I truly love
To be a pianist is what I've always dreamt of
Now that my dream is coming true,
I will pursue it with you

You are what inspires me to play
You are my glowing star day by day
I stay tangled in the past remembering you in my song
Waiting for your return I've got to stay strong

The melody of my songs get lonelier every day
Why did you have to leave and breakaway?
The new songs I write are like sad days with pouring rain
I continue to play to hide my inner pain

Without you it's like a world without an end
This is something you have to comprehend
It felt like an eternity when I finally saw you
We stood there in silence unsure of what to do

With tears streaming down my cheeks you hugged me
I felt a thousand different sensations of glee
We swore never again to fall apart,
For our music came only from our heart

Brenda Romero, Grade 8
John Adams Middle School

I Miss Loving You
I thought I liked you
I thought I loved you!
I thought that without you, I wouldn't be able
To live.
I cared for you.
I thought I wasn't going to let my
Love go to waste…
But it did, somehow.
I guess you don't find me attractive.
People keep saying there are lots more fishes in the sea,
But none of them will be
More interesting than you.
Already, I so miss loving you!
Gabriel Gutierrez, Grade 8
Corpus Christi School

Guess What I Am?
Passing by day and night
lighting up everything in its path with its eyes
with teeth that look like braces
just another everyday use
it rests every time it can
moves anywhere you want it to go
fast as the wind or as slow as a turtle
makes you happy when it does work
and when it does not work it makes you mad

What is it?
A car.
Alejandro Macias, Grade 8
August Boeger Middle School

What Is a Sister?
A sister will always be by your side
Even if you tell the worst lie
She will always have your back
Like when you argue with someone and that's a fact
She will always be around
Especially when your head is hanging down
A sister will always take care of you
When you are sick or have the flu
She will always have respect and love
Like the greatness of a dove
So what is a sister?
A person who will be there forever and ever
Dabrina Ray, Grade 8
Richard Merkin Middle Academy

Pieces of a Puzzle
Friends are two pieces of a puzzle
One without the other gets you into trouble.
Together we are like a title that can never be left behind
We always match each other like lemon and lime
Both of us together makes a puzzle that will last forever.
Cindy Do, Grade 7
Sarah McGarvin Intermediate School

My Mom
When my mom walks into a room,
My stomach jumps like a jumping bean.

When she kisses me goodnight,
I feel as safe as being in a vault.

She is my personal ray of sunshine that can light up any room.

She wears clothes that are as black as night.
Her hair is as beautiful as gold silk.

When she laughs I get a spark of joy,
Like car cables starting a car.

When she helps me study,
I feel like she is smarter than Plato.

She is as beautiful as a flower.
She makes biscuits like a professional cook.

She always wears heels as high as the Twin Towers.
I love her more than anyone in the world.
Daisy Moses, Grade 8
Junipero Serra School

Softball
Softball…
It's a sport
To people it's just a game,
But to me it's a passion
I play to achieve my goals,
Others play to have fun
Opportunities can arise from one single play,
One swing at the bat can bring joy or sorrow
My coach says my name
I'm up to bat
The crowd gets anxious as I walk up to the plate
I slowly look up, the crowd and everyone's eyes were upon me
I dig my foot into the dirt
The pitcher's and my eyes meet
She winks at me and then the pitch came…
Felicia Magana, Grade 8
Isbell Middle School

Sebastian
S ebastian is my bunny. Sweet, soft, and simply special.
E very day I look forward to seeing his squishy little face.
B ecause he always licks my nose as if to say…
" **A** lways, I'll be yours."
S ometimes he is rowdy and sometimes he is freaky.
T oday, he is cuddly and just a little sneaky.
I will forever love my little "Sabi."
A part of my family 'til the end.
N ever to be forgotten, ALWAYS to be my friend.
Taylor Fuller, Grade 7
Nobel Middle School

High Merit Poems – Grades 7, 8 and 9

Cancer Be Gone

My mom is a wonderful rainbow you see.
I love her more than a flower loves a bee.
Then God was evil and put a spell on her.
And my beautiful mother got breast cancer.

The car went vroom to the doctor we went.
To do a view of a biopsy we were sent.
Thankfully the mean, killing cancer had not yet spread.
Relief went crying happily through my head.

She began to go to chemotherapy.
My family was devastated with her health you see.
My mom's weak body was always in bed.
My heart was now always full of dread.

The ugly day of operation came.
The feelings that day was not the same.
We were all anxiously waiting in the waiting room.
All is well the flowers bloom.

My mom's cancer ran away and she is cured.
Her life is happy to be back and assured.
That her health will stay strong with mine.
We are all now doing just fine.

Magdalena Martinez, Grade 8
John Adams Middle School

Blissful Waters

As I walk along the calm seashore,
I am in utter bliss,
I wish to stay forevermore,
But it is pure — I have gone amiss,

The waves that wash are crystal clear,
But my wrongs have made me so opaque,
To me this place is so dear,
For such beauty no mortal could ever make,

I craft a vessel of the strongest, lightest wood,
For I wish to sail upon blue waters,
In the sea there is unthinkable good,
Better than intricate vases of experienced potters,

During my life I had dwelt among the trees,
Concealing my horrid past,
Now I'm on my hands and knees,
And tears are rolling fast,

I decide to board my magnificent ship,
Because it is for peace that I yearn,
So into the horizon I begin to slip,
And at time's end I will finally return.

Johnathan Ford, Grade 7
Arroyo Seco Jr High School

Broken

It was not so long ago,
When he first caught her eye
He seemed sweeter than apple pie
But he left her with a broken heart to sew.

They were both young at the time,
When he caught her eye,
But she fell for him harder than a rock.
But to him she was another girl from the block.

With time he started to like her back,
When he told her this her heart raced faster
They were happy together but it ended in disaster
He changed so much

He took everything for granted
It was like a love game.
But she thought it was lame
She felt disenchanted.

But she still sees him in her dreams,
He is like a melody it seems
That's stuck in her head
That with time will be dead.

Tiffany Tovar, Grade 8
John Adams Middle School

Only One

Sharing many similarities with my sister
Addressed with the same name as my friend
One within a sea of faces
Yet there is only one of me

Gradually developing in a cocoon
Shedding the old me and putting on the new
Created within the hands of love —
The love that imagined my heartbeat
And breathed my life into existence
He is my only artist

Hidden between the lines
Pages blown in the wind
Worn and tattered on the floor
Bound together by His unfailing love
He is my only author

Starving for acceptance
Betrayed and left behind in an endless desert
Searching for water but I come up dry
Finding a source of hope in His oasis
His dedication to me suddenly quenching my thirst
He is my only need

Annie Thweatt, Grade 8
Grace Lutheran School

My Friends at Home
Around the corner
Having fun just me
And my friends and
Our crazy times

Around the corner
Having fun riding
Our bikes and racing
In races

Around the corner
having fun playing
In football games,
Tackling each other,
And scoring touchdowns

Around the corner
Having fun playing pool
And being boys

Around the corner
Having fun oh the
Memories I had there
Ron Webb, Grade 8
Richardson PREP HI Middle School

Sunglasses
Sunglasses
meant to protect
but do more
hide personalities
behind walls
like shadows
beside someone
not in front
but alone
keep them covered,
camouflaged and hidden
from the world.
Taylor Peiton, Grade 8
Temecula Valley Charter School

Ode to Makeup
Putting on my blush
trying not to be in a rush
not trying to impress
but I've got to look my best
lips all red
curls on my head
ready for school
gonna make boys drool
my shoes are untied
oohh no I'm late
detention time
Alejandra Sanchez, Grade 8
August Boeger Middle School

Reflection on Edvard Munch's The Scream
Water strong, orange sky
I'm on a bridge with my mouth open.
Full of fear, I want to scream, but nothing
Nothing comes out. I'm all alone on a bridge
With no one to hear me
Oh wait, I see two other people coming towards me.
I scream for their help.
They don't hear anything,
My tensions building within me I scream again.
All they see is a strange person with his mouth open,
But that person is me, the scream.
I feel all alone with no one to help or care for me.
Wanting to cry, but have no feeling.
The only feeling I have is terror,
All because of what Edvard Munch painted into me.
If only someone could ask, "Is he okay,"
But they can't because I am only a painting.
I wish I could get out of this cursed painting and
Scream what I have felt for a long time when I couldn't in the painting.
All I have ever wanted was to be heard and to be cared for.
If only I could.
Megan Suzanne Hardin, Grade 7
Tenaya Middle School

Why, Oh Lord?
Why, oh Lord, would you have such dissension in the world?
Why, oh Lord, would you not have peace in this place you created?
Why, oh Lord, do we have sadness?
Why, oh Lord, did you let my grandfather go so young?
Why, oh Lord, do we have inequality?
Why, oh Lord, do you let Satan exist?
Why, oh Lord, are there wars, in which innocents die?
Why, oh Lord, do fires devastate California each year?
Why, oh Lord, must there be sickness?
Why, oh Lord, must there be murderers and other criminals?
Why, oh Lord, do people get away with heinous things?
Why, of Lord, do you allow loved ones to be snatched from our lives?
Why, oh Lord, must people live with disabilities?
Why, oh Lord, do we Americans not manufacture most of our products?
Why, oh Lord, do people not have faith in you, no matter what problem?
Tyler Gehl, Grade 7
Monte Vista Christian School

The Final Battle
A t some point in the future
R ighteousness shall do battle with sin.
M an shall fight alongside their leader, determined by their previous choice,
A nd sin shall be lost under the knee-deep lake of blood.
G od's people will rejoice in victory; Satan's shall mourn in defeat.
E ternity will be decided.
D eath shall be done away with, with varying circumstances,
D iscipleship shall gain a new meaning, along with pain
O nce this battle is over.
N ow many know this as: The Battle of Armageddon.
Ian Rosse, Grade 9
Lucerne Valley Jr/Sr High School

I Am From…

I am from a place where you fight to get in but you can't get out
I am from a place where you put a lot in but get nothing in return
The streets are dirty and the people are mean, they have no respect for anyone
better yet themselves and they walk around all day doing nothing
I am from a place where people struggle with low self-esteem and insecurities
I am from a place where everyone has a handle on them and they're fighting to be free
They have no hopes, for tomorrow is yesterday and it seems a new day will never come
They walk around trying to change the past and not the future
They love what is lost and lose what is forever and cherish what is a memory
I am from a place where education is a manifestation for no one is particular
A place where when the street lights are out it's not safe to roam about
A place where not even the birds and the bees roam around the trees
A place where one little secret can cause a whole lot of damage
A place where it's not safe to go outside for the fear of staying alive so people hide from themselves
I fight, I struggle, and I try to break free from all the drama, all the pain, and
the chain of never ending agony and what I do I do…I SUCCEED

Jermanay Webb, Grade 8
St Jerome Catholic School

Forest Is My Name

There is a tree in me…I am tall and majestic…fruit is nestled in my branches…there are squirrels sleeping in my trunk…
Shelter I give to those in need…I am strong as a bear and gentle as a feather…the wind blows my leaves…a calming sight…the forest gave me trees and I am grateful for that.

There is a rabbit in me…playful and kind…silky fur…soft to the touch…the calming breeze tickles my neck…the satisfying taste of ripe berries…I am quick and quiet…listening for sneaking predators…I was given a mind and soul.

There is a sun in me…shining brightly above…I awaken the birds to sing their song…sunny and cheerful…I light up the forest every day…looking down to observe the animals at play…I hand my soul to the moon at night…my job will stay important to life.

There is a bear in me…protector of the forest…smells of pine leaves and skunks…my nose knows best…look into my eyes and you will see understanding and truth…rubbing my back on the rough bark of a tree…I am very glad to be free.

My name is forest…I love my family, weak and strong…we work together as a team…I hold on tight to nature's reins…the future holds an adventure to be made…My heart is in the forest, where it will remain.

McKenna Friedman, Grade 7
Lindero Canyon Middle School

Broken Bones

Every week when I practice in that football field I use my helmet and my pads as a shield to protect me from all the hits
Though they may not protect you from broken bones or scrapes on your knees from falling on stones
One day in practice while working on a drill something went wrong and I took a spill
Someone came after me through the line they tackled me from the blind side
When I fell, you heard the smack of my broken bone when it cracked
The moment it cracked I felt the pain I nearly went insane
My teammates surrounded me to help me out but didn't know what it was about
The coaches examined my arm to see if I could play
Though the pain was so unbearable I didn't think I'd make it through the day
Then my parents rushed me to the hospital before I could say the doctors told me my bone was broken
We gave the results to my coaches when I came they smothered me like roaches
For I was their only star quarterback until I fell and I heard the crack
I was out for three months until our first game and I wished to be able to play the same

Jacob Torres, Grade 8
John Adams Middle School

It Could've Been Better

The death of Michael Jackson
Also known as the "King of Pop"
Led thousand to stress and grief,
Depression and sadness and broken hearts.

Many thought of him as a "God"
Some saw him as a "Legend"
I saw him as a normal person
Who needed help, but those around wouldn't.

Fans want to fill his shoes
For the fame or the money
Some just admire him for his moves
Others wanted to help but they couldn't

It was too late, that sad day
Eventually came and tore the
Hearts of many and to know that
Dear Jackson died in his sin.

— Or at least as far as we know —
Tugged at my soul just to know
The one who many admired has passed on
And he'll never have another chance.

Dayleon Bell, Grade 8
Richardson PREP HI Middle School

Broken Heart

The alarm clock can't defend itself'
I wake up with you on my mind;
I never know how to tell you this,
But I think about you all the time.

A broken heart is like a broken mirror:
It's better to leave it broken then hurt yourself trying to fix it,
But I'm dumb enough to do it anyways
Because I won't give up, I will not quit.

I feel my heart aching all the time,
I wish you could be mine, you are so perfect;
Sometimes I trick myself but I know it's not true
Because I always know what to expect.

Dreams lined up against the wall,
It's this path that I choose;
I don't know why I'm doing this
Because I know that I will lose.

With you on my mind I close my eyes;
I don't feel so alone;
I hope tomorrow will be different;
A heart that's so unknown.

Andy Warren, Grade 8
Joe Walker Middle School

Hooray for Today!

Hey you! Yeah you!
Why are you looking so sad?
We all make mistakes
But it can't be half bad.

Yesterday was yesterday
It's all in the past
Tell yourself to get back up
Tell yourself it won't last

Tomorrow is tomorrow
Let's not worry about it now
When troubles come and rain clouds form
You'll deal with it; you know how!

But today, ah today! Today's the day for you!
Take chances, ask for dances; do what you need to do.
It's the only day that matters it's the only day that counts
You can do so much today! You can break so many bounds!

Maybe yesterday was gloomy
Or tomorrow doesn't look pleasant
But today is a gift in itself
That's why it's called the present.

Kevin Lin, Grade 8
Joe Walker Middle School

An Impoverished Comparison

See they, the poor, huddled on the street,
With no shoes to warm their cold, bare feet,
Full of despair, full of dejection,
Against many horrors they have no protection.

See the lucky, like us, who have no worries or cares,
Wearing warm clothes with no wears or tears,
Eating every meal ambrosial food,
Dining, a time of merry mood.

See the many differences between us and they,
Both took separate, different ways,
Yet, both were born equally, first full of hope,
Now some are too tired of their life to cope.

See us, with much spirit and life,
Yet they still battle a woeful strife,
What have they done to deserve this malady?
For this is truly a heartbreaking tragedy.

See the many ways you can help they who are despairing,
Feeding them, leading them, giving a hand that is caring,
Maybe someday they will come out of their dreadful woe,
Maybe then, it shall be true happiness that us and they will know.

Lou Y. Chen, Grade 8
Richardson PREP HI Middle School

Stars

All day since the morning I've been worrying when it's going to be night. Everybody when I get home from school I sit and watch the sunset gosh, it's so beautiful it's like a rainbow color. There's red, yellow, blue, purple, and pink but when it gets darker I get excited because it's so soothing, there's the full moon, the bright stars, and myself. I wish I could be a star since they're so bright, pretty, and soothing. Also they seem so happy all the time, and I think that's why they're so bright.

Brandi Stewart, Grade 8
Charles Maclay Middle School

Jamaican Islands

I am like a vacation to the Jamaican Islands. I am fun, enjoyable, and exciting to the people who come to me. I am like a vacation. As a vacation, people will remember what I have done to make them happier. I can't last forever, but memories of me always will. I am like a vacation.

Will Galippo, Grade 8
Palm Desert Charter Middle School

The Dinosaur and the Whale

Many extraordinary fairy tales,
Where dinosaurs roar and roar,
They have big nails,
They love to play with whales.

A dinosaur and a whale,
Were climbing like some snails,
On a really little dale,
And they love each other with a love leaving trails.

They played and played,
Every day and night,
They would always glade,
And woke up on the bright.

A tremendous huge bright yellow sun,
Would always be there,
They would run and run,
Then talked about love and to beloved.

The dinosaur told the female whale,
I roar you,
What does that mean?
The dinosaur said,
I love you!

Karla Sanchez, Grade 8
John Adams Middle School

Love Story

When I first saw you, you caught my eye.
You were looking so cute.
I couldn't stop starring out you.
With your long brown hair.
I knew I would never have a chance with you.

You were popular, I was a no one
You hang out with a cheerleader.
I told you I had feelings for you.
You acted like you didn't care.

I figured out you had two different personalities.
I love one of them, hated the other one.
You cared about what others said.
You were embarrassed of me.

You told me you loved me.
You were a jerk, you promised you would change
You didn't even try to change.
You wrote love poems.

You learned to care for others.
You asked for another chance.
You changed your attitude.
You gave me your heart.

Lilibeth Cardozo, Grade 8
John Adams Middle School

Winter Is Coming

Shouts of soccer games fade away
Goodbye to flip flops and cutoffs that fray
Dew littering fields and nearby roads
Clouds hiding the sun and homework loads
Shops show turkeys and maybe a scarecrow
Temperature starts to feel like 40 below
School shows raincoats and boots
Home shows chocolate and dreams of Christmas loot
All say a single thing
Winter is coming, it's a long way 'til spring

Kasha LaRoche, Grade 7
White Hill Middle School

Reno

She is very old
She never sleeps
She wears snow pants in the winter
She loves Mt. Rose
Reno drives a snow mobile
Loves to listen to rock
Her best friend is Las Vegas
A lot of people visit her
Reno's favorite movie is *Frosty the Snow Man*
She wants to be a famous snowboarder.

Hannah Henson, Grade 8
Daniel Savage Middle School

Foods That Make Me Smile

Pork and fried burritos are foods that make me smile. I'll fight till the end so they don't fall on the kitchen tile.
Spam, fries, and brownies are my friends. I'll defend their delicious tastes to the end.
People say I talk about food too much. Of course I do, because I love them a bunch!
Burger King, Carl's Jr., Big Boy — they're all the same. I'll win for them like I'm playing a football game.
Healthy foods are also my friends that put a smile on my face.
But I gotta force myself to eat them like I'm running a marathon race.
Overall, all foods make me happy and safe. I'll store them in a secret hiding place.

Antonio Iosefo Gaxiola, Grade 7
Our Lady of Guadalupe School

Chains

I feel like I'm in chains…time and time again I feel wrapped up, held down by unknown forces. why am I living like this? people would say, but I just tell them to shut up, go away. I don't talk about my feelings for that would be a weakness for where there's weakness in myself I feel powerless. I hide the pains of hatred, anger…depression and sorrow with a simple smile…I know I'm not the only one in chains but when I'm hurt I feel like no one cares…like I feel like I am alone…I feel as though I'm in chains…

Jaime McCallon, Grade 8
Palm Desert Charter Middle School

I Am a Laptop Hear Me Reboot

I am a laptop, very easy to work. There are a lot of choices to make on a laptop, just like in life. My brain is similar to a central processor within any laptop although I show emotions to help guide me through life. If I do not treat my problems correctly, it can reflect those of my laptop and my life. I search for information to help me solve my everyday dilemmas. I can do many things at once, similar to a laptop which can have multiple tabs open at one time. I have many functions and work hard at everything I do. I am a laptop, and I can be very useful to many different types of people.

Michael Henry, Grade 8
Palm Desert Charter Middle School

Lost Person

People feel sad when they lose someone that they love. They either cry or talk about how much they loved them. But who can blame them they loved them so much and losing them is heartbreaking. They never think about nothing but them. The way they express themselves is powerful. It shows how much they cared about the person. All they want is them back. They pray for them that they stay well wherever they go.

Kevin Garcia, Grade 8
Richard Merkin Middle Academy

Moonlight Mirror

Upon the lake when moonlight wakes, there is a mirror of the sky. The open darkness of the night, moves as the slow current sways. The moon itself so blissful and so still, shows upon the mirror's thin but elegant glass. As the time passes the moonlight ends and the mirror begins to shatter. Without a trace and without a figure. The mirror sways out of place as day breaks. It waits until moonlight wakes, but until then waiting in the shadows of daybreak.

Jaylee Dawkins, Grade 7
Orville Wright Middle School

We Are Friends, Best Friends

We met in second grade at a new school. I was really scared, but no one knew. He walked up to me and said his name, I was so relieved of this scary pain. We became friends right away, playing on the yard everyday. I knew he could be a best friend. Our friendship has continued to grow, blossom and bloom. I still cannot believe that this is true. When we met we were seven and now we are twelve. We are friends, best friends.

Darielle Preston, Grade 7
Orville Wright Middle School

The Seasons

T here are four seasons in a year, so fill them with
H appiness and cheer.
E ach day is different than any other.

F all is when the earth turns to a calmer attitude than it had in summer,
O range, yellow and brown become the colors of life
U nderfoot is the old tree leaves, marking that autumn is here. The
R obust feel of fall is replaced soon by the chill of winter as

S now, the white wonder of winter, becomes the favorite toy of the children, but the work of adults.
E verything changes when life warms up in spring,
A ll of a sudden flowers pop out of everywhere on the ground, and the
S now melts in the warm air. After a while the sun gets hotter and hotter until summer arrives. Children are
O verjoyed when the school year ends.
N o one can resist the urge to jump into a pool.
S pring, Summer, Winter, and Fall are the four seasons, remember them all!

Chase Wilson, Grade 7
Willma Cavitt Jr High School

The Sadness of the Shoah

She lived her life, day by day, playing with her doll, till they took her away
The happiness, the smiles no longer there, now replaced with forsakenness, frowns and despair
The poor little darling, awaiting her death, wondering when she will take her last breath

An innocent child marked by what she believed in, now she's sitting in a barrack, growing feverish and thin
As the man in uniform cruelly marches past her stall, the young child sits and watches her own tears fall
She should be playing with her doll, at such a tender age, yet she's crying in a cage, confronting a never-ending rage

Hovering in the corner like a newborn calf, cowering in the corner, no longer able to laugh
Only nine years old, just days ago a heart of gold, now after all that she's been through, her heart is frozen cold
From the corner she looks up, for the sound of a knock, her time slipping away, tick tock tick tock

Her time has come, as sad as it may be, the suffering will end, her death is the key
Just as the leaves fade from green to fiery red, the innocent child lies, now lifeless and dead
It is now our job to remember this child, for she represents all the ones who once smiled

Mazelle Etessami, Grade 8
The Mirman School

Why?

"Live well." That's what he told me.
The U.S. Marine. His name was Paul. Told me his story.
Made me think of all the families that one man could pull apart.
But why is there war when you could sit down and have peace.

Sending millions of our youth to war when they are not guaranteed that they will come back.
Life is valuable according to law.
But they are still sending troops to fight and die for you and I when things might stay the same.

He died three months ago in Afghanistan. Paul's sister called me.
The sound in her voice made me want to break down and cry.
War is something that doesn't have to be done,
but we may as well give our thanks and respect for all the Marines who have fought for us for years.
But yet the question still remains in millions of Americans' hearts…
WHY?

Jonathan Castellanos, Grade 8
Richard Merkin Middle Academy

It Starts with Us
Change
It is a big word
What is change?
It is what you make it to be
It is how you adapt to something
People say we're too apathetic to change
Are we?
No, *we* are the *change*
We are the future
We are the next to prove that this is not apathetic
How do you change?
I cannot answer that, for I am not you,
Only you choose to change
Change, it is a big word
Some say you can't change
But we can if we try
We are the change, the future
We are leaders
We are as one
Change
Can you do it?

Morgan Caricchio, Grade 8
Roseland Accelerated Middle School

Friendship
Friendship is like a chain
It will never be broken in the rain
Even if it rusts
It will always stay strong with trust
You can play games or hang out
You could be in a fight and have to shout
Eventually you will give in
And you will always be as close as twins
Your friendship will last as long as you'll like
You can go out and sing karaoke with a mic
But you will always be tight
You can text late at night
You will have fun
Until your day is done

Hailey Mock, Grade 7
Carden Academy of Santa Clara

Good Bye...
I miss your absence, all I got is reminiscence,
When you walked out the door, it just wasn't the same anymore,
I haven't got a clue, I just miss you,
The days I spent with you, it all felt so true,
That you loved me, and you're all that I see,
Together watching the sunset, as I fell asleep on your chest,
Walking and holding hands, and your cute demands,
Your adorable singing, your kiddish jokings,
Has got my mind going crazy, the memories are getting hazy,
What made it go wrong, our love was so strong,
Forget all your lies, now I'll finally say good bye...

Lisa Khuat, Grade 9
La Quinta High School

Unsaid Excellence
Standing, staring, wondrous figures dancing in the frame
Gaping at the wonders within the depiction
Each passionate silhouette sets your mind aflame
Your mind is at a loss; there is no verbal description
For this overwhelming impression, this search is now an obsession
Blinded by love, the intensity fills your heart
Intrigued, the victim is pulled into love's realm
Enthralled forever, like an artist in his art
The subject is inarticulate; leaving him overwhelmed
Intensity so strong he can't bear to leave
The fervor he fears he will never receive
You try to speak; yet you are dumb, life is as dull as a cloudy night
The search for happiness makes you numb
For, you think that existence could not be bright
Finally, as if the sun bursts from secretion
Lyrics fill your head and your life is now in completion
Your mind fills with words but none exquisite enough
Speechlessness fills you leaving to ponder
Never believing that this quest could be this rough
Your brain begins to wander like a lost lover searching for affection
You are speechless; in a state of perfection

Danielle Wolf, Grade 8
The Mirman School

Ode to Darkness
It surrounds you with nothing but darkness.
You see no shadow,
Only capable of seeing the color, Black.
When the sun sets,
I then feel more belonged.
Darkness is like a place to be.
You never know what's going on,
Never know what's in those little corners in the wall.
Most of all,
Darkness is like a mystery.
You're always going to keep guessing and guessing what's there,
And then it surprises you.

With a whole different, unimaginable thing,
Darkness is just a whole 'nother story.

Teresa Ha, Grade 8
August Boeger Middle School

Streaked Pane
An exasperated sigh escaped from her lips
And the glass fogged from her breath
Outside the rain drenched the wet pavement
Puddles formed over the already sodden earth
Tear-like streaks of rain streamed down
And the color gray tinted the cool evening sky
Blankets of cloud concealed the sun
A cold blast of wind howled through the land
Sheltered back inside the warmth of her home
She was again witnessing the falling of the sky's tear

Michelle Nguyen, Grade 7
Sarah McGarvin Intermediate School

The Big Wave*
Extreme waves from sea,
Miles of water below:
The big wave will come.

Raging flames burst out
As the ashes fill the air.
The sky is soon clear.

Losing your loved ones:
Memories fill your heart now;
Making you speechless.

Disasters change lives.
Weak during disasters, but
Made stronger, with age.
Matthew Brajkovich, Grade 7
Tenaya Middle School
*Remembering the novel, The Big Wave

Edvard Munch's The Scream
Someone is screaming,
But no one hears him.
He is screaming, no one
Knows why. He is standing
On a bridge with a river going
Under with a boat. The people
behind him are calm,
But he is not. What's
Wrong with him, no one knows.
Do you?
Everything is calm,
But him.
Everyone is calm,
But him.
What's wrong with
Him?
Frankie Rosenthal, Grade 7
Tenaya Middle School

My Memory
My memory remains
In a place I call home.
Where I'd spent hours playing.
Even when the sun was fading

My memory remains
In a place where I ignored the whole world
A place to be creative, as I wanted to be
A place where I can be just me

My memory remains
In a place I call home.
As years go by in my mind
Those memories are getting harder to find.
Karla Gutierrez, Grade 8
Richardson PREP HI Middle School

Passion of Love and Nature
Love and nature are sweet;
Its differences are lovely,
Its two worlds to meet,
But none of them are ugly.

They are both a passion;
But each has their own thing,
Sometimes nature has tension,
And love is beautiful in everything.

Love and its passion;
Has hands to grab your heart,
Nature and its passion,
Has eyes to see its art.

Passion of love;
Passion of nature,
Passion of a dove,
Passion of Love and Nature.
Ruth Serrano, Grade 8
Charles Maclay Middle School

Dog Fights
Outside living conditions
Rainwater with algae for water,
No food bowls
So sad.

Along with very timid
Attention starved
Non-socialized
Human-friendly dogs,

Cowering in cages
Older dogs scarred
Malnourished
Simply skin and bone,

Puppy dead
Tossed aside
In used plastic bags,
So sad.
William Carter, Grade 8
Richardson PREP HI Middle School

Raindrops
I hear the sound soft and light
Then fast and hard I hear it fall
Down my window and to the ground
I listen to that oh so sweet sound
I watch the water wash away all
The things I used to hate while I
Watch and while I listened I became
Lost in the sound
Megan Velez, Grade 8
Shadow Hills Intermediate School

I Am Mean
I wonder why I yelled at you
I hear myself cry
I see the tears in your eyes
I want to slap myself for saying those words
I do hate my lies
I am mean

I pretend to say I hate you
I feel your sorrow
I touch the images of myself
I worry about someone's heart
I cry when I am heartless
I am mean
I understand myself clearly
I say I am sorry

I dream of making you happy
I try to aim for a perfect person
I hope you will accept my apologies
I am mean
Amy Vang, Grade 9
Hiram W Johnson High School

Lone Life
it's all inside
all bottled up
it clings to me for shelter.
where to put it
I don't know
on a shelf
behind a door.
can't let it go
I don't know why.
a gift for a friend
I think not.
they say to trust them,
but I cannot
my deepest secrets
give away
to a stranger
that I met along the way
so that is why
it's all inside
all bottled up.
Gloria Marin, Grade 8
Richardson PREP HI Middle School

Winter
Winter time is fun
I love it because there's hardly any sun.
The rain and snow are the best.
During winter you better wear a vest.
I love that you can always smell pine.
I wish it was winter all the time.
Colett Gonzales, Grade 8
St Francis de Sales School

Days to Remember and Nights to Forget
In the day we pretend
We ignore all our pain
On this show we depend
To forget the nights we disdain

The light hides the truth
Shows only what's needed
But we're cruel and uncouth
In the dark, our souls depleted

By the veil of darkness
Is shown what's unseen
Our essence in starkness
Grows unsatisfied and lean

The echoed howling tune
With packs, hunt the prey
To attack with the moon
Once allies from the day

This stays as forever
And thought we regret
All days to remember
And these nights to forget

Julien Ishibashi, Grade 8
St Rita School

The World Will End
The seas will become monsters,
flooding homes and hearts
People will die, people will cry
The end of the world will come.

The ground will shake beneath our feet,
cracking cities and lives
People will scream, people will dream
The end of the world will come.

Hurricanes and tornados will crowd the Earth,
destroying buildings and minds
People will run, people will be done
The end of the world will come.

Wars will break out all around
killing women and kids
People will thrash, people will clash
The end of the world will come.

As I think of all this
I wonder what to do
when the world comes to an end,
in the year 2012.

Rebecca Bennett, Grade 8
Richardson PREP HI Middle School

The Beach
The sun sets beyond the waves,
And the dolphins splash in the sea for days.
The palm trees' coconuts just out of reach,
And all of this happens at the beach.

From the sea spray to the seagull's cry,
To the giant, clear, blue sky.
It is a land that never snows,
But to it, people always go.

When the beach is all clear,
And most people have left,
The few who are near,
Watch the ocean sunset.

It is hot by day, yet cool by night.
And the waves roll onto the shore in the pale moonlight.
The nighttime is beautiful, but it is time to move on,
For the sun to rise into next morning's dawn.

Each day brings anew,
With the sea smell so sweet,
And each day my heart wanders
Away, to the beach.

Kyle Graham, Grade 8
Park View Middle School

Have You…?
Have you ever wondered, have you ever dreamed,
About a life before you?
You think to yourself what a wonderful world,
but has it always been that way?

Have you ever wondered, have you ever dreamed,
What others are thinking?
If they are, are they thinking of you?

Have you ever wondered, have you ever dreamed,
Of the beauty in life?
How there's another world under the sea?
How those creatures run freely,
Why don't we?

Have you ever wondered, have you ever dreamed,
Who you're going to be in the life ahead?
Whatever you choose now, will be the result.
Will you be happy?

Life is full of surprises, live it while you can.
Love someone with all your heart.
Ask questions, have answers,
Is this the life you wanted?

Jennifer Fisher, Grade 8
Carmel Valley Middle School

Hidden Emotions

I don't know why inside;
I have all these emotions, thoughts that I hide
Sealed up, buried somewhere in a pit,
But they can't all fit.

These confusing emotions, thoughts, a crazy whirlpool,
Like Hate is boiling lava and frozen over tears icy, cool.
The things that make me sad,
Or my thoughts running bloody mad.

I need to let out my feelings:
Like a singer needs to sing,
Or how a dancer moves to the beat,
Or a stuntmen with a daring feat.
To let it free!
For others to see
A piece of me inside
To see what I hide.

I must let it go!
My thought must flow!
Of what I'm hiding in my soul,
Or it'll rush out with an angry, crazy flow.

Diana Nguyen, Grade 8
McFadden Intermediate School

My Backyard

In the backyard I see the past
Where as a little girl I swung on
The T-shaped pole. Back and
Forth. Back and forth.
Memories lay in the backyard.

The garden my family and I planted.
Flourished beautiful and big the two
Sunflowers that grow too close to each other,
Smiles and laughs did it fill us with.
Memories lay in the backyard.

In the summer would my dad hose us
Down in the grassy green grass
But once winter, friends and family
Would gather round the fireplace outside.
Boy, do memories lie in the backyard.

Once the day ends the backyard gets locked up —
Locked up like a precious little gift
Filled with happiness and so much delight
And I wait for a new day to open the gift again
Oh how many memories lay in the backyard.

Lisette Lopez, Grade 8
Richardson PREP HI Middle School

You Are Like a Book

You are like a book to me
'Cause you have an attractive cover
'Cause you have a sweet name
Because you keep me company
'Cause you have many surprises
'Cause you have a bad guy
Because you have a story that eventually gets boring
'Cause you have an end that has already come.

You are like a book to me
'Cause I can predict your actions
'Cause I can hold you in my arms
'Cause I can understand you
'Cause I can question you without a reply
Because I can turn you, make you walk away
'Cause I can never forget you
Because I loved you and can never forget it!

You are like a book to me
Because you were my main character
'Cause I didn't get tired of you, till now
Because you were my favorite book, until you sold yourself
You are like a book to me, because the end is too inevitable.

Robert Nguyen, Grade 8
Richardson PREP HI Middle School

The Man on the Moon

Gyroscope generating G-force
Pitting physics against the will of man
Bone jarring rattle; astronauts stay the course
Exercising like peak climbers with a plan
Neil Armstrong trains to ascend the mountain of space

Hotter than habaneros; taste the engine fire
Rockets spitting, spewing, and screaming red flame
Operatically timed like a well-rehearsed choir
Reaching for unknown heights is the game
Neil Armstrong hopes to summit the mountain of space

Tickling the stars like a butterfly's wing
Desolate darkness an enveloping cocoon
Loading into the LEM, space bows to the king
Footprints on a dusty rockscape, the alien moon
Neil Armstrong first touches the mountain of space

American supremacy plants the flag
Wisps of sunlight in a waltzing dance
Celebrating the moment, a chance to brag
Mankind memorializes a magnificent advance
Neil Armstrong conquers the mountain of space

Shayne Bennington, Grade 8
The Mirman School

Love Is

Love is being in kindergarten,
And having a crush on that dimple faced boy, who smiled shyly at you.
Love is being in second grade,
And turning red when your mom mentions Timmy from math class.

Love is being in fourth grade,
And throwing food at the boy table, and then pushing down that special one.
Love is being in sixth grade,
And immediately denying knowing the boy who you saw put the love note in your desk, signed "Secret admirer."

Love is being in eighth grade,
When you get your first boyfriend, and having your first kiss under the sunset.
Love is being in high school,
And slyly passing your phone number to the nice boy from Spanish.

Love is being in college,
And experiencing your first true, real heartbreak, high school was nothing compared to this.
Love is on your wedding day,
Getting married to a man you'll never stop loving.

Love is holding your first newborn child for the first time,
And seeing that when he smiles, he has dimples.

Courtney Conlan, Grade 8
Easterbrook Discovery School

Just Say Hi

This goes out to the lonely kid sitting by himself on the side
Told his parents that he has so many friends as a new kid, but he lied
He wouldn't go up to any student to ask if they can be friends, I wish he tried

At least every day, I see him around school
Or at least sitting down while kids call him uncool or fool
Just because he doesn't have any friends
Doesn't mean he is a weird person or someone different

Wow, I wish I can just stand up for him one of these days
And I wish I can just tell those bullies off in so many ways
Every single day, I've been trying to at least say "what's up" or at least a "Hi"
But on the other hand I just hang out with my friends until the bell rings then walk right past by
I promise, next time I see you, I'll at least introduce myself or at least give my name
Even if the other kids may think I'm lame.

All in all, I think it's crazy how a stranger can suddenly become a friend,
He was too scared to stand up for himself but now I see him standing up for other new kids
Getting picked on and helping them defend
From sitting by himself because he was too shy
To becoming a good friend of mine just because I said "Hi."

Gabriel Hipol, Grade 8
August Boeger Middle School

Like a Rainbow

I'm like a rainbow. Every day I have different moods. All the colors represent me. Sometimes I would be blue as the sky. Or sometimes yellow like the sunshine. But watch out for the color red it's like fire. I will sometimes disappear for my hard times of my life. Happy times in my life I will always be shining my color yellow really bright for everybody.

Michelle Ruvalcaba, Grade 8
Palm Desert Charter Middle School

High Merit Poems – Grades 7, 8 and 9

Wind
Whoosh! It yells.
The wind dances around
to spread his gift.

Leaves and twigs swim
through the frosty air.

Wind jumps and runs through houses.
He goes to the forest and blows on
the poor dead leaves.

The leaves crackle as they begin to ignite.
Dead seedlings whisper their thanks
under the new present.

You're welcome, Wind blew back.
*Sarina Ortega, Grade 7
Sarah McGarvin Intermediate School*

Ode to the American Soldier
I want to thank you
From the bottom of my heart.
You risk your lives every day,
Just to give strangers freedom.
I can walk and run and play outside freely.
You rarely see your family
Yet I see mine every day.
I take advantage and don't realize
How lucky I am to have them
By my side.
I will think about
That the next time I go
To say hateful words
To one of my loved ones.
You make living in the U.S.
A good thing.
*Abaigeal McCormick, Grade 7
St Francis Parish School*

Flickering Light
Oh flickering light,
How you draw me in,
With your orange glow,
Flickering,
Dancing when
Someone walks by,
A gust of breath,
And you die,
Smoking as you leave earth,
Mysterious to all,
We stare into you,
Fascinated,
Then blow you out,
Oh flickering light.
*Ricquel Crouse, Grade 8
Temecula Valley Charter School*

Lucky Me
Deep within people an evil urge
Lurks, surfacing occasionally
Creating havoc…but this I lack
No such wicked monster breathes inside me
No mammoth mischief-maker
No satanic scoundrel!
Perhaps a few whispering voices
Urging me to stray from straight choices
Nasty sopranos echo and reverberate
But…so far my booming baritone
Drowns out the Sirens Songs
Like a tidal wave, engulfing them
Dragging them to the deepest ocean trench
My conscience, like a vigilant Hercules
Stays strong
Prepared to squelch those sopranos
Whenever they return
*Gabriel Rivas, Grade 7
The Mirman School*

Erasing Mistakes
The eraser might be small,
But it does its job well.
It can erase all sorts of mistakes.
Most of them are easy,
Especially the ones on paper.
But other mistakes are more
Difficult to fix.
Like the ones that are etched
In your heart
With permanent marker.
No eraser can fix that.
Instead, that mistake will
Become a mark,
And become a reminder
To never,
Ever,
Make that mistake in life again.
*Tatiana Martinez Navarro, Grade 8
Temecula Valley Charter School*

Can't Let Go
I can't let her go
She is my forever memory
I can't erase
Her video in my head
Playing over and over again
Maybe I'm just immature
But everything I do relates to her
She taught me how to love
She taught me how to hate
She taught me the pain of falling
In love. I still love her, and
I can't let her go
*Daniel Viray, Grade 8
Corpus Christi School*

Remember the Times
Remember when we hugged
And I comforted you

Remember I made you laugh
When you were feeling sad

Remember I said, "I love you,"
When I always needed you

Remember I always made you smile
When I kissed you on the cheek

Remember we were together
When I held your hand

Remember the love we had
When we were both kissing

Remember I was thinking about you
— When you were always missing me

Remember the times
We were always there for each other
We'll be remembering now and forever…
*Justin Lucas, Grade 8
Corpus Christi School*

The Challenge of Getting Good Grades
Studying, listening
keeping up with the class
trying your hardest
trying your best

Paying attention may be hard
but I guess it's the road to success
concentrating the toughest of all
the most important of them all

When it comes to me
in working hard
compared to the others
I'm as slow as a snail

Getting good grades
is hard for me
while for others
it just comes naturally.

If good grades
is what I want
then these are the things
I'll have to do.
*Scarlette Lopez, Grade 8
St Helen Catholic Elementary School*

A Piece of My Life
It was a cold day in
November…
A day I would always remember.
My family was crying.
It was as sad as if
The world was ending.
Someone important in our life
Has passed away.
The weather was cold.
The sky was gray.

I remember the tears.
The sad faces.
The comforting hush.
I wish the image
Would just fade away.
Yenyen Tran, Grade 7
Sarah McGarvin Intermediate School

The Big Wave*
An ocean angry:
The fiery sunset low,
The roaring waves high.

A deadly black wave;
All who lived are no more, now.
Harsh ocean tears gone.

Pale complexion
Heart broken by gloating waves,
Never to heal.

An empty plain beach
Beginning to house again.
A new start for all.
Dalia Dull, Grade 7
Tenaya Middle School
*Inspired by The Big Wave

iPod
O, iPod
You fill my ears with music
any time of the day.
You wake me up in the morning
so I can go to school.
You entertain me when I am bored.
I could play games on you all night long.
When I am stuck with no one around
I just turn you on and I am taken care of.
But the time I need you the most
is when my dad tells me to mow the lawn.
When he tells me to do that
I just pop you on
and I have music all night long.
Michael Vennard, Grade 8
Daniel Savage Middle School

The Big Wave*
Sun shines on ocean;
The ocean glitters orange,
Sea animals play.

Fear makes the man weak.
There is no need to have fear,
So have much courage.

How can Jiya live
Knowing that his dad is dead;
He is very brave.

Jiya and Kino:
The big wave is behind them,
Both are worried, still

Jiya and Setsu:
Marry and live happily.
They love each other.
Allan Cleveland, Grade 7
Tenaya Middle School
*Inspired by The Big Wave

I Am in Love
I wonder if you love me.
I hear your voice.
I see a beautiful day.
I want to be with you.
I do everything for you.
I am in love.

I pretend to be happy without you.
I feel lonely.
I touch your hand.
I worry how you are.
I cry when I am hurt.
I am in love.

I understand my destiny.
I say I miss you.
I dream about my future.
I try my hardest.
I hope you are the one.
I am in love.
Ying Vue, Grade 9
Hiram W Johnson High School

Light
Light is what wakes you up in the morning,
Heats your toast and keeps you exploring,
It lets you see and fuels the plants,
It lights up the moon and burns the ants,
It is the most important thing in life,
So don't give in to the nightlife.
Ryan Brobst, Grade 8
Carden Academy of Santa Clara

I Am Black Soldier
I am Black Soldier
I was whipped and beat
And still I stand strong
Force me to work in a place
For a man I call master
I am Black Soldier
He gives me no rights
Just the right to do what he says
I am forced to pick cotton
I am forced to pick crops
And I still get no respect
I am Black Soldier
But one day I will be free
No more picking crops for my master
Reunited with my family again
I am Black Soldier
Elyse Perez, Grade 7
Orville Wright Middle School

You and I
I can't remember
When you held my hand
When you made me dinner
When you made me laugh

And it's hard
To remember
To speak of you
To ever forget you

That's why *I* still see you
I see you in my father
I see you in my brother

And every day *I* see *You* and me.
TOGETHER
Ava Sims, Grade 7
Arcade Middle School

In A…
In a neighborhood that I call mine,
Quietness runs down the street
No excitement, none at all
But suddenly a beat

In a house that I call mine,
Family friends and the fun begins
As we all start playing games
Dancing and laughing with joy

In a place that I call mine,
My secrets hid away
Why don't you come in…
And maybe even stay
Gabby Morones, Grade 8
Richardson PREP HI Middle School

High Merit Poems – Grades 7, 8 and 9

I Am…

I am a sapling
I prosper and thrive when I see the light,
I am not a great big tree, which thrive so easily.
I have to struggle and push my way through each day,
But that's what I have to do, and because I want to,
I might be small now,
But I have the potential to be a tall great Redwood who is unlikely to fall,
I have strong deep roots and a small layer of bark.
I have two big guardians standing over me, and three other new trees growing beside me.
I have the will to grow and succeed and I can be anything I want to be, (however it is not a tree).

Scheridan Vorwaller, Grade 8
Palm Desert Charter Middle School

Drugs

Drugs take your life and can crush it in a second
It is like a merry-go-round; you just keep going 'round, 'round, and 'round…
Now it's going too fast; you want to get off but you can't
So you keep going 'round and 'round and 'round…
It is cold and weighs a thousand pounds
It is as addictive as food to an obese child
It is hot and burns an imprint on your face, hands, your speech, your family, and your friends
It grabs your hand and pulls you further, further into the naked darkness.
It is dull — there is no point
Drugs are unforgiving and make you start to question yourself.

Cat Silveira, Grade 7
Monroe Middle School

Where I'm From

I am from love, support, and never being judged for flaws
I am from a generation where fun is trying to be an adult and do what your older siblings do
I am from strong African American women who've withstood many trials and tribulations
From a city where ridicule is a habit and compliments are considered to be unusual and foreign
From a country where thousands of soldiers are sent to lay down their lives to fight wars
that aren't worth fighting
From constant labor in prayer
I am from persistent teaching and preaching of what's right and what's wrong
I am from spiritual stability
I am from constant reminding of who I am and to never get lost in who the world wants me to be

Trinity McGruder, Grade 8
Bret Harte Middle School

I Am an Unfinished Book

I am an unfinished book. I am not perfect therefore, I have my flaws and mistakes. The climax of my life wasn't so easy to solve and I am positive there is more on its way. I am still being written as you can see and by far it is tremendous. Some chapters of my life weren't the best but, the characters beside me helped me through it all. I have many pages and there is still many more to come. Don't judge me by my cover and come open me up and begin to read.

Arieanna Deshazo, Grade 8
Palm Desert Charter Middle School

By My Side

Probably I don't know the meaning of love, but I really want you to know that I want you I want you by my side forever and ever you're that person that gives me the energy of my day just by looking at that smile, that smile that makes me forget about everything, everything even my fear of being near you that fear that shows how much I love you that fear that is able to protect our love from anyone that fear that is together forever and ever not able to be broken apart

Stephanie Aguilar, Grade 8
Richard Merkin Middle Academy

My Parallel Universe

A parallel universe
A land of dreams and fantasies that are never turned down
Where whatever I wish for appears in the blink of an eye
Where I can be myself and not fear being mocked
Where criticism is criticized and everything stands out in its own way
Where laughter is heard in every corner
Where the smallest thoughts become the largest plans
And where the largest plans no longer stay plans
Where one can live to their own standards free of society's class system
Where helping hands reach out and find you at the first cry of help
Where our planet's atmosphere is free of harm
Where animals run free in the wild with no fear of hunters and poachers
Where rainforests are flourishing rather than fading
Where millions of innocent people can roam freely without being cruelly injured or murdered
Where friendship truly lasts forever and I never have to leave the ones that I love
Where I can have my own privacy and solitude to calm down and peacefully wait for serenity
Where childhood stories and novels come to life
Where those who have pained me feel the wrath of karma
Where I can show the world what I have to offer
And where my hard work pays off more than ever
Where there really is a happily ever after…

Jaslin Gosal, Grade 8
August Boeger Middle School

Cradle to Grave

When you come into this world as a baby, you're so cute and soft and love to explore your new world.
You age and age, then age some more, you learn to talk and learn to walk and off to preschool you go.
Remember how proud you were when you learned to count? One, two, four, oops!
You go to kindergarten, then first grade and learn your grammar.
Finally your parents let you watch the big boy shows like *Power Rangers*.
All those crazy shows make you play pretend, but be careful because it's all fun and games until someone gets hurt.
3rd, 4th, then 5th grade, life goes so fast and suddenly you get letter grades, A, B, F, uh-oh.
Here comes middle school, weren't you nervous?
Switching classes seems strange, but you soon see it isn't that bad.
You finish eighth grade, then go to high school.
You go mad about the clubs, then before you know it you're being yelled at in ROTC.
Wow, college! Look at how old you are, remember second grade, man you aged.
Time for the big decision, what job are you going to get? Being a lawyer sounds fun but teaching seems cooler.
Finally your boyfriend proposes and you say "yes."
You have a child and before you know it you're forty.
Twenty years pass and then you retire.
Look at how nice your life is.
Another year or two passes and you begin to have heart trouble so your doctor gives you medicine.
Now look, your child is twenty, they grow up so fast!
Before you know it you are ninety and on your death bed.
Looking back it's been quite a ride, and now you're left breathless.

Eric Claus, Grade 7
Monroe Middle School

Why

Am I not good enough? Am I not what you wanted? Why do you hold me in your arms like it's the last time you could? Why does it seem you have fallen for me but only to land on your knees at my feet? Why did you tell me you love me but never really mean it? What did you see in her that wasn't in me? What makes her better than me? I was your best friend. Was it her looks, her voice or her status? What did I do? Why did you do this to me? Was I not what you wanted? Was I not good enough?

Isabelle Richards, Grade 7
Letha Raney Intermediate School

Black and White

My life is a tornado of colors
How hard I try to fight if I'm still
Stuck in the eye
As the stormy wind passes me by, I think
"You see what you like, but not what you need."
The storm then takes me
And I let it, so easily
I don't fight it…don't struggle
Because I saw it coming my way
How colorful the world is
But in my mind, it's still black and white
As it twists and turns around me
Horrible thoughts start building up in my mind
But as quickly as they come, they start to fade away
As the storm takes me round and round,
I see what I need
And it's definitely not you
So I say goodbye to this day, seeing
The world in a colorful way.

Lilliana Ramirez, Grade 8
Valinda School of Academics

A Fall Afternoon

The pumpkins are out
The last light of day arrives
The sky, covered in a pink ribbon
Fireflies come out to greet the oncoming night
Trees covered in amber, orange, and red
Children running through the leaf paved streets

The wind whistles through the trees
It seems to sing to the world
Everything seems still
A glass of lemonade sits on an empty porch

The sun winks goodnight
Street lights flicker on
Night has come
A single star appears in the warm sky
If only the world could look like this forever
To watch the colors dance and swirl
The colors of fall

Alison Clifford, Grade 8
Monte Vista Christian School

Snow

Snow is fluffy and white,
the lightest shade of gray.
It melts when it lands on your tongue,
and tastes like water.
It's light as a feather,
and shaped like a crystal.
It falls from the sky,
and comes to rest on your outstretched hand.

Allysa Lui, Grade 8
Holy Name School

thoughtless

the big green tree
flowing in the wind
speaks to me
in a way i cannot explain
it understands all
but none understand it
in the hustle and bustle
of hum drum days
they passed it by
without a thought of it
but one day
before i died
i stood staring
at the tree
as i thought
the big green tree
flowing in the wind
speaks to me
in a way i cannot explain

Oliver Patterson, Grade 7
Los Angeles Center for Enriched Studies

Friends

Friends, people who help in the hardest of times;
They help even on the highest of climbs,
Friends will stay close;
No matter the foes

Friends will make beautiful remarks;
Yet still hang out at parks,
Friends can be hard to find;
But once found, they bring peace of mind

Friends can fight and fight;
Yet still make things right,
Good friends are hard to come by;
Still, it's always good to have someone to share the pie

Friends, someone who never has to be missed;
And will always exist,
Friends cannot just enlist;
They must be able to coexist.

Shad Baccus, Grade 7
Joe Walker Middle School

Ode to Sesame Street

Sesame Street, my ode to you:
For years you've taught me my one's and two's.
From ABC's and how to write,
You've kept me happy and feeling bright.
Elmo and Ernie, Cookie Monster, too,
You're like my family; I'm stuck on you!
Congratulations you're 40 years old,
Your episodes are just plain GOLD!

Madeline Hopson, Grade 8
Coronado Middle School

Halloween Costumes
Going with my mom and her friend
I try pick out material,
No, this isn't good,
That won't do,
That's perfect.
Busy days
Fittings for the costume
Making adjustments
Trying it on
Getting accessories
Last fitting
It's done!
It's perfect.
Shelby James, Grade 7
Tenaya Middle School

Goodbye Clock
School is like a clock
Tick Tock
It makes me yawn
Tick Tock
Time to study
Tick Tock
For the quiz
Tick Tock
Then it comes
Tick Tock
Thanks to the bell
Tick Tock
Goodbye clock
Antonio Ornelas, Grade 8
August Boeger Middle School

Friendship
Friendship is strong
Friendship is a chain
Friendship lasts very long
Friendship can never be a pain
Friendship can be found in shopping malls
Friendships can be found in games
Friendships can be found in winter, spring,
Summer, and fall
Friendship will never be lame
Friendship can be found anywhere
Friendship will never be shook
Friendship is strong as a bear
So, if friendship is near you, look!
Kim Luong, Grade 7
Carden Academy of Santa Clara

Stars
Bright and white at night
All over the sky tonight.
Will they disappear?
Gary Chan, Grade 8
St Mary's Chinese Day School

Autumn
Leaves are falling down
Twisting, spinning to the ground
The wind blows gently
Max Leon, Grade 8
St Martin-in-the-Fields School

Escher's Bond of Union
Looking back on life
I see me, so young, so free
What happened to me?
Mackenzie Samora, Grade 7
Tenaya Middle School

The Desert
A drop of rain is
A never-ending ocean
In a vast desert
Kendrick Nguyen, Grade 7
Sarah McGarvin Intermediate School

School Days
The morning bell rings
I dash to Pre-Algebra
the school day begins.
Gabriela Taylor, Grade 7
Sarah McGarvin Intermediate School

Ladybugs
The ladybugs small
It's covered with lots of spots
It's red like a rose
Gabriela Garcia, Grade 8
Almond Tree Middle School

The Choice
It ruins your life
Make the right choice don't do drugs
Or you will be dead
Dalton Mitchell, Grade 9
Foothill High School

A Book
It holds adventures.
It shows magnificent things.
Its name is a book.
Sophia Nguyen, Grade 7
Sarah McGarvin Intermediate School

Night
When the sun departs,
Then darkness spreads like a scourge.
Now engulfed in black.
Kelly Blasberg, Grade 8
Palm Desert Charter Middle School

Grades 4-5-6 Top Ten Winners

List of Top Ten Winners for Grades 4-6; listed alphabetically

Hailey Benesh, Grade 6
T J Walker Middle School, Sturgeon Bay, WI

Anne Cebula, Grade 6
Intermediate School 239 Mark Twain for the Gifted & Talented, Brooklyn, NY

Zari Gordon, Grade 5
Walker Elementary School, Evanston, IL

Helena Green, Grade 5
Hopewell Elementary School, Hopewell, NJ

Kristin Kachel, Grade 6
Discovery Canyon Campus, Colorado Springs, CO

Carrie Mannino, Grade 5
The Ellis School, Pittsburgh, PA

Mariah Reynolds, Grade 4
School for Creative and Performing Arts, Cincinnati, OH

Jeremy Stepansky, Grade 5
Hillside Elementary School, Montclair, NJ

Anne-Katherine Tallent, Grade 5
Providence Academy, Johnson City, TN

Claudia Zhang, Grade 6
Rolling Ridge Elementary School, Chino Hills, CA

All Top Ten Poems can be read at www.poeticpower.com

Note: The Top Ten poems were finalized through an online voting system. Creative Communication's judges first picked out the top poems. These poems were then posted online. The final step involved thousands of students and teachers who registered as the online judges and voted for the Top Ten poems. We hope you enjoy these selections.

Melancholy and Ecstasy

Trailing through the corridors
Of a place that holds happiness and sadness
Filled with people with stories to tell
The cheery background seems ironic
The floral décor in every corner
The bright yellow walls old
And yet reflecting the goal
To help those too old or too injured
Gloom fills my heart as I walk through
Yet for those who live here it's a relaxing abode
Where they can rest
While their pain decreases
Unless their thoughts are slowly fading
Everywhere is chatter
Nurses run about
Residents laugh and cry
Until life ends forever

Melanie Krassel, Grade 6
The Mirman School

Volleyball

I wonder if I will be a champion volleyball player
I hear my mom chanting
I see my team smiling
I am screaming with excitement
I am ready
I concentrate on my serve
I feel pumped
I touch the ball
I am worried that my ball won't make it over
I cry inside
I am nervous
I remember what my coach has said
He shouts "you can do it!"
I dream I make it to the championships
I try so hard
I hope we make it
We are the best

Gabrielle Wong, Grade 6
Chinese American International School

Green

Green is the taste of a fresh crunchy salad.
Green is the feeling of a crocodile's skin.
Green is the sound of a dewdrop plopping on a leaf.
Green is the smell of a tall redwood.
Green is a color that is friendly and growing.
Green is the feeling of desire and freshness.
Green is the color of living wildlife.
Green is the taste of grapes on the table.
Green is the sound of leaves rustling.
Green is the eyes of an unseen creature.
Green is the color of an enchanted forest.
And green is the feeling of a smooth lizard.

Sasha Dolgashev, Grade 4
Heather Elementary School

God's Creation

Trees give us oxygen and the
Sun gives us light as the
Rain gives us water to drink and the
Plants give us food to eat.
Plants, trees, fields, and bushes all gives us
Food that's delicious.
Yellow flowers give us honey to eat as
Fields give us crop seeds.
Parents give us love and care
Just as cows give us milk to share.
Teachers give us an education and
Family gives us love and care as
Planes give us an easier way to travel through air.
Houses give us shelter and
Clothes give us warmth just as
Parents give us life
They also teach us wrong form right
Show your appreciation of the world because
It is also God's Creation!

Brittnie Tapia, Grade 6
Our Lady of the Rosary School

My Mom

My mom, whose heart
Is red like a volcano's lava,
Who is so sweet like a
Newly-born puppy,
Whose eyes are brown
Like a puppy dog's sparking eyes —
I love my mom so much!
I would die for her,
Because she has given me everything.
Her brilliance is as if
She were the smarted person ever.
She is Salvadorian, and she is my mom.
I LOVE HER SO MUCH!
My mom is worth so much more than money,
she is a treasure sent from heaven.
My mom is everything to me.
Her hair sparkles in the sunlight.
My mom's great and loving.
She is more than a guardian angel to me.

Johanna Castaneda, Grade 6
Corpus Christi School

Lucky

The dog of my life
The dog that carried my heart in his
The dog that ran with me
The dog that laughed with me
The dog…that had a bone tumor
The dog that was carried away to heaven by a car
No time
No time to say good-bye

Elle McDougald, Grade 4
Prospect Sierra School

Just a Bird and Me: Inside a Two-Year-Old's Mind

Alone
Don't know where
They have gone.
Just a bird
And me
Alone.
Into the forest
Go I.
Quiet, I come back
Alone.
Bird flying to me.
No friends either; it's
Alone.
I hug it. I clutch it.
It's comfort
Just a bird and me, all
Alone.
Lost we are.
Don't know what to do.
Just know we're
Alone.

Christina Duval, Grade 6
Carlthorp School

A Breeze of Wind

Wind is yet but a single breeze
You cannot touch nor see it
But you can feel the warm or cool air
The wind surrounds the world with its delight
Wind goes wherever it pleases, north, south, east, west
You go here, you go there, you go ever so far
But it will go wherever you go

The wind moves the water, crashing it into the rocks
It also blows through the trees in many directions
The Breeze of Wind is like the breath of Earth
But to us, it is like a blanket…
A blanket that warms us and cools us with its breeze

Leslie Villatoro, Grade 6
Corpus Christi School

Aqua

Aqua looks like ripples in a lake when I throw rocks in the water
Aqua sounds like raindrops hitting the window
Aqua smells like my hair after I'm in the pool
Aqua tastes like popsicles on a summer day
Aqua feels like waves hitting my feet at the beach
Aqua sounds like the big splash when I jump in the water
Aqua smells like shampoo when I take a shower
Aqua tastes like ice cream after a long hot day
Aqua feels like the grass tickling my feet outside
Aqua looks like snow falling outside
Aqua sounds like water rushing down a river
And aqua feels awake and ready for a new day

Carly Comparato, Grade 4
Heather Elementary School

Bittersweet Winter

Cold and bittersweet, a lick of the first bite of frost,
Light, steaming clouds emitting,
Like the touch of a butterfly wing.
Gossamer bows, hanging from a leaf,
Leaden with dawn-flavored silver,
The tears of a tree.
The willow sighs in remembrance of birds,
Wondering if it will ever hear
The musical trills again.
The world is blue,
A transparent blue,
As clear as the sweat,
The sap of a tree.
The beauty of the cold, the coldness of beauty,
As the ice glimmers faintly,
Immersed in eager hope,
Delighted beyond elated ecstasy.
The bees don't hum,
The bear's lumber ceased,
All that is left,
Is the longing for spring.

Claudia Zhang, Grade 6
Rolling Ridge Elementary School

Darkness

In the dark
I see weird things.
In the dark I want to scream.

Please, I want to see the shimmer in the light,
But all I do is close my eyes in fright.

Now there's something here to hurt me,
All I want is my mommy.

Oh, look! There she is, right there!
Mommy, mommy, look! I'm scared.
But you're here!

Taylor Brown, Grade 5
Granada Elementary School

Community

A sense of community is a sense of pride
Unpredictable, unchangeable, like the thundering tide
Like a sense of support, like a metal base
Blending in with the crowd, just another face
A strength that always keeps you strong
A strength that makes you want to belong
A feeling to always keep you appeased
A feeling to keep others pleased
As cozy as being wrapped up in bed
A feeling you know isn't just in your head
Wherever we go, wherever we wander
Every friend will make us stronger

Danielle Egan, Grade 5
Strawberry Point Elementary School

Oatmeal

You may think that "OATMEAL" is a funny name for a pet,
It's certainly not a name you soon will forget!

She has light yellow fur and soft silky ears,
Out of which she hears from far or near.

When she wakes up in the morning she gives me a lick,
The smell of her doggie breath just makes me sick!

The funniest habit of my precious, sweet dog,
Is that she snorts through her nose just like a hog.

I am very sad that Oatmeal is so old,
She is my best friend and has a heart of gold.

I love my big and beautiful yellow lab.
I wish she could stay with me my whole life long.

Jessica Marelli, Grade 4
Mira Catalina Elementary School

Chocolate

Swirling pools of creamy goodness
rich and dark just makes you wanna eat it up
just take a bite
feels good right
take another
not too fast
don't spoil it
not too slow
you can't get the real taste
dark as the eyes of the one who is brown eyed
not brown eyed
chocolate eyed
got a sweet tooth
nourish it with chocolate
the world revolves around chocolate
the sweet, tasty chocolate
now don't you want to eat some?

Shayna Sternin, Grade 5
Laurence School

Gold

Gold is a yellow crayon pressed down hard on paper.
Gold is one million screams of glory after a long race.
Gold is a hot piece of bread not too done.
Gold is fresh lemons over done ones.
Gold is a treasure box from long ago near a salty sea.
Gold is lights in Las Vegas shining all night.
Gold is stars hung on the wall by the teacher.
Gold is a rare Corvette racing down the street.
Gold is a candle just lit to light your way.
Gold is dirty sand in your mouth.
Gold is the first day of summer bright and hot.
Gold is a tooth biting down on meatloaf.

Jaison Betsekas, Grade 4
Heather Elementary School

Perseverance

One more day
I think
One more day
Everyone is crying out in hunger
My taste buds eagerly await
The stale rotten food
The stench of sweat fills the air
Overpowering the smells of
Rotten potatoes and burning flesh
The Nazis' laughter grates against my eardrum
As they whip other helpless prisoners
"Slash, slash"
My clothes are tattered
My shoes are nearly soleless
The wounds on my legs are becoming infected
I wonder if
My people will survive
I do not know
One more day
I think
One more day

Alex Graden, Grade 6
Lindero Canyon Middle School

Pink

Pink smells like a lovely rose in the summer time.
Pink feels like a dress that was just put on a princess.
Pink tastes like a bubble gum bubble that just popped on your nose.
Pink smells like a book you read 4 times.
Pink feels like you're jumping in snow.
Pink smells like a perfume you just put on.
Pink sounds like a bird singing to you.
Pink tastes like a lollipop when you first lick it.
Pink looks like the cute teddy bear.
Pink feels like the softest blanket.
Pink smells like a pie you just made.
Pink tastes like a candy you love so much.

Henry Polaha, Grade 4
Heather Elementary School

Christmas

Christmas is full of joy
with all kinds of little toys.
Boys and girls running along the street
Fireplaces lit to bring up the heat.
Snowballs flying here and there
Christmas carolers everywhere.
People buying turkey, stuffing, and rolls
Others are making gumbo to put in bowls.
Parents don't go to work and children are out of school
No one will even think about going in a pool.
Santa on the roof with his flying reindeer
Oh how I love Christmas because it's full of cheer!

Jordyn Buchanan, Grade 6
St Pius X Elementary School

High Merit Poems – Grades 4, 5 and 6

If I Were in Charge of the World*
If I were in charge of the world
I'd have a ranch full of horses
All owned and ridden by me
And I would be famous for my skill in eventing

If I were in charge of the world
There'd be no war
Instead people would talk it out
And peace would settle in.

If I were in charge of the world
You wouldn't have cars
Everyone would use horses
And laugh attacks would be a sport
In the Olympic Games

If I were in charge of the world
A sugary snickerdoodle
With cookie dough ice cream
Would be a vegetable.
All mean teachers would suddenly disappear
If I were in charge of the world!

Sarah Leicht, Grade 6
St Raphael School
*Patterned after Judith Viorst

The Love That Was Never Meant to Be
A car that purrs like a lion, and grips the road as it is driven.
That's just the life that some people are liven.
To drive that car in less than four seconds is a thrill,
But you have to work hard to get your fill,
And first you have to pay the car payment bill.
After that you are ready for the ride of your life.
As you are going through the gears;
So fast you will be covered in tears.
If you get to the highest speed of thee;
You will see that your love of the car was meant to be.
Dream on. Dream on.
Life would be heaven with my Porsche 997,
But the only problem is, I'm only eleven.

Anthony Aquino, Grade 6
St Martin-in-the-Fields School

Endless Walk on the Clouds
As I leaped through the clouds
the insistent sun rays hit my eyes.
The crunch of each foot landing on them
made me realize the bumps, arches, and gaps.
My steps sliced the wispy clouds.
As I swayed, I noticed
the metallic night arrived.
Seeing the clouds no longer
I still knew I was walking endlessly
on the clouds.

Isabel Wiesenthal, Grade 5
Carlthorp School

Venice Beach, Always Busy with No Stops
Across the street a glass necklace stares at me
With its sparkly eyes that glow in the sun
A painting is being made within ten minutes
The freak show with its sword-eating lady,
Two-headed turtles and pigs
A man rollerblades while he sings and plays electric guitar
He plays a song for each person and hopes they will sing along
I walk past a brick wall,
It does not look like brick
It has graphite all over in different colors
And one wall dedicated to chewed up gum
The ocean breeze is so great on this hot summer day
But there are too many people
Some scattered across the road
At the little stand or waiting in line for ice cream
It's a one of a kind place
Always busy with no stops

Jessica Wolf, Grade 6
The Mirman School

Rain, the Foster Kid
Rain, you are covered in rain
Wet, soaked and dripping.
You have nothing to cover yourself.
I will name you Foster Boy,
Going round and round looking for a home.
You have no family
You have no place of your own.

Going to the beach,
A wave comes towards you
Snatches you to the other side of the shore
And you don't know how to swim.

Looking for your family
Rolling down the drains
Going back to the sea
From where once you came.

Nilarun Sanyal, Grade 4
Ruskin Elementary School

Camping Trip
Camping, camping, camping
my trip was so much fun!
All day having a blast, playing in the sun.

Roasting marshmallows, watching the stars,
I think this is better than a trip to Mars.

There are insects, bugs, and lots of trees.
They're fuzzy and buzzy, just like bees.

To have fun each and every day
a camping trip is the best way!!

Lauren Avila, Grade 5
Our Lady of Mount Carmel School

Until the Umbrella

Shuffling through the streets, I go nowhere.
Rain pummels me down to the ground
Shimmering like small cold shooting stars.

No one in sight, everyone gone, rushing home
To warm and dry
To big mugs of steaming hot chocolate.

All heat has abandoned me, left me, stranded me
In a world without warmth, whisked away
With the sun that is now swathed in clouds.

My plain collar flaps, flaps, flaps
Against my cheeks, my heavy coat
Even heavier from the isolating loneliness of rain.
My clomping boots sturdy, strong, rebelling against
The reign of a tyrant, the reign of the deluge.
It hits me, beats me down, forcing me to submit
To the cold icy sheets that swallow me in an
Enveloping chill.

I block the aqua bullets
With my umbrella, my noble umbrella.
Bright red, almost fluorescent, beating back the
Dark wet.

Genny Thomas, Grade 6
Carlthorp School

An Ocean in Me

There is a whale in me…
Roaming the oceans, majestic and free
Finding a path for its future,
Never knowing where it is going next

There is a sea lion in me…
Darting back and forth beating the competition
Entertained by new things,
Courageous, always looking for adventure

There is a sea turtle in me…
Calm and mellow
Taking life easy, observing its surroundings carefully
Finding a path to a great life

There is a dolphin in me…
Fun, energetic and playful
Always sticking with its friends
Never giving up no matter what the odds are

There is an ocean in me…
Having its ups and downs
There is no way of knowing the path I will take
Just follow the current and do what is right,
So I can enjoy a good long life.

Sara Passantino, Grade 6
Lindero Canyon Middle School

A Peek at My Soul

I am a typical naïve, curious little girl
I wonder about how Earth provides for the human race
I hear the sweet singing of holy angels
I see the sky caressing our planet with soft, blue hands
I want world peace so no one ever loses his home or family
I am a typical naïve, curious little girl

I pretend I rule over a tiny, pleasant island.
I feel the surprises of my future ahead of me
I touch the sky with almighty power
I worry about heartless scoundrels
I cry over people fighting for their own interests or beliefs
I am a typical naïve, curious little girl

I understand that nobody's perfect
I urge people to listen to their inner voice
I dream of happiness lasting forever
I try to look on the bright side of things
I hope for everyone on Earth to bond together
I am just a typical naïve, curious little girl

Catherine Pham, Grade 5
Dingeman Elementary School

Seasons on Top of the Mountain

In the fall, leaves fall on the ground
They crackle under my feet, the air is crisp
Woodpeckers go tappity, tap, tap on the trees
Squirrels scatter across the ground

In the winter, snow is falling on my nose
On the ground a thick sheet of snow shimmers
Animals are hibernating
All is quiet, the trees are bare and covered with snow

In the spring, all the snow melts to form a great river
Birds fly high up in the sky twittering and tweeting all the time
Flowers bloom into gorgeous colors
There is rain to nourish the plants

In the summer, all is hot and the river dries up
The pine trees are full and a rich green once again
Deer run free in the sunlight
There are small wild fires

Micaela Ruiz, Grade 4
Juarez Elementary School

A Busy Day

When the moon goes down
The sun comes up
A new working day is born
People are busy helping other people
And people are ready to be helped by other people
And people are working hard to keep the world shiny
And cleaner than ever

Karina Cardona, Grade 6
Lincoln Elementary School

Midnight
The midnight island sky would chime
Listen to the waves whisper with
The dark narrow blue stream
Clang the door shut with a chime
The willow tree as cold as an icicle
The water turns into mist with a twist
The children sleep in bed as
Their parents kiss them goodnight
Shamiya Pappas, Grade 5
Henry Haight Elementary School

Shopping
Oh shopping, oh shopping
I hate it so
GMC store, Macy's, and Fragrant store.
But only one store I like
Is the Lego store
Oh I wish, oh I wish
All the stores were Lego
Then maybe I'd like to shop.
Julian McKeon, Grade 5
Our Lady of Mount Carmel School

Flying Is Great
Up we go
And leave the ground
Up some more
Now look around
Across the country
Over the sea
Flying is great
For you and me
Gabriela Madrigal, Grade 6
Lincoln Elementary School

The Basketball Game
Basketball is fun
He throws the ball
He makes a score
He looks at his coach
He winks his eye
He believed he could do it
He threw the ball
And made a score
Juan Resendiz, Grade 6
Lincoln Elementary School

Fall
When summer is ending
It gets colder and colder every second
Leaves fall from the trees
Animals store food for the winter
People sleep peacefully in their beds
Then everything is quiet
Andrew Ahn, Grade 4
Carlthorp School

That Mouse!
That mouse is as small as a finger,
   but it won't stay and linger.
I would try to catch it,
   but he would go in such a fit.
As quick as a car,
   his limits stretch very far.
Taking cheese out of traps,
   right before it snaps!
Takes it to that hole of his,
   as fast as a soda's fizz!
Leaving hair everywhere,
   his food he won't share.
Catching the mouse is very tough,
   so I'll just get a little more rough.
While he is running around,
   he does not want to be found.
He will try to run away,
   but I will catch him…someday.
Shanmukh Kutagulla, Grade 6
Carden Academy of Santa Clara

The Midnight Sky
The
   Midnight
     Moon
Like   Shines

   a
    diamond
     while
Millions   the
  of
  stars
   dance
the   around
  moon
   while
    the wind
a   whispers
  poem…
Seung Bo Nam, Grade 5
Henry Haight Elementary School

Rainy Days
I see the birds swooping down
just to catch a worm or two
with its big talons
it's very easy to catch a worm
the enormous drops
upon their heads
look like falling golf balls
with everything wet
everything dripping
the puddles look like lakes
Spencer Davis, Grade 4
Carlthorp School

Thoughts of an Eraser
I am a useful thing in school,
   at home,
     and at work.
I like removing mistakes
   and leaving no marks at all.
I'm sad when I am dumped in
   desks and not cared for.
You can see me smile however
   when you hold me
     and wipe your wrongs.
I wish you use me more
   every time you forget
     what is right.
If I could speak aloud
   I would shout and say,
     "Hey I'm here,
     hold me, use me,
     and you will see,
     how useful I can be."
Raj Razon, Grade 4
Joseph M Simas Elementary School

Baseball
You catch me
and toss me
you roll me on the ground
you hit me with a stick
   I hate it when
   you hit me hard
   with that stick
   it makes a bing
   and it also stings
I like it when you just
toss me up and down.
     I want you to
     stop getting
     me dirty like
     a dirt ball.
I might be a ball
but I still have
feelings even though
they're small.
Conner Burkhalter, Grade 4
Joseph M Simas Elementary School

My Dog Blue
I have a dog and his name is Blue.
He likes to eat, but not my shoe.
He has fur on his face and fur on his legs.
When he wants a cookie, he begs and begs.
He likes to chase rabbits, his tail, and a ball.
He always comes when I call.
My dog Blue is my best friend.
He always will be until the end.
Braydon Evans, Grade 4
Mira Catalina Elementary School

Christmas Day
While I look out into the frigid snow,
I sip warm, sweet hot cocoa,
I then look to the Christmas tree,
And see huge presents waiting for me.

I hurry to the humungous tree,
So I can see what I've received.
Although the presents might be great,
For sure I will not hesitate.

Because I know that the best thing for me,
Is to spend time with my family.
I'm filled with glee when I go outside,
As I see the snow and ground collide.

I make a thousand snowman's,
All across the white chilly land.
I then go inside and I already know,
That on my face a smile shows.
Jessica DaMota, Grade 5
Lydiksen Elementary School

If You Knew Me…
If you knew me,
You would know
I dream of my Chihuahua,
Yoshi.
He is such a funny dog!
I wonder about him,
For, he is savvy
Sometimes.
I fear
When he falls off the couch.
I worry about him.
I giggle when he does tricks.
When he does his stunts,
He's very funny.
I think about
The times when he acts weird,
And smiles.
If you knew me,
Then you would know why…
Alexis Ordunez, Grade 5
Orange Glen Elementary School

The Storm
When lightning flashes
and thunder roars
it means it's time
to close the doors
wait till the storm dies
and when it does
run, not walk
into a wonderful day
Jack Cohen, Grade 4
Carlthorp School

If You Knew Me…
If you knew me,
You would know that
I dream of vacationing in Hawaii.
I like the ocean and
Hawaii is beautiful.
I wonder if I'll ever have
a baby sister?
I have brothers,
However
No sisters to play with.
I fear spiders.
I'm scared of them and fearful of
Getting bitten by them.
I giggle when something is funny.
Funny things just make me laugh!
I think about problems.
When I have one,
It saddens me.
If you knew me,
Then you would know why…
Issmene Flores, Grade 5
Orange Glen Elementary School

A Life of a Rock
I am a rock,
I get kicked
around a lot
as you can see
you're nothing
to me
I'm tired of being
stuffed in pockets
thrown away
scurried around
and kicked
being thrown in a lake
makes me feel
like I'm flying
through the waves
they never get a chance
to clean me
I really don't know why
what I say to the person
please don't make me die.
Oscar Escalera, Grade 4
Joseph M Simas Elementary School

My School
Ms. Hoang is super sweet,
From her head down to her feet,
I'm lucky I've got her this year,
As other teachers make kids fear!
She makes us study hard for every test.
She really is the best.
Taylor Pascua, Grade 4
Pulliam Elementary School

Christmas Time
Christmas Time
Christmas Time
Oh how I love Christmas time
Chestnuts roasting in the night
Opening presents under the tree
Having chocolate chip cookies
But once it's time to go to bed
We all get sad
Once we wake up we just can't wait
Until next year.
Makayla Natoli, Grade 4
Creek View Elementary School

Inspiration
Come on get up
You can do it
Just stand up
Don't let the snow falling bring you down
Just take a chance
And do all you can
Don't give up
You can do it
Just win the game
That's all there is to it.
Alejandra Castro, Grade 6
Lincoln Elementary School

Cars
I know cars
Cars roaring engines, cars driving
People cleaning cars, animals ruining cars.
I know cars
The sight of new cars, the sight of old cars.
The taste of oil "yuck!"
I know cars
"Fix that alternator," "use that screwdriver"
"I know that," I fixed the alternator
I know cars.
Johnny Vazquez, Grade 4
Lankershim Elementary School

China
Cherry blossoms
Chopsticks
Beautiful temples
Pandas
Bamboo
Peaceful forests
Buddha
Mysterious oceans
Heartwarming colors
Noodles
Maya Martynovich, Grade 6
Gardner Street Elementary School

High Merit Poems – Grades 4, 5 and 6

If You Knew Me…
If you knew me,
Then you would know
I dream of being
A baseball player
Because, I do that for a living!
I wonder,
If the world is going to end
In 2012?
I fear
Big pit bulls.
I think about my dogs
Because, they mean so much to me.
I giggle
When I hear a funny joke.
If you knew me,
Then you would know why…
Jaden Pabloff, Grade 5
Orange Glen Elementary School

My Lost Friend
There was a day when I was sad,
My life was really, really bad.
Then like the trick of a magic hat,
I had a friend, it was just like that.
We had our fun and it was good,
My friendship was as hard as wood.
Unknown a sad change would jump out,
And this change had given me new route.
Here is the action that had happened,
I changed my school and we were saddened.
We keep in contact, which is good.
So our friendship is still hard as wood.
Slowly we grow more apart,
But new friends need a chance to start.
And as this story meets its end,
The last three words are My Lost Friend.
Ryan S. White, Grade 6
St Linus School

School Uniforms
Summer, summer,
It's just so fun.

When I go into school,
I look like a fool.

But during summer,
I look so cool.

At the end of summer,
I go back to school.

And of course,
I will look like a fool.
Travis Ruso, Grade 5
Our Lady of Mount Carmel School

Finally, Thanksgiving
I wake up smelling the turkey roasting
I am ready for a feast
My friends will come to party with me
Oh frabjous day, caloo, callay!
Thanksgiving is finally here, oh yes!

I help make the pumpkin pie
For all of my excited guests
I can't wait for the evening to come
Oh frabjous day, caloo, callay!
Thanksgiving is finally here, oh yes!

The guests are here to party
And have a wild feast
The moment is finally here
Oh frabjous day, caloo, callay!
Thanksgiving is finally here, oh yes!

Now the guests must leave
It's getting very late
I have to go to bed now
Oh frabjous day, caloo, callay!
Thanksgiving is already over, awe man!
Edie Graber, Grade 4
The Mirman School

If I Were in Charge of the World*
If I were in charge of the world
I'd cancel eggs,
Waking up at 6 am,
Hard tests, and mean brothers.

If I were in charge of the world
There would be shorter school days,
No more chores and
Everyone would have a pet.

If I were in charge of the world
You wouldn't have anger,
There wouldn't be wars,
You wouldn't get homework.
There wouldn't be vegetables like broccoli.

If I were in charge of the world
A doughnut would be good for you.
Snakes would be extinct.
A person who wasn't yet in high school,
Or wasn't fifteen
Could still be in charge of the world.
Cameron Roberts, Grade 6
St Raphael School
*Patterned after Judith Viorst

I Am a Blanket
Spending my time,
tossed on the floor,
kicked off the bed,
it makes me feel sad,
when I bump my silk head.
It makes me happy when
you pick me up
for you save me from
lil' Scrappy, that mean brown pup.
It would be nice if,
there was kicking no more,
and that dog lil' Scrappy
out the doggie door.
Please look into,
me not being hung,
nor crumbled
nor stepped on,
nor children to
me clung.
Savanna Deavult, Grade 4
Joseph M Simas Elementary School

Chico
I miss you
we played since you could walk
you always make me happy
with your funny bark
when I am alone
you were there for me
I took care of you
when you were a pup
I always cared about you
and you cared about me
you used to lick my face
all of the time
and rub your belly
and you were happy
we'd always mess around
and play a lot together
we've got in trouble together
we went to sleep together
but why did you have to go
Rafael Gomez, Grade 6
Isbell Middle School

Halloween
for Halloween guess what I was
yea you guessed it Mrs. Claus
I know you're asking for the reason
why I am so out of season
but I just love Christmas so much
is that so strange is it such
candy for me is the theme
definitely Halloween
Gemma Sturgeon, Grade 4
St Raphael School

All About Me

There's a tennis shoe in me. I love to chase balls on the tennis court, kick a soccer ball down the field, and score the winning touchdown when I play football with my friends and family.

There's a flip flop in me. I enjoy traveling to white, sandy beaches where I swim with stingrays and dolphins and play in the warm soft sand.

There's a pink fuzzy slipper in me. I love to get comfortable on the couch and watch a funny movie with a big bowl delicious of popcorn in my lap.

There's a shoe store in me with many different kinds of footwear. I'm different in many ways. Just like each pair of shoes. This makes me unique.

Eva Schneider, Grade 6
Lindero Canyon Middle School

Miss Solorzano

Miss Solorzano is always there to support me
She is caring and loving
She is oh so funny
Her laugh will always remind the sleepy tired old sun to rise early in the morning
The way her pretty voice leads straight to my eardrums make the moon and the stars shine brighter
Her big wonderful smile brightens everybody's day even when it is dark
She is not just some teacher that teaches kids
She inspires people to follow their dreams and follow their hearts
She is like a lifesaver
Anyone would be very lucky to have her as their own

Sewit Tesfamicael, Grade 5
La Presa Elementary School

Rough Weather

It all starts with wind. Wind pounding the shoreline whistling through the canyons. It brings in rain.
With the wind and rain comes…hail. Huge hunks of hail hammer the ground with a pulsating beat.
And hail means one thing…
Thunder rolls through the silence of the rain, the beating of the hail, the whistling of the wind.
The storm goes on.
Flooding the plains burning the forests smashing the mountain…it is dangerous.
You think, safe in your home, why does this happen?
Then the lightning stops, the flood and rain recede, the hail's rampage breaks, the fires extinguish.
The sun comes out…
And it is beautiful.

Kai North, Grade 6
Grant Elementary School

My Heart

I got her when I was 2
I loved her to death
She was the first dog I ever had
Her name was Princess
She wasn't playful at all but something made her really special
She started to get old
When I didn't see it coming, she died
I cried my eyes out
I couldn't sleep
I missed her so much
I wanted to die.

Cristal Lopez, Grade 6
Isbell Middle School

Ode to Popcorn

Pop!
Your tastiness makes my stomach growl,
Your delicious flavors delight me.
Pop!
Your taste makes me want to have more,
Your great aroma makes everyone dying for some too.
Pop!
You're the one everyone loves,
Your taste is so delicious.
O' tasty popcorn.
Pop!

Nathan Wang, Grade 6
Chinese American International School

Soaring High

My dream is to be an astronaut
To soar high up into the sky
To hear those engines roar and people say bye
To see the moon dust which might seem like fuzz
And to see the boot prints of Neil Armstrong,
Michael Collins, and Buzz
And I hope to see a space ship and wave hi
To all the space life.

Nikolaos Karis, Grade 5
River City Christian Academy

Mother

Man, how she makes me smile!
O.M.G…she helped me get on the Honor Roll!
Taking me to multiple places…
Having the courage to protect me.
Everlasting love she gives me…
Rainy days turn into sunny days when I see her.

Mothers…aren't they great?

Marissa Nuñez, Grade 4
Creek View Elementary School

The Pig Eats Bugs

The pig was happy that he ate bugs.
The bugs were not happy that the pig ate bugs.
They were not happy, so the pig became sad.
So the pig quit eating bugs.
The pig and the bugs became friends forever.
The pig and the bugs were happy
That the pig didn't eat bugs anymore.

Sarai Chavez, Grade 5
Tipton Elementary School

I Know Christmas

I know Christmas
Families decorating, kids helping
Kids sleeping, parents working
I know Christmas
The sound of people cheering, the smell of cookies baking
The taste of eating cookies, the sound of people laughing
I know Christmas

Michael Guzman, Grade 4
Lankershim Elementary School

Sadness

I could cry as much as I hide.
We hide when we cry.
But don't worry, we could stop crying.
Just look at the bright side, we need to be happy.
Just remember, we should have good feelings.
Don't look at the dark side, try looking at the bright.
Try to be happy as much as you can.

Irving Sandoval, Grade 5
Granada Elementary School

Red

Red sounds like someone is angry.
Red looks like lava coming down.
Red smells like fire burning.
Red tastes like pepperoni.
Red feels like a hot day.
Red is the color of fire.
Red sounds like not doing homework.
Red looks like roses glistening.
Red smells like a freshly picked apple.
Red tastes like pizza sauce.
Red feels like hot soup in a bowl.
And red is the color of an apple when you eat it.

Kosta Prepoutse, Grade 4
Heather Elementary School

Adrenaline

Blood surging through your body
Sweat everywhere on your body, like crazy
Nervousness strikes your body over and over again
Your heart beats faster every second
You have a feeling there is a bomb ticking
Tick tock tick tock…then BAM
You freak out and run like crazy
Until you hit a wall
Knocked unconscious until the next day
You find yourself in a hospital
Calmed down and all drugged up
Resting peacefully, healing now at last, finally

Jonar Tanguilig, Grade 6
Corpus Christi School

My Eyes

Without my eyes
there would be nothing to see,
for they are the key,
to the beauty in me
with the purest white back,
red streaks like lightning
with bright rings like Saturn,
full of different patterns
in the apple of my eye,
there would be a figure you cannot deny,
look and see, I do not lie,
it is your reflection in my eyes.

Cassandra Bija, Grade 5
George Washington Charter Elementary School

Grandmother

My grandmother means more to me than you think.
She used to tuck me in bed, and sing a song in German.
She also cooked food for me, but most of all, she loved me.
When I was five, she got cancer and died.
But today I know she is looking over me.

Briawna Freeman, Grade 6
John Muir Elementary School

World Creation: Good and Bad

When I see the world
I see God's creation —
Mountains, trees, lakes, and rivers
In the lake there are fish
On the mountain there is snow
In the river there lie rocks
On the tree there grows fruit
There is the bad and there is the good
The colors of the world are not always bright
Thunderstorms, tornadoes, floods
Bring destruction
Summer, fall, spring, and winter —
The seasons are not all good
Winds blow hard, sunshine blazes
Day is light and night is dark
Here is cold, there is hot —
Extremes of everything
Creation is both good and bad
When I see creation
I seek healing redemption of God's world

Alyssa Balocating, Grade 6
Corpus Christi School

The Escapade

Crickitey crick, crickety crack,
The boats crash near the cataract.
A chariot race pursues.
Pharaoh is persecuting a man,
Because of his rebellious views.
A foot race across the desert,
A perilous journey indeed,
But it is not danger that this man bothers to heed.
Lawlessness and anarchism he prefers,
Sabotage and dissent.
When he began to protest,
It was to the extremes that he went.
They make their way up the Nile,
They know that they've traveled many a mile.
This man challenges the mighty Pharaoh,
Maybe for no reason?...
Nevertheless,
This man shall be tried for treason.
First he will be taken into the judge's hall.
And then be hung from the palace wall.

Alexander Gelland, Grade 6
Ashley Falls Elementary School

Drug Free

All of us will one day be drug free
That is how it's supposed to be.
I will give hugs instead of drugs.
We will support each other
Like a father and a mother.
One day, one will say, "NO MORE BAD DRUGS!"

Nicole Biley, Grade 6
St Linus School

A Cold Living

A single kettle sits alone,
apart, separate, away.
I feel alone, my one window
shows deep blue sky,
a swirling stretch of bluebird sea
blotched with stark clouds,
and I remember the times
when I would venture from
my dark lonely prison of a home,
but now I hide.

I hide myself away, like a crab in its shell.
I hide myself away from the faces, the places,
the rumble and bustle of the cruel,
unforgiving world.
Light from my window shines in on me,
but at the same time shines in on nothing,
shines in on an empty carcass of a man,
like a lantern's glow,
a shell of a man
who has already died
alone.

Nicholas Steele, Grade 6
Carlthorp School

The African Plain at Sunset

So silent
But at the same time
So loud
Bursting with fear and excitement
Becoming more alive every moment
Grass getting darker with the sky
Animals awakening everywhere
Elephants thumping
Tigers roaring
Making the ground shake like an earthquake
Feels like time stops
Smells new like the first awakening moment
Peaceful

Semaj Walker, Grade 6
LaVerne Elementary Preparatory Academy

The Monster

As the moon very softly plants a garden of stars
while the sun sleeps soundly
it's time for bed and my mom reads a book we can savor.

Then the monster comes out and silently makes a scary noise
that takes a bite out of my comfort.

I laugh to think the monster soft
and sing to give him kindness.

He is calm as we fall together into my dream.

Ruth Freiberger, Grade 6
Thomas Starr King Middle School

My Life

I am athletic and brave
I wonder how the earth was made
I hear the buzzer announcing the end of the hockey game
I see my family greeting me from home
I want world peace
I am athletic and brave

I pretend I'm flying an airplane
I feel joyful when the month December comes around
I touch warm hot chocolate
I worry about the wars in Iraq and Afghanistan
I cry about death
I am athletic and brave

I understand life isn't fair
I say everything is going to be all right
I dream I'm playing hockey
I try to make everybody happy
I hope I finish this
I am athletic and brave

Jesse Lycan, Grade 5
Dingeman Elementary School

A Quarterback's View

As I look out to the field
I see my wide receiver ready for the pass
I look to the left; nobody is there
I run out of the pocket trying to get away
The linebacker goes for the tackle!
He misses by an inch!
The line has been broken
The whole defense is coming at the quarterback
I scramble and throw the ball
With two seconds on the clock
The crowd stands
The whole stadium is screaming!
The wide receiver's running towards the end zone,
Reaching for the pass
The ball is up for grabs
BOOM!
The wide receiver catches it for a touchdown!
The crowd goes absolutely wild!
We won the game!
Now we celebrate!

Joshua Aguilera, Grade 6
Corpus Christi School

Lost

lone and weary
trudging along the road
sorrow washes over me
reducing me
slowly eating my
memories

Clelia Knox, Grade 6
Chinese American International School

Peace on Planet Earth

The skies that rise up above
A sign of peace, like a white dove
The sun that shines bright
The moon that gives light
The dew that drips in between flowers
The days and nights and countless hours
The earth that's in the solar system
The music, the beats, the songs, the rhythms
California, my home, my state
Peace is our goal, stop the hate!
I want peace! That's coming from me
I tell others,
So grow the family tree!
Trying to make a difference, peace
I'm not the only one you see
There are so many people who want to be heard, like me
So give this beautiful world what it deserves
It's time for the little people to be heard
For they have words that can change this world
Even the most unexpected girl
Peace on planet Earth

Lyric Quinto, Grade 5
Juarez Elementary School

Ode to My Tutor

I sit down in the chair
Trying to get comfortable
I hear the sound of wind blowing
I pick up my pencil to write
I read the comics that are taped on the lamp
I pick up my glass of water
And take a sip
I look at the rainbows
That comes from the reflection
Of a small diamond
Hanging on the window
I hear the phone ring
But it is not to be picked up
Class is in session
I look at the clock
But sadly its time to go
I say good-bye and drive away
Since I am having such an enjoyable time
I don't realize
How much I am learning

Bailey Lanman, Grade 6
Chinese American International School

Love

She is my love and I shall not abandon her
She is the light on my path leading me to the right future
Even when she is not around she is always in my heart
She is my soul
She is my life…my love

Jacen Doebler, Grade 6
Mountain View Elementary School

Bamba

Flavor, aroma, zest of culinary delicacies
Tempting spicy, tangy, sweet candies
10 o'clock dinners and refreshing night swims
The essence of an enchanted land

Floral dresses and colorful garments
Fervent sightseers visit ancient ruins
A kaleidoscope of colors fills the sky
Here come the monarch butterflies

A crystal clear sea caresses
The white sensitive sand
As she moans and complains
From the infinite tourists who walk upon her

Palm trees sway like dancers
To the tropical rhythms — Bam! Bam! Bamba!
Conquered by bliss
In the carefree Mexican Riviera

Laura Chavolla-Zacarias, Grade 6
The Mirman School

The Musical

I wonder why it's so great
I hear the wonderful music
I see the actresses and actors sing
I want to see the musical again
I dream of going back.

I pretend I am on the stage
I look around the theater
I stare at the gaping audience
I laugh and cry with them too
I am watching the musical

I understand the musical is phenomenal
I say "It's the best!"
I smooth my ticket stub between my fingers
I wish I could remember exactly how the musical sounded
I try to see their costumes
I love the musical *Wicked*!

Kelsey Rasmussen, Grade 6
Chinese American International School

Ode to the Forest

O' Forest,
I see the trees that make you,
Your colorful leaves stand out,
In the blue sky.
My shoes get wet when I walk on your grass.
And I lay down to admire the sunset.
As I walk along, I hear an owl hooting
As I lay down for the second time, exhausted,
I fall into a deep sleep.

Tiffany Poon, Grade 6
Chinese American International School

Longevity

I am old.
I have lived for hundreds,
Maybe even thousands, of years.
I have survived floods and earthquakes,
I have survived thunderstorms,
While others turned to ash.
I have given birth to baby saplings.
I have given food to hungry caterpillars,
And held generations of singing birds in my arms.

But,
Despite all the things I have done in my life,
It feels so short.
I am being struck down,
Blow by blow.
Golden sap pours from my cuts like blood.
My dead body will be used as lumber,
Just like generations of trees before me have been.
My stump will rot into the ground.

Even though nothing lasts forever, hopefully,
In my place, a new tree will grow.

Elizabeth Wu, Grade 6
Chinese American International School

Hershey

My cute dog Hershey
Hershey's always there for me
He makes me smile when I'm sad
He sits and whines for my food, especially meat

He gives me his paw when I put out my hand
I throw the ball and he runs after it
I throw the Frisbee and he jumps to catch it

He's very loyal to my mom
He even followed her car
He's black, white, cute, and furry
He's my dog Hershey

Sarah Carney, Grade 5
Ocean Air School

A Breathtaking Rollercoaster

Going through gigantic loops,
Flying down colossal drops,
Racing through crazy twists,
Feeling a rush of adrenalin,
On a breathtaking rollercoaster.

Riding through darkened tunnels,
Feeling a sense of anxiousness,
Visionless until your eyes burn from the scintillating sun,
As you halt to complete this journey
On a breathtaking rollercoaster.

Aaron Beckman, Grade 6
Viewpoint School

If I Were in Charge of the World*
If I were in charge of the world
I'd cancel Monday mornings,
School days, war, poverty
And all children's bedtimes.

If I were in charge of the world
There'd be free ice cream every day
Scary movies would be rated G
I would make a candy a vegetable
And take the word homework out of the dictionary.

If I were in charge of the world
I would make popcorn fall out of the sky,
And make sure no one starves.
I would have all video games in the world
I would sleep all day and party all night.

If I were in charge of the world
I would cancel OLDER sisters,
And crying babies wouldn't exist.
Only calmness would exist in my world.

If I were in charge of the world
Kids could be presidents
And babies could be kings.

Manny Rea, Grade 6
St Raphael School
*Patterned after Judith Viorst

If I Were in Charge of the World*
If I were in charge of the world
I'd throw away all the spinach in the house,
All the chores that have to be done,
And most of all the homework.

If I were in charge of the world
There'd be brownies for dinner every day,
Bike rides and playing sports more often,
And more time to sit and watch TV.

If I were in charge of the world
You wouldn't have a bedtime,
You wouldn't have to be 18 to drive a car,
You wouldn't have bad hair days at all,
You wouldn't have to take medicine when you're sick,
It would all just be in a candy bar.

If I were in charge of the world
A unicorn would be considered an animal,
Your birthday would come every two months,
You could have as many pets as you want,
And every single food in the world would be blue and green,
If I were in charge of the world!

Summer Soto, Grade 6
St Raphael School
*Patterned after Judith Viorst

Friend
A friend is kind and nice
A friend isn't mean or selfish

A friend says, "Good job!"
A friend doesn't say, "Give me your lunch money!"

A friend gives his time to play with you
A friend doesn't give you a mean look

A friend has a good smile
A friend doesn't have a bad heart

A friend hopes for the best for you
A friend doesn't hope for the worst in you

A friend isn't mean or selfish
A friend is kind and nice
And God is one of them!

Mark Barajas, Grade 6
Our Lady of Guadalupe School

A Spectacular Spider Web
A female spider spinning her web,
On a pine tree's branch, as she carefully makes it perfect.
She dangles from her accomplishment,
Waiting for a meal.
Droplets make her web sparkle in the sun,
Like a gemstone in the light.
Her body is black,
With gleaming spots
In the corner of her web is the male,
Her mate.
She has an egg sack full of 500 or more eggs,
That will soon be ready to hatch.
They will fly off their mothers web,
And leave their home.
They will be like leaves leaving the tree
By a great, strong wind.
A day will come when they will be spinning,
The same web as their mother did.

Madelyne Van Kirk, Grade 6
Heritage Christian School

My Dog
My dog is white. She doesn't bite.
She walks around and licks the ground.
She is so nice.
She is such a delight.
She never barks she never hides.
She always eats and always drinks.
She will sit down and whine aloud.
She will sleep in your arms and sit on her bed.
She licks your face in an uncomfortable way.
And always gives you a smile on your face.

Mia Gioiello, Grade 4
Mira Catalina Elementary School

Fall/Winter
Baseball ends and football begins
leaves start to die
the clouds start to cry
ski mountains open
the sun turns away
grass starts to hide
animals take a long nap
lakes start to freeze
presents are given
a new year comes
and life comes back
Connor Listen, Grade 4
Carlthorp School

Spring
The birds are chirping
The trees are blooming alive.

Gardens are lush
Soon enough,
School will be out.

Then all of us
Will run out,
In a shout.
That's what happens in spring.
Troy Koehn, Grade 5
Granada Elementary School

My Dog
I wash my dog.
He scratches me.
But I still love him.

I poured on the shampoo.
Then I rinsed him off.
He scratches me again.

I dry him off.
He runs away.
And he rolls in the dirt again.
Susana Navarrete, Grade 6
John Muir Elementary School

Stuck on a Problem?
When you're stuck on a problem
Don't take your time
Just think of figuring it out
Don't stress yourself
Once or twice is not enough
Repeat it like a ritual
So you'll end up that a problem
Is nothing more than a situation
You have overcome
Stephanie Delgado, Grade 6
Lincoln Elementary School

Halloween
On Halloween,
at night it comes,
some scary creatures
without a thumb.
Some are hairy,
some are fright,
some will ask
for a fight.

On Halloween,
it's like a ghost,
coming to you
and getting close.

You should be scared
on Halloween.
Natalie Durr, Grade 5
Granada Elementary School

My Fairy Tale Dream
I went to sleep at night,
I had a great dream,
All of the sudden I was a fairy,
Flying over a stream.

I flew to the flowers,
The trees and bees,
I gathered some honey,
And brought it to the Queen.

I met the prince at sunrise,
We had tea in the garden,
And we danced till noon,
He took me back to the Queen,
I said, "Good Day"
And that was my fairy tale dream!!
Blaire Goldberg, Grade 5
Carden Conejo School

Cheerleading
Cheerleading is so much fun
Even if we have to run!
Even at a long game
You never feel the losing shame!
Cheerleading practice is three hours long
You will always hear our song!
All the smiles and all the laughter
Makes the practice worthwhile after!
In the air or on the ground
You will always hear our sound!
So get ready to groove
'Cause we've got the moves!
1, 2, 3…
Go RC!!
Gracie Greco, Grade 5
Our Lady of Mount Carmel School

Seashells
S eashells, seashells
E verywhere
A long the beautiful
S and. Oh
H ow beautiful are they some are
E normous and some are
L ittle. Big or small I
L ike them they're pretty along the
S and.
Renee Moore, Grade 4
Heather Elementary School

Jellyfishes
Like leaves on a fall day,
Jellyfish just float away.
Their stingers can hurt very bad,
But it's not because they're mad.

These gooey blobs of gel,
Have no bones or a shell.
Because of this, I'd like to bet,
That no one has one as a pet.
Ajani Stamper and Dennis Mello, Grade 4
Pulliam Elementary School

California
Beaches
Seashells
Strawberries
Tall buildings
Sunny days
Sporting events
Luxurious weekends
Beautiful parks and
Clear blue sky
Anna Tabachnik, Grade 6
Gardner Street Elementary School

Thanksgiving
On Thanksgiving
I eat turkey and dessert
we pray in thanks to the Lord
and play games with family.
I LOVE THANKSGIVING!
Abrianna Renteria, Grade 4
St Raphael School

Alone
Alone is when my cousin died
Alone is when my cousin went to the sky.
Alone is when my dog left me alone.
Alone is when my mom is not here with me.
Alone is when I'm by myself.
Alone is when my grandmother dies.
Mario Rivera, Grade 4
Lankershim Elementary School

A Winter Day in Wisconsin
Snow slowly blanketing the ground from the cold, foggy sky
Footprints pressed against the soft, cushy pillows of white
Gleaming lights joining the holiday
Dressed up snowmen everywhere I go
Just remember the very first time you felt snow…
Remember those days…
Towering forest trees covered in ice
Wild animals getting ready to hibernate
Parties being heard every night
Snowball fights being seen during the day
Snow angels created by the little ones
Oh…when will I visit Wisconsin again?
Tori Lukasik, Grade 5
Juarez Elementary School

Drawing
D rawings are like a map
R unning through many cultures
A lways adding new things
W ashing away the old
I hope I'll find a new part
N o drawings are worthless
G oing on forever, leading new trails

Y ore when they first invented it
A nother generation past
Y ou'll never see drawings end
Jonah Tang, Grade 6
Chinese American International School

What If
What if I could fly
That would be wonderful to me
What if I can't die
That would be wonderful to me
What if I was the tallest kid in school
How cool that would be

All those things are cool but I like to stay on the ground
not be the tallest one around
and I would like to die when I die.
So everything is cool but I want to be myself today.
Colin Carnevale, Grade 6
Grant Elementary School

Holidays
H arvests and lights that bright up the night.
O n vacation, please don't disturb.
L aughing with friends at sleepovers.
I n the sun having a lot of fun.
D aring and mischievous acts all around the house.
A t home watching TV.
Y um, I smell delicious food at the table.
S o that is what I do when I have holidays!
Megha Mallya, Grade 6
Carden Academy of Santa Clara

Guys and Girlfriends
Guys are only for a little bit
Girlfriends are forever
Guys will betray you
Girlfriends have you back
Guys will lie to you
Girlfriends are your trusties
Guys blurt secrets
Girlfriends keep secrets
Guys give you tears
Girlfriends wipe them away
Guys say, "It's okay," when you want to talk
Girlfriends sit down and listen
Guys fight with you
Girlfriends can't stand fighting
Guys make you sad
Girlfriends can't stand to see you sad
Guys talk to you once in a while
Girlfriends talk to you 24/7
Guys make you smile now and then
Girlfriends make you smile every day
Guys can be jerks, but girlfriends are your besties
Karissa Miranda, Grade 6
Corpus Christi School

Music
I've been playing piano since I was four.
Music notes are one of the many things I adore.
I can sing,
And sometimes dance.
Music makes me feel great and proud.
The instrument I play has eighty-eight keys.
I can read the notes, it's such a breeze.
I can play and sing a bunch of songs,
Some of them are a tad bit long.
"Bless the Broken Road" is so sweet.
"Love Song" has a groovy beat.
I love listening to music,
Yes, it's true.
I love to play music too!
Danielle Bongulto, Grade 6
St Pius X Elementary School

Furry Friends
Cats are soft and furry.
They mew and meow all day long
It sounds like their purry song
Some cats are chubby some cats aren't
Some cats are beautiful some are playful
They are swift and sleek
They are also light on their feet
They are quiet and smooth
Most of them are cute
When you are mean they try to pounce away
They also have sharp claws for their prey.
Melinda Saadatnejadi, Grade 4
Mira Catalina Elementary School

The Ending World

As I walk down the street…
I see the carnage in front of me
The anarchy and death the ongoing fires
I see the destruction all around me.
As I walk down the street…
I smell burnt belongings
The leaking of gasoline
I smell old rotten foods
As I walk down the street…
I hear the screams of the roaring fires
The several alarms that have gone off
Sirens of police cars, I hear the pleas of the injured.
As I walk down the street…
I touch the destroyed objects all about
All that I love or cherish
My own face to make sure this is not a dream
I feel the walls to make sure I don't stumble and fall.
As I walk down the street…
I taste defeat, I have lost
The world has lost
All is lost.

Lucas Lagola, Grade 6
Lindero Canyon Middle School

Beauty

Beauty starts in Hawaii
Then going to the beach and having fun all day on the reefs
Being able to play in the water
Then walking along the shores
When the waves crash on the shore there is always a thousand more
When the waves go back out and rocks tumble with glory
Then sitting down and watching the sun set
Beauty starts over again when the stars come out
The sky is shining and the full moon is out
Shining stars everywhere there is no doubt
Watching them go from East to South
Shooting stars fly to give their last shot
Then it's your time to go snuggle up
Beauty starts over and life goes on

Karlie Grant, Grade 6
Miraleste Intermediate School

Green

Green looks like the grass that my dog rolls in.
Green looks like the leaves on a tree.
Green sounds like people running on the grass.
Green smells like mint.
Green smells like fresh soil at a green house.
Green tastes like a big, fat, sour, juicy, pickle.
Green tastes like ice cold limeade.
Green tastes like a mint chip milk shake.
Green tastes like a green apple that you crunch away.
Green feels like the grass on your back when you lay in the shade.
Green feels like the back of a snake.

Jeromey Klein, Grade 4
Heather Elementary School

I Am…

I am an adventurous girl who dreams of being in space
I wonder if meteors are harmful and scary
I hear strong noises that make my ears peel
I see a giant meteor aim straight at me
I want to feel the meteor and learn more about it
I am an adventurous girl who dreams of being in space

I pretend to run floating in space
I feel an asteroid blast past me
I touch imaginary tools to throw at the asteroid
I worry if I never get out of space and be out here forever
I cry for help but no words come out
I am an adventurous girl who dreams of being in space

I understand that the astronauts are in trouble
I say that space is a wonderful imaginary world
I dream of being inside a spaceship with my friends
I try to think about all my friends migrating to space
I hope I could explore this brand new land
I am an adventurous girl who dreams of being in space

Maryam Sayeed, Grade 5
Lydiksen Elementary School

My Teddy Bear*

I will never give my teddy bear away
I'll always want my teddy bear to stay
If I ever gave it away that would be wrong
Since my teddy bear is like a song.

It has a cute nose
It has a cute pose
It will always be mine
From time to time.

It has a scarf that's cute
Although my teddy bear is on mute
I love him every hour of every day
It is so very precious in many different ways.

My teddy bear belonged to my mom that's why it is precious to me
I love him so very much as well you can see
My mom passed away but I've had that teddy bear forever
And I could never give it away, never!

Genevieve McWilliam, Grade 6
St Martin-in-the-Fields School
*Dedicated to my mom

Into the Darkness

When you think of time,
when the light shines.
now the darkness has declined to shine.
when you talk about the darkness
you will come into the darkness with your soul.
oops…now is it declined?

Kayla Martain, Grade 5
Northside Elementary School

Lebanon

Sweet
Lebanon
Mountains
Beaches
Views
Foods
Old ruins
Rivers
Roller coaster
Music
People
William Mansour, Grade 6
Gardner Street Elementary School

The Walk

I walk down the street
with new shoes on my feet

Got the sun on my face
and I'm in the right place

As I get to school
I'm feeling cool

I would stand up and dance
if given the chance
Zane Palermo, Grade 5
Eastwood Elementary School

Summer Ends

Summer came…
Mountains in flames.
Because of the heat,
Everyone's in fear.
Summer is fun,
But not for everyone.
When it gets too hot
People could die.
September has come…
that means fall is almost here,
colder weather, and now summer ends…
Glenn De Guzman, Grade 6
Corpus Christi School

Mom

I know Mom
Mom cooking, Mom cleaning
Mom walking, Mom running
I know Mom
Mom working, Mom shopping
Mom smells like the rose in my room.
I know Mom
Mom singing to me when she's happy.
I know Mom.
Carl Burgess, Grade 4
Lankershim Elementary School

Soccer

Soccer is…
Running around
Getting kicked down
Scoring a goal
Hearing the coach's whistle blow
Getting tripped
Hitting your hip
Your team losing
Everyone booing
The coach yelling "You suck!"
I blame it all on my friend Buck
Francisco Reyes, Grade 4
Lankershim Elementary School

The Lone Wanderer

I am the Lone Wanderer
I walk through the rain
On whispering gray shoes
People think me mysterious
I wander through
The dreary streets
Of the city
Gray and cold
As they may be
I wander them in the night
I am the Lone Wanderer
Kate Planting, Grade 4
Carlthorp School

My Dog Cassie

My dog Cassie is a cocker
She can fit in my locker.
Cassie can see right through fog
She is my hunting dog.
Instead of chasing rats
She wants to play with cats.
Cassie begs for many treats
She can climb lots of trees.
Cassie is a great puppy
She makes me so happy.
Olivia Gonzales, Grade 5
Our Lady of Mount Carmel School

Fourth of July

Boom! Boom! Crackle! Pop!
I hearken the sounds.
Look at these diminutive explosives
Comparable to sparkling flames
Loud, resounding.
Discharging blasts enormous, exciting.
Hooray! Hooray! The grand finale!
Popping and shouting stops.
Now increasing roars, an enormous
Scintillation-like blaze.
Nolan Mitschke, Grade 6
Ocean Air School

Over on the Other Side

Over on the other side I lie,
dreaming and thinking about
the truths that lie.

Over on the other side you cry,
crying and sighing with that
soft, sad sigh.

Over on the other side she rides,
riding high into the big blue sky.

Over on the other side they climb,
climbing into their beds up high.

Over on the other side we say,
"Goodnight" and say "Goodbye."
Jordan Bobbitt, Grade 5
Carden Conejo School

Analisa Rillamas

A lot of caring
N ot a fan of spiders
A lways curious
L oves playing the piano
I s outgoing
S wimming is one of her favorite sports
A bsolutely loves the beach

R ice is one of her favorite foods
I ce cream is awesome to her
L aughable
L oves sushi
A lover of Jamba Juice
M eets standards in school
A truthful person
S inging is a skill she has
Analisa Rillamas, Grade 6
John Muir Elementary School

My Invention

I have a great idea that
Could really come in handy
Every healthy meal would
Really taste like candy

All the candy you could eat
Hershey bars, Milky Ways
For breakfast, lunch, and dinner
Every single day

I have just one problem
With this great invention
If I do it during school
I'll get sent to detention!
Sam Torgove, Grade 5
Sierra Canyon School

Thoughts of a Sad Eraser

I am an eraser
  wide and tall
    and you treat me like a ball
      you throw me to your neighbor
        and your rip me and poke
          and leave me in the dark

You leave me in the water and make me soggy and wet
  and you're breaking my really small heart you bend me a lot
    and throw me on the ground
      but I like it when you
        erase me on a mistake

I like who you are but please take care of me
  and don't throw me all around
    on the dirty ground.

Ronnie Reyes, Grade 4
Joseph M Simas Elementary School

Trees

Trees are green and brown,
They grow in forests and from seeds
Animals live in them too.
Birds build their nests in them
Monkeys climb up them.
Koalas do too.

Trees have leaves
And big branches.
There are maple trees, fir trees,
Pine trees and oak trees.
Just to name a few!

Trees help us in many ways,
So this poem is dedicated to the trees on Earth.
Thank you for all your help!

Isabella Alexander, Grade 6
St Pius X Elementary School

Grandma

She's neat, she's sweet, she's totally cool;
She's mine, she's fine, she helps me in school;

She's there when I am sad;
She's there when I am mad;

She's always there giving me a place to go;
When I cry, hurt myself or even stub my toe;

When I go to her house we get to bake;
My favorite is chocolate chip cookies and cake;

Sometimes we just sit around and watch TV;
I love my grandma and she loves me.

Sage Herndon, Grade 6
St Martin-in-the-Fields School

Just Around the Corner

There it is! Peace
Just around the corner
It's there and people know it
But why don't they acknowledge it
War, devastating death
Might all vanish into thin air
I can see the world with no violence
If everyone concentrates harder
Looks more thoroughly
And finds unabating peace, right there
Just around the corner
Just around the corner
Peace lies in everlasting sleep
Waiting for someone to awaken it
And cause it to spread like an epidemic
Friendships made with enemy nations
Happiness overcomes worry and hate
As peace flutters in the breeze, people will heed
Hearing the soft sound of joy
But for now it sits abandoned
Just around the corner

Dylan Schifrin, Grade 6
Laurence School

Celebrities!

Why are boys so obsessed with celebrity girls?
Why can't they go in their room and play with their toys
Every time they see them they just scream and make noise
They might have bling, can probably sing,
But in time this won't mean anything
Don't even like getting dirty
Probably won't change oil 'till they're thirty
Always concentrating on their looks
When they should be hitting the books
Can't look as good as me, it's irrational
Just look at me, I'm all natural
Looking at their life is a waste of time
When you should be looking at mine.

Jeanine Ojeda, Grade 6
St Linus School

Flowers

I like flowers.
Flowers are beautiful.
Some flowers are big and some are small.
I like yellow flowers and pink flowers.
Flowers come in many different shapes and sizes.
Some flowers smell sweet and some smell weird.
I also like to pick flowers.
And put them in vases.
Flowers can be very tiny.
Some can be huge.
You can flatten flowers and put them on paper.
Some flowers smell like perfume.

Natalie Covarrubias, Grade 6
St Pius X Elementary School

A Nightmare

I sit here alone, on the cold, hard, bloodstained ground, surrounded by wire fences
I wonder, will I ever wake from this horrible nightmare?

Will I ever replace the smell of rotting food, dead bodies, and the stink of sweat
from so many overworked Jews with the aromas of hot food and spring flowers?

Will I ever feel the warm sun on my face while I run and throw balls for my little puppy Benny?
Or feel tears run down my cheeks as I am reunited with my family?

Will I ever not wake up to the cracking of whips,
those screaming in pain,
and the sobbing of the other prisoners
who miss their families so terribly much?

Will I ever see the day the Nazis open the gates of this awful place
and say, "Go, go, be free!"

I touch my cuts, scars, and bruises,
and at first I am doubtful,
but then I think,
I have hope!
My people have hope!
Suddenly I don't feel so alone anymore.
I know that someday, sooner or later,
this nightmare will be over.

Devon Morris, Grade 6
Lindero Canyon Middle School

The Delight of Jessica Dang

I am a cloud on an airplane flying in the clear, blue sky.
I am a green, mighty alligator that hunts in the musty swamp.
I am a butterfly that follows trails through day and night in the flowing, beautiful plants.
I am the whistling wind that howls and goes nowhere.
I am the dark night, the white, shining moon of the sky.
I am a barking dog playing with a bouncy tennis ball.
I am a cluster of shelves of books waiting patiently to be opened.
I am the farthest, scaly fish swimming for adventure.
I am the cold of the shivering, white ice.
I am the moon of an angry, terrified tiger.
I am the glitter of the sparkling rain falling from above.
I am the long slithering, scaly snake of the bumpy, almond colored tree in the noisy, humid jungle.
I am a flower of four colors.
I am a coyote running away in the never-ending woods.
I am a field of flowers and grass waving in the air.
I am a herd of striped zebras in the wild Madagascar.
I am the hunger of an abandoned child.
I am the balance of these things. You see I am alive I am alive.
I stand in good relationship to my loving family. I stand in good relationship to the good earth.
I stand in good relationship to my loving friends. I stand in good relationship to the balance of the day.
You see I am alive I am alive.

Jessica Dang, Grade 6
John Muir Elementary School

I Am...

I am a motivated girl who loves to run
Wonder if I will be in the Olympics one day
I hear the crowd yelling on top of their lungs
I see the stadium with runners in line
I want to fill my room with medals so it can shine
I am a motivated girl who loves to run

I pretend to sprint as fast as the speed of light
I feel that I am running 100 miles per hour
I touch the hands of my family meaning that I can do it
I worry that someone will beat me right before the finish
I cry if I trip and fall in the middle of a race
I am a motivated girl who loves to run

I understand people saying that running is boring
I say that running is extremely entertaining
I dream of God encouraging me
I try to do my best without hurting myself
I hope I win 1st place in one of my races
I am a motivated girl who loves to run

Diana Guerrero, Grade 5
Lydiksen Elementary School

I Am...

I am an enthusiastic student who loves to learn.
I wonder about all of the complicated things I don't know.
I hear the quiet whispering of my classmates.
I see colossal piles of books in my room.
I want to know more about our amazing world.
I am an enthusiastic student who loves to learn.

I pretend I know all of the hidden secrets of the world.
I feel the things I know swirling around in my head.
I touch the awe-inspiring books I love.
I worry as I age this passion will slowly fade away.
I cry when I make a big mistake.
I am an enthusiastic student who loves to learn.

I understand things others don't, like my fervor to learn.
I say I love the awesome thing call math.
I dream of feeling the joy of winning the spelling bee.
I try my best always.
I hope to be a great student.
I am an enthusiastic student who loves to learn.

Grace Martin, Grade 5
Lydiksen Elementary School

Wonder About Me?

I am big-hearted and curious
I wonder how old the earth is?
I hear rain falling
I see pigs flying all around
I want fighting to stop
I am big-hearted and curious

I pretend to be a rocket ship flying all around
I feel sharp razor teeth of a shark
I touch blubber from a dolphin swimming in the sea
I worry to die young
I cry when I get teased
I am big-hearted and curious

I understand losing someone
I say "Don't give up"
I dream to be an angel floating in the sky with a shining halo
I try to finish work when it needs to be finished
I hope the earth gives peace and hope
I am big-hearted and curious

Reece Grodzicki, Grade 4
Dingeman Elementary School

A Finished Puzzle About Me

I am courageous and intelligent
I wonder whether I can get into Harvard University
I hear the faint scratching of glassy ink on a wrinkled piece of paper
I see my ancient ancestors from the past
I want the highest score in everything
I am courageous and intelligent

I pretend to sleep late into the cool, dark, peaceful night
I feel as though I could sleep a million years
I touch the wooden pencil as I write
I worry there will be a World War III
I weep when any of my family members die
I am courageous and intelligent

I understand we all die
I say there is evolution
I dream the world will explode
I try to do my best
I hope I can get first place in everything
I am courageous and intelligent

Daniel Sun, Grade 4
Dingeman Elementary School

Football

I'm a football
I get sad, and mad when they kick dirt in my face.
When it rains I get washed.
If they throw me like a rocket and don't catch me I get hurt.
When my team loses they get mad and throw me on the ground.
When they pop me I die.

Raymond Ybarra, Grade 4
Liberty Elementary School

The Voice of Freedom

The Earth is an endless maze,
Where anything can happen
Where we take our first step
Where we speak our first words
And where we hear
Our first voice of Freedom...

Emma Shleifer, Grade 6
Chinese American International School

High Merit Poems – Grades 4, 5 and 6

Love Will Always Last

Every day I hear a sound that says,
"I need to be found!"
By someone who will care and love me.

Then I say, "Okay, I'll come, so we can go away
together and always love."

Please give me a sign,
the one I need to find,
because you call me every night.

I have found you,
and you seem very bright.
We must run away in the shining light.
And remember one thing…
Everyone's love will always last.

Sandra Casarez, Grade 5
Granada Elementary School

The Sundown of a Beautiful Rainbow

Colors in the streams,
Floating in the air,
As a sundown arrives —
It can't compare to the colors of the rainbow

A light little pink flashes in a wink,
The blossoms bloom in the spring —
It can't compare to the colors of the rainbow

As I lay outside, a sundown arrives
It starts to sprinkle rain
It starts to pour then it just stops
A rainbow appears in the distance
I relax in peace, but from the rain —
It still can't compare to the colors of the rainbow

Chloe Kouyoumdjian, Grade 4
Laurence School

Being Different

I wonder what a normal person is like
I hear them talk, I observe
I see them do everyday things
I am different, but I don't want to be

I pretend to be like others
I feel so alone sometimes
I worry that nobody likes me
I cry when that sometimes seems true

I understand that being different isn't bad
I say I know I have to be myself
I dream to be important to the world
I try my best to achieve that
I am different, but I know that's normal

Yvonne Chen, Grade 6
Chinese American International School

Wonderful Dogs*

Dogs, dogs, what wonderful creatures
They're better than frogs with slimy features!
There's Rotties and Boxers, and Bulldogs, and Collies
Some are so cute, they look just like dollies.
There's hunting dogs and house dogs, but they all love to play.
I bet if you had a cute little puppy, it would make your day.
They might be a handful and might make a mess,
But if you treat them with care, they won't be such pests.
All dogs are special in each and every way,
I hope you have a dog to love each and every day.

Caelynn Hwang, Grade 5
Our Lady of Mount Carmel School
*Inspired by Shel Silverstein

Winter

Winter is a big snowball
As big as a mountain
Winter is joy and happiness
Like Santa in your house
Winter is warm when you sit around the fireplace
As hot as you sitting on the sun
Winter is cold
Like 20 degrees
Winter is windy
As strong as it can be
Winter is over and now it is spring

Peter Zhu, Grade 5
Ocean Air School

Life

Life
…is a rollercoaster.
…is a continuous adventure.
…is an un-asked question.
…is a complicated story.
…is a long difficult path that you have to take.
…is fun when you don't have any homework to do.
…is delightful when you can swim on a hot day in a lake.
…is free when you are dancing.
Life is a never-ending story.

Lihong Chan, Grade 6
Chinese American International School

The Many Sides of Me

I seem to be a dove, cooing and flying,
But really I'm a parakeet, screeching and annoying.
I seem to be an onlooker, silent and watching,
But really I'm a participant, running and tired.
I seem to be a cloud, taking my time,
But really I'm a hurricane, plowing through jobs.
I seem to be a duckling, small and frail,
But really I'm a bull, strong and quick.
I seem to be a pearl, glistening and smooth,
But really I'm a rock, rough and hard.

Kenny Abbott, Grade 6
Las Flores Middle School

The Lord

The Lord is good, the Lord is kind.
The Lord is in our hearts and mind.
The Lord is three persons in one.
God the Holy Spirit, God the Father, God the Son.
He tells us not to sin.
He tells us to do good and pray to follow Him.
The world is in His hands.
We should follow His commands.
We should always do right,
To make our relationship with Him tight.
We should go to church to hear His word.
So we can learn what His Son did for us, and the world.
His Son died on the cross to give us peace.
The Seven Sacraments we should receive.
We should never fuss.
If we do God will forgive us.
At the end of the day,
We should bow our heads to pray.

Taylor Lebahn, Grade 6
St Pius X Elementary School

The Library in Me

I have a librarian in me
Someone to teach and lead,
Someone to show others how
To find what they are looking for

I have books in me
I have an adventure, because I always love to explore
I have a romance, because I love my family and friends
I have a textbook, a symbol of knowledge and learning

I have a step stool in me
Helping others to reach higher shelves and harder books,
Enabling them to achieve greater goals

I have a library in me,
A quiet place to sit and rest
Or a place to explore other worlds,
Without even leaving your chair.

Joshua Pattiz, Grade 6
Lindero Canyon Middle School

Family

Family is very important in life
Family is very supporting in life
My family is wonderful
They are very caring and helpful
Cousins are always blubbing but loving
Brothers are cute, irresistible, and annoying
Aunts are there for you
Uncles are there to help you with difficult things
Mom is there when you have problems and
Dad is there to say no to boys

Briana Rojas, Grade 6
Isbell Middle School

Chocolate

I stare at you
So perfect and untouched
Your hard surface
So smooth and brown
I hear people chewing their's
Their lips closing and opening
They look so satisfied
I just can't wait to eat mine
I smell the sweetness
As it drifts into the air
I feel like nothing else matters
As you melt in my mouth
Without you I wouldn't exist
O' Chocolate

Julia Howard, Grade 6
Chinese American International School

Jesus' Birthday

Hooray! Winter Is Almost Here!
It's the time of the year when school is closed.
It is the time of the year when kids stay home and drink hot cocoa.
It is the time when kids make snowmen and have snowball fights.
Hooray! Christmas occurs in late December.
Christmas is when kids write letters to Santa Claus.
If you are nice, your gifts will be in your stocking.
But if you're naughty, Santa will put coal in there.
Christmas celebrates the birth of Jesus,
Our Savior, Friend, and Lord.
Happy Birthday, Jesus!
Christmas is my favorite time of the year!

William Bernardino, Grade 6
Corpus Christi School

I Know Christmas

I know Christmas
Cookies baking, Santas taking
Doorbells ringing, song singing
I know Christmas
The sound of doorbells ringing, the sound of people singing
The sound of snow falling, the sound of people calling
I know Christmas
Drinking eggnog, singing songs
Decorating trees and shopping in the mall

Christian Ramirez, Grade 4
Lankershim Elementary School

Halloween

You get lots of candy
you listen to scary stories
then you hardly sleep at all
then you eat all your candy
it tastes so good
but the next day you regret it
'cause you didn't get to eat any candy the next day

Tiffany Nguyen, Grade 4
St Raphael School

A Turkey Tale

I pause, outside a poor man's home
As I hear a noise
The noise I have long left
The noise of joy
I knock
A poor man answers
He invites me to sup with him
Though he has little
He has food, however
More food than ever seen
Around this four foot long table are children
Children who brought him food
And to us, the children and I
He told a story
The story that has changed me forever
The story that I wept upon hearing
"My father's great grandfather was
a priest upon the Mayflower"
His rugged face was lit by the firelight
As he told the tale

Savannah Weinstock, Grade 4
Carlthorp School

The Heavens

When I see the sky
It reminds me about heaven
God said, "Let there be light
And there was light."

I dream about the sky
I feel the wind blowing
I feel like I'm soaring
Through the sky
Like the eagle.

I see the mountains,
Lakes,
Oceans,
God's wonderful creation

God loves us with all His heart

Every night, stars shine brightly in the sky.
God created the stars to light our way to Heaven.

Karen Soto, Grade 6
Corpus Christi School

Powdery White

Snow, falling outside your cabin window, gorgeous
Mist, from the shimmering waterfall in the tropics
Calm, but also laughter
Everything vanilla, sweet and irresistible
March, cozy and warm in bed with my dog
Powdery white, the most well rounded color

Lorenzo Sampson, Grade 5
Laurence School

Rain

Drip-drop, drip-drop
I can hear the raindrops hitting my windowpane
I can see them drizzling from the cloudy sky
I can smell the fresh aroma of the fall
I can feel the slippery raindrops sprinkling on my face
I can taste the refreshing water tapping on my tongue
Rain
It gives life to nature
It brings us happiness, yet sometimes sorrow
Lakes, rivers, and trees
Cannot survive without you, rain
Human beings depend on you for life
Animals gather around the lake waters
Knowing you will satisfy their thirst
Rain
As you stop, silence surrounds us
The sun starts to appear
Rays of light are shining through
Red, orange, yellow, green, blue, indigo, and purple
Now you know: To get a rainbow...
You have to get past the rain

Gabriela Ramos, Grade 6
Corpus Christi School

Christmas Trees

What is Christmas without a tree?
I can answer that: Nothing.
It's like a missing piece of a puzzle
That completes its purpose — beauty.
Some trees are tall and some are short.
NO matter what size,
They all bring joy —
Whether green or maybe even white,
Decorating with family
Shows much love.
Those prickly needles that scratch our skin
Are sometimes a bit of surprise, but
The trees stand upright —
A beautiful star that sits on top of the tree
Reminds us all of our days of being a child, like Him.
We all listen to Christmas music
As we wrap up the presents,
As all the little ones scream and shout...
The anticipation, is that what it's all about?
O, we remember the story —
That Christmas is all about Jesus!

Briana Washington, Grade 6
Corpus Christi School

Summer

Summer is a season for fun and treats,
you laugh and play with your friends and family
drinking ice cold lemonade;
you swim and party all day.

Ally Watkins, Grade 6
John Muir Elementary School

How Many Ways Can Numbers Be Used
I can use them at Dairy Queen,
I can use them on street signs,
I can use them with sizes of my clothes,
I can use them when telling time,
I can use them when I'm trying to see
how much is in my juice box,
I can use them on license plates,
I can use them to calculate,
I can use them on birthday dates,
That's how many I can think of,
What about you?
Mia Weitz, Grade 6
John Muir Elementary School

Life
Life is life,
You should live it,
Even though it's not very good.

You should live day and night,
For as long as you can.

Life is all about happiness,
I hope you cherish it.
Don't be afraid to die.
That's life, so like it.
Diana Camacho, Grade 5
Granada Elementary School

Football
I can make a field goal,
I can make a touchdown.

I could throw a football,
with all my friends in town.

My favorite team is the Cowboys,
their jerseys are silver and blue.

Would you like to play with me?
I'd really like you to.
Evan Bremer, Grade 5
Eastwood Elementary School

Spring
Today came spring,
after long waiting.
Today came emerald meadows,
quiet, placid, peaceful.
Today came green trees,
leaves sprouting after winter.
Today came light, refreshing rain.
Today came spring,
green wet, moist spring.
Andrew Kim, Grade 5
Ocean Air School

Why?
Why are you endless?
As two mirrors reflect each other.
Stop pestering me,
To think people would use you,
Repeatedly — over and over.
Ask me, "Why not? Why bother?"
Funny, how you can be,
A letter itself, a vowel, a slingshot.
If something other, why not say so?
The slightest hint, was so simple,
yet, so unspecific.
And undescriptive,
And the blank, hollow answer is:
BECAUSE
Nicholas C. Braga, Grade 6
Gardner Street Elementary School

Things That Make Me Smile
Walking down the sandy beaches
Biting into fuzzy peaches
Music playing fairly loud
Standing out from all the crowd
Singing softly to my sister
Playing family games; like Twister
Going places near and far
Writing songs on my guitar
Laughing loud with all my friends
Trying on the newest trends
Reading books about a mystery
Finding out my family history
Jogging slowly for a mile
These are the things that make me smile
Litah Pechenkov, Grade 6
Gardner Street Elementary School

Fun on the Cruise
To place to place on the cruise
New friends, new faces
New things to do, new places to discover
Let's have some fun with each other

Dancing in the ballroom with fancy dinners
Dress to impress, and photo to be taken
Shiny stars for us to see
We laugh together all night

Between pools and clubs we fool around
We have funny weather all week
Sometimes lightning, sometimes very hot
After all it was a fun cruise
Fernanda Valdez, Grade 6
St Pius X Elementary School

The Window
When I am looking
Through the window, I see
Kids running outside
In raindrops and mist
Watching a movie
Cars splashing
Drinking hot Chocolate
Relaxing
Playing in the puddle
Watching the lightning
There are many things
To look at through a window
When it rains
Darren Huang, Grade 4
Carlthorp School

Around the World I Go
Guess who I am
Who might I be
I drift up above you
You eye me as you gaze
Into the beautiful, blue yonder
Gracefully I sail
As a boat touching every corner
The never ending sky
Children look up and stare
Imagining a puppy, cat or car
I repair dying plants
With power of rain
What am I? You can decide.
Madeline Song, Grade 5
Ocean Air School

You Are Almost There
Go, go, go
You can do it
Just two inches away
You are almost there
To home plate
Everyone believes in you
Yeah, yeah, yeah
You did it!
I'm so proud
Yeah, yeah
You're awesome
You can do anything
You set your mind to!
Rosa Guillen, Grade 6
Lincoln Elementary School

Art
A rt
R eally pleasant and fun
T errific and I love it.
Juliana Todesco, Grade 4
Heather Elementary School

My Fallen Leaf

My leaf is reddish, brown with a
Hint of golden orange and
Traces of faded green.
Its delicate, brittle edges curl
As its long tail
Looks like a graceful hook.
My tiny dancer
Swirls
Dips
Floats
Soars
Before bowing to the next
Gentle breeze
Or sudden gust.
The interesting stories
You could share,
Now in the autumn of your life.
My favorite fallen leaf.
Jennifer Ramos, Grade 4
Orange Glen Elementary School

Music

Music is there
When you are discouraged
It gives you hope
When you are angry
It calms you down
When you forget
Music is there

I bounce my head to "Biggie"
I rock my head to "Kiss"
No matter what you listen to…
Music is there

When you're sad
It cheers you up
When you're lonely
You could always turn to music…
'Cause music is always there
Leo Garcia, Grade 6
Isbell Middle School

Dreams

When you dream,
You have a good dream.
Sometimes when you dream,
You may also have a nightmare.
When you have a scary dream,
You wake up and cry.
When you have a good dream,
You lie down and sleep fine.
But remember,
It is all just a dream.
Keno Valdenor, Grade 6
St Linus School

White

White, an invisible color
It is there when I want to be alone

White is soft and cozy
My warm bed in the cold winter night

White is the wonderful snow saying "Hello"
White is a calm, relaxing color
Where nothing is

White is a happy color that only smiles
White is simple
And that's just that
Noah Chaouli, Grade 5
Laurence School

My Best Friend

My best friend was always there
She died when we were ten
I see her in my dreams
I haven't had a best friend since then
She will always be my best friend
When she died she told me one thing
Don't be afraid of your dreams
When I went to the park I fell asleep
I had a dream she was there with me
When I woke up I saw her there
But it was just my imagination
I miss her
I wish I was with her
Camille Martinez, Grade 6
Isbell Middle School

Video Games

Video games are awesome,
Video games are great,
I just wish I had the time to play.

Video games are cool
Video games are fun,
But first I have to get my homework done.

PS3, X-Box, Game Cube, and more,
But now I have to do all of my chores.

Oh how I wish and wait to play the games,
All I have to do is wait five days.
Kenneth Rivera, Grade 6
Our Lady of Guadalupe School

The Red Woods

Redwoods growing tall
Reaching, sprouting, thriving, grand
The majestic woods
Cooper H. Cullins, Grade 6
St Martin-in-the-Fields School

Friends

Friends stand up for each other.
Friends support one another.
Friends have love.
It's a special kind of love.
Love that goes away at times,
But always comes back.
Friends are people who
Will stick together
For all of eternity.

Friends are people
That are especially born
To be together.
God makes them with
A very special instinct.
Friends mean caring.
Friends are the closest
People in the universe.
Friends are forever.
Miranda Leibig, Grade 6
St Linus School

If You Knew Me…

If you knew me,
You would know
I dream of dogs,
So I can help them.
I wonder,
What I will be
When I grow up.
I hope that I can become
A veterinarian.
I fear most of all
Spiders!
I giggle when
Someone starts laughing.
It makes me chuckle!
I think about how
I can help dogs and puppies
Anywhere, everywhere
If you know me,
Then you would know why…
Haley Rood, Grade 4
Orange Glen Elementary School

Malibu Creek

Mini waterfalls everywhere
Sun beating down on my face
Rushing through rocks
Like cells through my body
No sound besides water
Knees dangling from a rock
Like feathers dangling from a bird's back
No sound
Grace Gagnier Guillod, Grade 4
Laurence School

Earth

Oh Earth, you give so much to us
Oh Earth, how can we pay you
Oh Earth, we must save you
You give us life
You give us clay
You tell us how
And we will play
Oh Earth, let us save you
Morgan McIntyre, Grade 5
Ocean Air School

Ocean Wave

I am an ocean wave.
I feel free as can be.
People riding all down my back.
I see depths no human has seen.
Crashing all day long.
Washing up on the warm sandy shore.
I am an ocean wave.
Liana Merk, Grade 5
Ocean Air School

Soccer

Soccer is fun
Soccer is cool
I play it every time
I'm in school
You score a goal
You get excited
You run around the playground
Edward Alvarado, Grade 6
Lincoln Elementary School

Good or Bad

Run, run, run
Into the sun
God is with you
No matter what you do
You have a choice
Good or bad
The things you do
Joshua Castro, Grade 6
Lincoln Elementary School

Alone

Alone is a time when you're stuck
and have no place to go.
You can't even go home.
Alone is when no one wants you.
You try and try to tell them
but they never listen to you.
Alone is when you feel like a servant.
Jamie Roark, Grade 4
Lankershim Elementary School

A Cloudy Night

I'm striding onto a long
endless cloud.
All alone, I feel the cold
metallic surface.
I've always expected clouds
to be like cotton candy.

My stomach growls
from hunger.
There is no food in the
tower that links me
to this cloud.

A sharp pain hits my stomach.
I can only think
of food.
I hear a crunching noise
coming from my feet.
It's my old cleats
puncturing the cloud.
Layla Moghavem, Grade 5
Carlthorp School

The Whip

Why did you whip me
Did I do something wrong
Every day I do what you say
I want to live, be free, have a home
As I lie down in bed
I feel the blood from that whip
As I wake up
The odor of sweat
The odor of blood
It fills the room
I am a Jew, not a criminal
I go outside and work
Only to be spit at
Beated
Jews did nothing wrong
I won't die though
I will feel pain
I will feel disgust
I will feel that whip again
But I will not die
Joshua Kuschner, Grade 6
Lindero Canyon Middle School

Sun

Bright, yellow
Blazing, shining, melting
Fire, light, beach, summer
Glaring, heating, sunbathing
Giant, beautiful
Star
Matthew Tran, Grade 5
Eastwood Elementary School

Pigeons

While sitting along park benches
And the top of my roof,
How are you feeling?

Why do you always seem to be
Anywhere I am?

When I'm busy
Living out my life,
What are you doing?

My feelings lie
In the atmosphere
That surrounds me.

We're somewhat
Social birds
And we have become part
Of the scenery to those around us.

We simply watch.
It is our instinct.
Madeline Krane, Grade 6
Gardner Street Elementary School

California

War and peace
Elegant flowers
Raging voices
All through the day
Wishes and dreams
Beautiful places
Streets and parks
Snow and rain
School and jobs
Never-ending laughter
Elizabeth Gusenov, Grade 6
Gardner Street Elementary School

Snowfire

It was midnight,
mist below ground,
a ripple in the stream
seemed to melt away slowly.
Icicles hanging dropped, splashed
and the ring finally came at last
I picked up a handful of snow.
Deep inside was a color like
ember, but I realized that it was fire
How could it be?
It surely would melt!
But just like
a flash,
The glittering red was gone...
Jessica Nguyen, Grade 5
Henry Haight Elementary School

High Merit Poems – Grades 4, 5 and 6

Seasons
Up in the sky, birds fly by.
Deep in the waters fish swim.
The clouds float above the trees.
Animals hop out to have breeds, flowers bloom,
As the first days of spring come by.
In the summer fruits grow.
Deep in the wilderness, rivers flow.
Different animals look for food.
Gulls fly across the ocean shore,
As people relax in the summer sun.
The leaves start falling, and multicolored
Autumn is coming.
People start their school year while
Animals store food for their families. It is a start for winter.
Winter comes, the trees are bare.
The birds fly south through the air.
Rain comes down from the sky and the butterflies,
Dragonflies say bye-bye.
Then, its spring again all so peaceful.
People have fun.
Wouldn't you like it too?
Toby Lam, Grade 5
Ocean Air School

My Broken Everything
As my heart beats…
(Though it feels like my last)
It doesn't mean anything to you,
It never did…
My heart feels as if it died of love,
Love that had no chance at all…
Down does my heart go,
Like torn-up pieces of paper falling —
I wish you'd stay and pick them up…
But you have a life of your own,
A life that I'm not part of,
And never will be…
People say they love you…
But do those words mean anything today?
You broke my heart…
YOU broke my…everything
Don't drown me in your lies.
Go ahead, play with my fragile heart.
Play with it like there's no tomorrow…
Because at least I have my solid self,
And not even you could ever break me down.
Abigail Vergara, Grade 6
Corpus Christi School

Thanksgiving
Thanksgiving is nice with turkey to eat,
The night goes on and we are having a feast,
Thanksgiving is cold, night is long,
Our family comes over and we are having a bomb.
Krissia Sanchez, Grade 6
St Linus School

Beware the Jumpaza
In the day you may not see
What's behind the Funnelberry trees.

But if you find some, don't be fooled.
For you may face death all too soon.

The jumpaza are cute, pink and fluffy,
With polka-dot ears that are bright and puffy.

They have blue eyes that stare with wonder,
But don't you dare go any closer.

For if you do, their eyes turn red.
If you look back, then you'll be dead!

They'll try once more if that doesn't work;
They'll sing a song you'll go berserk!

Then with one touch from the creature,
You'll be poisoned death through torture.
Katie Park, Grade 6
J L Academy

Butterscotch Brown
Butterscotch brown
A warm cozy hug from my family
Butterscotch brown
Love from everyone around me
Butterscotch brown
A sweet, creamy, delicious butterscotch bar jumping into my mouth
Butterscotch brown
The best dream ever
Butterscotch brown
The mellow ocean waves tickling my feet
Butterscotch brown
My bed swallowing me up
Butterscotch brown
The tube flips me off into heaven
Butterscotch brown
Caramel sauce slowly dripping down the cone
Butterscotch brown
A big fluff of light, sticky happiness
Butterscotch brown
The color of my life
Jessica Robinson, Grade 5
Laurence School

Dirt Bike
My dirt bike is bloody red, pitch black, and dark purple,
It sounds like a bee,
It tastes like dirt,
My dirt bike smells like gas,
It looks like a dirt bike,
My dirt bike makes me feel like a rock star.
Austin Silvers, Grade 4
Lankershim Elementary School

Competition

Tick, tick, tick
The time is running
Drip, drip, drip
Your palms are sweating
Go! Go! Go!
The fans are cheering
No one knows who'll win
But if you lose your name will go in the recycling bin
Time to announce the winner
Silence takes hold
Every one standing tall and bold
Congratulations!
The winner has been chosen
And he is thrilled with mixed emotions

Nayeli Vallecillo, Grade 5
Mark Keppel Elementary School

Mayans

The Mayans had great papayas with Chile!
Although they went through killing.
They did like bowling games that would let them live
The kings wanted blood sacrificed from every one!

They had great calendars of time,
The calendar would tell when they were due to the next world.
They said we were due on Sunday December, 2012.
What they thought was insane about this Earth.

Finally, they played this game for their lives.
Make it into a hoop no death, but honor.
But we have faith that we will live!
Their civilization traveled 'til 2009 A.D.

Fabrice Zugarazo, Grade 6
John Adams Middle School

Retreat

My fortress of privacy
A place as calming as a baby sleeping
Anger and frustration are blocked from my bedroom
As if a shield was blocking everything that tried to enter
I can lay on my bed with no disturbances
Watching my dog dream quietly
Under my blonde wood desk
Outside my window lemon tree leaves dance gracefully
Mirroring trees around the Great Salt Lake in my poster
An imperturbable breeze passes my face peacefully from my window
Then all is hushed as if I had cotton balls stuck into my ears
Secure from the outside world
Truly this is my sanctuary
My Retreat

David Rivas, Grade 6
The Mirman School

An Autumn's Night

The trees discard their leaves, throwing them to the wind.
Yet some appreciate their glowing colors.
Red leaves are like a crackling fire.
The yellow and pumpkin-orange leaves merge with the piles of red,
Giving them an almost lifelike effect.
Under a blue sky in the rosy-hued twilight they are lovely to behold.
The golden sun sets behind the mountains,
Staining their peaks with a fiery tinge, and
Spreading glorious colors through the sky.
Shimmering in the dusk's light they are as lovely as the leaves.
Night comes.
A cricket chirps in the lukewarm silence.
Every thing is still.
Perfect peace.

Isaac Schott-Rosenfield, Grade 5
Synergy School

The Future

The future is very different from the past
It might be better or worse
There might be better inventions
Some people think that there will be no more jobs

If things are worse people will suffer
They have to get better for a better future
Our economy has to get better to get jobs again
Many books tell stories about the future

Kids think there will be robots in the future
Flying cars is also a possibility
There might be better things that people might need
I can't wait to see how the future will be

Elizabeth Ortiz-Chavez, Grade 6
John Adams Middle School

A Special Place

Monstrous roaring waterfalls
And sweet, brilliant birdcalls
Cobalt lakes and azure streams
In a breathtaking land that seems like a dream
Here people scale towering peaks
And jubilantly frolic in placid creeks
Emerald green foliage is home for wolves and deer
A haven for animals to live without fear
Where people can bike-ride and relax
A protected forest not touched by axe
A place to catch fish and see lumbering bears
To hike up steep mountains and simply stare
At the majestic beauty of this verdant place
A look of great joy and pleasure on my face

Nathan Lee, Grade 6
The Mirman School

Dwarfed

As we line up I
realize that my new
classmates tower over me.
I end up at the
back of the line,
the teacher so distant,
as if she were a mile away.
Then a huge student that
looks as tall as a tree
steps in front of me
and I lose all hope
of understanding the
teacher's instructions.
Other immensely tall
students walk into
the line at my end.
I feel dwarfed
standing in line
with these giants,
just like a pebble
in a field of boulders.
Zachary Wieder, Grade 6
Carlthorp School

The Day Goes By

As the day goes by
From morning to evening
I look at the clock
It's got me listening
All I can hear is
Tick tock tick tock
Waiting for school to end
I look out the window
Before I knew it, I was caught
Not paying attention
The teacher warned me
And students laughed
I guess they never thought
Of their getting detention
Thinking and thinking
Of things I could do
Thought after thought
Idea after idea
Time goes by till the end of the school day
Everyone cheers, packs up
Walks away
Mayleah Panganiban, Grade 6
Corpus Christi School

Nature's Painting

Sunset is like a painting.
The sky which it truly is tainting.
The colors stand true and bright.
Against the sky of twilight light.
Srividya Seetharam, Grade 6
Carden Academy of Santa Clara

Sports

Sports are fun
When you're on the run.
If you win the game,
You'll gain a lot of fame.

Tennis is cool
Right after school,
Holding my racket
Getting ready to whack it!

Baseball is great.
I don't want to be late
When I slide into third base
Without hitting my face.

Football is tough
And very rough.
I like the action
And seeing everyone's reaction.

My goal in sports is always the same.
It is to reign in every game.
In baseball, football, and tennis, too,
I do my best, and I hope you do, too.
Brandon Holt, Grade 6
Miraleste Intermediate School

Fear

I feel fear
throughout my body
pain and sadness,
death and suffering
part of my everyday life.

I'm fearing death
but also life
I live in nothing but filth,
with my skin red and raw
my fear overcomes me
I think I'll die soon.

The sound of their footsteps
their evil laughs
make me shudder every time I hear them
for I fear these people,
these people who hate us so much.

I feel fear
throughout my body
pain and sadness,
death and suffering
part of my everyday life.
Kate Morris, Grade 6
Lindero Canyon Middle School

Untitled

At midnight
I listen
to the
wind whirling.
I see a faint
shadow I
stare at
the moon
my only
source of
light. I
think in
my mind
a spider
trembling on
its web.
I feel
my bones
shake to
a dreadful chime.
Rahsaan Wilson, Grade 5
Henry Haight Elementary School

Wonderful Me

I am wonderful and funny
I wonder if I can fly
I hear birds chirping
I see me relaxing
I want to have a special thing
I am wonderful and funny

I pretend to act like a princess
I feel a soft silk
I touch a hard rough rock
I worry when something is very dangerous
I cry when I get hurt
I am wonderful and funny

I understand when you're more busy
I say stuff that is funny
I dream of being famous
I try to make things better
I hope I am artistic
I am wonderful and funny
Tiffany Vo, Grade 4
Dingeman Elementary School

The Planet

The sky is blue
The sun is yellow,
But when it gets dark
We're all in this together
So help out our planet
So we can do much better.
Edwin Ocampo, Grade 6
Lincoln Elementary School

Ode to Mia
You sit there and wait
for a treat of beef, chicken, or cheese.

I love you and you love me.
You're the best dog in the world,
hug me please!

105, just passed away.
I'll miss her cute, loving smile. Mia.

You watched me grow up and
I watched you grow old.

She tap danced away
in her final days.
So if you're listening,
I LOVE YOU!
Zella Roth, Grade 4
Mira Catalina Elementary School

I Love God's Creation
I love dogs
Don't forget cats too
I love my family
Including you
I love the beautiful clouds in the sky
I also like seeing birds fly
I love playing in the rain that God made
I also like how the clouds give us shade
I love someone
Guess who
I love God
What about you?
I love all of God's creation
You should too
Love God always
And I'm telling the truth.
Amanda Estevane, Grade 6
St Pius X Elementary School

Soccer
Soccer is great,
it gets you energized.
Sometimes soccer can
be hard, but if you
get the hang of it,
you'll be like a pro.
Soccer is fun.
I recommend soccer
for many others.
So go ahead,
try to join soccer,
and the minute you do,
you will LOVE it!
Giovanna Downing, Grade 6
St Pius X Elementary School

Friendship Never Dies
Knowing that real friendship never dies
And friends are like the sky
Always waiting for you in the morning
And I'm sure that no one is ignoring
The signal that they send
Wanting us to comprehend
That they are waiting to comfort you
When you are feeling down or blue
So do not disdain the ones who care
And forever share
The pride within
To in the end win
The gifts of all gifts
Friendship
Lauren Powers, Grade 6
Las Flores Middle School

Time Travel
There is a wish I want to make
That is to go into the past
I want to go with the Spartans
Where I can see beautiful trees

So that's my wish
I want to go badly but it is impossible
The Athens is my second stop
I want to see the wars

I want to feel the pain
I also want to see the games
The past is what I want to see
That is the place I want to be
Diana Luna, Grade 6
John Adams Middle School

A Walk with Papa
Walking with Papa is just like a dream;
I feel like I'm on a movie scene.
It doesn't matter if I walk slow;
Papa will wait for me wherever I go.

I remember I used to walk slowly,
But Papa only said I was aglow.
Just like an angel with its wings,
Papa left me with other things.

Things like family and friends of mine;
Papa was sweet, loving, and kind.
Even though it is sad at times,
I know that Papa will always be mine.
Emma Jackson, Grade 6
St Martin-in-the-Fields School

If You Knew Me…
If you knew me
Then you would know that
I dream of being a singer.
I love singing!
I wonder if going to
Middle school
Will be scary?
I fear thunder,
It's loud and threatening!
It's the storm's language or song.
I giggle when someone
Tells a joke or
Something funny.
I think about what
I might get for
Christmas.
If you knew me
Then you would know why…
Claudia Ruelas, Grade 5
Orange Glen Elementary School

If You Knew Me…
If you knew me
You would know
I dream of being President,
Having gold.
I wonder about a lot of things
Like
Whether an asteroid
Will hit the Earth?
I fear that
I'm going to be attacked
By a snake!
I giggle when someone tells a joke
That's really humorous.
I think about cool things
Like mathematics.
Math is awesome, formidable, super!
If you knew me
Then you would know why…
Erick Pulido, Grade 4
Orange Glen Elementary School

Orchid
Oh, so tiny
Oh, so delicate,
Many beautiful hues to pick
A great gift,
But you must be aware,
It's just so tiny and so delicate,
Growing in a small pot
Next to a mighty rosebush, standing tall
Such a small flower
Might be in doubt.
Isabella Cutillo, Grade 5
Sakamoto Elementary School

Winter Holiday
Snow is falling down
Kids are calling out
It's very chilly outside
Snow, snow, let it snow
Temperature is 10 below

Drinking hot chocolate I say
Eating Christmas cookies all day
All day I wait and lay until
Christmas is almost here today

Stars fill the dark night
Santa is coming here tonight
Getting presents every Christmas
Having lots of love
And so much fun
Jesenia Alonso, Grade 5
Juarez Elementary School

Colors
Green is the poison of the devil's skin,
Glooming in Hell
And painted on the grass
But sleeping on a frog.

Black is flowing on the blackbird's wings,
Dancing in shadows,
But hiding from light.

Gold is the shiny light of the moon
Hiding in the river,
But swimming in the sun.

Red is the prisoner in a heart,
Digging in blood.
Colors are in your lungs.
Christy Moon, Grade 5
J L Academy

Who I Am
I am a person
Who wants to be better
I am a student
Who loves math
I am a child
Who plays activities
I am a strong kid
Who plays advanced wall ball
I am a boy
Who watches football
I am a player
Who no longer plays rough
I am someone
Who will be victorious at anything
Thitichon Viengpasertsay, Grade 4
Dingeman Elementary School

The Seasons
Winter, oh winter
You shine so bright
In the cold winter light
The snow so white

Spring, oh spring
The flowers color
The rain in the sky
The power of thunder

Summer, oh summer
Sun high in the sky
The water gleaming with light
The sun is up 'til midnight

Fall, oh fall
The leaves change color
The wind starts to blow
And the leaves start to go

Seasons, oh seasons
Will always go on
Madeline Hodges, Grade 5
Ocean Air School

The Philadelphia Phillies
Phillies,
Phillies,
Phillies.
Let's go Phillies
Howard is powered
Stairs hits it to the stars,
Chase gets on base,
To keep them in the race
The winners of late '08,
Let's go Phillies.
Jack Martin, Grade 5
Our Lady of Mount Carmel School

Thanksgiving Day
Thanksgiving is a lucky day
for all the girls and boys
it's not like Christmas
when your parents give you toys.
it's not like a joke
that seems funny
and it's not like your birthday
when your uncle sends you money
Thanksgiving is the day I like best
it is like Sunday
because Sunday is a day of rest
Thanksgiving is a lucky day
cause you're able to play
so always say thanks.
Stephen Magallanes, Grade 6
River City Christian Academy

Christmas Tree
They are trees
We use to celebrate
Christmas.
We decorate the tree,
And we put a big bright star
At the top.
We spend lots of time
Decorating the Christmas tree.
When we look
At it,
It looks beautiful.
We set the table,
Some milk,
And some cookies.
Next morning, we come
Out of bed to see what Santa ate,
And it was all eaten.
Nathan Lam, Grade 5
Top Kids Center

Guitars
Guitars make a ding
When you pluck the string.

When you wear the strap
There is a very big gap.

You always play with a pick
It's not even that thick!

You always need a stand
To form a great band.

When you make a strum
It doesn't sound like a drum.

You always play on the neck
So I hope it's not a wreck!
Zahraa Hijara, Grade 5
Eastwood Elementary School

McDonald's
I went to McDonald's and had
two Big Macs.
My dad kept telling me
I'm going to get fat!
I went to McDonald's and had
a vanilla shake.
My stomach did not feel well
and started to quake.
I went to McDonald's
and it was no big deal.
I should have stuck with a
Kid's Happy Meal!
Andrew LaRocca, Grade 4
Creek View Elementary School

Snow

Oh the snow from Lake Tahoe,
The soft white gentle powder,
Coming down from the sky the white powder flies,
Oh the beautiful snow blankets the way we go.

The magnificent snow comes down in a shower as the miracle of nature shows its true power,
As the bear hibernates in its lair, as the deer trot across the snow,
The snowbound citizens love this season for it is the happiest of all,
A fantastic shower of sunlight melts the snow and shows a vivid pink flower.

Everyone is stopping to enjoy the true beauty of nature,
While the children frolic in the snowbound meadows,
While the adults play poker and go skiing,
The freezing magic of nature works like an ice cold glacier.

The dogs yap and yap on and on,
As swimmers swim in Lake Tahoe's frigid waters,
The wolves have arrived at last,
But they will disappear at dawn.

Cliff Moran, Grade 5
Lydiksen Elementary School

A Mouse in a Lion's Eyes

I am but a tiny mouse in the eyes of a lion,
Nothing but a small, defenseless speck in front of a ruthless attacker,
Who wishes so hard for a miracle to come by and save us,
But probably will not live to ever see one,

In the four filthy walls of torture they call a concentration camp,
I wake up to the sound of whips cracking and wicked laughter,
Sounds that mean that the Nazis still haven't had their fill of suffering Jews,
A feeling that no ten year old girl would ever want to hear about in her life,

Hatred and sorrow exists all over this place,
Miserable, starved, thin-to-the bone bodies cramped into a filthy room with the stench of torture and despair,

While swarms of flies around freshly bloodstained clothes hanging from the barbed-wire fence carry the odor of hatred, death,
And sweat from innocent men who have been ordered so cruelly to work to their deathbeds,

I am but a mouse in a lion's eyes,
Nothing but a small, defenseless speck in front of a ruthless attacker, who wishes so hard for a miracle to come,
But will never live to see one.

Kathleen Gu, Grade 6
Lindero Canyon Middle School

Beauties of Winter

Snow, white and fluffy, finds its way into our lives. The shiny icicles strong and sturdy, fight among the bitter cold. It makes you smile, to see a left-behind snowman with a carrot for a nose, and mittens on his arms. One can feel bliss when watching little toddlers having a snowball fight. As well as the warm and tender fireplace burning and sparking up smoke, while you are wrapped inside a blanket sipping hot cocoa with three marshmallows. Although, the one true beauty of them all is the sparkly, snowflakes gently dancing to the untouched snow where they lay together, each one unique and special! Reminding us of our uniqueness and individualities!!!

Natalie Janett, Grade 6
Las Flores Middle School

Hungry Winter
I lie in the snow
gazing at the ocean
in the distance.
The wind howls around me.
I'm insignificant,
like one of the millions of ants
each human steps on every year.
I'm a little hungry fox in a big world.

Birds fly above me,
knowing they're safe
because I'm too weak
to grab their tails.

Fifty feet away
berries huddle together in the snow,
scared I'm going to gobble them up.
But I'm too weak to approach them.

I am alone, encircled by the cold,
encircled by loneliness, encircled by hunger.
The snow is my death waiting for me
slowly
to melt.
Hannah Kelson, Grade 6
Carlthorp School

A Steep Hike
I walk up the mountain
A beautiful sight in front of me
I walk up the slippery stairs
Made of stone

Water hitting my skin
As I climb to the summit
No handles or rails
I hope I don't tumble

Being sprayed with mist
As I ascend up the peak
I'm huffing and puffing
As I move further upward

I see the top!
My thighs are burning
Just a few more steps
And I won't be sorry

I've made it! I've made it!
I say to myself
I look down the cliff
The sight dazzles me
Freddy Mulbarger, Grade 6
The Mirman School

Book
I am a book.
I'm stared at.
It tickles when people
Turn my pages.
When you sit me on a shelf
I like to talk to my neighbors
Some have hard covers
Some have soft.
I don't like it
When you tear my pages
And when you leave me in a desk
I feel banished.
Tyson Reed, Grade 4
Liberty Elementary School

Shopping!
Shopping, shopping, shopping, ahhh
Let those bags fill up to the top
Shopping my favorite thing, sports, nahhh
Here I buy a skirt and a tank top
Nothing is a bore
I need to buy more!
I shop for my dog's sweaters
For the icy weather
My jeans are the greatest
My accessories the latest
Shopping is the absolute best
And I never rest!
Gianna Johnson, Grade 5
Our Lady of Mount Carmel School

My Morning
Gazing in wonder at the moon and stars,
I climb into bed,
my eyelids droop,
and I close my eyes to reality,
open my eyes to fantasy,
Anxious for a new morning.

I awake just in time for sunrise,
the wonderful colors fill up the sky,
I imagine I am flying around the world,
And not the world now,
the world filled with green.
Marie Shi, Grade 5
Ocean Air School

Fall
Each fall I go to the mall
To buy a dress for the ball
I go down the aisles I go down the stalls
I just can't find that dress for the ball
But then I go down one last stall
There it is the dress for the ball
Candy Raye Torrez, Grade 4
St Raphael School

Soccer
Soccer is my favorite sport
All I have to wear is shorts.
I kick the ball up in the air
From over here to over there.

I pass to the left and pass to the right
With the goal in my sight.
The defender from the other team
Is so big and very mean.
He took the ball away from me
And kicked me hard on the knee.

I ran so fast to get the ball
And stole it from a guy named Paul.
There was only one minute left to play
On such a beautiful sunny day.

I passed the ball to my teammate Geoff
Who kicked the ball at the ref.
It bounced off his head and hit the floor
I kicked so hard that I scored!
Kyle Serrano, Grade 5
Eastwood Elementary School

If You Knew Me…
If you knew me
Then you would know that
I dream of being
An Archeologist,
Like
Indiana Jones
My hero.
We wear the same fedora!
I wonder about
How they make Legos?
I fear
Explosives.
Sorry Indy
I giggle when
Someone says something comical,
Or
When Dad throws me in a swimming pool!
I think of the amazingly savvy
Indiana Jones.
If you knew me
Then you would know why…
Andruw Carriedo, Grade 4
Orange Glen Elementary School

Internet
Endless, entertaining
Quick, enjoyable, helpful
Lets me go anywhere
Web
Arman Ramezani, Grade 6
Miraleste Intermediate School

Myself

I am a young
Intelligent lady.
Learning is my passion,
I need an education,
To have a better life.
So my goals in life,
Are to keep a positive,
Attitude,
Work hard,
Stay focused,
Be the best that
I can be.

Aixa Fuller, Grade 5
PLACE @ Prescott

My Mom

My mom is kind of short
And she makes a really good apple torte
My mom is so pretty
And she's kind of witty
She is so funny
And she works hard for her money
She is very caring
And is always sharing
She is always sweet
And makes everything so neat
Everyone says she's lovable
And I think she is huggable

Baysia Ordaz, Grade 5
Eastwood Elementary School

The Blue Sky

In the morning after the
snowfall the sky was dark
and misty

Snow melts and the sky was blue
like a diamond

Flowers woke up and danced
to the violin of the wind

The blue sky glittered like
a million diamond icicles

Shu Wen Yan, Grade 5
Henry Haight Elementary School

Alone

Alone is being left home.
Alone is a broken heart.
Alone is when you are not friends anymore.
Alone is not going to see anyone.
Alone is when no one loves you.
Alone is no one is home with you.

Olivia Manzo, Grade 4
Lankershim Elementary School

Dreams and Reality

I am a dreamer and an explorer.
I wonder why the earth turns.
I hear flames burning.
I see a rainbow world.
I want a delightful life.
I am a dreamer and an explorer.

I pretend to touch the tender sky.
I feel asteroids cracking on my back.
I touch the slick air.
I worry if the earth will be destroyed.
I cry when I fail on something.
I am a dreamer and an explorer.

I understand that life is unfair.
I say that writing is a piece of art.
I dream that I can be a wizard.
I try to do well in school.
I hope I can make the world better.
I am a dreamer and an explorer.

Jonathan Lam, Grade 5
Dingeman Elementary School

Book

I am a book.
I am exquisite.
I feel scared when
I am put away.
I have plenty of stories.
There is trust
And hope in my stories.
Indeed I'm very happy
When you read
My pages.
In fact,
When you see
My pictures,
I feel like
Changing stories.
Furthermore
When my pages are old
I am going to die.
When my pages fall out
I am dead.

Dominique Wiley, Grade 4
Liberty Elementary School

The Amazing Lyrebird

Amazing lyrebird
Can speak any word
Have you heard
This amazing bird
Makes your ears leap
He can imitate any peep

Kardena Patricia Velasquez, Grade 6
Open Alternative Elementary School

Who Knew Kid?

There's a new kid
And he took my lid.
He has his own pen
And he likes to beat up my friend Ren.
He thinks he's so cool
But he pushed my friend in a pool.
He says his name is Max
Max really know his math facts.
Max says he fights with all his might
I hear he punches with his right.
Wow, he's nice
And he's as clean as dice.
Now Max is sweet
And he doesn't smell like feet.
Max is my friend
I never knew I'd like him at the end.

Chyanne Garcia, Grade 4
Kerman-Floyd Elementary School

Grandpa, I Miss You

Grandpa, Grandpa
Oh how I miss you
I wish you could be here with me
You always made me laugh,
So why must you be gone?
You used to call me Buttercup,
Oh how I wish to hear your voice
Just one more time
All I have is photos to remember you by
So why must you be gone?
Even though you passed four years ago,
It feels like just yesterday I saw your face
Oh how I wish you could come back
For just one day,
Because I never got to say good-bye.

Mia Bustillos, Grade 6
Isbell Middle School

Home and Outside

Spring is coming,
Birds are humming,
I am too,
As I walk in,
The sky is blue.

As I walk out,
I heard a shout,
I saw a vet,
With a pet.

I returned from night,
The moon is bright,
In the light,
My mom says, "Sleep tight."

Bryan Su, Grade 4
Top Kids Center

The End Is Coming

The end is coming
My time is running out
I've worked too hard
I'm weak and frail
I've been through too much, and I just want to disappear

The end is coming
Right before my eyes
Friends, family, the innocent are dying
There is nothing I can do

The end is coming
I'm not only sad
Anger flares through me because it is all their fault
My life is over because of them

The end is coming
Inside me there is fury but also emptiness
They have won, and I am almost gone

The end is coming
There is no hope
Every speck of light has been taken by them
There is no point in living
I give up because the end has come
Alexandra Scholefield, Grade 6
Lindero Canyon Middle School

What Will You Find at the Edge of the World

What will you find in sadness,
The raging ocean at bottom of a steep cliff at your toes,
A jug of water suspended just out of reach in the dessert,
Your dream on the other site of a never-ending fence,
The flight to happiness canceled.

What will you find in bliss,
A heavy rain after a bone-dry drought,
Gold at the end of a bright rainbow,
A pair of sunglasses on a blindingly sunny day,
The flight to happiness early.

What will you find in hope,
Bright words in a dull world,
A breeze on a hot summer day,
A drop of happiness in an ocean of sadness,
The flight to happiness delayed.

What will you find in disappointment,
Seemingly happy promises not kept,
Running a race and tripping just before the finish,
Being betrayed by someone you thought you knew,
The flight to happiness is next week.

What will you find at the edge of the world? Life.
Radu Andrei, Grade 6
Woodside Priory School

The Maui of Hawaii

With white sandy beaches
And perfect white clouds
As well as shimmering sunsets
Palm trees swaying in the breeze
With hammocks strung between them
But I do not want to relax in the shade of a palm
When there are sparkling blue seas
And waves with white crests
For me to glide over
Running down the beach
Kicking up sand in a flurry behind me
I run past a series of sand castles
As I dive into the ocean
That clear cold water
My breath is grabbed from my lungs
I can see dolphins and I swim out to join them
Sarah Ashdown, Grade 6
The Mirman School

School

School is…well, not my favorite place in the world.
It just makes me feel like my head is all swirled.
Math is essential, but sometimes just…BORING.
It just makes me feel like I'm trapped and outside it is pouring.
Science is not really science:
We just write down notes with a writing appliance.
There's history, of course, which is all right.
We learn about how things were made, like the world's first kite.
Literature's a breeze, just reading old stories:
They're all classics, those truly old glories.
French is a time when we have words to translate.
Wait…do we even need French to graduate?
Language arts is full of words and vocab.
It's also a time to write, not just gab!
When school is done, I am SO glad.
But when the day starts over again, I am so very, VERY sad.
Kai Hynes, Grade 6
Carden Academy of Santa Clara

The Lone Group

Beneath a dull and gloomy sky
A drumming boy passes by
Behind the steady, monotonous sound
A throng of children gather 'round
Throughout the children there is one loss
The adults are absent from an unknown cause
By night the unaccompanied minors rest
But at the break of day they resume their quest
Against the odds they march along
And feel the beat to remain calm
Then off a precipice they fly
Over the sea and into the sky
And thus our valiant story ends
Of brave little girls and courageous young men
Austin Veseliza and Joaquin Townsend, Grade 5
The Mirman School

Be Thankful for Your Senses

Oh, I'm so grateful for my sense of sight; being able to see tall, tall trees and radiant light.
How beautiful are the colors of the Earth; that I have seen ever since my birth.
I can see roses red and cornflowers blue, but also fresh, lush grass wet with dew.

Thank you for all I can hear; noises loud and soft, normal and queer.
I love to hear the voice of my teacher, but also I love the speech of the preacher.
Oh, my ears; they can hear everywhere; which is why I use them with great care.

Now, let's move on to the senses in my brain. There's so much information that I can gain.
My brain always tells me what to do: eat, write, think, and chew.

How wonderful it is to be able to smell. Whether it smells pleasant or not, I can tell.
There are things that are wonderful for my nose. Like the delicious, pungent, powerful scent of a rose.

My favorite sense is the sense of taste. Because food is good, I eat in haste.
Food like vegetables green, candies sweet; oh, my gosh, what good things to eat!

Jocelyn Leung, Grade 5
Westpark Elementary School

time and consequence

fate is dynamic; when choice and destiny come into play,
change ahead by changing now and behind, change your life by choosing a road
dream a very powerful word, believe
believe in yourself
those of the future sacrifice themselves for those of the past and their loved ones
the present alters itself when you neglect what is foretold and use a wise heart to make a new path.
a choice that is forced to achieve victory in the long run leads to glory, but then in order
to succeed in the past you must lose the future to gain wisdom and win.
never give up on yourself have faith and hope
give into the past what technology, wisdom, gift, experiences, and character you hold.
only by letting go can you bring victory from the future into the past.
to make the past better you have to be willing to lose your future and existence
only by traveling the path of least fame and glory will you find happiness

Kimberly Hernandez, Grade 6
John Adams Middle School

Sunset

Gigantic deep blue waves crashing over your head creating a sensation of icicles,
Soft grains of sand brushing delicately against your back as the fierce sun beams you with its rays,
Miniature sand crabs frantically digging into the damp sand below their tiny legs,
Towering sand castles by the shoreline while young children protect them as a mother bear would its cubs,
Strong, impatient surfers cutting you off to catch the perfect wave,
Adorable dolphins playfully entertain the swarm of foreign tourists dressed in flowery Hawaiian shirts,
Innocent toddlers happily digging small holes with their miniature plastic shovels,
The gentle ocean mist spraying the faces of giggling parents suddenly feeling like small children,
Weak, helpless mussels determinedly clinging onto the strong pier majestically standing tall in the sparkling ocean,
Beautiful shades of red, orange, purple, blue, and yellow as the mighty sun sets on the perfect day.

Pascal Schlee, Grade 6
The Mirman School

Good Bye

I remember looking back and seeing his yellow coat shine in the sun, him leap into the water,
then run back and spray me with water then came the day to say good bye, shot and killed
gone forever good bye I miss you.

Brooke Martinelli, Grade 5
Northside Elementary School

My Dog Chelvin

My dog is really sweet
She likes it when I give her treats
My dog likes to lick my face
Which makes her run all over the place
She could never be replaced
She is a big part of my heart
I hope were never apart

Paulina Garcia, Grade 6
Isbell Middle School

War

War
Precarious, despicable
Running, hiding, fighting
Contradiction, collision, capacity, injury
Collapsing, fading, vanishing
Fatal, inhumane
Disaster, atrocious

Gissel Ruiz, Grade 5
Mark Keppel Elementary School

When I Grow Up, I Want To…

When I grow up, I want to travel the world.
I want to fly a plane.
I want to climb a pyramid.
I can be whatever I want to be,
and no one can stop me,
so let me dream.

Anna Hilbert, Grade 6
Grant Elementary School

I Love Math

I think math is kind of fun
It's easy for me to get it done.
Long division takes so long
One mistake you'll get it wrong.
I try to do it all in my head
But sometimes I use my fingers instead.

Darlene Prom, Grade 4
Pulliam Elementary School

Making the Grade

Homework
Longlasting, forever
Writing, reading, researching
I get it every day
Assignments

Landon Ma'a, Grade 5
St Louis De Montfort School

Snow

Icy, freezing
Skiing, sledding, sinking
Wet, snowy, fun, tastes good

Francesca K., Grade 4
Proctor Elementary School

Sky Blue

Sky blue is the color of a baby's eyes when she is laughing.
Sky blue is the smell of a new-blossomed daisy in the spring.
Sky blue looks like a shimmering moon glowing in the night mist.
Sky blue is the taste of fresh water trickling down your throat.
Sky blue is the feeling of a fuzzy, warm blanket someone uses on a cold night.
Sky blue sounds like a stream flowing peacefully at day.
Sky blue looks like a waterfall rushing its water through the afternoon.
Sky blue is the color of tears dripping down my cheek when I sob.
Sky blue is the smell of a woman's fragrant perfume that lasts all day.
Sky blue is the taste of a raspberry lollipop waiting for someone to lick it.
Sky blue is the sound of birds singing beautifully in the morning.
Sky blue is the feeling of clothes made of soft silk.
Sky blue is the taste of picked blueberries with juice splattering everywhere.
Sky blue is the color of a girl's eyes twinkling in the light.
Sky blue looks like a blue jay's detailed feathers in its nest.
Sky blue is the feeling of a blanket of stars shining in the night sky.
Sky blue is the sound of the ocean's waves crashing and tumbling at shore.
Sky blue is the smell of rainy weather on a cloudy day.
And sky blue is a lovely color that is beautiful and unique.

Skylar Weiss, Grade 4
Heather Elementary School

The Future

Nobody knows what the future will be like.
It might be full of crazy gadgets,
Or maybe even hard work,
But I am certain it'll be good. What you do today will affect you tomorrow.
But you can make the future how you want it!
You can make the robots or the gadgets.
It may not even be hard!
People and things may come and go,
But hold onto your faith,
And for certain, your future will be full of laughs and joy!
Or future hope is exciting,
Bright with all God's promises.

Christian Aparicio, Grade 6
Corpus Christi School

The Nocturnal Prowler

As I step within range of the dark corner of my room,
Otherwise known as "kitty territory,"
I sense the stare of two icy, menacing eyes
Watching my every move
All of a sudden, the loud, piercing battle cry of the predator fills the still air
"MEOW!"
Sharp, piercing claws penetrate my socks as he attacks
I kick back at him gallantly but only to further encourage him
I fight him off as I back towards the light switch
My defenses melt to see kitty, playfully rolling over
Awaiting his belly rub.

Jeremiah Strang, Grade 6
Chinese American International School

Boy Scouts
Sometimes scouts are hiking,
Other times they're biking.

A scout is all about,
Finding life's best route.

At night when they retire,
They tell stories by the fire.

The fun never ends,
When you're camping with your friends.
Russell Smith, Grade 5
Eastwood Elementary School

Anger
Anger is in the air,
Yelling like mad commandos.

Anger is hidden in the grass,
Waiting like a cobra.

Anger is coming close,
Streaming like a river.

Anger is in the red hot,
Dancing like ferocious fire.
Natalie Pandher, Grade 5
Sakamoto Elementary School

Shadow
Sometimes your friend,
others your enemy,
but no matter what you do,
it will always be there,
and when it is,
it will be with you,
in your shadow.
It will always follow you
and become large or small,
old or young,
he will always be there.
Ian Ryan, Grade 6
Grant Elementary School

The Golden Tower
Groan, crunch, crack.
A gap appears
in the golden tower
high above the metallic clouds.
It's empty but dangerous.

The golden tower sways once again.
A final crack, and the majestic tower
finally falls.
Paige Thompson, Grade 5
Carlthorp School

Butterfly
Soft Wings
Small insect
Different colors
Gentle friend
Likes the flowers
Nice and sweet
Stands on your hands
They lie on the plants
Love to fly
See them most around trees
Kimberly Marroquin, Grade 6
Gardner Street Elementary School

Surgery
I'm having a scary ear and nose surgery.
I wish I were not eligible,
Red sparkling blood, sharp pointy needles,
Make me uncomfortable.
I will try not to shake,
Like an enormous earthquake.
I hope my bones will not break.
I am in fright!
I will not sit upright
It'll be all right!
Grace Schonfeld, Grade 5
Our Lady of Mount Carmel School

Rainy Day
Gloomy
Grey skies
Cold
Wet
windy
Slippery
Foggy
Thunder
Cloudy
Drip, drip.
Danyelle Salazar, Grade 6
Gardner Street Elementary School

A Search Under the Sea
Her goal is
To find an angelfish
Before she dives
She makes a wish
She hears her brother cheers
She dives into the water
She sees a school of fish
Closer to a coral reef
She knows she can find it
And she did!
Wendi Lara, Grade 6
Lincoln Elementary School

A Treasure
A treasure can be anything
Money, gold, or anything that pleases us
But the greatest treasure is a friend
A friend can't be bought
Nor forced to be one
A true friend is a companion
Someone who watches your back
Someone you can trust

A true friend doesn't judge you
By what kind of culture you came from
Or by your race, or how you dress
A true friend judges you by how you act
A friend helps you in need
When you're in trouble
Or when you stumble or fall

So don't abuse your friends
Don't put them in harm's way
Let the friendship last
Before you grow apart
And lose the treasure
Sean Ace Minerales, Grade 6
Corpus Christi School

Munch, Chew, Yum!
Crack, crack,
The chips fall down my throat
As I stuff them in my mouth
Munch munch,
Chew chew,
I hungrily stuff
My mouth
With turkey
Eagerly and happily,
Ahhhh…
Soft and chewy
Yummy and delightful,
Thump thump,
Back for seconds as my feet thump
On the rocky tile floor,
On the table,
There is a spread of squishy
Mashed potatoes,
Yummy turkey,
And vegetables of all shapes and sizes
Mmmmm…
Sarah Costanzo, Grade 4
Dingeman Elementary School

Sweet Apple
Sweet apple growing
on a beautiful oak tree
thinking about the fall.
Mark Rubinov, Grade 6
Gardner Street Elementary School

High Merit Poems – Grades 4, 5 and 6

Fun Bug
Bee
Black, yellow
Buzzing, stinging, pollinating
Flying around your garden
Insect
Brandon Cantor, Grade 5
St Louis De Montfort School

How to Have Fun
Skateboard
Awesome, fun
Grinding, rolling, flipping
Hard to get balanced
Longboard
Miranda Herrera, Grade 5
St Louis De Montfort School

The Sea Turtle
A gentle sea turtle
Crawling on the cold sand
On a peaceful fall morning
On the beach
To lay her eggs
Nikolas Ognjan, Grade 6
Gardner Street Elementary School

The Dandelion
A peaceful dandelion
Flying in the soaring wind
On a cool summer's night
In a mysterious forest
It enjoyed the flight
Sarah Contreras, Grade 6
Gardner Street Elementary School

Sports
Basketball
Round, brown
Bouncing, dribbling, shooting
Making a slam ball
Dunk
Meagan Armijo, Grade 5
St Louis De Montfort School

Candy on a Stick
Lollipop
Yummy, sour
Licking, swirling, crunching
Makes my hands very
Sticky
Giselle Carmona, Grade 5
St Louis De Montfort School

Who I Am…
I am an adventurous male, eager to be a pilot
I wonder how hard it is to be an honorable doctor
I hear the loving sounds of birds in the morning as I wake up
I see clouds shaped as stars and whales
I want to stay close to my family, especially when they are depressed
I am an adventurous male, eager to be a pilot

I pretend to love something even if I don't
I feel the sharp claws of a lion scratch me
I touch the sensitive skin of my baby brother
I worry when I hear a sudden knock at the door when everyone is asleep
I cry when someone I love dies, especially at a young age
I am an adventurous male, eager to be a pilot

I understand that life is not fair
I say goodbye to my mother when she leaves
I dream that I have a huge diamond piece to give to my mother
I try not to cry when I have to move to a new house
And miss the opportunity to see my friends
I hope that my family and me live for a good 100 years
I am an adventurous male, eager to be a pilot
Ahmad Nuhaily, Grade 5
Dingeman Elementary School

You
In your min, you rule your world
But are you perfect as you can be? No one is
Being someone else doesn't make you feel better
You are who you are; you don't have to change yourself
Everybody has something that they hate about themselves, but is it
Important enough to give away who you are instead of being yourself?
Loving and enjoying every moment of your life is what you should
Do other than losing yourself to change who you are
But the most important thing is to appreciate who you are in the inside,
Because the inside makes you who you are, not someone you're not
On the outside, sure it's important too, but faking a person inside of you
Is more difficult and challenging to hold on than to just being yourself
For once in your life, noticing that you have beauty is so much more important
Than knowing that you're ugly and hideous
You are all you could be
So learn how to appreciate yourself and you'll love yourself better…
Having a life like no other…
You
Jenny Nguyen, Grade 5
Juarez Elementary School

The Valley
As I walk on the grass I think of my past how painful but also so pretty.
I think of the tree back at home locked in its dreadful roots and I am free.
I see the wind hitting the bushes like it's mad.
I am cold. Oh how breezy it is. I feel sad.
It is bright and so beautiful. That's how the valley looks.
That is why I'm so hooked.
Ava Rae Summers, Grade 5
Eastwood Elementary School

My Dad
On the way to Red Wood Park
I got to see many things
and lots of wild life
deer, birds, and squirrels!
even a bald eagle!!
Matthew Hansom, Grade 4
St Raphael School

State Capitol
The State Capitol
Big, elegant
Working, debating, discussing
Important things happen here
Grand building
Kristen Sun, Grade 4
Proctor Elementary School

Sky Warrior
Jet
Quick, sleek
Flying, spying, disappearing
Used for dangerous missions
Plane
Ethan Ellickson, Grade 5
St Louis De Montfort School

Yummy Treats
Apples
Green, red
Sweetening, enjoying, growing
Healthy and very tasty
Fruit
Colby Woodside, Grade 5
St Louis De Montfort School

My Family
We went to Red Rock park for a reunion
my family was all there
my cousin Danny was there too
he is really nice and funny
he plays with me a lot!
Dax Galvan, Grade 4
St Raphael School

Halloween
It's scary it's creepy
no matter what time it is
loads of candy that equal 5 pounds
bound to get a cavity
bound to get scared
Wade Varesio, Grade 4
St Raphael School

I Am
I am a rainbow and I can mix colors so magical
I wonder if I mixed blue and orange what color it would make
I hear the sound of the thick blue brush as I paint
I see the blue calalillies that are shiny in the luscious green grass that I painted
I want an art easel with colors and majestic paints
I am an artist that is creative

I pretend to paint my dreams in the breezy air
I feel that art can paint my whole life
I touch the bristled brush as it sways, as I paint
I worry that someone won't like my precious art
I cry when I fail and no one likes my work I have created
I am an artist that is creative

I understand that colors mix like the beautiful blue sky
I say and say that I can paint what I say
I dream that one day I'll be in the museum looking at my art
I try to paint what I feel and my untapped emotions at my art
I hope that I'll be famous in the museum that I cherish
I am an artist that is creative
Christin Crawford, Grade 5
Lydiksen Elementary School

Blue
Blue looks like a castle in the sky.
Blue sounds like the birds chirping when the sun rises.
Blue smells like blueberries that have just been picked from their bush.
Blue tastes like bubble gum that just popped in your mouth.
Blue feels like the baby blanket you had when you were a toddler.
Blue is like the blue sky on a summer's day.
Blue tastes like blueberry muffins that just came out of the oven.
Blue smells like raindrops falling from the sky.
Blue is the feeling when you are lonely and without a friend.
Blue is the wind that flows through your hair.
Blue is the feeling when you walk along a sandy beach.
Blue is the feeling of your first Christmas.
Blue is a color that's friendly and fresh.
Florence Khalife, Grade 4
Heather Elementary School

Green
Green is the color of the first day of spring.
Green is the feeling of a sweet victory at a Ping-Pong game.
Green sounds like a fluttering butterfly, flapping its wings in the whistling wind.
Green tastes like a lime, fresh from the garden.
Green looks like a lush green forest.
Green smells like the sweet scent of a rose in full bloom.
Green is the sound of pine trees shaking in the chilly wind.
Green feels like the sun's warm rays beating on you when it first rises
Green smells like the fresh air that you inhale each morning when you're camping.
Green feels like a comforting hug, given to you by someone who cares.
Green sounds like a distant voice, calling you home.
Green is a color of nature.
Michelle Lytle, Grade 4
Heather Elementary School

High Merit Poems – Grades 4, 5 and 6

Snail
S tinky is my snail's name.
N ever touch his eyes.
A snail is slimy.
I like to play with my snail.
L ittle little snail.

Alexis Glow, Grade 4
Pine Street Elementary School

The Blue Bird
The miraculous blue bird,
Sitting on the oak tree
On a beautiful Saturday morning
At farmer Steve's farm
Is thinking about life's joys and wonders

Thomas Balin, Grade 6
Gardner Street Elementary School

Old School House
Old school house
Small, quiet
Learning, reading, drawing
The students were happy
Classroom

Sabrina Ma, Grade 4
Proctor Elementary School

Candy Shop
Candy shop
Yummy, sweet
Tasting, laughing, smiling
The kids are eating
Building

Madeline Albright, Grade 4
Proctor Elementary School

Railroad Museum
Railroad museum
Big, quiet
Learning, looking, walking
A big train museum
Building

Ester Fader, Grade 4
Proctor Elementary School

Indian Museum
Indian museum
Small, brown
Learning, shopping, listening
Looking for smallest basket
Museum

Felicia Wang, Grade 4
Proctor Elementary School

Mom, the Key to My Life and Heart
You're my heart, my smile, my life, and everything around me
Your smile is a mile wide that warms the world
Your heart melts everyone else's with love and compassion
You're the key that opens an everlasting gate to a better place
You shine as brightly as the sun more than anyone
Your pride and confidence are as strong as bricks
So no one can ever bring you down
You're my hero for the past, present and even the future
You should win a medal just for being you and of course the greatest mom for me
You're always there for me and I know you will always be there for me
You're the greatest role model to me and everyone while giving me the greatest power:
ENCOURAGEMENT
You cheer me on when I'm down even if I'm nearly on the ground
You always make me laugh with the funniest things
You make my life a ton easier by helping me through it
And also by giving the greatest advice that always works
You're the perfect mom and I would never change my mind about that for the world
I would do anything to be with you and be just like you
Most important…
You're the key to my life and heart
Mom I love you

Joely Weiner, Grade 5
Laurence School

Bravery
Don't say I'm a lion
I'm not brave
I'm not brave because I don't like taking that risk
I want to at times
But in the end I'm too afraid
In the end I'm too afraid to go off that jump
Or go on the biggest diving board
So please don't say I'm a lion for I'm not brave
I'm not brave
I can't make that last choice to go on the roller coaster
Or try to stand up to something that scares me
For I'm not brave
I can't compare myself to a great person
For I can't make it through that last few minutes of that scary movie
Please don't judge me for I'm not that brave
I'm not brave

Connor Cook, Grade 6
Grant Elementary School

Alone Is a Lot of Things
Alone is when I went to a party and I did not know anyone.
Alone is when someone in your family dies.
Alone is when you get sick the day of your birthday.
Alone is when your heart has been broken.
Alone is when your best friend doesn't want to be your friend anymore.
Alone is when people say you're ugly.
Alone is a lot of things but I'm just going to keep my head up high.

Alanze Scott, Grade 4
Lankershim Elementary School

Broken Dreams

Her dreams shatter to the ground,
Only pieces can be found,
It leaves a reminding mark,
To tell her what has made this spark,
Of ache and suffering,
And pain of the heart.

Jessica Bailey, Grade 4
Creekside Elementary School

I Like to Play with Clay

I like to play with clay all day
Black, blue, green and pink
Clay makes my day.
It's also a fun activity to play with all day.
What I can make out of clay is a flower
Or a big tall tower.

Tzirintzi Garcia, Grade 5
Renuevo School

Bubble

B umping, thumping thing
U nbeatable little ring.
B oring sphere of soap
B ouncing all around.
L ittle menace of soap
E ager thing wanting to fly.

Nicholas Russo, Grade 4
Heather Elementary School

Flying

F loating across the sky
L ying on your back.
Y awning as you go
I nto the clouds.
N ice cool air
G athering around your face.

Jill Albertson, Grade 4
Heather Elementary School

Pogo

Slimy, striped
Eating, sleeping, racing
Radula, tentacles, tail, optic nerve
Polka dotted, gooey
Mollusks

Sabrina Traynor, Grade 4
Pine Street Elementary School

Sutter's Fort

Sutter's Fort
Mighty, honor
Amazing, working, fighting
The fort is historical
Camp

Tyler Gormly, Grade 4
Proctor Elementary School

Inanimate Objects Conquer All

I am just a "thing" they say, I don't have a brain.
They don't think that I care about anything, so let me explain.
Although I don't go to school, I truly am smart!
I don't just have a brain, but I have a heart.
When you go around and act like I'm not there, it really does hurt.
When you disrespect me, you should be alert.
I am watching, you know, everything you do.
When you choose to damage me, we have an issue.
Can you please let us be!? You see, our lives aren't long.
Gosh! You darned humans are so headstrong!
Maybe someday we will have our chance.
So if I were you I would think in advance.
Don't chop that tomato or boil that water!
You shouldn't squeeze that bottle or crush that can!
Don't bounce that basketball or throw that baseball!
Because soon, we will have it all!
We will scream and holler, then hold you by the collar.
Then we will say, "We've had enough! We are now here and we are more tough!"
So, think before you act, people, 'cause we'll find a way to overcome you someday.
We're inanimate objects and we're here to stay!
Oh, and by the way, you really should be scared!

Juliana Mastro, Grade 6
St Anne Elementary School

Why?

Why?
Why can't we do anything?
No improvement at all.
Every day it makes me furious to think that even now,
with all the things we have achieved, we still can't find it!
I get a big lump of rage and shock stuck in my throat.
I don't know how to get it out!
So many people want it, or at least they say they do.
But do they really?
'Cause if they really had a thirst for it, perhaps they would do something.
Yet no one does.
But if one person starts, maybe,
just maybe, we can start a chain,
a chain of acts,
Acts that,
WILL!
Bring
Peace!

Greta Pasqua, Grade 6
Laurence School

Ocean

The ocean dreams of trash on dry land
The ocean remembers the tiny krill that disappeared in the big, blue whale's mouth
The ocean moves in an undulating motion with the waves
The ocean promises food to all the friendly fish,
while the unfriendly ones go to the sharks
The ocean vacations wherever it can find a warm spot
The ocean is a sign of life to all the sea critters of the world

Stephanie Vartany, Grade 4
Laurence School

High Merit Poems – Grades 4, 5 and 6

Time Traveling
If I had a time machine
I would fly to many different places
Maybe I would fly to the past.
If I flied to the past
I wouldn't be able to visit the future or present.
I'm already in the present
But I would like to visit the future.
Maybe I'll see what I will look like or how I would live.
Maybe I'll get married and have kids maybe.
Estefani Moreno, Grade 6
John Adams Middle School

Look Inside Your Heart
If life gives you one thousand reasons to cry,
Give life one thousand reasons to smile
During day or during night
Make your day bright
Hold the ones you love close and tight
Look inside your heart
So it won't be torn apart
You will be glad you did your part.
Mayted Hernandez, Grade 6
Lincoln Elementary School

Purple
Purple looks like a fish swimming in its tank.
Purple tastes like a juicy plum being eaten.
Purple sounds like a dress spinning around and around at the ball.
Purple is the color of grapes on a vine.
Purple feels like riding a bike down a path.
Purple looks like a blackberry smoothie in the blender.
Purple tastes like juice going down your throat.
Purple sounds like an opera person singing with a hat on her head.
Natalie Troglio, Grade 4
Heather Elementary School

Fires
Fires are so bright,
raining ashes from the sky,
a loud roaring sound like thunder,
it's a tidal wave of flames,
trying hard to rescue,
eyes blinded from the smoke,
destination unknown,
heroes gone, but will always be remembered.
Ashley Montgomery, Grade 5
Quail Valley Elementary School

New Dawn
The sun rose slowly
And the dark sky broke
Into a new dawn.
Fresh and crisp readying
Itself for the day.
Sarah Brosio, Grade 5
Sakamoto Elementary School

Tattoos
What are tattoos?
Are they permanent marks on your body?
Are they drawings, symbols, or letters that you will regret later?
Are they something that you'll wish you had not gotten?
Are they painful?
Will they cause problems later?
One should think long and hard before making this choice
Tiara Brown, Grade 5
PLACE @ Prescott

Shine and Spark
Beauty is like
Shining diamonds
And red rubies.
Beauty is like
Sparkling lightning,
Flashing with booming sounds
Striking the ground with sparks flying everywhere.
Jason Moon, Grade 4
J L Academy

Peace
Peace is a feeling
It's a sign of life
You can't live as great if you are not in a life of peace
Make peace move into your heart
You'll feel like you're in a better world
Peace is a feeling
Instead, make it a way of life
Hannah Chaouli, Grade 4
Laurence School

A Cover!
Sometimes I'm very thick
and sometimes very thin.
My home is in the library,
and I am always in.

There are different types of topics,
but the ones I like the best
are mysteries and fantasies,
much nice than the rest.

I make your brain go wild
with clues and many facts.
The world is yours to learn,
from knowledge on the racks.

I am many different colors,
I am smooth like wings on a dove,
a row of spectrum binders,
and pictures that you'll love.

What am I?
Eugenia Tzeng, Grade 6
Sage Canyon Elementary School

Snow
Snow
Fluffy, soft
Sledding, skiing, jumping
Sinking in the snow
Ice
Esther Punzel, Grade 4
Proctor Elementary School

Sutter's Fort
Sutter's Fort
Square, white
Guarding, training, working
Is also very interesting
Fort
Daniel Albright, Grade 4
Proctor Elementary School

Snow
Snow
Chilly, cold
Skiing, sinking, sledding
It is fun to go snowboarding
Ice
Katherine Tai, Grade 4
Proctor Elementary School

Steel Birds
Jet
Speedy, fast
Flying, lasting, hovering
Always on the move
Airplane
Logan Herrera, Grade 5
St Louis De Montfort School

Healthy Treat
Apples
Tasty, yummy
Crunching, munching, eating
They are really sour
Fruit
Nicolas Cash-Colón, Grade 5
St Louis De Montfort School

You Are My Love
You are my love
Because you are sweet
And you try your best at everything
Even if you cannot do it
You are my love
Erik Cuevas, Grade 6
Lincoln Elementary School

Waiting
I sat poised in a big blue chair waiting.
I tapped my fingers on the brown desk.
Then I took out a sheet of paper and started doodling on it.
I was waiting for:

Wars to stop.
Paint to dry.
Years to pass.
Books to be read.
Ice cubes to melt.
Food to be eaten.
Money to be spent.
Rain to fall.
Dust to gather.
Epidemics to end.

I sat poised in a big blue chair waiting.
Waiting for people to say, "That old man has sat in that chair so long,
That his beard is as long as a tape measure"
Waiting for time to fly.

Isaac Wilf, Grade 6
Shalhevet School

I Am…
I am a joyful comedian full of spirit
I wonder if my ancestors were anything like me
I hear tiny voices giving me inspiring advice
I see tiny figures following me
I want to be a comedian when I grow up
I am a joyful comedian full of spirit

I pretend I'm on a stage in front of millions keeping them entertained
I hear voices showing me the way to success
I touch the tiny figures that taunt me with their mysterious identity
I worry about what will become of me in the future
I cry about the grandfather of mine that I never got to see
I am a joyful comedian full of spirit

I understand that every living thing deserves a second chance
I say that everything has meaning in it
I dream that I can soar through the sky
I try to make people full of depression laugh
I hope that I can be a humorous comedian when I grow up
I am a joyful comedian full of spirit.

William Mattingly, Grade 5
Lydiksen Elementary School

Grandpa
He would take me to get ice cream.
He could eat two scoops.

He then took me to the store to find things.
When he was done he went home.
I miss him very much.

Sam Thomas, Grade 6
St Johns Lutheran School

Winter Days
A winter day, slow and cold
Snow covering the floor like powder
Cold snowflakes covering your body
Giant coats and boots keeping you warm
A touch of light fills the land
The snow is gone, like a tan

Elycia Guerrero, Grade 5
Granada Elementary School

Ocean

When I go to the
beach I feel the
ocean's mist when
the ocean's waves
ripple they look like
they're dancing I listen
to the waves splashing
they sound like whispers
the ocean is big and blue

Gina Vasquez, Grade 5
Henry Haight Elementary School

Whatif*

Whatif I don't make the team,
Whatif some of the players are mean,
Whatif I don't make a shot,
Whatif my passes get caught,
Whatif I don't get a fast break,
Whatif I do, that would be great,
All these thoughts creep in my head,
But all this time I'm sleeping in bed.

Drake Paretti, Grade 6
Grant Elementary School
Inspired by "Whatif" by Shel Silverstein

Halloween

H appy children
A live not dead
L aughing witches
L ovely angels
O h what fun to "Trick-or-treat"
W eeping werewolves
E vil devils
E vil vampire dogs
N o sunlight when vampires are awake

Taylor-Rose Viner, Grade 4
Carlthorp School

State Capitol

State capitol
Important, busy
Working, thinking, voting
Everybody is working hard
Important building

Alyssa Vigallon, Grade 4
Proctor Elementary School

Growing

First you plant your seed
Sun and water is what it will need
You give some water to your flower
It will make a misty shower
Next week it should be growing
Then you'll see something showing

Vanessa Barahona, Grade 5
Eastwood Elementary School

A Painful Hope

Crowds of people, surrounded by barbed-wire gates taunting us to escape,
Among those people, frail and diseased, suffering in need of assistance,
Wandering eyes of a child puzzled why Jews are disliked,
Helpless babies whining for relief, but there is still hope.
The faint smell of the delicious food of the Nazis,
Body odor and foul breath in the air, and the filthy, stinky stained beds,
With all that I have faith in my people. The laughter and giggles from the Nazis,
Mixed with the groans of sobbing children, chirping birds with free spirits,
Awful coughing voices from the infirmary, though I still have courage.
I had beautiful long hair, now rough and tangled,
I am cramped and uncomfortable when sleeping, having seven to a bed,
Feeling hot, stuffy and sweaty wearing black and white striped clothes,
Or cold, chilly and numb, while exhausted and tired from back-breaking work,
Hungry and eager for a variety of foods, I still love my religion.
I eat rotten potatoes with salty water, sometimes thin bitter tea,
Occasionally flavorless soup, maybe with a side of stale bread,
While the poor children say, "Not that icky broth again, Eema!"
I will always believe my people. I am a Jew, I am proud
There will be a time when I am free, when justice will prevail.

Sanika Ganesh, Grade 6
Lindero Canyon Middle School

Waffle

Put the butter on the iron, mix the flour and the milk
Put in the eggs and the vegetable oil. Mix it up.

Put the batter on the waffle iron.
Be careful! Do not spill the batter. Close the iron let it cook.

It is ready! Take it out. Watch out it is hot, hot, hot.
Put it on the plate give it a friend. His friend's name is syrup, syrup, syrup.

Sausage and bacon want to join the gang.
Put them in a pan and cook them until they're brown.

Chocolate chip and whipped cream want to join the fun.
Put them on the plate and let them dance around.
Orange juice is knocking on the refrigerator.
Put them in a glass and let him join the party.

Everyone is having fun. Now serve them up and let them be eaten.
As you watch them be eaten, save pancake for another day.

Matthew Engquist, Grade 6
St Linus School

Fall

Fall is here
ghosts come and go
leaves start to fall
red, gold, sometimes green
rake them up
jump in piles
fall has come
then gone for the year

Rachele Aurino, Grade 4
Carlthorp School

Lucy

There was a girl named Lucy who was blue
She didn't know how to tie her shoe
Then a ghost came and said, "Boo!"
Then an owl came and said, "Hoo!"
Lucy was scared and turned blue
She still didn't know how to tie her shoe
Lucy asked everyone around town
But ended up with a big frown

Vincent Veals, Grade 5
Top Kids Center

TV

Big ones, little ones
Thin ones, fat ones
Tall ones, small ones.
They are all the same.
You can see them and hear them.
You can see them everywhere.
They're up and down,
They're all around.
They're slanted, straight, or maybe upside down.

Erik Poole, Grade 5
Tipton Elementary School

The Owl

The owl is as silent as the night.
You would think he is not there.
He calls out hoo hoo,
As if taunting you to sleep.
As he swoops down from the trees,
He grabs a leaf in his claw.
As he flies for awhile, the leaf starts to fall.
The sun does just the opposite, it starts to rise.
It is time for the owl to go back to its tree.

Chris Gately, Grade 5
Ocean Air School

Blue

Blue is the color when you have a bad day.
Blue is the color of the great big sky.
Blue feels like a cold winter day.
Blue sounds like a rushing waterfall.
Blue tastes like a cold glass of water.
Blue feels like the fresh air.
Blue tastes like a juicy blueberry.
Blue smells like a pool on a hot summer day.
And blue sounds like rain falling on your deck.

Kevin McGee, Grade 4
Heather Elementary School

I Know My Mom

I know my mom.
Mom cleaning, mom buying.
Mom cooking, mom driving.
I know my mom.
Mom showering, mom dressing.
Mom taking me to school, mom protecting me.
I know my mom.
Mom vacuuming, mom washing dishes.
I know my mom.

Anthony Leon, Grade 4
Lankershim Elementary School

Alone Time

Alone is when you are grounded 2 months.
Alone is when you get embarrassed.
Alone is when they hit you for no reason.
Alone is when your grandmother dies.
Alone is when they get angry at your brothers.
Alone is when they forget about you.
Alone is when you stay at home alone.
But without the light and in the night.
Alone is when you don't get recess.

Diego Tinoco, Grade 4
Lankershim Elementary School

Dragon Fire

My thoughts were fierce,
The beast swept through my window.
Swift flight, fiery breath, eyes of pity.
Rough, scaly coat, and his sharp tail,
The dragon paced closer, closer.
I feared being captured into his fantasy world.
Escaping the wild beast,
Thankfully he flew out my chimney,
Leaving behind mystic, green footprints.

Julianne Uribe, Grade 5
Ocean Air School

Glorious Colors

Red is as hot as fire,
Blue is freezing as ice,
Yellow is as warm as sunshine,
Green is cool as grass.
Orange has a nice glow
Black is angry and fierce,
Pink is sweet and warm,
Purple is hot, cold, sweet, fierce, bright, and dull.
Colors, oh so glorious.

Taylor Albizati, Grade 5
Ocean Air School

My BFF

My BFF is Karina Orozco.
We have been best friends since 3rd grade.
I hope it never ends.
We tell each other secrets and stories we know.
We tell scary and funny stories.
Karina and I are best friends forever, for life.
We trust each other.
She is nice, smart, and pretty.
Now that's my poem of my BFF.

Natalie Sanchez, Grade 5
Tipton Elementary School

High Merit Poems – Grades 4, 5 and 6

I Am Me!

I am a person who works hard, is smart, and creative,
but when I can't think of anything I am stubborn as a troll.

I am as smart as Albert Einstein at math,
but sometimes I am as bad at math as a dinosaur in school.

I dream that I am as fast as Usain Bolt in track,
but in reality sometimes I stumble and fall.

I am a person who loves homework, school, and learning,
but at times I just want to play and be with friends.

I am a person who loves social studies and reading like a mad man,
but at times I just want to be a regular sixth grader!

Michael Abbott, Grade 6
Las Flores Middle School

10 Good Reasons to Stay Up Late

Here are 10 good reasons that you should stay up late
This is something that will surly start a big debate
I don't want it to, so look up and listen here
this is something you'll want to hear, so don't you break a tear

Playing on my computer or watching my big TV
making a nice snack or doing the laundry
sitting on the couch or making my messy bed
maybe I should read, oh wait, I already read

There's only two more, and I can't even speak
all of this talking is making me weak
doing your homework or writing a song
man, I am tired, maybe I was wrong

Jacob Frank, Grade 5
George Washington Charter Elementary School

California's Winter

California's winters are not snow and ice,
but foggy and misty overall nice.

No layered sweaters or gloved hands,
the children are playing in small bands.

Outside the wind hurts our ears and nose,
oh no, it's not time for playing with a garden hose.

Outside there's rainstorms here and there,
inside it is cozy and warm everywhere.

I am done describing winter here,
but just my luck, Christmas is near.

Katie Bui, Grade 6
Las Flores Middle School

Thanksgiving Turkey

Everyone's thankful, except one bird
He's the turkey that will be eaten, he's heard
No one's been thinking about his pain
Only about the food that they'll gain
He'll be served with stuffing, or even maybe plain!

It's hard to be glad when you'll be eaten tomorrow
The poor little fowl is filled with sorrow
Turkey's a tradition, but why not chicken or dove?
Not everyone's filled joy and love!
Thanksgiving's not a time for worries to be thought of...

You may be hungry but Turkey is not
We're thankful, but Turkey's not happy with his lot!
Yes, he's famous, but not with cheer
Because the time of the eating now is here
The turkey is filled to bursting with fear!

The turkey will be brave
Even when his feathers off they shave!
I'm sad for him but I'm hungry today
Can't wait till food's served on a tray
Thanksgiving is here now, yay!!!

Hannah Sherwindt, Grade 4
The Mirman School

Our Soldiers

Soldiers are brave
Soldiers unite
Soldiers are here to defend and fight for us
Soldiers are here to save the world
Soldiers are sent to protect our freedoms
Soldiers provide hope and justice to everyone
Soldiers are loyal to others

Soldiers fight for our country
Soldiers fight for our faith and freedom
Most soldiers have discipline
Most soldiers are warmhearted and considerate

Soldiers never back down
Soldiers have the strength to continue
Soldiers stick with friends to gain control
Soldiers have many things in life they have to go through
Many soldiers have fought and died
Many soldiers have been victorious

Soldiers fight against evil
Soldiers put their lives in danger
Soldiers love and trust God with all their heart

John Marvy C. Abiol, Grade 6
Corpus Christi School

Time Travel
I would like to go to the future.
I would like to meet the people.
I would like to see their religion.

Most of all I would like to see them.
And how they all look.
Maybe there are many men women.

I'll find out if they are nice or mean.
Maybe even both or none at all.
Or probably it will be the same.

I know there would be more technology.
And hopefully medical breakthroughs.
I can't wait to go to the future!
Aaron Linares, Grade 6
John Adams Middle School

Come Winter Come
Winter, winter
come to me
follow my footprints
and you'll see

Snow oh snow
fall from the sky
it's so beautiful
I can't believe my eye

The snow fell on my tongue
it gives me a shiver
and it makes me so cold
that I want to go ice skating
on the river!
Allison Mantikas, Grade 4
Mira Catalina Elementary School

Dance Class
A safe place to be,
in class or the lobby,
stretching out before class,
The teacher tip toes in,
every drop of sweat,
every tear drop,
All worth it,
Tired as a cheetah on
A high speed chase,
fragile as a vase,
feet shaking more than ever,
blood dripping like a waterfall,
Toes swollen, red, strained,
All worth it,
in dance class.
Sophia Tamrazian, Grade 6
Ocean Air School

Rainbows
Reaching, reaching up so high
Then arching over that pale blue sky
Red and orange
Yellow, green, blue
Do these colors satisfy you?
If not, if not, then look up now
Indigo, purple blend them all
Rainbow, rainbow brightening the gloom
Thanks to the rain
I can see you!
Kelsey Lyons, Grade 5
Our Lady of Mount Carmel School

Raptors
Sharp claws
Meat eater
Runs fast
sharp teeth
Small
Good eyesight
Different families
Different colors
Good swimmer
Scary
Brandon Watroba, Grade 6
Gardner Street Elementary School

Midnight Sky
In the middle
of the island
You can see the
beautiful mist and shadow.
The midnight moon in the
sky looked like a shining diamond
in the beautiful blue sky.
It sounded like I was listening
to the whisper from above.
Esther Feng, Grade 5
Henry Haight Elementary School

Who Am I?
I'm black and white
I have a red and white suit
I have a red hat with a fuzzy ball
I have a sleigh
I have seven deer
I have a black and gold belt
I don't bite a lot.
Who am I?
I am the penguin who stole Christmas.
Adam Pelaiz, Grade 5
Tipton Elementary School

If I Were in Charge of the World*
If I were in charge of the world
I'd cancel all school uniforms
Butternut squash, stale crackers,
And also prejudice and war.

If I were in charge of the world
There would be more peace
Less economic downturn,
And an Earth that won't melt
In the next million years.

If I were in charge of the world
You would always have friendship
You would always have fun
You could eat all the junk food you want
Without any cavities

If I were in charge of the world
Your book would always be in stock
Nobody would make fun of anybody
And everybody would love everybody

But only
If I were in charge of the world.
Madelyn Pixley, Grade 6
St Raphael School
**Patterned after Judith Viorst*

Sunsets
Different colors
In the sky
Beautiful nature
That no one can deny

Colors so peaceful
Painted over the Earth
No price can be placed
On what it is worth

It happens at dusk
Each and every night
It never gets old
Such an incredible sight

Big ball of fire
Sinking into the sea
Putting an end to our day
So safe and calmly

While it is sinking
The colors reflect
On the water's horizon
As the sun and sea connect
Gabriella Morrow, Grade 6
Miraleste Intermediate School

Thoughts of an Eraser

You poke me,
   You shake me,
      You use me every day.

You poke holes in me,
   You tear me apart,
      You make me all dirty,
         Oh how I wish I could shout!

You put me in the desk,
   You leave me overnight,
      You put me in your lap,
         I have so much fun.

But that's not all, no not at all,
   I want to say,
      I love you so much!
Keeley Rogers, Grade 4
Joseph M Simas Elementary School

I Love the Beach

I love the beach.
Hear the screeching seagulls,
feel the green slimy seaweed
and the hot steaming sand.
See the huge crashing waves
with cold water at your feet.
Smell the ocean smells.
Have a summer picnic
with warm melting s'mores.
Collect the shimmering colorful shells.
Feel the cool ocean breezes
or watch the crawling crabs.
Find the smooth sea glass.
Feel the stinging sunburn.
Watch the twirling umbrellas
and the golden sunset.
I love the beach!
Kathryn Shirley, Grade 4
Mira Catalina Elementary School

My Gray, Little Cat

I have a cute, gray, little cat
I show him some of my favorite hats.
He is very, very, very, very gray
He is even more so in the bright day.
My cat climbs tall trees
To see if there are any bees.
He always likes to destroy nests
So he could have a comfortable rest.
My cat is such a fun little pet
But he doesn't want to go to the vet.
If you give him a chicken bone
He would like to eat it alone!
Isaac Rodriguez, Grade 4
Lankershim Elementary School

Grandma

When you walk I see you smile
as you walk down the aisle.

You can't hear well but that's okay
because I see you every day.

Your dog is really cool
when I see it after school.

Where you live it is very hot
steam rises from your pot.

Our love is the best
just put us to the test.
Claire Mangold, Grade 5
Eastwood Elementary School

Shoes

Shoes have different brands
my favorite brand is Vans.

My shoes are so bright
it shines of the light.

When my shoes go across the street
they make a little beat.

When my shoes go in style
I always make a big smile.

When my shoes go with me to the store
they make a squeak on the floor.
Brittney Do, Grade 5
Eastwood Elementary School

Disappearing Winter

The winter days turn into sun
One by one
I watch them go
And when they do
The birds shall come
All at once
I watch them come
Frozen ponds betray the skates
And plunge them into iciness
That's when you know the winter's gone
As if in doubt; an icy qualm
As it creeps to other lands
One by one
I watch it go.
Abbie Hastings, Grade 6
Ada Harris Elementary School

If You Knew Me…

If you knew me
You would know that
I dream of having
A tiger sanctuary.
I like tigers.
They are big and awesome.
I think in black and orange
Great colors for tigers!
I wonder if tigers will become extinct?
They are already endangered.
I don't fear anything,
For I have confidence.
I giggle when I see
A tiger outsmart its prey.
Tigers are cool, magnificent, and excellent!
If you knew me,
Then you would know why…
Oracio Bernal, Grade 5
Orange Glen Elementary School

My Fallen Leaf

My leaf is like a
Butterfly
That has lost its way.
It's as delicate and temporary
As a piece of ice
Thin as a grain of sand.
Sharp as a knife
Strong as a piece of paper.
The butterfly's wings
Bend like rubber.
Its touch is rough and rocky
Yet, still so beautiful.
It floated down from its home
Onto the ground
Detached forever,
As the wind blows it further away.
Its adventure will never end.
Nhu Pham, Grade 4
Orange Glen Elementary School

Pencil

I taste like wood don't I?
I'm made from a tree.
I am bored with no arms or legs
To help me with having some fun.
I smell like grapes
Because I am purple.
The sound I make
Is the sound of being miserable
With no body parts to play with anyone.
People liking me is difficult
Because I've been ugly
Bitten by a dog.
Georgina Chamale, Grade 4
Liberty Elementary School

If I Was in Charge of the World*
If I was in charge of the world, I would
Cancel all news channels.
All school days would be canceled except for Friday.
I would cancel all war, and have peace over the whole world.
Vegetables would give you cavities.
If I was in charge of the world,
There would be cars for all kids.
Robots would do your homework and chores.
There would be bigger ice cream parlors.
If I was in charge of the world,
You'd have 10,000,000,000 friends.
You would not have to clean your room.
Your bedtime is 9:30 am.
You allowance would be $100.00 per week.
You could bring your dog to school every day.
A whole candy bar would be considered good for you.
Every Tuesday would be Taco Tuesday.
Nobody would ever catch a cold.
But, only if I was in charge of the world.

Allie McCoy, Grade 6
St Raphael School
**Patterned after Judith Viorst*

Wonder What I Am
I used to be a piece of silk
Feeble and minute
But now I am a shirt
Thick and long
I used to be a shirt
Gigantic and wide
But now I am in a trunk
Thick and chunky
I used to be in a trunk
Stubby and round
But now I am in a cargo ship
Impatiently waiting to go on an island
I used to be in a cargo ship
Dumpy and stumpy
But now I am on an island
Beating with heat
I used to be on an island
Stocky and squat
But now I am in a store
Waiting heartbroken for someone to buy me

Bryan Pan, Grade 4
Dingeman Elementary School

Daisy
I am a daisy
Full and beautiful, white or yellow, purple or pink
Daisies are not just beautiful they are as soft as silk
Or as puffy as a white cloud
It is me
A daisy full and beautiful, a daisy

Nina, Grade 6
Grant Elementary School

The Delight Song of Deborah Oliveira
I am a project on a desk being looked at
I am a green-eyed rabbit that moves on the table
I am a fragile cub that jumps, everywhere in the igloo
I am a newborn that follows the human mind
I am the sun and the stars of the sky
I am a panda playing with the grass
I am a group of people writing with a pencil
I am the farthest state from where you are
I am the cold of the ice; I am the drum beat of the drums
I am the glitter of the sparkles in your eyes
I am the long yellow meadow grass of the farm
I am a flag of four colors
I am a cheetah running away through the grass
I am the hunt of mixed animals in grassy meadows
I am the hunger of the animal-like beast
I am the whole humanity of these things
    You see, I am alive, I am alive.
I stand in good relation to my house in which I live
I stand in good relation to my family that takes care of me
I stand in good relation to the United States in which we stand
I stand in good relation to our God who formed us.

Deborah Oliveira, Grade 6
John Muir Elementary School

The Park
Have some fun at the park,
Where people bring their dogs that bark;
You can throw the Frisbee;
And hear all the buzzing bees.

Surrounded by grass and trees,
Play in the big piles of leaves;
See the cool brown squirrels,
And see the gophers dig their holes.

Hopping and jumping in the playground,
See and play on the seesaw that goes up and down;
You can also play baseball at the park,
And play in the light or dark.

Jonathan James, Grade 6
St Martin-in-the-Fields School

Nature
Sweet nature, wind, leafless trees swaying,
Blue skies, nice smells blowing through the air,
Little kids skipping home from school,
Humming birds singing loving songs,
Light drops of snow falling from the sky,
Delectable cinnamon buns I smell from the bakery,
Small salamanders eating, tadpoles to frogs, kittens to cats,
Puppies to dogs, fawn to deer,
Fox pups cuddling and playing together is a cute sight to see,
Beautiful sunsets at the beach,
Two love birds sitting in the sand, nature sweet nature.

Breanna Morris, Grade 4
Juarez Elementary School

Delightful Sound
The door is open;
And I could feel the cold breeze;
Coming from outside;
I could hear the hummingbirds;
Humming in the tree.
Tariq Smith, Grade 6
John Muir Elementary School

Puppies
Dogs
Furry, soft
Running, jumping, playing
My favorite fluffy pet
Canine
Malachi Robbins, Grade 5
St Louis De Montfort School

Scott
S porty
C areful
O bedient
T errific
T houghtful
Scott Miller, Grade 4
Heather Elementary School

Candy
C olorful candy it's
A wesome. Sometimes
N utty, very
D elicious and another word for it is
Y ummy!
Nathan Frojelin, Grade 4
Heather Elementary School

Reading
Reading strategies
Predict, visualize, question
Connecting, infer
Identification
Evaluate while reading
Erica Casares, Grade 6
John Muir Elementary School

Winter
Winter
Freezing, icy
Running, sledding, laughing
The snow is awesome
Season
Hervin Hernandez, Grade 4
Heather Elementary School

The Animated Galapagos Islands
Crystal blue ocean, streaking water
Swift, scaly angelfish dart in front of the exotic tiger shark
On the eroded beach
Giant crimson and indigo crabs scurry through the rocks
Hoping to stay away from the dreaded predator
The great frigate bird
On the overgrown field, the elusive frilled land iguana crawls to shelter
As the rainstorm awaits to strike
The valiant pelican darts from above to catch the frightened fish
As it tries to swim away
At the bottom of the sea
The sly ray suddenly springs up, catching its prey in shock
The minuscule jellies
Surprisingly lay their soft, pink tentacles on your skin
And terrorize you in pain
Trying to escape these treacherous waters
On the shoreline, massive sea lions lay inches away from you
Suddenly they jump up and take an aquatic ride
As you sorrowfully sit on the rocky boat you mourn inside
Spending your last few moments on the Galapagos Islands
When your exotic adventure comes to an end
Daniel Birnholz, Grade 6
The Mirman School

Under the Bridge
In the punting boats we go,
Gliding leisurely down the river.
Through the town that's stood the ages,
King's College shimmers in the dusk sun,
The church's illuminated stone façade glows in the fading orange light,
The students, studying between classes, smile as they see us.
With family we go.
Under the bridge again.

The sun passes away from our eyes.
The bridge, an astrolabe of architecture,
Fades as the sun retreats from the night.
The structure, in its own small corner of the world,
A nail-less assemblage,
Whispers to me of the proud carpenters' perseverance.
As the tranquil night moves over the sky.
Benjamin Goldsmith, Grade 6
The Mirman School

River
A river dreams of meeting the vast ocean
A river remembers the places it sees as it flows along its winding path
A river moves with youthful strength
A river promises to quench the thirst of nature
A river travels to new places, forever changing its route

A river is a sign of everlasting freedom
Batia Blank, Grade 4
Laurence School

Christmas
Fun, presents, happy, families
all together around the Christmas tree
having fun, giving presents
making good choices
Tiana Molony, Grade 4
St Raphael School

Puppies
Cute, fluffy
Barking, running, sleeping
Marisa is very lovable
Dogs
Maria Tabares, Grade 5
Our Lady of the Rosary School

Family
We laugh, play and have fun,
We sing with love,
We play board games,
AND I WIN EVERY TIME!!
Izabelle Ruehlman, Grade 4
St Raphael School

Football
Scoring a touchdown is so simple to me,
I fly down the field and I feel like I'm free.
Then when people try to tackle me
I juke them out and go for the T.D.
Lucas Dentoni, Grade 6
Grant Elementary School

Red Rose
Red rose blossom glow
They shine in the red sunlight
Roses light the day
Jacob Rivas, Grade 4
The Mirman School

A Bumble Bee
A bumble bee on
a bright sparkling daffodil
ready to fly off.
Gretchen L. Peckler, Grade 6
Gardner Street Elementary School

Spring
Spring rains trickle down
The rain makes some new flowers
It becomes summer
William Turner, Grade 4
The Mirman School

The Delight Song of Elaine Reyes
I am the sun in the dark galaxy, looking down on Earth
I am a white swan that swims peacefully on the glistening lake
I am the tiger that hunts, actively in the forest
I am the star that follows the moon
I am the kitten playing with a ball of yarn
I am a cluster of polished pebbles
I am the farthest planet
I am the cold of the winter's day
I am the chirp of the birds
I am the glitter of the crackling fireworks
I am the long piece of thread in the needle's eye
I am the Filipino flag of four colors
I am the pigeon flying away through the midnight sky
I am a field of rice and wheat
I am a herd of hyenas in the wide, free land of Africa
I am the whole life of these things

You see, I am alive, I am alive
I stand in good relation to my parents. I stand in good relation to my relatives.
I stand in good relation to my friends. I stand in good relation to my health.
You see, I am alive, I am alive
Elaine Reyes, Grade 6
John Muir Elementary School

Don't You Wish…?
Don't you wish the sky was always sunny, so we could always have fun outdoors?
Maybe not, nature needs rain to live on.

Don't you wish it was spring all the time, so the flowers were always blooming?
Maybe not, we'll always have to mow the lawn.

Don't you wish weekends were every day, and we could play all the time?
Maybe not, we need to learn writing, reading, and (in chess) how to move a pawn.

Don't you wish you had all the candy in the world to eat?
Maybe not, you'd get stomach aches every day and, if you bit the candy, your tooth might be gone.

Don't you wish everyone praised you even when you did something bad?
Maybe not, the truth is always worth as much light as the morning dawn.

Don't you wish everyone was always happy and laughing all day?
Maybe not, sometimes tears make you stronger for life later on.
Rachel Hong, Grade 5
Ocean Air School

Sunset
A sunset dreams of cool clouds to shelter it
A sunset remembers the day it came from the sky
A sunset moves slowly, taking in the last moments it has before tomorrow
A sunset promises that one day it will take cover under the clouds
A sunset vacations in a faraway beach, talking and laughing with its friends, the clouds

A sunset is a sign of beauty
Jaclyn Rothman, Grade 4
Laurence School

High Merit Poems – Grades 4, 5 and 6

Dreams Are Reality
I woke up Saturday morning
To a loud boom!
I look outside to see my dad's car
Crashed on the front lawn.
I go outside and see two cars wrecked
On the front lawn, and my mom's car destroyed.
I go inside and feel like I am going to cry.
The police came to make sure things are okay.
The guy who crashed "spun out of control" is what he said.
No one was hurt thankfully.
This is a true story
That happened to me and my family.
I feel like it was a dream
But it's not
It is reality.
Rebecca Swyers, Grade 6
St Johns Lutheran School

Red
Red looks like me on a summer day.
Red sounds like the wind blowing on my face.
Red smells like a pizza that just came out of the oven.
Red tastes like cherries when they're ripe.
Red feels really hot.
Red looks like me when I get mad.
Red sounds like a rose blowing away.
Red smells like a tomato.
Red tastes like a sundae with a cherry on top.
Red feels like a Friday rest.
Red looks like a color on somebody's jersey on a soccer team.
Red sounds like a flower moving on a hot day.
Red smells like a rose on a fantastic day.
Red tastes like an apple that is already ripe.
Red feels like a boy who is mad.
Victoria Mataele, Grade 4
Heather Elementary School

Green
I am green
I am a Chartreuse dress gliding across
The ballroom
I am grass stemming from the ground to see if
Children have come to play upon me
I am an emerald hanging around an elegant woman's neck.
I am the possession making people's lives fall
Apart and come together…
Money…
I am a frog on a green lily pad,
The melody of the creek flows through my
Ears trickle, trickle, plop
I am the color that will change our world
Use me wisely…
I am the color of life!
Aashni Purohit, Grade 6
Ocean Air School

Ode to My Grandfather
O' Ong Ngoai
Your flabby skin to ever play with,
Wrinkles turn to mini smiles,
Gardens rolls around in laughter,
When the moon is out
There you are to comfort me,
When tennis is on TV
You imagine you're John McEnroe,
You're so wonderful and funny
You're my Grandfather
Audrey Connell, Grade 6
Chinese American International School

Ode to Cookies
So sweet
Crunchy and chocolaty
Hot and sweet smelling
Cookies how you're loved
Mothers and children alike gobble you up
I do too
Great things come when I eat you
Chew…crunch…mmmm…
Your yummy goodness makes me feel great
Cookies are the best
Nicholas Yarbrough, Grade 6
Chinese American International School

Snakes
Snakes are scaly as scaly can be, scaly from head to tail.
(Much more scaly than a snail.)
If a snake is bright it cannot blend with night.
If a snake is gray it won't blend with day.
If it is neither it might blend with either.
Snakes scare some people, but they don't scare me.
Do snakes scare you? Probably not at a zoo.
Maybe if they are blue, they will scare you.
If you think of an animal that is quite unique,
a snake is what you should think.
Henry Norton, Grade 4
Mira Catalina Elementary School

Baseball
Wham! I hit the ball.
It's hard to hit because it's so small.
I run so I don't get out.
I hope my coach doesn't shout.
I am up to second base.
I hope I'm not being chased.
The other team has the ball.
It is impossible to catch me because I got it all.
I run up to third.
I made it to home. It was all a blur.
Billy Emery, Grade 5
Eastwood Elementary School

The Cloud Who Wanted to Get Out
    In the
        midnight snow
    a yellow
        spiral cloud
    sleeps in
        his bubble
    wanting to
        get out
    It twisted
        and it twisted
    Then all of a
        sudden a
    big reddish flame
        came and
    It popped
        the spiral cloud
    bubble out!
Christina Vera, Grade 5
Henry Haight Elementary School

Halloween Colors
The Halloween colors
Are Red, Orange, and Black

Red is for the
Juice that the vampires
Drink

Orange is the color of
A pumpkin

Black is the color of
The cats that roam
Around the night

Then if you stay up after 8 pm
This will give you a fright
That the witches roam the night
Maryana Adams, Grade 6
St Linus School

Baseball
When you
Step up to the plate
And look straight ahead
The pitch comes at you
Grip the bat
Get ready to swing
You swing the bat
Crack!
The ball goes over the
Fence you win the game
The crowd goes crazy
You are the world champion!
Javier Noriega, Grade 5
Juarez Elementary School

Animal
Reptiles slither
As armadillos crawl
In mating season
bears may brawl,
cats meow
as dogs bark
bats can even see in the dark,
Sharks swim below
as your plants grow
As lions stalk behind
All these animals have a purpose
Burrrp! Ah!
To feed us.
Juan Magana, Grade 6
Isbell Middle School

Indiana Jones
I ndiana Jones is
N ow looking in the
D angerous temple.
I nside lies the
A mazing golden idol.
N ow he must get the
A mazing idol. Go Indiana

J ones! Almost there,
O ops look out for the arrows.
N ow be careful as we
E xit the temple. What a
S urprise…a boulder! Go Indy Go!
Jacob Saunders, Grade 4
Heather Elementary School

Sharpener
I'm a lonely sharpener
in a dark scary desk.
Sometimes at night
I hear rats outside my desk.
I make roaring sounds
   like a hungry lion
I make your pencil
   small and tiny!
You empty me and
I get hungry again!
Feed me your pencil
for my hungry soul.
Jasmine Sias, Grade 4
Liberty Elementary School

Thanksgiving
Thanksgiving is a wonder
it's such a giving thing
to be with your family
and all living things!
Jenny Zaida, Grade 4
St Raphael School

Chicken and Friends
There was a chicken that had a hat
His friends always wanted a hat
His friends saw him
Wouldn't talk to him
And he wondered "why?"
His eyes lit up and he knew why
He flapped his wings to the store
And hats he bought more
When his friends saw him
They all ran happily to him
They put on the hats and started to play
They all became friends once again
Jennifer Cardenas, Grade 5
Renuevo School

I Know Christmas
I know Christmas
Deer flying and Santa "Ho Ho Hoing,"
cookies baking, Christmas music playing.
I know Christmas.
The smell of cookies, the sound of bells,
the sight of green and red lights,
the feel of presents, the taste of cookies
I know Christmas
"Ho Ho Ho"
"Open your present"
"Merry Christmas"
I know Christmas.
Abraham Pech, Grade 4
Lankershim Elementary School

War Hurts
War is unpleasant
   because it has violence.

War is unpleasant
   because it has gore.

Gore is unpleasant
   because it has pain.

Pain is unpleasant
   because it hurts.
War hurts.
Jesse Perez, Grade 5
Granada Elementary School

Cookies
C raving cookies
O r maybe cake
O reos, or a big huge chocolate shake
K iwis and strawberry tart
I nstead of fruitcake from Walmart
E njoy your desserts from the shopping cart
Aditi Mittal, Grade 6
Carden Academy of Santa Clara

Winter
There are frosty stars.
There are thick diamonds outside.
All snowflakes sparkle.
Hailey Wilson, Grade 4
Coyote Valley Elementary School

Snowflakes
Gold bells are ringing
Snowflakes are falling tonight
How I love snowflakes
Jennifer Stephens, Grade 4
Coyote Valley Elementary School

Cold and Icy
Outside is icy
Bells are everywhere I see
It is now winter
Amy Herrmann, Grade 4
Coyote Valley Elementary School

Frost and Snow
The snow is now here
So is the glittery frost
Winter is now here
Colleen Schimansky, Grade 4
Coyote Valley Elementary School

Winter Day
It's winter today
Snuggle by a fireplace
Hurray for winter!
Gabriella Farr, Grade 4
Coyote Valley Elementary School

Flowers
Flowers in a field,
moving with a gush of wind
swaying in sunlight.
Annie Kalantarian, Grade 4
Anderson Valley Elementary School

Spiders
Creepy eight eyed bug
busily building thin webs
in corners of walls
Omar Mendoza, Grade 4
Anderson Valley Elementary School

Sharks
giant animals
can smell blood a mile away,
looking for shelter
Gabriel Segura, Grade 4
Anderson Valley Elementary School

Dance vs Football
Football and dance are both considered a sport
Now that I've done both I must report
Which one is harder and requires the most attention
You must ask yourself, "What is my intention?"
The best part is, it's just common sense once you realize
You gotta do what makes you happy, that's the overall life prize

I'm trying to decide what I want to do
It's not that easy when you have 2 sports you are into
Which one will I get the most out of, that's what's up for debate
I love them both, I don't mean to exaggerate
The best part is, I don't have to decide right now
I can do them both and when you watch me you will say "WOW"

Football has a season and dance is all year-round
Anyone could do both you don't need a professional background
Don't worry if you are a girl or a boy
It matters what you want to do, do what you enjoy
The best part is, if I'm dancing on stage or running with the pig skin
Remember my name, because you're gonna hear it again!
Wm. Michael Porter, Grade 5
Highland Elementary School

About Me
My full name is David Roy Vasquez
And I just like to be called Roy
The animal inside of me is a fast and aggressive tiger
I have a toy in my heart because I am always playing
Strong and active is written on my forehead which describes just the way I am
I like the sound of my toy gun shooting, but I hate the sound of thunder
I love the pizza smell, but cigarette smoke, it hurts my nose
My favorite time of the day is after school daycare, where I can play with my friends
If my hands could speak, they would say, "Roy you are very smart"
When I was 5 years old I hugged a 6 foot long cat shark
No matter where I am or what I am doing,
my parents always come and tell me that they love me
Cool!
David Roy Vasquez, Grade 6
St Pius X Elementary School

I Can't Tell Who I'm Thinking Of
The stars are out — shining on my bedroom window.
I think to myself…who and why is the light shining on me?
It feels like a 30 pound weight on my heart.
I can't tell who I'm thinking of…
I wonder what that star is telling me.
I wonder who it is who I'm thinking of…tell me tell me why
I can't tell who I'm thinking of.
I prayed to God the last ten minutes ago —
I wonder why the danger is coming on!
Is it a boy? No, it's a girl.
What does this girl want from me?
It's all in my head but in my dreams I'm thinking of the only girl it could be…
And that's me.
Adelaide Brannan, Grade 4
American Martyrs School

The Bad Weather
One dark midnight
the moon was shining
like a huge diamond
suddenly the dark
clouds were coming
the wind was
whispering in my ears
the rain came pouring
down and invented puddles
I like to listen to the rain
the next morning
it was sunny again
Kha Hua, Grade 5
Henry Haight Elementary School

My Dog
My dog is so cute
When she fits in a boot
I am not that proud
That my dog is so loud
My dog wags her tail
When she sees the mail
My dog is so fun
When we go for a run
My dog is so fast
She's definitely not last
My dog is so fat
She looks like a cat
Kellie Kale, Grade 5
Eastwood Elementary School

Spring
i remember
when the flowers came
i remember
the new grass smell
i remember
playing games outside
i remember
when the wind blew
i remember
the new baby animals
i remember
Ashley Robertson, Grade 5
Northside Elementary School

Midnight Moon
The dark midnight sky creates
a dark shadow over the moon
The moon's diamond color
fades away from the midnight shadow
You can listen to it
whisper, "Goodnight, Earth"
as it dozes off to sleep
Taiyadi Espino, Grade 5
Henry Haight Elementary School

The Fisherman
Stroke, stroke, stroke.
I'm rowing out to sea
   In my small boat.

Fish, fish, fish.
I'm fishing for my supper
   In my small boat.

Pull, pull, pull.
I'm pulling up a net of herring
   Up into my small boat.

Shiver, shiver, shiver.
I feel a storm blowing
   In my sailor's bones.

Stroke, stroke, stroke.
I'm rowing away from a storm
   In my small boat.
Robbie Lowe, Grade 6
Carlthorp School

Artist
I am an artist.
I weave colors into
Vibrant shapes and sizes
That will amaze even the best.

Shades of red, yellow, and blue
Gracefully dance across the thick,
White pages filled with my intricate
Patterns, designs, and imagination.

I can create a roaring lion
As bright and golden as the sun,
Or a quiet evening on the plains,
The moon shining on the grasses.

Now what shall I create just for you?
A lifelike giraffe or maybe a dragon.
But perhaps a bed for you to rest in.
For I am an artist.
Marisa Shah, Grade 5
Lydiksen Elementary School

Colors
Pink is the color of a baby's nose.
Red is the color of a rose.
Orange is like pumpkin pie.
Yellow is for the sun in the sky.
Green is the color of a frog.
Blue is the color of water in a bog.
Indigo is mixed with purple and blue.
Violet has more of a reddish hue.
Darcy Brown, Grade 5
Eastwood Elementary School

Enchanting Poetry
Poetry are the words on my lips.
As I say it, it brings radiance to me.
It goes in every direction, every world
Forever it will stay.
Its beauty will come and go
With kindness, love, and maybe sorrow.
Enchantment flutters in the air
With passion and serenity.
Both will bind and become one
They will be magic like in a fairy tale.
It will go throughout the world
With everything you'll need
To create beautiful poetry.
Zinab Attia, Grade 6
Sierra Charter School

Ode to Rubber Feet
Oh, rubber feet, without you,
   Everything would…
      Slip and slide,
      And coast and glide
      Around the floor,
   And eventually…
      Be no more.

You give me stability,
Of motion and of mind.
Oh rubber feet,
On the bottom of my seat,
May you never slip.
Jamie Smith, Grade 5
Ocean Air School

Powerful Death
How do the dead spirits come back?
Death, you amaze me,
how hundreds of excited people rush
to celebrate you returning.
Death, you dance cleverly
around the precious gates of life
until we accidentally open the gates,
and let you in.
Death, you teach us,
to spend our time wisely,
so we don't waste precious time,
doing unproductive things.
Today we learn about death.
Emily Hou, Grade 5
Dingeman Elementary School

Thunderstorms
Loud noises from storm
Shocks little kids in the bed
Light in the dark sky.
Alexander Gonzalez, Grade 5
Our Lady of the Rosary School

Fall to Winter
In fall it's very cold
so I sit inside
on my cozy blue couch
while I watch cartoons
on my brand new TV
animals go back
to their houses
or start migration
then comes winter
when I like to go skiing
I must remember
to wear a heavy coat
don't forget
winter is also very cold
Aliza Walden, Grade 4
Carlthorp School

Think of Me
Feel my radiance…
Feel the sun
Think of me, as number one

I'm there for you
You're there for me
Think about us
What more can there be

I am me
You are you
Happiness will always be true
If I never have to miss you
Hannah Pittman, Grade 6
Grant Elementary School

Autumn
When Autumn comes
the leaves fall
the creatures migrate
people play
the dawn comes
and the sun rises
Ethan Knight, Grade 4
Carlthorp School

The World You See
A land below your feet,
Peaceful animals, many to meet,
The river sparkles in the sun,
Forests, the color of healthy green,
A place where endless resources roam,
The sky, a magical phase of blue,
Seashores with soft sounds of the waves,
Everything evolved from the past,
Organisms live at last.
Adeline Danielle Torres, Grade 5
Juarez Elementary School

Thoughts of a Pencil
I am a pencil
 a number 2 pencil
  and a very scrawny pencil
I spend my time drawing
 I write essays and letters
  It is boring times ten
I can't forget painful oh I can't
When I get my lead broken
 or get snapped in two
and getting gripped hurts too
When I get sharpened
oh it feels good,
but really I would want to
move away from this kid
or I will cry and fade away
Alex Pereyra, Grade 4
Joseph M Simas Elementary School

Blue
Blue is the color of the sky,
 And the cars passing by.
Blue is the color of a fish's fin,
 And the recycling bin.
Blue is the color of the sea,
And it's on the flag that makes us free.
Blue is the color of the bench,
 And the color of my wrench.
Blue is the color of my power cord,
It's also the color of my skate board.
Blue is supposed to symbolize sadness,
 But everyone owns something blue,
  And not everyone is sad.
   To me,
Blue is the greatest color.
Felix Hernandez, Grade 6
St Pius X Elementary School

American Flag
I'm red, white and blue
yes I'm talking to you.
I'm bright
like a light.
You talk to me
every morning.
Every day
you make gestures,
and put your hand
on your heart.
You talk to me
like I'm your king.
I hate it
when you sit down
and ignore me.
Jackie Pelayo, Grade 4
Liberty Elementary School

Backpack
I am a backpack
Full of trash
Please, please clean me out!

I don't want to be tossed at home
Or spend a day in the dark.

I beg and beg,
She still won't clean me out!

I beg and beg,
Then she finally cleans me out!

One day she left me at home.
I was feeling so sad.
The next day I said,
"Take me to school with you.
I don't like staying home!"

Please, please take me from now on.
I don't want to be left out.
Jeneva McDaniel, Grade 4
Joseph M Simas Elementary School

Dying
Why do we die?
Do we really go to a better place
where there are ice cream hats
and cotton candy clouds?
How do you want to die?
Some by bullets or bombs,
fighting for their rights.
Others by disease,
But I don't want to die sick.
I wish to die like a swan.
A graceful
Swan.
I wish to die like a
Slow,
Graceful,
Old,
Gorgeous
Swan.
DO others wish to?
Do
You?
Kragen Metz, Grade 5
Ocean Air School

Midnight Sky
I look upon the midnight sky
 laced in mist
I see my shadow from the moon
I feel the rain kiss my cheek
Isabel Tiaffay, Grade 5
Henry Haight Elementary School

Watch Me Fly
Watch Me Fly
Up way high in the sky
Too tall to reach
Just me, myself, and I
Watch Me Fly

I can follow my dreams
Like I already have
So just look
Up into the sky
And believe you can fly
Watch Me Fly

So now you know
What it's like to fly
Follow your dreams
And take off into
The sky
And Fly, Fly, Fly
Jessica Funke, Grade 6
Grant Elementary School

Time Travel
Time traveling is very fun
Wish I can do it every day
Slowly make my way to destination

I'm in my time machine
Pulling buttons checking trials
Testing digits moving dials
Will my dream come true?

My journey begins
Setting the year fixing the date
Choosing time finding a place to go
Does the future call me?

But I go to a time still far
The morning after today
As all now I meet my future
So what happens to me next?
Magdalena Mendoza, Grade 6
John Adams Middle School

Seasons
Winter is cold with lots of snow.
Ice is on top of the roof.
Fall is also cold with leaves
The colors of red, yellow, and orange
And all the leaves fall down from the tree.
Spring is fun with flowers growing
On trees and also flowers blooming.
Summer is hot, it is vacation
And time to swim in the pool.
Emily Lopez, Grade 5
Tipton Elementary School

Ball
I'm a ball
I taste like grass
I feel hard and tough
I smell like dirt
when people bounce me
on the ground
I go THUMP THUMP!
I am orange or red
with black thick lines.
It's not easy
being me.
Horrible horrible
human beings!
Adrianna Venegas, Grade 4
Liberty Elementary School

Beautiful Nature
Nature is beautiful
and so are you.
The forest is green,
the ocean is blue,
just like the color of your eyes.
Animals could be wild,
yet you are calm.
The desert is brown
like the opposite side of your palm.
But best of all,
you have the beauty of an angel.
Nature, oh nature;
It is so beautiful.
Mark Ponce, Grade 5
Renuevo School

Hiltie
Hiltie is my dog
She makes me smile
bringing me life, laughter, and happiness.
Hiltie helps me with doors.
She brings me toys and
much, much more.
Hiltie is there for me.
She protects me and plays.
Hiltie is my friend she walks with me,
and opens my door.
She knows when I am sad,
and jumps up when I am glad.
Hiltie is my dog.
Andrew Sipich, Grade 6
Grant Elementary School

Toucan
A black, striped toucan
resting on an old palm tree
ready to take off.
Nicole Savluk, Grade 6
Gardner Street Elementary School

My Fallen Leaf
My leaf is like a
Flower blooming
Yet, shaped like a star.
When my star spins
It looks so interesting,
Twisting,
Twirling,
Diving.
The jagged edges have pizzazz!
Luckily, saved
Before a car could run over him.
He's so flimsy
But not flexible.
My leaf is unyielding and fearless
As he soars and swirls
On invisible pathways.
Brown with hints of green,
My little star is not dense,
Able to shatter into little pieces,
So handle with care
My fallen leaf, my tarnished star.
Carlos Aparicio, Grade 4
Orange Glen Elementary School

If You Knew Me...
If you knew me
You would know that,
I dream of being a Veterinarian.
I love animals and
Care for my dog when he is hurt.
I wonder about school
Because, I might not pass to
6th grade.
I fear sharks now,
Ever since my dad
Made me watch a scary shark movie!
I giggle
When my parents and sister
Tickle me!
I often think about
My grandparents,
Who are in Mexico.
I miss them very much.
If you knew me
Then you would know why...
Alejandra Cazares, Grade 5
Orange Glen Elementary School

Rain
Rain creates many fun things to do
Play in puddles
have water fights
run around
But, it is also fun to stay inside
Tyler Kornguth, Grade 4
Carlthorp School

My Love

He is a love to me you know.
He's even better than winter snow.
You would think he's not the one for me.
But I tell you that he's the best you can be.

Through the dark and light we go.
He is my love and that you should know.
When he walks he has a stride.
Why did he have to say "goodbye?"

I think he still beats the rest.
But know he's not the best.
Maybe he wasn't for me.
I don't know if he still is for me.

I found a new love.
Now I'm certain he's for me.
And I'm very happy.
Plus he is my love and that you should know.

Kaylin Finley, Grade 5
Lydiksen Elementary School

I'm a Pencil

I am a pencil
I spend my time writing
And getting sharpened

I don't like it when you make me dull.
I like being sharp,
Not broken
And not too little.

I hate it when
You roll me all around on the rusty old ground.

But what makes me happy is that
You always write with me.
But I wish you would try not to break me.

I wish I could tell you to take care of me.
And not leave me lying around,
Or underneath your big books.

Alexa Lopez, Grade 4
Joseph M Simas Elementary School

Now I Am…

I used to be a bee
Bold and confident
But now I am a hive
Full of unforgetting confidence and pride
I used to be a hive
Enclosing secrets and surprises
But now I am honey
Sweet and warm-hearted
I used to be honey
Creamy and loving
But now I am a sandwich
Threatened to be eaten
I used to be a sandwich
A shell with a sensitive filling
But now I am a plate waiting to keep an important secret
I used to be a plate trustworthy and brave
But now I am a bee in a hive
Making honey to put in a sandwich
To put on a plate bold, confident, sweet, sensitive and trustworthy.

Veeda Movaghar, Grade 5
Dingeman Elementary School

The Forest

Crunching leaves on the forest floor
Slimy moss on the old enchanted trees
Poison oak rubbing against your cold pale leg
Tripping on old roots falling on your scabby knees

Small swamps covered with algae
Croaking of toads and frogs
Wolf packs hunting late at night
Chasing squealing hogs

Decaying branches laying on the ground
Hundreds of bugs crawling under there
Holes and stumps all over the ground
Ankles twisting and muscles tear

Rocks and logs sticking out of the ground
Lizards and frogs slipping in between your legs
If you ought to go again
You wouldn't even beg

Joshua C. Harger, Grade 5
Lydiksen Elementary School

Thanksgiving

Thanksgiving is a day we are thankful
We have enough food to make our stomach full
I like the meal, do you know why?
It ends with lots of pie
It is a highlight of fall
We'll play lots of games and watch football
I will spend it with my parents and siblings
They are my most special blessing

William Buxton, Grade 4
Carlthorp School

Creature

This creature makes me happy and sad
It is small but mighty
It acts like a spoiled princess
It plays with fire but doesn't get burned
I tried to play with it but it poked me in the eye
It showed me no pity, when a tear rolled down my cheek
Although the innocence is a blessing
If she is lucky she will stay this way forever

Gabriel Doynel, Grade 6
Gardner Street Elementary School

My Dad
Roses are red,
Violets are blue,
You smell like cologne and shampoo.

When you're off on a job,
I miss you.
I really do,
Even though you have to.

I want you to know
You sure make a lot of money.
But I miss you
Calling me honey.

You're coming back
In a couple of days.
And oh, you're going to be surprised
With the presents you've gained.
Natalie Vallin, Grade 5
Granada Elementary School

If I Were in Charge of the World*
If I were in charge of the world
I'd be in charge of myself
The weather'd be nicer
And breakfast would be served in bed

If I were in charge of the world
There'd be three-day weekends
You'd always be healthy
And there'd be holidays every week

If I were in charge of the world
You wouldn't have bedtimes
You wouldn't have homework
You wouldn't have lunch box food
Or school till 12:30

If I were in charge of the world.
Fritz Mora, Grade 6
St Raphael School
Patterned after Judith Viorst

Vegetables
Vegetables are very crunchy in my mouth.
Some are eaten by people in the south.
Most vegetables can be small.
Some like corn can grow very tall.
Carrots are very fun.
When they grow in the sun.
If you leave them outside they will get stale.
They might even get eaten by a snail.
Some vegetables have rotten ends.
But vegetables are our friends.
Reese Oliver, Grade 5
Eastwood Elementary School

Summer
I have lots of fun
in the blazing hot sun!

I have lots of crazy plans
on my busy hands.

With my sister I go about
and always go and hang out.

During summer I always take
a really long summer break!
Tricia Fukuzawa, Grade 5
Eastwood Elementary School

Football
Football is the sport I play,
I am really good they say.
When I run, I run with speed,
I juke and jive until I arrive,
In the end zone where I must be.
When I catch the ball, I do not drop it at all.
I hold it tight with all my might.
I have to be tough in order to play,
I have to have speed to go all the way.
Life without football is no life for me,
When I play, I set myself free.
Cobi Jay Ciolino, Grade 6
Miraleste Intermediate School

Rain Drop
As I
listen
to the
rain in my
mind water
splashing
Music on my
umbrella
Rippling rain
from the
blue sky
Serena Manalili, Grade 5
Henry Haight Elementary School

A Walk on the Beach
I enjoy walking on the beach
To feel the warm sand on my feet
I enjoy feeling the sun coming my way
To swim with all the little colorful fish
It's like the perfect wish

When it's time to go
I say good-bye and I know to say
"I'll be back soon so don't go away"
Amaya Luckie, Grade 6
St Martin-in-the-Fields School

Christmas
Receiving toys, presents, money
Giving presents and love
I love eating gingerbread houses
Throwing snowballs, making snowmen
Snowboarding, snow skiing
Sledding, ice-skating, snow angels
Time with family and friends
Christmas is the best holiday ever!
Ivan Pang, Grade 5
Juarez Elementary School

My Midnight Dream
My Midnight Dream
has clear blue rippling water
the moon sings
at night the stars begin
to dance
the trees slowly move back
and forth while
the plants begin to dance
Maricela Rojas, Grade 5
Henry Haight Elementary School

Summer
There's winter and spring
There's winter and fall
But summer is the one thing
I love most of all.
Though it gives me a tan
Though I will need a fan,
Once you have fun
You'll never be done.
Ebony Wilson, Grade 5
Eastwood Elementary School

Hungriness
Like hungry animals
Creatures hunt
They are trying to catch a small deer
He runs
He falls
And he fights for his life
And the sky winks
At his braveness
Jenifer Grado, Grade 6
Lincoln Elementary School

Thanksgiving
On Thanksgiving
I eat stuffing and rice
it's very nice.
We play games
please do stay
to play.
Nicolle Monreal, Grade 4
St Raphael School

High Merit Poems – Grades 4, 5 and 6

The Beauty of Night
You peer into the night filled with
stars while they twinkle at you.
The blackness of night vanishes.
The grayness of dark clouds disappear.
The darkness of fog is lifted.
Because the sparkling light of stars fill
the vast sky!

Leo Li, Grade 6
Ocean Air School

Leaves
Leaves are falling
Leaves are turning
The most beautiful sight in the night
When I look out the window
Red, green, yellow
I can't believe what I see under the moon
Under the shining stars comes fall!!!

Kaya Maxwell, Grade 4
Juarez Elementary School

Seasons
S ummer, it's nice and hot
E ach day, I sleep a lot
A utumn, it's nice and cool
S oon, I can't go to the pool
O n the leaves I dance
" **N** ot winter next!"
S pring, I think, is still the best

Caitlin Ou, Grade 6
Carden Academy of Santa Clara

No One Has a Perfect Life
No one has a perfect life.
You might not always enjoy your day.
It is not the end of the world.
There, the next day, you will start fresh.
But if you make a big mess,
You cannot freeze time.
Just live with it and you'll be fine.

Stephanie Salvador, Grade 6
St Linus School

My Inspiration
My inspiration is my mom.
She's short, she's tall,
She dreams, she loves,
She believes in me.
She thinks of me,
She has a heart the size of a tree.
She is the world to me.

Stephine Lanini, Grade 6
Linda Elementary School

Delight of Elena Reyes
I am a baby bird in a deep nest
I am a curious duck that wanders in the pond
I am a hyena that laughs, wildly in the grasslands
I am the cub that follows the lion mother
I am the sunrise, the bright light of the sky
I am the kitten playing with the ball of yarn
I am the cluster of freshly picked roses
I am the farthest rock skipped across the water
I am the cold of the snow in winter that falls from the sky
I am the plops of rain that falls
I am the glitter of the stars in the night sky
I am the long branch of the tree in the forest
I am the rainbow of four colors
I am the cheetah running through the grasslands
I am the field of tulips and roses
I am the herd of elephants on the dried grassland
I am the hunger of the mighty tiger, you see, I am alive, I am alive.
I am the whole of gracefulness of these things
I stand in good relation to my father. I stand in good relation to my mother.
I stand in good relation to my friends. I stand in good relation to my siblings.
You see, I am alive, I am alive.

Elena Reyes, Grade 6
John Muir Elementary School

Green
Green is the color of a small, sour lime waiting to be picked.
Green feels like a smooth ten-dollar bill of money in my hand.
Green looks like an emerald sparkling in the sun.
Green sounds like the waves crashing in the beach.
Green feels like a prickly cactus in the desert.
Green tastes like a big glass of green grape juice refreshing you.
Green is the color of my face when I'm on a boat in the choppy waves.
Green smells like newly cut grass on a fall evening.
Green sounds like leaves blowing in the wind.
Green smells like a freshly baked apple pie.
Green feels like the slimy skin on a frog's back.
Green tastes like delicious Granny Smith apples with juice dripping down your chin.
Green smells like the air in Hawaii after it rains.
Green sounds like a juicy delicious pear being eaten.
Green looks like a four-leaf clover bringing you good luck.
Green tastes like a pickle fresh out of the jar.
Green is the color of a large, sleeping iguana.
And green looks like spring leaves on a huge tree.

Tessa Bagby, Grade 4
Heather Elementary School

The Outdoors
I went camping, brought some gear, a knife, a backpack and a spear.
Camping is a big part of my heart, and I wish it were on every day of my chart.
Unfortunately, I go twice a year, off mountains, cliffs and a couple of piers,
To keep warm, my dad says grow a beard, but I think that is just a little bit weird.
Off the mountains and cliffs and peaks I stare, doing that when I have time to spare.
I always bring food so I never starve, when I am bored a stick I carve.
Some people like running, baseball or to farm, but camping for me has a special charm.

Erica Rennie, Grade 4
Brooks Elementary School

A Hot Summer Day

On a hot summer day,
Children went out to play.
They jumped, laughed, ran, and giggled,
As I watched the babies in the pool wiggle.
It was a perfect day to relax and enjoy the warm sun.
I quickly got ready to go out to have some fun.
At the park I sat under a tree and enjoyed the warm breeze.
I felt so relaxed and at ease.
This was the perfect hot summer day,
To enjoy with family, friends, and play.

Geraldo De La Cruz, Grade 4
Mira Catalina Elementary School

Halloween

Ghosts scaring, mummies wrapping tearing,
Vampires biting the skins, souls haunting the haunted inns,
Bride of Frankenstein married, to the green and scary,
Frankenstein greening, dead birds preening,
Werewolves gone a clawing, headless man a sawing,
Skeletons' bones cracking, Medusa's snakes are snapping,
Bats are flying, kids are crying,
Pumpkins have faces, spiders spinning laces,
Witches making potions, black cats making commotion,
Pirates got a hook, HA!, made you look!

Kiana David-Allison, Grade 4
Manchester GATE Elementary School

Winter

Winter has come and the bears are hibernating.
The holidays are here and people are decorating.

The snow is falling and people are skiing.
The birds fly south from the weather they are fleeing.

Kids are having snowball fights.
The days have gotten shorter and now there's more night.

That is what happens in the winter.

Adam Blagg, Grade 5
Ocean Air School

A Scaly Surprise

I'm startled, I scream,
Quickly covering my head
With a plain, white sheet.
A swift beautiful dragon capered
Like a ballet dancer twirling around.
Her great appearance ferocious, gigantic, long, scaly.
Breathing fire, protecting her newborn.
Fly away fierce dragon, don't scare me no more;
I looked out my window, no dragon,
Just burn marks on the floor.

Melissa Pelowski, Grade 5
Ocean Air School

Xbox 360

I love to play my game all day.
It's hard to put away when I have to go away.
When I go to bed it's stuck in my head.
When I open my eyes there it lies.
In the end it's like my best friend.
Sometimes I love it sometimes I hate it.
I would play all day if I had a say.
If you use cheat codes it's an epic fail,
But if you don't it's a win.
The Xbox 360!

Bobby Farrell, Grade 6
St Martin-in-the-Fields School

Christmas

C hristmas is the time for bells and chimes
' **H** appy holidays' is what people say during this time
R udolph to me is definitely not fake
I ce skating is fun to do on a frozen lake
S now covers the streets
' **T** is the time for lots of goodies and treats
M y room is filled with cards that are sent
A t midnight, we like to open presents
S itting by the fireplace, drinking hot chocolate is what I like to do

Neha Dhayanand, Grade 6
Carden Academy of Santa Clara

Nightmares

I am only scared when no one is there
No one there to hug me or comfort me

I am only scared when I see nothing
Only the blackness of the room

I am only scared when my nightmares come true
And I can't do anything but hide

Though I am not scared, I am only dreaming

Morgen Shattuck, Grade 6
Grant Elementary School

Christmas Dazzle

Twinkling stars in the midnight breeze.
Hot chocolate, fluffy mittens to make sure I don't freeze.
We hang ornaments with colors of all kinds.
Throughout the season I have thoughts of gifts in mind.
I hear melodies that are singing out.
The imaginable *White Christmas* is one of my favorites, no doubt.
Oozy chocolate cookies jumping out of the oven,
Each Christmas every relative give you that special lovin'.
Flashy outdoor lights shine with a warm feeling in my eyes.
When it's time for company to leave, I'm sad to say my good-byes.

Gabriella Sarrouh, Grade 5
Our Lady of Mount Carmel School

If I Were in Charge of the World*
If I were in charge of the world
I would cancel cavities,
Wars, tetanus shots,
And BROCCOLI! Ick!

If I were in charge of the world
There would be avocado trees all over,
Cats that wouldn't scratch,
And shorter school days from 10:00 to 1:00.

If I were in charge of the world
An animal would NEVER be eaten,
All the animals would be safe and never harmed,
And Taylor Lautner would live right next door to me.
And a person who hates to do homework
And who sometimes throws baby tantrums
Would still be in charge of the world!
Eden Rae Sedgwick, Grade 6
St Raphael School
*Patterned after Judith Viorst

Blue
Blue tastes like a juicy burger.
Blue looks like a bright sunny sky.
Blue sounds like a chomp of cake.
Blue is the color of a scoop of bubble gum ice cream.
Blue smells like a freshly seasoned steak.
Blue feels like a missed opportunity.
Blue tastes like a plate of pasta.
Blue looks like a cool swimming pool.
Blue sounds like an explosion of happiness.
Blue is the color of a blue whale.
Blue smells like a soda can just opened.
Blue tastes like a freshly baked pie.
Blue looks like a new friend.
Blue sounds like a rushing river in a quiet forest.
Blue is the color of a cool drink of water.
Blue smells like a warm evening.
Blue feels like a fish scale.
And blue is an overachieving color.
Corbin Balitactac, Grade 4
Heather Elementary School

A Day at the Park
My sister cries
My mother smiles
And we all play a game at the park
We get hurt but we get up
We get mad at each other and encourage one another
There are the ones who are poor sports
But we get over it and keep on playing
My grandma watches because she cannot play
While she is watching she starts to cry
Because she sees us all playing a game at the park as a family
Andrew Zepeda, Grade 6
Isbell Middle School

TV
O' TV
You are my life
As I touch the TV remote
The happy sensation
Sweeps through me
As I stare at the TV screen
And I watch
And watch
And watch
Yet the relaxation still fills me
As I watch the cooking channel
The fresh aroma of cookies
Blows by my nose
Suddenly my mom comes
Turns it off
And just by the press of the button
It's all gone
Ivan Jutamulia, Grade 6
Chinese American International School

My Dream
I had a dream,
That there was a stream,
Knitted out of blue silk.
The stream was so blue,
I thought it was all true!
And then came the raindrops from all around,
Oh! What a beautiful sound!
There were fish in the heaving waves,
Leaping up and down.
High green mountains loomed into the sky,
Oh! How beautiful and divine!
And then slowly the sun drifted into the sky,
The silvery gray clouds vanished out of sight.
Alas! My dream then faded away,
And there in my bed awake I lay,
Wondering what a wonderful way to begin a day!
Neilabjo Maitra, Grade 4
Manchester GATE Elementary School

Purple
Purple is the feeling when you find a good book.
Purple sounds like crickets chirping at night.
Purple tastes like warm hot chocolate.
Purple looks like the rainbow up in the sky.
Purple smells like the cold rain.
Purple is the taste of pancakes that just came out of the oven.
Purple is the smell of the ocean waves.
Purple is the feeling when you get 100% on a test.
Purple is the taste of fresh grapes in your mouth.
Purple looks like a beautiful sunset.
Purple smells like a rushing river.
Purple is the grape juice that cools your mouth on a hot day.
And purple is the feeling when you win a soccer game.
Jillian Stern, Grade 4
Heather Elementary School

A Chaotic Thanksgiving Eve

The turkey flew out of the window,
It became a stuffed statue no more.
I began to think it knew where to go,
I think it flew to the Atlantic shore.

We chased it until we were beat,
And my father told us not to feel defeat,
For even though the turkey had run away,
We could still eat ham on Thanksgiving Day.

When we reached the house,
We quietly opened the door,
And saw the potatoes being eaten by a mouse,
And the cranberry sauce was dumped onto the floor.

My mother stood in the kitchen with a look of scorn,
And changed the potatoes for some zucchini, radish, and corn,
And we knew that tomorrow we would have to eat,
Those silly vegetables and that snouted meat.

Zoe Beckman, Grade 5
Carden Conejo School

Lake Winnipesaukee Memories

The crisp morning air blows in our faces
Freezing water below shakes the swift craft
The aroma of ice cream fills the air
The dock comes closer

Surrounding islands give a sense of protection
As if we are the only ones
Lurking this lake of history
As water marks its time

Stories are shared
As the night comes to a close
In front of a crackling fire
Memories to hold

Grandfather's ashes lie there today
Irreplaceable memories with him
As the waves carry them away
Like petals along a spring breeze

Katherine Roush, Grade 6
Mirman School

Dancing

I wonder why the hard work isn't paying off.
I hear the teacher yelling at me for having my leg bent.
I see an exhausted girl in the mirror.
I want to end the class immediately.
I am not perfect.

I pretend the only thing I hear is the music.
I feel the beads of sweat dripping down my face.
I touch the smoothness of the wooden barre.
I worry about messing up a movement.
I cry about all the pressure.
I am not ready.

I understand the teacher is doing what's best for me.
I wish not everyone's eyes will be on me.
I dream I won't embarrass myself on stage.
I try my best.
I hope it is good enough.
I am a dancer.

Elaine Chen, Grade 6
Chinese American International School

Dandelion Seed

Here it comes, my sister gasps as the shadow of the hand
mockingly approached, fast, but gently,
the monster grabbed my…Momma…Pain…
as she screamed for all she was worth.
Her stem was no match
for the hand pulling Momma
out of the sweet, homely ground.
I stiffened then suddenly relaxed
as the owner of the hand spoke,
I wish for a puppy, childishly, with longing.
Then with no warning, a vast wind blew from the west.
I hung on Momma, never letting go all the memories, *never*.
Long ago when we were still unseasoned,
she would tell us about the untold future,
when we had to let go, and wait, 'till we grew, just like our momma.
Trembling, I saw that my white-headed friends had left,
Already, leaving me behind, desolate.
Finally the wind stopped, and I let go,
with no regrets.

Jane Jeong, Grade 6
Gale Ranch Middle School

Space

Space has a lot of secrets it does not tell.
    Do black holes lead to different dimensions?
    Where do comets land?
    How many galaxies are there beyond us?
    Are there other creatures there?
    Will we ever know?
Space is silent.
It does not answer us, but we ask.

Justin Lee, Grade 5
Granada Elementary School

My Puppy

I have a little puppy
It is cute, cuddly and green
Although he may be odd
He is not very mean
He plays all day
And sleeps all night
That is why
My puppy is all right

Karsyn Punt, Grade 5
George Washington Charter Elementary School

High Merit Poems – Grades 4, 5 and 6

Flying Friends
Birds
Tiny, colorful
Nesting, flying, eating
Landing on a branch
Pilots
Austin Adam, Grade 5
St Louis De Montfort School

Loving Animals
Dog
friendly, fun
licking, jumping, slobbering
always makes me laugh
Friend
Antoni Nunez, Grade 5
St Louis De Montfort School

A Pretty Thing
Diamond
Pretty, fancy
Sparkling, glowing, shining
A symbol of love
Jewel
Allison Luis, Grade 5
St Louis De Montfort School

Kings of the Jungle
Lions
Tough, strong
Roaring, growling, prowling
Rulers of the land
Beasts
Evan Vega, Grade 5
St Louis De Montfort School

Air Force Equipment
Jet
Fast, big
Flying, shooting, transporting
Helps us in war
Plane
Anthony Fuller, Grade 5
St Louis De Montfort School

In the Sky I See A…
Blue Jay
Navy, small
Flying, soaring, gliding
Passing through the sky
Bird
Will Pena, Grade 5
St Louis De Montfort School

The Delight Song of Lexi Zeyen
I am the moon in the shining sky
I am a black tiger that preys in the wild, waiting for food
I am a koala bear that sways on a tree trunk upside down
I am the afternoon, the light of the sky
I am a monkey playing with a banana
I am a pack of wolves hunting for food
I am the farthest planet
I am the cold of Alaska
I am the honk of a car
I am the glitter of a star
I am a long stick on the ground on the sidewalk
I am a stoplight
I am a monkey swinging away through the swamps
I am a field of sheep and cows
I am a group of snakes
I am the hunger of a black bear
I am the whole world of things
You see, I am alive, I am alive
I stand in good relationship to my family. I stand in good relationship to my friends.
I stand in good relation to my teachers. I stand in good relationship to myself.
You see, I am alive, I am alive
Lexi Zeyen, Grade 6
John Muir Elementary School

Purple
Purple tastes like a juicy plump grape.
Purple looks like a layer in a sunset.
Purple feels like a smooth eggplant.
Purple smells like a violet growing in the sunlight.
Purple sounds like a dewdrop dripping off a lush green leaf.
Purple tastes like a fresh glass of grape juice.
Purple looks like a plum in the tree making a big shadow on a hot summer day.
Purple feels like a squishy ripe plum.
Purple smells like an iris-scented candle burning.
Purple sounds like the pitter patter of rain on a cold autumn day.
Purple tastes like warm vegetable soup.
Purple looks like a cold winter day.
Purple feels like a soft, wool blanket.
Purple smells like a hot soothing cup of peppermint tea.
Purple sounds like someone threw a rock in a pond.
Alyn Seymour, Grade 4
Heather Elementary School

Beautiful Nature
Beautiful beaches
Clear blue skies
Huge moon that wakes up in the night
A butterfly with all her beauty flying far away from me
A golden sun that burns my eyes is hanging there up in the skies
A gorgeous flower growing there on the plain on the right
Huge towers sticking from the ground like they were already there
A bird is singing some mysterious songs, I wish I knew their language
Just look at this nature it's so bright
I wish I was a part of that
Olga Guseva, Grade 6
Gardner Street Elementary School

When It Rains
When it rains
the sky is gray;
it's a pain.
When it rains
drops fall down
to the ground
in the town.
I have a frown;
it's like everything's upside down!
Melanie Cortez, Grade 6
Renuevo School

My Brother, Daniel
My brother Daniel is a pain.
His attitude is very lame.
The only thing he gets an A in,
Is Physical Education.
Daniel never ever shares
He doesn't even really care
About the things I do and dare,
But I'll love him anywhere.
Fatai Heimuli, Grade 5
Our Lady of Mount Carmel School

My Brother
My brother Aaron
Loves rowing as a crewman.
Aaron is a college man,
Now he is in Washington.
It makes me blue because he is away.
Now Aaron is no longer a "Padre."
I know he must earn a degree,
But why do I miss him so badly?
Joshua Gonzales, Grade 5
Our Lady of Mount Carmel School

Trees
Trees, oh trees
They give us breeze
They even have some fruit to eat
That is what we have for a treat
Trees are green
And so are the leaves
Go ahead and grab some lemons
We'll make a stand of lemonade!
Lizzeth Lombera, Grade 5
Our Lady of Mount Carmel School

On a Branch
On a branch
The birdie sat
Oh, oh,
My gosh,
Is that a bat?
Sherry Ross, Grade 5
PLACE @ Prescott

This Awful Camp
For all the hardships we've suffered we never have hurt anyone or anything
The treacherous camp that I'm trapped in right now, where did my people go wrong

For all I see confined in this jagged barbed wire fence
The ribs of starving people, their faces longing to be free
The soldiers whipping and beating their prisoners, where did my people go wrong

The awful tastes that we don't deserve, just watery soup and a crust of bread
Some rotten potatoes and leftover meals, where did my people go wrong

My ears cannot stand what I'm witnessing, the sound of guns way too close to me
Awful whips thrashing at innocent Jews, where did my people go wrong

The bed that I lay in is sore to my back, we're way too cramped in this tiny camp
The papery clothes are our only source of heat, where did my people go wrong

For all the hardships we've suffered we never have hurt anyone or anything
The treacherous camp that I'm trapped in right now, where did my people go wrong
Rebecca Stelman, Grade 6
Lindero Canyon Middle School

Burnt Gold
Burnt gold is the color of the sun infinitely burning high in the sky
Burn gold is buddies uniting to make an unbreakable web
Burnt gold is the color of leaves fluttering to the cold ground in fall
Burnt gold is the color of sunflowers swaying softly in the morning breeze
Burnt gold is smooth, cool wood on your warm palm
Burnt gold is a sleek horse galloping in the pouring rain
Burnt gold is golden Christmas lights twinkling on a dense tree
Burnt gold is a Golden Retriever bolting through a field chasing his golden ball
Burnt gold is my loving mom hugging me tightly in her strong arms
Comforting me and assuring me everything is all right
Burnt gold is happiness with everyone sharing, caring and loving
Chris Roy, Grade 5
Laurence School

Eraser
I am an eraser
you poke and
leave me in the dark.
All of these things
are breaking my heart.
I like it when you use me
and share me with your friends.
I want to be treated nice
and not thrown in your desk.
All I want is to shout, shout, shout
when you throw me around.
It makes me sad
when you leave me in a desk.
Take me home
where I'm supposed to be,
if you don't
I will be in your desk for eternity.
Jorge Barba, Grade 4
Joseph M Simas Elementary School

If You Knew Me...
If you knew me, then
You would know why.
I dream of returning to
Arizona,
Because I like visiting the
Grand Canyon!
I wonder why,
Everybody kills,
Fears sharks?
I dread
The barracuda.
They have razor-sharp teeth!
I giggle when somebody
Tickles me.
On the belly!
If you knew me,
Then you would know why...
Byron Michael, Grade 4
Orange Glen Elementary School

A Special Person
She is very nice.
She is always precise.
She loves me very much.
Her answer is always a hunch.
She knows me very well.
I really think she's swell.
When she listens to Frankie Valli,
She says, "Oh he's wowie!"
She may brag about me a lot and
My birthdays she never forgot.
She loves to go shopping from store to store.
And she's always hopping from door to door.
Do you know this person?
No, she's not a sea urchin.
Her name is Diane and she is my gram.
Since this is the end,
Good bye all friends.

Celeste Fox, Grade 6
St Johns Lutheran School

White
White is the wind blowing on your face.
White tastes like ice cream.
White is the noise of beats on a drum
White is the beauty of skipping, of laying down, looking at clouds.
White is the feeling of skipping through a meadow.
White is the fun of playing baseball.
White is the fun of making art work.
White is the thing that makes old movies cool.
White is the fun of coloring blank paper.
White is the fun of having snowball fights.
White is the snowflakes falling from the sky.
White is what makes the white taste good.
White is what the White House is made of.
White is the fog high in the sky.
White is the chalk on a baseball field.
White is the flavor of whip cream.
White is what makes you able to write on white boards.

Ethan White, Grade 4
Heather Elementary School

Thoughts of a Pencil
You throw me in
your dark, stinky desk
full of goo and slime.
I feel alone in the desk.
I want to scream real loud.
I hate when you write with me hard
and break me on purpose
and it makes me cry so know I want to fly.
I like when you write with me every day.
I like when you tap me
and it makes a little tune.
I could never ask for a better owner like you.

Brianna Velez, Grade 4
Joseph M Simas Elementary School

If I Were in Charge of the World*
If I were in charge of the world
I'd cancel boy shows, Friday mornings,
Commercials, bedtimes and homework.
If I were in charge of the world
There'd be shopping malls everywhere
Less news and more kids shows on television,
And more places to eat good food.
In I were in charge of the world
Someone would cook you breakfast every day
You would have hot lunch every day
You wouldn't have to wake up at 7:00 am
And no consequences for our actions
If I were in charge of the world
Everyone would have a flat screen TV
You would be allowed to choose if you want to eat vegetables
You'd be allowed to eat all the candy you liked
If I were in charge of the world
Every outfit would cost $2.00
And a person who forgets to go to bed on time
And sometimes can't think of a rhyme
Would still be allowed to be in charge of the world.

Carlie Kuhns, Grade 6
St Raphael School
*Patterned after Judith Viorst

Thanksgiving
The leaves blush from yellow to red;
They fall upon a flower bed;
An interesting smell is in the air;
The tasty aroma, I cannot bear.
Set on the table are delightful foods;
As we all sit down with joyful moods.

Our mouths are enjoying the sensation of food;
The turkey and yams are oh so good;
Our conversations come with laughs;
Cheerful stories about the past;
Thanksgiving isn't about getting mad,
It's for thanking God for all we have.

Gabriella Perez, Grade 6
St Martin-in-the-Fields School

Christmas
I know Christmas
There are bells ringing and people singing
Elves working and reindeer sleeping
Santa ho ho hoing, kids snoring
I know Christmas
The taste of cookies, the sight of snow
The smell of a gingerbread houses, the sight of cookies
I know Christmas
"Merry Christmas," "Give me my present"
"Open your present," "Turn off the Christmas light."
I know Christmas

Norma Salazar, Grade 4
Lankershim Elementary School

My Hero
You have been with me night and day,
And you have protected me from all evil.
Hence, you are my hero.
As winter turned to spring,
You vanished from my sight.
But as summer turned to fall,
You reappeared so very bright.
I endured the hardships of the wintertime
With you right by my side.
Now, the time has come for you to leave,
But I know you will always be there for me.
Katrina Yap, Grade 6
St Linus School

Boogie Board
I love to boogie board at the beach,
And have a snack that's a juicy peach.

I get my boogie board and go in the ocean,
which has a lot of motion.

But when there are no waves, I get mad,
So I call him, and here comes dad!

Then I go very fast and ride
through the ocean tide!
Audrey Cope, Grade 5
Eastwood Elementary School

Life
Life goes by fast,
faster than you want,
for once is enough,
enough for you to see
that the world is tough.

It may just be your last day,
minute or breath.
So I tell you, friend,
do what you can,
while you can.
Nicholas Manjarres, Grade 5
Granada Elementary School

My Skin
My skin color
Is brown
It's not just any brown
It's one of a kind
It's unique
Sparkles
It's beautiful
I love me beneath
My skin.
Namiye People, Grade 5
PLACE @ Prescott

The Midnight Party
At midnight,
the dark
sky was
quiet, but
the
moon is
like a
fire that
lights the
sky and
the stars
are like a
million eyes
listen to
the
moon because
the moon is
singing a
song it
is a
midnight party
Bai Hao Deng, Grade 5
Henry Haight Elementary School

Time Travel
Time travel would be a fun adventure
I wish I could do it someday
I would go into the future and see
What it would be like
I wonder if Global Warming will
Be gone
Or if the planet Earth will be around
Will there be humans left alive?
What will we be doing?
How will we transport?
What would the past be like?
Time traveling would only ruin the
Past, future, and present
If you would like to change
The past it will affect you in the
Present and future
There is nothing like living in the moment
Life is a lesson
Either it makes you or breaks you
Why time travel, if it would only want
To make you change things
Ezmeralda Ocampo, Grade 6
John Adams Middle School

Cookies
Round, small
Eating, tasting, smelling
Delicious, good, and yummy
Cinnamon
Mia Molinar, Grade 5
Our Lady of the Rosary School

My Life
My name is Nicole,
I am going through a stage
when I can study something
for a half an hour
and when it comes to the test,
I have no idea what I was studying.
It's like not studying at all.
It bugs me all the time
because I would fail.
Luckily I'm seeing a therapist
to help me through the stress.
Before I knew what I had,
my mother would make me cry
because she would yell at me.
The subjects that are the
hardest are Language Arts,
Literature, and History.
Nicole Poch, Grade 6
Carden Academy of Santa Clara

Earth
Sun rises in the east…
Green grass growing;
Sun sets in the west…
Blue sky going;
Earth!

Sun rises in the east…
Flowers flourishing; blooming;
Sun sets in the west…
Dark shadows looming;
Earth!

Sun rises in the east…
Animals coming;
Sun sets in the west…
Birds humming;
Earth!
Simone Hernandez, Grade 6
St Martin-in-the-Fields School

A Big Race
My goal is to win the race
I make a faithful face
Look to my right and see
People cheering
Look to my left and hear screaming
We start to run as fast as we can
I know I can win
Closer and closer to the finish line
Open my eyes and see
A ribbon on my hand
And I knew
I made it!
Diana Palma, Grade 6
Lincoln Elementary School

High Merit Poems – Grades 4, 5 and 6

Tulip
I have a dog with one eye
the sight of her could make you cry
one day we went to the pound
and picked her up off the ground
and she smelled like a garbage mound
we put her in the car
thank goodness we didn't have to go far
a bath was on the list
of things that were certainly missed
when the bath was through
we got her a teddy bear to chew
she tore open poor teddy's back
and gave my mom a heart attack
but don't worry my mom is fine
and I am sorry but this is the last line
Adrian Ford, Grade 6
Heritage Christian School

Volleyball
When the ball hits the ground,
The crowd sure does make a sound.
But when they hit it out of bounds,
The other side sings real loud!
When they're on their second game
Everyone's cheering in any way.
Screaming shouting yelling things,
Things, things they always say.
When the referee calls it in,
The other team yells "WE WIN"
The team that lost said "It's all the same."
Then they shake and say "Good Game."
One side is happy but the other is not.
But that's OK
We all had fun a lot.
Haley Ferko, Grade 6
St Pius X Elementary School

If You Knew Me…
If you knew me
You would know that
I dream of being a veterinarian
To save the lives of animals,
All over the world.
I fear getting bitten by animals!
So this is causing me to wonder
About becoming a vet.
I also want to be a firefighter!
I giggle when my brother's snake
Goes around my neck.
I think about having a career
That helps others.
If you knew me
Then you would know…
Katheryne Mora, Grade 5
Orange Glen Elementary School

Rainy Days
When I hear the pitter patter on the window
It makes me feel cozy and warm
gloomy and relaxed
I love to watch the birds
swooping down to get worms
I like to see the raindrops
and watch the wind blow the trees
I like to sit on the couch
with hot chocolate
watch a movie
curl up
lie down to rest
Do you like rainy days?
I know I do
Georgia Pappas, Grade 4
Carlthorp School

Beauty Is…
Beauty is the delicate flower
Dancing in the breeze.
So small, yet so full of power
That is sometimes hard to meet.

Beauty is the lone wolf in the night,
The silvery figure standing in the moon.
It sings with all its might;
Those who hear it forget their boons.

Beauty is all the world
Without any troubles or plights,
Only the pulse of happiness
Sending dreams into the night.
Susie Lim, Grade 6
J L Academy

Flickering in the Darkness
The ground is wet and cold
And the air is like a blade
Flashes of white and blue
Bursting from the gray sky
Not a movement, anywhere
The world is frozen in time
But somewhere there is a church
Encrusted with ivy
Unused for years
Forgotten
Within it holds total darkness
Yet
There is a lone candle
Flickering in the darkness
Gabriel Jenkinson, Grade 6
The Mirman School

My Wonderful Leaf
My wonderful leaf's colors are
A ghostly brown and green.
Its long stem lets me
Spin and twirl it
Between my fingers.
Your jagged edges
Have attitude
Like a person.
Before the fall,
You always watched
While we walked along the street
Lined up,
Sauntered,
And
Played
At school.
Very passionate, artistic, and elegant,
My wonderful leaf
You are my dream maker!
Nicolas Smith, Grade 4
Orange Glen Elementary School

If You Knew Me…
If you knew me,
You would know
I dream of going home
To relax,
I'm tired!
I dream of my dog
When I'm in school,
He is so cute.
I wonder
What my pup is doing?
He is playful.
I fear when I have to clean up
Because I can make a big mess!
I giggle when something is funny.
I laugh a lot!
I think about my family.
I care deeply for them.
If you knew me,
Then you would know why…
Paola Hernandez, Grade 5
Orange Glen Elementary School

War Begins
One day the war began.
The families were screaming in fright.
I don't want to see the enemies tonight.
If I do I'll hold on tight
And not scream in fright.
All I have to do is lay calm
In my hiding spot
Where I'll be bombed.
Jack Schultz, Grade 5
Granada Elementary School

Yosemite National Park
An exciting ride
Beautiful fresh splashing waterfalls
Interesting mountains
Excitement of the biggest trees in North America

Get there and setting up the tent in the refreshing wind
Getting to hear the most beautiful sounds of singing birds
The pleasure to go rafting with your family
Seeing great views of waterfalls
Hiking up the mountains

Feeling the breeze while hiking up a waterfall
Glacier Point is the most beautiful mountain
Seeing the most gentle deer
Furious and roaring bears
Finally the beautiful night sky

Gilberto Pena, Grade 6
St Linus School

Singing Joy
Joy sings only sweet songs
And her brown eyes light up with each pure note
A short dress falls
Down to her knees
And an old pair of old, woven, brown sandals on her feet
And a content smile on her face

She spends her free time finding small sweet things to nibble upon
She has seen busy honeybees
Creating rich golden honey
And singing birds finishing nesting

But Joy remains naïve
She has never met Grief
And when he is spoken of
She quickly leaves the room

Megan Phelps, Grade 5
Hawthorne Elementary School

The Christmas Days
We hang the stockings next to the tree,
jumping around, filled with glee.
Hoping for candy and holiday joy,
asking for games and also some toys.
The tree is green with sparkling lights,
so it will be pretty during the night.
We had a healthy dinner in our tummies,
except for the cookies which are very yummy.
When we got tucked in to go to bed,
our mother calmed us by rubbing our heads.
The next day, we ran out of the sheets,
hoping for gifts and wonderful treats.
We ripped the paper, smiling the entire way,
and as it went on, it became a great day.

Justine Cooper, Grade 6
Carden Academy of Santa Clara

Crystal Clear
Its world starting out slowly
Quickly changing direction
Swerving and turning,
Moving like a snake
Frigid and ominous
Hidden secrets,
Breaking to the surface
Scenery slowly slipping by
A veil of trees, hidden from the sun
Gradually churning its water from crystal clear
Then dissolving into brown
The sound of my laughter
Silently slipping through cracks
Slapping against rocks, gaining speed
Pulling me farther and farther from where I began
Building up until the end
Then once again slowing down
Breaking its waves for the last time
Splash, splash
Then disappearing into the shadows
Becoming quiet and still once again

Megan Oppenheim, Grade 6
The Mirman School

Books
I wonder where I am
I hear creatures chattering, squawking
I see fairies dancing in the moonlight
I am in an unknown jungle
I pretend I know where I'm going
I feel lonely, afraid
I worry that I'm the only person here
I cry, waiting for someone to come
I am falling into a deep, dark slumber
I understand that my family must be worried about me
I try to not feel homesick
I hope the readers of this poem know that
I am not lost, just reading a book in bed

Megan Ho, Grade 6
Chinese American International School

My Dogs Joe and Jerry
When I got them they weren't too small,
But instead, very tall.
They didn't shrink,
But they did sing to the winking moon.
When we would go to the roaring beach
They would go wild to see the pouring water.
But then came a day, a very sad day.
They went to live in the mighty Santa Cruz.
Hope they enjoy their mornin' "cruz."

Oh how I miss you,
Joe and Jerry.

Dean Skinner, Grade 5
Our Lady of Mount Carmel School

Jorge Perez

Jorge Perez was kind;
He was mine;
He helped me shine.
Jorge Perez!

Jorge Perez was patient;
He was in the nation;
He was a sensation.
Jorge Perez!

Jorge Perez liked to read at night;
He had a short height;
He would enjoy riding a bike;
He liked to rest at night.
Jorge Perez!

Jorge Perez liked to read books;
He had some good looks;
He knew how to cook.
Jorge Perez!

Jorge Perez was my father;
He was my hero;
A person that I will love, care, miss, and remember forever.
Jorge Perez!

Astrid Perez, Grade 6
St Martin-in-the-Fields School

If I Were in Charge of the World*

If I were in charge of the world
I would protect stray animals,
Homeless families from the cold,
Soldiers from getting hurt and
Older people from feeling lonely.

If I were in charge of the world
There wouldn't be any homework,
Candy and toys wouldn't cost a cent,
No chores and
No alarm clocks to wake you.

If I were in charge of the world
You wouldn't have to read,
Study or do projects,
There wouldn't be any surprise quizzes or tests and
Recess would be extra long

If I were in charge of the world
Lunch would include a piece of chocolate and pizza every day,
School would have lots of short days,
We would have lots of movie passes,
We would have more holidays and vacations.

Adrianna Borgatello, Grade 6
St Raphael School
*Patterned after Judith Viorst

Ode to Poetry

I feel you are different animals
Each animal having its own personality
Haiku, chicks,
Small and short
Sonnets, snakes,
Big and long
Acrostic poems, giraffes
Standing tall and straight
Concrete poems, are the monkeys,
Making different shapes for the poem
Finally, the Odes, the dogs,
You'd probably have strong feelings about those poems.
O', we'll never run out,
Of different kinds of poetry to write
O', the wonders of poetry.

Justin Kim, Grade 6
Chinese American International School

My True Day

Summer days are warm,
Winter days are cold.
Bees will swarm as the days grow old.

I might play every day,
No matter what, I will play anyway.

Stars will come out at night,
Angels sing till it's bright.

Ladybugs might land on me,
I could be lucky can't you see.

When skies are gray or your day is blue,
Smile and make the day you would want to be true.

Sarah McGraw, Grade 6
Our Lady of Guadalupe School

When Christmas Is Near…

When Christmas is near,
Oh how the kids cheer!
To think about presents,
They'll get when Christmas is near.
They think about puppies, bunnies and birds,
All of them on the Christmas lists.
Oh Santa will be busy
Writing letters, grooming reindeers.
And so will his elves, making toys, and loading Santa's sleigh.
When Christmas Eve is here,
Children asleep, prancing reindeer on the roof,
But all is silent on Christmas Eve.
Christmas Day is here,
Opening presents, shouting for joy,
May all be merry on Christmas Day.

Angela Huang, Grade 4
CB Eaton Elementary School

Winter
Winter
Cold, cloudy
Slipping, skiing, sledding
Frosty weather is exciting
Season
Lucas Billot, Grade 4
Heather Elementary School

Snowflake
Snowflake
Freezing, delicate
Falling, settling, covering
Hides the whole city
Unique
Jasper Bodamer, Grade 4
Heather Elementary School

About Work at Home
Homework
Hard, easy
Learning, reading, doing
Math is a great
Subject
Alyssa Charette, Grade 5
St Louis De Montfort School

Snow
Snow
Snowmen lay
Sledding, snowball fighting, skiing
Making snowballs in snow
White
Lexi Brown, Grade 4
Proctor Elementary School

The Pollinators
Bees
Buzzy, ready
Flying, gliding, diving
Always pollinating a flower
Mighty
Matthew Reyes, Grade 5
St Louis De Montfort School

Cha-Ching!
Money
Green, paper
Buying, spending, earning
Save it for college
Cash
Matthew Wingerden, Grade 5
St Louis De Montfort School

I Am
I am an imaginative adventurer
I wonder how many places I will go to when I become an adventurer
I hear my heart pumping as I jump over the broken bridge
I see the crumbling rocks as the old temple collapses
I want the treasure and see the shining gold
I am an imaginative adventurer

I pretend that I am running from the people who want my gold that I found
I feel the sweat running down my skin from all the traps
I touch the golden treasure, smooth as silk
I worry that I will get trapped from the terrifying booby traps
I cry that I will not get the gold and get trapped there forever
I am an imaginative adventurer

I understand that being an adventurer is tiring work
I say that being an adventurer is so risky and exciting
I dream to be the best adventurer ever
I try to get the shimmering gold from the people who will steal it
I hope that I will also get someone to help me on my adventures
I am an imaginative adventurer
Timmy Wong, Grade 5
Lydiksen Elementary School

Blue
Blue
Blue is the feeling in your mouth after eating a blueberry muffin for a snack.
Blue sounds like the swirling wind on a hot summer day.
Blue is the sound of the water running in the shower.
Blue is the color of the peaceful and beautiful pond.
Blue is the taste of ice cream rolling into your mouth.
Blue is the feeling of when you're sad or when you lose a baseball game.
Blue smells like the fresh food from the farmer's market.
Blue looks like the never-ending sky up there.
Blue feels like the freezing ocean water splashing your feet.
Blue looks like my best friend's shirt shining proudly.
Blue is the coldness of an ice cube.
And *Blue* is the color that is peaceful and lovely.
Connor Lin, Grade 4
Heather Elementary School

The Forest
Peacefully, gracefully, and quiet
All you hear is water falling from a waterfall up high in the sky,
Get close, see and feel water crashing on rocks
And little drips of water on your face like mist feels refreshing
Birds chirping a wonderful song with good melodies as true as singers do
Animals making noises as they play along with each other,
Having the time of their life
You will see cuddly cute baby animals that are scaly and furry,
Trees growing, big and strong
Trees that give us oxygen to breathe
What a wonderful place to be, and cool place to explore,
You should not cut down trees because
They are a big part of the forest and help us breathe
Kyara White, Grade 5
Juarez Elementary School

High Merit Poems – Grades 4, 5 and 6

Yarn
Warm and fuzzy balls
comes from sheep that we adore
makes a lovely scarf
Evah Campbell, Grade 4
Anderson Valley Elementary School

Sharks
Sharks are very fast
They live in deep waters
They have gills to breathe.
Ryan Torrez, Grade 5
Our Lady of the Rosary School

Daisies
Daisies are pretty.
They are very colorful.
They also smell good.
Daisy Arauz, Grade 5
Our Lady of the Rosary School

Winter
Snowy and fluffy
White and cold and fun and nice.
Beautiful time.
Jozeph Ruelas, Grade 5
Our Lady of the Rosary School

It Is Christmas Time
It is Christmas time
I want it to be snowing
The ponds are frozen.
Joey Mattson, Grade 4
Coyote Valley Elementary School

Winter Is Here
Winter is here now.
I like the cold icicles.
I like hot cocoa.
Chloe Khoury, Grade 4
Coyote Valley Elementary School

Winter
Winter icicles
they're like crystals in the snow
then they melt away.
Sean MacDonell, Grade 4
Coyote Valley Elementary School

Winter
Winter time is here.
Snowflakes and frost are falling.
It is time to cheer.
Alejandra Pineda, Grade 4
Coyote Valley Elementary School

Endless Days
What is this now, my eighth month here?
Perhaps it does not even matter.
For soon, it will by my turn to be taken away on the stretcher of twenty.
What I need now is a shoulder to cry on.
But my parents are gone and my sister would think I am being a baby.
I know deep inside she feels the same way,
For no one can escape the sadness of this joyless hellhole.
Beth, my sister, is the only friend I have, even though I sleep on a bed with ten others.
They are all sick, and now I think I am coming down with something.
Oh what I would do to taste something other than a raw potato!
If I close my eyes, I can hear the tasty crunch of a ripe, firm apple, picked just for me.
Just the other day I saw a man beaten to death but he had done nothing wrong.
It really was a horrible sight to see blood squirting out everywhere.
I remember seeing his arm broken and twisted backwards.
Despite all of the cruelty that surrounds me each day,
I still have hope of getting out and going back to my home town.
The two of us, my sister and I, would be living a happy life.
We would not have to worry about the ruthless Nazis.
But that is just a "maybe" for now.
I wait here writing letters, hoping one day someone will read them and feel what I felt.
After what I think has been about eight months here.
Ryan Berkowitz, Grade 6
Lindero Canyon Middle School

Alpine Rime
A white that fills the sky, bone chilling, yet heart warming
Forests of plenty, mountains of majesty in this area they all reside
The green sprouts of life that penetrate the ivory shroud
Light catching the crystals of frost as they tumble down from the heavens
The wind blowing through the echoing forest
Clouds snuff out the sun like a candle and awaken the gelid adversary
Ancient trees, tall and wise whisper to the wild
Humanity and wilderness, a thin border in between
Chaotic yet calm in this enveloping region
The white shadow covering the lake as it tries to break through
It all comes together in harmonious symphony
The man on the moon looks down on this locale
And smiles at all of the brilliant splendor
Mammoth Mountain holds all this glory
Josh Friedman, Grade 6
The Mirman School

Orange
Orange is like a tiger searching for its prey.
Orange smells like my dad's remarkable pumpkin pie.
Orange tastes like the bubbles in your throat after a nice glass of orange juice.
Orange feels like the radiant silk of water flowing through my hands.
Orange sounds like music bouncing from one ear to the other.
Orange looks like a young little orange cricket pouncing through the long blades of grass.
Orange is the sun, moon and stars.
Orange is when you first wake up in the morning.
Orange is the feeling of my cat's soft, silky and welcoming fur.
Orange is the smell of a pizza that just came out of the oven.
Orange is me.
Summer Dow, Grade 4
Heather Elementary School

The Ocean
Shimmering blue water
Creatures of the sea
Luscious pearl in an oyster
Waves clashing on shore
Tiny pebbles patting the sea
Fish blowing out bubbles
Jellyfish as pink as a flamingo
Boats in the middle of the sea
Seagulls swooping down to fish
Dolphins swimming at sunset
Monica Meza, Grade 6
Gardner Street Elementary School

Alone Is Sad
Alone is sad.
I lost my dog when I was six.
We were going to move.
We left her at my grandmother's.
She left to find me.
Alone is sad.
A month after that my uncle died
Alone is sad
I lost my dog and my uncle
Alone is sad.
Jorge Peña, Grade 4
Lankershim Elementary School

The Mouse in the Basement
I was enjoying a warm summer day,
My family was quite gay,
I had a chore to do,
In the basement is where I was due,
I crept down the stairs,
It was by the chairs,
A small mouse as cute as a button,
Was nibbling on a piece of mutton,
He still lives there now,
By a small wooden cow
Devrath Das, Grade 6
Carden Academy of Santa Clara

Earth
Why so blue?
What have you been doing?
How can we make you feel new?

My surface is covered by water.
I'm floating here in space
With my other eight planet friends.

You can help me
By recycling.
Robert Vartazarov, Grade 6
Gardner Street Elementary School

If You Knew Me…
If you knew me
You would know
I dream of being a Veterinarian or
A Zoologist
Because some animals may become extinct!
How can I help preserve them?
I would love to take care of
All kinds of animals.
I wonder
How to become an animal doctor?
I adore animals
But fear mice, snakes, and spiders.
Some bite and
Others are poisonous!
I giggle
When tickled on my stomach.
If you knew me
Then you would know…
Lily Prado, Grade 5
Orange Glen Elementary School

If You Knew Me…
If you knew me,
You would know that
I dream of cotton candy.
It's sweet, fluffy, and sticky.
I wonder about stars,
Sometimes
I see constellations.
Sometimes,
I don't.
I fear
Spiders!
Like the big black one
On my wall
Yesterday
At home
Until, Mom eliminated it.
If you knew me,
Then you would know why…
Khloe Brinegar, Grade 5
Orange Glen Elementary School

Christmas
I remember
the snow falling
I remember
Santa coming
I remember
presents under the tree
I remember
family coming
I remember
CHRISTMAS
Alise Everton, Grade 5
Northside Elementary School

Book
Why are you so quiet?

What are you doing
In the dusty corner, all alone?

Don't you want to
Just let it out?

I'm quiet because
My friends are torn.
And it's like
No one cares and now I'm scared
To think the same
Will happen to me.

I'm in the corner all alone
Where no one can see me.

I do want to just let it out
To many people,
But they might not listen to me.
Sheree Mizell-Williams, Grade 6
Gardner Street Elementary School

If You Knew Me…
If you knew me
You would know that
I dream of being a teacher,
Because I love school.
Or I may be a teller in a bank,
For I love to count
Money and coins!
I wonder how we can
Protect the Earth?
I don't want our planet
Dirty and unhealthy.
I fear rats.
They are gross and ugly.
I giggle when people say
Funny things,
Especially hilarious jokes.
I think about what I will do
This vacation
Legoland or Disneyland?
Eeny, meeny, miney, moe!
If you knew me then you would know…
Yissel Reyna, Grade 5
Orange Glen Elementary School

Summer
Warm, breezy
Diving, roasting, swimming
Having fun in the pool.
Vacation
Jaime Mendoza, Grade 5
Our Lady of the Rosary School

Raining

The rain is falling
I escape from the wetness
See the rain drop down

Anna Hendrickson, Grade 5
Lydiksen Elementary School

Bulls

strong horns bucking loud
I ride them at rodeos
furious intense

Tanner Stone, Grade 4
Anderson Valley Elementary School

Sunflower

Exotic petals
on the tallest sunflower
dance on Western Winds.

Lester Balsells, Grade 6
Gardner Street Elementary School

White Diamonds

The white diamonds fall
during winter's riches, snow
covering the world.

Richard Ridjan, Grade 6
Gardner Street Elementary School

Butterfly

Butterfly flying
In the stormy blowing wind
Exploring the world.

Daniel Radilla, Grade 5
Our Lady of the Rosary School

Christmas

Birth of Jesus Christ.
The night on which He was born.
We all celebrate.

Javier Acevedo, Grade 5
Our Lady of the Rosary School

Sun

Shiny, yellow, ball
Surrounding my little home
Comes out right in time

Marlen Ferreyra, Grade 4
Anderson Valley Elementary School

Trees

strong, tall, climb for fun
green and brown oval orange leaves
food for animals

Blake Sanchez, Grade 4
Anderson Valley Elementary School

Chaos and Peace

Chaos and Peace
3:26PM
The hallway is silent, nothing moves
3:27PM
A growing feeling is rising in everyone
3:28PM
The feeling is stronger and it is becoming too powerful
3:29PM
The feeling is too strong to hold in
3:30PM
Suddenly, the doors open and students come flying out of everywhere
The original peace is then replaced by sudden chaos
Shouting and talking students rush to leave
Pushing and shoving is the only way out
3:40PM
The normal silence has overthrown the chaos
There is no sign of the earlier chaos
Chaos and Peace
Exact opposites
Yet intertwined in a unique way

Peter Huang, Grade 6
Chinese American International School

Elusive Island

I am Mauna Loa, passionate, fervent. Ideas surging within me
Fermenting, churning, building with intensity
Then flowing, unstoppable
'til quenched by the sea

I am the morning tide, a wave of calm, a constant cadence
A potent presence that pounds the sand, but knows to retreat from the shore
Challenging the surfer, tickling the toes
A tingle of turquoise, an invigorating spray

I am the Kohala cliffs, standing my ground, blessed with perspective
Tower of strength, guarding green meadows
Behind every rock, another surprise
With no stone unturned, no question unanswered

I have the irrepressible urge to create like Mauna Loa,
The steady strength of a refreshing morning tide,
The complexity of the Kohala Cliffs
I am an elusive island,
but accessible when earnestly explored

Benjamin Baraad, Grade 6
Lindero Canyon Middle School

Happiness

Happiness is when you see someone you love so much for the very first time.
When a miracle happens that no one can stop from becoming reality.
So never give up for what is bad now will become happiness soon.
When that day comes you will look up into the sky and smile.
You will remember all the bad things that happened.
Then you finally realize that it made you who you are today.

Theresa Partida, Grade 6
St Linus School

Sweet Rainforest
Fresh rainforest shines,
Spiders weave webs silently,
Sloths hang in deep sleep.
Alaman Diadhiou, Grade 4
The Mirman School

Kilimanjaro
Trees rustling in wind.
Ice pools fill with cool water.
Kilimanjaro.
Rane Tzeng, Grade 4
The Mirman School

Rainbows
Rainbows reflect light
Vapor hovers over lakes
Fog dissolves in air
Chaz Cotton, Grade 4
The Mirman School

The Sun
The sun warms the air.
Green grass sways gentle fields.
Kids play in water.
Alexandra Goldstein, Grade 4
The Mirman School

The Garden
Smiling oranges.
The hose runs, tickling pears.
Sun bakes bananas.
Nikolas Chapas, Grade 4
The Mirman School

Wolves
Wolves fierce and burly
They cannot be taken down
A great meat eater
Joe Meyerson, Grade 4
The Mirman School

Fall
Crispy crunchy leaves
Change colors through the season
Falling to the ground
Jordan Yadegar, Grade 4
The Mirman School

Imagination
Dreams its creation.
A source of entertainment.
A powerful tool.
Matthew Robinson-Wrobel, Grade 6
Carden Academy of Santa Clara

Gas Lamps and Stars
Gas lamps burning, neon eyes glaring,
Pools of harsh commanding beams, on the dunes of cement and broken dreams
Cars and a motorcycle rushing past, cat meows and a train does blast
The darkness, the pulsing veins of night, connecting the blaring pumpkins of light
My eyes, gazing up, up, up to the night, my mind, my heart, fleeing noise into flight,
Free of the bondage of the lights and the sounds,
Free to roam…
So many fading stars, so many scattered dreams,
Crushed hopes, dying, dying by harsh rules, so it seems
All the love and understanding,
Where is it?
Maybe this world that I have known — this world where love and hate are sown,
Maybe it's a jar, a jar where all
Love and Anger, Luxury and Slavery, Care and Neglect,
Maybe, this jar is where all souls are kept,
Where dreams are born and over promises wept
Maybe
Perhaps the moon, it's a hole to escape
Outside, who can tell? Is it another world like this?
Or is it heaven? It will not, it cannot be the same,
But maybe, just maybe, it can be better.
Grace Park, Grade 6
Jane Lathrop Stanford Middle School

Pink
Pink is the color of a piglet that was just born.
Pink feels like a pig that just took a mud bath.
Pink is the smell of a cupcake that just came out of the oven.
Pink sounds like a bee buzzing when a hungry bear attacks.
Pink tastes like watermelon when a wave of heat strikes.
Pink looks like a rabbit when it pops out of a magic hat when everyone is sad.
Pink is the color of a rose when it blooms from the ground.
Pink is the feeling when you won the spelling bee.
Pink is the smell when you take a cake out of the oven.
Pink is the sound when mice take your cheese.
Pink tastes like lemonade when a heat wave strikes.
Pink looks like a dragonfly's wings when the sun shines.
And pink is the feeling when a baby girl is born.
Sara McNevin, Grade 4
Heather Elementary School

Violet
Violet looks like a dove floating on a silver lake.
Violet sounds like the water faucet turning on.
Violet smells like fresh April flowers.
Violet tastes like fluffy white marshmallows.
Violet feels like sand under your bare feet.
Violet looks like cool water pouring into a tall glass.
Violet sounds like the flapping of a humming bird's tiny wings.
Violet smells like salad on a hot and humid summer day.
Violet tastes like juicy, sweet blackberries waiting for you in the fridge.
Violet feels like rain soaking into your boots.
Violet sounds like the soft pitter-patter of raindrops on a car window.
And violet is a color that is calm and peaceful.
Emma Petersen, Grade 4
Heather Elementary School

If I Were in Charge of the World*

If I were in charge of the world
I'd destroy all schools so all kids can have freedom
And stop all wars so there would be peace

If I were in charge of the world
There'd be more soccer
Dogs would be important
And no more bullies

If I were in charge of the world
You would have desserts for dinner
You would not have sickness
The economy would not be bad
No abortions or killing
And no stealing

If I were in charge of the world
Everything would be free
Video games would be everywhere
Nobody homeless or poor
No more loneliness
My world would be awesome
If I were in charge of the world

Nicolas Zepeda, Grade 6
St Raphael School
*Patterned after Judith Viorst

When the Pilgrims Came

When the Pilgrims came to town,
They all gathered around.
With many, many foods to eat,
They had a magnificent, enormous feast.
An amazing feast that couldn't be beat.

When the pilgrims came to town,
They set foot on the ground
That no one had ever seen,
For the ground was so green,
There was no trash, it was so clean.

When the pilgrims came to town,
In front of their eyes was the land they had found.
The first sound they heard was a beautiful sound,
A sound that had never been heard before
It was the wind but there was much more.

When the pilgrims came to town,
They had all smiles, no frowns.
For that land was theirs, for a short time,
But they were penniless no quarters, no dimes.
Thanksgiving, Thanksgiving.

Cypress Toomey, Grade 4
The Mirman School

Friends Are with You

When I first met you, I was happy.
You were nice, you were very friendly.
You were by my side when I stole from you.
You got angry,
but you were always by my side.
When you meet someone who you have a lot in common with,
you hope you stay friends forever.

Rashaud Johnson, Grade 5
Granada Elementary School

Sports

Playing sports is lots of fun
I like to spend time in the sun
After each game we all get a treat
Usually it is something delicious to eat
Then after it is done we all go home all stinky
Once I got home I heard my baby brother spit out his binky
So for next time I'll be sure to have fun in the sun and eat my treat.

Jared Gassman, Grade 6
Our Lady of Guadalupe School

Ocean

An ocean dreams of traveling across the world
An ocean remembers the animals that lived one million years ago
An ocean moves up and down with waves crashing
An ocean promises to be powerful
An ocean vacations in the clear blue sky

An ocean is a sign of undersea life

Ryan Ostrovsky, Grade 4
Laurence School

Mountain

I always like to see the snow blow.
It is so white and bright.
While I ski I feel free.
When we get up in the trees we began to freeze.
It's always fun in the winter sun.
When we go on trails we don't do the rails.
When skiing's done it's no fun.

Micah Ray, Grade 5
Eastwood Elementary School

I Wish

I wish I could fly, so high in the sky
I wish I could breathe in the sea
I wish I could talk to beautiful flocks, of geese and swans and ducks
I wish I could grab a wishing star
To make all these wishes come true
But I wish I was normal, and wishing these wishes come true
I wish wish wish wish

Emily Bakewell, Grade 5
Northside Elementary School

Railroad Museum
Railroad Museum
Big, interesting
Riding, steaming, moving
Railroad museum is interesting
Museum
Joshua Anguiano, Grade 4
Proctor Elementary School

Snow
Snow
Cool, fluffy
Snowboarding, sledding, skiing
Snow is extremely cold
Chilly
Caitlin McCuaig, Grade 4
Proctor Elementary School

Sutter's Fort
Sutter's Fort
Big, white
Walking, living, talking
The man was happy
Home
Aaron Lim, Grade 4
Proctor Elementary School

State Capitol
State Capitol
Really big
Learning, looking, touching
Everybody is happy
The Capitol building
Mario Martinez, Grade 4
Proctor Elementary School

Best Friends!!!
Best friends are funny.
Best friends are great people.
Best friends help you out.
Best friends will always be there for you.
Who's your best friend?
Elisabeth Roy, Grade 6
Grant Elementary School

Candy Land
Candy Land
Sweet, chewy
Yummy, tummy
It's fun with my buddies
Candy World
Esmeralda Prieto, Grade 4
Proctor Elementary School

Presidential Serenity
There is a certain magical experience when visiting this east coast territory
It is the birthplace of our evolving American story
Washington was the proprietor of this sprawling manor
To construct this democratic country, he was one of the primary planners

After leading the American Revolution to secure a new homeland
Washington became the father of our country on the ground where visitors stand
Feelings of awe swiftly embrace each spellbound guest
It is remarkable how one man successfully led the country to pass the ultimate test

Standing on the wharf of the peaceful Potomac is like stepping into a history book
The stunning rolling hills and natural beauty deserve a second look
It is now easy to see why Washington chose to reside here instead of D.C.
Among acres of green gardens and unspoiled land spotted with towering trees

The bed where Washington died is on display for all to see
It is dressed in fine linens, just as it used to be
It is easy to picture him lying there, gasping, as he took his last breath
On a wet, windy winter's day on December fourteenth

Inspirational thoughts descend upon all who admire the striking vistas that surround
Traversing the same worn paths that Washington once strolled around
The luxurious home is meticulously preserved for all to discover
Powerful personal feelings, this historic plot will uncover
Jadon Yariv, Grade 6
The Mirman School

An Aspect of Life
Once I took a walk in a park. It was a very extravagant day.
It was late but, not dark. On the horizon the sun lay.

Then I saw a lonely tree. So, I thought about it for a while.
What if that tree was me? I frowned I could not smile.

I soon would have to be cut down. Made into some wood.
I would soon be lying on the ground. Looking at the place where I once stood.

I thought that was not how it should be. It's evil and unfair.
You might think it's a useless tree. Nevertheless it gives us air.

You should never misjudge a living being. But, it is the circle of life.
Some might think it's mean. But, creatures, they are rife.

So when I stared at that tree today. I thought Earth is a beautiful place.
All I know that from this day, I will keep the Earth safe.
Allison McSwain, Grade 6
Montessori School of Coronna

My Little Brother
I always tell my brother I LOVE him more than TV.
I always tell my brother I LOVE him more than chocolate covered pizza.
I always tell my brother I LOVE him more than recess.
But, no matter how hard I try, I can't LOVE him more than GOD loves him.
Allison Garcia, Grade 6
St Johns Lutheran School

Ode to Calculator

O' calculator,
O' calculator,
You are my useful tool.

I can do incredibly hard equations on you,
Yet you still get the answer for me.

When I'm in doubt,
You are always there for me.

Sometimes friends ask me,
What is 10x10?
I can use you as my reference.

O' calculator,
O' calculator,
You make my best subject math.

Daryl Chen, Grade 6
Chinese American International School

Ode to Flowers

O' flower
You are the art produced by nature
You fill my nose with scrumptious scents
Your colors just blow me away
I pick many kinds of you
I admire your pretty colors
I perfume you
Then I tear you up
To make
Potpourri
I present you with a flourish
To the queen
She exclaims
"Oh my what pretty potpourri"
And puts you
In her
Socks drawer

Sophia Vann-Adibe, Grade 6
Chinese American International School

The Thing I Miss Most

The thing I miss most is when we would go in the trees.
Who's we you see, my grandpa and me.
We went to Train Town,
and we rode your bike,
we went to the park,
and we played and swung on the swings all night.
We washed our dog Spicy, and had a lot of fun,
but now it's all over it's all gone and done.
You left without a goodbye, a kiss or a hug.
You left me here, alone in the sun.
I will always love you and you know that,
but now it's my turn to leave it at that.

Sydney Starke, Grade 6
Grant Elementary School

Prisoner

Like a pearl in a clam I am a prisoner, trapped
Stuck behind a barbed wire fence in a concentration camp
I see people tortured and killed
Children, skin and bones, starving, stealing food
People sick because there is no medicine
I smell the dank air filled with hatred
The foul odor of filthy clothes crusted with sweat
The rancid smell of burning bodies
I hear the cries of babies, calling for their mothers
And the cracking of the whip tearing into bare flesh
I feel the cold, hard ground where I am forced to sleep
My hands callused and blistered from working
The throbbing of hunger in my stomach
I taste the dirt
The dirt which many before me have tasted
The dirt which holds memories of grief, sorrow, and despair
I feel cold, weak, and scared
My hope used to be a radiant candle
Shooting rays of light in every direction
But now it is feebly flickering out
I have such a longing to be home…home

Conrad Wahl, Grade 6
Lindero Canyon Middle School

Green

Green sounds like the Earth working together.
Green looks like grass bursting out of the ground.
Green smells like a flower at its ripest.
Green tastes like you are eating your fruits and vegetables.
Green is the color of money getting spent.
Green feels like bugs passing you in the spring.
Green tastes like a mint in your mouth.
Green sounds like trees whistling in the wind.
Green is the color of leaves on the ground.
Green smells like a freshly mowed lawn.
Green looks like the Earth becoming better.
Green feels like you're rich.
And green is friendly, safe, and alive.

Maia Helterbrand, Grade 4
Heather Elementary School

Best Friends

Best friends are people who are with you always.
Best friends will keep you by their side.
Best friends won't throw you out even if anyone else would.
Best friends will take you in if no one would,
Best friends will feed you if you are hungry,
Give you clothes if you are cold,
Shelter if you are lost, help if you are stuck,
But even if you don't give them a hand,
They always would to you,
Because that is what best friends do.
Best friends will stay together,
BFF = Best Friends Forever.

CaitlinMarie Smith, Grade 6
St Pius X Elementary School

If You Knew Me…
If you knew me
Then you would know why
I dream of going back
To Mexico.
I love their beaches,
The sand, surf, sun, and smiles.
I wonder about my cousin there.
I miss him.
I fear that the hurricane
Will hurt his home.
I often think about returning
To Mexico,
Seeing my family, and
Going to the beach.
If you knew me
Then you would know why…
Francisco Vicente, Grade 5
Orange Glen Elementary School

The Cold City of Gold
The tall, golden towers
stand in front of me
like a range of mountains.
The endless buildings stretch
for eternity.
The cold wind slices through my body.
The skyscrapers seem to sway
and totter in the harsh wind.
The snow crunches under
my feet.
My breath freezes in front of me.
I look up.
I see a forest of buildings and
an army of clouds.
This is my home in the
cold, cold city of gold.
Charlie Thompson, Grade 5
Carlthorp School

Life
Life can be a challenge
  or life can be managed.
Life can be something incredible
  or life can be something regrettable.
Life can be an achievement
  or life can be an agreement.
Life can be tragic
  or life can almost seem like magic.
Life can be something
  or life can seem like nothing.
Life for people is a wish
  it is just like a special gift.
Life is not sad so just be glad
  for what you really have.
Audrie Tapia, Grade 6
Our Lady of the Rosary School

I Don't Know
Why is the world like this
Why is nonsense always near
Why am I even asking
And the answer you get in
Your mind is…
I don't know
Your life like swirling colors
Ferocious angry colors
With calm swaying mellow colors
Always flipping like a pancake
I don't know…I don't know
Life is a question
Answers, beyond in mysteries…
I don't know…
But there's always a chance
And it all starts with I don't know…
Azriel Almera, Grade 5
Juarez Elementary School

A Book
I am a book
short
tall
slimey
and dirty
you shove me
in your backpack
you treat me like a dog
it makes me feel sad
just like a ball
it makes me feel
like your smelly feet
I, this book, would like
to change how you treat me
and if you do
I'll let you read me.
Tayler Perry, Grade 4
Joseph M Simas Elementary School

Thoughts of a Suitcase
I am just a suitcase
I don't like to be shoved
with all kinds of things
like a PSP or
a lot of clothes.
I want to be cleaned out
I am just a suitcase.
I don't want to have
junk or gunk
in the lunch or
with little toys.
I am just a suitcase.
I am sad
so clean me out!
Bryson Berna, Grade 4
Joseph M Simas Elementary School

Rainbows
Appearing with joy
Sparkling in bright sunlight
Disappearing fast
Isabella Soboleski, Grade 4
Anderson Valley Elementary School

Oceans
beautiful, vast, calm,
mysterious animals,
being discovered
James Carlin, Grade 4
Anderson Valley Elementary School

Halloween
Scary, fun, awesome
I love trick or treating WOW
cool, it's fun going out with friends
Grace Martin, Grade 4
St Raphael School

The Leaves
Leaves are lush and green
They are attached to the trees
In autumn they fall
Aleksandar Kalman, Grade 6
Carden Academy of Santa Clara

Index

Abalos, Frances 171
Abbott, Kenny 261
Abbott, Michael 287
Abiol, John Marvy C. 287
Abughrib, Sarah 183
Acevedo, Javier 315
Adam, Austin 305
Adams, Heather 15
Adams, Maryana 294
Addison, Shannon 89
Adeyeye, Adeola 54
Adhiambo, Dulcie 15
Adjei, Russell 179
Afanan, Patool 62
Aguado, Ericka 58
Aguilar, Lizzette 131
Aguilar, Stephanie 233
Aguilera, Joshua 251
Aguilera, Kassandra 161
Aguirre, Perla 183
Ahn, Andrew 245
Akbari, Dorrin 101
Ake, Yesenia 80
Alaniz, Jamie 169
Alarcon, Isaac 186
Albertson, Jill 282
Albizati, Taylor 286
Albor, Karina 169
Albright, Daniel 284
Albright, Madeline 281
Alejandro, Bella 192
Alexander, Caitlin 50
Alexander, Isabella 258
Alexander, Ms. Specialjoy . 176
Allen, Jonathan 130
Allison, Alexa 99
Almaraz, Catherine 102
Almera, Azriel 320
Alonso, Jesenia 271
Altieri, Madeline 94
Altimimi, Norhan 79
Altman, Angela 53
Alvarado, Citlali 72
Alvarado, Edward 266
Alvarado, Elizabeth 80
Alvarez, Beatriz 27
Alvarez, Jocelyn 139
Alvarez, Marcela 98
Alvarez, Samantha 42
Alvarez, Sarah 189
Alves, Maya 204
Amador, Brianna 121

Amarasekera, Kevin 184
Amaya, Alexander 140
Anderson, Daniel 98
Andre, Jeffrey 46
Andrei, Radu 275
Angel, Jessica 206
Anguiano, Joshua 318
Anwar, Zia 123
Aparicio, Carlos 298
Aparicio, Christian 277
Apitz, Alexander 191
Apodaca Morales, Armando 112
Aquino, Anthony 243
Aragon, Destiny 86
Arauz, Asalia 191
Arauz, Daisy 313
Areola, Alexia 118
Arevalo, Neftali 116
Arias, Alex 124
Armijo, Meagan 279
Armstrong, Amanda 127
Arreola, Aticza 45
Arreola, Rafael 65
Arroyo, Jacob 163
Arwine, Shannon 66
Ascencio, Anna 56
Ascencio, David 74
Ashdown, Sarah 275
Attia, Zinab 296
Aulakh, Ravi 175
Aurino, Rachele 285
Avalos, Jessica 158
Avila, Desiree 155
Avila, Lauren 243
Aviña, Daniel 40
Ayala, Leonard 192
Azizollahi, Ronnel 115
Baccus, Shad 235
Bagby, Tessa 301
Bahena, Ana 65
Bailey, Jessica 282
Bakewell, Emily 317
Bakotich, Geena 37
Balderas, Carina 125
Balin, Thomas 281
Balitactac, Corbin 303
Ballesteros, Fernando 177
Balocating, Allison 164
Balocating, Alyssa 250
Balsells, Lester 315
Band, Daniel 115
Banks, Rodney 125

Banovac, Nichole 173
Banuelos, Jazmin 41
Baraad, Benjamin 315
Barahona, Vanessa 285
Baraiya, Surya 214
Barajas, Mark 253
Barba, Edgar 38
Barba, Jorge 306
Barbosa, Alberto 112
Barcenas, Vanessa 172
Barnett, Haley 21
Barnett, Robert 83
Barnett-Magdaleno, Sarah . 42
Barocio, Caridad 176
Barranco, Emely 101
Barreto, Christian 157
Barrett, Allysa 173
Barrios, Jesus 66
Barron, Rachael 160
Barsi, Clint 176
Bartholomew, Brittany 27
Basa, Allison 150
Baskerville, Darion 88
Bayard, Chanel 168
Beall, John Paul 82
Bear, Katie 115
Beasley, Katie 116
Beckman, Aaron 252
Beckman, Zoe 304
Belardes, Caitlin 43
Bell, Dayleon 222
Bell, Gloria 147
Beltran, Fausto 47
Belvin, Jade 202
Bender, Kylie 68
Benitez, David 189
Benjamin, Annabell 141
Bennett, Hayley 159
Bennett, Rebecca 228
Bennington, Shayne 229
Benyam, Nahom 203
Berkowitz, Ryan 313
Berna, Bryson 320
Bernal, Oracio 289
Bernardino, William 262
Berry, Jason 200
Berry, Kasey 131
Betsekas, Jaison 242
Bigler, Hannah-June 123
Bija, Cassandra 249
Biley, Nicole 250
Billberry, Miriah L. 172

Billot, Lucas 312
Birnholz, Daniel 291
Blackwell, Nakia 196
Blagg, Adam 302
Blake, Viviane 209
Blando, Macarena 107
Blank, Batia 291
Blanks, Mya 214
Blasberg, Kelly 236
Bobbitt, Jordan 257
Bodamer, Jasper 312
Bonette, Andie 128
Bongulto, Danielle 255
Borda, Samantha 58
Borelli, Alan 128
Borgatello, Adrianna 311
Borunda, Brianna 109
Bowman, Brandy 143
Boyd, Chelsea 104
Boyer, Adam 84
Boylan, Bridget 139
Bradshaw, Christine G. 216
Braga, Ariana 57
Braga, Nicholas C. 264
Brajkovich, Matthew 227
Brannan, Adelaide 295
Brass, Taylor 68
Bratton, Arianna 180
Brayan, Olivia 68
Bremer, Evan 264
Brinegar, Khloe 314
Brobst, Ryan 232
Brooks, Andy 57
Brosio, Sarah 283
Brothers II, William 73
Brow, Gabby 168
Brown, Darcy 296
Brown, Hannah 198
Brown, Lexi 312
Brown, Luke 185
Brown, Shelby 184
Brown, Taylor 241
Brown, Tiara 283
Brownell, Amber 43
Bruce, James 156
Brunner, Katie 21
Bryan, Caitlin 75
Buchanan, Jordyn 242
Bueno, Karly 44
Bueno, Samantha 136
Bui, Huy 105
Bui, Katie 287

Bultsma, Alex 22
Burdick, Andrew 170
Burdick, Ashley 153
Burgess, Carl 257
Burke, Caitlin 92
Burkhalter, Conner 245
Bustillos, Mia 274
Butler, Brenna 48
Buxton, William 299
Caballero, Esmeralda 141
Cabanez, Jeffrey 60
Cabral, Juan 58
Cadle, Tucker 163
Cadwallader, Jenna 195
Cahill, Kendall 24
Cahn, Naomi 33
Cairns, Victoria 63
Calaustro, Katrina 76
Caldwell, Rebecca 98
Calhoun, Deion 30
Calhoun, Kendra 147
Camacho, Diana 264
Camacho, Miriam 189
Camarena, Joclyn 77
Camargo, Sofia 205
Campbell, Evah 313
Campbell, Kyla Alejandra ... 15
Campos, Kiona 146
Canada, Alyssa 144
Canela, Maria 90
Cantor, Brandon 279
Capilla, Diana 113
Capulong, Roland Theo P. 193
Cardenas, Jennifer 294
Cardona, Karina 244
Cardozo, Lilibeth 223
Caricchio, Morgan 226
Carlin, James 320
Carlon, Nicole 147
Carlson, Hannah 101
Carmona, Giselle 279
Carnevale, Colin 255
Carney, Sarah 252
Carriedo, Andruw 273
Carter, William 227
Carton, Halie 168
Casares, Erica 291
Casarez, Sandra 261
Cash-Colón, Nicolas 284
Castaneda, Cece 51
Castaneda, Johanna 240
Castellanos, Jonathan 225
Castellanos, Monica 206
Castillo, Ulises 23
Castillo, Victor 55
Castro, Alejandra 246
Castro, Joshua 266
Castro, Roy 18

Castro, Salvador 80
Cavin, Rikk 21
Cazares, Alejandra 298
Ceballos, Eric 82
Ceja, Ana Yuliana 198
Cendana, Christian 116
Cervantes, Stephanie 100
Cespedes, Leticia 56
Cespedes, Maricela 51
Cetera, Aislynn 146
Chacón, Amanda 110
Chagoya, Racquel 45
Chairez, Raylene 141
Chamale, Georgina 289
Chambers, Christina 12
Chan, Gary 236
Chan, Leonard 13
Chan, Lihong 261
Chang, Mindy 206
Chang, Vichai 132
Chaouli, Hannah 283
Chaouli, Noah 265
Chapas, Nikolas 316
Chaqueco, Rebecca 47
Charette, Alyssa 312
Chavez, Sarai 249
Chavira, Daniel 23
Chavolla-Zacarias, Laura .252
Chen, Cindy 94
Chen, Claire 201
Chen, Dandan 69
Chen, Daryl 319
Chen, Elaine 304
Chen, Kenny 217
Chen, Lou Y. 222
Chen, Melissa 119
Chen, Stephanie 63
Chen, Xing 23
Chen, Yvonne 261
Chernyetsky, Carolina 200
Chiong, Christopher 101
Chiu, Catharine 127
Chiu, Vivian 56
Christian, Maci 115
Christiansen, Cody 50
Chung, Richard 37
Cintron, Ricardo 190
Ciolino, Cobi Jay 300
Cirincione, KaSea 190
Civirjic, Serghei 99
Clark, Amber 163
Clark, Brandee 100
Clark, Braydon 112
Clark, Jack 98
Clark, Riley 142
Claus, Eric 234
Clausen, Sara 182
Clausen, Sara 210

Cleveland, Allan 232
Clew, Lilly 36
Clifford, Alison 235
Cline, Dallas 143
Clubb, Cesare 127
Cohea, Nicole 186
Cohen, Arick 129
Cohen, Jack 246
Cohen, Nicole 192
Colangelo, Nicole 191
Collins, Cheyenne 178
Colquhoun, Mac 133
Comparato, Carly 241
Compton, Sabrina 93
Conde, Guadalupe 136
Conklin Walker, Elizabeth .. 44
Conlan, Courtney 230
Connell, Audrey 293
Contreras, Adrianna 207
Contreras, Domanique 148
Contreras, Johanna 122
Contreras, Sarah 279
Cook, Connor 281
Coon, Richard 13
Cooper, Ashley 14
Cooper, Garrett 214
Cooper, Jaziah 212
Cooper, Justine 310
Cope, Audrey 308
Coppock, Jules 117
Correa, Lauren 74
Cortes, Lorraine Gail 98
Cortes, Meerlin 12
Cortes, Michael 89
Cortese, Molly 187
Cortez, Kathy 48
Cortez, Melanie 306
Cosimano, Andrew 127
Coson, Kelly 178
Costanzo, Sarah 278
Cotton, Chaz 316
Coughlin, Erin 82
Courtney, Samantha 203
Covarrubias, Natalie 258
Cowlishaw, Natalie 162
Cox, Caitlin 81
Cox, Shelby 169
Crawford, Christin 280
Crawford, Hannah 46
Crawley, Genevieve 27
Cron, Shelby 25
Crosby, Katrina 189
Crouse, Ricquel 231
Cruz, Alexandra 139
Cruz, Brian 25
Cruz, Christa 207
Cuadra, Brianna 40
Cuevas, Erik 284

Cuevas, Karla 131
Cullins, Cooper H. 265
Cutillo, Isabella 270
Czekaj, Natascha 175
d'Avignon, BridgeAnne 175
D'Souza, Angela 212
Daddino, Brendan 200
Damian, Vanessa 144
DaMota, Jessica 246
Dang, Caroline 65
Dang, Jessica 259
Dao, Steven 196
Das, Devrath 314
David, Madison 187
David-Allison, Kiana 302
Davis, Deja 55
Davis, Hannah 124
Davis, Spencer 245
Dawkins, Jaylee 224
De Guzman, Glenn 257
De Guzman, Mark 169
De La Cruz, Geraldo 302
De La Cruz, Magdalena 21
De La Mata, Patricia 39
De la Pena, Joselyn 62
De La Torre, Arturo 210
Deavult, Savanna 247
Delgado, Stephanie 254
Dempsey, Marissa 206
Deng, Bai Hao 308
Denier, Connor 166
Densing, Taylor 153
Dentoni, Lucas 292
Deoudes, Allison 161
Derby, Tiffinee 130
Deshazo, Arieanna 233
Dewan, Shoumyo 94
Dhayanand, Neha 302
Diadhiou, Alaman 316
Diaz, Lizbeth 165
Diep, Anthony 149
Dinh, Hali 147
Do, Brittney 289
Do, Cindy 218
Doebler, Jacen 251
DoLe, Leilani 211
Dolgashev, Sasha 240
Dominguez, Nancy 58
Donyanavard, Jessica 19
Dow, Summer 313
Downing, Giovanna 270
Doynel, Gabriel 299
Dragun, Victoria 129
Duarte, Neftali 103
Duarte, Tristin 149
Dubin, Alexis 75
Duke, Maricela 199
Dull, Dalia 232

Index

Duncan, Emily 120
Durr, Natalie 254
Duval, Christina 241
Earl, Semaj 77
Edmondson-Gooden,
  La Tricia 194
Edwards, Mariah 113
Egan, Danielle 241
Eichelberger, Jamika 108
Elledge, Lauren S. 94
Ellickson, Ethan 280
Elliott-Pope, Bridgid 126
Emery, Billy 293
Englert, Delaney 196
Engquist, Matthew 285
Enloe, Rozene 196
Ennon, Waltanisha 39
Eroles, Nathan 87
Escalera, Oscar 246
Escamilla, Gloria 28
Escobar, Jessica 163
Escobar, Michelle 15
Espino, Franchesca 186
Espino, Taiyadi 296
Espinosa, Erika 156
Espinosa, Maria 181
Esqueda, Johnny 20
Estevane, Amanda 270
Estrada, Robert 92
Etessami, Mazelle 225
Evans, Braydon 245
Evenhaim, Edan 214
Everton, Alise 314
Factor, Virgille 138
Fader, Ester 281
Fang, Jennifer 188
Farquar, Nicole 72
Farr, Gabriella 295
Farrell, Bobby 302
Farris, Madison 188
Fekadu, Abel 119
Fekkes, Cristina 130
Feng, Esther 288
Ferguson, Desiree 56
Ferko, Haley 309
Ferreyra, Marlen 315
Fetters, Katy 83
Fielding, Katey 46
Figueroa, Armando 61
Figueroa, Sua 13
Finley, Kaylin 299
Fisher, Jennifer 228
Flores, Issmene 246
Flores, Mario 28
Flores, Olivia 127
Flores, Raymond 56
Flowers, Walanda 149
Fong, Dion 145

Ford, Adrian 309
Ford, Audrie 158
Ford, Johnathan 219
Forte, Alexandra 126
Foux, Andreah 25
Fowler, Jamie 59
Fox, Autumn 88
Fox, Celeste 307
Franco, Joshua 66
Frank, Jacob 287
Frank, Maddie 107
Franklin, Nia 93
Fraser, Heather 124
Frayle, Estefania 20
Freeman, Briawna 249
Freiberger, Ruth 250
Freiling, Adriana 153
French, Dylan 133
Frichner, James 17
Friedman, Andrew 151
Friedman, Josh 313
Friedman, McKenna 221
Frojelin, Nathan 291
Fry, Emily 23
Fukuzawa, Tricia 300
Fuller, Aixa 274
Fuller, Anthony 305
Fuller, Taylor 218
Funke, Jessica 298
Furano, Olivia 98
Galeazzi, Kaitlyn 128
Galippo, Will 223
Galvan, Dax 280
Galvan, Gabriela 160
Gamez, Alice 203
Gamez, Jackie 129
Ganesh, Sanika 285
Gantman, Isabella 174
Gao, Edward 24
Garcia, Adam 134
Garcia, Alexa 197
Garcia, Allison 318
Garcia, Andy 89
Garcia, Chyanne 274
Garcia, Enoc 52
Garcia, Gabriela 213
Garcia, Gabriela 236
Garcia, Hugo 102
Garcia, Jasson 45
Garcia, Jesse 141
Garcia, Jessica 131
Garcia, Jessica 144
Garcia, Joseph 195
Garcia, Joshua 122
Garcia, Justine 110
Garcia, Kevin 224
Garcia, Ladislado 17
Garcia, Leo 265

Garcia, Maria 100
Garcia, Mark 110
Garcia, Paulina 277
Garcia, Priscilla 69
Garcia, Rosa 162
Garcia, Selena 187
Garcia, Shayla 141
Garcia, Tzirintzi 282
Garcia, Yazaira 127
Garcia, Yesenia 181
Garcia, Ysabella 199
Garibay, Brenda 42
Garman, Dani 134
Garrett, Christine 113
Garrido, Lorena 52
Garza, Hailey 103
Garza, Madeleine 156
Gasper, Braelynn 183
Gasper, Karissa 114
Gassman, Jared 317
Gaston, Melanie 35
Gately, Chris 286
Gattison, KeJae 199
Gaxiola, Antonio Iosefo ... 224
Gayle, Makeda 126
Gaytan, Cristina 109
Geary Lopez, Denis 37
Gehl, Tyler 220
Geldert, Amanda 116
Gelland, Alexander 250
Georgedes, Gabriella 188
Gerlach, Angela 41
Geronimo, Samantha 145
Gerritsen, Jasmine 55
Ghumman, Tinarpan 114
Gibson, Harley 112
Gilstrap, Taylor 66
Gimena, Anabell 201
Gioiello, Mia 253
Gip, Binh 63
Glow, Alexis 281
Gnessin, Talia 111
Gochenour, Dakota 85
Goldberg, Blaire 254
Goldsmith, Benjamin 291
Goldstein, Alexandra 316
Gomez, Adrian 212
Gomez, Audrianna 163
Gomez, Eric 145
Gomez, Rafael 247
Gong, Tiana 163
Gonsalves, Andrew 186
Gonzales, Breanna 113
Gonzales, Colett 227
Gonzales, Joshua 306
Gonzales, Olivia 257
Gonzalez, Alexander 296
Gonzalez, Andrea 50

Gonzalez, Brianna 204
Gonzalez, Fernanda J. 205
Gonzalez, Gabriela 54
Gonzalez, James 188
Gonzalez, Jonathan 76
Gonzalez, Maria 18
Gonzalez, Marisol 104
Gonzalez, Martha 126
Gonzalez, Martin 192
Gonzalez, Oscar 71
Gonzalez, Stephanie 197
Goodman, David 32
Gorder, John 167
Gormly, Tyler 282
Gosal, Jaslin 234
Graber, Edie 247
Graden, Alex 242
Grado, Jenifer 300
Graham, Kelli 199
Graham, Kyle 228
Grant, Karlie 256
Grasman, Autumlace 135
Graves, Isaiah 150
Greco, Gracie 254
Greig, Janessa 140
Griffith, Abriana 64
Grimaldo, Daniel 101
Grimes, Mitch 26
Grindeland, Andrew 180
Grissom, La Dra 16
Grodzicki, Reece 260
Gu, Emily 104
Gu, Kathleen 272
Guajaca, Joseph 140
Guerrero, Diana 260
Guerrero, Elycia 284
Guerrero, Ivan 67
Guerrero, Joseph 85
Guerrero, Savannah 106
Guido, Daniela 188
Guillen, Rosa 264
Guillen, Yesenia 68
Guillod, Grace Gagnier 265
Guintu, Allan 165
Gullen, Gracie 211
Gusenov, Elizabeth 266
Guseva, Olga 305
Gutierrez, Branden 17
Gutierrez, Gabriel 218
Gutierrez, Karla 227
Gutierrez, Katrina 57
Gutierrez, Milca 208
Guzman, Kayla 129
Guzman, Michael 249
Ha, Teresa 226
Haffermann, Kyle 187
Hager, Emma 100
Hajjali, Mirna 26

Hall, Kayley 129	Hong, Rachel 292	Judulang, Brandon 60	Lam, Nathan 271
Hamilton, Chloé 77	Hong, Rayson 45	Juinio, Marielle 209	Lam, Toby 267
Hanafi, Cassie 157	Hoops, Rachel 119	Julian, Jeffrey 120	Lambert, Charles 76
Hancock, Sierra 200	Hopson, Madeline 235	Julius, Lauren 204	Landers, Adrian Morgan 29
Hang, Caroline 132	Horner, Bryton 161	Jutamulia, Ivan 303	Langarica, Consuelo 173
Hansen, Mary-Frances 129	Horton, Christina 98	K., Francesca 277	Lanini, Stephine 301
Hansom, Matthew 280	Hosepian, Chandler 193	Kahly, Yasmine 206	Lanman, Bailey 251
Hardin, Megan Suzanne ... 220	Hou, Emily 296	Kalantarian, Annie 295	Lano, Janine 179
Harger, Joshua C. 299	How, Justine 145	Kale, Kellie 296	Lara, Nancy 165
Harmer, Elizabeth 205	Howard, Houston 49	Kalman, Aleksandar 320	Lara, Wendi 278
Harris, Sarah 111	Howard, Julia 262	Karis, Nikolaos 249	LaRocca, Andrew 271
Hart, Reya 91	Howard, Kezia 35	Karis, Samantha G. 202	LaRoche, Kasha 223
Hartley, Hudson 104	Howard, Sierra 165	Katz, Lauren 38	Lasater, Kyle 101
Harvey, Ashley 138	Hsieh, Olivia 142	Kayfez, Jaclyn 215	Lasconia, Mayson 105
Hastings, Abbie 289	Hu, Zoe 123	Kebbas, Nicholas Lee 49	Latch, Laura 180
Haynes, Brenton 35	Hua, Kha 296	Keil, Chabree 190	Laub, Shannon 113
Hearn, Kaitlin 108	Huang, Angela 311	Kelly, Courtney 128	Law, Beverlyn 187
Hechanova, Brian 19	Huang, Darren 264	Kelson, Hannah 273	Lawrence, Brittney 94
Hegwood-Kyle, Josh 25	Huang, Peter 315	Kerford, Colin 31	Lazos, Tiffanie 59
Heimuli, Fatai 306	Huatran, Sunny 81	Kessler, Brooke 216	Le, Alex 206
Helm, Brooke 42	Hudson, Hailey 27	Khalife, Florence 280	Le, Anna 46
Helterbrand, Maia 319	Hughes, Faith 174	Khoury, Chloe 313	Le, Davina 155
Hendrickson, Anna 315	Hulsey, Abby 152	Khuat, Lisa 226	Lebahn, Taylor 262
Henry, Michael 224	Hurtado, Cody 99	Khurana, Avneet 150	Lee, Angeline 76
Henson, Hannah 223	Hurtado, Sharleene 211	Khwaja, Huda 183	Lee, Erin 198
Hernandez, Denise 130	Hutt, Sarah 60	Kilgore, Larishia 20	Lee, Justin 99
Hernandez, Diana 99	Huynh, Victoria 184	Kim, Andrew 264	Lee, Justin 304
Hernandez, Ethan 149	Hwang, Caelynn 261	Kim, Christina 205	Lee, Kevin 215
Hernandez, Felix 297	Hynes, Kai 275	Kim, Hojun 175	Lee, Nathan 268
Hernandez, Gabriel 167	Ibarra, Lizette 153	Kim, Jason 17	Lee, Pheng 166
Hernandez, Hervin 291	Iida, Kate 191	Kim, Justin 311	Leibig, Miranda 265
Hernandez, Jessie 187	Isaac, Iesha 30	Kim, Stephanie 24	Leicht, Sarah 243
Hernandez, Jose 20	Ishibashi, Julien 228	Klein, Jeromey 256	Leiva, Michelle 169
Hernandez, Kimberly 276	Iskandar, Bree 152	Knight, Ethan 297	Leon, Anthony 286
Hernandez, Lily 137	Ivanovich, Katarina 199	Knott, Ryan 104	Leon, Max 236
Hernandez, Mayted 283	Jackson, Emma 270	Knox, Clelia 251	Leonard, Dana 154
Hernandez, Paola 309	James, Alyssa 33	Koehn, Troy 254	Lerias, Emily 211
Hernandez, Simone 308	James, Jessica 196	Koenig, Nicholas 51	Lerouge, Thomas 208
Hernandez, Stephanie 179	James, Jonathan 290	Kornguth, Tyler 298	Letson, Emma 212
Hernandez, Victoria 85	James, Shelby 236	Kouyoumdjian, Chloe 261	Leung, Jocelyn 276
Hernandez, Yadira 34	Janett, Natalie 272	Kovacevich, Jacob 206	Leung, Melinda 155
Herndon, Sage 258	Jang, Aram 47	Kozloyan, Elmast 83	Leung, Serina 104
Herrera, Crystal 102	Jaramillo, Evelyn 17	Krane, Madeline 266	Li, Leo 301
Herrera, Logan 284	Jardeleza, Veronica 114	Krassel, Melanie 240	Ligh, Kimmi 72
Herrera, Miranda 279	Jarvis, Eric 194	Krider, Gus 141	Lim, Aaron 318
Herrmann, Amy 295	Jenkinson, Gabriel 309	Kromrey, Alex 104	Lim, Susie 309
Herrmann, Chelsea 40	Jeong, Jane 304	Kuhns, Carlie 307	Limon, Nestor 19
Hicks, Lejon 86	Jesus, Nieto 136	Kulkarni, Niket 162	Lin, Connor 312
Hicks, Samantha 18	Jimenez, Martin 122	Kuschner, Joshua 266	Lin, Gavin 144
Hijara, Zahraa 271	Johnson, Emily 49	Kushell, Samuel Louis 192	Lin, Kevin 222
Hilbert, Anna 277	Johnson, Gianna 273	Kutagulla, Shanmukh 245	Linares, Aaron 288
Hipol, Gabriel 230	Johnson, Rashaud 317	Kwok, Jessica 204	Lindee, Brooke 114
Ho, Megan 310	Johnson, Richard 156	Lagola, Lucas 256	Lindsay, Desiree 75
Hoang, Nina 203	Jones, Amber 121	LaGuardia, Dereck 135	Listen, Connor 254
Hodges, Madeline 271	Jones, Eryn 150	Laguna, Cinthia 191	Little Turtle, Corina 134
Holmes, Raquel 147	Juarez, Irving 64	Lai, Archibald 193	Litvak, Maya 154
Holt, Brandon 269	Juarez, Jesse 215	Lai, Michael 29	Liu, Joyce 83
Honda, Christopher 132	Juarez, Joshua 126	Lam, Jonathan 274	LiVolsi, Thomas 131

Index

Lizama, Sabrina 90	Magana, Claudia................ 144	Mastro, Juliana 282	Mendoza, Jaime 314
Locke, Claire 107	Magana, Felicia.................. 218	Mataele, Victoria 293	Mendoza, Madison............138
Logan, Dylan..................... 196	Magana, Juan..................... 294	Matthews, Tyler 186	Mendoza, Magdalena........298
Logan, Kyle........................ 50	Mahan, Bethany 193	Mattingly, William 284	Mendoza, Mikala 164
Lombera, Lizzeth 306	Mahoney, Kaylin 57	Mattison, Lamarr 107	Mendoza, Omar 295
Loo, Beverley..................... 166	Maier, Devon...................... 36	Mattson, Joey.....................313	Mendoza, Rene..................124
Lopez, Alexa 299	Maisonet, Franky 214	Maxwell, Kaya 301	Mendoza, Veronica............215
Lopez, Andy 70	Maitra, Neilabjo..................303	Mayoral, Emely 213	Menke, Lee 28
Lopez, Caitlin 39	Malakian, Talar 51	Mazza, Jordan 177	Mera, Courtney 43
Lopez, Charlie 94	Maldonado, Brittany......... 124	Mazzella, Christina 13	Mercado, Jolly Mae 192
Lopez, Cristal..................... 248	Maldonado, Carina 202	Mazzuca, James 171	Mercado, Priscilla 149
Lopez, Emily...................... 298	Malik, Zaynab.................... 167	McCallon, Jaime.................224	Mercer, Niamh 79
Lopez, Esther...................... 33	Mallya, Megha.................... 255	McCallum, Jessica............... 69	Merk, Liana.......................266
Lopez, Jacqueline 13	Manalili, Serena 300	McClellan, Bryar 22	Mesa, Kristen M................. 44
Lopez, Jennifer 156	Mangold, Claire 289	McClure, Cameron..............93	Mesarch, Garin 208
Lopez, Lisette..................... 229	Manjarres, Nicholas........... 308	McCormick, Abaigeal 231	Metz, Kragen 297
Lopez, Miguel 176	Manjarrez, Ashley 130	McCown, Aidan 29	Meyerson, Joe 316
Lopez, Ryan 106	Manjarrez, Justine 110	McCoy, Allie 290	Meza, Monica 314
Lopez, Scarlette 231	Manley, Avery 161	McCuaig, Caitlin 318	Michael, Byron 306
Loughrey, Ryan 69	Mansour, William 257	McDaniel, Jeneva 297	Micheletti, Kimberly 35
Lowe, Robbie 296	Mantikas, Allison 288	McDaniel, Monique 207	Mighell, Sarah 104
Lucas, Justin 231	Manwarren, Justin 140	McDaniels, Korrena 67	Miles, Shontavia 25
Lucey, Sierra....................... 194	Manzo, Olivia..................... 274	McDougald, Elle................. 240	Millan, Alan 146
Luckie, Amaya................... 300	Marcelo, Carol.................... 156	McFarland, Analise 168	Miller, Austin 155
Lugo, Stephanie 133	March, Matthew.................. 81	McFate, Derek.................... 178	Miller, Brianna...................204
Lui, Allysa.......................... 235	Marelli, Jessica 242	McGee, Kevin..................... 286	Miller, Scott 291
Luis, Allison....................... 305	Mares, Ricardo 65	McGrath, Collin 85	Minerales, Sean Ace 278
Luk, Carmen 118	Marin, Gloria...................... 227	McGrath, Heather 69	Miranda, Karissa 255
Lukasik, Tori...................... 255	Marks, Bonnie Jean............. 86	McGraw, Sarah 311	Miron, Carly 214
Luna, Diana 270	Marmolejo, Lily 173	McGruder, Trinity 233	Mistry, Tina 210
Luna, Zaira 56	Marroquin, Kimberly......... 278	McIntyre, Morgan 266	Mitchell, Aaron 94
Luong, Holly 208	Marsh, Ty 118	McKay, Gregory 193	Mitchell, Dalton 236
Luong, Kim 236	Martain, Kayla 256	McKean, Chelsea 90	Mitschke, Nolan 257
Luu, Ai............................... 191	Martez, Maybelline 25	McKeon, Julian 245	Mittal, Aditi 294
Lycan, Jesse 251	Martin, Grace..................... 260	McKim, Samantha.............. 160	Mizell-Williams, Sheree....314
Lyon, Carmen.................... 172	Martin, Grace..................... 320	McKovich, Amanda 14	Mock, Hailey......................226
Lyons, Kelsey 288	Martin, Jack 271	McMahon, Jocelyn 36	Moghavem, Layla 266
Lysaythong, Allen............... 162	Martin, Katelyn 191	McMath, Paige 61	Molina, Angel 209
Lysaythong, Jennifer 39	Martindale, Kelsey 77	McNeill, Meihki 121	Molina, Jennifer 165
Lytle, Michelle 280	Martinelli, Brooke............... 276	McNevin, Sara 316	Molinar, Mia.....................308
Ma, Chris........................... 67	Martinez, Andrea 40	McPhail, Shelby 109	Molony, Tiana 292
Ma, Sabrina........................ 281	Martinez, Camille 265	McSwain, Allison................318	Monge, Elizabeth 24
Ma'a, Landon 277	Martinez, David 114	McTaggart, Marissa............. 181	Monjaras, Ana 172
Mabie, Danielle 76	Martinez, Elizabeth 26	McWilliam, Genevieve 256	Monreal, Nicolle 300
MacDonell, Sean 313	Martinez, Ian 142	Mears, Brandon 108	Montano, Anayeli 117
Macias, Alejandro 218	Martinez, Jonathan............. 41	Mecalco, Ana...................... 71	Montano, Barbara 215
Macias, Enrique 132	Martinez, Kassandra........... 83	Medina, Alondra 117	Montemayor, Samantha.....93
Macias, Savannah............... 103	Martinez, Lizet 106	Medina, Cristian 55	Montgomery, Ashley..........283
Madarang, Janessa.............. 181	Martinez, Magdalena......... 219	Medina, Elizabeth...............47	Montgomery, Audrey.........168
Maddox, Brittney................ 23	Martinez, Mario 318	Medina, Kimberly 134	Montiel, Oriana 116
Madison, Alley L................. 170	Martinez, Rosalinda 175	Mejia, Karina 202	Moody, Kate 182
Madison, Ambyr 28	Martinez, Sara 139	Mekuria, Christian.............. 16	Moon, Christy....................271
Madison, Chloe 14	Martinez, Selina.................. 132	Melancon, Jasmine 198	Moon, Jason 283
Madrigal, Gabriela.............. 245	Martinez Navarro, Tatiana231	Mello, Dennis 254	Moore, Neena 171
Madron, Saraé 209	Martynovich, Maya 246	Menchaca, Samantha........ 110	Moore, Renee 254
Maestas, Jason.................... 25	Mascarenas, Angella 13	Mendez, Carmen 31	Moorman, Keith................. 59
Magaling, Jemm 140	Massey, Mariah 182	Mendez, Crystal..................169	Mora, Fritz........................300
Magallanes, Stephen........... 271	Massimiano, Adam 33	Mendez, Kelly 136	Mora, Katheryne 309

Morales, Martha 16	Nguyen, Khanh 24	Oronoz, Rebecca 20	Pattiz, Joshua 262
Moran, Cliff 272	Nguyen, Mai 100	Orozco, Elsa 179	Pech, Abraham 294
Moran, Jaimie 15	Nguyen, Michelle 170	Orr, Brenna 130	Pechenkov, Litah 264
Morataya, Jorge 119	Nguyen, Michelle 226	Ortega, Alyssa 215	Pecka, Kaitlynn 32
Moreno, David 40	Nguyen, Robert 229	Ortega, Jasmine 204	Peckler, Gretchen L. 292
Moreno, Estefani 283	Nguyen, Sophia 236	Ortega, L. 205	Pederson, Natalie 131
Morones, Gabby 232	Nguyen, Thien Pham 127	Ortega, Patrick 112	Pehrson, Taira 76
Morrell, Annie 32	Nguyen, Tiffany 262	Ortega, Sarina 231	Peiton, Taylor 220
Morris, Breanna 290	Nguyen, Trung 106	Ortega, Spencer 34	Pelaiz, Adam 288
Morris, Devon 259	Nicks, Robert 106	Ortiz, Erika 81	Pelayo, Jackie 297
Morris, Kate 269	Nicolson, Ella 210	Ortiz, Jovanny Avila 43	Pelowski, Melissa 302
Morrisette, Samantha 147	Niehoff, Delaney 151	Ortiz, Kassandra 136	Peña, Diana 212
Morrow, Cameron 111	Nievera, Roni 177	Ortiz, Stephany 213	Pena, Gilberto 310
Morrow, Gabriella 288	Nina 290	Ortiz, Teresa 36	Peña, Jorge 314
Morton, Katherine 106	Nolasco Ramirez, Maria .. 120	Ortiz-Chavez, Elizabeth ... 268	Pena, Rafael 198
Moses, Daisy 218	Noriega, Javier 294	Ostrea, Rheanna 176	Pena, Will 305
Moss, Dean 109	North, Kai 248	Ostrea, Rheanna 206	People, Namiye 308
Moss, Natalie 123	Norton, Henry 293	Ostrovsky, Ryan 317	Pereyra, Alex 297
Mossino, Trent 194	Nossett, Miles 34	Otsuka, Koby 105	Perez, Abigail 50
Mostafavi, Yassmin 164	Nuhaily, Ahmad 279	Ou, Caitlin 301	Perez, Astrid 311
Movaghar, Veeda 299	Nunes, Bryan 85	Ovanessian, Chelsea 60	Perez, Elyse 232
Mulbarger, Freddy 273	Nunez, Antoni 305	Pabloff, Jaden 247	Perez, Gabriella 307
Muller, Kelly Lauren 177	Nunez, Joanna 84	Pacheco, Alex 41	Perez, Jasmine 34
Munoz, Alan 94	Nunez, Liliana 59	Pacheco, Katrina 203	Perez, Jason 196
Murdock, Michael 155	Nuñez, Marissa 249	Padilla, Anthony 64	Perez, Jesse 294
Murillo, Alex 44	Nunez, Rafael 175	Padilla, Bianca 158	Perez, Justin 116
Murillo, Lindsey 110	Nye, Chanel 137	Padilla, Nathalia 142	Perez, Melanie 207
Murphy, Mackenzie 193	Nystrom, Kristen 64	Pahl, McKenna 185	Perez, Micayla 143
Murry, Jean Sue 116	Nzeadibe, Krystal 177	Pahua, Karla 198	Perez, Mireya 119
Musleh, Mahmoud 209	O'Campo, Rosa Alexandra .. 48	Pakro, Daniela 71	Perez, Nayra 159
Myers, Paige 120	O'Hara, Garrett 212	Palacios, Jessica 135	Perez, Rene 189
Nadalet, Caitlin 54	O'Leary, Brianna 32	Palencia, Angelica 190	Perez, Samuel 190
Nadler, Zehava Dalia 196	O'Toole, Michael 181	Palencia, Briana 195	Perez, Veronica 216
Nagarajan, Pranav 112	Ocampo, Amber 143	Palermo, Zane 257	Perez-Stable Husni, Yaul 42
Nair, Nisha 155	Ocampo, Edwin 269	Palma, Diana 308	Perry, Raven 31
Nam, Seung Bo 245	Ocampo, Ezmeralda 308	Pan, Bryan 290	Perry, Tayler 320
Natanzi, Nima 184	Ocampo, Lesley 28	Panbechi, Kiana 164	Peternel, Nicole 112
Natoli, Makayla 246	Ochoa, Natali 109	Pandher, Natalie 278	Peters, Angelo 143
Navarrete, Susana 254	Ochoa, Tania 88	Pang, Christopher 113	Petersen, Emma 316
Navarro, Adrian 48	Ochoa, Vanessa 146	Pang, Ivan 300	Peterson, Selena 92
Near, Cody 26	Ochoa, William 113	Panganiban, Mayleah 269	Pham, An 138
Neimand, Cameron 217	Ognjan, Nikolas 279	Pappas, Georgia 309	Pham, Catherine 244
Nelson, Patrick 190	Ojeda, Jeanine 258	Pappas, Shamiya 245	Pham, My 119
Ng, Justin 153	Okamoto, Alexander 205	Paredes, Beatriz 99	Pham, Nhu 289
Ng, Michael 188	Olazo, Erika 180	Paresa, Kai 170	Pham, Tu 103
Ngan, Yen 167	Oliva, Miguel 58	Paretti, Drake 285	Phan, Jennifer 162
Ngo, Christina 203	Oliveira, Deborah 290	Paris, Jared 47	Phelps, Cole 112
Nguon, Armani 59	Oliver, Reese 300	Park, Grace 316	Phelps, Megan 310
Nguyen, Angelique 175	Oliver, Tyler 176	Park, Joseph 129	Phillips, Brianna 120
Nguyen, Anthony 107	Olvera, Daniel 194	Park, Katie 267	Phun, Gabriel 160
Nguyen, Belle 196	Olvera, Stephanie I 63	Parker, Cydney 202	Phung, David 121
Nguyen, Diana 229	Oppenheim, Megan 310	Partida, Theresa 315	Picho, Breshana 109
Nguyen, Dianna 215	Ordaz, Baysia 274	Partin-Majerus, Taylor 179	Pilarski, Caleb 62
Nguyen, Jennifer Tram ... 116	Ordunez, Alexis 246	Pascua, Taylor 246	Piña, Angel 125
Nguyen, Jenny 279	Oren, Leore 209	Pasqua, Greta 282	Piña, Miguel 170
Nguyen, Jessica 266	Ornelas, Antonio 236	Passantino, Sara 244	Pineda, Alejandra 313
Nguyen, Kendrick 236	Ornelas, Karina 188	Patlan, Cristina 35	Pineda, Kevin 208
Nguyen, Kevin 122	Orona, Nikki 26	Patterson, Oliver 235	Pinski, Amanda 178

Index

Piper, Paige 84
Pitti, Samantha................. 152
Pittman, Hannah............. 297
Pixley, Madelyn 288
Planting, Kate 257
Poch, Nicole 308
Polaha, Henry 242
Ponce, Mark 298
Ponnuswamy, Sakthi 173
Poole, Erik......................... 286
Poon, Tiffany..................... 252
Porfirio, Jossimar................ 40
Porter, Lucas 151
Porter, Wm. Michael 295
Portillo, Elmer 201
Powell, Caitlin.................... 82
Powers, Lauren 270
Prado, Daniel 156
Prado, Lily 314
Prepoutse, Kosta 249
Preston, Darielle 224
Prieto, Esmeralda 318
Prieto, Juan 44
Prom, Darlene 277
Pulido, Erick 270
Punt, Karsyn 304
Punt, Kody......................... 183
Punzel, Esther 284
Purohit, Aashni................. 293
Purviance, Ashley 114
Quevedo, Ryan 215
Quevedo, Sayre.................... 37
Quintana, Leylani 193
Quintero, Anissa............... 150
Quintero, Marlen................ 38
Quinto, Lyric 251
Quizon, Ma. Ariane 55
Radilla, Daniel 315
Raj, Raajan 146
Ramezani, Arman............. 273
Ramirez, Andrea 197
Ramirez, Christian 262
Ramirez, Gabriel................ 38
Ramirez, Gina 54
Ramirez, Lilliana............... 235
Ramirez, Maria................... 81
Ramirez, Tiana 130
Ramirez, Veronica 87
Ramirez, Yvonne............... 136
Ramos, Brianna................. 127
Ramos, Gabriela 263
Ramos, Jaimie 153
Ramos, Jennifer 265
Ramos, Taylor 195
Ramsey, Alexander.............. 46
Rangel, Timothy 50
Rasmussen, Kelsey............ 252
Raval, Parth........................ 29

Ray, Dabrina 218
Ray, Micah........................ 317
Rayas, Aldo 140
Raymundo, Jasmine 34
Razo, Alexandra.................. 22
Razon, Raj........................ 245
Rea, Manny 253
Reasin, Brenton A. 60
Redmoon, Sarah............... 168
Reed, Tyson 273
Reichenberger, Samantha 189
Reimann, Keren.................. 71
Reintegrado, Jada 130
Renderos, Enha................. 143
Rendon, Robert................. 161
Rennie, Erica 301
Renteria, Abrianna 254
Resendiz, Juan 245
Reyes, Bryan....................... 89
Reyes, Carmen 54
Reyes, Christopher 105
Reyes, Elaine 292
Reyes, Elena 301
Reyes, Francisco................ 257
Reyes, Jose Angel 41
Reyes, Kathleen Escusa..... 209
Reyes, Matthew 312
Reyes, Ronnie.................... 258
Reyna, Yissel 314
Reynolds, Brielle 167
Rhodes, Jazmine 82
Richards, Isabelle 234
Richardson, Severine.......... 66
Ridjan, Richard 315
Rillamas, Analisa.............. 257
Ritchie, Jessica 183
Rivas, David 268
Rivas, Gabriel 231
Rivas, Jacob 292
Rivera, Angel 146
Rivera, Edward................. 110
Rivera, Kenneth 265
Rivera, Mario 254
Roark, Jamie 266
Robbins, Malachi 291
Roberts, Cameron 247
Roberts, Jamesa 90
Roberts, Kari 110
Roberts, Kayla................... 117
Roberts, Kyleigh 146
Roberts, Maureen 137
Robertson, Ashley 296
Robinson, Danyelle........... 102
Robinson, Jessica 100
Robinson, Jessica 267
Robinson-Wrobel,
    Matthew 316

Rocha, Anthony 190
Rodewald, Rachel 101
Rodriguez, Alberto 19
Rodriguez, Amanda 128
Rodriguez, Claudia 136
Rodriguez, Isaac 289
Rodriguez, Manny 150
Rodriguez, Michael........... 165
Rodriguez, Paul 64
Rodriguez, Ricardo 105
Rogers, Keeley 289
Roh, Erin............................. 26
Rojas, Briana 262
Rojas, Crystal 143
Rojas, Eduardo 43
Rojas, Maricela 300
Roland, Rebecca 198
Romero, Alexia.................. 202
Romero, Beatriz 189
Romero, Ben 189
Romero, Brenda................ 217
Romero, Christian 131
Romero, Gabrielle............... 45
Romero, Silvia 207
Rood, Haley 265
Rosales, Nataly 107
Rosas, Raul 67
Rose, Catherine................. 127
Rose, Christian.................. 172
Rosemont, Colin 67
Rosenthal, Frankie 227
Rosenthal, Haley 192
Ross, Aliquon 153
Ross, Maurice...................... 65
Ross, Sherry 306
Rosse, Ian.......................... 220
Roth, Zella......................... 270
Rothman, Jaclyn 292
Roush, Katherine 304
Routhieaux, Luke 200
Rowland, Tawnya............... 23
Roy, Chris 306
Roy, Elisabeth................... 318
Ruan, Ryman...................... 85
Rubinov, Mark 278
Rubio, Destiny 160
Rubio, Felicia 145
Rubio, Jordan 121
Rudney, Brandon 135
Ruehlman, Izabelle 292
Ruelas, Claudia 270
Ruelas, Jozeph................... 313
Ruggeri, Taylure 119
Ruggiero,
    Giovanni Daniel........... 131
Ruiz, Ericela....................... 71
Ruiz, Francine 24
Ruiz, Gissel....................... 277

Ruiz, Micaela 244
Ruso, Travis 247
Russo, Nicholas................. 282
Ruvalcaba, Michelle 230
Ryan, Ian 278
Saadatnejadi, Melinda...... 255
Sabin, Susanna................... 27
Sablan, Jesenia................. 100
Saidawi, Alice 180
Salas, Daniel 171
Salazar, Astrid 179
Salazar, Danyelle 278
Salazar, Eric 65
Salazar, Norma 307
Salazar, Paul 156
Saleem, Junaid 53
Saleem, Mahnoor 102
Salgado, Edwin 80
Salgado, Roberta 140
Salinas, Tyler 40
Salvador, Stephanie 301
Sam, Stephanie 176
Samora, Mackenzie 236
Sampson, Lorenzo 263
San Diego, Samantha........ 108
Sanchez, Alejandra 220
Sanchez, Alexa 90
Sanchez, Aman 194
Sanchez, Anthony 16
Sanchez, Bianka 134
Sanchez, Blake.................. 315
Sanchez, Karla 223
Sanchez, Kevin.................... 91
Sanchez, Krissia 267
Sanchez, Laurisa 178
Sanchez, Natalie 286
Sanchez, Vanessa 117
Sanchez, Veronica............... 30
Sanders, Greg.................... 103
Sandoval, Andres 190
Sandoval, Genessa 209
Sandoval, Irving 249
Sandoval, Maria.................. 61
Sandoval, Miguel................ 89
Sandoval, Vicente............. 142
Santana, Liliana 63
Santander, Sebastian 195
Santos, Margie 109
Santoyo, Griselda C........... 182
Santoyo, Jesus 103
Sanyal, Nilarun................. 243
Sarale, Emily..................... 193
Sarrouh, Gabriella 302
Saunders, Jacob 294
Savluk, Nicole 298
Sayeed, Maryam................ 256
Sbrocca, Marie 19
Schardein, Alec 180

Schenck, Ketti 20	Slusser, Victoria Margaret. 215	Su, Mei Mei 71	Torres, Ashley 140
Schifrin, Dylan 258	Smart, Jennifer 157	Sullivan, John 165	Torres, Jacob 221
Schimansky, Colleen 295	Smith, Alex 130	Sullivan, Sammy 179	Torres, Justice 107
Schlee, Pascal 276	Smith, Brittany 79	Summers, Ava Rae 279	Torres, Mayra 169
Schmidt, Maddie 199	Smith, CaitlinMarie 319	Sun, Daniel 260	Torres, Miguel 58
Schneider, Eva 248	Smith, Diamante 77	Sun, Kristen 280	Torres, Mitzi 120
Scholefield, Alexandra 275	Smith, Jamie 296	Swan, Samantha 182	Torres, Paola 169
Schonfeld, Grace 278	Smith, Katelyn 164	Swatling-Holcomb, Jesse 38	Torrez, Candy Raye 273
Schott-Rosenfield, Isaac ... 268	Smith, Kenneth 137	Swyers, Rebecca 293	Torrez, Lauren 101
Schultz, Jack 309	Smith, Krystal 19	Sysol, Alexandra 33	Torrez, Ryan 313
Scott, Alanze 281	Smith, Nick 148	T., Alex 26	Tortorice, Heather 144
Scott, Madison 126	Smith, Nicolas 309	Tabachnik, Anna 254	Toussaint, Sara 150
Sealander, Brandi 47	Smith, Russell 278	Tabares, Maria 292	Tovar, Tiffany 219
Seaman, Kaitlyn 155	Smith, Tariq 291	Taber, Valerie 49	Townsend, Joaquin 275
Sedgwick, Eden Rae 303	Snell, Evan 205	Tabor, Austin 187	Tracy, Brandon 184
Seetharam, Srividya 269	Soberon, Hector 92	Tai, Katherine 284	Tran, Binh 58
Segura, Gabriel 295	Soboleski, Isabella 320	Takehana, David 78	Tran, Christine 166
Seifert, James 22	Sobon, Austin 197	Takeshita, Tamara 32	Tran, Justin 145
Serrano, Jorge 103	Soler, Luis 34	Tamrazian, Sophia 288	Tran, Matthew 266
Serrano, Kyle 273	Solis, Emigdio 137	Tanega, Rachelle 171	Tran, Megan 164
Serrano, Ruth 227	Solis, Laura 186	Tang, Jonah 255	Tran, Peter 121
Serrato, Jennifer 30	Song, Madeline 264	Tanguilig, Jonar 249	Tran, Phuc 36
Serrato, Korina 18	Soriano, Sabrina 168	Tansey, Joey 175	Tran, Sophia 62
Seymour, Alyn 305	Sormann, Danielle 157	Tanuwijaya, Joshua 209	Tran, Yenyen 232
Shah, Marisa 296	Soto, Karen 263	Tapia, Audrie 320	Travalini, Felicia 26
Sharif, Karim 187	Soto, Mayra 16	Tapia, Brittnie 240	Traynor, Sabrina 282
Shattuck, Morgen 302	Soto, Rudy 173	Tapia, Francisco Antonio .. 170	Trinh, Stephen 68
Shepherd, Audrey 214	Soto, Summer 253	Tatkar, Shweta 173	Troglio, Natalie 283
Sheppard, Courtney 174	Soultanian, Erica 59	Tavakoli, Hannah 54	Truong, Pauline 150
Sherwindt, Hannah 287	Souza, Steven 171	Taylor, Briana 166	Tsai, Catherine 207
Shi, Marie 273	Speece, Teal 182	Taylor, Caitlin 28	Tsai, Matthew 185
Shier, Sara 44	Spencer, Steffi 24	Taylor, Gabriela 236	Tsai, Samantha 149
Shies, B.L. 61	Spenhoff, Dylan 12	Tellez, Heidi Galisia 31	Tsang, Timothy 209
Shipherd, Olivia 105	Spivack, Sarah 154	Tellez, Juckilin 213	Tucker, Everett 80
Shirley, Kathryn 289	Splinter, Garrett 104	Tenenbaum, Harry 145	Tucker, Keionna 105
Shivaram, Kavya 118	Srirama, Druthi 102	Terzian, Alexandra 83	Tucker, Ryan 73
Shleifer, Emma 260	Stahler, Olleanna 124	Tesfamicael, Sewit 248	Tuigamala, Tuileva 57
Shoushtarizadeh, Bijan 53	Stamper, Ajani 254	Thao, Jessica 125	Turner, Kelsey 144
Shpall, Sam 160	Stamps, Elizabeth 61	Thomas, Genny 244	Turner, Nicole 31
Sias, Jasmine 294	Starck, Sienna 181	Thomas, Owen 158	Turner, William 292
Sigala, Sarah 202	Starke, Sydney 319	Thomas, Sam 284	Tustin, Connor 200
Silva, Annabell 78	Stasiuk, Aleks 36	Thompson, Charlie 320	Tzeng, Eugenia 283
Silva, Joshua 103	Steele, Nicholas 250	Thompson, Hannah R. 187	Tzeng, Rane 316
Silva, Teresa 53	Stefani, Sierra Christabel . 105	Thompson, Paige 278	Ufondu, Ifeoma 185
Silveira, Cat 233	Steindorf, Matt 197	Thrasher, Brianna 198	Umamoto, Lacey 171
Silvers, Austin 267	Stelman, Rebecca 306	Thweatt, Annie 219	Umpierre, Jada 210
Silvers, Jessica 37	Stepanova, Natasha 62	Tiaffay, Isabel 297	Uribe, Julianne 286
Simpson, Alaina 41	Stephens, Jennifer 295	Tibrewal, Neha 106	Urtiz, Edward 17
Sims, Ava 232	Stern, Jillian 303	Tiffee, Destiny 69	Uy, Kaela 132
Sims, Nicole 101	Sternin, Shayna 242	Tinoco, Diego 286	Uyong, David 192
Singh, Anisha 214	Stewart, Brandi 223	Tinsley, Shea 94	Vadhin, Sandra 188
Singh, Apeksha 160	Stoebe, Devyn 142	Todesco, Juliana 264	Vaghjiani, Niki 117
Singh, Gunita 70	Stone, Tanner 315	Tomlinson, Kyle 118	Vahl, Katie 135
Sipich, Andrew 298	Strang, Jeremiah 277	Ton, Thucdan 159	Valdenor, Keno 265
Skinner, Dean 310	Stroud, Valerie 87	Toomey, Cypress 317	Valdez, Fernanda 264
Slagoski, Brooklyn 125	Stucker, Jeremiah 211	Torgove, Sam 257	Valdizon, Shannon 32
Slate, Tria 171	Sturgeon, Gemma 247	Torres, Adeline Danielle 297	Valdovinos, Amparo 123
Slater, Ryan 113	Su, Bryan 274	Torres, Ariel 29	Valencia, Rosendo 91

Vallecillo, Nayeli 268
Vallin, Natalie 300
Valrie, Marshanna 70
Van Buren, Courtney 60
Van Kirk, Madelyne 253
Van Ness, Ray 12
Vandenibos, Alicia Ann 91
Vang, Amy 227
Vang, Cai 73
Vang, Doua 114
Vang, Tommy 167
Vann-Adibe, Sophia 319
Varesio, Wade 280
Vargas, Evelyn 82
Vartany, Stephanie 282
Vartazarov, Robert 314
Vasquez, David Roy 295
Vasquez, Gina 285
Vasquez, Kevin 50
Vaughan, Kyle 204
Vazquez, Christian 58
Vazquez, Jesse 119
Vazquez, Johnny 246
Veals, Vincent 285
Vega, Evan 305
Vegar, Johvani 61
Velasquez,
   Kardena Patricia 274
Velez, Brianna 307
Velez, Megan 227
Veloro, Kyle 166
Vemula, Ridhima 80
Venegas, Adrianna 298
Vennard, Michael 232
Vera, Christina 294
Verduzco, Vanessa 201
Vergara, Abigail 267
Verma, Neil 53
Veseliza, Austin 275
Vicente, Francisco 320
Viengpasertsay, Thitichon 271
Vigallon, Alyssa 285
Villa, Kelley 38
Villa, Nadia 46
Villa, Rafael 57
Villamil, Montana 122
Villarreal, Nicole 138
Villatoro, Leslie 241
Villegas, Rosa S. 43
Vincent, Erzsebet 85
Viner, Taylor-Rose 285
Vinson, Trudy 18
Viray, Daniel 231
Viray, Marielle 64
Virgen, Aubree 160
Vis, Collin 135
Vo, Tiffany 269
Vollers, Carly 67

Vong, Hing 89
Vorwaller, Scheridan 233
Vue, Meng 125
Vue, Ying 232
Wada, Madison 138
Wade, Taurean 42
Wagner, Justin Dennis 35
Wahl, Conrad 319
Walden, Aliza 297
Walker, Semaj 250
Walters, Corey 92
Waner, Elizabeth 146
Wang, Felicia 281
Wang, Liann 78
Wang, Nathan 248
Warren, Andy 222
Washington, Briana 263
Washington, Michael 38
Washington, Tamara 52
Waterman, Justin 131
Watkins, Ally 263
Watroba, Brandon 288
Webb, Jermanay 221
Webb, Ron 220
Webber, Hailey 153
Weberg, Ryan 153
Weiner, Joely 281
Weinstock, Savannah 263
Weiss, Skylar 277
Weitz, Mia 264
Wells, Andrue 128
Wesley, Xavier 134
Wessels, Kira 103
Wexler, Alison 81
Wheeler, Josh 211
White, Diamond 14
White, Emma 49
White, Ethan 307
White, Kyara 312
White, Ryan S. 247
Whitehead, Ciara 156
Whitley, Michael 21
Whitlock, Abbygail 174
Wieder, Zachary 269
Wiesenthal, Isabel 243
Wiley, Dominique 274
Wilf, Isaac 284
Will, Alayna 74
Williams, Amanda 194
Williams, Ash Lee 41
Williams, Lavett 45
Williams, Stephen 118
Wilson, Chase 225
Wilson, Ebony 300
Wilson, Hailey 295
Wilson, Rahsaan 269
Wingerden, Matthew 312
Winn, Andy 210

Winograd, Toby 142
Witherspoon, Aimee 14
Wolf, Danielle 226
Wolf, Jessica 243
Wollman, Troy 52
Wolman, Mira 111
Wong, Audrey 142
Wong, Elliot 208
Wong, Gabrielle 240
Wong, Pinky 62
Wong, Richard 29
Wong, Timmy 312
Woods, Mariah 31
Woodside, Colby 280
Woodward, Emily 137
Wright, Emily 48
Wright, Luis 109
Wu, Elizabeth 252
Wu, Iris 194
Wyse, Rose 205
Xu, Jacqueline 12
Yadegar, Jordan 316
Yan, Shu Wen 274
Yanez, Francisco 162
Yang, Andrew 51
Yang, Will 191
Yap, Katrina 308
Yarbrough, Nicholas 293
Yariv, Jadon 318
Yaseen, Mashal 172
Ybarra, Raymond 260
Ye, Tiffany 209
Yepez, Arianna 197
Ygloria, Ariel 154
Ygrubay, Pamela 178
Yin, Xian 180
Ynami, Sophia 188
Yoon, Sang 148
Young, Melissa 39
Young, Tammy 24
Yu, Marissa 172
Zaida, Jenny 294
Zalduondo, Ruby 195
Zamora, Sacramento 149
Zamora, Tiffanee 63
Zaragoza, Daniel 107
Zataray, Sergio 55
Zavala, Andrea 18
Zavala, Christopher 139
Zeiter, Sierra 129
Zepeda, Andrew 303
Zepeda, Nicolas 317
Zeyen, Lexi 305
Zhang, Claudia 241
Zheng, Tiffany 217
Zhu, Peter 261
Zhuang, Lucy 161
Zosimo, Marissa 168

Zubeidi, Noah 22
Zugarazo, Fabrice 268